voices of modern psychology ;

a collection of readings for
introductory psychology

edited by elliot aronson
the university of texas

ADDISON-WESLEY PUBLISHING COMPANY
reading, massachusetts
menlo park, california / london / don mills, ontario

voices of modern
psychology

contents

Why another collection of readings? Admittedly it is a good idea to expose students to the original writing of contemporary psychologists in addition to a textbook summary of the field, but I am about as aware as the average reader that there already exists a great number of collections of articles in psychology. Indeed, one might venture to say that if there is one thing the field can do without it is still another book of readings.

Existing collections vary widely. Some are more "focused" than others; some are more "representative" than others; some consist mainly of "classic" experiments; others concentrate on "controversial" studies; some claim to consist of "crucial" experiments; some represent "hard" psychology while others lean toward softer areas. But they have one thing in common: in each volume, a large proportion of the articles are incomprehensible to the average college sophomore. Let's face it; virtually all articles that appear in contemporary journals are written for professionals. Accordingly, the style, language, and syntax that are used presume a degree of sophistication that is far beyond that of the average undergraduate student enrolled in his first course in psychology. Moreover, the space limitations of most psychological journals preclude elaboration. Even seasoned and sophisticated professionals have difficulty following some journal articles written with such Western Union-like brevity.

How, then, do we provide undergraduates with the flavor of original writings in psychology in clear and understandable form? It occurred to me that when people (including psychologists) make public speeches,

introduction

they are usually more lucid than when they write. Perhaps the apprehension of facing a live audience of blank and uncomprehending faces is a sufficient goad toward clarity. Perhaps the freedom from severe time limitations which comes with an invited address allows for a pace and elaboration that enhances clarity. Whatever the reason, in my experience, most speeches are clear, contain helpful examples, and some are even resplendent with humor, style, and grace—in short, they are everything that most journal articles are not.

With this thought in mind, I decided to build a collection of readings based entirely on carefully selected addresses. This has an added advantage: the "written" spoken word contributes to the clarity and understandability of the presentation. In addition, since scholars who are invited to speak tend to be among the more visible in their profession, this procedure brings to center stage precisely those people who have attained a degree of eminence through being expert. Thus, hopefully, this collection provides the reader with a rare combination of clarity and expertise. As editor, I have tried to select those articles that are most clear, most expert, most contemporary, and most oriented toward theory and data. Moreover, I have tried to make certain that the major areas of psychology are represented and that no area is overrepresented. This last consideration has forced me to exclude many articles which would be plainly acceptable under the other criteria. In situations where one author has made more than one speech on the same topic, I have opted for understandability, even (on occasion) at the expense of recency.

It should be noted that a collection of speeches is not entirely free from problems of unclarity. Although the articles in this volume tend to be far more lucid than the average journal article, many of them contain technical terminology which is left undefined. But with very few exceptions, the terminology used by the contributors to this volume is of a kind that is defined and explained in introductory psychology textbooks. Thus, if this collection is to be employed in an introductory course, it would be most useful if it were assigned in conjunction with a textbook, and if the appropriate chapter or chapters of the text were read prior to any specific article in this collection. For the student's convenience, I have organized the articles in a manner that parallels the chapter organization of most introductory texts.

Some consideration has also been given to the finances of the student. In all probability, one of the major uses of this book will be as a supplement to texts in introductory psychology; accordingly, we felt that it would overburden the student financially if his instructor were to suggest that he purchase a thick, expensively bound tome in addition to the thick, expensively bound text he has already purchased for the course. For this reason, we have opted for a paper rather than a cloth binding and we have included only a few readings in each major area—to offer the student a taste of original writing and thinking rather than a complete (and expensive) meal.

I would like to express my appreciation to the contributors and to the American Psychological Association for releasing copyrighted material, and to the staff of Addison-Wesley for their splendid cooperation. I also wish to thank my secretaries, Judith Hilton and Donna Beard, for their assistance.

E. A.

No man can be acquainted with all of psychology today, as our convention program proves. The scene resembles that of a circus, but a circus grander and more bustling than any Barnum ever envisioned—a veritable week-long diet of excitement and pink lemonade. Three days of smartly paced performance are required just to display the new tricks the animal trainers have taught their charges. We admire the agile paperreaders swinging high above us in the theoretical blue, saved from disaster by only a few gossamer threads of fact, and we gasp as one symposiast thrusts his head bravely between another's sharp toothed jaws. This 18-ring display of energies and talents gives plentiful evidence that psychology is going places. But whither?

In the simpler days of psychology, the presidential address provided a summing-up and a statement of destination. The President called the roll of the branches of psychology—praising the growth of some youngsters, tut-tutting patriarchally over the delinquent tendencies of others—and showed each to his proper place at the family table. My own title is reminiscent of those grand surveys, but the last speaker who could securely bring the whole of psychology within one perspective was Dashiell, with his 1938 address on "Rapprochements in Contemporary Psychology" (15). My scope must be far more restricted.

I shall discuss the past and future place within psychology of two historic streams of method, thought, and affiliation which run through the last century of our science. One stream is *experimental psychology;* the

the two disciplines of scientific psychology[1]

lee j. cronbach
stanford university

other, *correlational psychology.* Dashiell optimistically forecast a confluence of these two streams, but that confluence is still in the making. Psychology continues to this day to be limited by the dedication of its investigators to one or the other method of inquiry rather than to scientific psychology as a whole.

A stream of thought is identified by many features: philosophical underpinnings, methods of inquiry, topical interests, and loci of application. The experimental and correlational streams have all these aspects, but I am concerned with them as disciplines within

1. Address of the President at the Sixty-Fifth Annual Convention of the American Psychological Association, New York, New York, September 2, 1957. Reprinted from *American Psychologist*, 1957, Vol. 12, pp. 671–684. Copyright 1957 by the American Psychological Association, and reproduced by permission.

scientific psychology. The job of science is to ask questions of Nature. A discipline is a method of asking questions and of testing answers to determine whether they are sound. Scientific psychology is still young, and there is rapid turnover in our interests, our experimental apparatus and our tests, and our theoretical concepts. But our methods of inquiry have become increasingly stable, and it is these methods which qualify us as scientists rather than philosophers or artists.

The Separation of the Disciplines

The experimental method—where the scientist changes conditions in order to observe their consequences—is much the more coherent of our two disciplines. Everyone knows what experimental psychology is and who the experimental psychologists are. Correlational psychology, though fully as old as experimentation, was slower to mature. It qualifies equally as a discipline, however, because it asks a distinctive type of question and has technical methods of examining whether the question has been properly put and the data properly interpreted.

In contrast to the Tight Little Island of the experimental discipline, correlational psychology is a sort of Holy Roman Empire whose citizens identify mainly with their own principalities. The discipline, the common service in which the principalities are united, is the study of correlations presented by Nature. While the experimenter is interested only in the variation he himself creates, the correlator finds his interest in the already existing variation between individuals, social groups, and species. By "correlational psychology" I do not refer to studies which rely on one statistical procedure. Factor analysis is correlational, to be sure, but so is the study of Ford and Beach (23) relating sexual behavior to differences along the phylogenetic scale and across the cultural spectrum.

The well-known virtue of the experimental method is that it brings situational variables under tight control. It thus permits rigorous tests of hypotheses and confident statements about causation. The correlational method, for its part, can study what man has not learned to control or can never hope to control. Nature has been experimenting since the beginning of time, with a boldness and complexity far beyond the resources of science. The correlator's mission is to observe and organize the data from Nature's experiments. As a minimum outcome, such correlations improve immediate decisions and guide experimentation. At

the best, a Newton, a Lyell, or a Darwin can align the correlations into a substantial theory.

During our century of scientific psychology, the correlators have marched under many flags. In perhaps the first modern discussion of scientific method in psychology (1874), Wundt (54) showed how "experimental psychology" and "ethnic psychology" (i.e., cross-cultural correlations) supplement each other. In one of the most recent (1953), Bindra and Scheier (4) speak of the interplay of "experimental" and "psychometric" method. At the turn of the century, the brand names were "experimental" and "genetic" psychology, although experimenters were also beginning to contrast their "general psychology" with the "individual psychology" of Stern and Binet.

In 1913, Yerkes made the fundamental point that all the correlational psychologies are one. His name for this branch was "comparative psychology."

Although comparative psychology in its completeness necessarily deals with the materials of the psychology of infant, child, adult, whether the being be human or infra-human; of animal or plant [!]—of normal and abnormal individuals; of social groups and of civilizations, there is no reason why specialists in the use of the comparative method should not be so distinguished, and, if it seems necessary, labelled (55).

Even in advocating research on animals (56), Yerkes is emphatic in defining the goal as correlation across species. In France, *la psychologie comparée* continues to include all of differential psychology; but in America, as Beach (2) has lamented, comparative psychology degenerated into the experimental psychology of the white rat and thereby lost the power of the correlational discipline.

Except for the defection of animal psychologists, the correlational psychologists have remained loosely federated. Developmental psychologists, personality psychologists, and differential psychologists have been well acquainted both personally and intellectually. They study the same courses, they draw on the same literature, they join the same divisions of APA.

Experimental and correlational psychologists, however, grew far apart in their training and interests. It is now commonplace for a student to get his PhD in experimental psychology without graduate training in test theory or developmental psychology, and the student of correlational branches can avoid experimental psychology only a little less completely. The journals of one discipline have small influence on the journals of the other (14). Boring even dares to say (5,

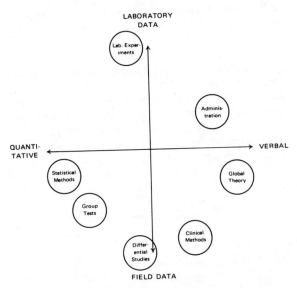

LABORATORY
DATA

Lab. Exper-
iments

Adminis-
tration

QUANTI-
TATIVE

VERBAL

Statistical
Methods

Global
Theory

Group
Tests

Differ-
ential
Studies

Clinical
Methods

FIELD DATA

Fig. 1
Factors accounting for esteem of leaders in psychology by American psychologists (based on correlations presented by Thorndike, 44, corrected for attenuation and refactored).

p. 578) that there is a personality difference between the fields: the distinction being that correlational psychologists like people!

Certainly the scientific values of psychologists are sharply divided. Thorndike (9, 44) recently asked American psychologists to rate various historic personages by indicating, on a forced-choice questionnaire, which have made the greatest contributions to psychology. A factor analysis of the ratings shows two distinct factors (Figure 1). One bipolar factor (irrelevant to our present discussion) ranges from verbal to quantitative psychologists. The other factor has at one pole the laboratory experimenters like Stevens, Dodge, and Ebbinghaus, and at the opposite pole those like Binet, May, and Goodenough who collect and correlate field data. A psychologist's esteem for the experimenters is correlated −.80 (−1.00, corrected for attenuation) with his esteem for scientists who use correlational methods.

There was no such schism in 1913 when Yerkes stated the program of correlational psychology. Genetic psychology and experimental psychology were hard at work on the same problems. Terman demonstrated in his 1923 presidential address (43) that the mental test was within the tradition of experimental, fundamental research in psychology, and had quotations to show

that the contemporary experimentalists agreed with him. Wells and Goddard, in 1913, had been asked to lecture on mental tests within the Holy Temple itself, the Society of Experimental Psychologists. And, in 1910, the High Priest Titchener had said:

Individual psychology is one of the chief witnesses to the value of experiment. It furnishes the key to many, otherwise inexplicable differences of result, and it promises to allay many of the outstanding controversies. . . . There can be no doubt that it will play a part of steadily increasing importance (46).

But when Terman spoke in 1923, the common front had already been fatally breached. Watson had announced that experimental treatment could make and unmake individual differences at will, thus stripping them of scientific importance. Thurstone had taken the first firm stride in the opposite direction:

I suggest that we dethrone the stimulus. He is only nominally the ruler of psychology. The real ruler of the domain which psychology studies is the individual and his motives, desires, wants, ambitions, cravings, aspirations. The stimulus is merely the more or less accidental fact . . . (45, p. 364).

The personality, social, and child psychologists went one way; the perception and learning psychologists went the other; and the country between turned into desert.

During the estrangement of correlational and experimental psychology, antagonism has been notably absent. Disparagement has been pretty well confined to playful remarks like Cattell's accusation that the experimental psychologist's "regard for the body of nature becomes that of the anatomist rather than that of the lover" (7, p. 152), or the experimentalist Bartlett's (1, p. 210) satire on the testers emerging from World War I, "chanting in unaccustomed harmony the words of the old jingle

'God has a plan for every man
And He has one for you.' "

Most correlationists have done a little experimenting in the narrow sense, and experimenters have contributed proudly to testing work under wartime necessity. But these are temporary sojourns in a foreign land. (For clear expressions of this attitude, see 5, pp. 570–578 and 52, p. 24.)

A true federation of the disciplines is required. Kept independent, they can give only wrong answers or no answers at all regarding certain important problems. It is shortsighted to argue for one science to discover the general laws of mind or behavior and for a separate enterprise concerned with individual minds, or for a one-way dependence of personality theory upon learning theory. Consider the physical sciences as a parallel. Physics for centuries was the study of general laws applying to all solids or all gases, whereas alchemy and chemistry studied the properties and reactions of individual substances. Chemistry was once only a descriptive catalogue of substances and analytic techniques. It became a systematic science when organized quantitative studies yielded principles to explain differences between substances and to predict the outcomes of reactions. In consequence, Mendeleev the chemist paved the way for Bohr the physicist, and Fermi's physics contributes to Lawrence's chemistry; the boundary between chemistry and physics has become almost invisible.

The tide of separation in psychology has already turned. The perceiver has reappeared in perceptual psychology. Tested intelligence and anxiety appear as independent variables in many of the current learning experiments. Factor analytic studies have gained a fresh vitality from crossbreeding with classical learning experiments (e.g., 18, 22). Harlow, Hebb, Hess, and others are creating a truly experimental psychology of development. And students of personality have been designing subtle combinations of experimental and correlational method (see, for example, 29) which may ultimately prove to be our parallel to the emergence of physical chemistry.

Characterization of the Disciplines

In the beginning, experimental psychology was a substitute for purely naturalistic observation of man-in-habitat. The experimenter placed man in an artificial, simplified environment and made quantitative observations of his performance. The initial problem was one of describing accurately what man felt, thought, or did in a defined situation. Standardization of tasks and conditions was required to get reproducible descriptions. All experimental procedures were tests, all tests were experiments. Kraepelin's continuous-work procedure served equally the general study of fatigue and the diagnosis of individuals. Reaction time was important equally to Wundt and to Cattell.

The distinctive characteristic of modern experimentation, the statistical comparison of treatments, appeared only around 1900 in such studies as that of

Thorndike and Woodworth on transfer. The experimenter, following the path of Ebbinghaus, shifted from measurement of the average mind to measuring the effect of environmental change upon success in a task (51). Inference replaced estimation: the mean and its probable error gave way to the critical ratio. The standardized conditions and the standardized instruments remained, but the focus shifted to the single manipulated variable, and later, following Fisher, to multivariate manipulation. The experiment thus came to be concerned with between-treatments variance. I use the word "treatment" in a general sense; educational and therapeutic treatments are but one type. Treatment differences are equally involved in comparing rats given different schedules of reinforcement, chicks who have worn different distorting lenses, or social groups arranged with different communication networks.

The second great development in American experimental psychology has been its concern with formal theory. At the turn of the century, theory ranged far ahead of experiment and made no demand that propositions be testable. Experiment, for its part, was willing to observe any phenomenon, whether or not the data bore on theoretical issues. Today, the majority of experimenters derive their hypotheses explicitly from theoretical premises and try to nail their results into a theoretical structure. This deductive style has its undeniable defects, but one can not question the net gains from the accompanying theoretical sophistication. Discussions of the logic of operationism, intervening variables, and mathematical models have sharpened both the formulation of hypotheses and the interpretation of results.

Individual differences have been an annoyance rather than a challenge to the experimenter. His goal is to control behavior, and variation within treatments is proof that he has not succeeded. Individual variation is cast into that outer darkness known as "error variance." For reasons both statistical and philosophical, error variance is to be reduced by any possible device. You turn to animals of a cheap and short-lived species, so that you can use subjects with controlled heredity and controlled experience. You select human subjects from a narrow subculture. You decorticate your subject by cutting neurons or by giving him an environment so meaningless that his unique responses disappear (cf. 25). You increase the number of cases to obtain stable averages, or you reduce N to 1, as Skinner does. But whatever your device, your goal in the experimental tradition is to get those embarrassing differential variables out of sight.

The correlational psychologist is in love with just those variables the experimenter left home to forget. He regards individual and group variations as important effects of biological and social causes. All organisms adapt to their environments, but not equally well. His question is: what present characteristics of the organism determine its mode and degree of adaptation?

Just as individual variation is a source of embarrassment to the experimenter, so treatment variation attenuates the results of the correlator. His goal is to predict variation within a treatment. His experimental designs demand uniform treatment for every case contributing to a correlation, and treatment variance means only error variance to him.

Differential psychology, like experimental, began with a purely descriptive phase. Cattell at Hopkins, Galton at South Kensington, were simply asking how much people varied. They were, we might say, estimating the standard deviation while the general psychologists were estimating the central tendency.

The correlation coefficient, invented for the study of hereditary resemblance, transformed descriptive differential research into the study of mental organization. What began as a mere summary statistic quickly became the center of a whole theory of data analysis. Murphy's words, written in 1928, recall the excitement that attended this development:

The relation between two variables has actually been found to be stable in other terms than those of experiment ... [Moreover,] Yule's method of "partial correlation" has made possible the mathematical "isolation" of variables which cannot be isolated experimentally. . . . [Despite the limitations of correlational methods,] what they have already yielded to psychology . . . is nevertheless of such major importance as to lead the writer to the opinion that the only twentieth-century discovery comparable in importance to the conditioned-response method is the method of partial correlations (35, p. 410).

Today's students who meet partial correlation only as a momentary digression from their main work in statistics may find this excitement hard to comprehend. But partial correlation is the starting place for all of factor analysis.

Factor analysis is rapidly being perfected into a rigorous method of clarifying multivariate relationships. Fisher made the experimentalist an expert puppeteer, able to keep untangled the strands to half-a-dozen independent variables. The correlational psychologist is a mere observer of a play where Nature pulls a thousand strings; but his multivariate methods make him equally an expert, an expert in figuring out where to look for the hidden strings.

His sophistication in data analysis has not been matched by sophistication in theory. The correlational psychologist was led into temptation by his own success, losing himself first in practical prediction, then in a narcissistic program of studying his tests as an end in themselves. A naive operationism enthroned theory of test performance in the place of theory of mental processes. And premature enthusiasm[2] exalted a few measurements chosen almost by accident from the tester's stock as the ruling forces of the mental universe.

In former days, it was the experimentalist who wrote essay after anxious essay defining his discipline and differentiating it from competing ways of studying mind. No doubts plagued correlationists like Hall, Galton, and Cattell. They came in on the wave of evolutionary thought and were buoyed up by every successive crest of social progress or crisis. The demand for universal education, the development of a technical society, the appeals from the distraught twentieth-century parent, and finally the clinical movement assured the correlational psychologist of his great destiny. Contemporary experimentalists, however, voice with ever-increasing assurance their program and social function; and the fact that tonight you have a correlational psychologist discussing disciplinary identities implies that anxiety is now perched on *his* windowledge.

Indeed, I do speak out of concern for correlational psychology. Aptitude tests deserve their fine reputation; but, if practical, validated procedures are to be our point of pride, we must be dissatisfied with our progress since 1920. As the Executive Committee of Division 5 itself declared this year, none of our latter-day refinements or innovations has improved practical predictions by a noticeable amount. Correlational psychologists who found their self-esteem upon contributions to theory can point to monumental investigations such as the *Studies of Character* and *The Authoritarian Personality*. Such work does throw strong light upon the human scene and brings important facts clearly

2.   This judgment is not mine alone; it is the clear consensus of the factor analysts themselves (see 28, pp. 321–325).

into view. But theories to organize these facts are rarely offered and even more rarely solidified (30; 31, p. 55).

Potential Contributions of the Disciplines to One Another

Perhaps it is inevitable that a powerful new method will become totally absorbing and crowd other thoughts from the minds of its followers. It took a generation of concentrated effort to move from Spearman's tetrad equation and Army Alpha to our present view of the ability domain. It took the full energies of other psychologists to move from S-R bonds to modern behavior theory. No doubt the tendency of correlationists to ignore experimental developments is explained by their absorption in the wonders and complexities of the phenomena their own work was revealing. And if experimentalists were to be accused of narrow-minded concentration on one particular style and topic of research, the same comment would apply.

The spell these particular theories and methods cast upon us appears to have passed. We are free at last to look up from our own bedazzling treasure, to cast properly covetous glances upon the scientific wealth of our neighbor discipline. Trading has already been resumed, with benefit to both parties.

The introduction of construct validation into test theory (12) is a prime example. The history of this development, you may recall, was that the APA's Committee on Psychological Tests discovered that available test theory recognized no way of determining whether a proposed psychological interpretation of a test was sound. The only existing theory dealt with criterion validation and could not evaluate claims that a test measured certain psychological traits or states. Meehl, capitalizing on the methodological and philosophical progress of the experimenters, met the testers' need by suggesting the idea of construct validity. A proposed test interpretation, he showed, is a claim that a test measures a construct, i.e., a claim that the test score can be linked to a theoretical network. This network, together with the claim, generates predictions about observations. The test interpretation is justified only if the observations come out as predicted. To decide how well a purported test of anxiety measures anxiety, construct validation is necessary; i.e., we must find out whether scores on the test behave in accordance with the theory that defines anxiety. This theory predicts differences in anxiety between certain groups, and traditional correlational methods can test those predic-

tions. But the theory also predicts variation in anxiety, hence in the test score, as a function of experience or situations, and only an experimental approach can test those predictions.

This new theory of validity has several very broad consequences. It gives the tester a start toward the philosophical sophistication the experimenter has found so illuminating. It establishes the experimental method as a proper and necessary means of validating tests. And it re-establishes research on tests as a valuable and even dispensable way of extending psychological theory.

We may expect the test literature of the future to be far less saturated with correlations of tests with psychologically enigmatic criteria, and far richer in studies which define test variables by their responsiveness to practice at different ages, to drugs, to altered instructions, and to other experimentally manipulated variables. A pioneering venture in this direction is Fleishman's revealing work (21, 22) on changes in the factorial content of motor skills as a function of practice. These studies go far beyond a mere exploration of certain tests; as Ferguson has shown (19, 20), they force upon us a theory which treats abilities as a product of learning, and a theory of learning in which previously acquired abilities play a major role.

Perhaps the most valuable trading goods the correlator can offer in return is his multivariate conception of the world.

No experimenter would deny that situations and responses are multifaceted, but rarely are his procedures designed for a systematic multivariate analysis. The typical experimental design and the typical experimental law employ a single dependent variable. Even when more than one outcome is measured, the outcomes are analyzed and interpreted separately. No response measure, however, is an adequate measure of a psychological construct. Every score mixes general construct-relevant variance with variance specific to the particular measuring operation. It is all right for the agriculturist to consider size of crop as the fundamental variable being observed: that is the payoff for him. Our task, however, is to study changes in fundamental aspects of behavior, and these are evidenced only indirectly in any one measure of outcome.

The correlational psychologist discovered long ago that no observed criterion is truly valid and that simultaneous consideration of many criteria is needed for a satisfactory evaluation of performance. This same principle applies in experimentation. As Neal Miller says in a recent paper on experiments with drugs:

Where there are relatively few facts it seems easy to account for them by a few simple generalizations. . . . As we begin to study the effects of a variety of drugs on a number of different behavioral measures, exceptions and complexities emerge. We are forced to reexamine and perhaps abandon common-sense categories of generalization according to convenient words existing in the English language. As new and more comprehensive patterns of results become available, however, new and more precise generalizations may emerge. We may be able to "carve nature better to the joint" and achieve the simplicity of a much more exact and powerful science (32, pp. 326–327).

Theoretical progress is obstructed when one restricts himself to a single measure of response (34). Where there is only one dependent variable, it is pointless to introduce intervening variables or constructs. When there are many response variables, however, it is mandatory to subsume them under constructs, since otherwise we must have a separate set of laws for every measure of outcome. Dealing with multiple response variables is, as Miller says (33), precisely the problem with which the factor analysts have been concerned. Factor analysis, by substituting formal for intuitive methods, has been of great help in locating constructs with which to summarize observations about abilities. It is reasonable to expect that multivariate treatment of response measures would have comparable value in experimental psychology.

Experimenters very probably have even more to gain from treating *in*dependent variables as a continuous multivariate system. The manifold treatment categories in a Fisherian design are established a priori. In agriculture, the treatment dimensions the farmer can manipulate are obvious: fertilizer, water, species of seed, and so on. In a more basic science, we require genotypic constructs to describe situations, constructs like the physical scientist's temperature and pressure. The conditions the psychologist most easily manipulates—stimulus form, injunction to the subject, strength of electric shock—are not chosen because we intend to apply these specific conditions when we get around to "controlling behavior." They are used because these conditions, we hope, embody scientifically useful constructs.

The experimenter has no systematic way to classify and integrate results from different tasks or different reinforcers. As Ferguson remarks (20, p. 130; see also 19,

p. 100): "No satisfactory methodology has emerged for describing particular learning tasks, or indicating how one task differs from another, other than by a process of simple inspection." We depend wholly on the creative flair of the theorist to collate the experiments and to invent constructs which might describe particular situations, reinforcements, or injunctions in terms of more fundamental variables. The multivariate techniques of psychometrics are suited for precisely this task of grouping complex events into homogeneous classes or organizing them along major dimensions. These methods are frankly heuristic, but they are systematically heuristic. They select variables with minimal redundancy, and they permit us to obtain maximum information from a minimum of experimental investment.

In suggesting that examining treatment conditions as a statistical universe is a possible way to advance experimental thinking, I am of course echoing the recommendations of Egon Brunswik (6, esp. pp. 39–58). Brunswik criticized the Fisherian experimenter for his ad hoc selection of treatments and recommended that he apply the sampling principles of differential psychology in choosing stimuli and conditions. A sampling procedure such as Brunswik suggests will often be a forward step, but the important matter is not to establish laws which apply loosely to a random, unorganized collection of situations. The important matter is to discover the organization among the situations, so that we can describe situational differences as systematically as we do individual differences.

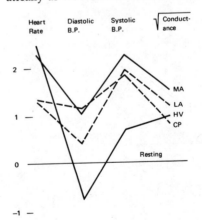

Fig. 2
Mean response to four stressors expressed in terms of resting standard scores (data from 50).

Research on stress presents a typical problem of organization. Multivariate psychophysiological data indicate that different taxing situations have different effects. At present, stressors can be described and classified only superficially, by inspection. A correlational or distance analysis of the data groups treatments which have similar effects and ultimately permits us to locate each treatment within a continuous multidimensional structure having constructs as reference axes. Data from a recent study by Wenger, Clemens, and Engel (50) may be used as an illustration. Figure 2 shows the means of standardized physiological scores under four different stress conditions: mental arithmetic, a letter association test, hyperventilation, and a cold pressor. The "profiles" for the four conditions are very significantly different. I have made a distance analysis to examine the similarity between conditions, with the results diagrammed in Figure 3. There is a general factor among all the treatments, which distinguishes them from the resting state, and a notable group factor among three of them. According to these data, a mental test seems to induce the same physiological state as plunging one's foot into ice water!

Much larger bodies of data are of course needed to map the treatment space properly. But the aptness of an attempt in this direction will be apparent to all who heard Selye's address to the APA last year. His argument (40) that all stressful situations lead to a similar syndrome of physiological changes is strongly reminiscent of Spearman's argument regarding a general factor linking intellectual responses. The disagreement between Selye and other students of stress clearly reduces to a quantitative question of the relative size of specific and nonspecific or general factors in the effects of typical stressors.

Applied Psychology Divided Against Itself

Let us leave for the moment questions of academic psychology and consider the schism as it appears in applied psychology. In applied psychology, the two disciplines are in active conflict; and unless they bring their efforts into harmony, they can hold each other to a standstill. The conflict is especially obvious at this moment in the challenge the young engineering psychology offers to traditional personnel psychology.

The program of applied experimental psychology is to modify treatments so as to obtain the highest average performance when all persons are treated alike—a search, that is, for "the one best way." The program of applied correlational psychology is to raise average performance by treating persons differently—different job assignments, different therapies, different disciplinary methods. The correlationist is utterly antagonistic to a doctrine of "the one best way," whether it be the heartless robot-making of Frederick Taylor or a doctrinaire permissiveness which tries to give identical encouragement to every individual. The ideal of the engineering psychologist, I am told, is to simplify jobs so that every individual in the working population will be able to perform them satisfactorily, i.e., so that differentiation of treatment will be unnecessary. This goal guides activities ranging from the sober to the bizarre: from E. L. Thorndike and Skinner, hunting the one best sequence of problems for teaching arithmetic, to Rudolf Flesch and his admirers, reducing *Paradise Lost* to a comic book. If the engineering psychologist succeeds: information rates will be so reduced that the most laggard of us can keep up, visual displays will be so enlarged that the most myopic can see them, automatic feedback will prevent the most accident-prone from spoiling the work or his fingers.

Obviously, with every inch of success the engineer has, the tester must retreat a mile. A slight reduction in information rate, accomplished once, reduces forever the validity and utility of a test of ability to process data. If, once the job is modified, the myopic worker can perform as well as the man with 20/20 vision, Snellen charts and orthoraters are out of business. Nor is the threat confined to the industrial scene. If tran-

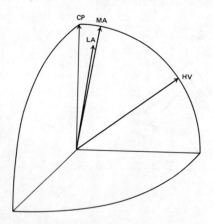

Fig. 3
Multivariate diagram showing similarity between four stressors.

quilizers make everybody happy, why bother to diagnose patients to determine which treatments they should have? And if televised lessons can simplify things so that every freshman will enjoy and understand quantum mechanics, we will need neither college aptitude tests nor final examinations.

It is not my intention to warn testers about looming unemployment. If test technology is not greatly improved, long before the applied experimentalists near their goals, testing deserves to disappear. My message is my belief that the conflicting principles of the tester and the experimenter can be fused into a new and integrated applied psychology.

To understand the present conflict in purposes, we must look again at historical antecedents. Pastore (36) argues with much justice that the testers and classifiers have been political conservatives, while those who try to find the best common treatment for all—particularly in education—have been the liberals. This essential conservatism of personnel pyschology traces back to the days of Darwin and Spencer.

The theory of evolution inspired two antagonistic movements in social thought (10, 42). Darwin and Herbert Spencer were real determinists. The survival of the fittest, as a law of Nature, guaranteed man's superiority and the ultimate triumph of the natural aristocrats among men. As Dewey put it, Spencer saw "a rapid transit system of evolution . . . carrying us automatically to the goal of perfect man in perfect society" (17, p. 66). Men vary in their power of adaptation, and institutions, by demanding adaptation, serve as instruments of natural selection among men. The essence of freedom is seen as the freedom to compete for survival. To Spencer, to Galton, and to their successors down to the present day, the successful are those who have the greatest adjustive capacity. The psychologist's job, in this tradition, is to facilitate or anticipate natural selection. He seeks only to reduce its cruelty and wastage by predicting who will survive in schools and other institutions as they are. He takes the system for granted and tries to identify who will fit into it. His devices have a conservative influence because they identify persons who will succeed in the existing institution. By reducing failures, they remove a challenge which might otherwise force the institution to change (49).

The experimental scientist inherits an interpretation of evolution associated with the names of Ward, James, and Dewey. For them, man's progress rests on his intelligence; the great struggle for survival is a struggle against environment, not against competitors. Intelligent man must reshape his environment, not merely conform to it. This spirit, the very antithesis of Spencerian laissez-faire, bred today's experimental social science which accepts no institution and no tradition as sacred. The individual is seen as inherently self-directing and creative. One can not hope to predict how he will meet his problems, and applied differential psychology is therefore pointless (39, p. 37).

Thus we come to have one psychology which accepts the institution, its treatment, and its criterion and finds men to fit the institution's needs. The other psychology takes man—generalized man—as given and challenges any institution which does not conform to the measure of this standard man.

A clearer view of evolution removes the paradox:

The entire significance of the evolutionary method in biology and social history is that every distinct organ, structure, or formation, every grouping of cells or elements, has to be treated as an instrument of adjustment or adaptation to a particular environing situation. Its meaning, its character, its value, is known when, and only when, it is considered as an arrangement for meeting the conditions involved in some specific situation (16, p. 15).

We are not on the right track when we conceive of adjustment or adjustive capacity in the abstract. It is always a capacity to respond to a particular treatment. The organism which adapts well under one condition would not survive under another. If for each environment there is a best organism, for every organism there is a best environment. The job of applied psychology is to improve decisions about people. The greatest social benefit will come from applied psychology if we can find for each individual the treatment to which he can most easily adapt. This calls for the joint application of experimental and correlational methods.

Interaction of Treatment and Individual in Practical Decisions

Goldine Gleser and the writer have recently published a theoretical analysis (11) which shows that neither the traditional predictive model of the correlator nor the traditional experimental comparison of mean differences is an adequate formulation of the decisions confronting the applied psychologist. Let me attempt to give a telescoped version of the central argument.

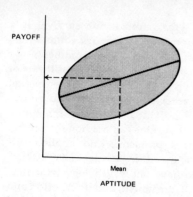

Fig. 4
Scatter diagram and payoff function showing outcome as a function of individual differences.

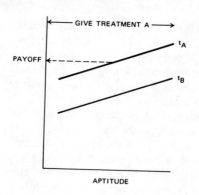

Fig. 6
Payoff functions for two treatments.

The decision maker has to determine what treatment shall be used for each individual or each group of individuals. Psychological data help a college, for example, select students to be trained as scientists. The aim of any decision maker is to maximize expected payoff. There is a payoff function relating outcome (e.g., achievement in science) to aptitude dimensions for any particular treatment. Figure 4 shows such a function for a single aptitude. Average payoff—if everyone receives the treatment—is indicated by the arrow. The experimentalist assumes a fixed population and hunts for the treatment with the highest average and the least variability. The correlationist assumes a fixed treatment and hunts for aptitudes which maxi-

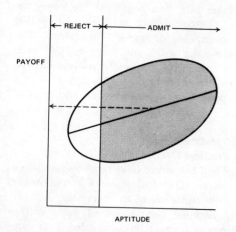

Fig. 5
Increase in payoff as a result of selection.

mize the slope of the payoff function. In academic selection, he advises admission of students with high scores on a relevant aptitude and thus raises payoff for the institution (Figure 5).

Pure selection, however, almost never occurs. The college aptitude test may seem to be intended for a selection decision; and, insofar as the individual college is concerned only with those it accepts, the conventional validity coefficient does indicate the best test. But from a societal point of view, the rejects will also go on into other social institutions, and their profit from this treatment must be weighed in the balance along with the profit or social contribution from the ones who enter college. Every decision is really a choice between treatments. Predicting outcome has no social value unless the psychologist or the subject himself can use the information to make better choices of treatment. The prediction must help to determine a treatment for every individual.

Even when there are just two treatments, the payoff functions have many possible relationships. In Figure 6 we have a mean difference between treatments, and a valid predictor. The predictor—though valid—is useless. We should give everyone Treatment A. In Figure 7, on the other hand, we should divide the group and give different treatments. This gives greater payoff than either treatment used uniformly will give.

Assigning everyone to the treatment with the highest average, as the experimentalist tends to recommend, is rarely the best decision. In Figure 8, Treatment C has the best average, and we might assign everyone to it. The outcome is greater, however, if we

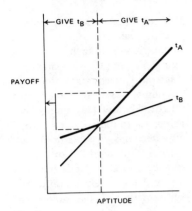

Fig. 7
Payoff functions for two treatments.

assign some persons to each treatment. The psychologist making an experimental comparison arrives at the wrong conclusion if he ignores the aptitude variable and recommends C as a standard treatment.

Applied psychologists should deal with treatments and persons simultaneously. Treatments are characterized by many dimensions; so are persons. The two sets of dimensions together determine a payoff surface. For any practical problem, there is some best group of treatments to use and some best allocation of persons to treatments. We can expect some attributes of persons to have strong interactions with treatment variables. These attributes have far greater practical importance than the attributes which have little or no interaction. In dividing pupils between college preparatory and noncollege studies, for example, a general intelligence test is probably the wrong thing to use. This test, being general, predicts success in all subjects,

therefore tends to have little interaction with treatment, and if so is not the best guide to differential treatment. We require a measure of aptitude which predicts who will learn better from one curriculum than from the other; but this aptitude remains to be discovered. Ultimately we should *design* treatments, not to fit the average person, but to fit groups of students with particular aptitude patterns. Conversely, we should seek out the aptitudes which correspond to (interact with) modifiable aspects of the treatment.

My argument rests on the assumption that such aptitude-treatment interactions exist. There is, scattered in the literature, a remarkable amount of evidence of significant, predictable differences in the way people learn. We have only limited success in predicting which of two *tasks* a person can perform better, when we allow enough training to compensate for differences in past attainment. But we do find that a person learns more easily from one *method* than another, that this best method differs from person to person, and that such between-treatments differences are correlated with tests of ability and personality. The studies showing interaction between personality and conditions of learning have burgeoned in the past few years, and the literature is much too voluminous to review in passing. Just one recent finding will serve in the way of specific illustration, a study done by Wolfgang Böhm at Vienna (38, pp. 58–59). He showed his experimental groups a sound film about the adventures of a small boy and his toy elephant at the zoo. At each age level, a matched control group read a verbatim text of the sound track. The differences in average comprehension between the audiovisual and the text presentations were trivial. There was, however, a marked interaction. For some reason yet unexplained, a general

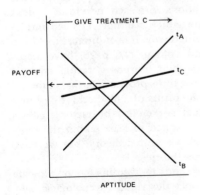

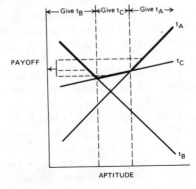

Fig. 8
Payoff functions for three treatments.

mental test correlated only .30 with text learning, but it predicted film learning with an average correlation of .77.[3] The difference was consistent at all ages.

Such findings as this, when replicated and explained, will carry us into an educational psychology which measures readiness for different types of teaching and which invents teaching methods to fit different types of readiness. In general, unless one treatment is clearly best for everyone, treatments should be differentiated in such a way as to maximize their interaction with aptitude variables. Conversely, persons should be allocated on the basis of those aptitudes which have the greatest interaction with treatment variables. I believe we will find these aptitudes to be quite unlike our present aptitude measures chosen to predict differences *within* highly correlated treatments.

The Shape of a United Discipline

It is not enough for each discipline to borrow from the other. Correlational psychology studies only variance among organisms; experimental psychology studies only variance among treatments. A united discipline will study both of these, but it will also be concerned with the otherwise neglected interactions between organismic and treatment variables (41). Our job is to invent constructs and to form a network of laws which permits prediction. From observations we must infer a psychological description of the situation and of the present state of the organism. Our laws should permit us to predict, from this description, the behavior of organism-in-situation.

There was a time when experimental psychologists concerned themselves wholly with general, nonindividual constructs, and correlational psychologists sought laws wholly within developmental variables. More and more, nowadays, their investigations are coming to bear on the same targets. One psychologist measures ego involvement by a personality test and compares the behavior of high- and low-scoring subjects. Another psychologist heightens ego involvement experimentally in one of two equated groups and studies the consequent differences in behavior. Both investigators can test the same theoretical propositions, and to the extent that their results agree they may regard both procedures as embodiments of the same construct.

3.   Personal communication.

Constructs originating in differential psychology are now being tied to experimental variables. As a result, the whole theoretical picture in such an area as human abilities is changing. Piaget (37) correlates reasoning processes with age and discovers a developmental sequence of schemata whose emergence permits operational thought; Harlow (24) begins actually to create similar schemata in monkeys by means of suitable training. It now becomes possible to pursue in the controllable monkey environment the questions raised by Piaget's unique combination of behavioral testing and interviewing, and ultimately to unite the psychology of intelligence with the psychology of learning.

Methodologies for a joint discipline have already been proposed. R. B. Cattell (8) has offered the most thorough discussion of how a correlationist might organize data about treatment and organism simultaneously. His factor analytic procedures are only one of many choices, however, which modern statistics offers. The experimenters, some of them, have likewise seen the necessity for a united discipline. In the very issue of *Psychological Review* where the much-too-famous distinction between *S-R* and *R-R* laws was introduced, Bergmann and Spence (3) declared that (at the present stage of psychological knowledge) the equation

$$R = f\,(S)$$

must be expanded into

$$R = f\,(S,T,D,I)$$

The added variables are innate differences, motivation, and past experience—differential variables all. Hull (26, 27) sought general laws just as did Wundt, but he added that organismic factors can and must be accounted for. He proposed to do this by changing the constants of his equations with each individual. This is a bold plan, but one which has not yet been implemented in even a limited way. It is of interest that both Hull (27, p. 116) and Tolman (47, p. 26) have stated specifically that for their purposes factor analytic methods seem to have little promise. Tucker, though, has at least drawn blueprints of a method for deriving Hull's own individual parameters by factor analysis (48). Clearly, we have much to learn about the most suitable way to develop a united theory, but we have no lack of exciting possibilities.

The experimenter tends to keep his eye on *ultimate* theory. Woodworth once described psychological laws

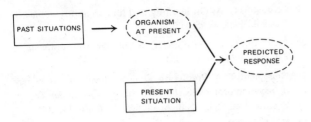

Fig. 9
Theoretical model for prediction from historic data.

in terms of the *S-O-R* formula which specifically recognizes the individual. The revised version of his *Experimental Psychology* (53, p. 3), however, advocates an *S-A-R* formula, where *A* stands for "antecedent conditions." This formulation, which is generally congenial to experimenters, reduces the present state of the organism to an intervening variable (Figure 9). A theory of this type is in principle entirely adequate to explain, predict, and control the behavior of organisms; but, oddly enough, it is a theory which can account only for the behavior of organisms of the next generation, who have not yet been conceived. The psychologist turns to a different type of law (Figure 10) whenever he deals with a subject whose life history he has not controlled or observed in every detail. A theory which involves only laws of this type, while suitable for prediction,

has very limited explanatory value. The theory psychology really requires is a redundant network like Figure 11. This network permits us to predict from the past experience or present characteristics of the organism, or a combination of the two, depending on what is known. Filling in such a network is clearly a task for the joint efforts of experimental and correlational psychology.

In both applied work and general scientific work, psychology requires combined, not parallel, labors from our two historic disciplines. In this common labor, they will almost certainly become one, with a common theory, a common method, and common recommendations for social betterment. In the search for interactions we will invent new treatment dimensions and discover new dimensions of the organism. We will come to realize that organism and treatment are an inseparable pair and that no psychologist can dismiss one or the other as error variance.

Despite our specializations, every scientific psychologist must take the same scene into his field of vision. Clark Hull, three sentences before the end of his *Essentials of Behavior* (27, p. 116), voiced just this need. Because of delay in developing methodology, he said, individual differences have played little part in behavior theory, and "a sizeable segment of behavioral science remains practically untouched." This untouched segment contains the question we really want to put to Nature, and she will never answer until our two disciplines ask it in a single voice.

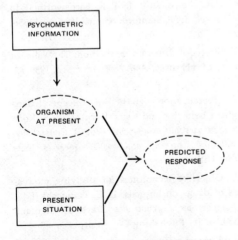

Fig. 10
Theoretical model for prediction from ahistoric data.

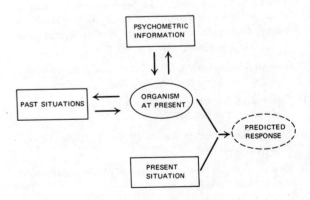

Fig. 11
Theoretical network to be developed by a united discipline.

References

1. Bartlett, F. C. Fifty years of psychology. *Occup. Psychol.*, 1955, *29*, 203–216.

2. Beach, F. A. The snark was a boojum. *Amer. Psychologist*, 1950, *5*, 115–124.

3. Bergmann, G., & Spence, K. W. The logic of psychophysical measurement. *Psychol. Rev.*, 1944, *51*, 1–24.

4. Bindra, D., & Scheier, I. H. The relation between psychometric and experimental research in psychology. *Amer. Psychologist*, 1954, *9*, 69–71.

5. Boring, E. G. *History of experimental psychology.* (2nd ed.) New York: Appleton-Century-Crofts, 1950.

6. Brunswik, E. *Perception and the representative design of psychological experiments.* Berkeley: Univer. California Press, 1956.

7. Cattell, J. McK. The biological problems of today: Psychology. *Science*, 1898, *7*, 152–154.

8. Cattell, R. B. *Factor analysis.* New York: Harper, 1952.

9. Clark, K. E. *America's psychologists.* Washington, D. C.: APA, 1957.

10. Corwin, E. S. The impact of the idea of evolution on the American political and constitutional tradition. In S. Persons (Ed.), *Evolutionary thought in America.* New Haven: Yale Univer. Press, 1950. Pp. 182–201.

11. Cronbach, L. J., & Gleser, Goldine C. *Psychological tests and personnel decisions.* Urbana: Univer. Illinois Press, 1957.

12. Cronbach, L. J., & Meehl, P. E. Construct validity in psychological tests. *Psychol. Bull.*, 1955, *52*, 281–302.

13. Cronbach, L. J., & Neff, W. D. Selection and training. In Com. on Undersea Warfare Panel on Psychology and Physiology, *Human Factors in Undersea Warfare.* Washington, D. C.: Nat. Res. Coun., 1949. Pp. 491–516.

14. Daniel, R. S., & Louttit, C. M. *Professional problems in psychology.* New York: Prentice-Hall, 1953.

15. Dashiell, J. F. Some rapprochements in contemporary psychology. *Psychol. Bull.*, 1939, *36*, 1–24.

16. Dewey, J. *Studies in logical theory.* Chicago: Univer. Chicago Press, 1903.

17. Dewey, J. *The influence of Darwin on philosophy and other essays.* New York: Holt, 1910.

18. Eysenck, H. J. Reminiscence, drive, and personality theory. *J. abnorm. soc. Psychol.*, 1956, *53*, 328–333.

19. Ferguson, G. A. On learning and human ability. *Canad. J. Psychol.*, 1954, *8*, 95–112.

20. Ferguson, G. A. On transfer and human ability. *Canad. J. Psychol.*, 1956, *10*, 121–131.

21. Fleishman, E. A. Predicting advanced levels of proficiency in psychomotor skills. In *Proc. Sympos. on Human Engng.* Washington, D. C.: Nat. Acad. Sci., 1956. Pp. 142–151.

22. Fleishman, E. A., & Hempel, W. E., Jr. Changes in factor structure of a complex psychomotor test as a function of practice. *Psychometrika*, 1954, *19*, 239–252.

23. Ford, C. S., & Beach, F. A. *Patterns of sexual behavior.* New York: Harper, 1952.

24. Harlow, H. F. The formation of learning sets. *Psychol. Rev.*, 1949, *56*, 51–65.

25. Harlow, H. F. Mice, men, monkeys and motives. *Psychol. Rev.*, 1953, *60*, 23–32.

26. Hull, C. L. The place of innate individual and species differences in a natural-science theory of behavior. *Psychol. Rev.*, 1945, *52*, 55–60.

27. Hull, C. L. *Essentials of behavior.* New Haven: Yale Univer. Press, 1951.

28. Laugier, H. (Ed.) L'analyse factorielle et ses applications. Paris: Centre National de la Recherche Scientifique, 1955.

29. Lazarus, R. S., & Baker, R. W. Personality and psychological stress—a theoretical and methodological framework. *Psychol. Newsletter*, 1956, *8*, 21–32.

30. McCandless, B. R., & Spiker, C. C. Experimental research in child psychology. *Child Develpm.*, 1956, *27*, 75–80.

31. McClelland, D. C. Personality. In P. R. Farnsworth (Ed.) *Annu. Rev. Psychol., 1956.* Stanford: Annual Reviews, 1956. Pp. 39–62.

32. Miller, N. E. Effects of drugs on motivation: The value of using a variety of measures. *Ann. N.Y. Acad. Sci.*, 1956, *65*, 318–333.

33. Miller, N. E. Liberalization of basic S-R concepts: Extensions to conflict behavior and social learning. In S. Koch (Ed.), *Psychology: A study of a science.* Vol. II. *General systematic formulations, learning, and special processes.* New York: McGraw-Hill, in press.

34. Miller, N. E. Objective techniques for studying motivational effects of drugs on animals. In E. Trabucchi (Ed.), *Proc. Int. Sympos. on Psychotropic Drugs.* Amsterdam, Netherlands: Elsevier Publishing Co., in press.

35. Murphy, G. *An historical introduction to modern psychology.* (3rd ed.) New York: Harcourt, Brace, 1932.

36. Pastore, N. *The nature-nurture controversy.* New York: Kings Crown Press, 1949.

37. Piaget, J. *Psychology of intelligence.* M. Piercy and D. E. Berlyne (Trans.). London: Routledge and Kegan Paul, 1950.

38. Rohracher, H. Aus der wissenschaftlichen Arbeit des Psychologischen Institutes der Universität Wien. *Wiener Z. Phil., Psychol., Pädag.,* 1956, *6,* 1–66.

39. Scoon, R. The rise and impact of evolutionary ideas. In S. Persons (Ed.), *Evolutionary thought in America.* New Haven, Yale Univer. Press, 1950. Pp. 4–43.

40. Selye, H. Stress and disease. *Science,* 1955, *122,* 625–631.

41. Shen, E. The place of individual differences in experimentation. In Q. McNemar and M. A. Merrill (Eds.), *Studies in personality.* New York: McGraw-Hill, 1942. Pp. 259–283.

42. Spengler, J. J. Evolutionism in American economics. In S. Persons (Ed.), *Evolutionary thought in America.* New Haven: Yale Univer. Press, 1950. Pp. 202–266.

43. Terman, L. M. The mental test as a psychological method. *Psychol. Rev.,* 1924, *31,* 93–117.

44. Thorndike, R. L. The psychological value systems of psychologists. *Amer. Psychologist,* 1954, *9,* 787–790.

45. Thurstone, L. L. The stimulus-response fallacy in psychology. *Psychol. Rev.,* 1923, *30,* 354–369.

46. Titchener, E. B. The past decade in experimental psychology. *Amer. J. Psychol.,* 1910, *21,* 404–421.

47. Tolman, E. C. The determinants of behavior at a choice point. *Psychol. Rev.,* 1938, *45,* 1–41.

48. Tucker, L. R. Determination of parameters of a functional relation by factor analysis. *ETS Res. Bull.,* 1955, *55,* No. 10.

49. Tyler, R. W. Can intelligence tests be used to predict educability? In K. Eells et al., *Intelligence and cultural differences.* Chicago: Univer. Chicago Press, 1951. Pp. 39–47.

50. Wenger, M. A., Clemens, T. L., & Engel, B. T. Autonomic response patterns to four stimuli. Unpublished manuscript, 1957.

51. Woodworth, R. S. *Dynamic psychology.* New York: Holt, 1918.

52. Woodworth, R. S. *Experimental psychology.* New York: Holt, 1938.

53. Woodworth, R. S., & Schlosberg, H. *Experimental psychology.* (2nd ed.) New York: Holt, 1954.

54. Wundt, W. *Principles of physiological psychology.* Vol. 1 (5th ed.) E. B. Titchener (Trans.) New York: Macmillan, 1904.

55. Yerkes, R. M. Comparative psychology: A question of definitions. *J. Phil. Psychol., and Sci. Methods,* 1913, *10,* 580–582.

56. Yerkes, R. M. The study of human behavior. *Science,* 1914, *29,* 625–633.

genetic, physiological, and sensory psychology

of flies and men[1]

theodosius dobzhansky
rockefeller university

One of the assertions which have gained acceptance by dint of frequent repetition is that science is competent to deal only with what recurs, returns, repeats itself. To study something scientifically, this something must be made representative of a class, group, or assemblage. A single *Drosophila* fly is of no interest whatsoever. A fly may merit some attention only if it is taken as a representative of its species. An individual person may, to be sure, merit attention. However, it is allegedly not in the province of science, but of insight, empathy, art, and literature to study and understand a person in his uniqueness.

1. Invited address presented at American Psychological Association, New York, September 1966. Some of the experimental work referred to in the text supported under Contract No. AT-(301)-3096, United States Atomic Energy Commission. Reprinted from *American Psychologist*, 1967, Vol. 22, pp. 41–48. Copyright 1967 by the American Psychological Association, and reproduced by permission.

I wish to challenge this view. Individuality, uniqueness, is not outside the competence of science. It may, in fact it must, be understood scientifically. In particular, the science of genetics investigates individuality and its causes. The singularity of the human self becomes comprehensible in the light of genetics. You may, of course, object that what science comprehends is not really a singularity but a plurality of singularities. However, an artist, no less than a biologist, becomes aware of the plurality because he has observed some singularities.

In the main, genetics is a study of differences among living beings. Genetics would be superfluous if all living beings were exactly alike. If all members of a species were exactly alike genetics could do very little. Since Mendel, the most powerful method of genetics is to observe differences among individuals in the progenies of parents which differed in some ways. Heredity and variation are the two sides of the same coin. Geneticists are always on the lookout for genetic diversity. Variety is said to be the spice of life. It is a staple necessity to geneticists. (This applies, of course, to Mendelian genetics proper. The great discoveries of the role of chromosomes in the development, and the relationships between DNA, RNA, and protein synthesis could conceivably have been made even if Mendel's laws remained unknown.)

That every person differs from every other person is so obvious that this is taken usually for granted. What continues controversial is to what extent the human differences are due to genetic and in what measure to environmental variations. Though in a new guise, the old nature-nurture problem is still with us. Now, the individuality of flies is rather less evident than human individuality. I do not claim to recognize every Drosophila by her face. The drosophiline individuality is nevertheless easier to analyze, and this analysis helps to throw some needed light on human individuality.

The theory of genetic individuality is simple enough. It stems directly from Mendel's second law, the law of independent assortment. An individual heterozygous for n genes has the potentiality of producing 2^n genetically different kinds of sex cells. Two parents, each heterozygous for the same n genes, can give rise to 3^n genotypes among the progeny, and parents heterozygous each for n different genes may produce 4^n genotypes. To be sure, not all of these genotypes are equally probable, because the linkage of genes in the same chromosome limits their independent assortment. Linkage disequilibrium delays but does not prevent eventual realization of the genetic variety. More important is the problem how large is n, that is, for how many genes an average individual is heterozygous, or how many genes are represented each by two or more variants in the populations of a species, such as man or a Drosophila.

The disagreement among geneticists on this point is rife. Those who espouse the classical theory of population structure believe that most genes are uniform, not only in all individuals of a species but even in different species not too remote in the biological system. The unfixed genes are a minority, perhaps of the order of some tens. Moreover, among the unfixed genes one variant, one allele, is normal and adaptively superior, while others are inferior and are maintained in populations by recurrent mutation. Though adherents of the classical theory are reluctant to admit this, the theory is a product of typological thinking. Lurking behind the facade of the variability, they like to envisage the Platonic archetype of the Normal Man, homozygous for all good with no bad genes.

The balance theory of population structure would assume numbers of variable genes of the order of hundreds, perhaps even thousands. An appreciable part of this variety is maintained in populations by several kinds of balancing natural selection. The kind most often discussed is the heterotic selection, operating because of hybrid vigor. There are, indeed, genetic variants which are adaptively favorable when heterozygous and unfavorable when homozygous. The gene which in homozygous condition causes sickle-cell anemia in man is a classical example; in heterozygous condition it confers a relative immunity to falciparum malaria. Perhaps even more important in evolution is diversifying natural selection. This can be explained most simply by pointing out that every living species faces not just one environment but a variety of environments. Human environments are certainly diverse, and moreover the diversity is growing. It is improbable that genes can be found to show optimal performance in all environments. More likely, different genes will be relatively more adaptive in different environments. Genetic variety is a method to cope with variety of environments.

Theoretical arguments cannot settle the questions for how many genes is an average individual heterozygous, and what proportion of the genes are represented by different alleles in different individuals of a species. Geneticists are busy working on these matters. I can cite here only the brilliant work of Lewontin and Hubby (1966), of the University of Chicago, as an example. Since the total number of genes is unknown, but is surely too large to have the whole set examined one by one, Lewontin and Hubby have decided to study what they believe is a random sample of genes. They chose a battery of enzymes that can be detected by electrophoresis in single individuals of the fly, Drosophila pseudoobscura. Some of these enzymes did and others did not show detectable genetic variations. The authors, after making a thorough examination of the possible biases and pitfalls, came to the conclusion that an individual fly was heterozygous for on the average between 10% and 15% of the genes in their sample. The numbers of kinds of genes in a sex cell can hardly be less than 10,000; an average fly may, then, be heterozygous for a number of genes of the order of 1,000.

Do these results have any bearing on man? Although man is not an overgrown Drosophila, he must have as many or more genes than Drosophila does. If the degree of heterozygosity in man is anything like it is in Drosophila, brothers or sisters are quite unlikely to inherit from their parents the same genes. The likelihood that any two unrelated persons are genetically identical is practically nil. Only identical twins may be genetically identical, since they arise by asexual division of a sexually produced fertilized egg. Even there the possibility of mutation and of cytoplasmic difference must be reckoned with. Human nature is, then, not unitary but multiform; the number of human natures is almost as great as the number of humans. Every person is unique, unprecedented, and unrepeatable.

The demonstration of the genetic uniqueness of individuals only opens, rather than solves, the problem as far as behavioral and social sciences are concerned. There seems little point in belaboring the truism that behavior as such is not inherited. Only genes can be inherited, in the sense of being handed down from parents to offspring. Even so, I have mostly division products, true copies of the genes I have inherited from my parents, rather than these genes themselves. The skin color is not inherited either, because the skin pigment is not carried in the sex cells. However, I am yet to meet anybody who would contend that one's genes have nothing to do with one's skin color. Human, as well as animal, behavior is the outcome of a process of development in which the genes and the environment are components of a system of feedback relationships. The same statement can be made equally validly with respect to one's skin color, the shape of one's head, blood chemistry, and somatic, metabolic, and mental diseases.

There are some authors who go so far as to question the existence of problems of genetics of behavior, distinct from genetics of anything else. They are right only inasmuch as there is not likely to exist a special brand of DNA concerned with behavior, different from that in other kinds of genes; moreover there are no genes "for" behavior, as there are no genes "for" the shape of one's nose. The problem is more subtle. It is the problem, or rather problems, of the genetic architecture of behavioral differences. We want to know how many genes are usually involved in such differences, the magnitude of their effects, the nature of their interactions, the parts played by mutation pressure, hybrid vigor, environmental heterogeneities, and by all forms of natural selection in the formation, in maintenance, and in normal and pathological variations of behavior. In this sense, the genetics and the evolution of behavior may well be different from, let us say, the genetics and the evolution of blood chemistry, or of metabolism, or of chromosomal polymorphism, or of concealing colorations, or mimetic resemblances. And in this sense, which is the only meaningful sense, the genetics of behavior, especially the experimental genetics of behavior, is not yet even a

Fig. 1
Dr. Dobzhansky and the classification maze for selection of *Drosophila* flies for geotactic behavior. (The starting tube is on the right. The terminal tubes are on the left, No. 1 being the uppermost, and No. 16 the lowermost.)

fledgling field, although it has recently begun to chirp rather lively.

In this article I can discuss only one example of a study of genetics of behavior, that made by my colleague B. Spassky and myself on phototaxis and geotaxis in *Drosophila pseudoobscura*. Hirsch and his students (Erlenmeyer-Kimling, Hirsch, & Weiss, 1962; Hirsch, 1962; Hirsch & Erlenmeyer-Kimling, 1962) have constructed a classification maze (Figure 1), and selected populations of *Drosophila melanogaster* which were clearly positively and others negatively geotactic in their behavior. They showed furthermore that the genetic basis of this behavior was polygenic, the three large pairs of chromosomes all influencing the result. Hadler (1964a, 1964b) made a similar maze for selection for phototaxis (Figure 2), and succeeded in obtaining positively and negatively phototactic strains of *Drosophila melanogaster*. Dobzhansky and Spassky (1962), using Hirsch's maze, selected positively and negatively geotactic strains of *Drosophila pseudoobscura*. Their starting population was polymorphic for some inverted

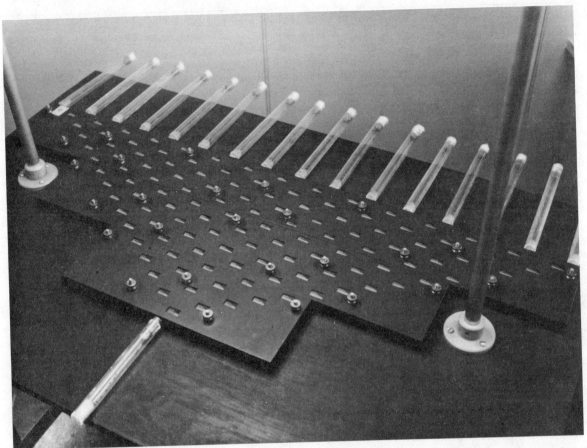

Fig. 2
The classification maze for selection of *Drosophila* flies for phototactic behavior. (The starting tube is on the lower left. The terminal tube No. 1, shown on the upper left, is reached by 15 dark passages. The terminal tube No. 16, the extreme right, is reached by 15 light passages.)

sections in the third chromosomes, and one of the variant chromosomes proved to favor negative geotaxis, while chromosomal heterozygosis favored positive geotaxis.

The results of newer experiments on selection for positive and negative phototaxis and geotaxis in *Drosophila pseudoobscura* are presented in Figures 3 and 4. The ordinates show the phototactic or the geotactic scores, i.e., the averages of the 16 terminal tubes of the mazes into which the flies distribute themselves. On the geotaxis maze the tube No. 1 is the uppermost and No. 16 the lowermost, on the phototaxis maze No. 1 is reached by 15 choices of dark passages and No. 16 by 15 choices of light passages. The selection is made by running through the maze 300 females or 300 males; the 25 most positive, or most negative, individuals of each sex are selected to be the parents of the next generation. The initial populations in our experiments were photo- and geotactically neutral on the average. Or, to be more precise, these initial populations had positive, neutral, and negative individuals in such proportions that the average scores were between 8 and 9 (an average of 8.5 is exact neutrality). After 15 generations of selection, the positively phototactic line had

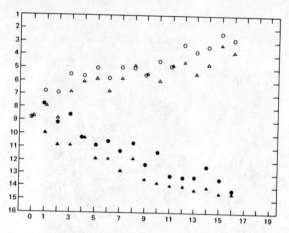

Fig. 3

Selection for negative (light symbols) and positive (dark symbols) phototaxis. (Circles—females, triangles—males. Abscissa—generations of selection, ordinate—the phototactic score.)

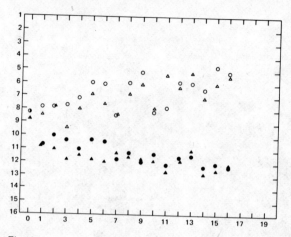

Fig. 4

Selection for negative (light symbols) and positive (dark symbols) geotaxis. (Circles—females, triangles—males. Abscissa—generations of selection, ordinate—the geotactic score.)

average scores 13.4 and 14.5 for females and males respectively, the negatively phototactic line 2.4 and 3.1, the positively geotactic line 12.1 and 12.5, and the negatively geotactic line 4.7 and 6.1. The frequency distributions overlap only slightly in the middle, i.e., only few flies of the selected strains end up in the terminal tubes Nos. 8 and 9.

Is it, then, the heredity which makes a *Drosophila* walk towards lights or darkness, climb up or descend? Even with flies, not only with men, the situation is more complex that that. From the effects of the selection in the first generation, the heritability of the photo- and geotactic responses can be calculated to lie between .15 and .20. This is somewhat oversimplifying the issue, but one can say that, as a first approximation, the genetic component of the behavior of the fly in our mazes is only 15% to 20%, while random chance and environment is responsible for 80% to 85%. Nor is this all. Taking the data for the 15 generations of selection as a whole, we can compute the so-called realized heritability, that is to say the efficiency of the response to the selection. This turns out to be very small, only about 9% for the phototaxis, and only about 3% for the geotaxis. In other words, a prediction of what the selection could accomplish in 15 generations, based on the initial heritability figure, would be a gross overestimate. There are several factors responsible for this situation, among which I shall single out just one, which seems most interesting.

In our first experiments (Dobzhansky & Spassky, 1962) we made selection in three populations of *Drosophila pseudoobscura* during 18 generations for positive and for negative geotaxis. After the positive and the negative populations have diverged about as much as the populations on Figure 4, the populations were split each into two. In one member of each pair the selection was reversed, i.e., a population formerly selected for the positive was now selected for a negative geotaxis, and vice versa. In another subpopulation the selection was relaxed, i.e., the subpopulation was propagated without selecting either the positive or the negative individuals. The selective gains obtained through 18 generations of the original selection were almost erased in 6 generations of the reverse selection. The simple relaxation of the selection resulted in a loss of about half of the selection gains.

A partial, or even complete, loss upon abandonment of selection of what had been gained by previous selection is a phenomenon well known to breeders of agricultural plants and animals. Lerner (1954) has called this the genetic homeostasis. Very simply, the average height, weight, speed of maturation, and many other characteristics of a population which are determined by cooperation of numerous polygenes, are held by natural selection at levels near optimal for the population in the environments in which that population usually lives. When a breeder selects toward higher or toward lower levels of certain characteristics, he does so for his benefit, not necessarily for the benefit of the animal or the plant in its original environments. In other words, the artificial selection is often pitted against natural selection. As the artificial selection progresses it becomes more and more frustrated by natural selection. When the artificial selection is stopped, natural selection is given an opportunity to undo what the artificial one had gained; and reverse selection is highly effective because the artificial and the natural selections then work in the same direction, in alliance rather than in opposition.

Biologically, adaptively, this is an excellent strategy for evolution to follow. It combines high adaptedness to the existing environmental conditions with high adaptability to environmental changes. This strategy is, however, not at all what the classical theory of genetic population structure envisages. If the environment were uniform, constant, and favoring phototactically and geotactically neutral Drosophilae, then the simplest solution of the adaptive problem would seem to be to make all members of the species homozygous for the genes favoring photo- and geotactic neutrality. "Normal" or "typical" flies would then be neutral, and positive and negative ones would be abnormal or atypical. But this is not what is observed. The populations, though neutral on the average, contain also positive and negative genetic variants.

The availability in the populations of this genetic variance confers upon them evolutionary plasticity. A change in the environment that favors a positive or a negative photo- or geotaxis makes the population respond rapidly by adaptive genetic changes. Such responses might occur also in a genetically uniform and homozygous population, but they would be much slower. They would have to wait for the occurrence of mutations. These mutations would have to produce genetic variants which were unfavorable in the old but adaptive in the new environments. The rapidity of the genetic adjustment is, however, not the whole story. A genetically polymorphic population not only responds adaptively to environmental challenges, but in so doing it does not, so to speak, burn the bridges for retreat. It is hedged against the contingency that the environmental change to which it is adapting may only be a temporary one. If it is indeed temporary, and the

original environment returns, the population can readapt itself speedily, by returning to its former genetic composition.

And yet genetic homeostasis does not stand in the way of permanent, irreversible, progressive evolutionary changes. If a new environment or a new way of life endures, a new genetic system becomes stabilized. This genetic system will be buffered against the vagaries of the new environments, but no longer able to retrace its steps to the conditions of the bygone age. If these conditions returned, the species would probably become adapted to them in some new way. One of the most interesting lessons that evolutionary biology teaches us is that there may be many more than a single method to eke out a living from an environment. Major evolutionary changes are irreversible and unrepeatable.

This point is so central that it must be reiterated: Man is not just an overgrown Drosophila. We reject the belief that man is nothing but an animal. Yet he is, among other things, also an animal. Like Drosophila, he is a sexually reproducing, outbreeding species, and his populations are abundantly provided with genetic variability. The genetic diversity affects all kinds of traits—morphological, physiological, and behavioral. The discrete, clear-cut, and usually pathological genetic variations of behavior, such as the so-called Mongoloid idiocy or phenylketonuria, need not be considered in the present discussion. The genetic variations among healthy persons are no less interesting, though much harder to study. The same situation exists also in Drosophila: sharp, easily distinguishable, and poorly viable mutants of classical genetics, versus slight, quantitative, polygenic variations. The difficulty, in human as well as in Drosophila genetics, arises because in the phenotypic variance of the second kind of traits the genetic and the environmental influences are intermingled.

Neither in the most highly selected, nor in the unselected, photo- or geotactic lines of Drosophila is the behavior of an individual rigidly determined. We have seen that the heritability of these behavioral traits is rather low. Whether at a given point of the maze an individual climbs upwards or downwards, takes a light or a dark passage, is in part a matter of environment, or simply of chance. The evidence is nevertheless conclusive that the genotype does bias the choices. Some flies are inclined to walk more often upward and others downward. Are the behavioral traits in human populations also conditioned by genetic variations? I shall be among the first to insist that the evidence is incomplete, and that more data must be collected. Yet the existing evidence, for a variety of traits ranging from IQ measurements to smoking habits, indicates that at least some genetic conditioning is involved, of course relatively more for some traits and less for others.

It is no secret that the study of the genetic conditioning of human behavior is hampered by the emotional reactions which this issue elicits in many people. Some wish to give an aura of scientific respectability to their race and class biases. Differences in material well-being and in social position are represented as just and necessary outcomes of the genetic differences. Others cling obstinately to the old tabula rasa theory. Man is a product of his environment and social conditions, and his genes are simply irrelevant. I submit that, irrespectively of your preconceptions, modern biology makes it necessary to state the problems of genetic conditioning of behavior in terms rather different from the traditional ones. This is because one of the most significant changes in the biological theory in the recent decades has been a shift from typological to populational models and concepts. This conceptual reformation has been discussed with admirable clarity and discernment, particularly by Simpson (1961) and by Mayr (1963), making it possible to state what is essential for us here very briefly.

To a typologist, what is real and important is the species or the race to which an organism belongs. Differences among individuals of the same species and race are, of course, too obvious to be denied. A typologist regards them, however, as merely a kind of troublesome noise in the biological system. He tries, as it were, to recognize the melody obfuscated by the noise; he seeks to identify, classify, and name the species and the races. He hopes that once he can determine to which species and race an individual belongs, that individual is thereby adequately described.

A populationist, on the contrary, regards the individuals and their diversity as the prime observable reality. The biological validity of species and races is not thereby refuted (although some extremists try to do just that, in my opinion ill advisedly). Species and races are, however, derivative from individuals, not the other way around. Species and races are Mendelian populations, reproductive communities of sexually reproducing organisms, forms of adaptive ordering of systems of individuals, evolved because they have

made the evolutionary feedback processes between the organisms and their environments most efficient and successful.

Man in the street is a spontaneous typologist. To him, all things which have the same name are therefore alike. All men have the human nature, and an alleged wisdom has it that the human nature does not change. All Negroes are alike because of their negritude, and all Jews are alike because of their jewishness. Populationists affirm that there is no single human nature but as many human natures as there are individuals. Human nature does change. Race differences are compounded of the same ingredients as differences among individuals which compose a race. In fact, races differ in relative frequencies of genes more often than they differ qualitatively, one race being homozygous for a certain gene and the other lacking it entirely. The extremists who deny that races exist are disappointed typologists who have discovered for themselves the gene gradients between race populations. They fail to understand that such gradients elucidate the nature of race as a biological phenomenon; the facts warrant the conclusion that Platonic types of races do not exist, not that races do not exist.

The typological and populational operational approaches are characteristically different. A race of typology is described in terms of means or averages of height, weight, cephalic index, intelligence, etc. Populationists regard variances at least as important as means. Genetic variance characterizes not only the status but also the evolutionary possibilities of a population. The *Drosophila* populations with which Hirsch and his colleagues as well as ourselves began our experiments were photo- and geotactically neutral on the average. Yet the experiments have shown that the average neutrality did not mean that all individuals were neutral. Selection has attested the presence in the populations of genetic elements for positive and negative photo- and geotaxis. This does not quite mean that the original populations contained individuals as sharply positive and negative as are individuals of the selected strains. Natural and artificial selection do not act as simple sieves which isolate genotypes which were there before selection. Selection creates novelty, because it compounds genotypes the origin of which without selection would be altogether improbable.

All human beings have certain universally recognized rights because they are members of the species Homo sapiens. Members of other species do not have the same rights. Cows are sacred to Hindus, but even in India cows are not treated exactly like humans. An imaginative French writer, Vercors, has given a thought-provoking discussion of legal and other problems that might arise if a hybrid of man and some anthropoid species were produced. Anyway, membership in a group, be that a species or a race, does not define all the characteristics of individuals. The notion that it does is implicit in race pride, exclusiveness, and bias.

Racists busy themselves attempting to scrape up any kind of evidence that Race X has a lower mean IQ, or smaller mean brain volume, or greater emotionality than Race Y. How large is the genetic component in such differences is questionable. The partitioning of the genetic and environmental variances obtained through studies on monozygotic and dizygotic twins cannot be used as a measure of the genetic and environmental components of the group differences. The basic assumption of the twin method is that the environments of the cotwins are uniform. This is obviously not true when different social classes, castes, and races are compared. Even if we had much more complete data on twins than are actually available, this would still leave the question of the magnitude of the genetic component in the group differences wide open. The argument that about one-half of the interracial variance in IQ must be genetic because this appears to be so among cotwins is a misinterpretation when it is not an intentional obfuscation.

To say that we do not know to what extent group differences in psychological traits are genetic is not the same as saying that the genetic component does not exist. It is a challenge to find out. If individuals within populations vary in some character, be that blood grouping, or stature, or intelligence, it is quite unlikely that the population means will be exactly the same. What matters is how great is the intrapopulational variance compared to the interpopulational variance. This is different for different characters. Skin pigmentation is individually variable in probably all races, but the interracial variance is evidently larger. Although precise data are not available, it is at least probable that the relation is reversed for psychological traits. In simplest terms, the brightest individuals in every class, caste, and race are undoubtedly brighter than the average in any other class, caste, or race. And vice versa—the dullest individuals in any of these groups are duller than the average of any group. There are sound biological reasons why this should be so. Very briefly, in the evolution of mankind the natural selection has worked, nearly always and everywhere, to increase and to maintain the behavioral plasticity and diversity, which are essential in all human cultures, primitive as well as advanced.

True enough, an individual taken from a population with a higher mean of some trait, say a higher intelligence, has a higher statistical probability to possess this trait more developed than an individual from a population with a lower mean. When we select *Drosophilae* for stronger or weaker photo- or geotaxis, we generally breed the high and the low selection lines separately. Spassky and myself have, however, some experiments in progress, in which pairs of populations exchange migrants in every generation. The migrants are selected for high or for low photo- or geotaxis or for some other genetically conditioned trait. This may be considered to represent to some extent an experimental simulation of social mobility in human populations. The preliminary results of these experiments are, at least to us, fascinating. Genetically selective social mobility seems to be a powerful evolutionary agent.

A day may conceivably arise when mankind will embark on some all-out eugenical breeding program. This day is not yet in sight, because mankind has not reached a level of wisdom when it could decide with anything approaching unanimity what combination of genetic qualities should the ideal man have. It is rather easier to agree what qualities he should not have. As for positive ideals, we can only recommend that a diversity of tastes, preferences, abilities, and temperaments should be preserved and perhaps even increased. Anyway, when we consider the social implications of the human genetic diversity we are not usually preoccupied with eugenical breeding programs. The genetic diversity is, for example, most relevant to educational problems. The students are, however, selected for study, not for stud.

Insofar as the genetic component is concerned, the intelligence, or temperament, or special abilities of the parents have little predictive value for these qualities in an individual child. This does not mean that such genetic components do not exist, as some authors have overhastily concluded. It means two things. First, the heritability is fairly low, as it is low in the photo- and geotactic behavior of our flies. In other words, the environmental variance is high, and in man the parent-offspring similarities in behavioral traits may well be due more to the cultural than to the biological inheritance. Second, one cannot too often be reminded of the fact that we do not inherit the genotypes of our parents but only one half of their genes. The genes do not produce their effects in development each independently of the others. The genes interact; the genetic "nature" of an individual is an emergent product of the particular pattern or constellation of the genes he carries. This is often the reason why a child is sometimes so strikingly dissimilar to his parents in some traits, even if the environment is kept constant.

How can I summarize the contents of this article, which is itself a summary of thinking concerning a variety of issues? Perhaps the best way is to say that genetics bears out John Dewey's emphasis of "the infinite diversity of active tendencies and combinations of tendencies of which an individual [human] is capable."

References

Dobzhansky, T., & Spassky, B. Selection for geotaxis in monomorphic and polymorphic populations of *Drosophila pseudoobscura. Proceedings of the National Academy of Science*, 1962, *48*, 1704–1712.

Erlenmeyer-Kimling, L., Hirsch, J., & Weiss, J. M. Studies in experimental behavior genetics. III. Selection and hybridization analyses of individual differences in the sign of geotaxis. *Journal of Comparative and Physiological Psychology*, 1962, *55*, 722–731.

Hadler, N. Genetic influence on phototaxis in *Drosophila melanogaster. Biological Bulletin*, 1964, *126*, 264–273. (a)

Hadler, N. Heritability and phototaxis in *Drosophila melanogaster. Genetics*, 1964, *50*, 1269–1277. (b)

Hirsch, J. Individual differences in behavior and their genetic basis. In E. L. Bliss, *Roots of behavior*. New York: Harper, 1962. Pp. 3–23.

Hirsch, J., & Erlenmeyer-Kimling, L. Studies in experimental behavior genetics. IV. Chromosome analyses for geotaxis. *Journal of Comparative and Physiological Psychology*, 1962, *55*, 732–739.

Lerner, I. M. *Genetic homeostasis*. Edinburgh & London: Oliver & Boyd, 1954.

Lewontin, R. C., & Hubby, J. L. A molecular approach to the study of genic heterozygosity in natural populations. *Genetics*. 1966, *54*, 595–609.

Mayr, E. *Animal species and evolution*. Cambridge: Harvard University Press, 1963.

Simpson, G. G. *Principles of animal taxonomy*. New York: Columbia University Press, 1961.

One of the basic problems in the psychology and physiology of sensation is that of the mechanism by which different sensory qualities are perceived. The classical dictum on this problem was propounded by Johannes Mueller in his doctrine of the Specific Energies of Nerves. Actually Charles Bell had enunciated (Carmichael, 1926) the principle somewhat earlier, but Mueller's version is better known. This doctrine made clear that "We are aware of the state of our nerves, not of the external stimulus itself." The eye, however stimulated, gives rise to sensations of light; the ear, to sensations of sound; and taste buds, to sensations of taste.

The further extension of the doctrine of Specific Nerve Energies to the different sensation qualities within a single modality was made by Helmholtz. According to his place theory of hearing, the perception of a particular pitch was attributed to the activity at a particular region of the basilar membrane of the inner ear; stimulation of individual nerve fibers at these specific locations gave rise to unique tonal qualities of pitch. *Pitch* depended upon *which* nerve fiber was activated (Boring, 1950). In the less complex modalities, like the cutaneous or gustatory senses, von Frey and his school propounded the view of "modalities within modalities." The cutaneous sense was said to consist of separate modalities: touch, pressure, warm, cold, and pain, each with their specific receptors. The history of research on cutaneous sensitivity is, in large measure, a history of the search for such receptors. In taste the "BIG FOUR" are familiar to all; the qualities, salty, sour, bitter, and sweet, were each mediated by a specific receptor type.

the afferent code for sensory quality [1]

carl pfaffmann
brown university

Implicit in these formulations is an isomorphism between receptor structure and phenomenology. Pure sensation as a basic psychological entity was to be reduced to a physiological entity. Psychology (at least a part thereof) was to be "explained" by the underlying physiology, hence, "Physiological Psychology." This formulation, simple and direct, dominated the field of sensory psychology from the beginning with only an occasional and sporadic dissenting voice. The fact that the psychological entities were only postulated and the question of whether they were, in fact, valid were almost forgotten in the search for the "real thing."

Many of the more recent findings in sensory psychology and physiology derive from the application of

1. Presented as part of the Presidential Address to the Division of Experimental Psychology at the APA Annual Convention, September 3, 1957. Reprinted from *American Psychologist*, 1959, Vol. 14, pp. 226–232. Copyright 1959 by the American Psychological Association, and reproduced by permission.

electrophysiology to the study of sensory processes. The publication of E. D. Adrian's *The Basis of Sensation* in 1928 opened a new era. The invention of the electronic tube, appropriate amplifying circuits, and recording instruments made it possible to study directly the activity of the sense organs and their nerves. Since 1928, the advances in technique and instrumentation have been so dramatic that there is almost no part of the nervous system that cannot be probed by the inquisitive microelectrode. Psychologists have played a significant role in this development. One of their best known early discoveries was that of Wever and Bray (1930), on the cochlea and VIIIth nerve.

This paper will review some experiments with this procedure on another sense, that of taste, and will discuss their general implications for the theory of afferent coding.[2] It should be emphasized that sensation itself is not being studied. Rather the investigator "taps in" on the "basis of sensation" by recording and amplifying the nerve impulse traffic in the sensory fibers "en route" to the brain.

The sense of taste is particularly well suited to this problem because it consists of well defined differentiated structures, the taste buds, which are capable of mediating quite different sensory qualities, but the array of qualities and dimensions is not too complex for interpretation. The afferent message from receptor to brain can be studied directly in the afferent nerve fibers from the tongue, for the primary sensory nerve fibers from the receptive organs are relatively accessible with no synaptic complexities in the direct line from the receptors except for the junction between sense cell and sensory fiber.

The taste stimulus, like all stimuli, acts first upon a receptor cell. Changes in the receptor cell in turn activate or "trigger" impulses in the nerve fiber. Both the sense cell, as well as the nerve fiber, and in fact all living cells are like tiny batteries with a potential difference across the cell membrane. When stimulated, this membrane is depolarized, and it is this depolarization that can be recorded. Figure 1 schematizes such recording from a single sensory nerve fiber shown in contact with a receptor cell to the left of the figure and entering the central nervous system (CNS) to the right. The recording electrodes on the fiber connect with an

2. Many of our experiments on taste were supported by a contract with the Office of Naval Research.

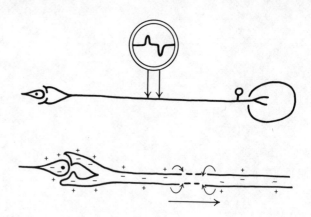

Fig. 1

Diagram of electrophysiological recording from a single sensory nerve fiber. Upper diagram shows a single fiber in contact with a single sense cell to the left. A diphasic response on the cathode ray tube is shown as an impulse passes the recording electrodes en route to the central nervous system schematized to the right. The lower figure shows in more detail the positive and negative charges around the cell membranes associated with the passage of the nerve impulse.

appropriate recording device such as a cathode ray oscillograph shown schematically. As the impulse passes the first electrode, there is an upward deflection; as it passes the second electrode, there is a downward deflection. By an appropriate arrangement, a single or monophasic deflection only may be obtained so that at each passage of an impulse there will be a "spike" on the oscillograph tracing. The lower figure shows schematically the electrical activity associated with the passage of a nerve impulse. The message delivered along any single nerve fiber therefore consists of a train of impulses; changes in excitation of the receptor are signaled by changes in the frequency of this train. Thus, changes in strength of solution bathing the tongue change the frequency of impulse discharge per second. In any one fiber, the size of the impulse is nearly constant. The sensory nerve message, therefore, is a digital process.

Figure 2 shows a typical series of oscillograph tracings obtained from a *single* nerve fiber when different concentrations of sodium chloride are applied to the tongue of the rat. The "spikes" signal the passage of each impulse past the recording electrode. With stronger stimuli there is a higher frequency of dis-

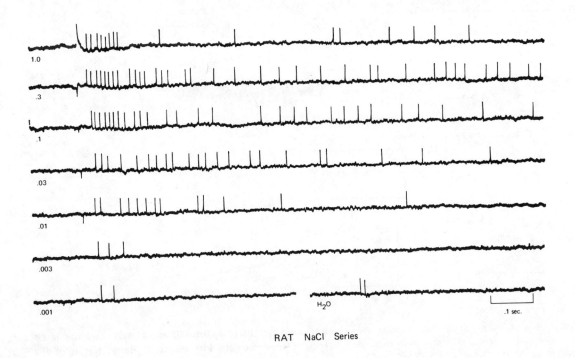

1.0

.3

.1

.03

.01

.003

.001   H₂O   .1 sec.

RAT NaCl Series

Fig. 2
A series of oscillograph tracings obtained from a single taste nerve fiber when different concentrations of salt solution are placed on the tongue. Note that water as well as .001 M NaCl will elicit two impulses. A concentration of .003 M NaCl will elicit three impulses and may be considered as threshold. (Reproduced from the *Journal of Neurophysiology*.)

charge. Threshold for this fiber lies at approximately 0.003 M. Other fibers will show similar behavior, but may possess higher thresholds for the tongue contains a population of taste receptors with thresholds of differing value.

This description applies to the impulse in the single sensory nerve fiber. Actually, the sensory nerve is a cable, made up of many different fibers each connected with one or more receptor cells. The single fiber recordings shown were obtained after the nerve cable had been dissected to a strand containing just one functional unit. Sometimes, the same effect is achieved by using microelectrodes.

The nerve fibers subserving taste travel in three nerves from the mouth region: the lingual, glossopharyngeal, and vagus nerves which contain touch, temperature, pressure, and pain fibers as well as those concerned with taste. The taste fibers from the anterior tongue branch off from the lingual nerve to form the

chorda tympani nerve where it is possible to record almost exclusively from taste nerve fibers. This nerve can be exposed by appropriate surgery in the anesthetized animal and placed on the electrodes leading to the recording apparatus.

A block diagram of the apparatus together with sample records is shown in Figure 3. The integrated record is readily adapted to quantitative treatment by measuring the magnitude of the deflection at each response and so provides a measure of the total activity of all the fibers in the nerve. An index of over-all taste sensitivity can be obtained from such recordings. The curves in Figure 4 are such measures for the cat for quinine, hydrochloric acid, sodium chloride, potassium chloride, and sucrose solutions (Pfaffmann, 1955).

The basic taste stimuli can be arranged in order of thresholds from low to high as follows: quinine, hydrochloric acid, sodium chloride, potassium chloride,

The Afferent Code for Sensory Quality   29

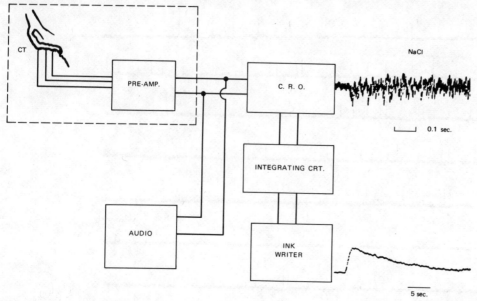

Fig. 3
A block diagram of the recording apparatus showing two types of record. The upper trace shows a typical asynchronous, multifiber discharge from a large number of active fibers; the lower trace shows the integrated record of such activity. (Reproduced from the *American Journal of Clinical Nutrition*.)

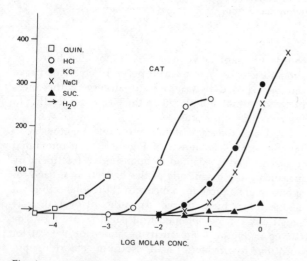

Fig. 4
Curves of taste response in the cat to four different taste stimuli as indicated by the integrated response method. (Reproduced from the *Journal of Neurophysiology*.)

and sucrose. In this animal, as in man, quinine is effective in relatively low concentrations. Sugar at the other end of the scale requires relatively high concentrations, and the electrolytes are intermediate. Sugar produces a nerve response of small magnitude compared with that to other stimuli. Differences in response magnitudes are found from one species to another. In the hamster or guinea pig, for example, sugar will elicit a strong discharge, and other species differences with quinine and the salts have been observed (Beidler, Fishman, & Hardiman, 1955; Pfaffmann, 1953). Recently, Carpenter (1956) has correlated certain of these species differences with behavioral data using the preference method.

The representation in Figure 4 does not show that the animal can distinguish one substance from another. Actually an animal like the rat will avoid quinine and acid, but will show a preference for NaCl and sucrose. To find how the animal can discriminate among different chemicals the single fiber analysis is required.

In the early study of the single gustatory fibers in the cat (Pfaffmann, 1941), three different kinds of fiber were found. One was responsive to sodium chloride and acid, another to quinine and acid, and a third to acid alone. Thus, acid stimulated all receptor-neural units found. This established not only that the gustatory endings were differentially sensitive to different chemicals but that the physiological receptor "types" *did not* correspond to the phenomenal categories as reported by man. In view of the more recently demonstrated species difference, this might not appear to be surprising. But, regardless of what the cat "tastes," these findings pointed to an important principle of sensory coding. This is that *the same afferent fiber may convey different information depending upon the amount of activity in another parallel fiber.* To illustrate, suppose A represents an acid-salt unit and C, an acid sensitive unit, then activity in A only would lead to salty; but activity in that same fiber, A, plus discharge in C would lead to sourness. Recent studies emphasize still another important point, namely, that some stimuli may decrease or inhibit the frequency of sensory discharge. Certain receptors, which can be stimulated by water (as well as other agents), may be inhibited by the application of dilute salt solutions (Liljestrand & Zotterman, 1954). Taste stimuli, therefore, may either increase or decrease, i.e., modulate, the amount of afferent nerve traffic. A diminution in activity may signal, not merely the withdrawal of a particular stimulus, but the application of a different one.

Table 1 taken from a recent paper from Zotterman's laboratory (Cohen, Hagiwara, & Zotterman, 1955) illustrates the afferent code or pattern which may be described for the cat based on a compilation of the "types" so far discovered for that species.

But the use of the term "fiber type" harks back to some of the errors of classical thinking. Types are defined only by the range of stimuli sampled; the wider the range, the more difficult will it be to define pure "types." "Taste types" may turn out to be as varied and individual as "personality types." Figure 5 shows the variety of response patterns of nine single fiber preparations to the following standard test solutions: .03 N HCl, .1 M KCl, .1 M NaCl, .01 M quinine hydrochloride, and 1.0 M sucrose (Pfaffmann, 1955).

The bar graph shows the magnitude of response in each of the single fiber preparations in impulses per second of discharge. The central crosshatched bar graph shows the relative magnitude of response to these same solutions in the integrated response of the whole nerve. It is apparent that the individual fibers do not all have the same pattern. The sum of activity of all fibers is shown by the crosshatched diagram. Furthermore, fiber types are not immediately apparent in this array.

The fact that the individual receptor cells possess combined sensitivity as salt plus acid, or salt plus sugar, cannot be dismissed as the result of multiple innervation of more than one receptor cell by a single fiber. Kimura (Beidler, 1957; Kimura & Beidler, 1956) has studied the sensitivity patterns of the individual taste cells by inserting micropipette electrodes directly into the sense cells themselves. The pattern of sensitivity found in the individual sensory cell is like that already described for the single afferent fiber. Thus, within the individual sense cell there must be different sites which are selectively sensitive to different taste stimuli. These sites on the membrane may be determined by molecular configuration, the shape and size of pores in the membrane, or some such microcellular feature.

One additional principle must be introduced. This is that the relative rather than the absolute amount of activity in any one set of afferent fibers may determine the quality of sensation. Figure 6 shows frequency of discharge as a function of stimulus intensity for two units labelled A and B. Both are stimulated by both stimuli sugar and salt, but it is apparent that A is more sensitive to salt and B to sugar (Pfaffmann, 1955). Once each stimulus intensity exceeds the threshold for a particular receptor unit, the frequency of discharge increases with concentration. Thus the afferent pattern as the code for sensory quality must take account of the changing frequency of discharge with stimulus intensity. The pattern concept may be retained by recognizing that "pattern" is still apparent in the relative amount of activity of different fibers. In the two-fiber example shown in Figure 6, low concentrations of salt

TABLE 1*
Fiber Type Response in the Cat

Stimulus	"Water" fiber	"Salt" fiber	"Acid" fiber	"Quinine" fiber	Sensation evoked
H_2O (salt < 0.03M)	+	0	0	0	→ water
NaCl (0.05M)	0	+	0	0	→ salt
HCl (pH 2.5)	+	+	+	0	→ sour
Quinine	+	0	0	+	→ bitter

* Cf., Cohen, Hagiwara, & Zotterman, 1955.

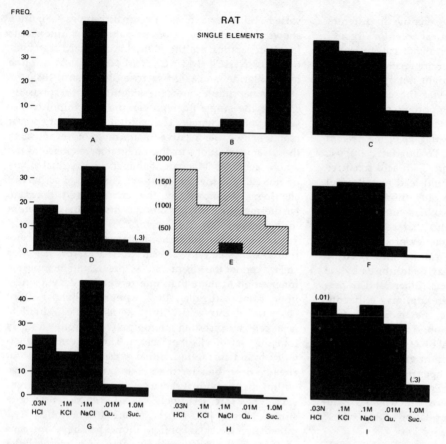

Fig. 5
The pattern of taste responses in nine different single sensory nerve fibers of the rat. The solid bar graphs show the frequency of response in impulses per second for different taste stimuli (indicated along the abscissa). The crosshatched bar graph shows the relative response of the total nerve (integrated response) to these same solutions. (Reproduced from the *Journal of Neurophysiology*.)

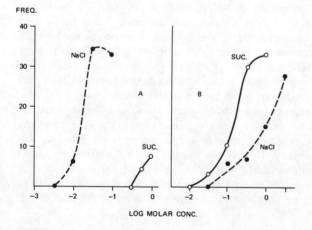

Fig. 6
The relation between frequency of discharge and concentration in two fibers both of which are sensitive to sugar and salt. (Reproduced from the *Journal of Neurophysiology*.)

will discharge only A, higher concentrations will discharge both A and B, but activity in A will be greater than that in B. Low concentrations of sugar will activate only B, higher concentrations will activate both B and A, but B will be greater than A. Thus the sensory code might read:

Frequency Code
A > B = salty
B > A = sweet

where A or B may go to zero. It is not only the activity in parallel fibers that is important; it is the *relative amount* of such parallel activity.

Studies of the other senses indicate that these principles are not unique to taste. In the cutaneous senses there is a variety of different endings which overlap two or more of the classical skin modalities (Maruhashi, Mizuguchi, & Tasaki, 1952). For example, some pressure receptors in the cat's tongue are activated by cold (Hensel & Zotterman, 1951), and there are several different pressure, temperature, and nociceptor endings, some serving large or small areas, some adapting slowly, others rapidly to give a variety of temporal as well as spatial "discriminanda." These findings are reminiscent of Nafe's (1934) quantitative theory of feeling, and the recent anatomical studies of Weddell (1955) and his group are of similar import.

In audition, selective sensitivity among the individual primary afferent fibers is very broad. Those fibers arising from the basal turn of the cochlea respond to tones of any audible frequency; those arising in the upper part respond only to a band of low frequency tones (Tasaki, 1954). Further, it has been suggested (Wever, 1949) that the temporal patterning of the discharge, especially in the low frequencies, provides a basis for pitch discrimination. In vision, Granit (1955) has suggested that different impulse frequencies in the *same* third order neuron from the retina may signal different spectral events at the periphery.

These electrophysiological results should not have been surprising to us. That a particular sensory dimension is not isomorphic with a particular physical dimension is well known. Auditory loudness, functionally dependent upon sound pressure level, is not synonymous with physical intensity. Pitch is not the same as frequency, although the latter is its major determinant (Stevens & Davis, 1938). Visual brightness is not the same as physical luminance. It would, indeed,

have been surprising if similar nonidentities had not been found at the physiological level.

And so in attacking Mueller's classic problem with modern techniques, we have found, at least, within the modalities, a solution different from that which was first anticipated. Differential sensitivity rather than specificity, patterned discharges rather than a mosaic of sensitivities is the form of our modern view. Mueller's principle did not answer a problem so much as it posed one. In the answers that I have attempted to suggest, we see, not only the details of the mechanism for which we have searched, but we can discern broader implications for the principles governing the relation between psychology and physiology. Psychology cannot rest content with a pseudophysiology based solely upon phenomenology. So long as the receptor surface was conceived to be a static mosaic where phenomenal qualities were reified (in some instances in the form of specific anatomical structures), sensory psychology and physiology were reduced to the study of how the "little pictures" were transmitted via the sensory nerves to the "sensorium" located presumably somewhere "inside the head." Such a view is not only out of date, but it diverts our attention from the proper study of the afferent influx, its dynamic properties and interactions and its relevance for all levels of neural intergration and behavioral organization.

References

Adrian, E. D. *The basis of sensation.* New York: Norton, 1928.

Beidler, L. M. Facts and theory on the mechanism of taste and odor perception. In *Chemistry of natural food flavors.* Quartermaster Research and Engineering Center, 1957. Pp. 7–47.

Beidler, L. M., Fishman, I. Y., & Hardiman, C. W. Species differences in taste responses. *Amer. J. Physiol.,* 1955, *181,* 235–239.

Boring, E. G. *A history of experimental psychology.* New York: Appleton-Century-Crofts, 1950.

Carmichael, L. Sir Charles Bell: A contribution to the history of physiological psychology. *Psychol. Rev.,* 1926, *33,* 188–217.

Carpenter, J. A. Species differences in taste preferences. *J. comp. physiol. Psychol.,* 1956, *49,* 139–144.

Cohen, M. J., Hagiwara, S., & Zotterman, Y. The response spectrum of taste fibers in the cat: A single fiber analysis. *Acta. physiol., Scand.,* 1955, *33,* 316–332.

Granit, R. *Receptors and sensory perception.* New Haven: Yale Univer. Press, 1955.

Hensel, H. & Zotterman, Y. The response of mechanoreceptors to thermal stimulation. *J. Physiol.*, 1951, *115*, 16–24.

Kimura, K., & Beidler, L. M. Microelectrode study of taste bud of the rat. *Amer. J. Physiol.*, 1956, *187*, 610.

Liljestrand, G., & Zotterman, Y. The water taste in mammals. *Acta physiol., Scand.*, 1954, *32*, 291–303.

Maruhashi, J., Mizuguchi, K., & Tasaki, I. Action currents in single afferent nerve fibers elicited by stimulation of the skin of the toad and the cat. *J. Physiol.*, 1952, *117*, 129–151.

Nafe, J. P. The pressure, pain and temperature sense. In C. Murchison (Ed.), *Handbook of general experimental psychology.* Worcester: Clark Univer. Press, 1934. Chap. 20.

Pfaffmann, C. Gustatory afferent impulses. *J. cell. comp. Physiol.*, 1941, *17*, 243–258.

Pfaffmann, C. Species differences in taste sensitivity. *Science,* 1953, *117*, 470.

Pfaffmann, C. Gustatory nerve impulses in rat, cat, and rabbit. *J. Neurophysiol.*, 1955, *18*, 429–440.

Stevens, S. S., & Davis, H. *Hearing.* New York: Wiley, 1938.

Taski, I. Nerve impulses in individual auditory nerve fibers of guinea pigs. *J. Neurophysiol.*, 1954, *17*, 97–122.

Weddell, G. Somesthesis and the chemical senses. *Ann. Rev. Psychol.*, 1955, *6*, 119–136.

Wever, E. G. *Theory of hearing.* New York: Wiley, 1949.

Wever, E. G., & Bray, C. W. Action currents in the auditory nerve in response to acoustical stimulation. *Proc. Nat. Acad. Sci.*, 1930, *16*, 344–350.

Reward and drive processes are intricately related to those of learning. Therefore brain studies of reward can be expected to provide a basis or at least an introduction to the study of physiological mechanisms underlying learning. Rewards and drives have been studied with lesions and electric stimulations which usually affected many hundreds of neurons at a time. While the grossness of these methods was not a clearly insuperable obstacle in the study of motivational processes, the methods have not yet proved fruitful in the study of the more detailed aspects of learning. It is possible to suppose that the root of the difficulty lies in our inability, with these methods, to study neurons one at a time or in very small families. Newer single unit studies are therefore currently pursued with the hope of finding by their use a key to the mnemonic aspects of brain function. However, in view of the large number of neurons and areas that might be sampled it has seemed that certain guidelines might be provided if we organized the newer pursuits on the basis of the more solid generalizations distilled from the data obtained with the older methods.

A long and reasonably happy research program was launched in 1953 when a rat fortuitously evidenced a neuronal rewarding effect (see Figure 1) by returning to the place on a table top where it had been when an electrical stimulus was applied to the brain via chronically implanted electrodes (Olds, 1955). The ensuing studies provided not only a neural substrate as a focal point for further study of a key psychological concept, namely the law of effect, but also a stable

the central nervous system and the reinforcement of behavior[1]

james olds
university of michigan

method for studying many brain behavior relationships. On the basis of accomplishments to date, the method bodes well in its own way to prove as fruitful as other well-known landmarks in the behavioral sciences such as Skinner's method for studying operant behavior or Lashley's method for studying discrimination and choice on a jumping stand.

The initial observation led to studies which showed that electrical excitation in a restricted region of the central nervous system caused rats to work

1. Reprints available from author, Brain Research Laboratory, 1121 Catherine Street, University of Michigan, Ann Arbor, Michigan. Reprinted from *American Psychologist*, 1969, Vol. 24. Copyright 1969 by the American Psychological Association and reproduced by permission.

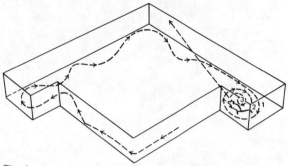

Fig. 1
The accidental discovery of brain-stimulated reward. (A rat exploring the edges of this table-top enclosure was electrically brain stimulated in one small subdivision and repeatedly came back for more. The dotted line pointing upward represents the connection to the stimulator.)

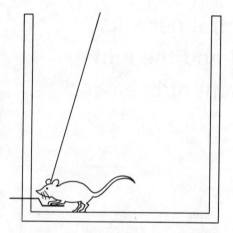

Fig. 2
The self-stimulation experiment. (By depressing a lever the animal delivers a brief electric shock to the appropriate point in the brain.)

steadily at arbitrarily assigned tasks (see Figure 2) in order to obtain the electric stimulus (Olds & Milner, 1954). The behavior was easily reproducible from animal to animal, it was sustained during extended periods of testing, and it was not accompanied by any other obvious pathological signs. It seemed, therefore,

possible to view this self-stimulation behavior as evidence of an artificial activation of the brain's normal positive reinforcement mechanism. This discovery has led to much research in our laboratory and has instigated parallel investigations in many other laboratories. At first much of this work was related to the question of whether we were being fooled by the data (see Figure 3). Was this a psychologically valid reward or merely a sham having the appearance but not the substance of a positive emotional effect? Experiments showed that animals would improve performance in a maze, running faster and eliminating errors from trial to trial, in order to arrive at the goal point where stimulation was administered (Olds, 1956). Twenty-three hours after a previous brain stimulation they would run purposefully through the maze without errors and without dalliance. In an obstruction box animals repeatedly crossed an electrified grid which applied aversive shock to the feet in order to obtain brain rewards (Olds, 1961). In performance tests when a choice between food and brain stimulation rewards was presented to hungry rats, they often chose brain rewards and underwent the danger of starvation (Routtenberg & Lindy, 1965). In a Skinner box animals would press one bar 50 or even 100 times in order to gain access to a second bar with which they could stimulate their brains (Pliskoff, Wright, & Hawkins, 1965). In extinction experiments, animals which had learned to press one of two pedals for brain rewards continued to press that pedal in preference to the other for days after the brain rewards were discontinued (Koenig, 1967). All of these tests fostered a positive answer to the question of whether this was a psychologically valid reward.

The anatomical study of brain rewards showed a relatively unified system to be involved (see Figure 4) consisting of the "old" olfactory cortex, nearby nuclear masses, and the hypothalamus which is a descending extension of this system connecting it to parts of the midbrain (Olds & Olds, 1963). The upper or cortical parts of this system had previously been correlated by neurological evidence and speculation with "emotional experience" (Papez, 1937). The lower part, that is, the hypothalamus, had been connected by experimental work with the control of consummatory responses and basic drives related to food, water, sex, temperature, and so forth (Miller, 1958; Stellar, 1954).

The pattern of anatomical distributions of brain reward effects was the same in many different animals

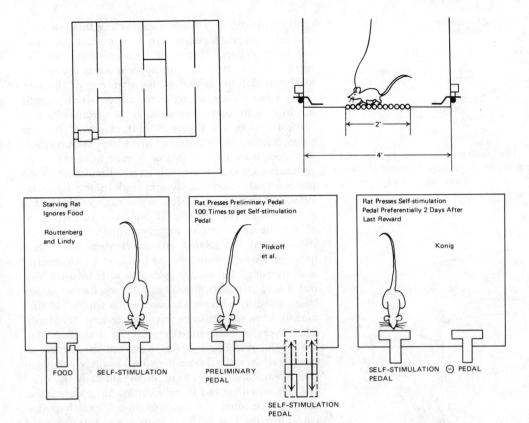

Fig. 3
Methods for validating the brain reward. (Animals learned to run from the apron to the pedal of the maze without errors in order to stimulate their brains. They repeatedly crossed the foot-shock grid in order to obtain brain stimulation. Hungry rats—Routtenberg & Lindy, 1965—chose brain stimulation over food and starved. In ratio tests—Pliskoff et al., 1965—rats pressed one pedal many times in order to acquire a self-stimulation pedal. In extinction tests—Koenig, 1967—rats pressed the self-stimulation significantly more than the non-self-stimulation pedal even two days after the last reward.)

including cats, monkeys, and man:

Self-Stimulation in Various Animals

1. Fish   Boyd and Gardner, 1962
2. Chick   Andrew, 1967
3. Rat   Olds and Olds, 1963
4. Rabbit   Bruner, 1967
5. Cat   Wilkenson and Peele, 1963
6. Dog   Stark and Boyd, 1963
7. Goat   Persson, 1962
8. Monkey   Bursten and Delgado, 1958
9. Dolphin   Lilly and Miller, 1962
10. Human being Bishop, Elder, and Heath, 1963

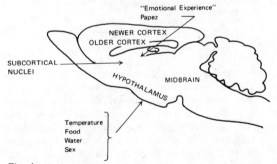

Fig. 4
Brain map with arrows indicating the parts of the brain involved in reward and titles indicating other functions ascribed to these areas.

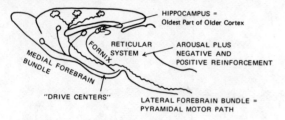

Fig. 5
Map showing the two main pathways connecting the self-stimulation areas, the medial forebrain bundle, and the fornix, and their relation to the descending motor pathway and the reticular "arousal" areas.

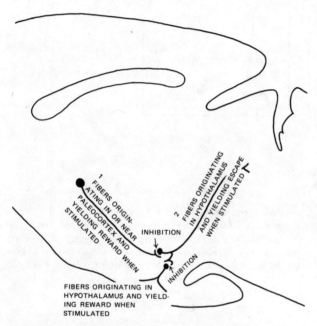

Fig. 6
Partly speculative picture of the connections in the posterior nucleus of the hypothalamus. (Fibers of the medial forebrain bundle, one,—from paleocortex—inhibit neurons of the periventricular system, two,—which project toward the reticular systems. The two fibers give off collaterals which inhibit a group of neurons originating in hypothalamus whose axons travel in the medial forebrain bundle—side by side with those coming down from paleocortex. These axons might carry integrated motivational messages—with positive reinforcements added and negative reinforcements subtracted—toward behavioral control mechanisms.)

The main two pathways connecting this relatively unified system together are the medial forebrain bundle (Kappers, Huber, & Crosby, 1936) and the fornix (Nauta, 1956). In the hypothalamus the medial forebrain bundle, which is the main one of the two, forms a relatively compact lateral hypothalamic bundle but in anterior parts it fans out to the various olfactory cortical centers (see Figure 5). In it, messages from the paleocortex seem to converge upon hypothalamus and messages from hypothalamus diverge to cortex. After rewarding effects were obtained by stimulating in the paleocortical emotional system and in the hypothalamic drive system which were connected by the medial forebrain bundle, it was not surprising to obtain the same effects by stimulating some parts of the anatomically related reticular system which had been previously shown to be involved in awakening and arousing the animal (Moruzzi & Magoun, 1949). But it was paradoxical to obtain these positive effects by stimulating some of the same areas which had previously been shown to be involved in neurally stimulated aversive behavior (Delgado, Roberts, & Miller, 1954). The rewarding effects were not very stable or intense when evoked from the mixed positive and negative areas, and they were often similarly mild or variable when evoked in paleocortex. They were stable and intense when evoked from the lateral hypothalamic bundle, that is, the compact part of the medial forebrain bundle. These are some of the same areas which have been called drive centers on the basis of other investigations. Therefore, we have thought that the hypothalamic drive centers are the main focus of the brain-stimulated reward effect.

The relations between brain-stimulated positive reinforcement and similarly stimulated negative reinforcement or pain behavior were clarified to some degree in a series of experiments.

In one hypothalamic center (see Figure 6) with three connecting pathways, stimulation of the first yielded positive reinforcement, stimulation of the second yielded negative reinforcement, and stimulation of the third yielded positive reinforcement again (Olds & Olds, 1963; Roberts, 1958). Stimulation of the center itself yielded mixed positive-negative effects. It was appealing to suppose that such a center receiving plus and minus emotional inputs might give rise to a set of output messages which would reflect the integrated sum of the organism's emotional state at a

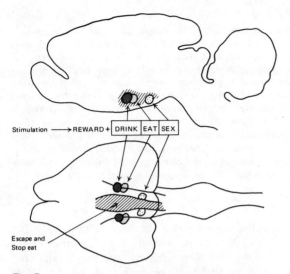

Fig. 7
Schematic map of medial area where stimulation causes eating to stop, and lateral areas where stimulation causes eating, drinking, and sexual behaviors.

given time and which would be effective in determining later behavior.

In keeping with the theory that interaction occurred, we found that stimulation of reward pathway number one inhibited behavior driven by escape pathway number two (Routtenberg & Olds, 1963). Stimulation of escape pathway number two inhibited behavior induced by stimulating reward pathway three (Olds & Olds, 1962). Stimulation at number three did not inhibit anything, but lesions here impaired both self-stimulation and escape behavior so we supposed that this might be the common pathway between reward and punishment (Olds & Olds, 1964). Because stimulation in this pathway itself yielded self-stimulation, we concluded that reward was an active excitatory or incremental process in these neurons, and negative reinforcement might be a negative inhibitory process in the same group.

Because of time limitations I will bypass details and go on to a discussion of the second important series of interaction studies, namely, those relating neural rewards to the basic drives. In midline hypothalamic centers (see Figure 7), lesions have been found by previous investigators to cause overeating and obesity (Brobeck, 1946). Here also, electric stimulation

caused cessation of eating (Wyrwicka & Dobrzecka, 1960). Because this stimulus terminated feeding it seemed that it might be drive reducing and rewarding. In fact, there were only aversive effects of stimulating this part of the hypothalamus (Krasne, 1962). In a more lateral area, lesions caused starvation (Anand & Brobeck, 1951) and electric stimulation caused animals to work for food and to eat even when satiated (Miller, 1960). Because this seemed to be a drive-inducing stimulus it was expected to have aversive properties. The finding again was quite the opposite. Stimulating at these feeding center points was often rewarding (Margules & Olds, 1962). Our first interpretation of this was to guess that the stimulation induced not a drive but a consummatory response and therefore might well be rewarding. However, stimulation here caused not only eating of food when food was available but also working for food when food was absent (Miller, 1960). This belied the supposition that these were mere consummatory centers and suggested that there was the induction by stimulation at these points of something very much like the hunger drive itself. The association of neural reward in its strongest form with brain points where basic drives were also induced was later confirmed by other experiments which found drinking and self-stimulation to be induced by stimulation in some nearby brain areas (Mogenson & Stevenson, 1966) and sexual responding and self-stimulation in others (Caggiula & Hoebel, 1966; Herberg, 1963). Thus, the common denominator between many drive-inducing points was the fact that their stimulation was quite often rewarding to the animal.

In trying to make sense out of the feeding data, it was easy to imagine that medial hypothalamic satiety caused an aversive condition of the organism which brought eating to a halt. While this reversed a priori notions about relations between satiety and reward, it was not out of harmony with everyday experience which indicates that eating ceases to be rewarding and even becomes aversive when the animal eats too much. Second, during a meal or between meals there might be a middle condition in which eating would induce rewarding effects and these might induce further eating. This also might be out of harmony with the a priori notions about connections between hunger and negative factors, but it was in harmony with experience which shows that food often is positively reinforcing and simultaneously induces further

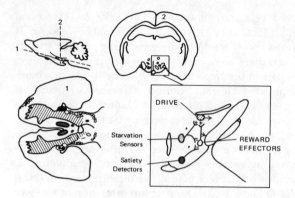

Fig. 8

Horizontal and transverse sections of rat brain with indications on a midline sagittal section showing where slices were made to get the two sections. (On the horizontal section—one—the medial forebrain bundle is cross-hatched, the so-called medial hypothalamic satiety center is black, and the lateral hypothalamic "feeding center" is shown by an open circle. On the enlarged part of the transverse section—two—a medial "satiety" neuron is shown in black, a lateral "food reward" neuron is shown as an open circle, a medial "starvation" neuron is colored gray, and a dorsal "drive" neuron is dotted. Minus signs indicate supposed inhibitory relations, and plus signs indicate supposed excitatory relations.)

hunger. What was missing was a center representing the other extreme from satiety, namely starvation. It seemed that we should find somewhere in the hypothalamus an area where stimulation would be aversive but would also induce eating. In recent research we believe we have found this center in the dorsal part of the medial hypothalamic area (see Figure 8). Here, not too far from the lateral hypothalamic feeding center, instrumental and consummatory feeding responses were induced by electric stimulation together with aversive behavior. In another dorsal area, not too far from this, stimulation induced eating with no reinforcing side effects at all. We have thought that both satiety and starvation centers might inhibit a lateral hypothalamic food-reward center. And both the lateral hypothalamic food-reward center and the starvation center might excite a dorsal drive center.

Hypothalamic reward centers related to other drives such as sex or temperature regulation might have equally complex relations but they would not need to be parallel to these. Each drive must have its own problems.

Studies which involved lesions were aimed at finding the input and output pathways of the hypothalamic reward areas.

In our laboratory we (Olds & Olds, 1964) found that lesions in or near the lateral hypothalamic fiber bundle or the neighboring parts of the descending pyramidal tract impaired or abolished self-stimulation behavior provoked by other electrodes far away but in the same bundle (see Figure 9).

Similar lesions in or near this bundle have been found in other laboratories to abolish feeding, drinking, and instrumental avoidance behaviors (Ba-

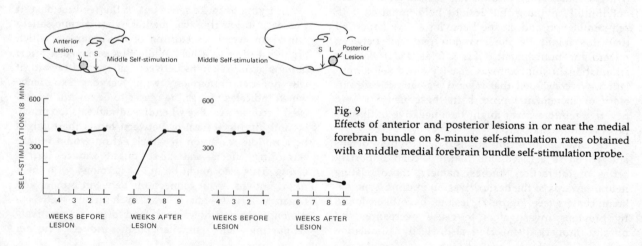

Fig. 9
Effects of anterior and posterior lesions in or near the medial forebrain bundle on 8-minute self-stimulation rates obtained with a middle medial forebrain bundle self-stimulation probe.

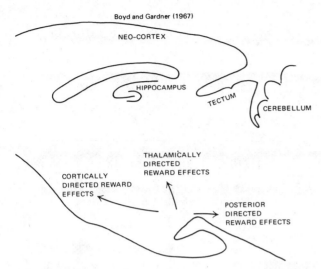

Fig. 10
Lesion studies of Boyd and Gardner (1967) showed that lesions at each of the three arrows caused attenuation of hypothalamic self-stimulation suggesting the possibility of rewarding effects directed in three directions away from the lateral hypothalamic area.

linska, Romaniut, and Wyrwicka, 1964; Teitelbaum & Epstein, 1962). In fact, animals with bilateral lesions in these areas often performed no instrumental behaviors and sometimes died. I believe that the only reason our animals survived was that lesions were placed only on the self-stimulated side of the brain, the other half remaining to support necessary feeding and drinking behaviors.

Another set of recently reported experiments (Boyd & Gardner, 1967) suggested that there are three significant pathways passing out of the hypothalamus (see Figure 10); one downstream through the midbrain, one frontward toward the paleocortex or neocortex, and one directly upward toward the thalamus. Lesions in any of these three caused marked attenuation but not total abnegation of hypothalamic self-stimulation behavior. These observations suggested the view that there might be several different areas in the brain where reward traces might cause critical neural events in behavior modification and that all of these areas might function simultaneously and redundantly.

The second set of methods that were applied to the problem of the significant inputs and outputs to the supposed reinforcing centers were electrophysiological ones.

In a set of newly reported electrophysiological studies (Kawamura, Funakoshi, & Kasahara, 1968), neurons have been recorded from medial hypothalamus during aversive stimulation of the tongue by means of 6% salt solution and during aversive stimulation of the animal by means of electric shock (see Figure 11). Medial hypothalamic neurons in the posterior nucleus of hypothalamus where aversive effects were obtained from electrical stimulation were augmented in their firing rate by aversive stimuli. In the same studies, neurons in lateral hypothalamus were slowed by the aversive gustatory and electric shock stimuli.

Two reports from other laboratories (Ball, 1968; MacDonnell & Flynn, 1966) have appeared which suggest that hypothalamic stimulation might have its effect by modulating the influence of peripheral reflex-inducing stimuli. One might guess from these that hypothalamic stimulation in some cases attenuated aversive effects of peripheral stimulation, and in the other case the hypothalamic stimulation perhaps lowered the threshold of consummatory responses.

My own belief is that before one ascribes the reinforcing effects of hypothalamic stimulation to a modulating effect on peripheral stimulation it would be wise to look further for direct hypothalamic influences on other mechanisms of the brain in the supposition that the internal influences themselves might often mediate reinforcement more directly.

With a view to demonstrating such internal processes, we have carried out experiments in which we have tried to reward the animal for making responses with its brain (see Figure 12). The most recent experiments (Olds, 1965, 1967) were carried out in freely behaving animals with chronically implanted microelectrodes used for recording the responses of single brain neurons. Several probes were implanted in each animal and sometimes action potentials were recorded simultaneously from more than one probe. Hungry animals were rewarded with food pellets. The operant response required was first that the animal should stand quite still. While standing still the animal was required to generate a drastically increased firing rate of a particular neuron. A discriminative stimulus (often a light)

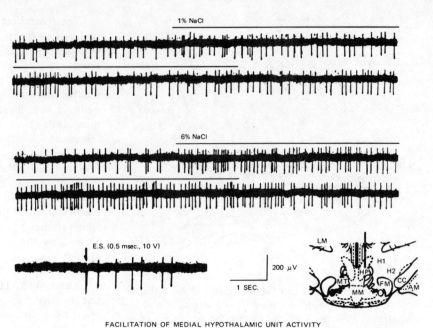

1% NaCl

6% NaCl

E.S. (0.5 msec., 10 V)

200 μV

1 SEC.

FACILITATION OF MEDIAL HYPOTHALAMIC UNIT ACTIVITY

Fig. 11
Unit experiments of Kawamura (Kawamura et al., 1968). (A neuron in medial hypothalamus is excited by an aversive salt-solution and by an aversive shock; a neuron in lateral hypothalamus is suppressed by the same two aversive stimuli.)

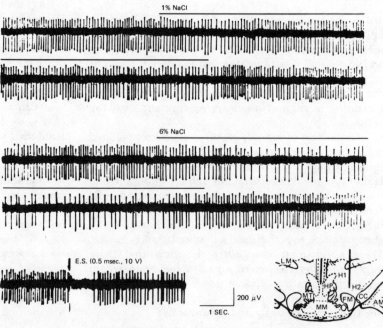

1% NaCl

6% NaCl

E.S. (0.5 msec., 10 V)

200 μV

1 SEC.

SUPPRESSION OF LATERAL HYPOTHALAMIC UNIT ACTIVITY

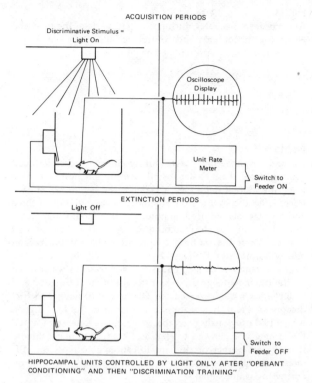

Discriminative Stimulus = Light On

Oscilloscope Display

Unit Rate Meter

Switch to Feeder ON

EXTINCTION PERIODS

Light Off

Switch to Feeder OFF

HIPPOCAMPAL UNITS CONTROLLED BY LIGHT ONLY AFTER "OPERANT CONDITIONING" AND THEN "DISCRIMINATION TRAINING"

Fig. 12

Animal firing a hippocampal unit at a high rate during acquisition period, indicated by a light as SD, and stopping this behavior during an extinction period, indicated by light off as S delta). When the feeder switch was "on" during SD periods high unit rates caused pellets to be dispensed.

was used to separate acquisition periods (which made up 2 of every 10 minutes) from extinction periods (which made up the remaining 8 minutes). It was found that animals could stand still and during the quiet period maintain a heightened rate of activity in many different neurons. It quickly became apparent that from the animal's viewpoint the responses being reinforced encompassed a great range including the adoption of certain postures or certain orientations and that quite often the responses observed in the brain resulted from sensory feedback from these responses. Neuron responses derived from some hippocampal areas, however, appeared to be modifiable with especial ease in these experiments even in cases where there was no obvious conditioning of a posture or of

an orientation. However, it was not unusual to find that hippocampal neurons fired faster while animals were waiting for rewards even though no attempt was made to condition this heightened level of hippocampal activity.

This made it seem likely that to some degree the apparent conditionability of hippocampal neuron responses might indicate either that the hunger drive or the anticipatory representation of the food object was innately represented in hippocampus.

The fact that some neurons in hippocampus appeared to respond in anticipatory fashion when animals were waiting for rewards led to the question of whether neurons which responded during rewards would be the same or different from neurons which responded in anticipatory fashion. In experiments to study this, recordings were made during pedal-pressing responses while animals were waiting for food or water (Olds, Mink, & Best, in press). In order to enhance the quietness of behavior, animals were trained to depress a pedal and then to remain motionless for a period of time in order to obtain the

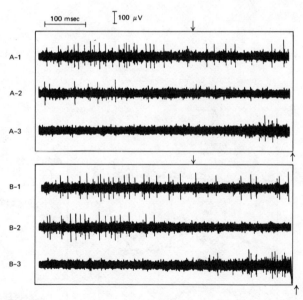

100 msec   100 μV

A-1

A-2

A-3

B-1

B-2

B-3

Fig. 13

A midbrain unit firing during an extended pedal press for food. (Each set of three traces represents a continuous 2-second waiting interval. Units fired rapidly when pedal was first depressed, and then fired rapidly again just prior to the presentation of the reward.)

CNS and Reinforcement of Behavior   43

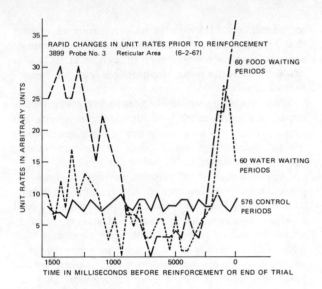

Fig. 14
Average response rates during different parts of the food and water waiting periods and control periods. Each average response-rate curve represents 60 or more trials.

Fig. 15
Average response-rate curves during an extended experiment (lasting more than 13 days) with a midbrain unit. (In these tests, the animal depressed a pedal at the beginning of each trace. After the first period of about one second, one of three auditory signals occurred, announcing that food, water, or no reward would be forthcoming after another one second period. When the training commenced, the stimuli had no effect on unit rates. On Days 2 and 3 the food signal evoked a large excitatory response, and some suppression was caused by the other two signals. When the meaning of the food and water signals was reversed, on Day 6, the difference at first disappeared and then reappeared in favor of the food signal, which had previously been the water signal. Later, on Day 12, the animal was allowed to feed ad lib and was made thirsty. During the course of this modification of drives, the difference disappeared again and then reappeared, this time favoring the water signal.)

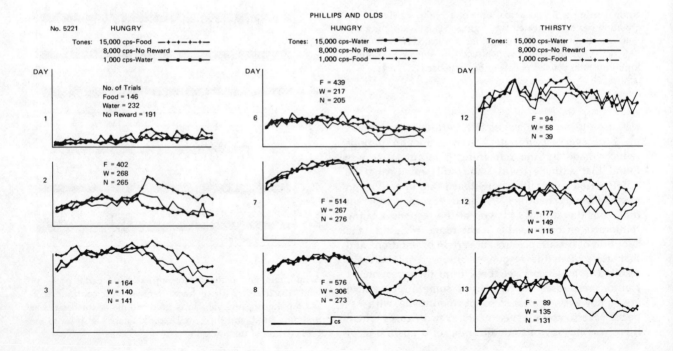

PHILLIPS AND OLDS

reward. The reward was forfeited if even a slight move occurred. Two pedals were provided at first, one for food and one for water. Action potentials were recorded simultaneously from reticular formation, from several points in the hypothalamic drive and reward systems and from hippocampus. Interesting neural correlates of instrumental behavior were observed both in the reticular formation and in the hippocampus but not in the hypothalamic drive and reward areas. Therefore, we now suppose that hypothalamic reward centers may be involved in representation of rewards but not in their anticipatory representation.

Large neurons recorded in reticular formation (see Figure 13) provided us with the most interesting patterns during anticipatory periods. There were large increments in neuronal activity which seemed to be correlated with the degree of expectancy on the one hand and with the desirability of the goal on the other. Reticular neurons fired rapidly at the beginning of the waiting period when expectancy was initiated and just prior to reinforcement when expectancy was again high (see Figure 14). The amount of firing was always more pronounced when the animal was working for food for which motivation was very high than when the animal was working for water for which motivation was lower. That the degree of motivation made the difference was proved in later studies where it was found that by feeding the animal on an ad-lib basis so that there was no particular food motivation, the response could be made to occur for water but not for food.

In the later studies[2] it was also possible to separate the level of expectancy and the level of motivation from the mere response characteristics of holding the pedal and waiting (see Figure 15). This was accomplished by having the animal press a single pedal without knowing what it would get. Then during the latter half of the waiting period one of three auditory signals was presented, one announcing that food would be presented, another announcing that water would be presented and a third announcing that there would be no reward. The firing rate of reticular neurons would often become augmented just prior to the point in time when the auditory signal appeared, then the auditory signal would cause either an added or sustained increment if food was announced, a pronounced decrement in firing if no reward was announced, or a less pronounced decrement if water was announced.

2.   M. I. Phillips and J. Olds, in preparation.

In these experiments, the responses to all three stimuli were quite similar before learning. Then a clear difference appeared favoring the food signal. Then when the significance was reversed so that the water signal became the food signal and vice versa, the difference first disappeared and then reappeared, again favoring food. Finally, when the animal was given free food but remained thirsty, the difference gradually shifted and finally favored water. Thus the high rate of firing did not depend on the auditory stimulus, it did not depend on the behavior, and it did not depend on the quality of the goal but only on its motivating power.

While these relatively rapid declines and increments in reticular formation neuronal firing rates were occurring there were often quite different neuronal patterns recorded from hippocampus (see Figure 16).

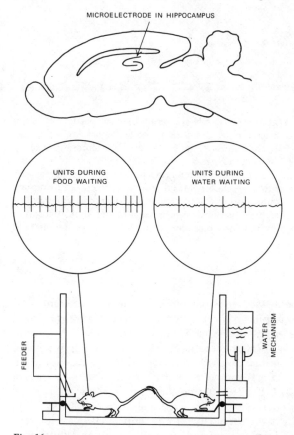

Fig. 16
A unit in hippocampus that fired rapidly during food waiting but at control levels during water waiting.

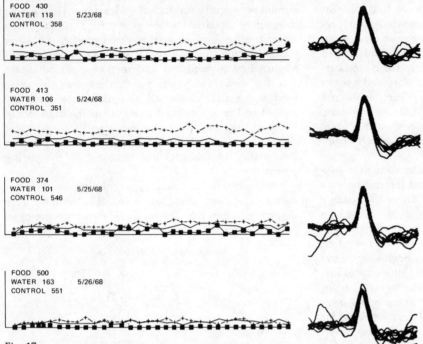

Fig. 17

Averaged response-rate curves on four successive days for a large hippocampal unit during food (+) and water (■) waiting periods and control periods. (The abscissa represents a series of 50-millisecond periods starting about ½ second after the pedal response and terminating just prior to reinforcement. The ordinate of each point represents the averaged firing rate of the unit during that particular 50-millisecond interval. The full height of the y-axis represents a rate of about 100 spikes per second. The spike rate was 10–20 per second in food periods, less during water and control periods. The food, water, and control numbers, at the left, indicate the number of trials averaged to make the respective traces. Each of the pictures on the right portrays 10 overlapped tracings of the unit being counted; the time base in this case is about 1.4 milliseconds and the amplitude of each tracing is about 200 microvolts. [These computer transcriptions were made with a method developed in our laboratory by P. J. Best; they provide assurance that real neuron spikes are being counted.])

These were relatively unrelated to the different temporal phases of the waiting period and correlated instead with the nature of the goal object. In several cases, hippocampal neurons were quite active while the animal awaited food but relatively inactive while the animal waited for water or vice versa (see Figures 17, 18, 19). This did not happen equally in all parts of hippocampus but occurred mainly in the "CA-3 field" which is a set of large hippocampal neurons with very well-known input and output connections. While these anticipatory responses in hippocampus were originally interpreted as suggesting that hippocampus might be innately wired to factors controlling food or water behavior, later experiments made it equally likely that temporary memories of food and water behaviors were being stored in hippocampus. Two kinds of evidence made this likelihood seem reasonable. The first was that the differential neuronal activity patterns favoring food or water behavior would often appear repeatedly for several days but they did not continue to be exhibited indefinitely. They would often disappear or even be reversed even in cases where it appeared that the action potential was recorded from the same neuron before and after the change. Thus it seemed

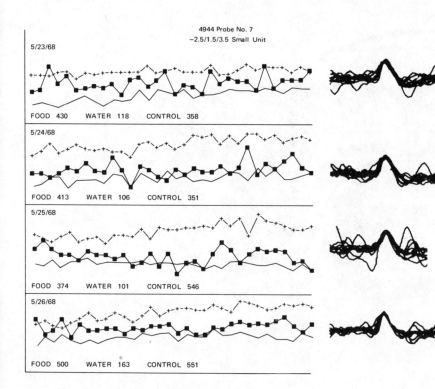

4944 Probe No. 7
−2.5/1.5/3.5 Small Unit

5/23/68

FOOD 430   WATER 118   CONTROL 358

5/24/68

FOOD 413   WATER 106   CONTROL 351

5/25/68

FOOD 374   WATER 101   CONTROL 546

5/26/68

FOOD 500   WATER 163   CONTROL 551

Fig. 18
Average response-rate curves for a smaller hippocampal unit than that shown in the preceding figure. (This unit was derived simultaneously with the same probe. It is presented to show that two neighboring units counted simultaneously from the same probe showed the same phenomenon, firing more rapidly during food-waiting than during water-waiting periods. Details are the same as in the preceding figure.)

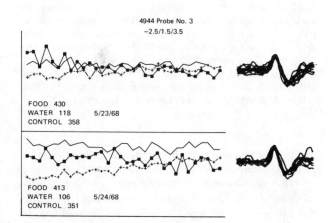

4944 Probe No. 3
−2.5/1.5/3.5

FOOD 430
WATER 118   5/23/68
CONTROL 358

FOOD 413
WATER 106   5/24/68
CONTROL 351

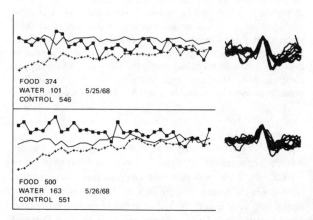

FOOD 374
WATER 101   5/25/68
CONTROL 546

FOOD 500
WATER 163   5/26/68
CONTROL 551

Fig. 19
Average response-rate curves for another hippocampal unit. (This unit was derived simultaneously but with a different probe, placed 1–2 millimeters away from the probe whose data were shown in the two preceding figures. It is presented to show that the more rapid firing during food behavior which characterized the two neighboring units in this animal did not characterize the whole hippocampus. In this case, the neuron regularly fired at a higher rate at the beginning of the water waiting periods and then there was a convergence of the rates toward the reinforcement end of the waiting period. Details are the same as in the two preceding figures.)

CNS and Reinforcement of Behavior

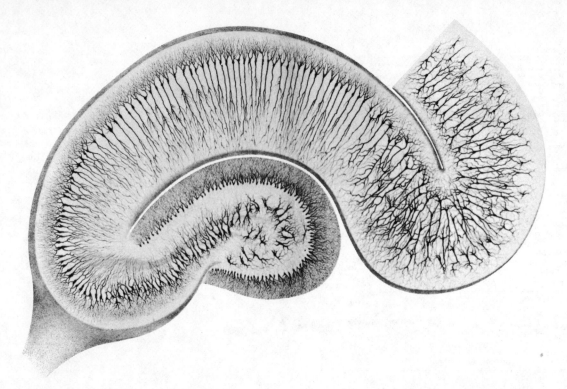

Fig. 20

A drawing of the mouse hippocampus made by Golgi in 1884. (Shown in ghostly gray are the "mossy" fibers. They originate in the very small "dentate granule" cells which are arrayed in the form of a horseshoe surrounding these fibers at their right-hand side. The mossy fibers pass through the dendrites of two sets of much larger neurons. One of these, scattered in disarray far inside the horseshoe is the CA-4 field of the hippocampus. The other set, more orderly, half inside and half outside of the horseshoe, is the CA-3 field of hippocampus.

Each mossy fiber makes an "en passant" synapse with many or all of the dendrites through which it passes. The very orderly arch extending from the end fibers along the top of the picture is the CA-1 field of hippocampus; through its dendrites pass axons, known as the Shaffer collaterals, from the CA-3 and CA-4 neurons. Beyond the CA-1 field on the far right is a less orderly field, the "subiculum." It gives rise to fibers which innervate mainly the dentate granules, but also to a lesser degree the other fields of the hippocampus.)

that the neuron firing was not a permanent anticipatory representor of food but only a temporary one which could be changed from day to day. The second thing which made the notion of temporary memory appealing was that differential activity patterns favored food about three to five times as often as they favored water and this was about the proportion of the two kinds of activity in this experimental environment. Both the relative impermanence and the correlation of probabilities between brain events and behavior in an artificial environment suggested that this might be a relatively temporary neuronal reflection of recent be-

havioral events and stimulus sequences rather than an a priori correlate of instrumental food or water behavior.

The well-known neuroanatomy of the hippocampus (see Figure 20) made an appealing focal point for interpretive schemes related to the problem of learning and reinforcement. This older section of cortex is esthetically arranged and clearly portrayed by histological methods so that the organization is well understood. Therefore, if some aspects of reinforcement processes may be observed in recordings from hippocampus, this might well make it a "Rosetta Stone" that is a key to the code, to guide our unraveling of the reward process in particular, and higher functions in general.

Organized grids which look like hippocampus are regularly used in computers as the main piece of hardware for solving the problem) of memory (see Figure 21). The main requirement in a good and reasonably fast computer memory is this: that all the information input lines should have reasonably quick access to all

of the memory storage elements, and vice versa. This is often accomplished in a random access memory by a simple grid. There is a large number of relatively short wires which make up the memory elements; all of these are crossed by a small number of relatively long digit wires. Each digit wire is connected to each memory wire by a magnetic core which functions much like a labile synapse (a bidirectional synapse in this case). At the time of storage, a memory address is activated, and at the same time a pattern of digit wires (carrying the code to be stored) is also activated. This simultaneous activation causes the code to be stored in the address (see Figure 22). Future activation of the address reactivates the digit lines and the same code which was previously stored now becomes the output. It is the grid on the one hand and the rapidly modifiable magnetic core "synapse" on the other which works much of the magic in the modern computer.

There are four problems in biological memory that are not immediately resolved by computer memories. The first is that a computer remembers when we call an address; the biological memory remembers instead when a new input pattern matches a remembered one to some degree. To make a computer memory do this is technically feasible and I will not go into details (see Figure 23). The second problem is that a biological

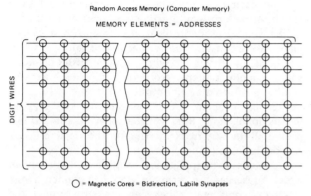

Fig. 21
Schematic drawing of a random-access computer memory. (The circular objects are "magnetic cores." They function as "labile bidirectional synapses," being "set" by simultaneous activation of intersecting wires; once "set" they form a temporary communications link between the two wires.)

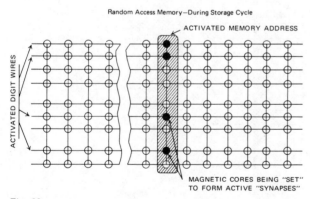

Fig. 22
Storing a trace. (When currents of proper type flow simultaneously through the two wires that pass through a single magnetic core, they reset it in such a fashion that an appropriate current passed later through one of the wires will cause a pulse to occur in the other.)

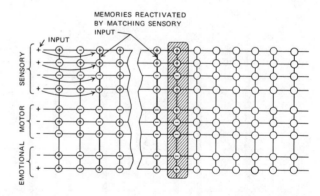

Fig. 23
Scanning a random-access memory with the digit wires. (Ordinarily a random-access memory is "read" by passing an appropriate current through the word lines and recording the output from the digit lines. Technically it would be simple to scan it by passing appropriate currents through the digit lines and looking then to see which word lines were most activated, that is which ones had the most nearly matching pattern.)

CNS and Reinforcement of Behavior   49

memory seems to record the temporal sequence of events in succession like a movie camera or a tape recorder. To make a computer memory do this we would arrange to store successive events in successive memory elements in order that the memory apparatus would convert a sequential array of events into a spatial array of elements (see Figure 24). That is, succeeding events would be written on adjacent memory lines. They would be "played back" in the same order.

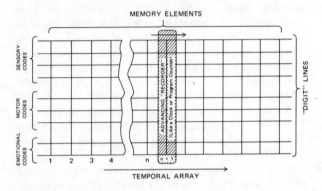

Fig. 24
Utilization of a random access memory as a sequential recorder by recording successive events on successive memory addresses.

The device would then remember not only the particular pattern which matched the input but also the events which followed it last time. The third problem is that if there was a reward among the events that followed last time, the biological memory would yield an output which would instigate remembered behaviors. Superficially at least this does not seem to be an impossible problem (see Figure 25). The general idea of the solution is (a) that digit lines would be divided into three categories, sensory, motor, and motivational; (b) that each memory when it was reactivated by a matching pattern would activate a series of successors in the spatial array until a successor with a special "motivating" inscription was activated, and (c) when this occurred, it would switch behavior from off to on and the motor pattern recorded on the first successor would be released as an output.

The last problem is that the computer synapses are bidirectional and this violates the accepted view passed all the way from Sherrington and Cajal to Eccles and de Robertis.

A relatively simple logical solution to this problem which preserves the accepted view has yielded a surprisingly good match between the structure of the computer model and the neuroanatomy of the hippocampus (see Figure 26). The interesting fact is that

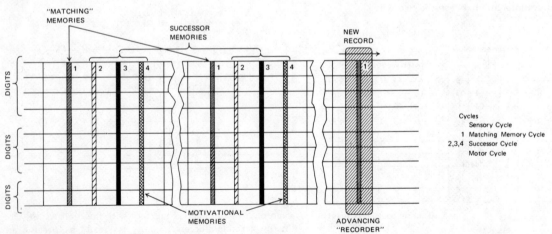

Fig. 25
Repeated record of a recurring event sequence. (If sensory aspects matching the first element were applied a third time, this might activate previous matching memories during a "matching memory cycle" and these in turn might activate their successors—2, 3, 4—during a "successor memory cycle";

finally, if one of the successors had a strong link to emotional digits, this might activate the motor components—of memory number—during an ensuing "motor cycle." Using gating and timing hardware currently available it would be relatively easy to build an electronic equivalent of this device.)

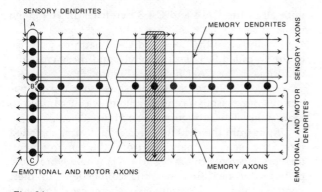

SENSORY DENDRITES

MEMORY DENDRITES

SENSORY AXONS

EMOTIONAL AND MOTOR DENDRITES

EMOTIONAL AND MOTOR AXONS

MEMORY AXONS

Fig. 26

A random-access memory device using neurons and unidirectional labile synapses rather than wires and magnetic cores. (The black circles represent the neuron somata, the lines tipped with arrow head pointing toward somata are dendrites, those tipped with arrow heads pointing away are axons. Sensory axons cross memory dendrites, memory axons cross motor and emotional dendrites. Functions would be the same as those in the previous figure.)

bidirectional synapses are not needed because sensory processes are the only ones that need to be afferent to the memory elements, and motor processes are the only ones that need to be efferent. That is, sensory inputs reactivate memories, and memories reactivate the previous motor processes. The memory element itself has to be a single line, with all the sensory elements crossing its afferent side or its dendrites, and all the motor elements crossing its efferent side or its axons. Sensory axons cross memory dendrites, memory axons cross motor dendrites. The structure required is the structure of the hippocampus (Lorente de Nó, 1934).

In hippocampus, the input comes along the perforant pathway, across the hippocampal cleft, and innervates the dentate granule cells (see Figure 27); the dentate cells might, therefore, be the sensory array. These give rise to large "mossy fibers."

So far as the eye can see, each large mossy fiber makes a very large number of "club-footed" synapses

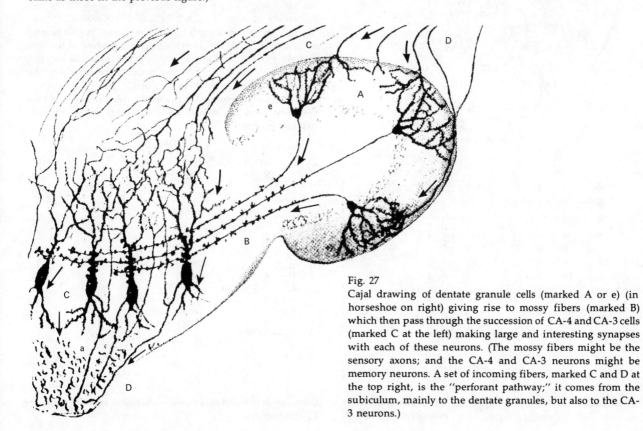

Fig. 27

Cajal drawing of dentate granule cells (marked A or e) (in horseshoe on right) giving rise to mossy fibers (marked B) which then pass through the succession of CA-4 and CA-3 cells (marked C at the left) making large and interesting synapses with each of these neurons. (The mossy fibers might be the sensory axons; and the CA-4 and CA-3 neurons might be memory neurons. A set of incoming fibers, marked C and D at the top right, is the "perforant pathway;" it comes from the subiculum, mainly to the dentate granules, but also to the CA-3 neurons.)

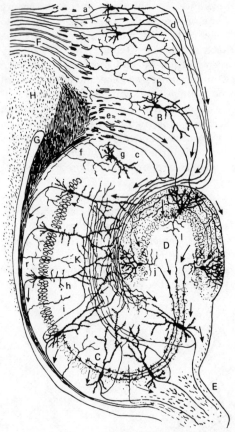

with all of the CA-4 and CA-3 dendrites in any given plane of section.

Finally, all of the CA-4 and CA-3 neurons give rise to the so-called Schaffer collaterals, and these cross the dendrites in the CA-1 field (see Figure 28).

It takes only redrawing to show that the hippocampus, for reasons I cannot fathom, was organized in exactly the manner required (see Figure 29).

Input from the dentate gyrus would carry in coded form the sensory patterns from the environment, memory elements in CA-4 and CA-3 would store these patterns by modified synaptic connections in their dendrites and would simultaneously monitor and store concomitant motor patterns by modified synaptic connections along their Schaffer collaterals. Patterns of

Fig. 28

Cajal drawing of mouse hippocampus. (In this case, the dentate gyrus is just above the D, the mossy fibers pass downward through the CA-3 field which is marked C. Each CA-3 neuron gives rise to a bifurcating axon; one part goes off and away at E, but the other part crosses upward to form the pathway marked K. These are the Schaffer collaterals and they pass through the CA-1 dendrites in much the same way that the mossy fibers pass through the CA-3 dendrites. These might form the memory axons, and the CA-1 field might form the motor and emotional outflow aspects of a temporary memory system.)

The Hippocampus Viewed as a Data Processing Grid

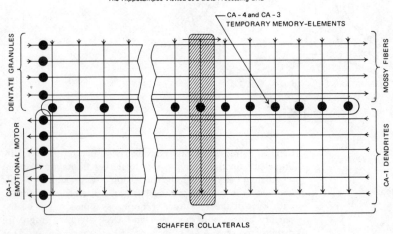

Fig. 29

A schematic drawing of the hippocampus, showing only the dentate granules sending mossy fibers through the CA-4 and CA-3 dendrites, and those sending Schaffer axons through the CA-1 dendrites.

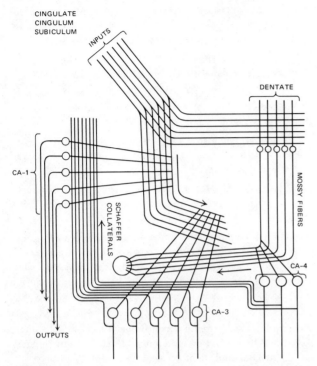

Fig. 30

A more complete schematic drawing of hippocampus. (This shows how the inputs, perforant pathway, sometimes bifurcate to innervate the dentate on one side, and the CA-1 and CA-3 fields on the other.)

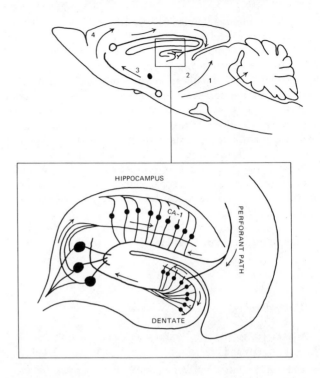

Fig. 31

Schematic drawing of an hypothetical relation between a reward system and four supposed learning grids. (Messages from reward areas are supposed to originate in hypothalamus and take Pathway 1 toward a grid in cerebellum, Pathway 2 toward a grid in tectum, and Pathway 3 toward a paleocortical—hippocampal—grid, and Pathway 4 toward a neocortical grid. In each grid a different kind of "learning" might occur; and all kinds might occur simultaneously. In the hippocampus, reward input would be funneled in with other inputs along the perforant pathway, passing on one side into dentate, and on the other side into the CA-1 and CA-3 fields, the latter being indicated by the very large black circles on the left.)

CA-1 activity would later carry the output codes of appropriate motor behaviors.

If it worked this way, then recordings from dentate should follow the sensory input, recordings from CA-4 and CA-3 should reveal patterns arbitrarily and temporarily related to significant and repeated features of an experimental environment, and recordings from CA-1 would be related somehow to behaviors and therefore they might be conditionable by operant techniques. We are at present in a position to make the appropriate tests and to find out whether these things are so.

A reward stimulus might make a motivational inscription on both the afferent and the efferent sides of the memory elements. Therefore we might find some family of fibers which simultaneously innervated the dentate and the CA-1 fields, and we might even find that its stimulation would be rewarding.

Both Cajal and Lorente de Nó made it clear that some parts of the perforant pathway bifurcate to go partly across the hippocampal cleft into dentate and partly along the cleft into the CA-1 field (see Figure 30). Recent self-stimulation studies of Mahut[3] seem to indicate that self-stimulation can be obtained by stimulating some parts of this pathway in both of these areas and at its root in the subiculum.

3.   Helen Mahut, personal communication, 1968.

In summary, it seems likely to me that emotional integrators of the subcortex and lateral hypothalamus might project into gridlike structures in places like the cerebellum, tectum, hippocampus, and neocortex (see Figure 31). The path to hippocampus would likely follow medial forebrain bundle forward to cingulate cortex and then follow cingulum into the perforant pathway. In these grids, rewarding messages would either (a) directly augment the frequency of ongoing responses, (b) reinforce in Hullian fashion certain ongoing synaptic relations, or (c), as I have just suggested for hippocampus, be recorded on temporary memory elements, to serve a motivating function in relation to remembered behavior patterns. It seems to me quite likely that all of these different kinds of processes (and others) might occur redundantly and simultaneously.

References

Anand, B., & Brobeck, J. R. Hypothalamic control of food intake in rats and cats. *Yale U. Biol. Bed.*, 1951, 24, 123–140.

Andrew, R. J. Intracranial self-stimulation in the chick. *Nature*, 1967, 213, 847–848.

Balinska, M., Romaniut, A., & Wyrwicka, W. Impairment of conditioned defensive reactions following lesions of the lateral hypothalamus in rabbit. *Acta Biol. Exper.*, 1964, 24, 89–97.

Ball, G. G. Cited in T. Trabasso & G. Bower, *Attention in learning: Theory and research*. New York: Wiley, 1968.

Bishop, M. P., Elder, S. T., & Heath, R. G. Intracranial self-stimulation in man. *Science*, 1963, 140, 394–396.

Boyd, E., & Gardner, L. Positive and negative reinforcement from intracranial self-stimulation in teleosts. *Science*, 1962, 136, 648.

Boyd, E. S., & Gardner, L. C. Effect of some brain lesions on intracranial self-stimulation in the rat. *American Journal of Physiology*, 1967, 213, 1044–1052.

Brobeck, J. R. Mechanisms of the development of obesity in animals with hypothalamic lesions. *Physiological Review*, 1946, 26, 541–559.

Bruner, A. Self-stimulation in the rabbit: An anatomical map of stimulation effects. *Journal of Comparative Neurology*, 1967, 131, 615–629.

Bursten, B., & Delgado, J. M. R. Positive reinforcement induced by intracranial stimulation in the monkey. *Journal of Comparative and Physiological Psychology*, 1958, 51, 6–10.

Caggiula, A. R., & Hoebel, B. G. "Copulation-reward site" in the posterior hypothalamus. *Science*, 1966, 153, 1284–1285.

Delgado, J. M. R., Roberts, W. W., & Miller, N. E. Learning motivated by electrical stimulation of the brain. *American Journal of Physiology*, 1954, 179, 587–593.

Herberg, L. J. Seminal ejaculation following positively reinforcing electrical stimulation of the rat hypothalamus. *Journal of Comparative and Physiological Psychology*, 1963, 56, 679–685.

Kappers, C. U. A., Huber, G. C., & Crosby, E. C. *The comparative anatomy of the nervous system of vertebrates*. New York: Macmillan, 1936.

Kawamura, Y., Funakoshi, M., & Kasahara, Y. A role of oral afferents in aversion behavior to salt and tannic acid solutions. In N. Yoshii & N. W. Buchwald (Eds.), *Japan-US Joint Seminar on Neurophysiological Basis of Learning and Behavior*, July 22–26, 1968, Kyoto International Conference Hall, Kyoto, Japan.

Koenig, J. D. V. The reinforcment value of intracranial stimulation and its interaction with arousal level. Cited in Berlyne, D. E., Arousal and reinforcement. *Nebraska Symposium on Motivation*, 1967, 1–110.

Krashe, F. B. General disruption resulting from electrical stimulus of ventro-medial hypothalamus. *Science*, 1962, 138, 822–823.

Lilly, J. C., & Miller, A. M. Operant conditioning of the bottlenose dolphin with electrical stimulation of the brain. *Journal of Comparative and Physiological Psychology*, 1962, 55, 73–79.

Lorente de Nó, R. Studies on the structure of the cerebral cortex. II. Continuation of the study of the ammonic system. *Journal f. Psychologie und Neurologie*, 1934, 46 (2 & 3), 113–177.

MacDonnell, M. F., & Flynn, J. P. Control of sensory fields by stimulation of hypothalamus. *Science*, 1966, 152, 1406–1408.

Margules, D. L., & Olds, J. Identical "feeding" and "rewarding" systems in the lateral hypothalamus of rats. *Science*, 1962, 135, 374–375.

Miller, N. E. Central stimulation and other new approaches to motivation and reward. *American Psychologist*, 1958, 13, 100–108.

Miller, N. E. Motivational effects of brain stimulation and drugs. Fed. Proc., 1960, 19, 846–854.

Mogenson, G. J., & Stevenson, J. A. F. Drinking and self-stimulation with electrical stimulation of the lateral hypothalamus. *Phys. and Behav.*, 1966.

Moruzzi, G., & Magoun, H. W. Brain stem reticular formation and activation of the EEG. *Electroencephalography and Clinical Neurophysiology*, 1949, *1*, 455–473.

Nauta, W. J. H. An experimental study of the fornix system in the rat. *Journal of Comparative Neurology*, 1956, *104*, 247–271.

Olds, J. Physiological mechanisms of reward. *Nebraska Symposium on Motivation*, 1955, *4*, 73–138.

Olds, J. Runway and maze behavior controlled by basomedial forebrain stimulation in the rat. *Journal of Comparative and Physiological Psychology*, 1956, *49*, 507–512.

Olds, J. Differential effects of drives and drugs on self-stimulation at different brain sites. In D. E. Sheer (Ed.), *Electrical stimulation of the brain.* Austin: University of Texas Press, 1961.

Olds, J. Operant conditioning of single unit responses. Excerpta Medica International Congress Series No. 87. *Proceedings of the XXIII International Congress of Physiological Sciences*, Tokyo, 1965, 372–380.

Olds, J. The limbic system and behavioral reinforcement. In W. R. Adey & T. Tokizane (Eds.), *Progress in brain research: (Structure and function of the limbic system).* (Vol. 27) Amsterdam: Elsevier, 1967.

Olds, J., & Milner, P. Positive reinforcement produced by electrical stimulation of septal area and other regions of rat brain. *Journal of Comparative and Physiological Psychology*, 1954, *47*, 419–427.

Olds, J., Mink, W. D., & Best, P. J. Single unit patterns during anticipatory behavior. *Electroencephalography and Clinical Neurophysiology*, in press.

Olds, J., & Olds, M. E. The mechanisms of voluntary behavior. In R. G. Heath (Ed.), *The role of pleasure in behavior.* New York: Hoeber Medical Division, Harper & Row, 1964.

Olds, M. E., & Olds, J. Approach-escape interactions in rat brain. *American Journal of Physiology*, 1962, *203*, 803–810.

Olds, M. E., & Olds, J. Approach-avoidance analysis of rat diencephalon. *Journal comp. Neurol.*, 1963, *120*, 259–295.

Papez, J. W. A proposed mechanism of emotion. *A.M.A. Neurol. Psychiat.*, 1937, *38*, 725–743.

Persson, N. Self-stimulation in the goat. *Acta Physiologica Scandinavica*, 1962, *55*, 276–285.

Pliskoff, S. S., Wright, J. E., & Hawkins, D. T. Brain stimulation as a reinforcer: Intermittent schedules. *Journal of the Experimental Analyses of Behavior*, 1965, *8*, 75–88.

Roberts, W. W. Both rewarding and punishing effects from stimulation of posterior hypothalamus of cat with same electrode at same intensity. *J. comp. physiol. Psychol.*, 1958, *51*, 400–407.

Routtenberg, A., & Lindy, J. Effects of the availability of rewarding septal and hypothalamic stimulation on bar-pressing for food under conditions of deprivation. *Journal of Comparative and Physiological Psychology*, 1956, *60*, 158–161.

Routtenberg, A., & Olds, J. The attenuation of response to an aversive brain stimulus by concurrent rewarding septal stimulation. Fed. Proc., 1963, *22*, (No. 2, Part I), 515. (Abstract)

Stark, P., & Boyd, E. S. Effects of cholinergic drugs on hypothalamic self-stimulation response rates of dogs. *American Journal of Physiology*, 1963, *205*, 745–748.

Stellar, E. The physiology of motivation. *Psychological Review*, 1954, *61*, 5–22.

Teitelbaum, P., & Epstein, A. The lateral hypothalamic syndrome: Recovery of feeding and drinking after lateral hypothalamic lesions. *Psychological Review*, 1962, *69*, 74–90.

Wilkinson, H. A., & Peele, T. L. Intracranial self-stimulation in cats. *Journal of Comparative Neurology*, 1963, *121*, 425–440.

Wyrwicka, W., & Dobrzecka, C. Relationship between feeding and satiation centers of the hypothalamus. *Science*, 1960, *132*, 805–806.

affective arousal: some implications[1]

paul thomas young[2]
university of illinois

In this paper I will consider two closely related problems. First, what is the nature of affective arousal? Second, how are affective arousals related to motivation, learning, cognition, evaluation? What are some of the implications?

The Nature of Affective Arousal

Affective arousals, like other complex events in nature, can be examined from various points of view. I will

1. Editorial note. This address was presented via sound film since Paul Thomas Young could not deliver it in person. Several paragraphs in the section entitled "Affective Arousal and Cognition," omitted in the film edition, have been restored. Reprinted from *American Psychologist*, 1967, Vol. 22, pp. 32–40. Copyright 1967 by the American Psychological Association, and reproduced by permission.

2. Retirement address: 336 Notre Dame Road, Claremont, California 91711.

consider them from three main points of view: First, the point of view of conscious experience. Second, the behavioral point of view. Third, the point of view of neuropsychology.

PLEASANTNESS AND UNPLEASANTNESS IN CONSCIOUS EXPERIENCE

Subjective methods have been unpopular for several decades, but there is one form of report that is thoroughly reliable and useful in the study of affective experience. That is the functional, or conative, type of report in the form: "I like it" or "I dislike it." The report "I like it" means "let it continue," "let it repeat." The report "I dislike it" means "stop," "no more." Almost everyone (with or without the benefit of psychological training) can report his likes and dislikes.

A sample of data obtained with the functional type of report is shown in Figure 1 (Kniep, Morgan, & Young, 1931). In one study, affective reactions to odors were tested with children and college students. Chemically stable substances were presented under standard conditions. Each subject was instructed to smell a substance and report immediately whether he liked or disliked the odor.

The odorous substances are shown at the base of Figure 1, ranked from the most frequently liked (vanillin, a synthetic vanilla) to the least frequently liked (heptyl aldehyde). The solid line shows percentage of adults *liking* the odors. The other lines show percentage of children *liking* the odors.

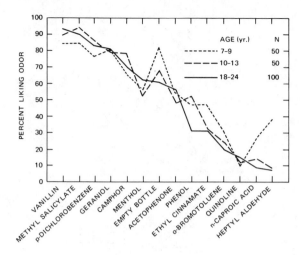

Fig. 1
Affective reactions to odors for three age groups (from Kniep, Morgan, & Young, 1931).

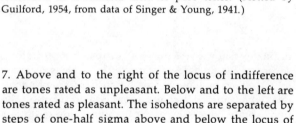

Fig. 2
Isohedons in a stimulus field of pure tones. (Plotted by Guilford, 1954, from data of Singer & Young, 1941.)

Coefficients of correlation among the three age groups are exceedingly high—in the range of .91 to .96. The high coefficients indicate that whatever determines the hedonic value of odors is relatively independent of age. Moreover, since most of the smells were unfamiliar to the subjects and since each odor was presented only once, we can assume that these hedonic values are independent of prior experience. The data suggest that the likes and dislikes of odors depend upon built-in mechanisms.

Another study was made with auditory stimuli (Singer & Young, 1941). A group of 39 adults rated the pleasantness and unpleasantness of pure tones with a graphic rating scale. Each tone sounded 5 to 8 seconds and was immediately rated for pleasantness or unpleasantness.

From our data, Guilford (1954) plotted the chart of isohedons shown in Figure 2. Guilford (1939) defined an isohedon as a line of constant affective value in a stimulus field. This stimulus field is determined by the frequency and intensity of relatively pure tones.

Note the locus of indifference—the curve marked 0.0. This curve starts with a tone of 100 cycles per second whose intensity level is at the arbitrary value 19 and ends, by extrapolation, with a tone of approximately 2,600 cycles per second whose intensity level is

7. Above and to the right of the locus of indifference are tones rated as unpleasant. Below and to the left are tones rated as pleasant. The isohedons are separated by steps of one-half sigma above and below the locus of indifference.

BEHAVIORAL STUDIES OF TASTE PREFERENCES
A laboratory rat cannot report his feelings of pleasantness and unpleasantness but he shows in no uncertain terms *absolute* likes and dislikes. *Relative* likes and dislikes are shown in tests of preference. A preference is an evaluative choice. Preference implies that one response is better, in some way, than another. When offered a choice between two sucrose solutions the rat prefers the sweeter (Young & Greene, 1953). In a series of choices he develops a habit of selecting the sucrose solution with higher concentration.

The lawfulness and predictability of taste preferences in the rat will be illustrated briefly by findings in three experiments. I will not pause for technical details, since they have been recorded elsewhere (for references see Young, 1966).

Palatability ratings with a sucrose scale. Figure 3 shows the hedonic equivalence of saccharin and sucrose solutions (Young & Madsen, 1963). The scale on the axis of

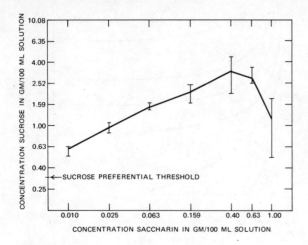

Fig. 3
Hedonic equivalence of saccharin and sucrose gustatory stimuli (from Young & Madsen, 1963).

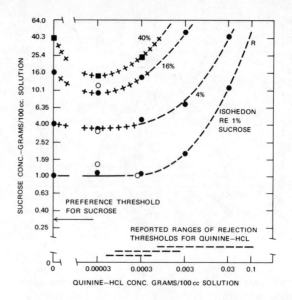

Fig. 4
Isohedons in a bitter-sweet stimulus field (from Kappauf, Burright, & DeMarco, 1963).

ordinates shows a series of sucrose concentrations separated by equal log distances. This scale is regarded as a scale of hedonic values because, as noted above, rats, when offered a choice between two sucrose solutions, prefer the solution with higher concentration. Figures along the base line show concentrations of seven standard saccharin solutions that were tested for palatability with a sucrose scale. (On palatability see Young, 1967a.) Each vertical cross line shows the range of mean sucrose concentrations that are isohedonic to a saccharin standard. The range is for a group of eight need-free rats, tested individually.

The curve reveals uniform and consistent relations between palatability of saccharin and sucrose solutions. The optimal concentration of saccharin (about .5%) is hedonically equivalent to a sucrose concentration of about 3.5%.

Isohedons. Figure 4 shows a family of isohedons mapped for need-free rats in a gustatory stimulus field (Kappauf, Burright, & DeMarco, 1963). The field represents an infinite number of compound solutions containing sucrose and quinine hydrochloride.

Each isohedon shows what bitter-sweet compounds are hedonically equal to a sucrose standard. The isohedons are roughly parallel; they follow similar courses and do not intersect. Plus (+) signs indicate

quinine concentrations that enhance palatability and minus (−) signs, concentrations that impair palatability relative to a pure sucrose standard.

If an isohedon dips below the standard level at low concentrations of quinine and rises above the standard level at higher concentrations, there is implied an indifference concentration which is hedonically equal to the standard but which differs from the standard in sensory quality. The locus of indifference concentrations has been plotted in another stimulus field.

Hedonic indifference. Figure 5 shows the locus of hedonic indifference within a sour-sweet stimulus field defined by the concentration of tartaric acid and sucrose in compound solutions (Young & Schulte, 1963). The locus was determined by preference testing with the up-and-down psychophysical method. In each test the sucrose concentration was the same in standard and comparison solutions. The acid concentration in the comparison solution was varied up and down from trial to trial to determine what acid concentrations made the compound hedonically equal to the sucrose standard. The range of acid concentrations employed in each test is indicated by a horizontal arrow.

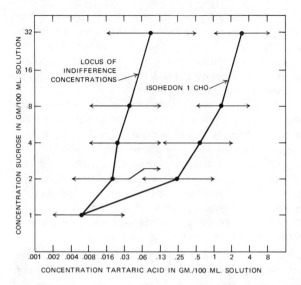

Fig. 5
Locus of hedonic indifference in a sour-sweet stimulus field (from Young & Schulte, 1963).

The locus of hedonic indifference divides the stimulus field into two regions. Compounds to the left of the locus are tart. They are preferred, by a group of 30 rats, to the sucrose standards. Compounds to the right of the locus are sour. The standards are preferred to them. Compounds on the locus are hedonically equal to the standards at the same sucrose level but differ from the standards in sensory quality.

Incidentally, the curve at the right is part of an isohedon in the sour-sweet area with a constant sucrose standard of 1%.

NEURAL BASIS OF PLEASANTNESS AND
UNPLEASANTNESS

Now let us approach the problem of affective arousal from the point of view of neuropsychology and ask: What goes on within the nervous system when pleasantness and unpleasantness are felt and when rats exhibit positive and negative behavior?

During the past 10 or 15 years there has been an explosion of interest in the neuropsychology and neurophysiology of affective arousal. Current interest began with the work of Olds and Milner (1954). They found that rats repeatedly pressed a lever that yielded intracranial stimulation through electrodes implanted in the septal area of the limbic system. In the same year, Delgado, Roberts, and Miller (1954) reported that cats form habits of avoiding intracranial stimulations in hypothalamic structures. Subsequently, positive and negative behavior have been elicited repeatedly through intracranial stimulations in the brains of rat, cat, dog, monkey, guinea pig, goldfish, bottlenose dolphin, and man.

Heath (1964) observed human patients with electrodes permanently implanted in the septal area of the limbic system. Equipment was arranged so that a patient could obtain intracranial self-stimulation by pressing a button. With stimulation in the septal area of the limbic system patients reported pleasant, good, happy feelings, pleasant memories, and some reported sexual feelings. With electrodes implanted at other limbic locations, self-stimulation produced distress and unhappy thoughts; but distress could be relieved and comfort restored by pressing the septal button. These observations are theoretically important because they demonstrate a direct relation between subjective feelings of pleasantness and unpleasantness, and intracranial self-stimulations.

The exact structure of the neural mechanism that mediates affective arousal is not known. Available evidence suggests that pleasantness is related to nonspecific excitation and unpleasantness to nonspecific inhibition. Magoun (1963) has shown that, in addition to nonspecific excitation produced through the famous reticular activating system, there is also nonspecific inhibition.

Olds and Olds (1964) have shown that in the lateral hypothalamus there is an area where intracranial self-stimulation is continued indefinitely. When self-stimulated in this area, rats continued bar pressing at the rate of about 10,000 responses per hour until physically exhausted. Near the positive area is another where self-stimulation is strongly negative. Olds demonstrated that nonspecific excitatory and inhibitory systems are connected by nuclei. Self-stimulation of the interconnecting nuclei produced dramatic behavior in which positive and negative tendencies appeared to be mixed.

Under normal conditions the nonspecific excitatory and inhibitory processes are reciprocally related (Stein, 1965). Obviously, the commands to go and stop are incompatible. The integrative action of the nervous system within limbic structures appears to be similar to that described by Sherrington (1911) as "reciprocal innervation," in reflexes of the spinal dog.

The concept of a single regulatory mechanism in which nonspecific excitatory (+) and inhibitory (−) processes are reciprocally related, fits in perfectly with what is now known about positive and negative affective arousals. Details of the neural mechanism of affective arousal are being rapidly discovered but there is much to be learned. We do not yet know why sugar solutions are immediately accepted and quinine immediately rejected, nor how positive and negative processes summate algebraically. We do not yet know how this neural mechanism works during the organizing of regulative dispositions which develop at the cerebral level.

THE HEDONIC CONTINUUM

I have now briefly considered from the points of view of conscious experience, animal behavior, and neuropsychology, facts relating to affective arousal. These facts supplement each other and do not contradict. All are congruent. Some of the basic principles of affective arousal that are apparent from all three points of view can be represented upon a bipolar hedonic continuum.

The continuum, Figure 6, extends from extreme distress (represented by a minus sign) to extreme delight (represented by a plus sign). The continuum is bipolar. It is incorrect to represent hedonic values upon a single scale of attractiveness because foul odors, bitter tastes, painful burns, etc., are not at all attractive; they are repulsive. Nor is it correct to regard pleasantness as merely the letting up of pain; many pleasant experiences exist apart from pain and the release of tension.

Arbitrary units of positive and negative intensity are marked off along the continuum. Arrows indicate four directions of hedonic change: toward and away from maximal intensity at the positive and negative poles. In this diagram the arrows are separated by a rather wide gap in the middle of the range to represent the fact that with habituated animals (including sophisticated human beings) a great many activities are neutral or nearly neutral. It is only occasionally that intense affective arousals occur.

The bipolar continuum implies that pleasantness and unpleasantness are antagonistic and incompatible. Hedonic changes cannot occur in opposite directions at the same instant. Felt pleasantness and unpleasantness, in fact, do not coexist in experience; they alternate (Young, 1918). A similar antagonism exists in the behavior of laboratory rats. A foodstuff is either accepted or rejected. Figure 7 shows what happens when substances with positive and negative valences are combined in a single compound solution.

Alegebraic summation of hedonic values. It is known that sucrose solutions are accepted by rats at all concentrations and that quinine solutions are rejected. Quinine solutions, however, can be made acceptable by adding sugar. There is thus an algebraic summation of hedonic values.

Figure 7 is based upon results from a group of 32 need-free rats (Young & Trafton, 1964). The solid lines at the top of the figure describe a three-dimensional

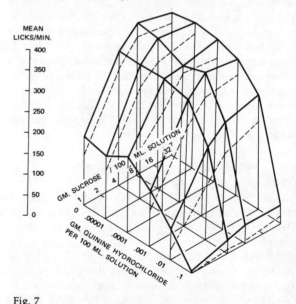

Fig. 7
Tridimensional activity surface showing rates of accepting bitter-sweet solutions (from Young & Trafton, 1964).

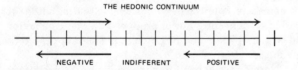

Fig. 6
A bipolar hedonic continuum showing wide indifferent range and four directions of hedonic change.

surface which shows how rates of acceptance (measured by mean numbers of licks per minute) vary with composition of the bitter-sweet compounds. Twenty-four solutions were tested with concentrations indicated by cross lines at the base of the figure.

It can be seen at a glance that the rate of ingesting a bitter-sweet compound increases with sucrose concentration and decreases with quinine concentration. Positive and negative values thus summate algebraically. The rate of ingesting a bitter-sweet solution depends upon two factors—an excitatory sweet factor and an inhibitory bitter.

The rates of acceptance vary from maximum to zero. Each rate depends upon the simultaneous arousal of positive and negative factors, and reflects the algebraic resultant. Below the zero point, I assume, there are degrees of negativity but these hypothetical differences of inhibitory strength are all represented by zero acceptance of the compounds. The figure shows only levels of positive acceptance.

Some Implications of Affective Arousal

I have now considered, somewhat sketchily, the nature of affective arousal and some of the basic hedonic principles. It is time to turn to the main problem: How are affective arousals related to motivation, learning, cognition, evaluation? What are some of the implications?

AFFECTIVE AROUSAL AND MOTIVATION

Homeostatic regulation. The physiological doctrine of homeostasis is firmly established. The biological necessity of maintaining homeostasis cannot be disregarded.

Pribram (1963) has pointed out that around the midline ventricular system are specialized areas sensitive to temperature, osmotic pressure, estrogen, glucose, and the partial pressure of carbon dioxide. These areas are embedded in the reticulum (the reticular activating systems). They act as homeostats which can be biased to accelerate or check the intake or output of agents to which the homeostats are sensitive.

Of special interest for the homeostatic theory of regulation is evidence concerning specific hungers. To illustrate: It is known that need-free rats prefer sucrose to casein and protein-starved rats prefer casein to sucrose. If, however, a sugar preference is established prior to protein starvation, rats hold stubbornly to this sugar preference despite a steadily increasing need for

casein. If the protein-starved rats are placed on a different apparatus which forces them to develop a new preferential habit, they promptly develop a preference for casein in agreement with their homeostatic need while still holding to the established sugar-eating habit on the original apparatus (Young & Chaplin, 1945). New habits tend to form in agreement with metabolic needs but established habits persist as independent regulators of food selection.

It is clear from this and similar observations that a homeostatic need increases the acceptability of a needed substance. It is also clear that a preferential habit, established prior to the development of a need, is an independent determinant of dietary selection.

Activation and arousal. Current research upon motivation has turned away, temporarily, from homeostatic needs and drives to investigate incentives and environmental conditions.

In current theorizing, the concept of activation, or arousal, is very much to the front. The work of Lindsley (1951), and others, upon the reticular activating system is well known. We know that every receptor stimulation contributes a bit of nonspecific excitation that tones up the cerebral cortex. The process of activation gives a physiological basis for the Hullian concept of a general, nonspecific drive—the D factor. The fundamental importance of activation, or arousal, has been recognized in the writings of Berlyne, Brown, Duffy, Hebb, and others. The activation concept, of course, does not vitiate earlier research upon homeostatic needs and drives; it simply supplements this work by pointing to a neurogenic source of nonspecific excitation, or drive (Young, 1967b).

One weakness of the activation concept is that it is one-dimensional. A one-dimensional continuum of activation, or arousal, lacks a directing, regulating, evaluating principle. This lack restricts the concept of motivation to the energizing aspect of behavior and places too heavy a burden of explanation upon habit and homeostatic regulation. The one-dimensional theory of activation is also incomplete in that it ignores diffuse inhibition which is known to exist and which, in integrated activities, is reciprocally related to diffuse excitation.

It is right here that the concept of affective arousal is important. This concept recognizes both positive and negative forms of activation, or arousal, and thus provides a directing, evaluating, regulating principle which *extends* the homeostatic doctrine of regulation, and *corrects* a weakness in the one-dimensional theory of drive.

In view of the total evidence, I am not convinced by the cogent arguments of Judson S. Brown (1955) that we can explain "pleasure-seeking behavior" without pleasure!

AFFECTIVE AROUSAL AND LEARNING

If a need-free rat runs down a straightaway to a cup of sugar water and is allowed 1 second of contact with the fluid, he will, on repeated trials, run more directly and quickly to the reward. If instead of sugar water, the cup contains a quinine solution, the rat will turn away upon initial contact with the fluid and, on repeated trials, appears actively to avoid the cup. In this situation there are two factors: (*a*) Upon first contact with fluid there is an immediate reaction of continuing or terminating ingestion, accepting or rejecting the fluid. (*b*) Upon repeated trials the animal *learns* to approach or to avoid the cup.

Consider the four arrows shown in Figure 6. According to hedonic theory, an organism behaves in such a way that positive affective arousals are continued and repeated (upper right arrow). An animal organizes and learns, if possible, behavior that maintains and regains positive affective arousals. After an animal has learned a rewarding pattern of behavior, removal of the reward is disturbing, disorganizing (lower right arrow). If, for example, a rat has learned to run to a cup of sugar water, removal of the reward extinguishes the learned behavior and leads to a change, or reorganization, of the animal's activity. A noxious stimulus is disturbing, disorganizing (lower left arrow). The normal animal organizes, if he can, and repeats any pattern of behavior that minimizes distress (upper left arrow). Distress reduction is the hedonic substitute for Hullian drive reduction. In general, animals *learn* behavioral patterns that lead to hedonic changes in the positive direction—that minimize distress and maximize delight. Changes in the negative direction are disturbing, disorganizing. Such changes require reorganization of behavior and relearning.

Conditions of learning. It is pertinent to ask: Under what conditions does learning occur? According to contiguity theory, learning occurs when one response is contiguous in space and time with another. The learned response is contingent upon some previous response or stimulation. I agree completely and wholeheartedly with the contiguity theory of associative learning. I will point out, however, that contiguity *as such* is neither positive nor negative. Contiguity lacks a directing regulating principle.

It is right here that hedonic theory comes to the rescue. Affective arousals are directive, regulative, evaluative. Animals are observed to organize, repeat, and learn adaptive patterns of behavior that maximize the positive and minimize the negative. There is clearly a steering, controlling principle.

On the basis of primary affective arousals, organisms develop dispositions which are variously called habits, motives, attitudes, traits, expectancies. There is considerable evidence (which cannot be reviewed here) that dispositions are organized hedonically during the early stages of development and, further, that the directive role of primary hedonic processes is taken over gradually by developing cerebral dispositions.

AFFECTIVE AROUSAL AND COGNITION

I have considered the dependence of affective arousals upon sensory processes—upon odors, tones, tastes, etc.—but this is only part of the story. Affective arousals are elicited not only from below—from receptor stimulations—but also from above—by the cerebral processes involved in cognition. Consider the feelings that are evoked by good news or bad news, by victory or defeat, by jokes, stories, and many other complex experiences that involve meaning and understanding.

In technical psychology it is widely recognized that feelings and emotions depend upon the cognitive awareness of events and situations. Festinger (1957), for example, pointed out that uncomfortable feelings arise from imcompatible cognitive elements. Knowledge, opinions, beliefs, do not always agree with each other. Nonfitting relations among the cognitive elements give rise to uncomfortable feelings with pressures to reduce the cognitive dissonance by changes of behavior, of cognition, and circumspect exposure to new information and opinion.

Again, Arnold (1960, p. 171) emphasized that emotions originate in the appraisal, or estimation, of an inducing situation. This cognitive origin of emotion distinguishes emotion from simple feelings of pleasantness and unpleasantness that depend upon receptor stimulations. Arnold regards sense-bound pleasantness and unpleasantness as rudimentary appraisals (rudimentary evaluations) that depend upon built-in bodily mechanisms. And so they are.

Emotional disturbance. When the organism behaves in a calm, undisturbed manner the limbic and cerebral systems function as a unit to produce behavior that is smooth, integrated, well motivated. Then one speaks of working with enthusiasm, interest, zeal, conviction, with high intrinsic motivation or, perhaps, indifferently.

Occasionally, however, there is emotional upset and the normal integration of behavior is temporarily reduced or lost. For example, one hears a good joke and laughs uproariously. The pleasant disturbance soon quiets down and leaves one with a pleasant mood and an inclination to recall the joke and tell it to a friend. Frequently the emotional disturbance is unpleasant, arising from frustration, disappointment, insult, failure. Emotional disturbances (apart from reflexive emotional patterns) originate in cognitive events that involve meaning and understanding.

At all times there is two-way traffic between the limbic structures and the cerebral mechanisms. Whenever an affective arousal occurs the information that it is occurring is relayed upward to the cerebral cortex where habits, attitudes, motives, and similar dispositions, are organized and registered.

Affective meanings. Emotional events are registered and recalled as pleasant or unpleasant. Innumerable objects, situations, and aspects of experience acquire affective meanings. In a small study (Young, 1937) I found that the affective meanings of words can be readily recalled and stated verbally. Subjects were instructed to recall words that had pleasant and unpleasant meanings. The subjects had no difficulty in doing so. Examples of pleasant words are: *love, beautiful, sweet, happy, sunshine.* Examples of unpleasant words are: *hate, ugly, death, stink, vomit.* Such pleasant and unpleasant words were recalled with little or no sign of genuine affective arousal. Whether or not conscious feelings of pleasantness and unpleasantness accompanied the recall is a moot question. There is no doubt that subjects can be aware of the cognitive *meanings* of pleasantness and unpleasantness apart from, and independently of, affective arousal.

It is important in systematic psychology to distinguish between affective meanings (which are cognitive) and genuine feelings and emotions (affective arousals). The cognitive and affective components of experience often fuse; they are interrelated.

AFFECTIVE AROUSAL AND EVALUATION

Is a science of value possible? It has frequently been said that science deals with facts and not with values. I doubt it. The preferential behavior of my rats is definitely evaluative and indicative of built-in evaluative mechanisms. These mechanisms can be studied objectively, quantitatively, experimentally, critically. Although complex human evaluations are largely cognitive processes, the primary evaluations of lower animals are mainly affective. At least some evaluative processes can be dealt with scientifically.

The primary evaluations of accepting or rejecting a foodstuff depend upon bodily structures that are the final products of evolution. During the long course of evolution, structures have developed that associate unpleasantness with biological harm and pleasantness with biological welfare of individual or species.

The physical basis of evaluation lies within the organism and is revealed by a dynamic organism-environment relation. Value does not reside within the physical stimulus object. Attempts to describe value as a physical attribute of the stimulus are doomed to failure. For example, stimulus intensity does not correlate perfectly with hedonic value. I have found that rats prefer salt solutions of low concentration to those of high concentration. And, as we have seen, human observers rate faint tones of low pitch as pleasing more frequently than loud, high-pitched tones. Nor is preference wholly a matter of size. A diamond is preferred to a boulder! Values are biologically and psychologically determined.

Moralists have distinguished between two kinds of hedonic values: pleasure and happiness. Pleasure is regarded as sensual. Happiness, contrastingly, is more lofty and a chronic state of affairs. Happiness is slowly achieved through progressive gain in control over one's surroundings. The happy individual is persistently well adjusted to his life situation.

What is happiness? There are numerous popular (sometimes humorous) and philosophical answers. While preparing this paper I encountered, among others, these two examples: "Happiness is not a destination but a daily way of traveling." And from a member of this Association: "Happiness is an uninhibited hypothalamus. . . ." Now, whatever happiness may be, it is something of positive value and unhappiness is something of negative value. We believe that free men everywhere have an inalienable right to life, liberty, and the pursuit of—an uninhibited hypothalamus!

Conclusion

I have tried to show that the role of primary affective arousal is to sustain or terminate activities according to the hedonic principle of maximizing the positive and minimizing the negative, and to organize dispositions which themselves become regulative. I have tried to demonstrate that a multiple-aspect, eclectic, approach to problems of affective arousal is useful. And, finally, that the concept of affective arousal is central in importance for a possible science of value and for psychology as a whole.

References

Arnold, M. B. *Emotion and personality.* Vol. 1. *Psychological aspects.* New York: Columbia University Press, 1960.

Brown, J. S. Pleasure-seeking behavior and the drive-reduction hypothesis. *Psychological Review,* 1955, *62,* 169–179.

Delgado, J. M. R., Roberts, W. W., & Miller, N. E. Learning motivated by electrical stimulation of the brain. *American Journal of Physiology,* 1954, *179,* 587–593.

Festinger, L. *A theory of cognitive dissonance.* Evanston, Ill.: Row, Peterson, 1957.

Guilford, J. P. A study of psychodynamics. *Psychometrika,* 1939, *4,* 1–23.

Guilford, J. P. System in the relationships of affective value to frequency and intensity of auditory stimuli. *American Journal of Psychology,* 1954, *67,* 691–695.

Heath, R. G. Pleasure response of human subjects to direct stimulation of the brain: Physiologic and psychodynamic considerations. In R. G. Heath (Ed.), *The role of pleasure in behavior—a symposium by 22 authors.* New York: Harper & Row, Hoeber Medical Division, 1964. Pp. 219–243.

Kappauf, W. E., Burright, R. G., & DeMarco, W. Sucrose-quinine mixtures which are isohedonic for the rat. *Journal of Comparative and Physiological Psychology,* 1963, *56,* 138–143.

Kniep, E. H., Morgan, W. L., & Young, P .T. Studies in affective psychology: XI. Individual differences in affective reaction to odors. XII. The relation between age and affective reaction to odors. *American Journal of Psychology,* 1931, *43,* 406–421.

Lindsley, D. B. Emotion. In S. S. Stevens (Ed.), *Handbook of experimental psychology.* New York: Wiley, 1951. Pp. 473–516.

Magoun, H. W. Central neural inhibition. In M. R. Jones (Ed.), *Nebraska symposium on motivation: 1963.* Lincoln: University of Nebraska Press, 1963. Pp. 161–193.

Olds, J., & Milner, P. Positive reinforcement produced by electrical stimulation of septal area and other regions of rat brain. *Journal of Comparative and Physiological Psychology,* 1954, *47,* 419–427.

Olds, J., & Olds, M. E. The mechanism of voluntary behavior. In R. G. Heath (Ed.), *The role of pleasure in behavior—a symposium by 22 authors.* New York: Harper & Row, Hoeber Medical Division, 1964. Pp. 23–53.

Pribram, K. H. Reinforcement revisited: A structural view. In M. R. Jones (Ed.), *Nebraska symposium on motivation: 1963.* Lincoln: University of Nebraska Press, 1963. Pp. 113–159.

Sherrington, C. S. *The integrative action of the nervous system.* New Haven: Yale University Press, 1911.

Singer, W. B., & Young, P. T. Studies in affective reaction. II. Dependence of affective ratings upon the stimulus-situation. *Journal of General Psychology,* 1941, *24,* 303–325.

Stein, L. Facilitation of avoidance behavior by positive brain stimulation. *Journal of Comparative and Physiological Psychology,* 1965, *60,* 9–19.

Young, P. T. An experimental study of mixed feelings. *American Journal of Psychology,* 1918, *29,* 237–271.

Young, P. T. A study upon the recall of pleasant and unpleasant words. *American Journal of Psychology,* 1937, *49,* 581–596.

Young P. T. Hedonic organization and regulation of behavior. *Psychological Review,* 1966, *73,* 59–86.

Young, P. T. Palatability: The hedonic response to foodstuffs. In C. F. Code et al. (Eds.), *Handbook of Physiology.* Section 6. *Alimentary Canal.* Vol. 1 Baltimore: Williams & Wilkins, 1967, in press. (a)

Young, P. T. Physiological drives. In D. L. Sills (Ed.), *International Encyclopedia of the Social Sciences.* New York: Macmillan, 1967, in press. (b)

Young, P. T., & Chaplin, J. P. Studies of food preference, appetite and dietary habit: III. Palatability and appetite in relation to bodily need. *Comparative Psychology Monographs*, 1945, *18* (3, Whole No. 95).

Young, P. T., & Greene, J. T. Quantity of food ingested as a measure of relative acceptability. *Journal of Comparative and Physiological Psychology*, 1953, *46*, 288–294.

Young, P. T., & Madsen, C. H., Jr. Individual isohedons in sucrose-sodium chloride and sucrose-saccharin gustatory areas. *Journal of Comparative and Physiological Psychology*, 1963, *56*, 903–909.

Young, P. T., & Schulte, R. H. Isohedonic contours and tongue activity in three gustatory areas of the rat. *Journal of Comparative and Physiological Psychology*, 1963, *56*, 465–475.

Young, P. T., & Trafton, C. L. Activity contour maps as related to preference in four gustatory stimulus areas of the rat. *Journal of Comparative and Physiological Psychology*, 1964, *58*, 68–75.

pain as a puzzle for psychology and physiology[1]

ernest r. hilgard
stanford university

Pain is so familiar that we take it for granted, but this does not lessen its importance. The medical profession may be thought of as dedicated to two tasks, the preservation of life and the reduction of pain and suffering. The ubiquity of pain is clear enough from our TV commercials, which pit one pain-killer against another.

While pain is thus a problem for the physician and surgeon, it is also a problem for the psychologist and

1. The preparation of this paper, and the investigations here reported, have been supported by the National Institutes of Health, Public Health Service, Grant MH-3859, and by a contract with the U.S. Air Force Office of Scientific Research (Contract AF 49[638]-1436). Reprinted from *American Psychologist*, 1969, Vol. 24. Copyright 1969 by the American Psychological Association and reproduced by permission.

for the physiologist. As psychologists we are familiar with the ancient dichotomy between pain and pleasure, and the affective and motivational significance that these terms imply. For the physiologist or psychophysiologist we have the task of discovering the events in the nervous system that produce a relationship between noxious stimulation and the reported experience of pain.

What is Puzzling About Pain?

The very familiarity of pain reduces our curiosity about it. Pain appears to warn us of tissue damage, and we may therefore dismiss it as "the cry of an injured nerve." Before going on to report some experiments I wish to reduce complacency about pain by raising a few questions about it, to point out the mysteries that remain to be unraveled.

1. *Is pain a sensory modality?* The first of these questions is this: Shall we consider pain to be a sensory modality like vision or audition? If you cut your finger or stub your toe, pain behaves very much as if it were an ordinary sensory modality. That is, there is a stimulus, there are receptors in the fingers and toes, there is an afferent transmission of impulses, a central processing of data, a perceptual response appropriate to the stimulus, and perhaps some verbal accompaniment—"Ouch." The perceptual response of felt pain localized in a finger or a toe is analogous to seeing a light off to the left or of hearing a sound off to your right. Perceptual responses give knowledge of environ-

mental events, and you guide your actions accordingly. Furthermore, the stimulus to pain can be graduated, as by an electric shock of varying intensity, or by water at different degrees of hot or cold, with subsequent changes in felt pain. All that I have said thus far qualifies pain as a sensory modality.

But there are other considerations which make it less easy to assign pain the status of a sensory modality. Most defined sensory modalities have definite stimuli, definite receptors, specific sensory tracts, and localized receptive areas within the cortex. Not so for pain. Any stimulus can qualify to produce pain, if it is intense enough; loud sounds and very bright lights are painful. The receptors are unspecified, despite the role traditionally assigned to free nerve endings. While there are pathways for cutaneous pain, there are at least two afferent systems, and they operate quite differently (Melzack & Wall, 1965). And there is no one pain center that has been localized in the brain.

A further problem arises in that there are so many differences in the quality of felt pain that it may be as dubious to consider pain a single sense as to consider all cutaneous experiences as belonging to a single sense of touch. Even the attempt to define pain has met numerous obstacles (e.g., Beecher, 1959; Melzack, 1968). One of the puzzles is how to deal with the distinction between mild sensory pain and the intense pains that are described as suffering or anguish; under frontal lobe operations, for example, the anguish may be reduced even though the pain remains.

We must therefore give a qualified answer to the question whether or not pain can be counted as a sensory modality.

2. *Are there any satisfactory physiological indicators of pain?* We know about pain through a subject's verbal reports, but if we expect to objectify the amount of pain he feels we would be happy to have some physiological indicators by which to compare his pain with that of others who suffer. Our second question is, then: Do satisfactory indicators exist?

A satisfactory physiological indicator of pain is one which is present (or increased) when pain is felt, and absent (or reduced) when pain is not felt. The correlation between the physiological indicator and the verbal report has to be established both positively and negatively if the indicator is to be used in confidence in the absence of supplementary verbal report. Without attempting at this time a literature review, may I simply summarize the state of our knowledge of the physiological correlates of pain by saying that there is at present *no single accepted indicator of pain* that can be counted to vary in an orderly way with degrees of pain and absence of pain.[2] While in many experiments some kind of average difference in a physiological response can be detected with increase in pain, individual differences in the patterning of responses, and some individual response stereotypy to different kinds of stress, complicate the problem.

3. *Where is the pain that is felt?* My third question about the puzzle of pain is this: Where is the pain that the subject reports? A subject locates the pain of an injury at the site of the injury or noxious stimulation by the same sorts of local signs and environmental references that he uses in localizing other sources of stimulation. I say: "I feel pain in my finger." My listener sees that the finger is bleeding, and replies: "No wonder you feel pain in your finger; you cut it." The pain is in my finger just as the word I read is on the printed page. The psychoneural *conditions* of feeling pain and of seeing words are within me, but it would be as uninformative to say that the pain is in my head as to say that the word I read is in my head. We have to distinguish between the *conditions* of the perception and the *informative aspect* of the perception itself. The *information* is of a pain in my finger and of a word on the printed page.

The trouble about pain as informative is that there are at least three kinds of pain which make us wonder whether or not to accept the information conferred by the localized pain. The first of these is *referred* pain, in which the source of irritation is one place and the pain is felt at another place, as in heartburn as a result of indigestion. The second is *psychosomatic* pain, in which the stimulus conditions may be vague, as in a headache following a political argument. The third kind is *phantom limb* pain, where the pain is felt in a part of the body which has been amputated from it. Of these, phantom limb pain is particularly interesting. Our tendency to revert to a strict sensory analogy is very strong; hence we would expect phantom limb pain to be the result of referring the stimulation of a cut nerve

2. There have been a great many reviews of the literature on pain, of which Melzack (1968) and Sternbach (1968) can serve as recent representatives and as sources of citations of earlier reviews.

in the stump to the limb from which it originally received its impulses. However, phantom limb pain probably has more to do with body image than with local signs (Melzack, 1968; Szasz, 1957; Sternbach, 1968). The reply to our question must then be that, *as information* (even if it be false) the best we can do is to accept that the pains are where they are felt, including the phantom limb pains; as *conditions* for pain, there are many complex events within the nervous system.

4. How to account for the great individual differences in felt pain? My fourth and final question about the puzzle of pain has to do with the *lack* of relationship between the conditions of noxious stimulation and the amount of pain that is felt. This is primarily a matter of individual differences, but they are very impressive. I am not talking about the extreme cases of people who are born with practically complete lack of sensitivity to cutaneous or other pains. These people correspond in their own way to the totally blind or the totally deaf. Within the normal population, however, there are widespread differences, and it is these which concern us now.

In the relief of postsurgical pain through morphine, Beecher and his associates (Beecher, 1959) have found results that may be summarized roughly as follows: about a third of the patients gain relief of pain through morphine that is greater than the relief following a placebo; about a third get as much relief from a placebo as they do from morphine; the final third are relieved neither by placebo nor by morphine in doses considered safe to use.

Differences in pain response are found to be related to cognitive styles by Petrie (1967). She reports that subjects selected on the basis of a test of kinesthetic aftereffects can be classified as *augmenters* or *reducers:* the augmenters exaggerate their pain responses and the reducers tend to inhibit theirs.

Differences in pain responsiveness, particularly complaints about pain, have been found to be associated with social class, ethnic groups, and family constellation. For example, Gonda (1962a, 1962b) found that those from the working class complain more to the nurses in hospitals than do those from white collar classes, an observation confirmed in England as well as in the United States.

Finally, pain responses in the laboratory appear to follow some of the theories of cognitive consistency, in that the pain corresponds to the amount of reward of-

fered for participating in pain experiments; the greater the reward the greater the pain, as though more suffering is consistent with the higher pay for participation (Lewin, 1965; Zimbardo & others, 1966).

By raising these four questions, about pain as a sensory modality, about the physiological indicators of pain, about where pain is felt, and about individual differences in pain responsiveness, I hope that you will now agree that there are sufficient unsolved problems to make a concerned attack on pain a fruitful scientific enterprise.

Pain as a Sensory Modality: Cold Pressor Response and Ischemic Pain in the Normal Waking State[3]

We have used two sources of noxious stimulation in the experiments I am about to report. In the first of these we produce pain by placing the subject's hand and forearm in circulating cold water at several temperatures. This arrangement is commonly referred to as the *cold pressor test* (Hines & Brown, 1932; Wolf & Hardy, 1941; Greene & others, 1965). In the second method we produce the pain by first placing a tourniquet just above the elbow, and then asking the subject to squeeze a dynamometer a standard number of times. After he quits working and is quiet, the pain begins to mount. This we call *ischemic pain,* following the practice of Beecher and his associates (Beecher, 1966; Smith & others, 1966). Their method is a modification of the method initiated by Lewis and others (1931).

First, the cold pressor test. I shall not report here the details of experimental arrangements, which will appear in due course in the form of journal articles. Suffice it to say that there are baseline conditions: first, a *vigilance* condition in which the subject keeps alert by pressing the appropriate one of a pair of buttons, to

3. Among the professional workers in the Laboratory of Hypnosis Research who have contributed most directly to the pain studies reported here I wish to mention Leslie M. Cooper, Arthur Lange, John Lenox, Arlene H. Morgan, Lewis B. Sachs, Toshimasa Saito, and John Voevodsky. A number of others have assisted in the record reading and data analysis. I wish to express my appreciation to these coworkers for permitting me to make use of the results of our joint efforts as they have appeared in reports already published, and as they will appear in other reports in which the participants will be coauthors.

turn off that one of two discriminable sounds which happens to be sounding; this is followed by a condition of *relaxation* for several minutes prior to the immersion of the hand and forearm in the cold water; the *immersion period,* usually of 40 seconds; then, after the hand and arm are removed from the water and dried, a repetition of the vigilance and relaxation conditions. Except as part of the situational background, the baseline conditions are not important for the present psychophysical account, but they are important for the physiological measures which were taken concomitantly with the verbal reports. While the hand and forearm are immersed in the cold water, the subject reports his felt pain on a scale of 0 to 10, 0 being no pain, and 10 being a pain so severe that he would wish to remove his hand. We refer to this as a *critical level,* for it is the tolerance level for the pain, without special encouragement to continue to suffer. If a subject has reached the pain level of 10 before the immersion period is over, we persuade him to keep his hand in the water a little longer and to keep on counting. This he is able to do, and the result is of course a number of pain reports beyond 10.

That such verbal pain reports yield an orderly relationship to the conditions of stimulation, both to the temperature of the water, and to the time in the water, is shown by the mean results for 0°, 5°, 10°, and 15° C. as plotted in Figure 1. The means of the pain-state reports in each of the temperatures differ significantly from each of the other temperatures by *t*-tests, with significances of at least $p = .05$.

These data appear orderly enough to provide a test of standard psychophysical models. The model chosen is Stevens' power function (e.g., Stevens, 1966) because it proves to fit better than the standard Fechner logarithmic function. The test is quite simple. If both the numerical pain report and some measure of the intensity of stimulation are plotted logarithmically, the power function fits if a straight-line function results.

We have the single scale for verbal pain reports, but we have two possibilities for describing the intensity of stimulation: one, the *temperature* of the water, on the simple assumption that the colder the water the greater the pain; two, the *time* in the water, on the assumption that the pain mounts the longer the hand and forearm are exposed to the cold. The two measures have a common intermediary, which is the relationship between cold and pain, but there is no *a*

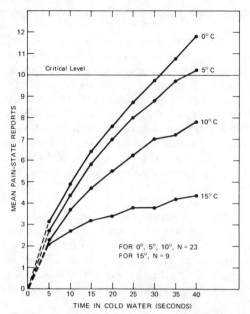

Fig. 1
Reported pain as a function of time in water at temperatures of 0°, 5°, and 15° C.

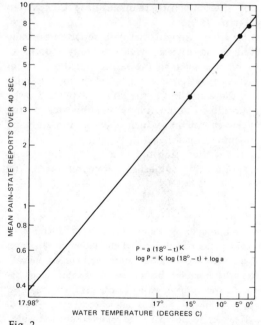

Fig. 2
Pain as a power function of the difference in water temperature from the threshold value of 18° C.

Pain as a Puzzle for Psychology and Physiology   69

priori reason for both of them to fit the same mathematical function.

Let us first see how pain varies as a function of water temperature. Other workers have found that the threshold for cold pressor pain is near 18° C. This is well below skin temperature, but water can feel cold without feeling painful. If we then plot the average pain-state reports at 15°, 10°, 5°, and 0° on a scale which assumes that as the water gets colder the pain will be a power function of the difference in water temperature from the threshold value of 18° we get the plot shown in Figure 2. The four plotted points fall quite well along a straight line, and the line projects to a threshold value of pain near 18°.

Now we may ask whether a similar result will be obtained if we plot pain as a power function of the time in water of a given temperature. Because we have four temperatures, we have a family of four lines, as shown in Figure 3. Again the straight lines fit well enough to indicate the appropriateness of the power function.[4]

Turning now to ischemia, as our second form of laboratory pain, and using the same scale of pain reports, we again find a power function with time, although now the time units are in minutes rather than in seconds (Figure 4).

Thus far I have shown that pain reported verbally on a simple numerical scale yields not only orderly results, but valid results, in the sense that the pain reported bears a systematic relationship to the temperature of the water and to the time of exposure to the noxious stimulus. The lawfulness is supported by the fit of the power function which holds within so many other perceptual modalities.

I emphasize these findings as a reply to those who would degrade the subject's statements as being

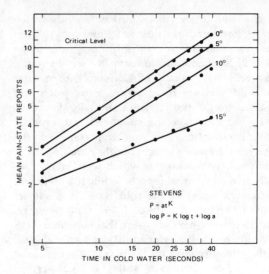

Fig. 3
Pain as a power function of time in cold water.

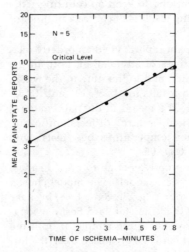

Fig. 4
Pain as a function of time in ischemia.

4. There are limitations in the fit of the power functions for both the cold pressor response and the ischemic response, when the stimulating condtions endure too long. In the cold pressor response numbing begins to set in at about 60 seconds for 0° C. water; in the case of ischemia there may be a sudden upturn of pain as the critical tolerance level is passed. We have elsewhere proposed a more complex function which can be used when there are inflections in the rate of change of pain or when the pain change is not monotonic (Voevodsky, Cooper, Morgan, & Hilgard, 1967).

"merely" verbal reports, as though some sort of physiological response would be sounder. I wish to assert flatly that there is no physiological measure of pain which is either as discriminating of fine differences in stimulus condtions, as reliable upon repetition, or as lawfully related to changed conditions, as the subject's verbal report.

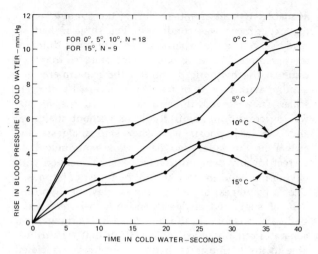

Fig. 5
Blood pressure as a function of time in water at four temperatures.

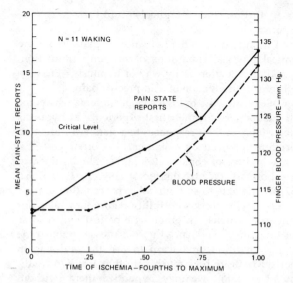

Fig. 6
Pain reports and blood pressure as a function of time in ischemia.

Physiological Accompaniments of Pain

If I seem to disparage physiological indicators of pain, it is not because we have not studied them, nor indeed because results are negative, for I shall have some positive results to report. We have studied a number of measures, but I shall confine my discussion to one indicator, systolic blood pressure as measured from a finger on the hand opposite to that which is suffering the pain. We place a small inflatable cuff around one finger, with a plethysmographic transducer on the finger tip to indicate when the pulse is occluded. Another plethysmograph on an adjacent finger helps us to monitor heart responses. An automatically operated air pump inflates the finger cuff until the circulation is cut off, as indicated by the record from the plethysmograph on that finger, and then a device automatically releases the air from the cuff until the pulse again appears and is restored to normal, when the cycle automatically repeats itself. Thus a record is obtained on the polygraph of the systolic blood pressure every 10 seconds or so. By connecting these measurements as they appear on the polygraph we have an essentially continuous record of the blood pressure.

The rise in pain in the cold water is accompanied by a rise in blood pressure, and the rise in ischemic pain is also accompanied by a rise in blood pressure. Thus, under appropriate conditions, blood pressure appears to be the kind of indicator of pain for which

we have been searching. A record of the blood pressure rise within cold water at four temperatures is given in Figure 5, which corresponds closely to the verbal pain reports earlier shown in Figure 1. The average results hold also for individual subjects. That is, those who suffer less at a given temperature also show less rise in blood pressure. Thus, for water at 0° C., a correlation between mean pain reports and blood pressure rise for 22 subjects reaches $r = +.53$, a satisfactorily significant correlation $r(p=.02)$. Others have reported similar findings (e.g., Tétreault & others, 1964).

Blood pressure also rises as pain rises in ischemia. Rise in pain reports and rise in blood pressure yield the curves shown in Figure 6. These are means for 11 subjects. The abscissa has been converted to ratios of time in ischemia in order to plot the several subjects in comparable units. The time to maximum tolerable pain (at which the tourniquet had to be removed) fell between 12 and 32 minutes, by contrast with the water pain which was measured over a fraction of a minute only.

Thus we have established blood pressure as a candidate to serve as an indicator of pain. At least, in two stressful situations, it mounts as the pain mounts. As we shall see later, this does not satisfy all the requisites for a physiological pain indicator.

Pain Reduction Under Hypnosis: Cold Pressor Response

Now I wish to turn to the reduction of pain, under the identical physical conditions of stressful stimulation, when that reduction is by way of hypnosis.[5] First we shall consider reduction of cold pressor pain.

College students or high school students who come to the laboratory for their first experience of hypnosis differ widely in their responses to a standard induction procedure followed by a standard list of suggestions. By making use of some scales earlier standardized in our laboratory (Weitzenhoffer & Hilgard, 1959, 1962, 1967) we are able to sort our subjects according to their degree of hypnotic susceptibility before they take part in the experiments concerned with pain. Then, at some later time, they experience the cold pressor pain in the waking condition, and learn to use the verbal pain report to indicate how much pain they feel. On a subsequent occasion we may hypnotize them, without suggesting any pain reduction, and then expose them to immersion in the cold water, or we may hypnotize them and tell them that they will feel no pain in the cold water. This is the condition which we call attempted hypnotic analgesia. The subjects who entered the ice water experiments had had very little experience of hypnosis, and they were not trained in pain reduction. Our purpose was not to see how completely we could wipe out pain, but rather to see what individual differences in pain reduction would appear under standard conditions.

Because we did not have blood pressure measures on the subjects of our first reported experiment,[6] I shall turn to our second experiment which was partially a replication of the first one, but also introduced some modifications. We used high school students as subjects in this second investigation, instead of college students, largely because they were conveniently available in large numbers during the summer when the experiment was conducted. The subjects had already served in the experiment with water at different temperatures, in the normal waking state, so that they came to the hypnotic portion of the experiment well familiar with reports of pain on the verbal pain-state scale. They served three days, one in the normal waking condition, one in hypnosis without analgesia, and one in hypnosis with suggested analgesia; the orders of the latter two days were randomized, to correct for any demand characteristics associated with having the hand in ice water in the midst of hypnosis. The advantages of comparing a day of hypnosis *without* suggested analgesia and hypnosis *with* analgesia are two fold. In the first place, this arrangement separates out any physiological effects that are attributable to the hypnosis as distinct from those associated with the stressful stimulus, and, in the second place, it rules out the effect upon pain of whatever relaxation is associated with hypnotic induction. It is well known that relaxation may itself reduce pain. The results for the three days are shown in Figure 7, plotted separately for the subjects low in hypnotic susceptibility and for those high in susceptibility. What we see from the figure is that hypnosis alone did not reduce pain appreciably for either group, but the suggested analgesia did indeed produce a reduction in verbally reported pain, slightly for the low hypnotizables, more for the high hypnotizables. In Figure 7 the high and low susceptibles are the extremes of a larger distribution, so that a correlational analysis is not appropriate. For a smaller group of 19 subjects, unselected for hypnosis, and including moderates as well as highs and lows, the correlation between hypnotic susceptibility as tested prior to the pain experiment and the pain reduction under hypnosis turned out to be $r = .60$ ($p = .01$).

5. The experimental literature on pain reduction (and pain production) in hypnosis is very confused, despite the well-established clinical successes in childbirth, dentistry, major surgery, and the successful relief of pain through hypnosis in severe burns and terminal cancer. A few of the major reports from other laboratories of experimental studies are listed here for the benefit of those who may care to explore this literature: Barber & Hahn (1962, 1964), Brown & Vogel (1938), Doupe, Miller & Keller (1939), Dudley & others (1964, 1966), Dynes (1932), Levine (1930), Sears (1932), Shor (1962), Sutcliffe (1961), West, Neill & Hardy (1952), Wolff & Goodell (1943).

6. Hilgard (1967). In this first experiment of the series with the cold pressor response, reactions from 55 college students were reported. The correlation between the amount of pain reduction under hypnotic analgesia and susceptibility to hypnosis was reported as $r = .37$ ($p = .01$). If one very discordant subject is eliminated, this rises to $r = .46$. See also Hilgard & others (1967).

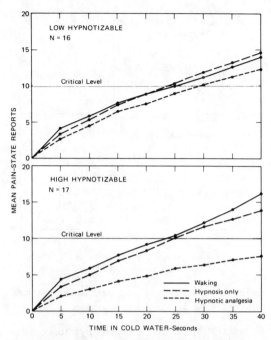

Fig. 7
Pain as a function of time in water of 0° C. in waking state, and following attempted hypnotic induction without analgesia instructions and with analgesia instructions. Low subjects, scores of 0–9 on combined forms A and C (mean=7.1); high subjects, scores of 18–24 on combined forms A and C (mean = 21.6).

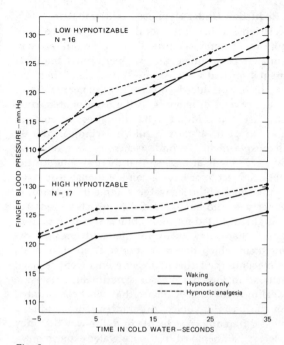

Fig. 8
Blood pressure as a function of time in water of 0° C. in waking state, and following attempted hypnotic induction without analgesia instructions and with analgesia instructions. Same subjects as in Figure 7.

The verbal pain reports thus yield an orderly picture of pain reduction under hypnotic analgesia, with the greatest reduction found for those who are the most hypnotizable. Now what of the blood pressure measures? Will they continue to correlate with pain reports under these conditions? To our surprise, the blood pressure *rises* under hypnosis and is highest under the analgesic condition, for both high and low hypnotizable subjects (Figure 8). It may be noted that, particularly for the high hypnotizable subjects, the blood pressure rises before the hands are placed in the ice water, so that the initial readings are above those of the less hypnotizable.

We are thus led to two propositions about the relationship between blood pressure and pain:

1. *When pain is felt there is a tendency for blood pressure to rise in an amount correlated with the amount of experienced pain,* and

2. *Blood pressure may rise in a stressful situation independent of the amount of felt pain.*

The second of these statements is my reason for asserting that blood pressure is not a completely satisfactory physiological indicator of pain. It works in some situations, but not in others. There is nothing very surprising about this, because we know that there are many controls over blood pressure of which pain is but one. The two propositions, taken together, show that we have to be careful not to identify a *correlate* of pain, found in some special arrangement, with the pain itself. We may note also that we have to avoid a superficial interpretation of pain reduction under hypnosis by claiming that the effects of hypnotic analgesia rest entirely on the reduction of anxiety; it appears that excitation, possibly with some anxiety over the impending stress, may keep the blood pressure high, even while the pain is reduced.

Pain Reduction Under Hypnosis: Ischemic Pain

The relationship between blood pressure and pain reduction under hypnosis turned out quite differently in ischemia. It is fortunate that we performed both experiments, for had we performed only one of them we might have produced misleading generalizations. There are several differences in the experiments to be noted. First, the cold water has the stress of cold, in addition to pain, while the cold is lacking in the ischemia experiment. Second, ischemic pain tends to mount very slowly at first, so that there is time for the hypnotic subject to achieve a confident analgesic state, while the shock of the ice water is immediate. Third, in the experiments to be reported the subjects were much more highly selected for their ability to reduce pain in hypnosis than they were in the cold pressor experiment, in which they were not selected at all. Still, the subjects in the ischemia experiments were selected from those in the cold pressor experiment, so we are not dealing with idiosyncrasies that can be accounted for on the basis of subject differences. These subjects behaved differently in ischemia from the way that they themselves had behaved in the ice water experiment.

It turns out that in the ischemia experiment these highly responsive subjects were able not only to rid themselves completely of pain for a matter of 18 to 45 minutes, but their blood pressure, which rose sharply in the waking state, *did not rise in ischemia or rose very little* even though the stressful condition was continued for many minutes beyond the time, in the waking condition, when the pain was too severe to be further endured. Results for six subjects, all of whom suffered greatly in the waking state but were able to maintain their analgesia throughout in the hypnotic state, are shown in Figure 9. The time to unbearable pain in the waking state is taken as unity; under hypnotic analgesia the tourniquet was kept on well beyond the time at which the intolerable pain would have been found in the waking state. Two subjects were unable to remain analgesic throughout; their blood pressures showed changes beyond the subjects reported in Figure 9. While they were eliminated from Figure 9, statistical treatment with them left in shows a significant difference (t=3.12, df=7, p=.01) between the rise in blood pressure in the waking state over hypnotic analgesia for the whole group of subjects tested.

The three additional subjects whose responses to ischemia in the waking state were reported earlier (in

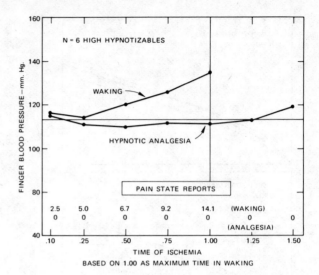

Fig. 9

Blood pressure in ischemia, in waking state and in hypnotic analgesia (mean 6 subjects).

Figure 6) were subjects refractory to hypnosis, who were intended to be used as simulators in the hypnotic analgesia experiment, according to the experimental design recommended by Orne (1959, 1962). It turned out that the stress was too great, however, and none of them could tolerate the pain for the time required to parallel the behavior of the "true" hypnotic analgesia subjects. While this in some respects spoiled the experimental design, the conclusions are the same regarding the reality of the hypnotic analgesia for the "true" subjects, substantiated by the lack of any appreciable rise in blood pressure.

We are now prepared to add a third proposition regarding the relationship between blood pressure and pain:

3. *When stressful conditions which normally lead both to pain and to an increase in blood pressure do not lead to an increase in blood pressure, it may be assumed that pain is absent.*

This now brings us to a conclusion regarding the reality of hypnotic analgesia and to a summary assertion about the role of blood pressure. The absence of pain, reported by the hypnotically analgesic subject, is confirmed by the absence of a rise in blood pressure. Thus we have a physiological validation for the reality of hypnotic analgesia, but the validator works in one direction only. That is, *absence* of the blood pressure rise may be taken as an indication of absent pain under specified conditions, but pain may be absent *even if blood pressure rises.* This is a logical problem which has caused a good deal of confusion in earlier efforts to deal with the question of pain reduction under hypnotic analgesia (see especially Sutcliffe, 1961; Barber, 1963; Barber & Hahn, 1962).

The Clinical Relevance of the Laboratory Study of Pain and Hypnotic Analgesia

I wish to close my remarks with a few comments on the practical implications of the kind of experiments I have reported. There are continuing arguments over the relative amounts of money and energy to be expended on basic research and on research aimed at the applications of science. There are those who take the position that basic research is an end in itself, designed to satisfy curiosity, to seek the truth, to discover and order knowledge for its own sake. There are others who take the position that basic science will ultimately pay off in its contributions to society, although immediate payoff is not to be expected; this is the essence of the position that "there is nothing so practical as a good theory." On the more general issues, I take a moderate position: I believe that science has multiple aims, that there is a division of labor along the spectrum from pure science to the arts of practice, that there should be mutual respect and encouragement for those who work at any point along this spectrum, so long as their work is imaginative and sound.

When, however, there is an evident application for laboratory results I believe there is an obligation on the scientific enterprise as a whole to provide the bridging investigations that move from the laboratory to the real world. Thus the psychology of learning is incomplete if it is not reflected in educational practices, and the study of pain is incomplete if it does not contribute to the relief of pain outside the laboratory.

One may well ask how the experiments which I have reported bear upon the relief of pain through hypnosis by dentists, obstetricians, surgeons, and others who are confronted with the practical problems of suffering people. The answer is that the studies alone will not make much of a contribution unless they are extended to deal with the practical problems, either by those within laboratories such as ours, or by others who build upon our findings.

The potential contributions fall along the following lines:

1. First, our hypnotic susceptibility scales make it possible to determine what kinds of responsiveness to hypnosis are essential if a patient is to profit from the use of hypnosis in pain reduction. Not all people can be helped, and one obligation upon science is to be diagnostic regarding those who can be served by particular applications. It must be pointed out, however, that until normative data are obtained in the practical setting, the scales cannot be used effectively.

2. Second, the further study of the physiological consequences of pain, and the alterations of these consequences by hypnotic analgesia, can yield better understanding of what is happening in otherwise stressful conditions, such as the preparation for surgery or surgery itself. If hypnosis can reduce surgical pain or postoperative shock, it is important to know what is happening inside the body. Again, unless these studies are carried out eventually in the hospital, the information gained in the laboratory will tend to be idle and useless.

We have accepted this as part of the responsibility of our own laboratory, and have undertaken studies of some patients suffering the pains of terminal cancer, others with migraine headaches. Clinicians are at present far ahead of our laboratories in the hypnotic reduction of pain, but the laboratory worker has a contribution to make. The contribution will be made, however, only if he takes his obligation seriously, and goes to the necessary trouble to tailor his findings to the needs of the world outside the laboratory.

References

Barber, T. X. The effects of "hypnosis" on pain: A critical review of experimental and clinical finding. *Psychosomatic Medicine*, 1963, 24, 303–333.

Barber, T. X., & Hahn, K. W., Jr. Physiological and subjective responses to pain-producing stimulation under hypnotically suggested and waking-imagined "analgesia." *Journal of Abnormal and Social Psychology*, 1962, 65, 411–418.

Barber, T. X., & Hahn, K. W., Jr. Experimental studies in "hypnotic" behavior: Physiologic and subjective effects of imagined pain. *Journal of Nervous and Mental Disease*, 1964, *139*, 416–425.

Beecher, H. K. *Measurement of Subjective Responses*. New York: Oxford University Press, 1959.

Beecher, H. K. Pain: One mystery solved. *Science*, 1966, *151*, 840–841.

Brown, R. R. & Vogel, V. H. Psychophysiological reactions following painful stimuli under hypnotic analgesia contrasted with gas anesthesia and Novocain block. *Journal of Applied Psychology*, 1938, *22*, 408–420.

Doupe, J., Miller, W. R., & Keller, W. K. Vasomotor reactions in the hypnotic state. *Journal of Neurology and Psychiatry*, 1939, *2*, 97–106.

Dudley, D. L., Holmes, T. H., Martin, C. J., & Ripley, H. S. Changes in respiration associated with hypnotically induced emotion, pain, and exercise. *Psychosomatic Medicine*, 1964, *24*, 46–57.

Dudley, D. L., Holmes, T. H., Martin, C. J., & Ripley, H. S. Hypnotically induced facsimile of pain. *Archives of General Psychiatry*, 1966, *15*, 198–204.

Dynes, J. B. Hypnotic analgesia. *Journal of Abnormal and Social Psychology*, 1932, *27*, 79–88.

Gonda, T. A. The relation between complaints of persistent pain and family size. *Journal of Neurology, Neurosurgery, and Psychiatry*, 1962a, *25*, 277–281.

Gonda, T. A. Some remarks on pain. *Bulletin, British Psychological Society*, 1962b, *47*, 29–35.

Greene, M. A., Boltax, A. J., Lustig, G. A., & Rogow, E. Circulatory dynamics during the cold pressor test. *American Journal of Cardiology*, 1965, *16*, 54–60.

Hilgard, E. R. A quantitative study of pain and its reduction through hypnotic suggestion. *Proceedings of the National Academy of Sciences*, 1967, *57*, 1581–1586.

Hilgard, E. R., Cooper, L. M., Lenox, J., Morgan, A. H., & Voevodsky, J. The use of pain-state reports in the study of hypnotic analgesia to the pain of ice water. *Journal of Nervous and Mental Disease*, 1967, *144*, 506–513.

Hines, E. A., & Brown, G. E. A standard stimulus for measuring vasomotor reactions: Its application in the study of hypertension. *Proceedings of Staff Meetings, Mayo Clinic*, 1932, *7*, 332.

Levine, M. Psychogalvanic reaction to painful stimuli in hypnotic and hysterical anesthesia. *Bulletin Johns Hopkins Hospital*, 1930, *46*, 331–339.

Lewin, I. The effect of reward on the experience of pain. *Dissertations in Cognitive Processes*. Detroit, Michigan: Center for Cognitive Processes, Wayne State University, 1965.

Lewis, T., Pickering, G. W., & Rothschild, P. Observations upon muscular pain in intermittent claudication. *Heart*, 1931, *15*, 359–383.

Melzack, R. Pain. *International Encyclopedia of the Social Sciences*. New York: Macmillan and Free Press, 1968, *11*, 357–363.

Melzack, R., & Wall, P. D. Pain mechanisms: A new theory. *Science*, 1965, *150*, 971–979.

Orne, M. T. The nature of hypnosis: Artifact and essence. *Journal of Abnormal and Social Psychology*, 1959, *58*, 277–299.

Orne, M. T. On the social psychology of the psychological experiment: with particular reference to demand characteristics and their implications. *American Psychologist*, 1962, *17*, 776–783.

Petrie, A. *Individuality in Pain and Suffering*. Chicago: University of Chicago Press, 1967.

Sears, R. R. Experimental study of hypnotic anesthesia. *Journal of Experimental Psychology*, 1932, *15*, 1–22.

Shor, R. E. Physiological effects of painful stimulation during hypnotic analgesia under conditions designed to minimize anxiety. *International Journal of Clinical and Experimental Hypnosis*, 1962, *8*, 151–163.

Smith, G. M., Lawrence, D. E., Markowitz, R. A., Mosteller, F., & Beecher, H. K. An experimental pain method sensitive to morphine in man: The submaximum effort tourniquet technique. *Journal of Pharmacology and Experimental Therapeutics*, 1966, *154*, 324–332.

Sternbach, R. A. *Pain: A Psychophysiological Analysis*. New York: Academic Press, 1968.

Stevens, S. S. Matching functions between loudness and ten other continua. *Perception and Psychophysics*, 1966, *1*, 5–8.

Sutcliffe, J. P. "Credulous" and "skeptical" views of hypnotic phenomena: Experiments on esthesia, hallucination, and delusion. *Journal of Abnormal and Social Psychology*, 1961, *62*, 189–200.

Szasz, T. S. *Pain and Pleasure*. New York: Basic Books, 1957.

Tétreault, L., Panisset, A., & Gouger, P. Étude des facteurs, émotion et douleur dans la réponse tensionnelle au "cold pressor test." *L'Union Médicale du Canada*, 1964, *93*, 177–180.

Voevodsky, J., Cooper, L. M., Morgan, A. H., & Hilgard, E. R. The measurement of suprathreshold pain. *American Journal of Psychology*, 1967, *80*, 124–128.

Weitzenhoffer, A. M., & Hilgard, E. R. *Stanford Hypnotic Susceptibility Scales, Forms A and B.* Palo Alto, California: Consulting Psychologists Press, 1959.

Weitzenhoffer, A. M. & Hilgard, E. R. *Stanford Hypnotic Susceptibility Scales, Form C.* Palo Alto, California: Consulting Psychologists Press, 1962.

Weitzenhoffer, A. M., & Hilgard, E. R. *Revised Stanford Profile Scales of Hypnotic Susceptibility, Forms I and II.* Palo Alto, California: Consulting Psychologists Press, 1967.

West, L. J., Neill, K. C., & Hardy, J. D. Effects of hypnotic suggestions on pain perception and galvanic skin response. *Archives of Neurology and Psychiatry,* 1952, *68,* 549–560.

Wolf, S., & Hardy, J. D. Studies on pain: Observations on pain due to local cooling and on factors involved in the "cold pressor" effect. *Journal of Clinical Investigation,* 1941, *20,* 521–533.

Wolff, H. G., & Goodell, H. The relation of attitude and suggestion to the perception of and reaction to pain. *Proceedings of the Association for Research in Nervous and Mental Disease,* 1943, *23,* 434–448.

Zimbardo, P. G., Cohen, A. R., Weisenberg, M., Dworkin, L., & Firestone, I. Control of pain motivation by cognitive dissonance. *Science,* 1966, *151,* 217–219.

the surprising simplicity of sensory metrics[1]

s. s. stevens
harvard university

If you shine a faint light in your eye, you have a sensation of brightness — a weak sensation, to be sure. If you turn on a stronger light, the sensation becomes greater. Clearly, then, there is a relation between perceived brightness and the amount of light you put in the eye. The visual sense organ behaves as a transducer with an operating characteristic of some kind — an imput-output function. But how, precisely, does the output of the system (sensation) vary with the input (stimulus)? Suppose you double the stimulus, does it then look twice as bright?

The answer to that question happens to be no. It takes about nine times as much light to double the

1   Reprinted from *American Psychologist*, 1962, Vol. 17, pp. 29–39. Copyright 1962 by the American Psychological Association, and reproduced by permission.

apparent brightness, but this specific question, interesting as it may be, is only one instance of a wider problem: what are the input-output characteristics of sensory systems in general? Is there a single, simple, pervasive psychophysical law?

Unlikely as it may seem, there appears to be such a law. Its form is a power function, and not the logarithmic relation that is almost universally cited in textbooks. The power law, although not yet widely known, is becoming so well fortified with evidence that it may someday replace the older law in all discussions of sensory dynamics. The wonder is, in fact, how we could have missed finding the power law for so long, especially since it is so surprisingly simple to demonstrate.

I pause at this point to pay respect, as is the custom, to the engrossing pursuit we call science — that relentless intellectual scrimmage which means such diverse things to its many devotees. Some regard it as a quest, a nomological quest, wherein the quarry reveals itself from time to time in the form of simplicities and uniformities in the complex of nature. Others regard the canons of impersonal, nomothetic endeavor as oppressive strictures against the free-wheeling development of an ideographic, personal science. These two polar points of view have always been with us — the tough- and tender-minded, as William James called them; the hircine and the ovine, as E. G. Boring suggests they be named — and the clash of their differing value systems will no doubt resound until the final éclat. My own guess is that even a phenomenological existentialist would cherish a natural law if he found one. Perhaps the psychologists' questing for nomological principles ought to get extinguished for lack of frequent reinforcement, but obviously it does not. Maybe it comes with the organism, like native curiosity, wired in from the start. Whatever it is that motivates inquiry, we can be sure that psychologists will not renounce the experimental search for simple and powerful principles of behavior.

The discovery of a law does not put an end to the nomological pursuit. At least it never has. There seems in fact to exist a meta-nomological principle, a kind of higher law, which says: the announcement of a presumed law in science will trigger prompt and vigorous attempts at its refutation. This higher law holds in all the sciences, but it sometimes appears to enjoy its freshest expression in psychology, where, by precept and performance, we often set criticism above creation.

As regards the psychophysical power law, criticism must be left to others. My task is to explain why I think it is a law. A pleasant enough task, to be sure, but one that gives rise to a curious sense of embarrassment. Why, if the power law is so simple, obvious, and easy to confirm, did we fumble around for so long without noting its existence?

It is difficult to account for acts of unobservant oversight, for they are essentially empty and neutral. What can you say about what you did not see? One can only try to lessen the embarrassment by describing those matters that diverted attention from the proper object, or that led from seemingly sound premises to wrong conclusions.

In a larger sense, psychophysical metrics got sidetracked for a hundred years, mainly by Fechner's diligence in behalf of his famous logarithmic law. I will not dwell on that diversion, for it has been dealt with at length in another place (Stevens, 1961). To many of us who worked in audition in the 1930s there was no question that Fechner's law was awry, for did not the sone scale of loudness issue from experiments that had been undertaken simply because it was so obvious to the acoustical engineers that loudness is not proportional to decibels, as Fechner's law would make it? Yes, a quarter of a century ago we knew better than to rely on Fechner's law, but, for reasons that I will try to ex-

plain, we did not know what to put in its place. All that has now changed.

Evidence for the Power Law

Within a first-order approximation, there appears to be no exception to the principle that equal stimulus *ratios* correspond to equal sensation *ratios*. (Fechner proposed, 101 years ago, that equal stimulus *ratios* correspond to equal sensation *differences*, and it is this hypothesis that the ratio rule denies and that the evidence refutes.)

The psychophysical power law relating the psychological magnitude ψ to the physical stimulus φ can be written

$$\psi = k(\varphi - \varphi_0)^n$$

where k is a constant determined by the choice of units. The exponent n varies with the modality, and also with such parameters as adaptation and contrast. Generally speaking, each modality has its characteristic exponent, ranging from about 0.33 for brightness to about 3.5 for electric shock. The value of φ_0 is determined by the effective "threshold" that obtains under the circumstances of the experiment. It is the point on the physical scale from which we must start if we want to measure the effective stimulus.

The power function has the happy virtue of describing a straight line in a log-log plot—a line whose slope is determined by the exponent. How this works for three different continua is shown in Figure 1,

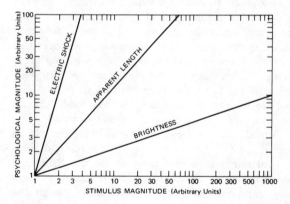

Fig. 1
In log-log coordinates the power function plots as a straight line. The exponent determines the slope. These exponents are: electric current through the fingers, 3.5; apparent length of short lines, 1.1; brightness of luminous spot, 0.33.

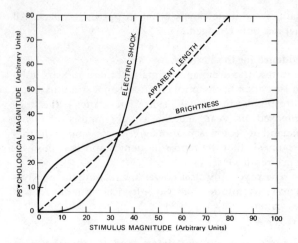

Fig. 2

The straight lines in Figure 1 become curved in linear-linear coordinates. The curvature is upward or downward, depending on whether the exponent is greater or less than one.

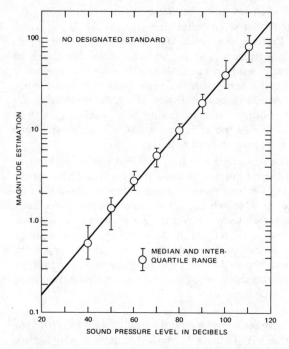

Fig. 3

Loudness function for 1,000-cycle tone. The points are the median magnitude estimations obtained when the tone was presented twice at each of eight levels in irregular order to 26 listeners. The listener assigned to the first loudness he heard any number he deemed appropriate and tried to assign proportional numbers to the succeeding loudnesses.

where we see how different the slopes (exponents) can be. In linear-linear coordinates these same three functions take the forms shown in Figure 2. Slope in the log-log plot becomes curvature in the linear-linear plot.

By much trial and error—*after* it had become plain that a power function governs the growth of sensation—we learned how to get reasonably clean data from observers by asking them to estimate numerically the subjective magnitudes of a succession of stimuli. This procedure, called the method of magnitude estimation, is only one of four numerical procedures that have been elaborated, but it is perhaps the simplest to execute. In this business, simplicity and validity seem not unrelated, but it has been hard for us psychophysicists to forsake the complex, indirect procedures in favor of a plain, straightforward, direct approach.

Consider, for example, the results in Figure 3. In an effort to see how far one could go in removing all biasing constraints from the task set for the listener, I gave each listener an irregular series of loudnesses and asked only one thing: to each loudness assign the number that seems most appropriate (Stevens, 1956). That was in 1954, long before J. C. Stevens (no relation of mine) had convinced me that the geometric mean usually gives an unbiased measure of location with data of this kind. I was still using the median, a

measure that is somewhat less efficient than the geometric mean.

Incidentally, the arithmetic mean is wholly unsuitable for averaging magnitude estimations. If space permitted we could examine the plausible argument that, in all scientific work where the *relative* error tends to be constant (Weber's law), the arithmetic mean is not as appropriate as the geometric mean. In a rigorous sense, the arithmetic mean has little legitimate use in science, for its proper domain is limited to metathetic continua and the like.

The International Standards Organization has recently fixed on a function of the form shown in Figure 3 as the relation between loudness and sound pressure to be used for engineering calculations. Thus the psychophysical law is coming to have practical uses in the market place.

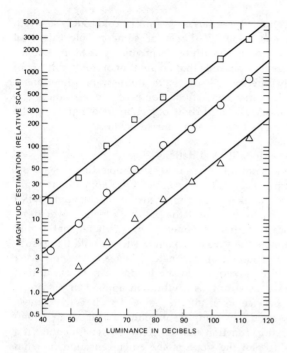

Fig. 4
Brightness functions for white light, based on geometric means of magnitude estimates made in three different experiments. *Squares:* as in Figure 3, there was no designated standard; each of the 18 observers used numbers of his own choosing. *Circles:* a standard called 10 was presented once at the beginning of each run. *Triangles:* the standard called 10 was repeated 10 seconds before each stimulus to be judged. These procedural variations made little difference to the outcome. Except where otherwise stated, the reference value for decibels of luminance is 10^{-10} lambert.

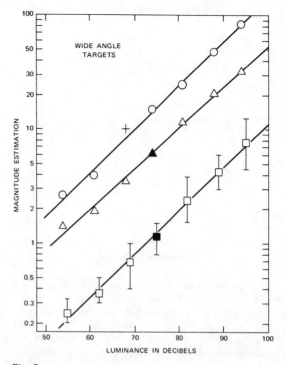

Fig. 5
Brightness functions for targets subtending large visual angles. The *circles* and *triangles* are for experiments in which the observer sat close to a large illuminated screen. The *squares* show the data obtained with a more nearly ideal *Ganzfeld.* Pieces of milk glass held close to the eyes were illuminated from in front of the observer. The standard, called 10, was the stimulus shown by the filled symbols and the cross. Each point is the geometric mean of 20 judgments (10 observers), except that the cross was not actually presented for judgment after it had served to define the modulus 10.

Meanwhile other modalities have been explored with equally good results. Figure 4 shows three different functions determined for brightness by J. C. Stevens. Each curve was determined with a different version of the method of magnitude estimation. The observers (previously dark adapted) viewed a luminous disk of light in a dark field and made judgments of its apparent brightness. We call this the standard viewing condition (S. S. Stevens & J. C. Stevens, 1960).

Interestingly enough, the power function is little affected when the area of the target is made to fill the entire field of view. The results of three experiments by

Gordon Bermant with wide-angle fields are shown in Figure 5. At the other extreme, when the target is reduced to a point source, the power function still holds, but the value of the exponent increases from about ⅓ to about ½. The squares in Figure 6 show how the line in the log-log plot grows steeper when the observer estimates the brightness of a very small target. The circles, giving an intermediate slope, are from an early experiment by E. G. Heinemann, who used a target of an intermediate size (28 minutes).

There exist dozens of functions like these, compiled by several different experimenters, and covering such sense modalities as vision, hearing, taste, smell,

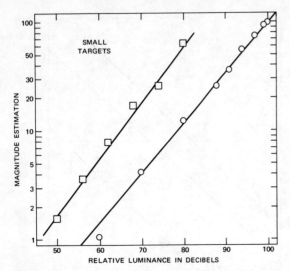

Fig. 6
Brightness functions for small targets subtending visual angles of 1.5 minutes of arc (*squares*) and 28 minutes (*circles*). The abscissa gives relative levels only. The highest level for the smaller target was about 110 db re 10^{-10} lambert. The larger target had a different highest value in each of four different experiments, all of which were averaged to obtain the circles.

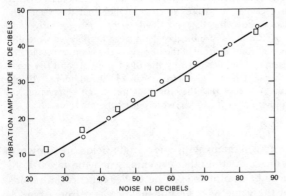

Fig. 7
Equal-sensation function produced by the cross-modality matching of loudness to vibration (60 cps on fingertip). *Circles:* the loudness was adjusted to match the vibration. *Squares:* the vibration was adjusted to match the loudness. Each procedure determines a slightly different slope, but the two experiments together define a power function whose exponent is equal to the ratio between the exponents for loudness and vibration.

vibration, kinesthesis, warmth, cold, and so forth (Stevens, 1960). Perhaps for some people this total array would constitute a convincing exhibit, but for others it is possible that no amount of this recording of verbal behavior—subjective numerical estimations—would carry conviction. Some of my esteemed colleagues make forthright objection to our treating the observer's utterances as measurements.

Cross-Modality Validations

There is nothing like a colleague's objection to send the scientist back to his apparatus. With hope that it might work, coupled with apprehension that it might fail, I decided to try to test the validity of the power functions, and their exponents, by methods that would eliminate the verbal behavior. There would be no subjective numerical estimates. Instead, the observer would be asked to adjust a loudness in his ear until it seemed as strong as a vibration applied to his finger tip, or vice versa. If the power law is correct, these cross-modality comparisons must result in an equal-sensation function that is also a power function. In a log-log plot the slope of the equal-sensation function should be given by the ratio of the exponents of the two modalities under comparison (Stevens, 1959).

The results of the first experiment are shown in Figure 7. The function is linear in the log-log plot as it should be, and the slope lies nicely where it belongs.

Other cross-modality comparisons followed, but the huge task of comparing each sensory continuum with every other continuum has not been completed. Thus far we have had to settle for a collection of interesting samples. Much to my surprise, and that of many observers, the matching of a sound to a vibration is satisfyingly easy—certainly no harder than the task of matching two disparate sounds in loudness, or two colored lights in brightness. Furthermore, the variability is reasonably well behaved, so that geometric averaging is clearly appropriate.

The largest number of cross-modality comparisons made thus far have been with handgrip. Instead of vocalizing, the observer merely squeezes a precision dynamometer (Fig. 8) to indicate his judgment of the apparent strength of the sound, or the light, or the electric shock. First we must ask what happens when the experimenter names numbers in irregular order and the observer squeezes what he judges to be a proportional amount (method of magnitude production).

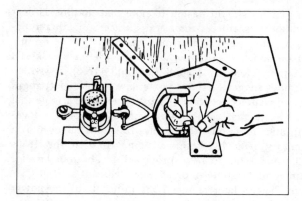

Fig. 8
One of the hand dynamometers.

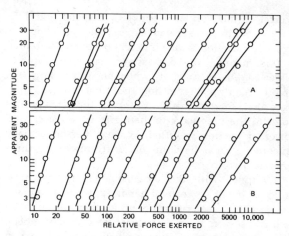

Fig. 9
Functions for apparent force of handgrip obtained by magnitude production. The experimenter designated certain numerical values (ordinate) in irregular order, and the observer produced proportionate squeezes (abscissa). Each curve is for a single observer. Plots A and B are for two different kinds of dynamometer. Points are medians of 7 squeezes (A) and 10 squeezes (B).

Fig. 10
Equal-sensation functions obtained by matching force of handgrip to various criterion stimuli. Each point stands for the median force exerted by 10 or more observers to match the apparent intensity of the criterion stimulus. The relative position of a function along the abscissa is arbitrary. The dashed line shows a slope of 1.0 in these coordinates.

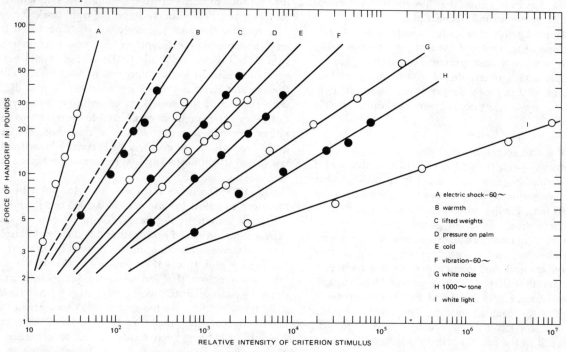

A electric shock–60~
B warmth
C lifted weights
D pressure on palm
E cold
F vibration–60~
G white noise
H 1000~ tone
I white light

Typical results, obtained by J. C. Stevens and J. D. Mack (1959) in two separate experiments, are shown in Figure 9. Each line is for a different observer. Presented in this manner, the data show that each observer follows a power function when he judges apparent force of handgrip. From this and other studies it appears that, for the median observer, the sensation of strain in the production of handgrip grows as the 1.7 power of the force exerted. When a person actually squeezes twice as hard, he judges it to be about three times as hard.

Equipped with this dynamometer and the measured exponent for force of handgrip, we have gauged the growth of sensation on nine other continua by asking observers to emit squeezes instead of numbers. The resulting equal-sensation functions are shown in Figure 10. When the exponents determined by the slopes of these functions are multiplied by the factor 1.7, the resulting values agree remarkably well with the exponents measured directly by magnitude estimation (Stevens, Mack, & Stevens, 1960).

The largest discrepancy between the exponent determined by verbal report and the exponent determined indirectly by squeezing turned out to be 0.07. We regard it as rather good that the greatest difference occurs only in the second decimal place.

Confronted with this richly interconnected evidence, some of us find it difficult to escape the belief that there exists a general principle of psychophysics — a principle that governs to a good approximation throughout all the prothetic perceptual domain. Psychophysics, we venture to suggest, has found itself a law.

Difficulties and Impediments

If the growth of sensation is so easy to measure, and if a single equation relates all sensory magnitudes to the stimulus magnitudes that produce them, why then did it take so long for the nomological quest to corner its prize? The reproach inherent in this question engenders chagrin mainly because the power law seems now so obvious, and ample data supporting it have long been at hand. But many experimenters have produced data that accord with a power law, without seeming aware of it, so that I find my own chagrin well tempered with companionship. The psychophysical power function has had to rise up, as it were, and strike us full in the face for acknowledgment. Why was this so?

First I should hasten to note that nothing is ever without its antecedents, and like certain other functions the power function has had its occasional champion. It begins perhaps with a letter by Gabriel Cramer, cited by Daniel Bernoulli (1738), in which Cramer suggested that a power law (square root) might govern subjective value—a psychological variable that the economist calls *utility*. Bernoulli favored a logarithmic function, the same function advocated a century later by Fechner. Some time in the 1850s Plateau seems to have proposed a cube-root law for apparent brightness, or at least Delboeuf says he did, but Plateau later changed his mind about the power law. He defected, as it were, when he was confronted with some of Delboeuf's data. Then there were various theories regarding differential sensitivity, two of which, Brentano's and Guilford's, took forms that led, via different sets of questionable assumptions, to a power law. So we see that the power function was certainly not unheard of (Stevens, 1957). Indeed, it was like many other mathematical functions that are constantly being tried out here and there. For instance, the power function was one of three equations tried out in 1932 by Ham and Parkinson when they were looking for a formula to fit their results on loudness estimation.

Ham and Parkinson were on the right track, it now appears, but the *piste* promptly got itself obscured by an unfortunate experiment on loudness fractionation by Laird, Taylor, and Wille (1932) whose results have ever since eluded explanation and repetition. Stevens, Rogers, and Herrnstein (1955) even tried to repeat them with the aid of the same kind of antique audiometer. But other experimenters continued to worry about the rather obvious fact that loudness does not seem to grow proportional to decibels (as Fechner's logarithmic law says it should), and experiments continued to accumulate.

In 1938 Davis and I were able to publish the loudness function for the standard 1000-cycle tone in the form shown in Figure 11. There we see an empirical function based on considerable data, but plainly it is not a power function, for it does not lie straight in the log-log plot. It was the curvature in that 1000-cycle loudness function that led us astray for more than a decade—indeed until work was begun on visual brightness in 1953. By the end of 1953 I was ready at last to advocate the power function (Stevens, 1954), but I would still have been hard pressed to convince a skeptic, for the evidence was not overwhelming. Not yet. But then began a long, ebullient period of proving and testing the law on a score of continua, and by every means we have been able to devise.

Reasons for Curvature in the Loudness Function

Why did we not obtain a clean power function when we plotted the loudness data in 1938? If the truth is so simple, how could we have missed? In retrospect there appear to be three causes. Three different sources of bias combined to hide the naked simplicity of the psychophysical law.

1. Fractionation, the setting of one loudness to half the value of a standard, has the built-in bias of an unbalanced experimental design. In those days it was a widely used method for scaling, but sometimes *halving* was not complemented by *doubling*. The underlying power function can be obscured by the resulting bias.

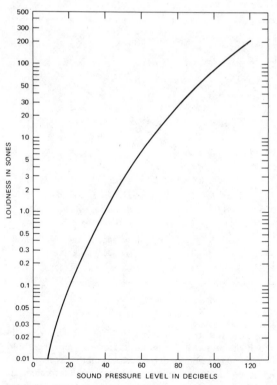

Fig. 11
An early form of the loudness function for the 1,000-cycle tone. The curvature may be ascribed to three factors, none of which was suspected in 1938.

2. Much of the data available in 1938 was based on binaural vs. monaural loudness balances. This was because Fletcher and Munson, two important pioneers in loudness measurement, had made the assumption that a sound in two ears is twice as loud as the same sound heard in only one ear. Furthermore this simple and engaging rule seemed to be nicely confirmed by fractionation experiments. That, indeed, is the unfortunate aspect of it: the assumption of perfect binaural summation turns out to be *almost* correct. It is, in fact, so nearly correct that it required a many-pronged attack to prove that the rule is false (Reynolds & Stevens, 1960). Samples of some of this work are shown in Figures 12 and 13. These and many other observations have shown that binaural loudness grows with an exponent of 0.6, whereas monaural loudness grows with an exponent of 0.54. At one sound pressure level (90 db) the binaural loudness happens to be exactly double the monaural loudness, but at no other level does this simple ratio appear to hold. The false assumption that the 2-to-1 ratio holds throughout the scale was a factor that helped

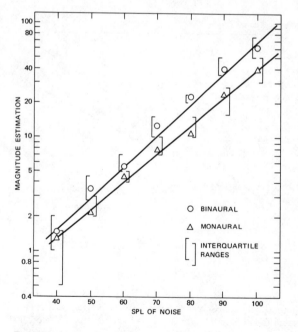

Fig. 12
Loudness functions for binaural and monaural listening. The signal was a band of noise 250 to 2,000 cps. Levels were presented at random to right, left, or both ears and the observer estimated the apparent loudness.

The Surprising Simplicity of Sensory Metrics

put curvature into the loudness function, which caused us to look for a complicated equation when a simple one would do.

3.   Even when all biases in the procedures and all false assumptions regarding the binaural-monaural relation have been cleared away, there still remains some residual curvature near the lower end of the loudness function. That is the reason for the constant φ_0 in the equation above. In order to get a power function one must measure the stimulus beginning at threshold, not at the conventional zero of the physical scale. This need for a threshold correction was most dramatically evident in our work on the perception of warmth and cold, because absolute zero on the temperature scale is far removed from "physiological" zero (J. C. Stevens & S. S. Stevens, 1960). With the temperature senses it would seem silly to measure from absolute zero—and indeed it is.

With sufficient care one can also show the need for φ_0 in the loudness equation, even though its value is small. A careful exploration of the low end of the loudness function by B. Scharf and J. C. Stevens (1961) gave the data in Figure 14. The unfilled points that curve downward are the uncorrected values. The subtraction of a constant φ_0 from each of the experimental points makes them all lie reasonably close to the same straight line and thereby restores the power function.

It was against the foregoing three sources of obfuscation that the power law had to fight its way into clarity. Curiously enough, it was only by working on other sense modalities that we found out what was wrong with the early form of the loudness function. If knocking your head against one wall produces no answers, it sometimes pays to knock against another wall.

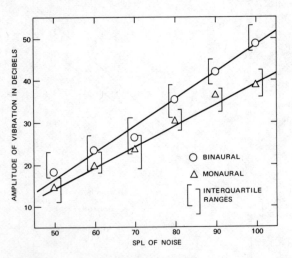

Fig. 13

Equal-sensation functions for loudness vs. vibration on the fingertip. The observer adjusted the vibration (60 cps) to match the apparent loudness of the band of noise (250 to 2,000 cps) presented to right, left, or both ears. Cross-modality matching confirms the evidence in Figure 12 that monaural loudness grows less rapidly than binaural loudness.

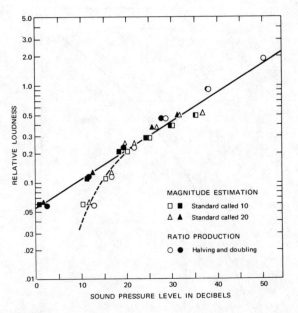

Fig. 14

Showing how the low end of the loudness function can be rectified if the stimulus is measured starting from threshold. The original data, obtained by various methods, follow the dashed curve (unfilled symbols). When a constant value, approximately equal to threshold, is subtracted from each experimental value, the filled points are obtained. The corrected points fall close to the sone function, represented by the straight line with a slope of 0.6.

Perturbations

I do not mean to imply by the foregoing remarks that loudness can now be shown to follow a perfect power function. It is probably not quite that simple—at least not for sounds of all spectra (Stevens, 1955). The scientific leverage that accrues from having an equation adequate to the first-order sensory transductions is simply this: once the first-order effect is reduced to a formula, the second-order departures from the basic law may conceivably lead to new and deeper understanding.

One is reminded, for example, that the discovery of the planet Neptune resulted from the stubborn refusal of the planet Uranus to follow precisely the law of the heavens, as ordained by Newton. Do perturbations in the power law foretell the discovery of new factors in the sensory process? That question sets a task for the future.

Parametric Explorations

Another task for the future has already been begun. It calls for the enlargement of the psychophysical law to embrace the principal parameters that affect the sensory transducers. There is time for only one example of what I have in mind.

Consider adaptation as it affects the eye. Dramatic changes in brightness can be observed when you follow a simple procedure. Hold your hand over one eye for 5 to 10 minutes, and then look around at the world first with one eye, and then with the other. To the eye that was closed, everything looks brighter and perhaps a little different in hue. That simple experiment sets the problem: how does the state of adaptation of the eye affect the brightness function?

First I should mention that all the brightness functions described above were determined with the eyes "dark adapted," that is to say, adapted to a level well below the level of the stimulus presented. That procedure we take as the standard or reference condition. One has to start somewhere. In the dark-adapted state the visual system responds to luminous stimuli in accordance with a power law having an exponent of about 0.33. We define a *bril*, the unit of the brightness scale, as the brightness seen by the dark-adapted eye when it views a 5-degree target at a luminance that is 40 decibels above the reference level 10^{-10} lambert.

Our next concern is to measure the effect of changing the state of the eye by adapting it to a prescribed level of luminance. In order to measure these effects we take advantage of the fact that we have two eyes: we light adapt one eye and dark adapt the other. With the two eyes thus differently adapted, we can do two kinds of experiments. We can measure the brightness function for each eye separately by the method of magnitude estimation. We can also compare these two functions directly by *matching* the brightness seen by the dark-adapted eye to that seen by the light-adapted eye. This interocular matching procedure has been used by Hering and many other workers.

Results of both procedures, matching and magnitude estimation, are shown in Figure 15. Each curve is for a different level of adaptation. In each of the many experiments (carried out mainly by J. C. Stevens), the left eye was dark adapted and the right eye was light adapted. (The right eye stared at a large white cardboard illuminated at various levels.) When the eyes were fully and differently adapted, the test target, subtending about 5.7 degrees, was presented briefly to one eye or the other.

The experimental data in Figure 15 show two things. Under different levels of adaptation, the "operating characteristic" of the visual system con-

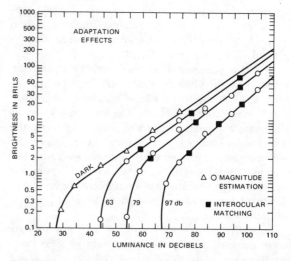

Fig. 15

Results of determining brightness functions under different states of adaptation. The upper curve is the "standard" bril function for the "dark-adapted" eye. Each of the other curves is for the eye adapted to a given luminance, indicated in decibels re 10^{-10} lambert.

The Surprising Simplicity of Sensory Metrics

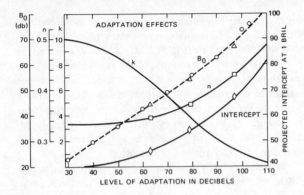

Fig. 16

Parameters of the brightness equation as a function of level of adaptation of the eye. The exponent values (*squares*) were read from Figure 15, as were the 1-bril intercepts (*diamonds*). The values of k were then calculated on the assumption that the luminance B is measured in millilamberts. The threshold values of B_0 were estimated from Figure 15 and plotted as triangles. The *circles* show the threshold values directly measured by P. G. Nutting.

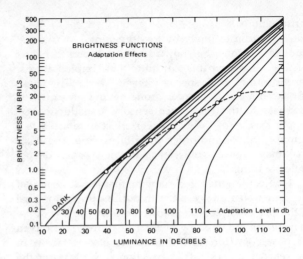

Fig. 17

Family of brightness functions for a wide range of adaptation levels. The dashed line is the terminal brightness locus—the level of sensation reached when the eye comes into full equilibrium with the luminance it is viewing.

tinues to be a power function, but both the "operating point" and the "gain function" are affected by light adaptation. Stated in another language, light adaptation alters each of the parameters in the equation $\psi = k(\varphi - \varphi_0)^n$. For each level of adaptation the parameters k, φ_0, and n take on a characteristic value.

How the parameters of the brightness function depend upon the state of the eye can best be seen in Figure 16. As the level of the light adaptation increases, the following changes occur: the constant k grows smaller, the exponent n grows slightly larger, and the threshold (labeled B_0) grows very much larger. All these changes accord well with common, everyday observation. There is nothing very new or mysterious about it—except perhaps that what everyone knows in a vague and general way has here been reduced to quantitative order.

When the parameters depicted in Figure 16 are used to generate a complete family of brightness functions, like those shown in Figure 17, a basis is laid for a new and fuller understanding of the visual transducer. These functions tell us how any given target, exposed for a second or two, will look to an eye in any of several states of adaptation (S. S. Stevens & J. C. Stevens, 1960).

The implications of these functions could be spelled out in a long chapter, but we have time for only one of the more interesting details. A series of circles appears in Figure 17 connected by a dashed line. These circles mark the locus of the equilibrium function—the brightness seen when the eye, adapted to a given level, is shown a stimulus at that same level. Another name we give the dashed curve is the "terminal brightness function," because it is the function that tells us how bright a target will look after the observer has stared at it for a long period of time—long enough to reach full adaptation. This terminal brightness function does *not* follow a power law.

We note another interesting feature: the dashed curve becomes horizontal at the upper end. If the viewer becomes fully adapted to the level of the stimulus, does he then see a maximal brightness regardless of the stimulus intensity? The answer is yes. This remarkable prediction accords with a result by K. J. W. Craik (1940), who pursued this question to the heroic level of 75,000 foot-lamberts (119 db re 10^{-10} lambert). Levels like that are about ten times greater than the luminance of snow under the noonday sun. The equilibrium brightness function measured by Craik was still flat at the high level.

Much more could be said, and no doubt will be said, about the varied and exciting principles that regulate the input-output functions of the sensory transducers. Tortuous and delayed as may have been the discovery of the basic law — the psychophysical power function — the way is now clear, even for the potential usefulness of proven discrepancies, when such there are.

One final note. The power function has asserted itself not only on continua that involve well-known stimulus variables, but also on a continuum, tactual roughness, for which we had at first thought there would be no metric stimulus-correlate (Stevens & Harris). Our first guess proved delightfully in error, for we found that apparent roughness grows as the 1.5 power of the diameter of the abrasive particles on standard emery cloths. When the observers judged the apparent smoothness of the same emery cloths, the exponent turned out to be nearly equal in magnitude, but opposite in sign. We thereby demonstrate the observer's remarkable ability to judge a continuum in terms of its reciprocal function. Judging the inverse aspect is not as easy, it seems, but people do remarkably well at it. Furthermore, reciprocal functions were produced rather exactly in two cross-modality experiments in which ten observers matched loudness to roughness, and ten others matched loudness to smoothness. Here again the measured exponents were equal in magnitude but opposite in sign. The testimony of these reciprocal judgments adds another dimension to the network of evidence supporting the power law.

References

Bernoulli, D. Exposition of a new theory on the measurement of risk. Originally published in Latin in 1738. Translation in *Econometrica*, 1954, 22, 23–35.

Craik, K. J. W. The effect of adaptation on subjective brightness. *Proc. roy. Soc.*, 1940, *B128*, 232–247.

Fletcher, H., & Munson, W. A. Loudness, its definition, measurement and calculation. *J. acoust. Soc. Amer.*, 1933, *5*, 82–108.

Ham, L. B. & Parkinson, J. S. Loudness and intensity relations. *J. acoust. Soc. Amer.*, 1932, *3*, 511–534.

Laird, D. A., Taylor, E., & Wille, H. H., Jr. The apparent reduction of loudness. *J. acoust. Soc. Amer.*, 1932, *3*, 393–401.

Reynolds, G. S. & Stevens, S. S. The binaural summation of loudness. *J. acoust. Soc. Amer.*, 1960, *32*, 1337–1344.

Scharf, B., & Stevens, J. C. The form of the loudness function near threshold. In *Proc. 3rd Int. Congr. Acoustics*. Amsterdam: Elsevier, 1961. Pp. 80–82.

Stevens, J. C. & Mack, J. D. Scales of apparent force. *J. exp. Psychol.*, 1959, *58*, 405–413.

Stevens, J. C., Mack, J. D., & Stevens, S. S. Growth of sensation on seven continua as measured by force of handgrip. *J. exp. Psychol.*, 1960, *59*, 60–67.

Stevens, J. C. & Stevens, S. S. Warmth and cold: dynamics of sensory intensity. *J. exp. Psychol.*, 1960, *60*, 183–192.

Stevens, S. S. Biological transducers. *Convention Record, I.R.E.*, 1954, Part 9, 27–33.

Stevens, S. S. The measurement of loudness. *J. acoust. Soc. Amer.*, 1955, *27*, 815–829.

Stevens, S. S. The direct estimation of sensory magnitude — loudness. *Amer. J. Psychol.*, 1956, *69*, 1–25.

Stevens, S. S. On the psychophysical law. *Psychol. Rev.*, 1957, *64*, 153–181.

Stevens, S. S. Cross-modality validation of subjective scales for loudness, vibration, and electric shock. *J. exp. Psychol.*, 1959, *57*, 201–209.

Stevens, S. S. Psychophysics of sensory function. *Amer. Sci.*, 1960, *48*, 226–252; also in W. A. Rosenblith (Ed.), *Sensory communication*, New York: M.I.T. Press and Wiley, 1961.

Stevens, S. S. To honor Fechner and repeal his law. *Science*, 1961, *133*, 80–86.

Stevens, S. S., & Davis, H. *Hearing*. New York: Wiley, 1938.

Stevens, S. S., & Harris, Judith R. The scaling of tactual roughness and smoothness. *J. exp. Psychol.*

Stevens, S. S., Rogers, M. S., & Herrnstein, R. J. The apparent reduction of loudness: a repeat experiment. *J. acoust. Soc. Amer.*, 1955, *27*, 326–328.

Stevens, S. S. & Stevens, J. C. The dynamics of visual brightness. Psychophysical Lab. Rep., Harvard University, August 1960, PR–246.

current trends and issues in adaptation-level theory[1]

harry helson
kansas state university

To discuss current trends and issues in adaptation-level theory I shall have to limit myself to a few of the highlights in selected areas that range from psychophysics to social psychology. This discursive treatment is not due to personal choice but is dictated by the fact that the theory has found application in widely separated areas.

1.   Preparation of this paper was supported in part by the Office of Naval Research under Contract Nonr-3634(01) with Kansas State University. The studies of reaction time, contrast and assimilation, and anchor effects in recall were supported by grants from the Bureau of General Research of Kansas State University. Reprinted from *American Psychologist*, 1964, Vol. 19, pp. 26–38. Copyright 1964 by the American Psychological Association, and reproduced by permission.

Let me begin by recalling an episode in the early 1930s when I gave a demonstration before the Optical Society of America of the inadequacy of the CIE (Commission Internationale de l'Éclairage) method of color specification. In this demonstration, although the stimulus qua stimulus did not change with change in surround, its color could be made anything we pleased by appropriate choice of the luminance and hue of the background color. In the discussion that followed, the late Selig Hecht, perhaps the leading worker in visual science at that time, arose and said: "Why do you complicate the problems of color vision by introducing background effects? Why can't you wait until we have solved the simpler problems before we go on to the more complicated ones?" Had my co-workers and I taken this advice the principle of color conversion, which accounts for the Bezold-Brücke phenomenon and the Land colors (Judd, 1951, 1960), would not have been formulated in 1938; we would not have shown that with proper choice of background all the psychological primaries can be seen in monochromatic illumination (Helson, 1938); we would not have found that neutral backgrounds induce chromatic changes as well as lightness contrast in object colors; and we would not have devised formulae predicting the colors of objects in non-daylight sources of illumination (Helson, Judd, & Warren, 1952; Helson, Judd, & Wilson, 1956). In all these cases adaptation, conceived as something more than mere loss of sensitivity from long-continued stimulation, was found to be the key concept in our attempts to understand and predict experimental findings.

For the past decade or so we have been faced with essentially the same situation in the field of psychophysics which existed in the field of visual science during the early 1930s. Workers in the tradition of classical psychophysics have tried to establish pure scales relating physical and psychological magnitudes by ruling out series, anchor, and order effects. In this approach each sense modality is presumed to have its own fixed sensitivity predetermined by the nature of the receptor mechanism. Each scale is supposed to have unique constants giving rise to negatively or positively accelerated functions. According to this view the organism acts only as a meter or transducer of energy; any variations due to series, contextual, background, or residual stimuli are considered errors that must be gotten rid of at all costs.

In contrast to the classical approach, adaptation-level theorists believe that complex factors determining psychophysical judgments must be taken into account, and a broader base must be incorporated in psychophysical laws. Contrasted with classical psychophysics, or the psychophysics of stimuli, is the psychophysics of classes, or frame of reference psychophysics. In this approach stimuli are regarded not as isolated events but as members of classes, and interest centers in the way stimuli are ordered in the classes to which they belong. Each class of stimuli is judged with respect to internal norms which can be objectively and quantitatively specified. Judgments are relative to prevailing norms or adaptation levels. Thus a 4-ounce fountain pen is heavy, but a baseball bat to be heavy must weigh over 40 ounces. What is called heavy or light cannot be attributed merely to a change in scale modulus or to semantic set or to judgmental relativity because different bodily members, different sets of muscles, and a different stance are used to swing a baseball bat and to write with a fountain pen. Even within the same sense modality different scales have to be used for different classes of objects if they are referred to different internal norms. Thus a single scale will not suffice for judging the sizes of rectangles or cubes under laboratory conditions, and judging the sizes of houses. A large house is judged according to a different internal norm from that used in judging large rectangles. Functional considerations also influence internal norms: A house that is large for a family of

three is small for a family of eight. Psychophysics cannot ignore the role of internal norms except at its own peril. By internal norms we refer to the operationally defined concept of adaptation level.

The concept of adaptation level may be defined by at least three different sets of operations:

1. Adaptation levels appear as neutral or indifferent zones in bipolar responses. The bipolar nature of behavior has been recognized in almost all systems of psychology, e.g., by Lewin (1951) in his positive and negative valences; by Pavlov (1927) in his concept of facilitation and inhibition; by Koffka (1935) in his concept of the "demand" character of objects which Boring (1936) put into behavioral terms as "that which attracts or repels us"; by N. E. Miller (1959) in his concept of approach-avoidance gradients; and in the concepts of positive and negative reinforcers used by learning theorists. Descriptively, we find positive and negative afterimages in sensory processes, and pleasant and unpleasant feelings in the domain of affects. If we measure bipolar properties of behavior on continua, then it is immediately evident that there are neutral zones between opposite qualities and opposed modes of behavior. Operationally, the stimuli or conditions eliciting neutral responses furnish a measure of prevailing levels. Long ago (1924), Hess pointed out that the earthworm, *Lumbricus terrestris*, avoids certain intensities of light above a certain level, approaches weaker intensities, and remains quiescent at some intermediate intensity. In the most primitive responses objects are grossly dichotomized into approach-ignore-avoid, good-indifferent-bad, pleasant-neutral-unpleasant. This is the simplest form of categorizing or scaling, and all scaling methods, whether they require the use of language or some other type of response, are fundamentally bipolar rating scales in which the neutral or zero is fixed by the organism. Adaptation levels are revealed in all forms of behavior whether they are sensory, motor, or cognitive verbal in nature.

2. We may deduce the concept of adaptation level (AL) from a set of assumptions regarding the nature of psychophysical judgments as was done by Michels and Helson (1949) in reformulating the Fechner law. Less strict than the derivation of AL by logico-mathematical reasoning is the incorporation of a parameter in empirical equations to make the organism's functional zero the zero of psychological continua. In such cases

the best values of AL can be determined from all judgments of a set of stimuli by curve fitting, linear interpolation, and so on. This has been done both by means of the reformulated Fechner law and also in using other types of equations, e.g., in the determination of the loci of achromatic points in strongly chromatic illuminances (Helson & Michels, 1948).

3. We may arrive at the concept of AL in the time-honored way found so fruitful in mathematics, physics, and chemistry, i.e., by definition. There are many advantages in defining a concept besides the important one that we then know what we are talking about. AL as a weighted log mean derives much of its value, like many concepts in physics, in being defined so that constants appropriate to specific cases can be determined. Like the general diferential equation relating resistance, capacitance, and inductance in electrical circuits, which can be used to solve any number of specific problems, so the definition of AL as a weighted mean can be used to obtain quantitative answers to many different questions.

This definition has provided a number of deductions such as the pooling or integrative nature of most types of responses, the decentered position of stimuli eliciting neutral psychophysical judgments, the non-linearity of stimulus-response functions, and AL as the moving zero of psychophysical and other functions. In addition it has accounted for such experimentally determined facts as the tendency of organisms to match level of output with level of input, variability of response with constant stimulation, and effects of anchors, context, and residual factors in perception and judgment.

We have found that the weighted log mean definition of AL is the best approximation to the neutral or indifferent region for sensory magnitudes. In estimates of the averages of series of numbers, Parducci, Calfee, Marshall, and Davidson (1960) have stressed the role of mid-, median, and end points of the series in determining AL. I prefer the weighted log mean because it brings in all the stimuli, not just the mid- and end stimuli, because of its greater theoretical power and greater generality, and because this definition requires fewer arbitrary constants than any other definition so far proposed. As an example, let us consider a recent application by Bevan, Barker, and Pritchard (1963) of this definition to handle an effect Stevens has called hysteresis, which means "lagging behind." These

writers point out:

When one asks what it is that lags, the concept of adaptation level presents itself for consideration. According to this point of view, the apparent difference in magnitude between two successively presented stimuli depends not simply upon a difference between the intensive processes representing the first (standard) and the second (variable), but upon the difference between an internal norm evolved from a combination, on the one hand, of all of the relevant prior inputs including the standard and, on the other, the process representing the variable. If a sequence of inputs is non-random (i.e., ascending or descending), then we may expect that there will be a lag in the shift of the internal norm in contrast to the shift in standard stimuli. If the norm evolves from successive presentations of an ascending series, it may be expected that the bowing will be upward; if a descending series is used, the expected bowing is downward [pp. 103–104].

Using lifted weights, Bevan, Barker, and Pritchard obtained concave upward curves in light-to-heavy order and concave downward curves in heavy-to-light order. Stevens' assumption (1957) that bowing is due to poorer discrimination at the higher end of the scale, resulting in greater use of upper categories, cannot, they show, explain positively accelerated curves because in these cases discrimination is better at the high than at the low end of the continuum. Hence this argument can apply only to *negatively* accelerated curves. Excellent fits were obtained to experimental data by taking as the effective stimulus not the physical value of the stimulus being judged, but the difference between the stimulus judged and the adaptation level, calculated as a weighted log mean of preceding stimuli, with the immediately preceding stimulus as standard. On this basis upward bowed curves were obtained for ascending series and downward bowed curves for descending series. No new assumptions had to be made in this application of the weighted mean definition to explain upward and downward bowing with ascending and descending orders of stimulus presentation.

Let us now turn to some other studies that reveal current trends and bear on fundamental issues in adaptation-level theory:

1. *Anchoring effects of subliminal stimuli.* In this connection it was found by Black and Bevan (1960) that experimental subjects judged a set of five electric shocks ranging from 1,500 to 2,700μa. as more intensive following a subliminal anchor shock than did a control group which received the five supraliminal

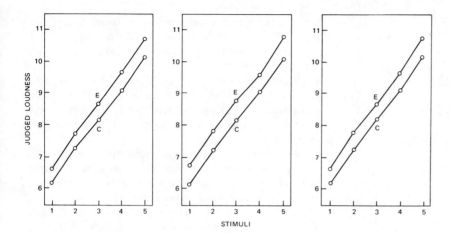

Fig. 1
Effects of a subliminal sound stimulus in raising judged intensity of series stimuli. (The control group, C, was not given the subliminal stimulus. The three plots are for subliminal sound introduced at varying intervals between successive series stimuli. From Bevan & Pritchard, 1963.)

shocks without the subliminal anchor. Since the subliminal shocks were not detected by GSR measures it appears that a behavioral measure, judgment, may be more sensitive to the influence of stimulation than a widely used physiological indicator. Similar results were found by Goldstone, Goldfarb, Strong, and Russell (1962) in judgments of shock with subliminal anchors, and by Bevan and Pritchard (1963) with sound stimuli.[2] As shown in Figure 1, subjects given a subliminal sound anchor preceding each series stimulus reported higher loudnesses than did a control group not given the subliminal anchor. Reinforcing effects of 2,300 μa. shocks were found by Bevan and Adamson (1960) to be most effective when the preadaptation electric shock was below 2,300 μa., least effective when the preadaptation shock was above, and intermediate in effectiveness when the preadaptation shock was the same as in the learning series. These findings were replicated with rat subjects in a subsequent study by Black, Adamson, and Bevan (1961) using running speed to escape shock as the criterion. It is difficult to believe that rats are subject to semantic sets, judgmental relativity, or change in scale modulus, as proposed by Stevens (1958) as alternatives to adap-

2. Boardman and Goldstone (1962) have shown that subliminal visual figures also affect supraliminal judgments of size.

tation-level theory. It seems simpler to assume that shocks following preadapting weak shocks are effectively more intense, and shocks following preadapting strong shocks are effectively less intense because of their effects on prevailing adaptation levels.

2. Residual effects of anchors in memory and recall. Using a null method that did not require judgment in terms of language responses, Steger and I (unpublished study) have found that effects of anchors persist over a period of time and influence recall as well as conditions during immediate impression of stimuli. In the first study four groups of subjects judged a series of black squares on white background during the impression or learning series. The squares ranged from 1.0 to 3.82 in. on a side and were judged in terms of a rating scale from very, very small to very, very large. The initial conditions for the four groups were as follows: (*a*) without anchor stimulus; (*b*) with an anchor at the geometric center of the series (1.96 in.); (*c*) with a 9.0-in. anchor; and (*d*) with a .30-in. anchor. The average size judgments are shown in Figure 2 and are in line with expectations from known anchor effects: The squares were judged smallest with the largest anchor, largest with the smallest anchor, and intermediate with the anchor at the center of the series and with the no anchor condition. One week later subjects were called back to the laboratory and asked to identify the smallest, middle, and largest stimuli in the

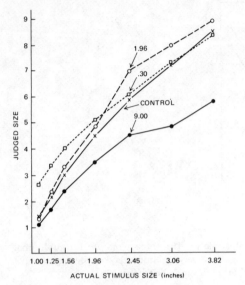

Fig. 2
Judged size of stimuli in the impression phase showing expected anchor effects with small (.30 in.), intermediate (1.96 in.), and large (9.0 in.) anchors and under the control condition in which no anchor was employed.

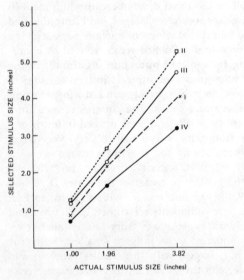

Fig. 3
Smallest, middle, and largest stimuli of the series recalled 1 week after initial presentation.

series from a much more extended series that ranged from .10 in. to 14.56 in. on a side presented in ascending and descending orders. As shown in Figure 3, the residual effects of the anchors in the impression trials are evident after 1 week: The 9.0-in. anchor group picked the smallest set of three; the .30-in. group picked the largest set of three; while the two control groups picked sets intermediate in size between those of the other two groups.

The first experiment was replicated and extended in a second experiment with four new groups of subjects to determine the relative potency of anchors as residuals, i.e., anchors given during the impression phase, versus anchors present during the recall phase. Two control groups were not given anchors during the impression phase but were exposed to the .30- and 9.0-in. anchors during the recall phase. One experimental group was given the 9.0-in. anchor during the impression phase and the .30-in. anchor during the recall phase; conversely, the other experimental group was given the .30-in. anchor in the impression session and the 9.0-in. anchor in the recall session. The results again show expected effects of anchors as seen in Figure 4 where the stimuli recalled with the 9.0-in. anchor present were smaller (curves coded V and VIII in Figure 4) than stimuli recalled with the .30-in. anchor (curves coded VI and VII in Figure 4). Comparison of the curves for Groups VI and VII show that the .30-in. anchor during recall was more effective if it followed 9.0-in. anchor during the impression phase 1 week earlier than if no anchor was present during the impression phase. However the 9.0-in. anchor in the recall phase following .30-in. anchor in the impression phase did not yield significantly lower recall choices than under the control condition (Groups V and VIII).

The clear effects of earlier levels operative later in recall argue against semantic set or judgmental relativity as an explanation since a matching-from-memory technique rather than verbal response was employed in these experiments. It is usually agreed that null or matching methods are freer from higher-order biases than are any other psychophysical methods and indeed are regarded by many physicists and engineers as the only valid psychophysical methods. In this study the most stringent psychophysical criterion was employed to rule out higher-order involvements. The basic nature of anchor and contextual effects in recall seems amply established.

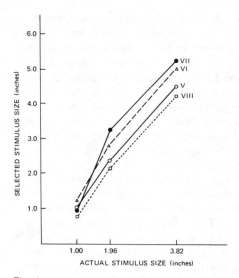

Fig. 4
Smallest, middle, and largest stimuli recalled 1 week after initial impression with large (small) anchor if small (large) anchor was employed during the impression phase.

3. *Series effects with an absolute, extraexperimentally anchored language.* Still further evidence against the theory of judgmental relativity comes from a study by Campbell, Lewis, and Hunt (1958) in which subjects rendered judgments of pitch of tones in low and high contexts by identifying them on a simulated piano keyboard after having been made acquainted with the pitch of middle C. In high context, pitches were designated lower than in low context as we would expect. These authors concluded that the shifting judgments of a common tone in different contexts was independent of the specific semantic details of the usual method of single stimuli assessment, since the response language was anchored outside the experiment and hence was not relative to the situation. Furthermore, the response language, they pointed out, was absolute in that it referred to invariant aspects of the stimulus, thus disposing of the explanation of shifts in scale values of stimuli in different contexts in terms of judgmental relativity.

4. *Neutral zones in unexpected places.* For the benefit of those who may feel that the concept of adaptation level does not have as wide a range of application as some of us have claimed for it, I would like to cite the

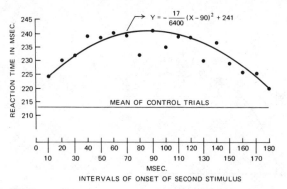

$$Y = -\frac{17}{6400}(X - 90)^2 + 241$$

Fig. 5
Showing increase in reaction time to a light stimulus when it is followed by a second light at intervals ranging from 10 to 180 msec. (From Helson & Steger, 1962.)

discovery of neutral points in an unsuspected area. In a study of reaction time (Helson & Steger, 1962) we found that when a second light followed the primary light signal at intervals ranging from 10 to 170 msec. the reaction time was significantly lengthened as shown in Figure 5 with maximum inhibition in the neighborhood of 100 msec. What is difficult to explain in this finding is how stimuli coming so long after the primary stimulus, when the reaction is presumably almost complete, can nevertheless delay the consummatory response. When asked by one of my students what relation this phenomenon might have to adaptation-level theory, I was obliged to answer that I did not see any relation although I secretly felt that it would indeed be extraordinary if a neutral set of stimulus conditions did not exist for this phenomenon also. Later work, using heteromodal stimuli, confirmed my belief. Using a light stimulus followed by a tone, or a tone stimulus followed by a light, we found that from simultaneous presentation of the two stimuli up to about 25–35 msec., response to the first stimulus was facilitated, i.e., quickened, and at 50 msec. up to about 175 msec. response to the first stimulus was inhibited, i.e., slowed (cf. Figure 6). The neutral or equilibrium condition in which the second stimulus neither facilitated nor inhibited response to the first stimulus proved to be in the region of 25–35 msec. We have thus demonstrated the bipolar nature of simple spot reactions and the presence of neutral zones of stimulation in this area. Added to the difficulty of finding a physio-

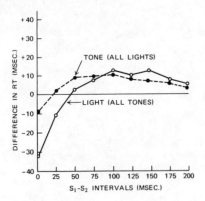

Fig. 6
Showing facilitation (shortening) of reaction time to a light (tone) when followed by a tone (light) up to about 25 msec., with little or no effect between 25 and 50 msec., and inhibition (lengthening) of reaction time from 75 to 175 msec.

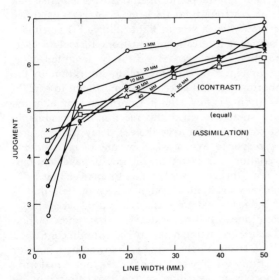

Fig. 7
Contrast and assimilation as a function of line width for various line separations. (From Helson & Joy, 1962.)

logical explanation of how a stimulus following an earlier one can lengthen reaction time, we now have to explain the neutral intervals during which a later stimulus neither facilitates nor inhibits response to an earlier one. We seem to have here a tool for the investigation of phenomena of central facilitation, equilibrium, and inhibition.

5. *Assimilation and contrast in sensory and social-judgmental processes.* It has been maintained by a number of workers that there are two independent processes at work both in judgments of sensory stimuli (Sherif, Taub, & Hovland, 1958), in judgments of social issues (Sherif & Hovland, 1961), and in judgments of clinical materials (Campbell, Hunt, & Lewis, 1957) one of which results in assimilation of greater likeness, and the other results in contrast, or greater difference in judged stimuli. Perhaps the most striking examples of assimilation in the field of sensory processes are the von Bezold designs in which *white arabesques lighten* and *black arabesques darken* chromatic backgrounds. It has been maintained by these workers that while contrast effects may follow from adaptation-level theory, assimilation effects do not. In a series of studies (Helson, 1963; Helson & Joy, 1962; Helson & Rohles, 1959) we have been able to show that far from being mutually exclusive processes, assimilation and contrast lie on a single continuum and are complementary in nature. Instead of using the artistic designs of von Bezold and others, we resorted to straight, ruled black and white lines on gray ground which give as striking assimilation effects as the von Bezold figures. By using straight lines it is possible to vary the width of the lines and to vary the ratios of line width to width of intervening gray. Systematic variation of line width and width of medium gray area shows (cf. Figure 7) that assimilation is found up to about 10-mm. line widths with all line separations. Then, as the black and white lines become wider, assimilation gives way to contrast: The gray areas between the white stripes are darkened and between the black stripes are lightened in accordance with expectations from classical contrast. In Figure 8 are shown the conditions that yield assimilation on the one hand and contrast on the other. The line separating the two regions denotes the conditions under which neither contrast nor assimilation appears. It is therefore evident that assimilation and contrast are complementary processes which plot on a single continuum separated by a neutral zone in which white and black lines neither lighten nor darken intervening gray areas.

Had we stopped our investigations after using the middle gray background we would not have realized that our generalizations were valid only for this condition because in a subsequent study (Helson, 1963), using near-white and near-black (very light and very dark) backgrounds, only assimilation was found as

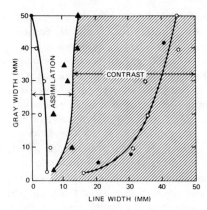

Fig. 8
Domains of assimilation and contrast. Each point in the plane represents the combination of line width and line separation that yields either assimilation or contrast. (From Helson & Joy, 1962.)

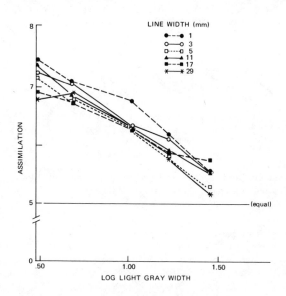

Fig. 9
Showing that only assimilation is found with backgrounds of high (80%) reflectance. (Assimilation is shown as a function of line separation—width of white.)

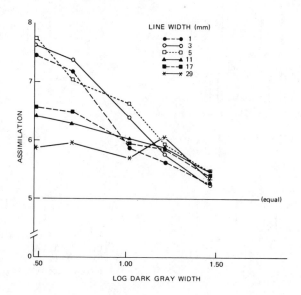

Fig. 10
Showing that only assimilation is found with background of low (14%) reflectance. (Assimilation is shown as a function of line separation—dark gray width.)

shown in Figures 9 and 10. This finding follows from a physiological hypothesis I advanced to account for assimilation and contrast (Helson, 1963) which was as follows: Small differences in excitation in neighboring areas (either in the retina or the brain) summate to produce assimilation while larger differences result in inhibition of the weaker impulses to produce contrast. It follows at once there are intermediate differences in excitation which give rise neither to summation (assimilation) nor inhibition (contrast). This consequence of the theory was verified experimentally. Only one additional assumption is needed to handle all cases: We assume that area functions for luminance in such a way that larger areas are equivalent to higher luminances. This assumption explains the cases where assimilation gives way to contrast as the white and black lines are widened relative to the intervening gray areas. The failure of contrast to appear with near-white and near-black backgrounds is easily explained on the basis that the differences in excitation between the white lines and light backgrounds, on the one hand, and the black lines and the dark backgrounds, on the other, are small and therefore summate, giving rise to assimilation. It is immediately apparent that for contrast to be perceived the adaptation level must have a value *between* contiguous areas; for assimilation to be perceived AL must be *below* or *above* the neighboring areas.

With a satisfactory account of assimilation and contrast at the sensory level we have a model with

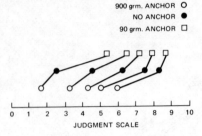

Fig. 11
Assimilation and contrast effects in judgments of lifted weights when extreme anchors are introduced.

which to envisage these phenomena at the social-judgment level. In social judgments small differences in items from an individual's own position are minimized (assimilation), while larger differences are magnified (contrast) (Sherif & Hovland, 1961). Suffice it to say here it does not now seem necessary to regard contrast and assimilation as opposed, independent processes. Their complementary nature appears as clear in the field of social judgments as in the field of sensory processes. Plots of scale values of lifted weights (Figure 11) as a result of the introduction of extreme anchors are similar to the plots of scale values of statements concerning attitudes toward the Negro by those having moderate and extreme pro- or anti-Negro biases (Figure 12, from Hovland & Sherif, 1952). The complementary nature of assimilation and contrast in social judgments arises from the fact that in finite

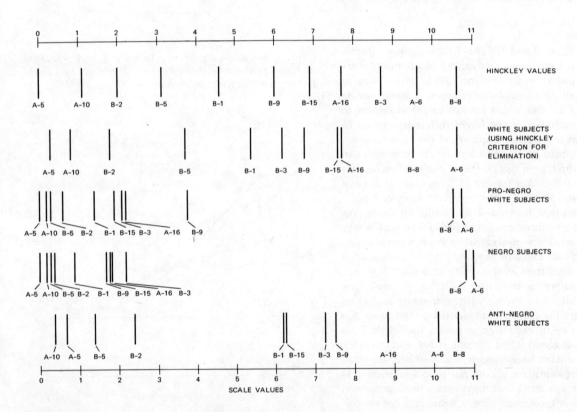

Fig. 12
Contrast and assimilation effects as shown by shifts in scale values of attitude items by those holding extreme positions. (Effects of extreme positions with respect to social issues are formally similar to shifts in judgments of lifted weights when extreme anchors are introduced. From Hovland & Sherif, 1952.)

98

scales if some scale items are spread apart (contrast), others will be crowded together (assimilation). By taking neutral or indifferent zones into account in attitude scaling we find there are two kinds of contrast: In the first type an item on one side of the scale (e.g., the favorable side) moves to the other side (unfavorable), thereby involving a change in *sign* or *quality* in the attitude. In the second type of contrast which was stressed by Sherif and Hovland, separations in scale values of items are increased without changing from positive to negative or vice versa and are therefore matters of *degree*. The difference between changing an individual's position from pro to con, or vice versa, and creating a more favorable or more unfavorable attitude can be very great and may have considerable practical significance, for example in changing voters' attitudes or consumer preferences.

6. *The methodological importance for social psychology of studies leading to functional relations between variables.* In applying the AL paradigm to social phenomena we hoped to show that it is possible to establish functional relations between intensity of stimulation and magnitude of response. Most of the basic information in the quantitative sciences is contained in equations expressing the variation in magnitude of dependent variables as functions of independent variables. In the study of personality and interpersonal interactions most studies have been concerned with correlations of responses to various tests or response-response correlations, rather than with the establishment of functional relations between situational and behavioral variables through variation and control of the intensity of stimulation. In the studies with Blake and our colleagues on the effects of social pressures on expression of attitudes and on other types of response, we varied the intensity of stimulation in accordance with the paradigm shown in Table 1. By combining weak, moderate, or strong focal stimuli with negative, neutral, or positive background stimuli, we were able to study behavior as a function of as many as nine "intensities" of stimulation.

Systematic variations of intensity of social stimulation revealed that with strong social pressures to conform, most individuals conform; with strong pressures against conformity, most individuals do not conform; and with intermediate pressures, frequencies of conforming and nonconforming reactions divide about equally. Thus in Table 2 it is seen that when a weak request was made for volunteers to take part in a

TABLE 1

Paradigm of Strengths of Focal and Background Stimuli Acting Upon Subjects in the Texas Action Studies

Background model	Strength of focal stimuli		
	Strong	Moderate	Weak
Agrees	++	0+	−+
Absent	+0	00	−0
Refuses	+−	0−	−−

Note. Code: + indicates strong condition; 0 indicates moderate condition; − indicates weak or negative condition.

psychology experiment, and a planted subject was heard to refuse, almost everybody refused. As the stimulating conditions were intensified with stronger requests to volunteer, and when planted subjects responded positively, more individuals agreed to take part in the experiment. In what was designed to be the neutral condition, the group split as near 50–50 as was possible with an odd number of subjects (Rosenbaum, 1956).

TABLE 2

Volunteering as a Function of Stimulus and Background Factors

Social background	Stimulus strength								
	High			Moderate			Low		
	Yes	No	W	Yes	No	W	Yes	No	W
Positive	12	3	(9.4)	12	3	(9.1)	6	9	(9.5)
Neutral	12	3	(9.1)	7	8	(7.4)	0	15	(4.6)
Negative	11	4	(8.6)	1	14	(5.5)	1	14	(5.3)

Note. Numbers in parentheses are average ratings on a scale from 0 to 15 of willingness to participate in the task (from Rosenbaum, 1956).

It is also possible to determine the role of personal factors in behavior as shown in a study of petition signing by Helson, Blake, and Mouton (1958). When subjects were asked to sign popular or unpopular petitions just after other (planted) individuals agreed or refused to sign, it was found that those who signed also had higher submissive scores on the Allport-

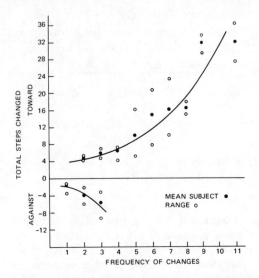

Fig. 13

Extent of movement toward or against group position as a function of frequency of yielding to, or resisting, group pressures. (From Helson, Blake, Mouton, & Olmstead, 1956.)

Allport A-S reaction study than did those who refused, the difference between scores of the two groups being highly significant ($p < .01$). Submissive subjects, as judged by the A-S reaction scores, were also found to yield to group pressures to a greater extent than ascendant subjects, in reporting number of metronome clicks, giving answers to arithmetic problems, and in expressing attitudes toward statements concerned with war and peace.

One of the advantages of performing experiments with systematic variation of conditions is that we not only find what we may have been looking for, but often something unexpected turns up which may be more interesting than the initial hypotheses. Thus in the study of expression of attitudes under social pressures previously referred to, we found, as shown in Figure 13, that the more frequently individuals were influenced by the group, the greater was their agreement with the group and conversely, the more frequently subjects differed from the group, the greater was their disagreement. There is thus a functional relation between frequency and extent of conformity to social pressures.

I must confess that the methodological importance of systematic variation of situational conditions does not seem to have been conveyed to social psychologists

by the studies that Blake and I, and our colleagues, did at the Univeristy of Texas, for the number of publications reporting response-response or test-test correlations has not diminished. Granting the value of such studies for some purposes, it is my belief that we shall not develop a *science* of personality or interpersonal relations until we have laws expressing the degree to which variation in one variable, whether situational or personal, is related to variation in other variables. When this happens we shall have a truly experimental social psychology and an experimental, as contrasted with a test, approach to personality and clinical psychology.

7. *An adaptation-level model for reinforcement and performance.* The need for a theory to reconcile conflicting empirical data in the area of reinforcement and performance is shown by a cursory review of studies in which reinforcement is the independent variable (cf. Hall, 1961; Logan, 1960). Thus questions concerning absolute versus relative amounts of reward, efficacy of continuous versus intermittent patterns of reinforcement, resistance to extinction, and effects of reinforcement following extinction are given various answers, sometimes in terms of specific models, sometimes with ad hoc assumptions. It is well to remember that there are an infinite number of correct theories, as well as an infinite number of incorrect ones, for any fact or class of facts, as Bertrand Russell (1948) has pointed out. What is needed are not ex post facto theories, but theories that account for facts in advance and can also accommodate new findings. There is a difference between legitimate extensions of theories and bending or twisting theories to save them from untoward facts. I believe a significant step forward has been taken in the Bevan and Adamson quantitative model for reinforcement which is based on the analogue of sensory adaptation levels. I can give only a very brief account of the theory and an even briefer statement of the classes of facts it brings together. One must consult the original sources (Bevan, 1963; Bevan & Adamson, 1960; Black, Adamson, & Bevan, 1961) for the evidence and reasoning supporting their interpretations.

The Bevan-Adamson reinforcement model rests upon the five following assumptions:

a. Organisms differentiate between primary (s_p) and background (s_b) stimuli.

b. Organisms create norms, ($\bar{s}$), by averaging stimuli over time. These norms may be defined as weighted averages:

$$(\bar{s}) = \frac{(s_{p1} + s_{p2} + \cdots s_{pn})^x}{N_p} \cdot \frac{(s_{b1} + s_{b2} + \cdots s_{bn})^y}{N_b}$$

where N_b and N_p refer to the number of background (s_b) and primary (s_p) stimuli respectively, and x and y are weighting coefficients denoting the relative contributions of the s_{pj} and s_{bi} to the internal norm.

c. Magnitude of reinforcement, R_{ji}, must be distinguished from magnitude of the reinforcing agent, S, the former depending upon the distance of the reinforcing stimulus from the already established norm, $\bar{s}$, and equal to $s_p - \bar{s}$ or Δs. This differential may be large, denoting strong reinforcement, or small, denoting weak reinforcement, or zero.

d. In addition to the effects of reinforcement as such, the tension level ($\bar{t}$) must be taken into consideration in assessing the effects of reinforcement and this, like $\bar{s}$, has temporal continuity and is affected by many factors, e.g., physiological state, amount of deprivation, etc. The relation between $\bar{t}$ and performance is curvilinear, performance being best at intermediate levels of $\bar{t}$ and poorer at both low and high levels.

e. The effectiveness of reinforcers is thus a function of both Δs and $\bar{t}$ concurrently.

The implications of these assumptions for nine classes of phenomena associated with reinforcement are as follows:

a. *Reinforcing agents as psychophysical stimuli.* Evidence that reinforcing agents behave like psychophysical stimuli in being scalable on continua having neutral or indifferent regions and in being subject to both series and anchor effects supports a pooling model which is applicable on the basis of experimental as well as a priori considerations.

b. *Effective intensity of reinforcement and performance efficiency.* From the definition of Δs, it follows that the effectiveness of a reinforcing stimulus is not a fixed value. This value changes with variations in $\bar{s}$ as new stimuli are added, as effects of old stimuli diminish, and with changes in internal norms due to other factors. Like sensory stimuli, reinforcing stimuli derive their effectiveness from their relation to prevailing levels: If the reinforcing agent is above its background level, it will appear intense; if below level, it will appear weak; and if it is near or at level, it will be medium or neutral. Performance efficiency will vary in accordance with some function of reinforcing effectiveness.

c. *Effectiveness of reinforcement and distinctiveness of the reinforcing agent.* From 2 above it follows that the greater the difference between a reinforcer and the general level, the more distinctive it will be and the greater will be its effectiveness as a reinforcer.

d. *Adaptation to repeated reinforcement.* The loss in effectiveness of stimuli as reinforcers with repetition may be accounted for on the assumption, supported by evidence from sensory adaptation, that reinforcing stimuli pull level in their own direction thus reducing the differential between s_p and $\bar{s}$ with resultant loss in reinforcing power. The loss in effectiveness can presumably be counteracted by changing the intensity of the reinforcer to preserve the same differential between s_p and $\bar{s}$ during successive presentations of reinforcing stimuli.

e. *Patterns of intermittent reinforcement and performance efficiency.* From what has been said it follows that certain patterns of intermittent reinforcement have a greater effect upon performance than continuous stimulation. If nonreinforced trials can be viewed as having zero intensity, then such trials should have the effect of reducing $\bar{s}$ and thus of enhancing the magnitude of Δs. In addition to the intensive level, the tension level must also be taken into account in accordance with the fact that intermediate levels of reinforcement, e.g., 50% and 75%, as against 25% and 100%, in eye-blink conditioning (Grant & Schipper, 1952), are more effective than low or high levels of reinforcement.

f. *Temporal spacing of reinforced trials.* Since each application of a fixed value of reinforcement is assumed to bring its effective value nearer to the indifference level, rapid repetition should be accompanied by relatively rapid neutralization of stimulation with consequent decrement in performance. In accordance with the assumption of a curvilinear relationship between tension level and performance, it follows that too wide spacing of reinforcements will also result in poorer performance. Extended periods of zero reinforcement cannot support optimal tension levels for performance. Experimental evidence for these deductions can be found in the original publication (Bevan, 1963).

g. *Performance with shifts in reinforcement magnitude.* Contrast effects in differential reinforcement support the assumption that subjects integrate reinforcements over time and/or trials with establishment of levels such that the effectiveness of succeeding reinforcers depends on their relation to prevailing level. Although more quantitative data are needed to determine the exact relationships between stimulus differentials and response differentials, the model proposed here seems to account for effects of relative or contrasting, as well as absolute, magnitudes of reinforcement.

h. Performance with combinations of different types of reinforcement. In this discussion no distinction has been made between types of reinforcers, e.g., rewards versus punishments, since both may act as either positive or negative reinforcers, depending upon the specific conditions of their use. As Bevan (1963) points out, both may be scaled in terms of their effectiveness and, while their respective ranges of influence may not coincide, they overlap to a marked degree. We assume that it is their intensity relative to the norm, not their bene- or nociceptive quality, that determines effectiveness in altering behavior. Since rewards and punishments lie on opposite sides of affective continua, this fact must be taken into consideration when they are used in combination, e.g., a positive reinforcer may be enhanced if employed following a negative one, or vice versa.

On the assumption that effectiveness depends upon arousal value of reinforcers or their ability to change tension level, it follows that whether correct responses or errors should be reinforced has little theoretical consequence. This conclusion is supported by experimental evidence, e.g., Muenzinger's (1946) study showing that when shock was given on correct turns in a brightness-discrimination problem, it required 49 trials to criterion, and when given for both correct and incorrect responses, it required 40 trials to criterion. Again, it should be pointed out that further work is necessary to determine the exact relations between positive and negative reinforcers on the one hand and performance on the other.

i. Resistance to extinction and reinforced performance following extinction. In this connection Bevan states that if the period of extinction is considered a sequence of zero or minimum reinforcements, then tension may be expected to return toward its initial level, with a consequent reduction in performance efficiency. On the other hand, the usual period of deprivation between extinction sessions should enhance tension level and thus make possible spontaneous recovery and the disinhibitory effect of "irrelevant" stimuli. Still other implications of this model regarding reinforcement levels and extinction are discussed by Bevan (1963).

From the foregoing exposition of the Bevan-Adamson model, brief as it has been, it appears to be capable of application to a variety of complex reinforcing situations. In addition, it possesses the great advantage of bringing reinforcement theory, and hence learning theory and motivation, nearer to psychophysical theory in its insistence on evaluating reinforcing stimuli by reference to internal norms.

The reinforcement model of Bevan and Adamson is essentially an attempt to account for effects of stimulation over time with certain variations in conditions of stimulation. Parducci (1964), interested in trial-to-trial variations in adaptation level, is testing a number of quantitative models to account for variations in judgment of stimuli from moment to moment. In a similar vein Rambo and Johnson (in press) have found that with repetition of the same series stimuli the value of adaptation level rises in a negatively accelerated curve and approaches asymptote after 30 to 40 cycles. They find that an inverse hyperbolic function fits the obtained ALs very closely.

Last but not least among the current trends are investigations by Bevan and his co-workers (Behar & Bevan, 1961) of cross-modal judgments, applications to Rorschach testing by Block (1964), to TAT tests by Dollin and Sakoda (1962), effects of context on scaling traits by Young, Holtzman, and Bryant (1954) and Podell (1961), and investigations by Goldstone and his co-workers (Goldstone & Goldfarb, 1964) in their experimental-psychophysical approach to psychiatric disorders.

While much has been accomplished, I believe that much more remains to be done both in refining present applications and in extending AL theory to new areas. I have great faith in the value of experimental-quantitative approaches to psychological problems. Perhaps the chief value of AL theory has been its encouragement of such approaches in the areas where it has been applied.

References

Behar, I., & Bevan, W. The perceived duration of auditory and visual intervals: Cross-modal comparison and interaction. *Amer. J. Psychol.,* 1961, 74, 17–26.

Bevan, W. The pooling mechanism and the phenomena of reinforcement. In O. J. Harvey (Ed.), *Motivation and social interaction*. New York: Ronald Press, 1963.

Bevan, W., & Adamson, R. Reinforcers and reinforcement: Their relation to maze performance. *J. exp. Psychol.*, 1960, *59*, 226–232.

Bevan, W., Barker, H., & Pritchard, Joan F. The Newhall scaling method, psychophysical bowing, and adaptation level. *J. gen. Psychol.*, 1963, *69*, 95–111.

Bevan, W., & Pritchard, Joan F. Effect of "subliminal" tones upon the judgment of loudness. *J. exp. Psychol.*, 1963, *66*, 23–29.

Black, R. W., Adamson, R., & Bevan, W. Runway behavior as a function of apparent intensity of shock. *J. comp. physiol. Psychol.*, 1961, *54*, 270–274.

Black, R. W., & Bevan, W. The effect of subliminal shock upon the judged intensity of weak shock. *Amer. J. Psychol.*, 1960, *73*, 262–267.

Block, W. A conceptual framework for the clinical test situation. *Psychol. Bull.*, 1964, *61*, in press.

Boardman, W. K., & Goldstone, S. Effects of subliminal anchors upon judgments of size. *Percept. mot. Skills*, 1962, *14*, 475–482.

Boring, E. G. Koffka's *Principles of Gestalt psychology. Psychol. Bull.*, 1936, *33*, 59–69.

Campbell, D. T., Hunt, W., & Lewis, Nan A. The effects of assimilation and contrast in judgments of clinical materials. *Amer. J. Psychol.*, 1957, *70*, 347–360.

Campbell, D. T., Lewis, Nan A., & Hunt, W. A. Context effects with judgmental language that is absolute, extensive, and extra-experimentally anchored. *J. exp. Psychol.*, 1958, *55*, 220–228.

Dollin, Adelaide, & Sakoda, J. M. The effect of order of presentation on perception of TAT pictures. *J. consult. Psychol.*, 1962, *26*, 340–344.

Goldstone, S., Goldfarb, Joyce L., Strong, J., & Russell, J. Replication: The effect of subliminal shock upon the judged intensity of weak shock. *Percept. mot. Skills*, 1962, *14*, 222.

Goldstone, S., & Goldfarb, Joyce L. Adaptation level, personality theory, and psychopathology. *Psychol. Bull.*, 1964, *61*, in press.

Grant, D. A., & Schipper, L. M. The acquisition and extinction of conditioned eyelid responses as a function of the percentage of fixed-ratio random reinforcement. *J. exp. Psychol.*, 1952, *43*, 313–320.

Hall, J. F. *Psychology of motivation*. Philadelphia: Lippincott, 1961.

Helson, H. Fundamental problems in color vision. I. The principle governing changes in hue, saturation, and lightness of non-selective samples in chromatic illumination. *J. exp. Psychol.*, 1938, *23*, 439–476.

Helson, H. Studies of anomalous contrast and assimilation. *J. Opt. Soc. Amer.*, 1963, *53*, 179–184.

Helson, H., Blake, R. R., & Mouton, Jane S. Petition-signing as adjustment to situational and personal factors. *J. soc. Psychol.*, 1958, *48*, 3–10.

Helson, H., Blake, R. R., Mouton, Jane S., & Olmstead, J. A. Attitudes as adjustments to stimulus, background, and residual factors. *J. abnorm. soc. Psychol.*, 1956, *52*, 314–322.

Helson, H., & Joy, V. Domains of lightness assimilation and contrast effects in vision. *Psychol. Beit.*, 1962, *6*, 405–415.

Helson, H., Judd, D. B., & Warren, Martha H. Object-color changes from daylight to incandescent-filament illumination. *Illum. Engr.*, 1952, *47*, 221–233.

Helson, H., Judd, D. B., & Wilson, Martha. Color rendition with fluorescent sources of illumination. *Illum. Engr.*, 1956, *51*, 329–346.

Helson, H., & Michels, W. C. The effect of adaptation on achromaticity. *J. Opt. Soc. Amer.*, 1948, *38*, 1025–1032.

Helson, H., & Rohles, F. H., Jr. A quantitative study of reversal of classical lightness-contrast. *Amer. J. Psychol.*, 1959, *72*, 530–538.

Helson, H., & Steger, J. A. On the inhibitory effects of a second stimulus following the primary stimulus to react. *J. exp. Psychol.*, 1962, *63*, 201–205.

Hess, W. Reactions to light in the earthworm, *Lumbricus terrestris. J. morphol. Physiol.*, 1924, *39*, 515–542.

Hovland, C. I., & Sherif, M. Judgmental phenomena and scales of attitude measurement: Item displacement in Thurstone scales. *J. abnorm. soc. Psychol.*, 1952, *47*, 822–832.

Judd, D. B. Basic correlates of the visual stimulus. In S. S. Stevens (Ed.), *Handbook of experimental psychology*. New York: Wiley, 1951.

Judd, D. B. Appraisal of Land's work on two-primary color projections. *J. Opt. Soc. Amer.*, 1960, *50*, 254–268.

Koffka, K. *Principles of Gestalt psychology*. New York: Harcourt, Brace, 1935.

Lewin, K. *Field theory in social science*. New York: Harper, 1951.

Logan, F. H. *Incentive.* New Haven: Yale Univer. Press, 1960.

Michels, W. C., & Helson, H. A reformation of the Fechner law in terms of adaptation-level applied to rating-scale data. *Amer. J. Psychol.*, 1949, *62*, 355–368.

Miller, N. E. Liberalization of basic S-R concepts: Extensions to conflict behavior, motivation, and social learning. In S. Koch (Ed.), *Psychology: A study of a science.* Vol. 2. New York:

McGraw-Hill, 1959.

Muenzinger, K. F. Reward and punishment. *U. Colo. Stud., gen. Sec.*, 1946, *27* (4), 1–16.

Parducci, A. Sequential effects in judgment. *Psychol. Bull.*, 1964, *61*, in press.

Parducci, A., Calfee, R. C., Marshall, Louise M., & Davidson, Linda P. Context effects in judgment: Adaptation level as a function of the mean, midpoint, and median of the stimuli. *J. exp. Psychol.*, 1960, *60*, 65–77.

Pavlov, I. P. *Conditioned reflexes.* (Ed. & Trans. by C. V. Anrep.) London: Oxford Univer. Press, 1927.

Podell, J. E. A comparison of generalization and adaptation level as theories of connotation. *J. abnorm. soc. Psychol.*, 1961, *62*, 593–597.

Rambo, W. W., & Johnson, E. L. Practice effects and the estimation of adaptation level. *Amer. J. Psychol.*, in press.

Rosenbaum, M. The effect of stimulus and background factors in the volunteering response. *J. abnorm. soc. Psychol.*, 1956, *53*, 118–121.

Russell, B. *Human knowledge.* New York: Simon & Schuster, 1948.

Sherif, M., & Hovland, C. I. *Social judgment.* New Haven: Yale Univer. Press, 1961.

Sherif, M., Taub, D., & Hovland, C. I. Assimilation and contrast effects of anchoring stimuli on judgments. *J. exp. Psychol.*, 1958, *55*, 150–155.

Stevens, S. S. On the psychophysical law. *Psychol. Rev.*, 1957, *64*, 153–181.

Stevens, S. S. Adaptation level vs. the relativity of judgment. *Amer. J. Psychol.*, 1958, *71*, 633–646.

Young, H. H., Holtzman, W. H., & Bryant, W. D. Effects of item context and order on personality ratings. *Educ. psychol. Measmt.*, 1954, *14*, 499–517.

A number of years ago we instituted at the University of Iowa a series of experiments concerned with the role of aversive motivational factors in learning situations. In addition to the more usual direct manipulation of variables influencing the motivational state of an individual, such, for example, as varying the intensity of a noxious stimulus, degree of motivation was also varied in these studies by employing selected subjects who differed in terms of their performance on a so-called scale of emotional responsiveness or manifest anxiety (31). That these experiments have aroused considerable interest among both clinical and experimental psychologists is readily evident, not only from the large number of published studies that have attempted either to check or to extend our experimental findings, but also from the not infrequent critical reactions they have elicited. Now, while some of the criticisms directed against our studies undoubtedly have merit, it has been rather dismaying to discover the extent to which many of them reflect a serious lack of understanding of the structure and purpose of the basic theoretical framework underlying the experiments.

While some of the responsibility for this failure to understand the nature and objectives of the theory can be assigned to the critics, I hasten to acknowledge that our theoretical treatments have been quite inadequate. The major difficulty is that the studies have appeared only in experimental journals in which space limitations have required that theoretical discussions be kept to a minimum. Since each article tended to limit the discussion to those portions of the theory relevant to

a theory of emotionally based drive (*D*) and its relation to performance in simple learning situations[1]

kenneth w. spence (1907–1967)
the university of texas at austin

the particular phenomena being reported, the theory has been presented only in a very piecemeal fashion. Apparently our hope that the interested reader, particularly the critic, would familiarize himself with the theory as a whole by considering all of the articles has not been realized.

Theoretical Schema

One of the purposes of this paper is to provide a more systematic presentation of our basic theory, or, to use

1   Reprinted from *American Psychologist,* 1958, Vol. 13, pp. 131–141. Copyright 1958 by the American Psychological Association, and reproduced by permission.

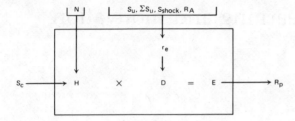

Fig. 1

Diagram representing portion of theoretical schema relevant to data for classical conditioning. (See text for explanation of symbols.)

an expression recently introduced by Cronbach and Meehl (4), of the nomological network underlying our studies. Following this the experimental evidence bearing on the theory will be presented and discussed. Fig. 1 presents the main concepts employed, at least in so far as one kind of learning situation, classical conditioning, is concerned. At the top of the figure are shown the experimentally manipulated independent variables such as N, the number of paired conditioning trials; S_u, the unconditioned stimulus; ΣS_u, the number of previous presentations of the unconditioned stimulus; R_A, score on the anxiety or emotional responsiveness scale. The empirical response measure at the lower right-hand corner is the dependent variable. Inside the rectangle are represented the several theoretical concepts (intervening variables) and the interrelations assumed among them. The arrows indicate the functions relating the dependent response measure to the intervening variables, and the latter to the experimentally manipulated variables. Details of the portion of the theory between the intervening variable E and the empirical response measure (R_p), involving such theoretical concepts as oscillatory inhibition and response threshold, have been omitted since our present purpose does not require them. It is sufficient to state that response frequency (R_p) is some positive monotonic function of excitatory potential E.

That the schema presented in Fig. 1 conforms to the Cronbach and Meehl concept of a nomological net is readily apparent. Thus to quote these writers: "The laws in a nomological network may relate (a) observable properties or quantities to each other; or (b) theoretical constructs to observables; or (c) different theoretical constructs to one another" (4, p. 290). One may readily find examples in our schema of each of these

"laws," or as I would prefer to call them, "relations," since the term "law" typically has a narrower meaning than these authors have given it.

The theory takes its start from Hull's basic assumption that the excitatory potential, E, determining the strength of a response is a multiplicative function of a learning factor, H, and a generalized drive factor, D, i.e., $E = H \times D$ (9). We have assumed, further, that the drive level, D, in the case of aversive situations at least, is a function of the magnitude or strength of a hypothetical response mechanism—a persisting emotional response in the organism, designated as r_e, that is aroused by any form of aversive stimulation. That is, aversive, stressful stimulation is assumed to arouse activity under the control of the autonomic nervous system, which, according to some neurophysiological evidence, may act as an energizer of cortical mechanisms. Those of you who are familiar with the theoretical writings of Miller (13) and Mowrer (14) will recognize that this mechanism is similar to one these writers have postulated in connection with their investigations of acquired motivation. Thus they assumed that aversive stimuli arouse a hypothetical pain (emotional) response which, when conditioned to previously neutral stimulus events, provides the basis for an acquired drive of fear.

On the basis of analogy with overt reflexes to noxious stimulation, there were a number of properties that could be assigned to our hypothetical response mechanism. Three, in particular, will be discussed here. The first and most obvious is based on our knowledge that the magnitude or strength of observable reflexes to noxious stimulation (e.g., the corneal reflex to an air puff, the GSR to an electric shock) varies directly with the intensity or degree of noxiousness of the stimulus. Assuming our hypothetical emotional response, r_e, would exhibit the same property, it followed that the level of drive, D, present in classical defense conditioning would be a positive function of the intensity of the US. From the remaining portion of the theory, it could be deduced that the performance level, e.g., frequency of CR's, would vary positively with the intensity of the US employed. At the time of the original formulation of our theory there was some evidence, in particular an experiment by Passey (15), which supported this implication of the theory.

A second implication of our hypothetical mechanism was based on the adaptive property of observable reflexes to noxious stimuli: namely, that such responses characteristically exhibit adaptation or weakening with repeated stimulation. On the assumption that our hypothetical emotional response would behave in an analogous manner, it followed that, if a series of trials employing the US alone were given *prior* to conditioning, a lower level of D would be present during the subsequent conditioning than if no such adaptation trials were given. But if D were lower, the level of performance in the conditioning situation would also be lower following such adaptation trials than without them. This assumption or hypothesis, if you wish, is represented in Fig. 1 by $r_e = f(\Sigma S_u)$. At the time of formulation of the theory, we found a study by MacDonald (12) that gave results precisely in line with this implication.

The third implication of our theoretical mechanism was based on the well-known fact or observation that individuals differ in the magnitude of their reflex responses to a given intensity of stimulation. By analogy, again, we were led to assume that individuals would differ characteristically in the magnitude of this response, r_e, to the same intensity of stressful stimulation. If now there were available some means of assessing differences in this emotional responsiveness of individuals, our theoretical schema would lead to the prediction that highly emotional subjects, as assessed by the measuring device, would exhibit a higher level of performance in aversive forms of conditioning than subjects who scored low on the device.

The problem thus became one of attempting to develop a test for identifying individual differences in the responsiveness of this hypothetical emotional mechanism. Such a test, of course, would have to be defined independently of the measures that were to be employed in testing the theoretical network, i.e., the measures of performance in conditioning and other learning situations. It was in connection with this portion of our theory that the Manifest Anxiety or A-scale was developed. The idea of using a self-inventory test that would differentiate subjects in terms of the degree to which they admitted to possessing overt or manifest symptoms of emotionality was suggested by Taylor in a doctoral dissertation (30).

At this point I should like to make a methodological digression and comment on a criticism recently made concerning this aspect of our research. One pair of critics, inspired, but unfortunately not too enlightened, by the excellent article of Cronbach and Meehl (4) on construct validity, insisted that we should have developed our scale for measuring D on the basis of a theory so that, and I quote them "performance on it might be a basis for inferring drive (differences) independently of the outcome of subsequent experiments" (10, p. 162). While there are a number of highly questionable methodological points in the arguments of these critics, I should like to call attention here merely to the fact that it is simply not true that no theorizing guided us in the development of the A-scale. As has just been recounted, we did have some very definite theoretical notions as to what lay behind differences in level of generalized drive, D, especially in the case of classical defense types of conditioning.

This theory, that D is a function of the strength of the emotional response made by the organism to the noxious stimulation, had already received considerable support. Its extension in the present instance to the individual difference variable logically demanded that we measure the emotional responsiveness of individuals under comparable environmental conditions. Naturally, so-called physiological indices of emotionality, such as, for example, changes in pulse rate or in the GSR, were indicated; and we have conducted some research along this line. However, it occurred to Taylor that it might be both interesting and valuable to investigate the possibility of making use of the presumed behavioral symptoms of emotionality that clinicians have described. That the questionnaire type of test developed turned out as well as it apparently has is to the credit, I think, of the clinical psychologists who selected the behavioral items as indicative of emotionally over-reactive individuals.

In this connection a further comment is in order concerning a surprising question that was asked by these same critics. Thus the problem was posed as to what the consequences would have been for either the theory or the test had the experiments using the A-scale been negative. The answer to the question, at least as regards the theory, should be obvious. The implications of the other portions of our theory with respect to our response mechanism, r_e, were sufficiently well confirmed that we would have had no hesitancy about abandoning the A-scale as being related to D in our theory. Since, however, the implications of this aspect of our theoretical net were confirmed, we have continued to employ the A-scale as one operational definition of this emotional responsiveness variable. That a more satisfactory scale, even one of this questionnaire type, can be developed, I have no doubt. Indeed, I

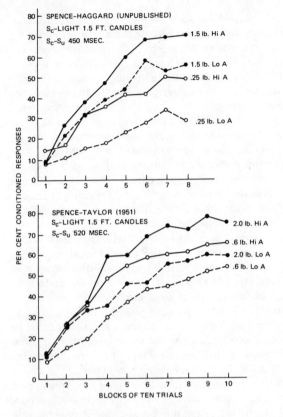

Fig. 2
Performance in eyelid conditioning as function of A-score and intensity of US.

would recommend that some of the time and energy now being squandered in the many distorted, even mendacious, criticisms that seem to find such ready acceptance in our current discussion-type journals be directed at this more constructive task. If the main purpose of these attacks is to discredit and eliminate the theory, they will fail in this objective, for the history of science clearly reveals that a theory is usually discarded only when a better theory is advanced. The same goes for the constructs within a theory.

Experimental Evidence

With these methodological remarks out of the way, let us turn now to the experimental evidence bearing on our theoretical schema. I shall spend the major part of my limited space presenting and discussing the findings of our eyelid conditioning experiments, for it

was in connection with data from this type of learning situation that the schema was originally formulated. With regard to performance curves of conditioning, e.g., frequency curves, the implications of the theory are, as we have seen, that level of performance will be a positive function of (a) the intensity of the US, (b) the level of score on the A-scale, and (c) the intensity of an extra stressful stimulation. We shall take up the first two of these variables together; since space is so limited, I shall present only those studies which had the largest sample of subjects and hence have provided the most reliable and stable data.

EYELID CONDITIONING EXPERIMENTS

In Fig. 2 are presented the findings of two experiments (one unpublished; the other, 27), one of which involved 120 subjects and the other 100 subjects. Both studies employed two levels of puff intensity, .6 lb. and 2.0 lbs./sq. in., in the one represented in the lower graph; .25 lb. and 1.5 lbs./sq. in., in the upper graph. Each study also involved two levels of emotionality (upper and lower 20% of subjects on the A-scale). Examination of the curves in both graphs shows clearly that at each of the four puff intensities, the High A group (shown by solid curves) was well above the Low A group (broken curves). Statistical analysis over all of the conditioning trials revealed the differences were significant at the .01 level in the lower graph and at the .025 level in the upper.[2]

A second point to be noted in these data is relevant to the assumption that the learning or habit factor (H) and the drive factor (D) combine in a multiplicative manner to determine response strength. This assumption leads to the further implication that frequency curves of conditioning for different values of the anxiety variable will exhibit a gradual divergence over the course of training.[3] That this prediction was borne out may be seen be inspecting the graphs. Statistical confirmation of the divergence is revealed by the fact

2. Since unequal numbers of each sex were used in both of these studies and because women consistently exhibit a greater difference than men, the curves have been weighted equally for male and female subjects.

3. This prediction must be qualified to the extent that the frequency measure has a ceiling of 100% and thus may not always reflect the continued growth of E. This is particularly the case at high levels of D in which E also is high.

that the trials-×-anxiety interaction for both sets of data were highly significant (.005 and .025 levels).

The findings with respect to the intensity of US variable also supported the implications of our theory. Thus it may be seen in both studies that the subjects that had the strong puff performed at a higher level than those with the weak puff. The divergence between the curves is also apparent.

As an indication of the stability of our findings involving these two experimental variables, Fig. 3 presents data from these same two studies along with some relevant data from four other investigations recently conducted in our laboratory (26). Shown on the ordinate of this graph are the percentage of CR's given in the block of Trials 41–80 as a function of the intensity of the unconditioned stimulus employed. The uppermost curve in this graph represents the results for subjects selected from the high end of the A-scale; the lowest curve, subjects selected from the low end. The middle curve represents data obtained in four different experiments in which unselected subjects, so far as A-score, were conditioned under highly comparable conditions to those used with the selected subjects (i.e., similar visual CS and very comparable S_c-S_u intervals). The consistency of the results from experiment to experiment, particularly the relation of the curve for the unselected subjects to those for the High and Low A subjects, is, I believe, quite impressive.

In addition to the data presented in these graphs, four other investigations have reported finding that High A subjects responded at a significantly higher level than Low A subjects in eyelid conditioning (21, 22, 28, 30). One additional study (8) also found superior performance by High A subjects, although the difference in this instance was not significant. A reasonable interpretation of the failure to obtain a significant difference in this latter study, especially to anyone familiar with the variability of individual conditioning data, is that there were only ten subjects in each group.

Mention was made earlier of the fact that in addition to the anxiety scale we have also attempted to employ a number of physiological measures as further operational definitions of our emotional responsiveness variable. One of the most discouraging aspects of this work has been the lack of consistency, i.e., unreliability from day to day, of such measures. Especially has this been the case with the GSR, on which, unfortunately, we concentrated most of our time and

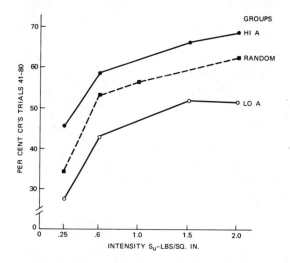

Fig. 3

Showing relation between conditioning performance and intensity of US for unselected and high and low A-score subjects.

energy. Recently, however, we have obtained results (to be published) with these measures that are rather more promising. Using changes in GSR and heart rate made to a mildly noxious stimulus and converting the measures into a so-called autonomic lability score by means of a formula suggested by Lacey (11), two groups of subjects who fell in the upper and lower third of the distribution of such scores were subsequently conditioned. Shown in Fig. 4 are the frequency curves of eyelid conditioning for these two groups of subjects. As may be seen, the subjects with the high autonomic lability index performed at a higher level than those with a low index. The difference is significant at the .02 level.

In addition to varying performance by manipulating the A-scale and US variables, it should be possible to produce a higher level of conditioning performance by presenting a strong extra stimulus, such as an electric shock, during the course of conditioning. Similarly, after a subject has experienced a strong electric shock just prior to conditioning, the mere threat of further shocks during the conditioning should arouse a strong and persisting emotional response that would raise the level of D and hence the level of performance. We have already published the results of one such experiment with unselected subjects which corroborated, in part, these theoretical expectations (25).

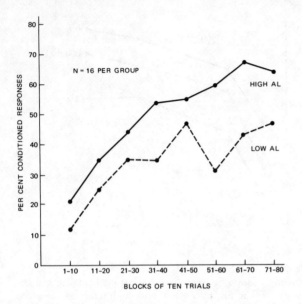

Fig. 4

Percentage of CR's for the high and low autonomic lability (AL) groups in blocks of ten trials.

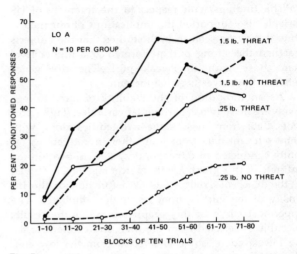

Fig. 5

Percentage of CR's in blocks of ten trials as a function of shock or no-shock threat and intensity of the US for subjects who score low on A-scale.

Recently a further experiment (to be published) studying the effects of shock threat on High and Low A subjects was completed in our laboratory. Some idea of the nature of the findings can be gained from Fig. 5 which presents the frequency curves of conditioning for four groups of Low A subjects (20th percentile). The two top curves in this graph are for subjects conditioned with a relatively strong air puff (1.5 lbs./sq. in.); the lower two, for subjects who had a weak puff (.25 lb./sq. in.). It will be seen that at both puff levels the threatened group (solid curve) was consistently above the nonthreatened group (broken curve) throughout the whole 80 trials. A similar experiment with high anxious subjects revealed a difference between the threat and nonthreat groups throughout the conditioning in the case of groups which had a weak puff. In the strong puff groups, however, the curves for the threat and nonthreat group, after separating in the early trials, came together in the later stages of the conditioning (last 40 trials). This latter effect undoubtedly results, in part, from the ceiling imposed by the frequency measure.

Space will not permit a detailed presentation of the experimental evidence with respect to that portion of our theory concerned with the assumption that the

emotional response to the noxious US would be weaker if adaptation trials are given prior to conditioning. It is sufficient to state that the original finding of MacDonald (12), that such preadapted subjects exhibited a lower level of performance in conditioning than nonadapted subjects, has been corroborated by Taylor (32). The latter experimenter also found that conditioning performance was inversely related to the intensity of the US employed during the preconditioning adaptation period. Thus the implications of this part of the theoretical network have also received further support.

The final set of conditioning data that I would like to present are concerned with the effect of level of D on differential conditioning. Without going into the theoretical derivation, it may be shown that one of the implications of our theory is that the higher the drive level, D, of the subjects, the greater should be the differentiation between the positive and the negative, i.e., nonreinforced, stimulus in such differential conditioning. Two studies from our laboratory have reported finding that, in five separate comparisons, high anxious subjects showed better discrimination than low anxious subjects (21, 23). Although none of the differences were significant, four closely approached be-

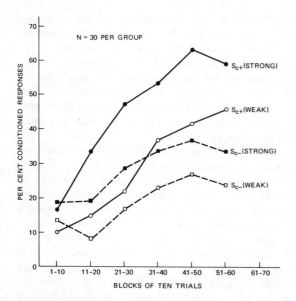

Fig. 6

Percentage of CR's to the positive and negative stimuli for groups conditioned with a strong and weak US.

ing so. More recently we have investigated the effect of varying the level of D on differential conditioning by direct manipulation of the intensity of the US. The graph in Fig. 6 presents the findings of this study (17) in terms of the frequency of CR's given to the two stimuli, positive and negative. As may be seen, the subjects conditioned with the strong US not only showed a higher level of response to the positive and negative stimuli, but, as predicted from our theory, the difference between the conditioned responses to the two stimuli was greater in the case of the group that had the strong US. Again this latter difference approached, but did not quite reach, statistical significance. Unfortunately, conditioning data are plagued by high individual variability, produced in part by a few subjects who show very little or no conditioning. In an effort to ascertain what the finding would be for subjects who showed considerable conditioning, a separate analysis was made of the upper two-thirds of each of the two groups run in the experiment. In the case of these subjects discrimination was significantly better for the high drive group at the .05 level.

So much for the findings in our eyelid conditioning studies. On the whole, we believe they are in fair accord with our theoretical schema, including the

portion of it that involves the A-scale. While not all of the results have met acceptable levels of significance, the fact that the direction of the differences in such instances has almost invariably been in accord with the theory has encouraged us to continue to hold to it. Attention might also be called here to the fact that this theoretical model, particularly the hypothetical emotional response mechanism, has also been quite successful in connection with a wide variety of other behavioral situations involving noxious stimulation with animals. Examples are to be found in the many studies cited by Miller (13) on the motivating and reinforcing roles of acquired fear in learning situations. The experiments of a number of investigators on the persisting motivational effects of emotionality aroused by electric shock on the consummatory behavior of rats provide yet another example (1, 2, 18, 19).

COMPLEX HUMAN LEARNING

Turning now to our studies involving the more complex types of human learning, let me begin by saying that it is in this area that the limitations of space in experimental journals for theoretical elaboration have been most unfortunate. Certainly we recognize that these treatments have been quite inadequate, particularly from the point of view of discussing the many factors that complicate efforts at theorizing in this area. By way of example let me mention two important points that need to be recognized but, unfortunately, have not always been so.

First, it should be realized that in order to derive implications concerning the effects of drive variation in any type of complex learning task, it is necessary to have, in addition to the drive theory, a further theoretical network concerning the variables and their interaction that are involved in the particular learning activity. It is perhaps unnecessary to point out here that theoretical schemas for such types of learning are as yet in a very primitive state of development, indeed almost nonexistent. As a consequence of this, one has considerable difficulty in drawing conclusions about the motivational part of the new, combined theory from supposedly negative findings, for the defect may be in the part of the network specifying the action of the variables in the complex learning situation.

The second point is that our theory of the mechanism underlying D was developed in connection with experimental situations involving some form of noxious stimulation. Complex human learning tasks, on the other hand, typically do not involve the use of a noxious stimulus. Whatever stress is present in these situations is usually produced by instructions that aim to create in the subject the desire or need to make as good a showing as possible. While it is true that this stress may be greatly augmented by introducing failure or punishment into the situation, so far as the usual type of human learning experiment is concerned, the question as to whether High A subjects would be more emotional than Low A subjects, and hence have a higher D level, is a moot one. In this connection two alternative subhypotheses have been proposed: (a) the chronic hypothesis: that High A subjects react emotionally in a chronic manner to all situations, whether stressful or not; and (b) the emotional reactivity hypothesis: that High A subjects have a lower threshold of emotional responsiveness and react with a stronger emotional response than Low A subjects to situations containing some degree of stress (16, 20, 25). As may be seen, according to the first of these hypotheses, mild nonthreatening situations would produce a differential drive (D) level in subjects scoring at extremes of the scale; whereas according to the second, there would not be a difference. These two examples are sufficient, I believe, to point up the fact that the problems involved in the extension of the theory to these more complex types of learning are quite formidable and that at this stage there necessarily must be a considerable amount of trial and error in our theorizing.

Now it will be recalled that the theoretical schema presented in Fig. 1 assumed that in classical conditioning habit strength to but a single response was established to the CS. In this circumstance, as we have seen, an increase in drive level implied an increase in response strength. In more complex, selective learning tasks, on the other hand, there are, typically, a hierarchy of competing response tendencies. Actually most of the complex learning situations employed with humans involve a number or sequence of such response hierarchies which involve competing responses, e.g., a number of choice points in the maze, whether verbal or spatial. To show what the implications of variation of drive level will be in such competing response situations, let us begin by considering the simplest conceivable case: one in which there is but a single response hierarchy involving two alternative responses. The single choice point maze involving turning left or right is one example of such a situation. If now the habit strength of the correct to-be-learned response is, at the beginning of the learning, somewhat stronger than that of the incorrect response, it may be shown that the higher the drive level, D, the greater will the difference between the competing excitatory potentials be and, *neglecting all other considerations*, the higher should be the percentage of correct responses at the start of learning, the sooner should the learning criterion be attained, and the smaller should be the total number of errors.[4]

The reverse situation, that in which the correct response is at the outset weaker than the incorrect one, is, from the theoretical viewpoint, even more complex. In this instance the stronger the drive, the greater will be the percent choice of the wrong response, or, in other words, the poorer will be the performance at this initial stage. But, as training proceeds, sooner or later the habit strength of the correct, reinforced response will overtake that of the wrong, unreinforced response and from this point on the percent choice of the correct response should in general be higher for the high drive group than for the low drive group. In other words, the performance curves should be expected to cross. Precise predictions about the total number of errors, number of trials, etc. in this situation will depend to a considerable extent upon the particular functions and parameter values assigned to the assumed habit and

4. As discussed in my Silliman Lectures (21), there are a number of other considerations that need to be taken into account in extending the theory to such competing response situation. Thus the particular composition rule (law) assumed in these lectures to describe the manner in which the competing responses interacted with each other led to the implication that the percentage of occurrence of the competing responses is a function, not only of the magnitude of the difference between the competing Es, but also of their absolute level above the threshold L. As a consequence in the low range of E values, there may actually be an inverse relation between performance level (percent choice of the response with stronger E) and the level of drive. Still other considerations involve whether habit strength (H) in learning situations is or is not assumed to be dependent on the reinforcer and whether drive strength (D) determines the inhibitory factor (I_n). Different combinations of these alternative assumptions, including even other possible composition rules, lead to different behavior consequences. Critical evaluation of the different conceivable theoretical models will require considerably more empirical data obtained under a wide variety of experimental conditions than is now available.

inhibitory factors. Actually we have never got around to working out in detail the implications of the various possibilities for the total learning period even in this simplest case.

Recalling now that such a learning task as the serial verbal or spatial maze involves a number of such competing response hierarchies, we see that the problem of predicting the effect on performance of variation of the drive in such situations becomes even more complicated. On the assumption that anticipatory and perseverative associative tendencies would develop in such a manner as to make the incorrect response the stronger in the case of many of the choice points of a maze, it was hoped that it would be possible to demonstrate that high drive (i.e., High A) subjects would perform more poorly in such serial learning situations than low drive (i.e., Low A) subjects. Two experiments, one with a verbal form of maze (35) and one using a finger maze (5) actually did provide results in agreement with this theoretical expectation. However, as was pointed out at the time, there was a serious discrepancy between the theory and the obtained results in these studies in that the anxious subjects made more errors at all but one of the choice points in both studies. In view of the ease of learning many of these choice points, and hence evidence for little or no strong competing response tendencies, the theory would have led us to expect that the High A subjects would have made fewer errors on them than the Low A subjects. Obviously the theory was wrong in some respect, but just in what way—an incorrect assumption or failure to include an important relevant variable—was not clear.

At this point in our work we realized that such serial learning tasks are, for a variety of reasons, quite unsatisfactory. Among the most important from our viewpoint was the fact that one has little or no knowledge of the relative strengths of the competing responses in each of the hierarchies. Accordingly we abandoned this type of situation and attempted to develop learning tasks in which it would be possible to specify or manipulate in some known manner the relative strengths of the competing responses in each hierarchy. Probably the chief value of these earlier experiments is that they did point up the fact that a higher anxiety score (and hence possibly a higher drive level) does not necessarily always lead to a higher level of performance.

Among the types of learning problems that we turned to was paired-associates learning. This type of

learning task may be conceived of as consisting of the formation of a set of more or less isolated S-R associations or habit tendencies. In one type of list, which we have referred to as a noncompetitive list, an attempt is made to isolate as much as possible the paired items by minimizing the degree of synonymity or formal similarity among both the stimulus and response words. As learning proceeds and the habit strengths of the stimulus words to their paired response words increase, high drive subjects should, according to our theory, perform at a higher level than low drive subjects. An important condition in this derivation is that the associative connections between each stimulus word and the nonpaired response words are lower than that to the paired response word.

Two lists of this type have been employed. In one the associative connections between the paired words were initially zero or at least very low. In this type of list it would be predicted that there would be little or no difference between high and low drive subjects at the start of learning, but that as learning progressed the curve of correct responses would diverge, that for the high drive group being the higher. Using nonsense syllables of low association value and low intralist similarity, Taylor has reported two experiments in which this type of list was employed (33, 34). The lower pair of curves in Fig. 7 present the data from one of these

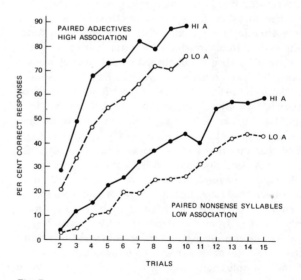

Fig. 7

Paired-associates learning as a function of A-score under conditions of unusual interword pair competition.

studies (34). Both curves, it will be observed, began at a very low level with the curve for the High A group (solid line) rising above that for the Low A group (broken line). An unpublished study from our laboratory employing nonassociated paired adjectives has given similar results, although the superiority of the High A over the Low A subjects was significant only on a single tailed hypothesis.

The second type of noncompetitive list differs from the first in that the associative strengths of the paired words are, as the result of past experiences, considerably above zero. Under this condition it would be predicted that the performance curves would, on the first anticipation trial, be considerably above 0% and that the curve for the high drive group would be above that for the low drive group. Employing paired adjectives that had been scaled by Haagen (7) as having high "closeness of association" values, two studies (24, 29) have reported results which support these implications. The upper pair of curves in Fig. 7 shows the findings of one of these studies (29). As may be seen, the initial level of performance was well above 0 and the High A subjects started out and continued at a higher level than the Low A subjects. On the other hand, a recently completed doctoral dissertation (6) using this type of list failed to obtain results in accord with the theory. There was little or no difference between the two groups at any stage of practice.

In contrast to these noncompetitive type lists we have also designed a competitive list which includes some paired items in which the initial habit strength of the stimulus word to call out the paired word is weaker than the habit strengths to one or more other response words in the list. In the case of these items it would be predicted from our theory that high drive subjects would at the start of learning perform more poorly than low drive subjects. Here again we should have emphasized that the theory of paired-associates learning has as yet not been developed sufficiently to predict what will happen beyond the first few trials, and it would have been more appropriate, as far as implications for our drive theory are concerned, if we had used at most only the data from the first four or five trials. Precise predictions concerning performance beyond this point must await the development of a more adequate theory of the variables determining the weakening of these stronger, incorrect responses in paired-associates learning. Two published studies (24, 29) and one doctoral dissertation (6) have reported data with respect to the implication of our theory for this type of list; while

all three found, as predicted, that the High A subjects were inferior to Low A subjects in the first four trials, none of the results was statistically significant. However, the implication of the theory that there would be an interaction between level of A-score and performance on the two kinds of lists, competitive and noncompetitive, was confirmed.

Summarizing the results with these paired-associates lists, I would say that the batting average of our theory is fairly high but by no means perfect. It is clearly evident from the data that differences in level of A-score (and hence level of D), if it is a factor determining performance on such tasks, is a relatively unimportant one. Certainly individual differences in verbal learning ability play a much more decisive role. Moreover, there are as yet many factors that play important roles in such complex behavior situations, about which we have as yet little or no knowledge. Among those of a motivational nature is the type of task-irrelevant response that Child and his group have studied (3). We think of these interfering responses as being elicited by drive stimuli (s_D), and hence they would be incorporated in a more complete motivational theory of learned behavior. On the basis of evidence in the literature and some recently completed studies of our own, we believe this factor is especially important when shock is introduced into verbal learning situations.

I should like to conclude this presentation by stating very briefly the purpose of such theoretical schemas as has been presented here. As I conceive them, their primary function is to provide for the unification of what, without the theory, would be a multiplicity of isolated or unconnected facts and laws. Thus, in the present instance, such phenotypically different phenomena as behavior in eyelid conditioning under various stimulus conditions, degree of emotionality as revealed by a personality questionnaire and physiological measures, and such opposite performance differentials in paired-associates tasks as just described have been interrelated by means of the theory. That much work, both of a theoretical and experimental nature, remains to be done in this area of behavior study is clearly revealed by the many gaps and deficiencies in the present attempt. It is my firm belief, however, that progress in the development of this, as in any other scientific field of knowledge, is greatly facilitated by such theoretically oriented research endeavors.

References

1. Amsel, A. The effect upon level of consummatory response of the addition of anxiety to a motivational complex. *J. exp. Psychol.*, 1950, *40*, 709–715.

2. Amsel, A., & Maltzman, I. The effect upon generalized drive strength of emotionality as inferred from the level of consummatory response. *J. exp. Psychol.*, 1950, *40*, 563–569.

3. Child, I. L. Personality. *Annu. Rev. Psychol.*, 1954, *5*, 149–170.

4. Cronbach, L. J., & Meehl, P. E. Construct validity in psychological tests. *Psychol. Bull.*, 1955, *52*, 281–302.

5. Farber, I. E., & Spence, K. W. Complex learning and conditioning as a function of anxiety. *J. exp. Psychol.*, 1953, *45*, 120–125.

6. Fredenburg, Norma C. Paired-associates learning as a function of anxiety level and shock. Unpublished doctoral dissertation, State Univer. of Iowa, 1956.

7. Haagen, C. H. Synonymity, vividness, familiarity, and association value ratings of 400 pairs of common adjectives. *J. Psychol.*, 1949, *27*, 453–463.

8. Hilgard, E. R., Jones, L. V., & Kaplan, S. J. Conditioned discrimination as related to anxiety. *J. exp. Psychol.*, 1951, *42*, 94–99.

9. Hull, C. L. *Principles of behavior.* New York: Appleton-Century, 1943.

10. Jessor, R., & Hammond, K. R. Construct validity and the Taylor anxiety scale. *Psychol. Bull.*, 1957, *54*, 161–170.

11. Lacey, O. L. The evaluation of autonomic responses toward a general solution. *Ann. N.Y. Acad. Sci.*, 1956, *67*, 123–164.

12. MacDonald, Annette. The effect of adaptation to the unconditioned stimulus upon the formation of conditioned avoidance response. *J. exp. Psychol.*, 1946, *36*, 1–12.

13. Miller N. E. Learnable drives and rewards. In S. S. Stevens (Ed.), *Handbook of experimental psychology.* New York. Wiley, 1951. Pp. 435–472.

14. Mowrer, O. H. A stimulus response analysis of anxiety and its role as a reinforcing agent. *Psychol. Rev.*, 1939, *46*, 553–565.

15. Passey, G. E. The influence of intensity of unconditioned stimulus upon acquisition of a conditioned response. *J. exp. Psychol.*, 1948, *38*, 420–428.

16. Rosenbaum, G. Stimulus generalization as a function of clinical and experimentally induced anxiety. Unpublished doctoral dissertation, State Univer. of Iowa, 1950.

17. Runquist, W. N., Spence, K. W., & Stubbs, D. W. Differential conditioning and intensity of the US. *J. exp. Psychol.*, in press.

18. Siegel, P. S., & Brantley, J. J. The relationship of emotionality to the consummatory response of eating. *J. exp. Psychol.*, 1951, *42*, 304–306.

19. Siegel, P. S., & Siegel, Helen S. The effect of emotionality on the water intake of the rat. *J. comp. physiol. Psychol.*, 1949, *42*, 12–16.

20. Spence, K. W. *Behavior theory and conditioning.* New Haven: Yale Univer. Press, 1956.

21. Spence, K. W., & Beecroft, R. S. Differential conditioning and level of anxiety. *J. exp. Psychol.*, 1954, *48*, 399–403.

22. Spence, K. W. & Farber, I. E. Conditioning and extinction as a function of anxiety. *J. exp. Psychol.*, 1953, *45*, 116–119.

23. Spence, K. W., & Farber, I. E. The relation of anxiety to differential eyelid conditioning. *J. exp. Psychol.*, 1954, *47*, 127–134.

24. Spence, K. W., Farber, I. E., & Mc Fann, H. H. The relation of anxiety (drive) level to performance in competitional and noncompetitional paired-associates learning. *J. exp. Psychol.*, 1956, *52*, 296–305.

25. Spence, K. W., Farber, I. E. ·& Taylor, Elaine. The relation of electric shock and anxiety to level of performance in eyelid conditioning. *J. exp. Psychol.*, 1954, *48*, 404–408.

26. Spence, K. W., & Ross, L. E. Experimental evidence on the relation between performance level in eyelid conditioning and anxiety (drive) level. USN Office of Naval Research Tech Rep., 1957, No. 5 (Contract N9 onr-93802).

27. Spence, K. W., & Taylor, Janet A. Anxiety and strength of the US as determiners of the amount of eyelid conditioning. *J. exp. Psychol*, 1951, *42*, 183–188.

28. Spence, K. W., & Taylor, Janet A. The relation of conditioned response strength to anxiety in normal, neurotic, and psychotic subjects. *J. exp. Psychol.*, 1953, *45*, 265–272.

29. Spence, K. W., Taylor, J., & Ketchel, Rhoda. Anxiety (drive) level and degree of competition in paired-associates learning. *J. exp. Psychol.*, 1956, *52*, 306–310.

30. Taylor, Janet A. The relationship of anxiety to the conditioned eyelid response. *J. exp. Psychol.*, 1951, *41*, 81–92.

31. Taylor, Janet A. A personality scale of manifest anxiety. *J. abnorm. soc. Psychol.*, 1953, *48*, 285–290.

32. Taylor, Janet A. Level of conditioning and intensity of the adaptation stimulus. *J. exp. Psychol.*, 1956, *51*, 127–131.

33. Taylor, Janet A. The effects of anxiety level and psychological stress on verbal learning. *J. abnorm. soc. Psychol.*, in press.

34. Taylor, Janet A., & Chapman, J. P. Paired-associate learning as related to anxiety. *Amer. J. Psychol.*, 1955, *68*, 671.

35. Taylor, Janet A., & Spence, K. W. The relationship of anxiety level to performance in serial learning. *J. exp. Psychol.*, 1952, *44*, 61–64.

36. Taylor, Janet A., & Spence, K. W. Conditioning level in behavior disorders. *J. abnorm. soc. Psychol.*, 1954, *49*, 497–502.

I want to present some recent research which my students and I have been pursuing. These studies are interrelated, but they reflect a variety of my own interests as well as those of different students who have contributed greatly to them. Therefore, they cover quite a range, beginning with some purely behavioral studies, and ending with a combination of behavioral and physiological techniques.

In order to put these studies into proper context, I shall from time to time briefly summarize certain earlier work from my laboratory. For the benefit of those who have not had extensive experience with research, I shall mention a few of the difficulties and failures, as well as those successes which ordinarily are all that is published and hence give a false impression of the actual process of groping forward into the unknown. But, even so, I shall not begin to do justice to the arduous exploration, only some of which has led forward.

While I realize all too well the difficulties of trying to prove the null hypothesis, I believe there should be more mention of negative results in publications, not only to give a truer picture of scientific research, but also to prevent later investigators, one after another, from proceeding in the same way into the same quagmires.

At the purely empirical level, drives and rewards obviously are important in the performance of learned behavior, be it individual or social, normal or abnormal. Thus all behavior theorists from Thorndike (1898) on have used the empirical law of effect in some

analytical studies of drive and reward[1]

neal e. miller
rockefeller university

form or other. Many advances have been made, and many more can be made, by staying at this level and applying the empirical law of effect to behavior in the laboratory and in the home, in the classroom, factory, and clinic. As you may know, I have made some such applications (Dollard & Miller, 1950; Miller, 1957b,

1. Address of the President to the sixty-ninth Annual Convention of the American Psychological Association, New York City, September 3, 1961. Reprinted from *American Psychologist*, 1961, Vol. 16, pp. 739–754. Copyright 1961 by the American Psychological Association, and reproduced by permission.

Work on the studies cited in this paper was supported by Grants MY647 and MY2949 from the National Institute of Mental Health of the National Institutes of Health; United States Department of Health, Education, and Welfare; Bethesda, Maryland. The work of Angus A. Campbell and Donald Novin was supported by Grant G5818 from the National Science Foundation, Washington, D.C.

1959; Miller & Dollard, 1941). My present purpose, however, is to try to analyze some of the fundamental mechanisms involved in drive and reward.

Effect of Drive on Reward and Learning

Everyone agrees that the level of drive can affect performance, but there has been a long, vigorous controversy over whether it also affects learning. As you know, Tolman (1932) initiated this controversy which has been carried on by other expectancy theorists (Hilgard, 1956). He contended that animals exposed to a learning situation without any motivation learn "what leads to what," but do not display this "latent learning" until they are motivated to perform. One of the difficulties in resolving this controversy has been that in the complete absence of any motivation it is hard to get animals to expose themselves to the mazes and other types of learning situations commonly used. A completely unmotivated rat would be expected to sit completely still. But for the learning theorist there is not much future in watching rats sitting still. How can we surmount this difficulty?

As a means of exposing unmotivated rats to water, I asked one of my students, Donald Jensen, to try to develop a fistula into the mouth. With considerable ingenuity, he developed the polyethylene fistula illustrated in Figure 1. This enters in the back of the rat's neck (where it is hardest for him to bite or scratch it out), passes under the skin, is anchored by a blob of dental cement, plunges down through the snout, and emerges into a little metal tip on the top of the palate. With further perspicacity, Jensen suggested that this fistula might be used to elicit and record conditioned tongue licks. The tongue completes an electrical circuit with the little metal tip. This technique was further developed with the help of another student, Richard C. DeBold, who performed with me the following experiment on the effects of thirst on conditioned tongue licks.

Fig. 1
The oral fistula used to elicit and record conditioned tongue licks.

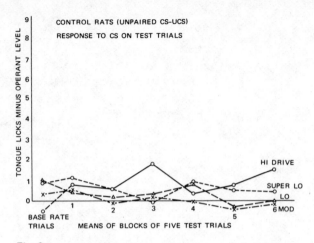

Fig. 2
The four control groups for pseudoconditioning show a low level of spontaneous licking which is not consistently related to number of training trials or level of thirst.

During the first, or learning, phase of the experiment, 64 male albino rats were given a total of 150 trials during which a flickering light was a signal for an injection of water into the mouth. Every fifth trial was an unpaired test trial. All rats were on a schedule of 22-hour water deprivation. Four experimental groups were run with different strengths of thirst achieved by the following treatments immediately before each day's training: (a) *strong thirst* with no drinking before training; (b) *moderate thirst*, allowed to drink before training 70% of amount usually consumed; (c) *satiated* by drinking ad lib. one hour before training; (d) *supersatiated* by preceding procedure plus injection via the mouth fistula of an additional 70% of daily water consumption, most of which the rat allowed to drool out of his mouth. We wanted to be absolutely sure that this last group was completely satiated. And it really was.

As a control for spontaneous level of licking and for pseudoconditioning, four similar control groups were run with exposure to the same number of lights and injections which never were paired with each other. Figure 2 shows the results for these control rats. There is a low level of spontaneous licking which does not change throughout the training and is not markedly or consistently related to the level of thirst.

Figure 3 shows that, during test trials, the performance of the satiated (LO) and supersatiated animals was approximately the same as that of the pseudocon-

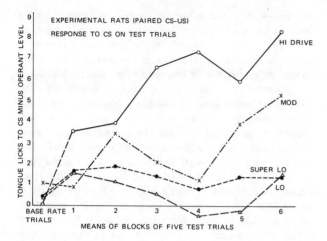

Fig. 3
Performance during conditioning as a function of level of drive.

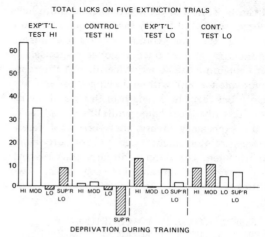

Fig. 4
Performance during testing under high drive (22-hour water deprivation) or low drive (normal satiation), as a function of deprivation during training.

ditioning controls. The moderately thirsty animals showed definitely better conditioning, and the highly thirsty ones obviously were the best of all. There seems to be a clear relationship between drive and learning. However, it is possible that the two nonthirsty groups actually were learning that the light led to the water, but were not performing because they were not motivated.

In order to test for such latent learning, half of the rats in each group were given five trials of exposure to the light alone (without water) when they were motivated by 22 hours of thirst. The other half were tested following normal satiation. The results are presented in Figure 4. Between the dotted lines just right of the center, we see that, when the experimental test is under low drive (actually satiation), the performance is within the range of the control test at the extreme right for spontaneous level and for pseudoconditioning. These results are yet another demonstration that performance is low under low drive.

On the left-hand side we see that when experimental animals were tested with high drive in order to bring out any latent learning, those originally conditioned with high drive gave many conditioned licks; those originally conditioned with moderate drive gave approximately half as many conditioned licks; and those conditioned with low or superlow drives were within the range of spontaneous licks, as indicated by

the control groups. Thus, when the effects of drive on learning are separated from those on performance by tests designed to bring out any latent learning, a clear-cut relationship between strength of drive and learning remains. This result is contrary to the prediction from Tolman's (1932) expectancy theory. It emphasizes the importance of drive.

Figure 5 shows the effect of strength of drive on the unconditioned licks to the water during the training

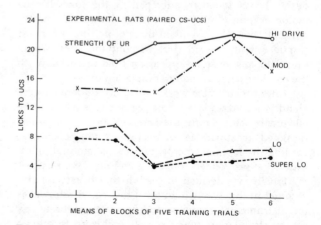

Fig. 5
Unconditioned licks during conditioning as a function of training trials and strength of drive.

trials. It can be seen that the water elicited more licks in the thirstier rats. Contiguity theorists, following the Guthrie (1952) tradition, could use this relationship between the drive and the unconditioned response as a basis for explaining the superior learning of the more highly motivated group, without having to assume any relationship between the strength of thirst and the *rewarding* effects of water. Thus, while the results went against the expectancy theory, they did not differentiate between reinforcement based on contiguity alone and reinforcement based on contiguity plus reward. How can we differentiate between these two possibilities?

UNSUCCESSFUL ATTEMPTS TO CONDITION
RESPONSES ELICITED BY ELECTRICAL STIMULATION
OF MOTOR CORTEX OF RAT
If one could elicit a response without motivation and reward, one might test between the contiguity and the reward theories of reinforcement. A considerable number of years ago, Roger Loucks (1935) apparently did this by implanting electrodes in the motor cortex of dogs. He paired a cue for over 600 trials with leg lifting elicited by stimulation of the motor cortex in three dogs without producing any conditioning. But by adding a food reward, he produced conditioning in two other dogs. This result seemed to show that contiguity alone was not sufficient for learning, while contiguity plus reward was.

I wanted to repeat this highly significant experiment and, in addition, to try a latent learning design to see whether, after pairing the cue with the motor response elicited by stimulating the cortex without reward, subsequent trials of pairing the motor response with reward (but without the cue), would cause the response to appear on final test trials with the cue but without motor stimulation or reward.

After considerable work, one of my students, Derek Hendry, found a place where leg movements could be elicited by stimulating the cortex of the rat, and also designed an apparatus for restraining the rat and recording the leg movements. But a large amount of additional effort yielded confusing and negative results.

Finally, we decided to see whether thirsty rats restrained in this way would learn the leg withdrawal as an instrumental response to get water without any central stimulation, much as they will learn to press a bar. They did not. Apparently rats react badly to restraint and are poor at learning discrete leg-retraction

responses. We had achieved no results from almost a year of work on this project. Perhaps some radical, or even minor, change would make the procedure work, but it was time for Hendry to concentrate on a PhD thesis, so he prudently changed to a safer problem.

Meanwhile, I found that Giurgea (Doty & Giurgea, 1961) had been able to establish conditioning in an animal by pairing electrical stimulation of a sensory area with electrical stimulation of the motor cortex, provided the trials were very widely distributed. But did the motor stimulation which he used serve as a reward, either like the Olds and Milner (1954) stimulation in subcortical structures, or by relieving boredom? The latter hypothesis would explain the need for the wide distribution of trials since the novelty effect of a stimulus is known to be subject to rapid habituation by massed trials and, as would be expected from this fact, Arlo Myers and I (1954) have found that widely distributed trials favor learning rewarded by weak exploration. Furthermore, Bower and I (1960) have found that strong reinforcement is required the more resistance a response must overcome. Thus if massed trials generate more reactive inhibition, they should require more reward. Such considerations suggest that Giurgea might get conditioning, even with less widely distributed trials, provided he added a reward.

I have just speculated that stimulating the motor cortex might have a mild rewarding effect. One could test for such a reward by determining whether the cortical stimulation will help to maintain some other response, such as bar pressing originally learned for food. If the cortical stimulation is rewarding, it should help to prevent the extinction of such a response (Miller, 1961a).

On the other hand, it is possible that the elicitation of an arousal response, rather than reward, is the basic requirement for effective learning. It is also possible that contiguity alone is sufficient, or that where an additional resistance must be overcome, a central excitatory state must also be conditioned by contiguity to serve as a booster.

CAN RESPONSES IN THE SENSORY CORTEX BE
STRENGTHENED BY REWARD?
At the moment I am shifting my efforts on this problem somewhat. I still am attempting to secure evidence on the effectiveness of contiguity alone compared with contiguity plus reward. But at the same

time, I am exploring the possibility of objectively studying certain phenomena which may be relevant to imagery, hallucinations, and mediating responses. Various investigators have electrophysiologically recorded so-called sensory conditioning. For example, if a tone is a cue for a distinctive rhythm of flashes of light, the evoked potential to the flashes originally recorded from the visual cortex can sometimes be recorded to the tone alone. But such conditioning characteristically is variable and does not persist for a large number of trials. We are trying to see whether it can be strengthened by adding a reward after the flashes. Will anticipatory evoked potentials from the visual cortex be learned if they are rewarded by giving food to a hungry animal? Can the flashes then be omitted and the distinctive rhythm of cortical potentials be made instrumental to securing reward? If so, will the activity producing these potentials have all of the functional properties of a cue producing response, such as a visual image (Miller, 1961a)? I had hoped to have answers for you, but as often happens, the solution to various technical problems has required more time than I anticipated. It is also possible that this will be one of the trials that, instead of leading to a break through the barrier mountains, leads into a box canyon.

WHAT DETERMINES THE EFFECTIVE POINT OF REINFORCEMENT IN A TEMPORAL SEQUENCE?

To summarize our position so far, we have succeeded in securing a clear-cut demonstration of the effects of drive on learning, but have failed to solve a second problem and to complete a related third one. Let us now turn to a fourth problem. At what point in a temporal sequence does reward occur?

Experiments by Thorndike (1933) purported to demonstrate a bidirectional gradient of reinforcement affecting acts occurring both before and after the reward. Probable sources of artifact in his data were discovered and his interpretation was seriously questioned (Jenkins & Sheffield, 1946). Looking for a simpler, more direct, test, one of my students, Mohammed Nagaty (1951), trained hungry rats some years ago to press a bar as soon as it was inserted. Next he habituated them to receive a pellet immediately before, as well as immediately after, pressing the bar. Then he found that rats with only the pellet *after* pressing omitted, extinguished at the same rate as those with the pellet omitted *both* before and after pressing the

bar. These results, and various controls, showed that the pellet before pressing the bar was not an effective reward. But under these conditions some of the food probably still was being chewed and swallowed, the taste lingered in the mouth, and food certainly was entering the stomach and being digested *after* the bar was pressed. In short, part of the chain of events of food ingestion and digestion followed pressing the bar. Why did these later events in the chain have no rewarding effect?

In a recent attempt to answer this question, David Egger and I (1962) advanced the hypothesis that reward occurs primarily at the point at which new information is delivered. Normally, delivery of food to the cup, and certainly food in the mouth, invariably means that it can be chewed, tasted, swallowed, will reach the stomach, and be digested. Therefore, feedback from these subsequent links in the sequence conveys no new information; it is completely redundant. According to our hypothesis, in Nagaty's experiment all of the new information, and hence the reward, came when the food was delivered.

In order to test this hypothesis, we worked on the learning of secondary reinforcement. We chose the learning of secondary reinforcement instead of the learning of a movement, since it is easier to control the interval between a cue and reward than it is the timing of a movement made by an animal. Our specific hypothesis was that the secondary reinforcement value of a cue is a function of its information value.

Figure 6 summarizes the experimental situation. Look at the diagram next to the bottom labeled "redundant." The first single pellet always predicts the delivery, 2 seconds later, of the trio of pellets. This is analogous to delivery of food predicting the taste, chewing, swallowing, and entry of food into the stomach. Thus, although the intervening stimulus is followed by additional pellets, it is redundant.

In the top diagram of simple conditioning, which represents the usual situation for learning secondary reinforcement, the stimulus is not redundant because there is no other way of predicting the trio of pellets.

But is there any other way of rendering the stimulus informative, while still having it always preceded by a pellet in order to control for any possible inhibitory aftereffect of the first bit of reward? Suppose we present unpredictably between trials a number of single free pellets, as is indicated in the diagram next to the top, labeled "informative." Then the stimulus is

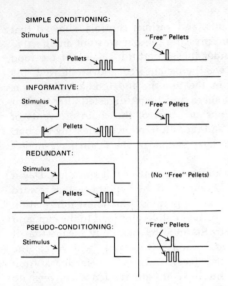

Fig. 6
Diagrammatic representation of the conditions in the first experiment on secondary reinforcement as a function of the information value of the CS.

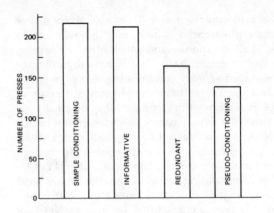

Fig. 7
Food administered immediately before a CS does not interfere with the acquisition of secondary reinforcement, provided the stimulus is an informative predictor of additional food, but does produce a substantial reduction if it makes the CS redundant.

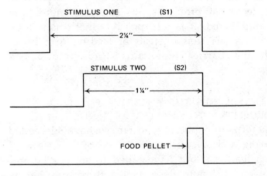

Fig. 8
Design of stimulus sequence used in second experiment on secondary reinforcement as a function of the information value of the CS.

no longer redundant: it is a more reliable predictor of the trio of pellets than is the single pellet. From our hypothesis, we predict that with such a group the stimulus should become a stronger secondary reinforcer than it will in the redundant group given exactly the same treatment in all other respects, but without the additional presentation of some free pellets not followed by the trio of pellets.

Finally, the bottom diagram represents a control for pseudoconditioning in which presentations of the stimulus and the pellets never were paired.

In order to achieve the most sensitive test for secondary reinforcement, we first trained rats to press a bar for pellets, then extinguished them by disconnecting the pellet feeder mechanism, and finally gave them test trials during which every third press delivered the stimulus, but no pellets. Thus the measure of secondary reinforcement was relearning after extinction and is shown by the amount of bar pressing for the stimulus in excess of that shown by the pseudoconditioning, control group.

Figure 7 presents the results. You can see that the informative group did as well as the group with the conventional simple conditioning procedure. The pellet of food a half-second before the stimulus had no ob-

vious inhibitory aftereffect. Furthermore, as demanded by our hypothesis, the informative group performed significantly better than the redundant one.

Figure 8 summarizes the design of a similar experiment on the same problem. Since Stimulus 1 always precedes Stimulus 2, the latter is redundant and should acquire less secondary reinforcement value, even though it always precedes food. But there is a way to make S_2 informative. Present S_1 unpredictably a number of times without either S_2 or food. Then S_2 is a

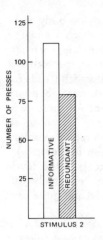

Fig. 9
Results of a second experiment showing that a cue is a stronger secondary reinforcer when it is informative.

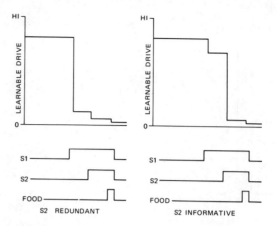

Fig. 10
Diagram showing how the difference in acquisition under the redundant and informative conditions might be explained by the drive-reduction hypothesis of reinforcement.

more reliable predictor of food than S_1 and is no longer redundant. From our hypothesis we predict that with a group given such training S_2 will be a stronger reinforcer than it will in a group given exactly the same number of identical pairings of S_1 plus S_2 with food, but without the additional presentations of S_1 alone.

Figure 9 presents the results of such an experiment (Egger & Miller, 1962). The ordinate is the number of bar presses, followed by S_2 as a secondary reinforcer for relearning after experimental extinction. You can see that there were more bar presses for S_2 under the informative than under the redundant conditions. The results of this second experiment also are in line with the information hypothesis.[2]

But it is quite possible to interpret these results at a different level of analysis, using the drive-reduction hypothesis, which I have found it extremely fruitful to investigate, although I am not at all certain that it is true. According to the strong form of the drive-reduction hypothesis, the secondary reinforcer must produce a reduction in that part of the drive which can

2. Since the measure was the ability of the cue to substitute for food in inducing recovery from experimental extinction, only the difference between the informative and redundant condition is relevant; the performance under the redundant condition may have represented disinhibition or spontaneous recovery.

be modified by learning. Figure 10 presents a diagram of the theoretical analysis. On the left-hand side of this diagram you can see that, if most of the learnable drive already has been reduced by S_1, little drive-reduction remains to be conditioned to S_2. On the other hand, if S_1 often fails to predict food, much of the conditioned drive-reduction to it should be extinguished. Hence, as is illustrated on the right-hand side of the diagram, more of the drive-reduction should occur to, and be conditioned to, S_2.

As you can see from the diagram, this type of an analysis demands that, if the secondary reinforcing value of our hitherto neglected stimulus, S_1, is tested, it should be greater under the conditions on the left-hand side when it is the reliable predictor (making S_2 redundant) than under those on the right-hand side when it is an unreliable predictor (making S_2 informative). Figure 11 shows that this is indeed the case.

Although the preceding experiment is in line with the deduction made by applying the drive-reduction hypothesis, it would be much more satisfying if we could test the hypothesis in this and in other situations by some more direct, independent measure of the moment-to-moment level of the drive. The need for such a measure in this and in many other experiments is one of the things that has motivated me to explore physiological techniques. My original hope was that, if the neural centers controlling hunger and satiation

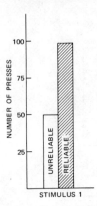

Fig. 11
Confirmation of the prediction based on the theoretical analysis summarized in Figure 10. (Stimulus 1 is a stronger secondary reinforcer when it is a reliable than when it is an unreliable predictor.)

could be located, it might be possible to use direct recordings from such centers as a measure of drive. While I am less optimistic about this than when I started, the experimental program initiated by this hope has produced many interesting results.

EXPERIMENTS ON SENSORY FEEDBACK FROM THE MOUTH AND STOMACH

Before investigating the brain, however, I worked on some more peripheral mechanisms: the sensory feedback from the mouth and the stomach which I had speculated might be sources of reinforcement in puzzling over the results of Nagaty's experiment. Please fasten your seat belts while I summarize this old work quickly, in order to give the background for some new experiments.

If drive-reduction is the basis of reward, it is obvious that it must occur promptly after the food is received, or else it will be too late to reinforce the responses leading to food. Therefore, the reduction in hunger must occur long before digestion and absorption have restored the cellular deficit. In order to study the effect on hunger of feedback from various links in the chain between the eating and absorption of food, Martin Kohn and I spent the better part of a year trying to develop a simple fistula through which food could be injected directly into the stomach of the rat. After trying many different techniques, we ended up with a great respect for the rat's incredible ability to

extrude various foreign devices from his body even though these were held in by flanges which seemed to make such extrusion impossible. Fortunately, we eventually heard that Evelyn K. Anderson of the National Institutes of Health had developed a stomach fistula for the rat. Now that various workers in our laboratory have made a few minor improvements of their own, this technique, which originally gave us so much trouble, can be taught to a good undergraduate student in a couple of days. Our experience in this particular case is representative of what often occurs in the development of new techniques. They are extremely difficult before certain problems are solved and quite easy afterwards.

Experiments by Kohn (1951), Berkun, Marion Kessen, and myself (1952) showed that food injected directly into the stomach produced a prompt reduction in hunger, and taken normally by mouth produced an even greater reduction. Similarly, Woodrow, Sampliner and I (Miller, Sampliner, & Woodrow, 1957) found that water injected directly into the stomach produced a prompt reduction in thirst, but water taken normally by mouth produced an even greater reduction. With each of these drives the same results were secured by two different techniques for measuring drive: volume of food or water consumed, and rate of working for food or water by pressing a bar on a variable-interval schedule. Thus we were confident of the results which showed that the drive was regulated by immediate feedback from both the stomach and the mouth (Miller, 1957a). These prompt effects avoided the delay that would have been embarrassing to the drive-reduction hypothesis.

Meanwhile, Sheffield and Roby (1950) had shown that a nonnutritive but sweet substance, namely saccharine, could act as a reward for hungry animals even though all of it was excreted, so that it served no nutritional need. This finding has been used as an argument against the strong form of the drive-reduction hypothesis. But Edward Murray, Warren W. Roberts, and I showed that saccharine taken by mouth reduces the amount of food consumed immediately thereafter, which suggests that it temporarily reduces hunger as would be demanded by the drive-reduction hypothesis, and supplies additional evidence for an oral feedback controlling hunger (Miller, 1957a).

Recently, a student of mine, Derek Hendry, has observed that thirsty rats will lick at a cooling stream of air, and then has found that they will learn to press a

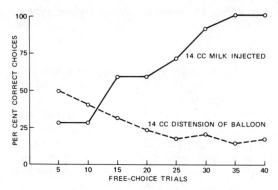

Fig. 12

One group of hungry rats learns to choose the side of **T** maze where their stomachs are distended by milk injected directly via fistula; another group learns to avoid the side where their stomachs are distended by injection of liquid into a balloon. (From Miller, 1957a)

bar to turn on the air briefly. Since the air increased evaporation, and hence the water deficit, he thought that this was evidence against the drive-reduction hypothesis. However, when at my suggestion he made the test for the effect of licking air on thirst, he found that a period of licking air not only reduced the immediately subsequent consumption of water, but also caused thirsty rats to reduce their rate of working for water by pressing a bar on a variable-interval schedule. Thus it appears that the feedback from the mouth produced by licking a jet of air may temporarily somewhat reduce thirst (Hendry & Rasche, 1961).

But to return to our original story, if food injected directly into the stomach produces a prompt reduction in hunger, it should serve as a reward. And indeed Marion Kessen and I (Miller & Kessen, 1952) found that rats would learn to turn to the side of the **T** maze in which they received milk via fistula directly into the stomach rather than isotonic saline.

Soon after that, we found that inflating a balloon in the rat's stomach would reduce the rate of bar pressing for food (Miller, 1955). We concluded that stomach distension probably reduced hunger. In that case, stomach distension should serve as a reward. But when we made the test, as Figure 12 shows, we found that the animals learned to avoid the side where their stomachs were distended by the balloon, in contrast to learning to go to the side where the stomach was distended by milk. This was nice in that the behavioral test showed

up a qualitative difference, which otherwise might not have been suspected. But it complicated the theoretical picture (Miller, 1957a).

DESIGN TO TEST INTERVENING VARIABLE

Now for some time I had been advocating and also practicing the use of a variety of behavioral tests to cross-check each conclusion in order to avoid being misled by side-effects which might be specific to a given type of test (Miller & Barry, 1960). Indeed, I insistently pointed out (1959) that an intervening variable is meaningful only when one secures the expected type of agreement in experiments designed to use a variety of techniques to manipulate the assumed intervening variable and a variety of techniques for measuring it.

Recently, I have completed an experiment of this type to compare the effects of three methods of manipulating thirst—water by mouth, by fistula, and in a stomach balloon—on three different measures of thirst: the volume drunk immediately afterwards, the amount of quinine in the water required to stop drinking, and the rate of working at pressing a bar rewarded by water on a variable-interval schedule.

Figure 13 presents the results of this experiment. Let us look at the two diagrams to the left and in the center showing results for measuring thirst by the volume of water drunk and by the amount of quinine

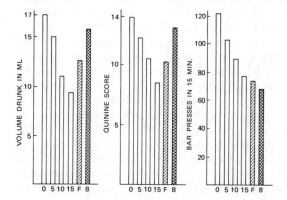

Fig. 13

Comparison of three different measures of the effect on thirst of three different types of pretreatment: Water drunk normally by mouth (0, 5, 10, or 15 milliliters); 15 milliliters of water injected via stomach fistula (F); 15 milliliters of water injected into stomach balloon (B). (The patterns of results measured by volume consumed or by quinine score are highly similar; the results measured by rate of bar pressing are different.)

required to stop drinking. In the open bars you can see that prefeeding increasing amounts of water—0, 5, 10 or 15 milliliters—produced progressive decrements in the scores on both tests. These decrements serve as a basis for calibrating the other effects.

Looking at the bar with single crosshatching and labeled F, you can see that using the fistula to inject 15 milliliters of water directly into the stomach produced an effect roughly comparable to that of drinking 10 milliliters normally by mouth. Allowing for sampling errors, the effects are roughly comparable in both the left and middle diagrams. Now looking at the double crosshatched bars labeled D, you can see that injecting into the balloon 15 milliliters of water to distend the stomach produced less effect than drinking 5 cubic centimeters normally by mouth. The effect is highly similar in both the left and middle diagrams. The general picture of agreement in these two diagrams is what might be expected if the different experimental operations—water via mouth, fistula, and in the balloon—all were manipulating a single intervening variable, namely, thirst, which was being measured by both of the tests: volume of water drunk, and amount of quinine required to stop drinking.

Now, shifting to the right-hand figure for results of the test which used rate of bar pressing as a measure, you can see that the effect of prefeeding various amounts of water was much like that in the preceding tests. The effect of injecting water by fistula was somewhat off. But the effect of inflating the balloon was grossly different. Instead of being almost negligible *less* than drinking 5 cubic centimeters of water by mouth, it was *greater* than that of drinking 15 cubic centimeters of water by mouth.

From this result we draw two conclusions: First, in my previous work by relying on bar pressing as the sole test, I probably had been trapped into greatly overestimating the reduction in drive, if any, produced by inflation of a balloon in the stomach. Second, when the bar pressing test is also included, the overall results cannot be explained by the assumption of a single intervening variable, since the results of all three tests are not perfectly correlated, as they would have to be if they were all pure measures of the same unitary thing, namely, strength of thirst. Perhaps the bar pressing test is especially susceptible to distraction, pain, and nausea, possibly produced by inflating the balloon in the stomach. If so, this pain or nausea would be a second intervening variable.

In any event, the need for this particular type of experimental design is obvious. As I have pointed out before (Miller, 1957b), we have great confidence in the electron as an intervening variable, because electrons produced by a great variety of experimental operations: rubbing a cat's fur against amber, heating a metal in a vacuum, putting zinc and carbon in acid, or cutting a magnetic field with a wire, all have exactly the same charge when measured by a variety of techniques— repelling like charges on a droplet of oil, depositing silver in an electroplating bath, or creating magnetic lines of force when they move. It is this kind of agreement which gives us confidence.

In the behavioral sciences we need to make much more use of such cross-checking of hypotheses. With sufficient ingenuity, it is possible, not only in simple situations of the kind I have been describing, but also in dealing with many other problems. For example, in the area of personality development, certain clinical observations on children can be checked against controlled experiments on animals and also against anthropological observations on the effects of different conditions of child rearing in other cultures.

Brain Electrolytes and Thirst

To recapitulate briefly, I have described evidence that drive is important for learning. I have shown that the point in a temporal sequence, at which maximum reward effect is concentrated, can be described in terms of information theory and possibly explained in terms of the drive-reduction hypothesis of reinforcement. I have shown that the drives of both hunger and thirst are promptly reduced by feedback from both the mouth and the stomach. Now let me carry on the main story a bit further.

For some time, it has been believed that there are osmoreceptors in the brain which could be an additional mechanism involved in controlling thirst. A few years ago, Andersson (1953), in Stockholm, added convincing evidence by showing that minute injections in the region of the third ventricle of a satiated goat's brain, would elicit drinking if the solution injected (2% NaCl) had slightly more effective osmotic pressure than is normal for body fluids. My students and I confirmed this in the cat, and in addition showed that minute injections of pure water, which has less osmotic pressure than the body fluids, would have the opposite effect of reducing thirst. For both the increase and the reduction, we got the same results with two

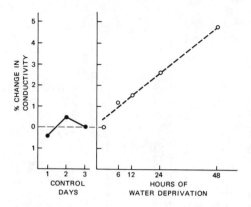

Fig. 14
Electrolyte concentration, as measured by conductivity, increases with hours of water deprivation. (From Novin, 1962)

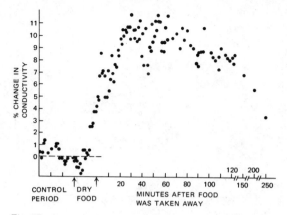

Fig. 15
Feeding dry food to a hungry rat increases electrolyte concentration, as measured by conductivity, which then decreases during the subsequent interval without access to water. (From Novin, 1962)

different measures: volume of water consumed and rate of performing a learned response to get water on a variable-interval schedule (Miller, 1961b). Thus we see that, in addition to being controlled by feedbacks from the mouth and stomach, thirst is controlled by receptors in the brain which respond to the state of the body fluid around them.

Still more recently a student of mine, Donald Novin (1962), has devised an ingenious technique for recording electrolyte concentration in the body fluids of normal rats free to move around in a small chamber. This is significant to our story because electrolyte concentration in the body is almost entirely due to the concentration of NaCl which in turn determines the effective osmotic pressure to which the "osmoreceptors" in the brain presumably respond.

Two platinum-black electrodes are chronically implanted in the rat's brain so that they can be connected to flexible leads. Since the electrolyte concentration of various body fluids presumably is the same, the placement in the brain is for convenience, rather than having crucial significance. With suitable bridge circuits, the resistance between these two electrodes is used to measure electrolyte concentration. Let us see some of the results which he has secured in our laboratory.

Figure 14 shows the results of water deprivation. As the animal becomes dehydrated, we expect the concentration of electrolytes (primarily salt) in his blood to increase, so that the conductivity should increase. We can see that this is exactly what occurred.

If a hungry animal is fed dry food, it makes him thirsty. Figure 15 shows that this procedure also increases the electrolyte concentration as measured by conductivity. But looking at the right-hand side of the figure, we see a peculiar thing. Several hours after eating dry food, and without any opportunity to drink, the conductivity begins going down. According to this, the animal should be less thirsty even though it is longer since his last drink. Figure 16 shows the results

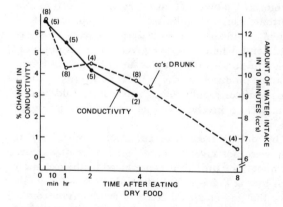

Fig. 16
After thirst is induced by feeding dry food to hungry rats, longer rest intervals without water produce a great reduction in thirst as measured either by conductivity or by volume of water drunk. (Separate tests are given at the end of each interval.) (From Novin, 1962)

Analytical Studies of Drive and Reward

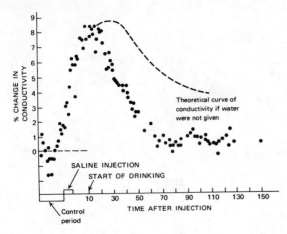

Fig. 17

An intravenous injection of hypertonic saline (1 milliliter of 12%) into a satiated rat increases thirst as measured by conductivity, so that when water is introduced, the rat starts drinking which restores conductivity to the baseline level for satiation. (From Novin, 1962)

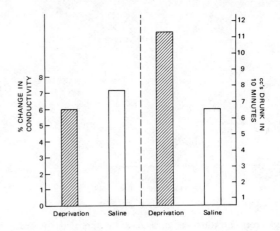

Fig. 18

An injection of hypertonic saline which produces a greater increase in conductivity than does a period of water deprivation, elicits less drinking than does the deprivation. Therefore, the change in effective osmotic pressure, measured by conductivity, cannot be the sole factor involved in thirst. (From Novin, 1962)

of separate tests for thirst, administered at different times after dry food without water. You can see that the rats do indeed drink less after the longer times. There is a striking parallelism between the curves of conductivity as a measure of electrolyte concentration and water-intake as a measure of thirst.

Figure 17 shows that an intravenous injection of a hypertonic saline (1 milliliter of 12%) solution into a satiated rat increases conductivity as would be expected, and when water is given after 10 minutes, causes him to start drinking as an indication of thirst. Drinking produces a drop in conductivity, which begins to occur rapidly enough so that it could be one of the factors involved in the eventual stopping of drinking.

The dotted theoretical curve of conductivity if water were not given is based on results of another experiment; the drop in it is produced by the excretion of salt by the kidneys. You should note for future reference that the empirical curve of conductivity comes back approximately to the same baseline level it had before the hypertonic saline was injected.

Looking at one type of experimental manipulation at a time, we have seen good qualitative agreement between the two measures: electrical conductivity and the volume of water drunk. If electrolyte concentration

is the only intervening variable involved, we must expect a perfect positive correlation between these measures when the effects of different manipulations are compared. In order to test this, Novin performed an experiment, comparing the effects of normal deprivation and of intravenous injection of saline upon both measures.

Figure 18 shows the results. Looking to the left of the dotted line, we see that the water deprivation used produced a slightly *lower* level of conductivity than did the saline injection. But on the right-hand side of the dotted line, we see that the water deprivation induced considerably *more* drinking than did the saline injection. This is not a perfect positive correlation; in fact, it is a negative one. Thus the results show that electrolyte concentration, which produces effective osmotic pressure, cannot be the sole factor involved.

Additional evidence of a discrepancy comes from the effect of drinking on conductivity. In Figure 17 we have seen that, after an injection of saline, drinking brings conductivity back approximately to the baseline of the preceding satiated state. Figure 19 shows that, after normal deprivation, drinking brings conductivity far below the satiation baseline level depicted by the solid horizontal line out from the little square on the ordinate. This is the kind of result that would be

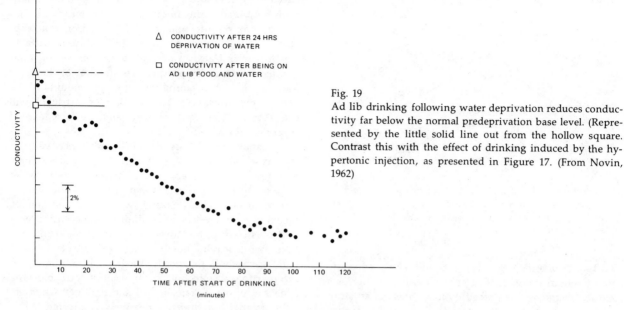

△ CONDUCTIVITY AFTER 24 HRS
   DEPRIVATION OF WATER

☐ CONDUCTIVITY AFTER BEING ON
   AD LIB FOOD AND WATER

Fig. 19
Ad lib drinking following water deprivation reduces conductivity far below the normal predeprivation base level. (Represented by the little solid line out from the hollow square. Contrast this with the effect of drinking induced by the hypertonic injection, as presented in Figure 17. (From Novin, 1962)

expected if the animal is drinking to restore a water deficit, rather than to bring electrolyte concentration back to a given level. Perhaps the so-called osmoreceptors are reacting not solely to effective osmotic pressure, but to total amount of dehydration. Perhaps there are some other receptors that react to the volume of body fluid. At least we know that electrolyte concentration cannot be the whole story.

Again we see the advantage of testing an intervening variable with a design comparing the effects of at least two different experimental manipulations upon at least two different measures.

UNSUCCESSFUL TESTS ON PARABIOTIC RATS

There has been a good deal of speculation that, in addition to the osmoreceptors, the brain contains receptors which respond to a hunger hormone, or the state of nutrients in the blood. In an attempt to locate some such humoral factor, Angus A. Campbell worked with me on parabiotic rats, or in other words, surgically created Siamese twins. But an extensive amount of labor failed to secure any evidence for a hunger hormone, or indeed for the transfer of appreciable amounts of nutrients across the parabiotic barrier. Since then I have learned that Teitelbaum also has secured somewhat similar negative results with such

rats.[3] Perhaps we need some other type of preparation to study this problem.

BEHAVIORAL ANALYSIS OF EFFECTS OF ELECTRICAL STIMULATION OF THE "FEEDING AREA" OF THE BRAIN

Now let us turn to a somewhat different approach to the problem. It has been known for some time that electrical stimulation of certain areas of the hypothalamus will cause a satiated animal to eat. Ted Coons and I have devised a series of behavioral tests to show that such stimulation does not merely arouse a gnawing reflex, but has many of the properties of normal hunger. Since these results have been summarized elsewhere (Miller, 1960), I shall merely mention them briefly as background for some new

3. Our observation was that having a well-fed partner did not appreciably increase the starvation time of the unfed one or increase the food consumption of the fed one. In a personal communication, P. Teitelbaum has told us that, in a similar experiment, the food intake of the fed member of the pair did not increase during the first several days, although it perhaps may have increased approximately 24 hours before the unfed member died of starvation.

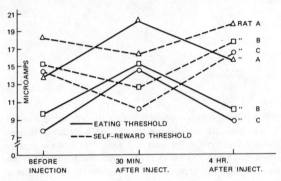

Fig. 20
An injection of dexedrine (2 mg/k) raises the threshold for eating, but lowers it for self-reward. (Twenty-five tests were given to each rat at each point.) (Experiments by E. E. Coons from Miller, 1960)

work. Stimulation of this area will elicit not only eating, but also will cause a satiated animal to perform learned responses reinforced by food. Such stimulation will cause a satiated rat to bite food, but not to lap up pure water. However, the rat will lap up sugar water or milk. Therefore the response is not defined primarily by the motor movements, but rather by a sensory feedback, namely, the taste of food. As would be expected from the drive-reduction hypothesis of reinforcement, turning *off* such stimulation will act as a reward to produce the learning of a **T** maze. But paradoxically, turning *on* such stimulation also will serve as a reward. This result is contrary to the prediction from the drive-reduction hypothesis of reinforcement.

In Figure 20 the center points of the solid lines show that the appetite reducing drug, dexedrine, *increases* the threshold (in microamperes) for eliciting eating. But as the center points of the dotted lines show, the same injection of the same drug *reduces* the threshold for bar pressing rewarded by a brief burst of stimulation. Both results are highly reliable for each of the three rats tested. Since the same drug has opposite effects on the two thresholds, perhaps the eating and rewarding effects are produced by different systems which are indiscriminately stimulated by the same electric current. If so, predictions from the drive-reduction hypothesis must be held in abeyance.

A CHEMICAL CODE IN THE BRAIN?
Another one of my students, Peter Grossman (1961), recently has devised a double cannula technique for

stimulating the same "feeding area" of the rat's brain with minute amounts of crystalline substances. He has found that minute amounts of the adrenergic substances, adrenalin or noradrenalin, will cause satiated rats to eat and also to perform a learned response rewarded by food. By contrast, stimulation of the same area via the same cannula, by minute amounts of the cholinergic substances, acetylcholine or carbachol, will cause satiated rats to drink and also to perform learned responses rewarded by water.

Various control tests with other substances rule out Ph, vasoconstriction or vasodilation, and osmotic pressure as the primary sources of these effects. More convincing still is the fact that an intraperitoneal injection of ethoxybutamoxane, which is an adrenergic blocking agent, practically eliminates the eating elicited by inserting the adrenergic noradrenalin into the brain, while leaving the drinking elicited by the cholinergic carbachol, practically unaffected. Similarly, an intraperitoneal injection of the cholinergic blocking agent, atropine sulfate, leaves the eating to centrally administered noradrenalin relatively unaffected, while practically eliminating the drinking to carbachol. These effects of the blocking agents are an elegant control to show that the drugs elicit eating and drinking via their adrenergic and cholinergic effects, respectively.

In rats with a cannula into this area of the hypothalamus, we apparently have a good method of investigating new compounds suspected to have central, adrenergic, or cholinergic effects, or to function as central blocking agents.

But are the effects we have just described involved in normal hunger and thirst? That they probably are is indicated by the fact that administering the appropriate blocking agent, either peripherally by intraperitoneal injection or centrally via the cannula into the brain, produced the appropriate differential effects on rats made hungry or thirsty by deprivation of food or water. The effects of the blocking agents on normal hunger and thirst are somewhat less complete than those on eating and drinking elicited centrally, but they are unmistakable. The adrenergic blocking agent produces a reliably greater decrement in food consumption than does the cholinergic one; the cholinergic blocking agent produces a reliably greater decrement in water consumption than does the adrenergic one. Thus adrenergic and cholinergic effects seem to be involved in normal hunger and thirst, respectively. In short, this evidence, along with that of other more

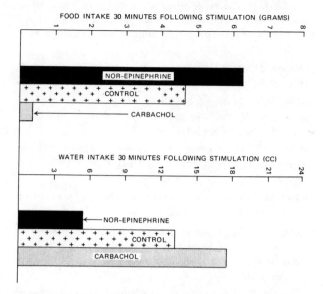

FOOD INTAKE 30 MINUTES FOLLOWING STIMULATION (GRAMS)

NOR-EPINEPHRINE

CONTROL

CARBACHOL

WATER INTAKE 30 MINUTES FOLLOWING STIMULATION (CC)

NOR-EPINEPHRINE

CONTROL

CARBACHOL

Fig. 21

When introduced into the "feeding area" of the lateral hy-pothalamus, minute amounts of adrenergic norepinephrine potentiate food intake induced by 24-hour deprivation, while cholinergic stimulation by carbachol interferes with food consumption. The same substances via the same cannula have opposite effects in similar tests for water consumption. (From Grossman, 1961)

purely physiological studies, suggests a chemical code in the brain.

BASIS OF ANTAGONISM BETWEEN HUNGER AND THIRST

The effects we have just described give us an opportunity to answer a theoretically interesting question. It is known that water deprived animals stop eating dry food. Is this because the drive of thirst is centrally incompatible with the drive of hunger, or because bodily dehydration interferes with peripheral aspects of the hunger mechanism—for example, a dry mouth making it difficult to eat dry food?

Similarly, food deprived animals drink less water. Is this because the mechanism of the hunger drive is antagonistic to thirst or merely because animals not eating dry food do not require as much water?

In an attempt to answer these questions, Grossman secured the results shown in Figure 21. In the upper graph, you can see that direct stimulation of the hy-

pothalamus by norepinephrine increased the food intake of normally hungry rats exposed only to food, while stimulation by carbachol markedly decreased it. Similarly, the lower graph shows that carbachol increased the drinking of normally thirsty rats exposed only to water, while norepinephrine decreased it. These results strongly suggest that there is some central way, analogous to reciprocal innervation, in which the drive mechanisms of hunger and thirst tend to inhibit each other.

These discoveries are being followed up in our laboratory. We have investigated the effects of injecting minute quantities of blood serum from hungry and satiated animals directly into the brain. Our preliminary results are negative. We are investigating the effects of other hormones and drugs, both in the feeding area and in the ventromedial nucleus, which is believed to be a satiation area. We are studying the effects of a bacterial toxin which seems to interfere with drinking (Dubos, 1961), and also we find with eating. We are testing the effects of adrenergic and cholinergic blocking agents on direct electrical stimulation of the brain. We are confronted with many more interesting problems than there possibly is time to investigate.

A NEW CONCEPTION OF THE BRAIN

The work that I have just described on drive and reward as well as the work on other topics by our Past President, Donald Hebb (1958), and by other laboratories in a number of nations, is opening up a new conception of the brain.[4] We no longer view the brain as merely an enormously complicated telephone switchboard which is passive unless excited from without. The brain is an active organ which exerts considerable control over its own sensory input. The brain is a device for sorting, processing, and analyzing information. The brain contains sense organs which respond to states of the internal environment, such as osmotic pressure, temperature, and many others. The brain is a gland which secretes chemical messengers, and it also responds to such messengers, as well as to various types of feedback, both central and peripheral. A combination of behavioral and physiological techniques is increasing our understanding of these processes and their significance for psychology.

4. For an illuminating overview see Magoun (1958); for a comprehensive series of authoritative summaries, Field, Magoun, and Hall (1960).

References

Andersson, B. The effect of injections of hypertonic NaCl solutions into different parts of the hypothalamus of goats. *Acta physiol. Scand.*, 1953, *28*, 188–201.

Berkun, M. M., Kessen, M. L., & Miller, N. E. Hunger-reducing effects of food by stomach fistula versus food by mouth measured by a consummatory response. *J. comp. physiol. Psychol.*, 1952, *45*, 550–564.

Bower, G. H., & Miller, N. E. Effect of amount of reward on strength of approach in an approach-avoidance conflict. *J. comp. physiol. Psychol.*, 1960, *53*, 59–62.

Dollard, J., & Miller, N. E. *Personality and psychotherapy*. New York: McGraw-Hill, 1950.

Doty, R. W., & Giurgea, C. Conditioned reflexes established by coupling electrical excitation of two cortical areas. In J. Delafresnaye (Ed.), *Brain mechanisms and learning*. London: Blackwell, 1961.

Dubos, R. J. The effect of bacterial endotoxins on the water intake and body weight of mice. *J. exp. Med.*, 1961, *113*, 921–934.

Egger, M. D., & Miller, N. E. Secondary reinforcement in rats as a function of information value and reliability of the stimulus. *J. exp. Psychol.*, 1962, in press.

Field, J., Magoun, H. W., & Hall, V. E. *Handbook of physiology. Sect. 1. Neurophysiology*. Washington, D.C. American Physiological Society, 1960. 3 vols.

Grossman, S. P. Behavioral effects of direct adrenergic and cholinergic stimulation of the hypothalamic mechanisms regulating food and water intake. Unpublished PhD thesis, Yale University, 1961.

Guthrie, E. R. *The psychology of learning*. (Rev. ed.) New York: Harper, 1952.

Hebb, D. O. *A textbook of psychology*. Philadelphia: Saunders, 1958.

Hendry, D. P., & Rasche, R. Analysis of a new nonnutritive positive reinforcer based on thirst. *J. comp. physiol. Psychol.*, 1961, *54*, 477–483.

Hilgard, E. R. *Theories of learning*. (Rev. ed.) New York: Appleton-Century-Crofts, 1956.

Jenkins, W. O., & Sheffield, F. D. Rehearsal and guessing habits as sources of the "spread of effect." *J. exp. Psychol.*, 1946, *36*, 316–330.

Kohn, M. Satiation of hunger from food injected directly into the stomach versus food ingested by mouth. *J. comp. physiol. Psychol.*, 1951, *44*, 412–422.

Loucks, R. B. The experimental delimitation of neural structures essential for learning: The attempt to condition striped muscle responses with faradization of the sigmoid gyri. *J. Psychol.*, 1935, *1*, 5–44.

Magoun, H. W. *The waking brain*. Springfield, Ill.: Charles C Thomas, 1958.

Miller, N. E. Shortcomings of food consumption as a measure of hunger: Results from other behavioral techniques. *Ann. N.Y. Acad. Sci.*, 1955, *63*, 141–143.

Miller, N. E. Experiments on motivation: Studies combining psychological, physiological and pharmacological techniques. *Science*, 1957, *126*, 1271–1278. (a)

Miller, N. E. *Graphic communication and the crisis in education. Audiovis. commun. Rev.*, 1957, *5*, 3. (b)

Miller, N. E. Liberalization of basic S-R concepts: Extensions to conflict behavior, motivation and social learning. In S. Koch (Ed.), *Psychology: A study of a science*. Vol. 2. New York: McGraw-Hill, 1959.

Miller, N. E. Some motivational effects of brain stimulation and drugs. *Fed. Proc.*, 1960, *19*, 846–854.

Miller, N. E. Integration of neurophysiological and behavioral research. *Ann. N.Y. Acad. Sci.*, 1961, *92*, 830–839. (a)

Miller, N. E. Learning and performance motivated by direct stimulation of the brain. In D. E. Sheer (Ed.), *Electrical stimulation of the brain: Subcortical integrative systems*. Houston: Univer. Texas Press, 1961. (b)

Miller, N. E., & Barry, H. Motivational effects of drugs: Methods which illustrate some general problems in psychopharmacology. *Psychopharmacologia*, 1960, *1*, 169–199.

Miller, N. E., & Dollard, J. *Social learning and imitation*. New Haven: Yale Univer. Press, 1941.

Miller, N. E., & Kessen, M. L. Reward effects of food via stomach fistula compared with those of food via mouth. *J. comp. physiol. Psychol.*, 1952, *45*, 550–564.

Miller, N. E., Sampliner, R. I., & Woodrow, P. Thirst-reducing effects of water by stomach fistula vs. water by mouth measured by both a consummatory and an instrumental response. *J. comp. physiol. Psychol.*, 1957, *50*, 1–5.

Myers, A. K., & Miller, N. E. Failure to find a learned drive based on hunger: Evidence for learning motivated by "exploration." *J. comp. physiol. Psychol.*, 1954, *47*, 428–436.

Nagaty, M. O. Effect of food reward immediately preceding performance of an instrumental conditioned response on extinction of that response. *J. exp. Psychol.*, 1951, *42*, 333–340.

Novin, D. The relation between electrical conductivity of brain tissue and thirst in the rat. *J. comp. physiol. Psychol.*, 1962, in press.

Olds, J., & Milner, P. Positive reinforcement produced by electrical stimulation of septal area and other regions of rat brain. *J. comp. physiol. Psychol.*, 1954, 47, 419–427.

Sheffield, F. D., & Roby, T. B. Reward value of a non-nutritive sweet taste. *J. comp. physiol. Psychol.*, 1950, 43, 471–481.

Thorndike, E. L. Animal intelligence: An experimental study of the associative processes in animals. *Psychol. Rev., Monogr. Suppl.*, 1898, 2 (4, Whole No. 8).

Thorndike, E. L. A proof of the law of effect. *Science*, 1933, 77, 173–175.

Tolman, E. C. *Purposive behavior in animals and men.* New York: Appleton-Century, 1932.

all-or-none processes in learning and retention[1]

w. k. estes
rockefeller university

If I should pull a match from my pocket and strike it, no one in the audience would be surprised at the sudden appearance of fire and smoke. The reason is not simply that we are all accustomed to predicting and controlling the behavior of matches, but rather that we have available a satisfying account of what occurs during the short interval when a bit of sulphur disappears and the air around it bursts into flame. To less

1. Preparation of this paper was supported in part by the Personnel and Training Branch, Office of Naval Research, under Contracts 908 (16) with Indiana University and 225 (73) with Stanford University, and by a grant from the Carnegie Corporation of New York to Stanford University. Reprinted from *American Psychologist*, 1964, Vol. 19, pp. 16–25. Copyright 1964 by the American Psychological Association, and reproduced by permission.

civilized individuals, unprepared to visualize what happens during the kindling of a fire in terms of the breakdown of molecules into their constituents and recombination into new molecules, the same phenomenon remains a perpetual source of mystery. But despite all our sophistication concerning molecules and atoms, the situation contains fully as much mystery for us. Although we may feel that we adequately understand the lighting of the match, we can offer no comparable account of the events that occur when an individual is learning to strike one. Eliminating this conceptual blind spot is one of the tasks, indeed to my mind the principal task, of learning theory.

How may we best direct our efforts if we hope to achieve an adequate picture of the processes and events involved in any instance of learning? Simply to the industrious accumulation of parametric data? This seems rather dubious when the mazes and memory drums, the cumulative recorders and variance analyzers already are producing data at a rate well exceeding our capacity to absorb them. When our purpose is to understand a complex system, sheer quantity of information may obstruct more than it illuminates. Suppose we were set the task of comprehending the workings of a metropolitan telephone system. We would make a slow job of it if we proceeded by determining the additive and interactive effects of factorially combined independent variables upon dollar volume of telephone bills.

Perhaps we could more strategically concentrate attention on particular types and aspects of data that seem likely to be of special diagnostic value. If, as a start in this direction, we consider analogies between properties of the learning organism and those of other organized systems that we know rather more about, such as communication networks and computing machines, we can scarcely fail to be impressed by the fact that it is of the very nature of organized systems to exhibit discontinuities—that is, sharp departures from proportionality of causes and effects. Thus locating discontinuities, despite the fact that they are normally masked by noise, i.e., experimental error, may well be one of our principal objectives. Even in our earliest efforts toward deciphering the organization of the learning process, one clear bit of evidence for a quantal change of state of the system may be of more diagnostic value than a mountain of data exhibiting gradual changes in output as a function of input.

These introductory remarks are intended, not as a prescription or admonition to anyone else, but as a brief reconstruction of the line of thinking that has led some colleagues and me to find special fascination in the uncovering of new sources of evidence for discontinuous changes in the organism's system of behavioral dispositions during learning.

The particular bit of evidence which seemed most compelling to me when I had occasion to address a division of this Association some 4 years ago (Estes, 1960) resulted from detailed analyses of the changes in response probabilities effected by a single reinforced trial in several standard learning situations. The observed pattern of changes uniformly agreed closely with that expected on the assumption of all-or-none association. The experiments were of the RTT design, that is, a single reinforcement followed by two successive unreinforced test trials. The results indicated that a single reinforcement left an item in one or the other of two quite distinct states: a learned state in which the correct response had a high probability on both tests, or an unlearned state in which the correct response had only chance probability on either test.

This is not to say that the observed pattern of test data could not at the same time agree with any other conception. Alternative interpretations of data can always be produced; consequently, the massive demonstrations (see, e.g., Postman, 1963; Underwood & Keppel, 1962) that such exist in the present instance have impressed me as being useful, but not necessarily of great theoretical import. Certainly we need to find ways of purifying experimental situations: for example,

in the case of paired-associate learning, by reducing individual differences in conditioning rates and differences of item difficulty. But no one investigator can do everything, and I have been inclined to leave this purification to individuals expert in the particular areas while I look in other directions that I personally find more congenial.

Sometimes one can make most rapid progress in differentiating among possible theoretical interpretations by looking for many alternative sources of evidence. If the same type of assumption continues to generate simple and satisfying accounts of results within a wide variety of situations, or in the same situation with a wide variety of variations in procedure, we naturally come to believe that the scheme is essentially correct. And long-term scientific experience seems to indicate that this is not a bad strategy even though it cannot be fully justified to the satisfaction of logicians.

When, in particular, we are engaged in analyzing the effect of a single learning trial, we can expect to obtain independent sources of evidence concerning the process involved by looking in different temporal directions from the point of reinforcement. Thus it seemed natural to follow up the studies of response shifts immediately following the reinforcement by examining the effects of events immediately *preceding* the point of reinforcement.

To the extent that the process of learning a response is basically akin to the flipping of a binary switch, we might expect the effect of a single learning

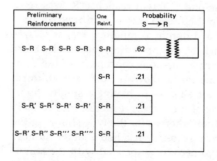

Fig. 1

Effect of a single learning trial in relation to differing reinforcement histories. (Probability of a response R to a stimulus S is assessed following five reinforcements of R, one reinforcement of R, four reinforcements of a single competing response and one of R, or one reinforcement of each of four competing responses in one reinforcement of R.)

trial to be relatively independent of the immediate reinforcement history. This expectation is quite in contrast with that of strong dependence which would, for example, be entailed by an interpretation in terms of thresholds and oscillation distributions of competing responses.

One type of experiment designed to yield evidence pertinent to these disparate expectations is schematized in Figure 1. This experiment was conducted at Indiana University with the assistance of Judith Crooks. Forty subjects, undergraduate students, were run on two paired-associate items under each condition (the stimuli being consonant trigrams and the responses English words). The common focus for all conditions was a single reinforcement of a response to a particular stimulus followed by a test to assess the effect of the reinforcement.

For items of the type illustrated in the second row of the figure, neither the stimulus nor the response member of the item had been involved in the experiment in any way prior to this single reinforced trial. In the type shown in the first row, the only difference in procedure was that the given response was reinforced four times in the presence of the same stimulus on preceding trials so that this item had five reinforcements of the correct response prior to the test trial. Inclusion of this condition provides a baseline measure of the effectiveness of additional reinforcements of the same item.

The item type exhibited in the third row of the figure differs from the last described only in that on the four trials preceding the reinforcement of the given response R, some one different response R' was reinforced. Finally, in the fourth row is exhibited an item type for which a different competing response was reinforced on each of the preceding four trials. From the standpoint of an all-or-none conception of the associative process, the items shown in the second, third, and fourth rows are all alike in having a single opportunity for learning of the correct response immediately prior to the test trial; whereas for the type shown in the top row, the correct response has had a larger number of opportunities to become associated with the stimulus present on the test trial.

The results portrayed in the figure speak quite well for themselves. I might add that, being properly impressed with the dangers of accepting null hypotheses, we replicated the second and fourth conditions as part of a later study with a larger number of observations and obtained quite comparable results (correct response probabilites of .25 and .24 based on Ns of 160 and 320, respectively, on the test trial). The charm of these data for me is not that they confirm any one previously formulated model, or even that they raise problems for other extant theories, but that they provide a relatively direct experimental demonstration of an independence-of-path property which has hitherto been assumed in stimulus sampling theories (see, for example, Bush & Mosteller, 1955; Estes, 1959) almost solely on grounds of mathematical simplicity.

It is only natural that new information concerning all-or-none processes should often come from especially contrived experiments, such as the one just discussed. A more surprising, and in some ways even more rewarding, development of the last few years has been the uncovering of previously unsuspected, or at least undemonstrated, evidence for the existence of steady states and discontinuities in the data of standard experiments. The methods of quantitative analysis largely responsible for these findings have grown directly out of attempts to formulate mathematical models of the associative process based on assumptions derived, in part, from the "one-trial" experiments.

Individuals who have been imprinted in the classical tradition of schools and systems of psychology seem to have almost insuperable difficulty in appreciating the function of models in this type of research enterprise. According to the conventional view, a model is chosen to represent a theoretical postion; then the representatives of different positions are pitted against each other in crucial experiments, the winner being "accepted" and the losers fading gracefully into oblivion, all much in the spirit of a Miss America contest.

But for those who actually use them in scientific research, the function of models is quite different. The set of theoretical ideas suggested by an array of experimental facts can never be adequately represented by any one formal model. On the contrary, to bring originally vague and incompletely defined theoretical notions to fruition, it is necessary to go through a series of successive approximations. At each stage, a specific, usually highly simplified and idealized realization of the general assumptions, that is, a particular mathematical model, is examined for its theoretical implications.

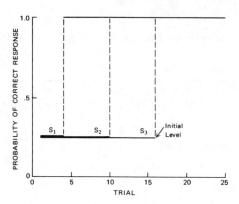

Fig. 2

Illustrative learning functions for individual subjects as conceived in the one-element model.

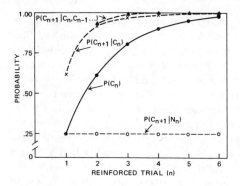

Fig. 3

Theoretical functions derivable from the one-element model, the indicated statistic in each case representing data pooled over subjects on each trial. (The conditioning parameter is taken equal to .50.)

its successes or shortcomings in describing data, its suggestiveness in guiding further experimental and quantitative analysis.

Since standard learning situations characteristically (perhaps universally) include important sources of variation in performance other than the effects of the reinforcing operation, raw data can be expected to reveal the outlines of underlying behavioral processes only if examined on the viewing screen, so to speak, of a model which selectively filters signal from noise. Thus, in the case of all-or-none learning theory, a major step conceptually, though a minor one from a mathematical viewpoint, was the formulation of what has been termed the one-element model.

The mathematical formalism of the one-element model evolved independently in the hands of several different investigators: Bower (1961a), Bush and Mosteller (1959); Estes, Hopkins, and Crothers (1960). But it was Bower who first saw the full potentiality of the model for analyzing verbal learning experiments and spelled out its implications in such detail as to make it a workable tool of analysis.

The assumptions of this model are illustrated in Figure 2. The graph represents probability of correct response versus number of training trials for a number of individual subjects. It is assumed for simplicity that all subjects begin at the same initial level of correct response probability (operant level, or guessing rate), and that on each training trial the subject has some fixed

probability of having his correct response probability jump from the initial level to unity. Because of the probabilistic nature of the process, different subjects jump to unity on different trials. Thus if data are pooled for a group of subjects, even though all have identical initial levels and identical probabilities of conditioning on each trial, a curve representing proportion of correct responses per trial should average out to something like the familiar growth curve. In some experiments the initial level of response probability may be expected to be zero; but in many, for example multiple-choice or paired-associate experiments, the initial probability of a correct response by guessing may have some value other than unity, frequently simply the reciprocal of the number of available response alternatives.

Some predictions derivable from this simple model are immediately obvious upon consideration of the assumptions; others are not so obvious until one has done some actual calculations and may even be missed by experts. In Figure 3 we show a sample of predictions derivable from the model. Assuming that all subjects start from an initial response probability of .25 and the probability of forming a correct association is .50 on each trial, we readily derive the mean curve for proportion of correct responses per trial which is shown as the heavy line, and which has the form that we anticipated.

The probability that a correct response will occur on any trial if the given subject made an incorrect response to the same item on the preceding trial is constant, as indicated by the horizontal dashed line toward the bottom of the graph. This prediction follows from the model, of course, only if experimental conditions and previous experience of the subjects are such that there are no learning-to-learn effects which would cause the probability of conditioning to change over trials. In the upper part of the graph is shown the curve representing probability of correct recalls as a function of trials, that is, the probability that a correct response to a given stimulus on one trial will be followed by a correct response to the same stimulus on the next trial. This result is of special interest because many investigators have believed it intuitively evident that this function should be constant over trials; and, in fact, data which follow quite nicely the trend of the dashed line in the figure have been taken to refute the one-element learning model. Such quaint illogicalities point up quite sharply the need for checking our intuitive ideas as to the consequences of theoretical assumptions by embodying the assumptions in specific models and deriving their implications by exact methods.

Finally, at the top of the graph, is shown the function representing probability of correct response on any trial given that it has been correct on the entire sequence of preceding trials; this function again has sometimes been assumed by the unwary to be constant if the one-element model holds; but that is true only in the special case when the initial level of response probability is zero. In all other cases, one has, following the first reinforced trial, a mixture of subjects who are attaining correct responses by guessing and subjects who have learned; as trials proceed, the balance shifts in the direction of the latter, thus giving rise to the rising curve for probability of correct recalls.

Now, having a model clearly formulated, what should we do with it? Proceed to apply it to various experiments with the plan of retaining it as long as it succeeds and rejecting it upon the first failure? This course would entail an absurd waste of time, for we can be certain in advance that no simple model will fit all sets of data even within a relatively limited area.

It is, however, of interest to see whether the model fits any data at all. Even the laws of motion rarely provide highly accurate predictions of the behavior of real objects; but in specially contrived situations, where perfect vacuums and frictionless planes are approximately realized, the Newtonian model comes off

TABLE 1

Bower Verbal Discrimination Data Compared with Predictions from One-Element Model

	Error distribution	
	M	SD
Observed	1.99	1.94
Predicted	(c = .25)	1.98

	Reset on error[a]					
n	1	2	3	4	5	Aver.
Observed	1.52	1.40	1.56	1.46	1.48	1.48
Predicted	1.49 ←——————— (constant) ————————→ 1.49					

	Constancy of learning parameter[b]			
k	1	2	3	4–5
p	.60	.62	.56	.60

	Precriterion stationarity[c]	
	First half	Second half
Observed	.492	.521
Predicted	.500	.500

[a] Mean errors to criterion after error on trial n.
[b] Proportion correct on trial following k successive errors.
[c] Proportion correct over precriterion sequence.

well enough to convince us that its abstract properties represent more than figments of our imagination.

In the case of the one-element model the first thorough-going applications were made by Gordon Bower (1961a, 1961b, 1962) and with successes far exceeding any expectations that I, at least, would have considered realistic.

A small sample of data from one of Bower's studies (1961b) is summarized in Table 1. The situation giving rise to the results summarized here was a simple verbal discrimination learning task, in which the materials were cards each containing a pair of nonsense syllables, one of which was arbitrarily designated as correct; and the subject's task on each trial was to guess which member of the pair shown on the given trial was correct. With knowledge of results following each correct or incorrect guess, subjects continued to cycle through the cards until they reached a criterion of correct performance. Estimating the value of the conditioning parameter, c, that is the probability that an association between stimulus and correct response would occur on a given trial for a given item, from the observed mean total errors, Bower proceeded to predict quantitative values for numerous statistics of the data. An example, shown on the top line of Table 1, is the prediction of the standard deviation of total errors per item. Investigators who are familiar by much experience with the difficulties of predicting variances as opposed to means may be somewhat impressed by the correspondence between the predicted and observed values. Similar agreement was found by Bower for a large number of statistics, including distribution of trials before the first success, frequencies of error runs of various lengths, and autocorrelations of errors with various lags.

Some additional results which point up particular aspects of the model are shown in the remainder of this table. The heading "reset on error" refers to the important property of the one-element model that the entire process starts over after each error. That is, the occurrence of an error on any trial signifies that up to that point no learning has occurred for that subject on that item. Consequently it is predicted that such statistics as mean errors to criterion after an error on trial n should be constant over trials. For the present data we can even see readily what the constant value should be. Since mean observed total errors, shown at the top, were 1.99, and the probability of an error on the first trial before the subject had received any reinforcements must have been .50 on the average, we can subtract the .50 from the total of 1.99 and arrive at a prediction of 1.49 for the constant mean errors to criterion following an error on any trial. The observed values seem to vary around this prediction with little indication of any systematic trend. If it is the case not only that learning is occurring on an all-or-none basis but that probability of learning is constant over trials, then the proportion of correct responses on any trial following a sequence of preceding errors should be independent of the number of preceding errors. The next to last row of the table shows the value of this proportion following one, two, three, etc., successive preceding errors (the data for 4 and 5 preceding errors being pooled since the number of cases was falling off).

The remaining type of analysis represented in the table arises from a valuable insight growing out of the reset-on-error property. The gist of the idea, developed fully by Suppes and Ginsberg (1963), is that despite the fact that one cannot observe directly the point at which learning occurs, one can define unequivocally a last point before which learning certainly has not occurred

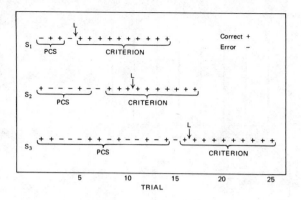

Fig. 4

Illustrative protocols for individual subjects, with the precriterion sequence (PCS), the point of learning (L), and the criterion sequence indicated for each.

if the one-element model holds. Referring to the illustrative protocols in Figure 4, one can see that this critical point in each protocol is the trial of the last error. If the learning process is correctly described by the model, then on all trials prior to the last error, the subject's responses are in effect being generated by a Bernoulli process with all the properties of coin tossing. Correct responses and errors during this precriterion sequence should occur at random with constant probability (not necessarily one-half except in certain two-choice situations) and independence from trial to trial. Thus cogent evidence concerning the existence of an initial steady state of random responding in any situation may be obtained by analyzing individual protocols, locating the last error in each, and performing various analyses on the data of the precriterion sequence.

One of the coarsest, though at the same time most intuitively appealing, of these analyses is a test for precriterion stationarity, that is, constancy of the probability of correct responding over the precriterion sequence, illustrated in the remaining section of the table for Bower's data. Because learning was rather rapid, the data have been pooled into observed and predicted proportions of correct responses in the first and second halves of the precriterion sequence. Departures from the predicted constancy at .5 do not seem great.

Many other results comparable to these have been reported during the last 2 or 3 years. Following are a

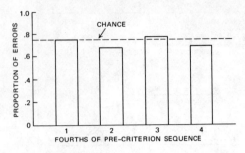

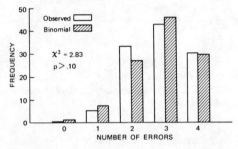

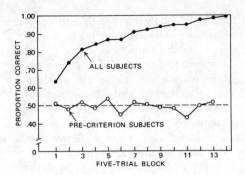

Fig. 6
Learning curve averaged over all subjects and items and curve representing precriterion data only, from Trabasso's (1963) study of concept identification.

Fig. 5
Precriterion analysis of data from Suppes' study of the learning of mathematical proofs by a group of 50 young children. (The upper diagram exhibits relative constancy of error probability; the lower diagram compares the distribution of error frequencies per four-trial block with the corresponding binomial distribution.)

few illustrations showing some of the situations in which these results arise. Figure 5 shows an analysis of precriterion data from an experiment by Suppes on the learning of mathematical proofs by young school children.[2] The upper portion of the figure shows the constancy of proportion of errors over successive fourths of the precriterion sequence predicted by the one-element model; the lower panel shows close agreement between the data and the binomial distribution of different numbers of errors predicted when data are pooled by four-trial blocks over the entire precriterion sequence. Up to the point when they are able to give several correct responses in a row, the behavior of these children in trying to provide successive steps of proofs in a miniature logical system are much like the data that would be obtained by tossing so many biased pennies.

In Figure 6 are shown data from a study of concept identification (Trabasso, 1963). This figure shows the dramatic contrast between the curve representing proportion of correct responses per trial block for all subjects over all trials and the plot for the same statistic limited to data from precriterion sequences. Whereas the overall mean curve rises steadily and smoothly, the proportion of correct responses per trial block is about as constant as one could ask for over the precriterion sequences. These data are of especial interest since it has sometimes been suggested that data conforming to predictions from all-or-none models arise only in situations where learning is very rapid; it can be seen that in this situation learning was rather slow, yet precriterion stationarity was nicely realized.

I shall not go on giving examples of all but perfect fits of the one-element model to data because these, although perhaps impressive, cease being particularly instructive.

For an example of a case in which a rather interesting deviation occurs, we may consider Figure 7, which shows pooled data from a series of eyelid conditioning experiments with human subjects.[3] The curve for proportion of conditioned responses per trial is again nicely negatively accelerated, but this time, when a stationarity analysis is performed, it is found immediately that proportion of correct responses does *not*

2.   I am indebted to Patrick Suppes for making available these unpublished data.

3.   This analysis was made possible by the cooperation of I. Gormezano, who provided protocols from a series of studies conducted in his laboratory. For the details of apparatus and procedure, see Moore and Gormezano (1961).

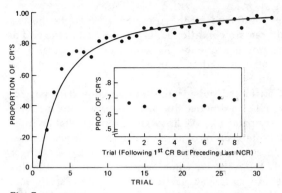

Fig. 7

Acquisition curve for eyelid conditioning data. (The inset shows stationarity of conditioned response proportion on trials following the first CR, but preceding the last non-CR.)

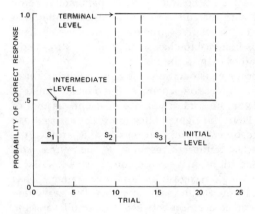

Fig. 8

Illustrative learning functions for individual subjects as conceived in three-state model.

avoidance situation, and led him to consider the extension of the one-element model illustrated in Figure 8. Here each subject begins at some initial level of response probability and learning occurs by discrete jumps, but subjects may go to an intermediate level before going to the final level of perfect performance. Bower and Theios (1963) investigated the properties of this three-state model and found that predictions from it provided excellent accounts of the data from the learning of rats in a shuttle box and also of the data on eyelid conditioning from which the preceding illustration was drawn.[4]

Now what is one to conclude from results such as these concerning "one-trial versus incremental learning"? The learning can scarcely be characterized as "one trial," and thus I suppose some will be happy simply to label it as "incremental" and let the matter rest. But if our interest is in understanding the behavior rather than in defending a position, we may wish to pursue the fact that this evidence points to the existence of all-or-none processes even in cases where the structure of the learning process is evidently more complex than that of simple paired-associate or verbal discrimination learning.

From even the brief sketch I have been able to give here, I think it must be evident that the investigators currently working constructively with notions of all-or-none learning have not formed a committee to set down a new theory. Rather they have been largely preoccupied with the always rewarding business of following up some unexpectedly fruitful research leads. At the same time a body of new theory has begun to take form, although only irregularly, and jagged in outline, much like the crystallization of rock candy in a saturated sugar solution. At some stage in this process one begins to raise questions of a broader character

remain constant over the precriterion sequence; rather the curve exhibits a steady rise, thus showing at once that the one-element model cannot give an adequate representation of the data. However, upon further analysis, stationarity reappears in a rather interesting way. If we truncate the precriterion sequence by considering only trials following the first conditioned response for each subject, then, as shown in the inset, the proportion of correct responses per trial is found to be relatively stationary between the first conditioned response and the last precriterion trial.

A similar observation had been made previously by Theios (1963), working with data from rats in an

4.   The intermediate state of conditioned response probability has a natural interpretation in stimulus sampling theory (Atkinson & Estes, 1963) on the assumption that the stimulus situation associated with onset of the CS overlaps only in part with the stimulus situation existing at the point of reinforcement (onset of the US). Theios and Bower's analyses bear out the prediction that, although the organism has constant probability of leaving the initial, "unlearned," state on any reinforced trial, it can go from the intermediate to the terminal state only on a trial when the conditioned response occurs at CS onset.

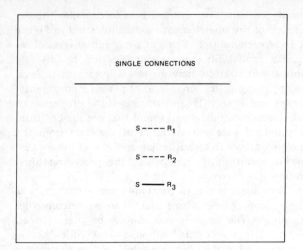

Fig. 9

Schema for stimulus-response associations according to the one-element pattern model. (Effective reinforcement of response R_3 to pattern S establishes an association — heavy line — supplanting the associations previously existing between S and R_1 or R_2 .)

than those having to do with the ability of specific models to fit specific data. In particular, one may begin to wonder whether a body of theory based on all-or-none conceptions could ever be extended and elaborated enough to guide research on forms of learning more complex than conditioning and verbal association without becoming unwieldy and unmanageable.

Some recent researches suggest that, to the contrary, theory based on stimulus sampling and all-or-none associaton may offer some special virtues in this respect. The one-element process, abstracted from the original context, may constitute a conceptual pattern which can be identified by similar methods at many different levels of behavioral organization.

The first few published studies involving new techniques for revealing all-or-none acquisition have, understandably, dealt only with simple, unitary responses (usually spoken letters or digits) to discrete stimulus patterns. In Figure 9 is shown the paradigm for individual learned associations assumed in applications of the one-element pattern model at this elementary level of behavioral organization. A stimulus pattern S can be conditioned to one response at a time only. Thus, if first R_1, then R_2, then R_3 were succes-

sively reinforced in the presence of S, only the last would remain conditioned. On a test trial at the end of this training sequence, R_3 would be evoked, and no trace of the earlier learned experiences could be detected.

Considered outside the limited context of paired-associate experiments, this last property of the model is not very palatable. We know, for example, that an individual often can recognize a previously learned, correct response to a stimulus even when he can no longer supply the response when presented with the stimulus alone. An earlier suggestion on my part (Estes, 1960) that association theory should allow for the learning and unlearning of recognition and recall responses as independent, even though often correlated, processes has met a chorus of complaints about lack of parsimony (see, e.g., Postman, 1963), parsimony being identified with the conception of a unitary underlying construct of associative strength. However, I believe that in this instance the lack of parsimony is in the organism, rather than in the theory.

Numerous considerations[5] suggest modification of the unitary-connection schema to the one illustrated in Figure 10 for the same sequence of events as that of Figure 9. Here the lighter lines represent associations established by earlier reinforcements of R_1 and R_2 (the one to the last reinforced response, R_3, being masked). These associations may be demonstrable by suitable procedures, e.g., recognition tests, even after R_3 has later been learned to the same stimulus. The heavy line represents an association between the stimulus and the response of recalling (selecting, emitting, retrieving) a particular one of the previously reinforced responses upon presentation of the stimulus. In this conception, the formation of each of the associations and the "switching" of the recall, or retrieval tendency, from one response to another are independent one-element processes. A currently active line of research in my laboratory is concerned with the experimental separation of these processes (DaPolito, Casseday, Kegel, McCollum, & Estes, 1961; Estes, 1964).

Departing in another direction from the elementary schema of Figure 9, we encounter numerous possible

---

5. Including recent work on information storage and retrieval in relation to short-term memory (Broadbent, 1958; Sternberg, 1963) and on nonassociative factors in recall (Asch & Ebenholtz, 1962).

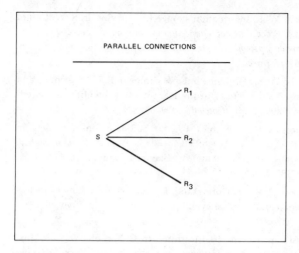

Fig. 10
Schema permitting coexisting associations (light lines) between a stimulus pattern, S, and successively, reinforced responses, R_1, R_2, and R_3. (The tendency to recall, or retrieve, a previously learned association—represented by the heavy line—is assumed to be governed by an independent, one-element learning process.)

levels of response complexity: The behavior segment which is counted as a single "response" in a learning experiment may be a single spoken digit, a multisyllable word in a new or artificial language, a combination of words, a rule or strategy. When a learning situation involves both the development of a relatively complex response unit and the association of this unit with particular cues or stimulus properties, one must expect that, regardless of the nature of the learning process, the probability of "correct responses" will change gradually over learning trials. However, some current researches are yielding encouraging signs of progress toward analyzing such complex forms of learning into simpler constituent processes. For example, the development of response compounds via the chaining of initially distinct component responses has been investigated by Crothers (1962, 1963) and the formation of chains of observing and instrumental responses by Atkinson (1961). In each of these instances, evidence has been forthcoming in support of the notion that the constituent associative processes conform to the one-element, all-or-none model. Once established, even complex response chains, rules, or strategies (Restle, 1962, 1963) may become associated

with, or dissociated from, stimulus patterns on an all-or-none basis.

From the general tenor of this report, you might suspect that I think of *all* learning in terms of the pyramiding and branching of simple component all-or-none processes. This would not be far from the truth. But at the same time, I hasten to add, I have no intention of giving up such time tested theoretical devices as linear operator models (Bush & Mosteller, 1955; Estes & Suppes, 1959) even though these are based on different underlying conceptions. However much we might prefer things to be otherwise, learning, as measured by available techniques, appears sometimes to be an essentially continuous, sometimes a sharply discontinuous process. Thus in current research we need models suitable to represent both kinds of data, while we await further evidence to determine which aspect is the more fundamental and which the derivative. There may turn out to be no basic inconsistencies between what at present appear to be extremely different mathematical models. This will, for example, be the case if we find that in situations involving numerous concurrent one-element processes, the overall functioning of the system should be expected to conform approximately to a continuous model.

While awaiting more definitive clues concerning underlying properties, I myself have come to operate on the working assumption that all instances of apparently incremental changes in behavioral dispositions during learning are simply cases of incomplete analysis. I am well aware that this assumption is untestable in a formal sense. Nonetheless, by following through its implications for a variety of learning situations, we are beginning to evolve quantitative techniques which may even come to rival the scalpel and the electrode as tools for exploring the organization of behavior.

References

Asch, S. E., & Ebenholtz, S. M. The process of free recall: Evidence for non-associative factors in acquisition and retention. *J. Psychol.*, 1962, 54, 3–31.

Atkinson, R. C. The observing response in discrimination learning. *J. exp. Psychol.*, 1961, 62, 253–262.

Atkinson, R. C., & Estes, W. K. Stimulus sampling theory. In R. D. Luce, E. Galanter, & R. R. Bush (Eds.), *Handbook of mathematical psychology*. Vol. 2. New York: Wiley, 1963. Pp. 121–268.

Bower, G. H. Application of a model to paired-associate learning. *Psychometrika*, 1961, *26*, 255–280. (a)

Bower, G. H. All-or-none theory applied to verbal discrimination learning. *Amer. Psychologist*, 1961, *6*, 466. (b) (Abstract)

Bower, G. H. A model for response and training variables in paired-associate learning. *Psychol. Rev.*, 1962, *69*, 34–53.

Bower, G. H., & Theios, J. A learning model for discrete performance levels. In R. C. Atkinson (Ed.), *Studies in mathematical psychology*. Stanford: Stanford Univer. Press, 1963. Pp. 1–31.

Broadbent, D. E. *Perception and communication*. London: Pergamon Press, 1958.

Bush, R. R., & Mosteller, F. *Stochastic models for learning*. New York: Wiley, 1955.

Bush, R. R., & Mosteller, F. A comparison of eight models. In R. R. Bush & W. K. Estes (Eds.), *Studies in mathematical learning theory*. Stanford: Stanford Univer. Press, 1959. Pp. 293–307.

Crothers, E. J. Paired-associate learning with compound response. *J. verb. Learn. verb. Behav.*, 1962, *1*, 66–70.

Crothers, E. J. All-or-none paired-associate learning with compound responses. In R. C. Atkinson (Ed.), *Studies in mathematical psychology*. Stanford: Stanford Univer. Press, 1963. Pp. 95–115.

DaPolito, F., Casseday, J., Kegel, P., McCollum, K., & Estes, W. K. Acquisition of paired-associates under differential instructions with recall and recognition tests. Paper read at Midwestern Psychological Association, Chicago, May 1961.

Estes, W. K. Component and pattern models with Markovian interpretations. In R. R. Bush & W. K. Estes (Eds.), *Studies in mathematical learning theory*. Stanford: Stanford Univer. Press, 1959. Pp. 9–52.

Estes, W. K. Learning theory and the new "mental chemistry." *Psychol. Rev.*, 1960, *67*, 207–223.

Estes, W. K. Information storage in behavior. In R. W. Gerard (Ed.), *Proceedings of symposium on information processing in the nervous system*. Amsterdam: Excerpta Medica Foundation, 1964, in press.

Estes, W. K., Hopkins, B. L., & Crothers, E. J. All-or-none and conservation effects in the learning and retention of paired-associates. *J. exp. Psychol.*, 1960, *60*, 329–339.

Estes, W. K., & Suppes, P. Foundations of linear models. In R. R. Bush & W. K. Estes (Eds.), *Studies in mathematical learning theory*. Stanford: Stanford Univer. Press, 1959, Pp. 137–179.

Moore, J. W., & Gormezano, I. Yoked comparisons of instrumental and classical eyelid conditioning. *J. exp. Psychol.*, 1961, *62*, 552–559.

Postman, L. One trial learning. In C. N. Cofer & B. S. Musgrave (Eds.), *Verbal behavior and learning*. New York: McGraw-Hill, 1963. Pp. 295–320.

Restle, F. The selection of strategies in cue learning. *Psychol. Rev.*, 1962, *69*, 329–343.

Restle, F. Sources of difficulty in learning paired-associates. In R. C. Atkinson (Ed.½, *Studies in mathematical psychology*. Stanford: Stanford Univer. Press, 1963. Pp. 116–172.

Theios, J. Simple conditioning as two-stage all-or-none learning. *Psychol. Rev.*, 1963, *70*, 403-417.

Trabasso, T. R. Stimulus emphasis and all-or-none learning in concept identification. *J. exp. Psychol.*, 1963, *65*, 398-406.

Sternberg, S. Retrieval from recent memory: Some reaction-time experiments and a search theory. Paper read at Psychonomic Society, Bryn Mawr, Pennsylvania, August 1963.

Suppes, P., & Ginsberg, Rose. A fundamental property of all-or-none models, binomial distribution of responses prior to conditioning, with application to concept formation in children. *Psychol. Rev.*, 1963, *70*, 139–161.

Underwood, B. J., & Keppel, G. One-trial learning? *J. verb. Learn. verb. Behav.*, 1962, *1*, 1–13.

This is the history of a crackpot idea, born on the wrong side of the tracks intellectually speaking, but eventually vindicated in a sort of middle class respectability. It is the story of a proposal to use living organisms to guide missiles—of a research program during World War II called "Project Pigeon" and a peacetime continuation at the Naval Research Laboratory called "ORCON," from the words "organic control." Both of these programs have now been declassified.

Man has always made use of the sensory capacities of animals, either because they are more acute than his own or more convenient. The watchdog probably hears better than his master and in any case listens while his master sleeps. As a detecting system the dog's ear comes supplied with an alarm (the dog need not be taught to announce the presence of an intruder), but special forms of reporting are sometimes set up. The tracking behavior of the bloodhound and the pointing of the hunting dog are usually modified to make them more useful. Training is sometimes quite explicit. It is said that sea gulls were used to detect submarines in the English Channel during World War I. The British sent their own submarines through the Channel releasing food to the surface. Gulls could see the submarines from the air and learned to follow them, whether they were British or German. A flock of gulls, spotted from the shore, took on special significance. In the seeing-eye dog the repertoire of artificial signaling responses is so elaborate that it has the conventional character of the verbal interchange between man and man.

pigeons in a pelican[1]

b. f. skinner
harvard university

The detecting and signaling systems of lower organisms have a special advantage when used with explosive devices which can be guided toward the objects they are to destroy, whether by land, sea, or air. Homing systems for guided missiles have now been developed which sense and signal the position of a target by responding to visible or invisible radiation, noise, radar reflections, and so on. These have not always been available, and in any case a living organism has certain advantages. It is almost certainly cheaper and more compact and, in particular, is especially good at responding to patterns and those classes of patterns called "concepts." The lower organism is not used because it is more sensitive than man—after all, the kamikaze did very well—but because it is readily expendable.

1. Reprinted from *American Psychologist*, 1960, Vol. 15, pp. 28–37. Copyright 1960 by the American Psychological Association, and reproduced by permission.

Project Pelican

The ethical question of our right to convert a lower creature into an unwitting hero is a peacetime luxury. There were bigger questions to be answered in the late thirties. A group of men had come into power who promised, and eventually accomplished, the greatest mass murder in history. In 1939 the city of Warsaw was laid waste in an unprovoked bombing, and the airplane emerged as a new and horrible instrument of war against which only the feeblest defenses were available. Project Pigeon was conceived against that background. It began as a search for a homing device to be used in a surface-to-air guided missile as a defense against aircraft. As the balance between offensive and defensive weapons shifted, the direction was reversed, and the system was to be tested first in an air-to-ground missile called the "Pelican." Its name is a useful reminder of the state of the missile art in America at that time. Its detecting and servomechanisms took up so much space that there was no room for explosives: hence the resemblance to the pelican "whose beak can hold more than its belly can." My title is perhaps now clear. Figure 1 shows the pigeons, jacketed for duty. Figure 2 shows the beak of the Pelican.

At the University of Minnesota in the spring of 1940 the capacity of the pigeon to steer toward a target was tested with a moving hoist. The pigeon, held in a jacket and harnessed to a block, was immobilized except for its neck and head. It could eat grain from a

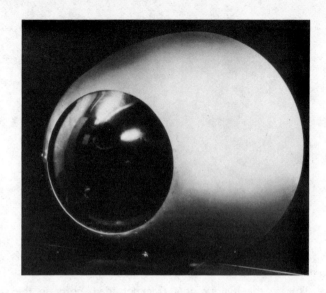

Fig. 2
Nose of the Pelican, showing lenses.

dish and operate a control system by moving its head in appropriate directions. Movement of the head operated the motors of the hoist. The bird could ascend by lifting its head, descend by lowering it, and travel from side to side by moving appropriately. The whole system, mounted on wheels, was pushed across a room toward a bull's-eye on the far wall. During the approach the pigeon raised or lowered itself and moved from side to side in such a way as to reach the wall in position to eat grain from the center of the bull's-eye. The pigeon learned to reach any target within reach of the hoist, no matter what the starting position and during fairly rapid approaches.

The experiment was shown to John T. Tate, a physicist, then Dean of the Graduate School at the University of Minnesota, who brought it to the attention of R. C. Tolman, one of a group of scientists engaged in early defense activities. The result was the first of a long series of rejections. The proposal "did not warrant further development at the time." The project was accordingly allowed to lapse. On December 7, 1941 the situation was suddenly restructured; and, on the following day, with the help of Keller Breland, then a graduate student at Minnesota, further work was planned. A simpler harnessing system could be used if the bomb were to rotate slowly during its descent, when

Fig. 1
Thirty-two pigeons, jacketed for testing.

the pigeon would need to steer in only one dimension: from side to side. We built an apparatus in which a harnessed pigeon was lowered toward a large revolving turntable across which a target was driven according to contacts made by the bird during its descent. It was not difficult to train a pigeon to "hit" small ship models during fairly rapid descents. We made a demonstration film showing hits on various kinds of targets, and two psychologists then engaged in the war effort in Washington, Charles Bray and Leonard Carmichael, undertook to look for government support. Tolman, then at the Office of Scientific Research and Development, again felt that the project did not warrant support, in part because the United States had at that time no missile capable of being guided toward a target. Commander (now Admiral) Luis de Florez, then in the Special Devices Section of the Navy, took a sympathetic view. He dismissed the objection that there was no available vehicle by suggesting that the pigeon be connected with an automatic pilot mounted in a small plane loaded with explosives. But he was unable to take on the project because of other commitments and because, as he explained, he had recently bet on one or two other equally long shots which had not come in.

The project lapsed again and would probably have been abandoned if it had not been for a young man whose last name I have ungratefully forgotten, but whose first name — Victor — we hailed as a propitious sign. His subsequent history led us to refer to him as Vanquished; and this, as it turned out, was a more reliable omen. Victor walked into the Department of Psychology at Minnesota one day in the summer of 1942 looking for an animal psychologist. He had a scheme for installing dogs in antisubmarine torpedoes. The dogs were to respond to faint acoustic signals from the submarine and to steer the torpedo toward its goal. He wanted a statement from an animal psychologist as to its feasibility. He was understandably surprised to learn of our work with pigeons but seized upon it eagerly, and citing it in support of his contention that dogs could be trained to steer torpedoes he went to a number of companies in Minneapolis. His project was rejected by everyone he approached; but one company, General Mills, Inc., asked for more information about our work with pigeons. We described the project and presented the available data to Arthur D. Hyde, Vice-President in Charge of Research. The company was not looking for new products, but Hyde thought that it might, as a public service, develop the pigeon system to the point at which a governmental agency could be persuaded to take over.

Breland and I moved into the top floor of a flour mill in Minneapolis and with the help of Norman Guttman, who had joined the project, set to work on further improvements. It has been difficult to induce the pigeon to respond to the small angular displacement of a distant target. It would start working dangerously late in the descent. Its natural pursuit behavior was not appropriate to the characteristics of a likely missile. A new system was therefore designed. An image of the target was projected on a translucent screen as in a camera obscura. The pigeon, held near the screen, was reinforced for pecking at the image on the screen. The guiding signal was to be picked up from the point of contact of screen and beak.

In an early arrangement the screen was a translucent plastic plate forming the larger end of a truncated cone bearing a lens at the smaller end. The cone was mounted, lens down, in a gimbal bearing. An object within range threw its image on the translucent screen; and the pigeon, held vertically just above the plate, pecked the image. When a target was moved about within range of the lens, the cone continued to point to it. In another apparatus a translucent disk, free to tilt slightly on gimbal bearings, closed contacts operating motors which altered the position of a large field beneath the apparatus. Small cutouts of ships and other objects were placed on the field. The field was constantly in motion, and a target would go out of range unless the pigeon continued to control it. With this apparatus we began to study the pigeon's reactions to various patterns and to develop sustained steady rates of responding through the use of appropriate schedules of reinforcement, the reinforcement being a few grains occasionally released onto the plate. By building up large extinction curves a target could be tracked continuously for a matter of minutes without reinforcement. We trained pigeons to follow a variety of land and sea targets, to neglect large patches intended to represent clouds or flak, to concentrate on one target while another was in view, and so on. We found that a pigeon could hold the missile on a particular street intersection in an aerial map of a city. The map which came most easily to hand was of a city which, in the interests of international relations, need not be identified. Through appropriate schedules of reinforcement it was possible to maintain longer uninterrupted runs than could conceivably be required by a missile.

We also undertook a more serious study of the pigeon's behavior, with the help of W. K. Estes and Marion Breland who joined the project at this time. We ascertained optimal conditons of deprivation, investigated other kinds of deprivations, studied the effect of special reinforcements (for example, pigeons were said to find hemp seed particularly delectable), tested the effects of energizing drugs and increased oxygen pressures, and so on. We differentially reinforced the force of the pecking response and found that pigeons could be induced to peck so energetically that the base of the beak became inflamed. We investigated the effects of extremes of temperature, of changes in atmospheric pressure, of accelerations produced by an improvised centrifuge, of increased carbon dioxide pressure, of increased and prolonged vibration, and of noises such as pistol shots. (The birds could, of course, have been deafened to eliminate auditory distractions, but we found it easy to maintain steady behavior in spite of intense noises and many other distracting conditions using the simple process of adaptation.) We investigated optimal conditions for the quick development of discriminations and began to study the pigeon's reactions to patterns, testing for induction from a test figure to the same figure inverted, to figures of different sizes and colors, and to figures against different grounds. A simple device using carbon paper to record the points at which a pigeon pecks a figure showed a promise which has never been properly exploited.

We made another demonstration film and renewed our contact with the Office of Scientific Research and Development. An observer was sent to Minneapolis, and on the strength of his report we were given an opportunity to present our case in Washington in February 1943. At that time we were offering a homing device capable of reporting with an on-off signal the orientation of a missile toward various visual patterns. The capacity to respond to pattern was, we felt, our strongest argument, but the fact that the device used only visible radiation (the same form of information available to the human bombardier) made it superior to the radio controlled missiles then under development because it was resistant to jamming. Our film had some effect. Other observers were sent to Minneapolis to see the demonstration itself. The pigeons, as

usual, behaved beautifully. One of them held the supposed missile on a particular intersection of streets in the aerial map for five minutes although the target would have been lost if the pigeon had paused for a second or two. The observers returned to Washington, and two weeks later we were asked to supply data on (a) the population of pigeons in the United States (fortunately, the census bureau had some figures) and (b) the accuracy with which pigeons struck a point on a plate. There were many arbitrary conditions to be taken into account in measuring the latter, but we supplied possibly relevant data. At long last, in June 1943, the Office of Scientific Research and Development awarded a modest contract to General Mills, Inc. to "develop a homing device."

At that time we were given some information about the missile the pigeons were to steer. The Pelican was a wing steered glider, still under development and not yet successfully steered by any homing device. It was being tested on a target in New Jersey consisting of a stirrup shaped pattern bulldozed out of the sandy soil near the coast. The white lines of the target stood out clearly against brown and green cover. Colored photographs were taken from various distances and at various angles, and the verisimilitude of the reproduction was checked by flying over the target and looking at its image in a portable camera obscura.

Because of security restrictions we were given only very rough specifications of the signal to be supplied to the controlling system in the Pelican. It was no longer to be simply on-off; if the missile was badly off target, an especially strong correcting signal was needed. This meant that the quadrant-contact system would no longer suffice. But further requirements were left mainly to our imagination. The General Mills engineers were equal to this difficult assignment. With what now seems like unbelievable speed, they designed and constructed a pneumatic pickup system giving a graded signal. A lens in the nose of the missile threw an image on a translucent plate within reach of the pigeon in a pressure sealed chamber. Four air valves resting against the edges of the plate were jarred open momentarily as the pigeon pecked. The valves at the right and left admitted air to chambers on opposite sides of one tambour, while the valves at the top and bottom admitted air to opposite sides of another. Air on all sides was exhausted by a Venturi cone on the side of the missile. When the missile was on target, the

Fig. 3
Demonstration model of the three-pigeon guidance system.

pigeon pecked the center of the plate, all valves admitted equal amounts of air, and the tambours remained in neutral positions. But if the image moved as little as a quarter of an inch off-center, corresponding to a very small angular displacement of the target, more air was admitted by the valves on one side, and the resulting displacement of the tambours sent appropriate correcting orders directly to the servosystem.

The device required no materials in short supply, was relatively foolproof, and delivered a graded signal. It had another advantage. By this time we had begun to realize that a pigeon was more easily controlled than a physical scientist serving on a committee. It was very difficult to convince the latter that the former was an orderly system. We therefore multiplied the probability of success by designing a multiple bird unit. There was adequate space in the nose of the Pelican for three pigeons each with its own lens and plate. A net signal could easily be generated. The majority vote of three

pigeons offered an excellent guarantee against momentary pauses and aberrations. (We later worked out a system in which the majority took on a more characteristically democratic function. When a missile is falling toward *two* ships at sea, for example, there is no guarantee that all three pigeons will steer toward the same ship. But at least two must agree, and the third can then be punished for his minority opinion. Under proper contingencies of reinforcement a punished bird will shift immediately to the majority view. When all three are working on one ship, any defection is immediately punished and corrected.)

The arrangement in the nose of the Pelican is shown in Figure 3. Three systems of lenses and mirrors, shown at the left, throw images of the target area on the three translucent plates shown in the center. The ballistic valves resting against the edges of these plates and the tubes connecting them with the manifolds leading to the controlling tambours may be

Pigeons in a Pelican

149

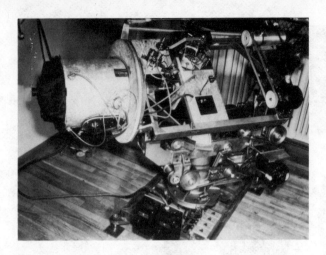

Fig. 4
Simulator for testing the adequacy of the pigeon signal.

seen. A pigeon is being placed in the pressurized chamber at the right.

The General Mills engineers also built a simulator (Figure 4) — a sort of Link trainer for pigeons — designed to have the steering characteristics of the Pelican, insofar as these had been communicated to us. Like the wing steered Pelican, the simulator tilted and turned from side to side. When the three-bird nose was attached to it, the pigeons could be put in full control — the "loop could be closed" — and the adequacy of the signal tested under pursuit conditions. Targets were moved back and forth across the far wall of a room at prescribed speeds and in given patterns of oscillation, and the tracking response of the whole unit was studied quantitatively.

Meanwhile we continued our intensive study of the behavior of the pigeon. Looking ahead to combat use we designed methods for the mass production of trained birds and for handling large groups of trained subjects. We were proposing to train certain birds for certain *classes* of targets, such as ships at sea, while special squads were to be trained on special targets, photographs of which were to be obtained through reconnaissance. A large crew of pigeons would then be waiting for assignment, but we developed harnessing and training techniques which should have solved such problems quite easily.

A multiple unit trainer is shown in Figure 5. Each box contains a jacketed pigeon held at an angle of 45°

to the horizontal and perpendicular to an 8″ × 8″ translucent screen. A target area is projected on each screen. Two beams of light intersect at the point to be struck. All on-target responses of the pigeon are reported by the interruption of the crossed beams and by contact with the translucent screen. Only a four-inch, disk shaped portion of the field is visible to the pigeon at any time, but the boxes move slowly about the field, giving the pigeon an opportunity to respond to the target in all positions. The positions of all reinforcements are recorded to reveal any weak areas. A variable-ratio schedule is used to build sustained, rapid responding.

By December 1943, less than six months after the contract was awarded, we were ready to report to the Office of Scientific Research and Development. Observers visited the laboratory and watched the simulator follow a target about a room under the control of a team of three birds. They also reviewed our tracking data. The only questions which arose were the inevitable consequence of our lack of information about the signal required to steer the Pelican. For example, we had had to make certain arbitrary decisions in compromising between sensitivity of signal and its integration or smoothness. A high vacuum produced quick, rather erratic movements of the tambours, while a lower vacuum gave a sluggish but smooth signal. As it turned out, we had not chosen the best values in collecting our data, and in January 1944 the Office of Scientific Research and Development refused to extend the General Mills contract. The reasons given seemed

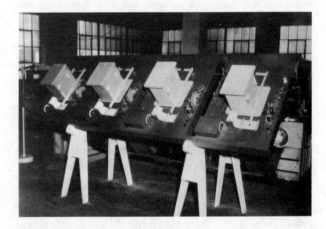

Fig. 5
A trainer for four pigeons.

to be due to misunderstandings or, rather, to lack of communication. We had already collected further data with new settings of the instruments, and these were submitted in a request for reconsideration.

We were given one more chance. We took our new data to the radiation lab at the Massachusetts Institute of Technology where they were examined by the servospecialists working on the Pelican controls. To our surprise the scientist whose task it was to predict the usefulness of the pigeon signal argued that our data were inconsistent with respect to phase lag and certain other characteristics of the signal. According to his equations, our device could not possibly yield the signals we reported. We knew, of course, that it had done so. We examined the supposed inconsistency and traced it, or so we thought, to a certain nonlinearity in our system. In pecking an image near the edge of the plate, the pigeon strikes a more glancing blow; hence the air admitted at the valves is not linearly proportional to the displacement of the target. This could be corrected in several ways: for example, by using a lens to distort radial distances. It was our understanding that in any case the signal was adequate to control the Pelican. Indeed, one servo authority, upon looking at graphs of the performance of the simulator, exclaimed: "This is better than radar!"

Two days later, encouraged by our meeting at MIT, we reached the summit. We were to present our case briefly to a committee of the country's top scientists. The hearing began with a brief report by the scientist who had discovered the "inconsistency" in our data, and to our surprise he still regarded it as unresolved. He predicted that the signal we reported would cause the missile to "hunt" wildly and lose the target. But his prediction should have applied as well to the closed loop simulator. Fortunately another scientist was present who had seen the simulator performing under excellent control and who could confirm our report of the facts. But reality was no match for mathematics.

The basic difficulty, of course, lay in convincing a dozen distinguished physical scientists that the behavior of a pigeon could be adequately controlled. We had hoped to score on this point by bringing with us a demonstration. A small black box had a round translucent window in one end. A slide projector placed some distance away threw on the window an image of the New Jersey target. In the box, of course, was a pigeon—which, incidentally, had at that time been harnessed for 35 hours. Our intention was to let each member of the committee observe the response to the target by looking down a small tube; but time was not available for individual observation, and we were asked to take the top off the box. The translucent screen was flooded with so much light that the target was barely visible, and the peering scientists offered conditions much more unfamiliar and threatening than those likely to be encountered in a missile. In spite of this the pigeon behaved perfectly, pecking steadily and energetically at the image of the target as it moved about on the plate. One scientist with an experimental turn of mind intercepted the beam from the projector. The pigeon stopped instantly. When the image again appeared, pecking began within a fraction of a second and continued at a steady rate.

It was a perfect performance, but it had just the wrong effect. One can talk about phase lag in pursuit behavior and discuss mathematical predictions of hunting without reflecting too closely upon what is inside the black box. But the spectacle of a living pigeon carrying out its assignment, no matter how beautifully, simply reminded the committee of how utterly fantastic our proposal was. I will not say that the meeting was marked by unrestrained merriment, for the merriment was restrained. But it was there, and it was obvious that our case was lost.

Hyde closed our presentation with a brief summary: we were offering a homing device, unusually resistant to jamming, capable of reacting to a wide variety of target patterns, requiring no materials in short supply, and so simple to build that production could be started in 30 days. He thanked the committee, and we left. As the door closed behind us, he said to me "Why don't you go out and get drunk!"

Official word soon came: "Further prosecution of this project would seriously delay others which in the minds of the Division would have more immediate promise of combat application." Possibly the reference was to a particular combat application at Hiroshima a year and a half later, when it looked for a while as if the need for accurate bombing had been eliminated for all time. In any case we had to show, for all our trouble, only a loftful of curiously useless equipment and a few dozen pigeons with a strange interest in a feature of the New Jersey coast. The equipment was scrapped, but 30 of the pigeons were kept to see how long they would retain the appropriate behavior.

In the years which followed there were faint signs of life. Winston Churchill's personal scientific advisor,

Lord Cherwell, learned of the project and "regretted its demise." A scientist who had had some contact with the project during the war, and who evidently assumed that its classified status was not to be taken seriously, made a good story out of it for the *Atlantic Monthly*, names being changed to protect the innocent. Other uses of animals began to be described. The author of the *Atlantic Monthly* story also published an account of the "incendiary bats." Thousands of bats were to be released over an enemy city, each carrying a small incendiary time bomb. The bats would take refuge, as is their custom, under eaves and in other out-of-the-way places; and shortly afterwards thousands of small fires would break out practically simultaneously. The scheme was never used because it was feared that it would be mistaken for germ warfare and might lead to retaliation in kind.

Another story circulating at the time told how the Russians trained dogs to blow up tanks. I have described the technique elsewhere (Skinner, 1956). A Swedish proposal to use seals to achieve the same end with submarines was not successful. The seals were to be trained to approach submarines to obtain fish attached to the sides. They were then to be released carrying magnetic mines in the vicinity of hostile submarines. The required training was apparently never achieved. I cannot vouch for the authenticity of probably the most fantastic story of this sort, but it ought to be recorded. The Russians were said to have trained sea lions to cut mine cables. A complicated device attached to the sea lion included a motor driven cable-cutter, a tank full of small fish, and a device which released a few fish into a muzzle covering the sea lion's head. In order to eat, the sea lion had to find a mine cable and swim along side it so that the cutter was automatically triggered, at which point a few fish were released from the tank into the muzzle. When a given number of cables had been cut, both the energy of the cutting mechanism and the supply of fish were exhausted, and the sea lion received a special stimulus upon which it returned to its home base for special reinforcement and reloading.

Orcon

The story of our own venture has a happy ending. With the discovery of German accomplishments in the field of guided missiles, feasible homing systems suddenly became very important. Franklin V. Taylor of the Naval Research Laboratory in Washington, D.C. heard about our project and asked for further details. As a psychologist Taylor appreciated the special capacity of living organisms to respond to visual patterns and was aware of recent advances in the control of behavior. More important, he was a skillful practitioner in a kind of control which our project had conspicuously lacked: he knew how to approach the people who determine the direction of research. He showed our demonstration film so often that it was completely worn out— but to good effect, for support was eventually found for a thorough investigation of "organic control" under the general title ORCON. Taylor also enlisted the support of engineers in obtaining a more effective report of the pigeon's behavior. The translucent plate upon which the image of the target was thrown had a semiconducting surface, and the tip of the bird's beak was covered with a gold electrode. A single contact with the plate sent an immediate report of the location of the target to the controlling mechanism. The work which went into this system contributed to the so-called Pick-off Display Converter developed as part of the Naval Data Handling System for human observers. It is no longer necessary for the radar operator to give a verbal report of the location of a pip on the screen. Like the pigeon, he has only to touch the pip with a special contact. (He holds the contact in his hand.)

At the Naval Research Laboratory in Washington the responses of pigeons were studied in detail. Average peck rate, average error rate, average hit rate, and so on were recorded under various conditions. The tracking behavior of the pigeon was analyzed with methods similar to those employed with human operators (Figure 6). Pattern perception was studied, including generalization from one pattern to another. A simulator was constructed in which the pigeon controlled an image projected by a moving-picture film of an actual target: for example, a ship at sea as seen from a plane approaching at 600 miles per hour. A few frames of a moving picture of the pigeon controlling the orientation toward a ship during an approach are shown in Figure 7.

The publications from the Naval Research Laboratory which report this work (Chernikoff & Newlin, 1951; Conklin, Newlin, Taylor, & Tipton, 1953; Searle & Stafford, 1950; Taylor, 1949; White, 1952) provide a serious evaluation of the possibilities of organic control. Although in simulated tests a single pigeon occasionally loses a target, its tracking characteristics are surprisingly good. A three- or seven-bird unit with the same individual consistency should yield a signal with a reliability which is at least of the order of mag-

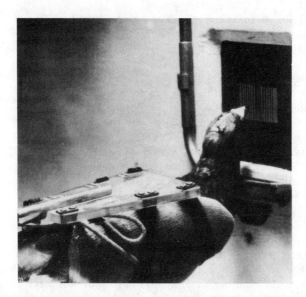

Fig. 6
Arrangement for studying pursuit movements.

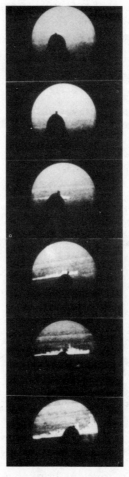

Fig. 7
Frames from a simulated approach.

nitude shown by other phases of guided missiles in their present stage of development. Moreover, in the seven years which have followed the last of these reports, a great deal of relevant information has been acquired. The color vision of the pigeon is now thoroughly understood; its generalization along single properties of a stimulus has been recorded and analyzed; and the maintenance of behavior through scheduling of reinforcement has been drastically improved, particularly in the development of techniques for pacing responses for less erratic and steadier signals (Skinner, 1957). Tests made with the birds salvaged from the old Project Pigeon showed that even after six years of inactivity a pigeon will immediately and correctly strike a target to which it has been conditioned and will continue to respond for some time without reinforcement.

The use of living organisms in guiding missiles is, it seems fair to say, no longer a crackpot idea. A pigeon is an extraordinarily subtle and complex mechanism capable of performances which at the moment can be equalled by electronic equipment only of vastly greater weight and size, and it can be put to reliable use through the principles which have emerged from an experimental analysis of its behavior. But this vindication of our original proposal is perhaps the least important result. Something happened during the brief

life of Project Pigeon which it has taken a long time to appreciate. The practical task before us created a new attitude toward the behavior of organisms. We had to maximize the probability that a given form of behavior would occur at a given time. We could not enjoy the luxury of observing one variable while allowing others to change in what we hoped was a random fashion. We had to discover all relevant variables and submit them to experimental control whenever possible. We were no doubt under exceptional pressure, but vigorous scientific research usually makes comparable demands. Psychologists have too often yielded to the temptation to be content with hypothetical processes and intervening variables rather than press for rigorous experimental control. It is often intellectual laziness rather than necessity which recommends the *a posteriori* statistical treatment of variation. Our task forced us to emphasize prior experimental control, and its success in revealing orderly processes gave us an exciting glimpse of the superiority of laboratory practice over verbal (including some kinds of mathematical) explanation.

The Crackpot Idea

If I were to conclude that crackpot ideas are to be encouraged, I should probably be told that psychology has already had more than its share of them. If it has, they have been entertained by the wrong people. Reacting against the excesses of psychological quackery, psychologists have developed an enormous concern for scientific respectability. They constantly warn their students against questionable facts and unsupported theories. As a result the usual PhD thesis is a model of compulsive cautiousness, advancing only the most timid conclusions thoroughly hedged about with qualifications. But it is just the man capable of displaying such admirable caution who needs a touch of uncontrolled speculation. Possibly a generous exposure to psychological science fiction would help. Project Pigeon might be said to support that view. Except with respect to its avowed goal, it was, as I see it, highly productive; and this was in large measure because my colleagues and I knew that, in the eyes of the world, we were crazy.

One virtue in crackpot ideas is that they breed rapidly and their progeny show extraordinary mutations. Everyone is talking about teaching machines nowadays, but Sidney Pressey can tell you what it was like to have a crackpot idea in that field 40 years ago. His self-testing devices and self-scoring test forms now need no defense, and psychomotor training devices have also achieved a substantial respectability. This did not, however, prepare the way for devices to be used in verbal instruction—that is, in the kinds of teaching which are the principal concern of our schools and colleges. Even five short years ago that kind of instruction by machine was still in the crackpot category. (I can quote offical opinion to that effect from high places.) Now, there is a direct genetic connection between teaching machines and Project Pigeon. We had been forced to consider the mass education of pigeons. True, the scrap of wisdom we imparted to each was indeed small, but the required changes in behavior were similar to those which must be brought about in vaster quantities in human students. The techniques of shaping behavior and of bringing it

under stimulus control which can be traced, as I have suggested elsewhere (Skinner, 1958), to a memorable episode on the top floor of the flour mill in Minneapolis needed only a detailed reformulation of verbal behavior to be directly applicable to education.

I am sure there is more to come. In the year which followed the termination of Project Pigeon I wrote *Walden Two* (Skinner, 1948), a utopian picture of a properly engineered society. Some psychotherapists might argue that I was suffering from personal rejection and simply retreated to a fantasied world where everything went according to plan, where there never was heard a discouraging word. But another explanation is, I think, equally plausible. That piece of science fiction was a declaration of confidence in a technology of behavior. Call it a crackpot idea if you will; it is one in which I have never lost faith. I still believe that the same kind of wide-ranging speculation about human affairs, supported by studies of compensating rigor, will make a substantial contribution toward that world of the future in which, among other things, there will be no need for guided missiles.

References

Chernikoff, R., & Newlin, E. P. ORCON. Part. III. Investigations of target acquisition by the pigeon. *Naval Res. Lab. lett. Rep.*, 1951, No. S-3600-629a/51 (Sept. 10).

Conklin, J. E., Newlin, E. P., Jr., Taylor, F. V., & Tipton, C. L. ORCON. Part IV. Simulated flight tests. *Naval Res. Lab. Rep.*, 1953, No. 4105.

Searle, L. V., & Stafford, B. H. ORCON. Part II. Report of phase I research and bandpass study. *Naval Res. Lab. lett. Rep.*, 1950, No. S-3600-157/50 (May 1).

Skinner, B. F. *Walden two.* New York: Macmillan, 1948.

Skinner, B. F. A case history in scientific method. *Amer. Psychologist*, 1956, *11*, 221–233.

Skinner, B. F. The experimental analysis of behavior. *Amer. Scient.*, 1957, *45*, 343–371.

Skinner, B. F. Reinforcement today. *Amer. Psychologist*, 1958, *13*, 94–99.

Taylor, F. V. ORCON. Part I. Outline of proposed research. *Naval Res. Lab. lett. Rep.*, 1949, No. S-3600-157/50 (June 17).

White, C. F. Development of the NRL ORCON tactile missile simulator. *Naval Res. Lab. Rep.*, 1952, No. 3917.

First, an introduction: I will attempt to achieve three goals today. (*a*) I will summarize some *empirical generalizations and problems* concerning the effects of punishment on behavior; (*b*) I will give some demonstrations of the *advantages of a two-process learning theory* for suggesting new procedures to be tried out in punishment experiments; and (*c*) finally, I shall take this opportunity today to *decry some unscientific legends* about punishment, and to do a little pontificating—a privilege that I might be denied in a journal such as the *Psychological Review,* which I edit!

Now, for a working definition of punishment: The definition of a punishment is not operationally simple, but some of its attributes are clear. A punishment is a noxious stimulus, one which will support, by its termination or omission, the growth of new escape or avoidance responses. It is one which the subject will reject, if given a choice between the punishment and no stimulus at all. Whether the data on the behavioral effects of such noxious stimuli will substantiate our common-sense view of what constitutes an effective punishment, depends on a wide variety of conditions that I shall survey. Needless to say, most of these experimental conditions have been studied with infrahuman subjects rather than with human subjects.

Sample Experiments

Let us first consider two sample experiments. Imagine a traditional alley runway, 6 feet long, with its delineated goal box and start box, and an electrifiable grid floor. In our first experiment, a rat is shocked in

punishment[1]

richard l. solomon
university of pennsylvania

the start box and alley, but there is no shock in the goal box. We can quickly train the rat to run down the alley, if the shock commences as the start-box gate is raised and persists until the rat enters the goal box. This is *escape* training. If, however, we give the rat 5 seconds to reach the goal box after the start-box gate is raised, and only then do we apply the shock, the rat will usually learn to run quickly enough to avoid the shock entirely. This procedure is called *avoidance* training, and the resultant behavior change is called *active* avoidance learning. Note that the response required, either to terminate the shock or to remove the rat from the presence of the dangerous start box and alley, is well

1. This is a slightly revised text of the author's Presidential Address to the Eastern Psychological Association, New York City, April 1963. The research associated with this address was supported by Grant No. M-4202 from the United States Public Health Service. Reprinted from *American Psychologist,* 1964, Vol. 19, pp. 239–253. Copyright 1964 by the American Psychological Association, and reproduced by permission.

specified, while the behavior leading to the onset of these noxious stimulus conditions is left vague. It could be any item of behavior coming *before* the opening of the gate, and it would depend on what the rat happened to be doing when the experimenter raised the gate.

In our second sample experiment, we train a hungry rat to run to the goal box in order to obtain food. After performance appears to be asymptotic, we introduce a shock, both in the alley and goal box, and eliminate the food. The rat quickly stops running and spends its time in the start box. This procedure is called the *punishment procedure,* and the resultant learning-to-stay-in-the-start-box is called *passive* avoidance learning. Note that, while the behavior *producing* the punishment is well specified, the particular behavior *terminating* the punishment is left vague. It could be composed of any behavior that keeps the rat in the start box and out of the alley.

In the first experiment, we were teaching the rat *what to do,* while in the second experiment we were teaching him exactly *what not to do;* yet in each case, the criterion of learning was correlated with the rat's receiving *no* shocks, in contrast to its previous experience of receiving several shocks in the same experimental setting. One cannot think adequately about punishment without considering what is known about the outcomes of both procedures. Yet most reviews of the aversive control of behavior emphasize active avoidance learning and ignore passive avoidance learning. I shall, in this talk, emphasize the similarities, rather than the differences between active and passive avoidance learning. I shall point out that there is a rich store of knowledge of active avoidance learning which, when applied to the punishment procedure, increases our understanding of some of the puzzling and sometimes chaotic results obtained in punishment experiments.

But first, I would like to review some of the empirical generalities which appear to describe the outcomes of experiments on *punishment* and passive avoidance learning. For this purpose, I divide the evidence into 5 classes: (*a*) the effects of punishment on behavior previously established by *rewards* or positive reinforcement, (*b*) the effects of punishment on *consummatory* responses, (*c*) the effects of punishment on complex, sequential patterns of *innate* responses, (*d*) the effects of punishment on discrete reflexes, (*e*) the effects of punishment on responses previously established by punishment—or, if you will, the effects of punishment on active escape and avoidance responses. The effectiveness of punishment will be seen to differ greatly across these five classes of experiments. For convenience, I mean by *effectiveness* the degree to which a punishment procedure produces *suppression* of, or facilitates the *extinction* of, existing response patterns.

Now, let us look at punishment for *instrumental responses or habits previously established by reward or positive reinforcers.* First, the outcomes of punishment procedures applied to previously rewarded habits are strongly related to the *intensity* of the punishing agent. Sometimes intensity is independently defined and measured, as in the case of electric shock. Sometimes we have qualitative evaluations, as in the case of Maier's (1949) rat bumping his nose on a locked door, or Masserman's (Masserman & Pechtel, 1953) spider monkey being presented with a toy snake, or Skinner's (1938) rat receiving a slap on the paw from a lever, or my dog receiving a swat from a rolled-up newspaper. As the intensity of shock applied to rats, cats, and dogs is increased from about .1 milliampere to 4 milliamperes, these orderly results can be obtained: (*a*) *detection* and *arousal*, wherein the punisher can be used as a cue, discriminative stimulus, response intensifier, or even as a secondary reinforcer; (*b*) *temporary suppression*, wherein punishment results in suppression of the punished response, followed by complete recovery, such that the subject later appears unaltered from his prepunished state; (*c*) *partial suppression*, wherein the subject always displays some lasting suppression of the punished response, without total recovery; and (*d*) finally, there is *complete suppression*, with no observable recovery. Any of these outcomes can be produced, other things being equal, by merely varying the intensity of the noxious stimulus used (Azrin & Holz, 1961), when we punish responses previously established by reward or positive reinforcement. No wonder different experimenters report incomparable outcomes. Azrin (1959) has produced a response-rate *increase* while operants are punished. Storms, Boroczi, and Broen (1962) have produced long-lasting suppression of operants in rats.[2] Were punishment intensities dif-

2. Since the delivery of this address, several articles have appeared concerning the punishment intensity problem. See especially Karsh (1963), Appel (1963), and Walters and Rogers (1963). All these studies support the conclusion that shock intensity is a crucial variable, and high intensities produce lasting suppression effects.

ferent? Were punishment durations different? (Storms, Boroczi & Broen, 1963, have shown albino rats to be more resistant to punishment than are hooded rats, and this is another source of discrepancy between experiments.)

But other variables are possibly as important as punishment intensity, and their operation can make it unnecessary to use *intense* punishers in order to produce the effective suppression of a response previously established by positive reinforcement. Here are some selected examples:

1. *Proximity* in time and space to the punished response determines to some extent the effectiveness of a punishment. There is a response-suppression gradient. This has been demonstrated in the runway (Brown, 1948; Karsh, 1962), in the lever box (Azrin, 1956), and in the shuttle box (Kamin, 1959). This phenomenon has been labeled the gradient of temporal delay of punishment.

2. The conceptualized *strength* of a response, as measured by its resistance to extinction after omission of positive reinforcement, predicts the effect of a punishment contingent upon the response. Strong responses, so defined, are more resistant to the suppressive effects of punishment. Thus, for example, the overtraining of a response, which often decreases ordinary resistance to experimental extinction, also increases the effectiveness of punishment (Karsh, 1962; Miller, 1960) as a response suppressor.

3. *Adaptation* to punishment can occur, and this *decreases* its effectiveness. New, intense punishers are better than old, intense punishers (Miller, 1960). Punishment intensity, if slowly increased, tends not to be as effective as in the case where it is introduced initially at its high-intensity value.

4. In general, resistance to extinction is decreased whenever a previously reinforced response is punished. However, if the subject is habituated to receiving shock together with positive reinforcement during reward training, the relationship can be reversed, and punishment during extinction can actually increase resistance to extinction (Holz & Azrin, 1961). Evidently, punishment, so employed, can functionally operate as a *secondary reinforcer*, or as a cue for reward, or as an arouser.

5. Punishments become extremely effective when the response-suppression period is tactically used as an aid to the reinforcement of new responses that are topographically *incompatible* with the punished one. When new instrumental acts are established which lead to the old goal (a new *means* to an old *end*), a punishment of very low intensity can have very long-lasting suppression effects. Whiting and Mowrer (1943) demonstrated this clearly. They first rewarded one route to food, then punished it. When the subjects ceased taking the punished route, they provided a new rewarded route. The old route was not traversed again. This reliable suppression effect also seems to be true of temporal, discriminative restraints on behavior. The suppression of urination in dogs, under the control of *indoor stimuli*, is extremely effective in housebreaking the dog, as long as urination is allowed to go unpunished under the control of *outdoor stimuli*. There is a valuable lesson here in the effective use of punishments in producing *impulse control*. A *rewarded alternative*, under discriminative control, makes passive avoidance training a potent behavioral influence. It can produce a highly reliable dog or child. In some preliminary observations of puppy training, we have noted that puppies raised in the lab, if punished by the swat of a newspaper for eating horsemeat, and rewarded for eating pellets, will starve themselves to death when only given the opportunity to eat the taboo horsemeat. They eagerly eat the pellets when they are available.

It is at this point that we should look at the experiments wherein punishment appears to have only a temporary suppression effect. Most of these experiments offered the subject *no* rewarded alternative to the punished response in attaining his goal. In many such experiments, it was a case of take a chance or go hungry. Hunger-drive strength, under such no-alternative conditions, together with punishment intensity, are the crucial variables in predicting recovery from the suppression effects of punishment. Here, an interesting, yet hard-to-understand phenomenon frequently occurs, akin to Freudian "reaction formation." If a subject has been punished for touching some manipulandum which yields food, he may stay nearer to the manipulandum under low hunger drive and move farther away from it under high hunger drive, even though the probability of finally touching the manipulandum increases as hunger drive increases. This phenomenon is complex and needs to be studied in some detail. Our knowledge of it now is fragmentary. It was observed by Hunt and Schlosberg (1950) when the water supply of rats was electrified, and we have seen it occur in approach-avoidance conflict experiments in our laboratory, but we do not know the precise conditions for its occurrence.

Finally, I should point out that the attributes of effective punishments vary *across species* and *across stages in maturational development* within species. A toy snake can frighten monkeys. It does not faze a rat. A loud noise terrified Watson's little Albert. To us it is merely a Chinese gong.

I have sketchily reviewed some effects of punishment on *instrumental* acts established by *positive reinforcers*. We have seen that any result one might desire, from response enhancement and little or no suppression, to relatively complete suppression, can be obtained with our current knowledge of appropriate experimental conditions. Now let us look at the effects of punishment on *consummatory acts*. Here, the data are, to me, surprising. One would think that consummatory acts, often being of biological significance for the survival of the individual and the species, would be highly resistant to suppression by punishment. The *contrary* appears to be so. Male sexual behavior may be seriously suppressed by weak punishment (Beach, Conovitz, Steinberg, & Goldstein, 1956; Gantt, 1944). Eating in dogs and cats can be permanently suppressed by a moderate shock delivered through the feet or through the food dish itself (Lichtenstein, 1950; Masserman, 1943). Such suppression effects can lead to fatal self-starvation. A toy snake presented to a spider monkey while he is eating can result in self-starvation (Masserman & Pechtel, 1953).

The interference with consummatory responses by punishment needs a great deal of investigation. Punishment seems to be especially effective in breaking up this class of responses, and one can ask *why*, with some profit. Perhaps the intimate temporal connection between drive, incentive, and punishment results in drive or incentive becoming conditioned-stimulus (CS) patterns for aversive emotional reactions when consummatory acts are punished. Perhaps this interferes with vegetative activity: i.e., does it "kill the appetite" in a hungry subject? But, one may ask why the same punisher might not appear to be as effective when made contingent on an *instrumental* act as contrasted with a consummatory act. Perhaps the nature of operants is such that they are separated in time and space and response topography from consummatory behavior and positive incentive stimuli, so that appetitive reactions are not clearly present during pun-

ishment for operants. We do not know enough yet about such matters, and speculation about it is still fun.

Perhaps the most interesting parametric variation one can study, in experiments on the effects of punishment on consummatory acts, is the *temporal order* of rewards and punishments. If we hold hunger drive constant, shock-punishment intensity constant, and food-reward amounts constant, a huge differential effect can be obtained when we reverse the order of reward and punishment. If we train a cat to approach a food cup, its behavior in the experimental setting will become quite stereotyped. Then, if we introduce shock to the cat's feet while it is eating, the cat will vocalize, retreat, and show fear reactions. It will be slow to recover its eating behavior in this situation. Indeed, as Masserman (1943) has shown, such a procedure is likely, if repeated a few times, to lead to self-starvation. Lichtenstein (1950) showed the same phenomenon in dogs. Contrast this outcome with that found when the temporal order of food and shock is *reversed*. We now use shock as a discriminative stimulus to signalize the availability of food. When the cat is performing well, the shock may produce eating with a latency of less than 5 seconds. The subject's appetite does not seem to be disturbed. One cannot imagine a more dramatic difference than that induced by reversing the temporal order of reward and punishment (Holz & Azrin, 1962; Masserman, 1943).

Thus, the effects of punishment are partly determined by those events that directly precede it and those that directly follow it. A punishment is not just a punishment. It is an event in a temporal and spatial flow of stimulation and behavior, and its effects will be produced by its temporal and spatial point of insertion in that flow.

I have hastily surveyed some of the effects of punishment when it has been made contingent either on rewarded *operants* and instrumental acts or on *consummatory* acts. A third class of behaviors, closely related to consummatory acts, but yet a little different, are *instinctive act sequences*: the kinds of complex, innately governed behaviors which the ethologists study, such as nest building in birds. There has been little adequate experimentation, to my knowledge, on the effects of punishment on such innate behavior sequences. There are, however, some hints of interesting things to come. For example, sometimes frightening events will produce what the ethologists call displacement reactions—the expression of an inappropriate behavior pattern of an innate sort. We need to experiment with such phenomena in a systematic fashion. The best example I could find of this phenomenon is the imprinting of birds on moving objects, using the locomotor following response as an index. Moltz, Rosenblum, and Halikas (1959), in one experiment, and Kovach and Hess (1963; see also Hess, 1959a, 1959b) in another, have shown that the punishment of such imprinted behavior sometimes depresses its occurrence. However, if birds are punished prior to the presentation of an imprinted object, often the following response will be energized. It is hard to understand what this finding means, except that punishment can either arouse or inhibit such behavior, depending on the manner of presentation of punishment. The suggestion is that imprinting is partially a function of fear or distress. The effectiveness of punishment also is found to be related to the critical period for imprinting (Kovach & Hess, 1963).

However, the systematic study of known punishment parameters as they affect a wide variety of complex sequences of innate behaviors is yet to be carried out. It would appear to be a worthwhile enterprise, for it is the type of work which would enable us to make a new attack on the effects of experience on innate behavior patterns. Ultimately the outcomes of such experiments *could* affect psychoanalytic conceptions of the effects of trauma on impulses of an innate sort.[3]

A fourth class of behavior upon which punishment can be made contingent, is the simple, discrete reflex. For example, what might happen if a conditioned or an unconditioned knee jerk were punished? We are completely lacking in information on this point. Can subjects be trained to inhibit reflexes under aversive motivation? Or does such motivation sensitize and enhance reflexes? Some simple experiments are appropriate, but I was unable to find them in the published work I read.

3. Since the delivery of this address, an article has appeared on this specific problem. See Adler and Hogan (1963). The authors showed that the gill-extension response of *Betta splendens* could be conditioned to a previously neutral stimulus by a Pavlovian technique, and it could also be suppressed by electric-shock punishment. This is an important finding, because there are very few known cases where the same response can be both conditioned and trained. Here, the gill-extension response is typically elicited by a rival fish, and is usually interpreted to be aggressive or hostile in nature.

A fifth class of behavior, upon which punishment can be made contingent, is behavior *previously established by punishment procedures:* in other words, the effect of passive avoidance training on existing, active avoidance learned responses. This use of punishment produces an unexpected outcome. In general, if the same noxious stimulus is used to punish a response as was used to establish it in the first place, the response becomes strengthened during initial applications of punishment. After several such events, however, the response may weaken, but not always. The similarity of the noxious stimulus used for active avoidance training to that used for punishment of the established avoidance response can be of great importance. For example, Carlsmith (1961) has shown that one can increase resistance to extinction by using the same noxious stimuli for both purposes and yet decrease resistance to extinction by using equally noxious, but discriminatively different, punishments. He trained some rats to run in order to avoid shock, then punished them during extinction by blowing a loud horn. He trained other rats to run in order to avoid the loud horn, then during extinction he punished them by shocking them for running. In two control groups, the punisher stimulus and training stimulus were the same. The groups which were trained and then punished by different noxious stimuli extinguished more rapidly during punishment than did the groups in which the active avoidance training unconditioned stimulus (US) was the same as the passive avoidance training US. Thus, punishment for responses established originally by punishment may be ineffective in eliminating the avoidance responses they are supposed to eliminate. Indeed, the punishment may strengthen the responses. We need to know more about this puzzling phenomenon. It is interesting to me that in Japan, Imada (1959) has been systematically exploring shock intensity as it affects this phenomenon.

Our quick survey of the effects of punishment on five classes of responses revealed a wide variety of discrepant phenomena. Thus, to predict in even the grossest way the action of punishment on a response, one has to know *how* that particular response was originally inserted in the subject's response repertoire. Is the response an instrumental one which was strengthened by reward? Is it instead a consummatory response? Is it an innate sequential response pattern? Is it a discrete reflex? Was it originally established by means of punishment? *Where*, temporally, in a behavior sequence, was the punishment used? How *intense* was it? There are but a few of the relevant, critical questions, the answers to which are necessary in order for us to make reasonable predictions about the effects of punishment. Thus, to conclude, as some psychologists have, that the punishment procedure is typically either effective or ineffective, typically either a temporary suppressor or a permanent one, is to oversimplify irresponsibly a complex area of scientific knowledge, one still containing a myriad of intriguing problems for experimental attack.

Yet, the complexities involved in ascertaining the effects of punishement on behavior *need not* be a bar to useful speculation ultimately leading to experimentation of a fruitful sort. The complexities should, however, dictate a great deal of caution in making dogmatic statements about whether punishment is effective or ineffective as a behavioral influence, or whether it is good or bad. I do *not* wish to do that. I would like now to speculate about the data-oriented theories, rather than support or derogate the dogmas and the social philosophies dealing with punishment. I will get to the dogmas later.

Theory

Here is a theoretical approach that, for me, has high pragmatic value in stimulating new lines of experimentation. Many psychologists today consider the punishment procedure to be a special case of avoidance training, and the resultant learning processes to be theoretically identical in nature. Woodworth and Schlosberg (1954) distinguish the two training procedures, *"punishment for action"* from *"punishment for inaction,"* but assume that the same theoretical motive, a "positive incentive value of safety" can explain the learning produced by both procedures. Dinsmoor (1955) argues that the facts related to both procedures are well explained by simple stimulus-response (S-R) principles of avoidance learning. He says:

If we punish the subject for making a given response or sequence of responses—that is, apply aversive stimulation, like shock—the cues or discriminative stimuli for this response will correspond to the warning signals that are typically used in more direct studies of avoidance training. By his own response to these stimuli, the subject himself produces the punishing stimulus and pairs or correlates it with these signals. As a result, they too become aversive. In the meantime, any variations in the subject's behavior that interfere or conflict

with the chain of reactions leading to the punishment delay the occurrence of the final response and the receipt of the stimulation that follows it. These variations in behavior disrupt the discriminative stimulus pattern for the continuation of the punished chain, changing the current stimulation from an aversive to a nonaversive compound; they are conditioned, differentiated, and maintained by the reinforcing effects of the change in stimulation [p. 96].

The foci of the Dinsmoor analysis are the processes whereby: (*a*) discriminative stimuli become aversive, and (*b*) instrumental acts are reinforced. He stays at the quasi-descriptive level. He uses a peripheralistic, S-R analysis, in which response-produced proprioceptive stimuli and exteroceptive stimuli serve to hold behavior chains together. He rejects, as unnecessary, concepts such as fear or anxiety, in explaining the effectiveness of punishment.

Mowrer (1960) also argues that the facts related to the two training procedures are explained by a common set of principles, but Mowrer's principles are somewhat different than those of either Woodworth and Schlosberg, or Dinsmoor, cited above. Mowrer says:

In both instances, there is fear conditioning; and in both instances a way of behaving is found which eliminates or controls the fear. The only important distinction, it seems is that the stimuli to which the fear gets connected are different. In so-called punishment, these stimuli are produced by (correlated with) the behavior, or response, which we wish to block; whereas, in so-called avoidance learning, the fear-arousing stimuli are not response-produced—they are, so to say, extrinsic rather than intrinsic, independent rather than response-dependent. But in both cases there is avoidance and in both cases there is its antithesis, punishment; hence the impropriety of referring to the one as "punishment" and to the other as "avoidance learning." Obviously precision and clarity of understanding are better served by the alternative terms here suggested, namely, passive avoidance learning and active avoidance learning, respectively. . . . But, as we have seen, the two phenomena involve exactly the same basic principles of fear conditioning and of the reinforcement of whatever action (or inaction) eliminates the fear [pp. 31–32].

I like the simple beauty of each of the three unifying positions; what holds for punishment and its action on behavior should hold also for escape and avoidance training, and vice versa. Generalizations about one process should tell us something about the other. New experimental relationships discovered in the one experimental setting should tell us how to predict a new empirical event in the other experimental setting. A brief discussion of a few selected examples can illustrate this possibility.

Applications of Theory

I use a case in point stemming from work done in our town laboratory. It gives us new hints about some hidden sources of effectiveness of punishment. Remember, for the sake of argument, that we are assuming many important similarities to exist between active and passive avoidance-learning processes. Therefore, we can look at active avoidance learning as a theoretical device to suggest to us new, unstudied variables pertaining to the effectiveness of punishment.

Turner and I have recently published an extensive monograph (1962) on human traumatic avoidance learning. Our experiments showed that when a very reflexive, short-latency, skeletal response, such as a toe twitch, was used as an escape and avoidance response, grave difficulties in active avoidance learning were experienced by the subject. Experimental variations which tended to render the escape responses more emitted, more deliberate, more voluntary, more operant, or less reflexive, tended also to render the avoidance responses easier to learn. Thus, when a subject was required to move a knob in a slot in order to avoid shock, learning was rapid, in contrast to the many failures to learn with a toe-flexion avoidance response.

There are descriptions of this phenomenon already available in several published experiments on active avoidance learning, but their implications have not previously been noted. When Schlosberg (1934) used for the avoidance response a highly reflexive, short-latency, paw-flexion response in the rat, he found active avoidance learning to be unreliable, unstable, and quick to extinguish. Whenever the rats made active avoidance flexions, a decrement in response strength ensued. When the rats were shocked on several escape trials, the avoidance response tended to reappear for a few trials. Thus, learning to avoid was a tortuous, cyclical process, never exceeding 30% success. Contrast these results with the active avoidance training of nonreflexive, long-latency operants, such as rats running in Hunter's (1935) circular maze. Hunter found that the occurrence of avoidance responses tended to produce more avoidance responses.

Omission of shock seemed to reinforce the avoidance running response. Omission of shock seemed to extinguish the avoidance paw flexion. Clearly the operant-respondent distinction has predictive value in active avoidance learning.

The same trend can be detected in experiments using dogs as subjects. For example, Brogden (1949), using the forepaw-flexion response, found that meeting a 20/20 criterion of avoidance learning was quite difficult. He found that 30 dogs took from approximately 200–600 trials to reach the avoidance criterion. The response used was, in our language, highly reflexive—it was totally elicited by the shock on escape trials with a very short latency, approximately .3 second. Compare, if you will, the learning of active avoidance by dogs in the shuttle box with that found in the forelimb-flexion experiment. In the shuttle box, a large number of dogs were able to embark on their criterion trials after 5–15 active avoidance-training trials. Early escape response latencies were long. Resistance to extinction is, across these two types of avoidance responses, inversely related to trials needed for a subject to achieve criterion. Conditions leading to quick acquisition are, in this case, those conducive to slow extinction. Our conclusion, then, is that high-probability, short-latency, *respondents* are not as good as medium-probability, long-latency operants when they are required experimentally to function as active avoidance responses. This generalization seems to hold for rats, dogs, and college students.

How can we make the inferential leap from such findings in active avoidance training to possible variations in punishment experiments? It is relatively simple to generalize across the two kinds of experiments in the case of CS-US interval, US intensity, and CS duration. But the inferential steps are not as obvious in the case of the operant-respondent distinction. So I will trace out the logic in some detail. If one of the major effects of punishment is to motivate or elicit new behaviors, and reinforce them through removal of punishment, and thus, as Dinsmoor describes, establish avoidance responses incompatible with a punished response, how does the operant-respondent distinction logically enter? Here, Mowrer's two-process avoidance-learning theory can suggest a possible answer. Suppose, for example, that a hungry rat has been trained to lever press for food and is performing at a stable rate. Now we make a short-duration, high-intensity pulse of shock contingent upon the bar press. The pulse elicits a startle pattern that produces a release of the lever in .2 second, and the shock is gone. The rat freezes for a few seconds, breathing heavily, and he urinates and defecates. It is our supposition that a conditioned emotional reaction (CER) is thereby established, with its major stimulus control coming from the sight of the bar, the touch of the bar, and proprioceptive stimuli aroused by the lever-press movements themselves. This is, as Dinsmoor describes it, the development of acquired aversiveness of stimuli; or, as Mowrer describes it, the acquisition of conditioned fear reactions. Therefore, Pavlovian conditioning variables should be the important ones in the development of this process. The reappearance of lever pressing in this punished rat would thus depend on the extinction of the CER and skeletal freezing. If no further shocks are administered, then the CER should extinguish according to the laws of Pavlovian extinction, and reappearance of the lever press should not take long, even if the shock-intensity level were high enough to have been able to produce active avoidance learning in another apparatus.

Two-process avoidance theory tells us that something very important for successful and durable response suppression was missing in the punishment procedure we just described. What was lacking in this punishment procedure was a good operant to allow us to reinforce a reliable avoidance response. Because the reaction to shock was a respondent, was highly *reflexive*, and was quick to occur, I am led to argue that the termination of shock will *not* reinforce it, nor will it lead to stable avoidance responses. This conclusion follows directly from our experiments on human avoidance learning. If the termination of shock is made contingent on the occurrence of an operant, especially an operant topographically incompatible with the lever press, an active avoidance learning process should then ensue. So I will now propose that we shock the rat until he huddles in a corner of the box. The rat will have learned to *do* something arbitrary whenever the controlling CSs reappear. Thus, the rat in the latter procedure, if he is to press the lever again, must undergo *two* extinction processes. The CER, established by the pairing of CS patterns and shock, must become weaker. Second, the learned huddling response must extinguish. This combination of requirements should make the effect of punishment more lasting, if my inferences are correct. Two

problems must be solved by the subject, not one. The experiments needed to test these speculations are, it would appear, easy to design, and there is no reason why one should not be able to gather the requisite information in the near future. I feel that there is much to be gained in carrying on theoretical games like this, with the major assumptions being (a) that active and passive avoidance learning are similar processes, ones in which the same variables have analogous effects, and (b) that two processes, the conditioning of fear reactions, and the reinforcement of operants incompatible with the punished response, may operate in punishment experiments.

There is another gain in playing theoretical games of this sort. One can use them to question the usual significance imputed to past findings. Take, for example, the extensive studies of Neal Miller (1959) and his students, and Brown (1948) and his students, on gradients of approach and avoidance in conflict situations. Our foregoing analysis of the role of the operant-respondent distinction puts to question one of their central assumptions—that the avoidance gradient is unconditionally steeper than is the approach gradient in approach-avoidance conflicts. In such experiments, the subject is typically trained while hungry to run down a short alley to obtain food. After the running is reliable, the subject is shocked, usually near the goal, in such a way that entering the goal box is discouraged temporarily. The subsequent behavior of the typical subject consists of remaining in the start box, making abortive approaches to the food box, showing hesitancy, oscillation, and various displacement activities, like grooming. Eventually, if shock is eliminated by the experimenter, the subject resumes running to food. The avoidance tendency is therefore thought to have extinguished sufficiently so that the magnitude of the conceptualized approach gradient exceeds that of the avoidance gradient at the goal box. The steepness of the avoidance gradient as a function of distance from the goal box is inferred from the behavior of the subject *prior* to the extinction of the avoidance tendencies. If the subject stays as far away from the goal box as possible, the avoidance gradient may be inferred to be either displaced upward, or if the subject slowly creeps up on the goal box from trial to trial, it may be inferred to be less steep than the approach gradient. Which alternative is more plausible? Miller and his collaborators very cleverly have shown that the latter alternative is a better interpretation.

The differential-steepness assumption appears to be substantiated by several studies by Miller and his collaborators (Miller & Murray, 1952; Murray & Berkun, 1955). They studied the displacement of conflicted approach responses along both spatial and color dimensions, and clearly showed that the approach responses generalized more readily than did the avoidance responses. Rats whose running in an alley had been completely suppressed by shock punishment showed recovery of running in a similar alley. Thus the inference made was that the avoidance gradient is steeper than is the approach gradient; avoidance tendencies weaken more rapidly with changes in the external environmental setting than do approach tendencies. On the basis of the analysis I made of the action of punishment, both as a US for the establishment of a Pavlovian CER and as a potent event for the reinforcement of instrumental escape and avoidance responses, it seems to me very likely that the approach-avoidance conflict experiments have been carried out in such a way as to produce inevitably the steeper avoidance gradients. In other words, these experiments from my particular viewpoint have been inadvertently biased, and they were not appropriate for testing hypotheses about the gradient slopes.

My argument is as follows: Typically, the subject in an approach-avoidance experiment is trained to perform a specific sequence of responses under reward incentive and appetitive drive conditions. He runs to food when hungry. In contrast, when the shock is introduced into the runway, it is usually placed near the goal, and no specific, long sequence of instrumental responses is required of the subject before the shock is terminated. Thus, the initial strengths of the approach and avoidance instrumental responses (which are in conflict) are not equated by analogous or symmetrical procedures. Miller has thoroughly and carefully discussed this, and has suggested that the avoidance gradient would not have as steep a slope if the shock were encountered by the rat early in the runway in the case where the whole runway is electrified. While this comment is probably correct, it does not go far enough, and I would like to elaborate on it. I would argue that if one wants to study the relative steepnesses of approach and avoidance responses in an unbiased way, the competing instrumental responses should be established in a *symmetrical* fashion. After learning to run down an alley to food, the subject should be shocked near the goal box or in it, and the shock should not be termi-

nated until the subject has escaped all the way into the start box. Then one can argue that two conflicting instrumental responses have been established. First, the subject runs one way for food; now he runs the same distance in the opposite direction in order to escape shock. When he stays in the start box, he avoids shock entirely. Then the generalization or displacement of the approach and avoidance responses can be fairly studied.

I am arguing that we need *instrumental*-response balancing, as well as *Pavlovian*-conditioning balancing, in such conflict experiments, if the slopes of gradients are to be determined for a test of the differential-steepness assumption. Two-process avoidance-learning theory requires such a symmetrical test. In previous experiments, an aversive CER and its respondent motor pattern, not a well-reinforced avoidance response, has been pitted against a well-reinforced instrumental-approach response. Since the instrumental behavior of the subject is being used subsequently to test for the slope of the gradients, the usual asymmetrical procedure is, I think, not appropriate. My guess is that, if the symmetrical procedure I described is actually used, the slopes of the two gradients will be essentially the same, and the recovery of the subject from the effects of punishment will be seen to be nearly all-or-none. That is, the avoidance gradient, as extinction of the CER proceeds in time, will drop below the approach gradient, and this will hold all along the runway if the slopes of the two gradients are indeed the same. Using the test of displacement, subjects should stay in the starting area of a similar alley on initial tests and when they finally move forward they should go all the way to the goal box.

The outcomes of such experiments would be a matter of great interest to me, for, as you will read in a moment, I feel that the suppressive power of punishment over instrumental acts has been understated. The approach-avoidance conflict experiment is *but one* example among many wherein the outcome *may have been* inadvertently biased in the direction of showing reward-training influences to be superior, in some particular way, to punishment-training procedures. Now let us look more closely at this matter of bias.

Legends

Skinner, in 1938, described the effect of a short-duration slap on the paw on the extinction of lever pressing in the rat. Temporary suppression of lever-pressing rate was obtained. When the rate increased, it exceeded the usual extinction performance. The total number of responses before extinction occurred was not affected by the punishment for lever pressing. Estes (1944) obtained similar results, and attributed the temporary suppression to the establishment of a CER (anxiety) which dissipated rapidly. Tolman, Hall, and Bretnall (1932) had shown earlier that punishment could enhance maze learning by serving as a cue for correct, rewarded behavior. Skinner made these observations (on the seemingly ineffective nature of punishment as a response weakener) the basis for his advocacy of a positive reinforcement regime in his utopia, *Walden Two*. In *Walden Two*, Skinner (1948), speaking through the words of Frazier, wrote: "We are now discovering at an untold cost in human suffering—that in the long run punishment doesn't reduce the probability that an act will occur [p. 260]." No punishments would be used there, because they would produce poor behavioral control, he claimed.

During the decade following the publication of *Walden Two*, Skinner (1953) maintained his position concerning the effects of punishment on instrumental responses: Response suppression is but temporary, and the side effects, such as fear and neurotic and psychotic disturbances, are not worth the temporary advantages of the use of punishment. He said:

In the long run, punishment, unlike reinforcement works to the disadvantage of both the punished organism and the punishing agency [p. 183].

The fact that punishment does not permanently reduce a tendency to respond is in agreement with Freud's discovery of the surviving activity of what he called repressed wishes [p. 184].

Punishment, as we have seen, does not create a negative probability that a response will be made but rather a positive probability that incompatible behavior will occur [p. 222].

It must be said, in Skinner's defense, that in 1953 he devoted about 12 pages to the topic of punishment in his introductory textbook. Other texts had devoted but a few words to this topic.

In Bugelski's (1956) words about the early work on punishment: "The purport of the experiments mentioned above appears to be to demonstrate that punishment is ineffective in eliminating behavior. This conclusion appears to win favor with various sentimentalists [p. 275]." Skinner (1961) summarized his position most recently in this way:

Ultimate advantages seem to be particularly easy to overlook in the control of behavior, where a quick though slight advantage may have undue weight. Thus, although we boast that the birch rod has been abandoned, most school children are still under aversive control—not because punishment is more effective in the long run, but because it yields immediate results. It is easier for the teacher to control the student by threatening punishment than by using positive reinforcement with its *deferred, though more powerful,* effects [p. 36.08, italics mine].

Skinner's conclusions were drawn over a span of time when, just as is the case *now*, there was no conclusive evidence about the supposedly more powerful and long-lasting effects of positive reinforcement. I admire the humanitarian and kindly dispositions contained in such writings. But the scientific basis for the conclusions therein was shabby, because, even in 1938, there were conflicting data which demonstrated the great effectiveness of punishment in controlling instrumental behavior. For example, the widely cited experiments of Warden and Aylesworth (1927) showed that discrimination learning in the rat was more rapid and more stable when incorrect responses were punished with shock than when reward alone for the correct response was used. Later on, avoidance-training experiments in the 1940s and 1950s added impressive data on the long-lasting behavioral control exerted by noxious stimuli (Solomon & Brush, 1956). In spite of this empirical development, many writers of books in the field of learning now devote but a few lines to the problem of punishment, perhaps a reflection of the undesirability of trying to bring satisfying order out of seeming chaos. In this category are the recent books of Spence, Hull, and Kimble. An exception is Bugelski (1956) who devotes several pages to the complexities of this topic. Most contemporary *introductory psychology* texts devote but a paragraph or two to punishment as a scientific problem. Conspicuously, George Miller's new book, *Psychology, the Science of Mental Life,* has no discussion of punishment in it.

The most exhaustive textbook treatment today is that of Deese (1958), and it is a thoughtful and objective evaluation, a singular event in this area of our science. The most exhaustive journal article is that by Church (1963), who has thoroughly summarized our knowledge of punishment. I am indebted to Church for letting me borrow freely from his fine essay in prepublication form. Without this assistance, the organization of this paper would have been much more difficult, indeed.

Perhaps one reason for the usual textbook relegation of the topic of punishment to the fringe of experimental psychology is the wide-spread belief that punishment is unimportant because *it does not really weaken habits;* that it pragmatically is a *poor controller* of behavior; that it is extremely *cruel* and unnecessary; and that it is a technique leading to *neurosis* and worse. This legend, and it is a legend without sufficient empirical basis, probably arose with Thorndike (1931). Punishment, in the time of Thorndike, used to be called punishment, not passive avoidance training. The term referred to the use of noxious stimuli for the avowed purpose of discouraging some selected kind of behavior. Thorndike (1931) came to the conclusion that punishment did not really accomplish its major purpose, the destruction or extinction of habits. In his book, *Human Learning,* he said:

Annoyers do not act on learning in general by weakening whatever connection they follow. If they do anything in learning, they do it indirectly, by informing the learner that such and such a response in such and such a situation brings distress, or by making the learner feel fear of a certain object, or by making him jump back from a certain place, or by some other definite and specific change which they produce in him [p. 46].

This argument is similar to that of Guthrie (1935), and of Wendt (1936), in explaining the extinction of instrumental acts and conditioned reflexes. They maintained that extinction was not the weakening of a habit, but the replacement of a habit by a new one, even though the new one might only be sitting still and doing very little.

When Thorndike claimed that the effects of punishment were indirect, he was emphasizing the power of punishment to evoke behavior other than that which produced the punishment; in much the same manner, Guthrie emphasized the extinction procedure as one arousing competing responses. The competing-response theory of extinction today cannot yet be empirically chosen over other theories such as Pavlovian and Hullian inhibition theory, or the frustration theories of Amsel or Spence. The Thorndikian position on punishment is limited in the same way. It is difficult to designate the empirical criteria which would enable us to know, on those occasions when punishment for a response results in a weakening of performance of that response, whether a habit was indeed weakened or not. How can one tell whether competing responses have displaced the punished response, or whether the punished habit is itself weakened by punishment? Thorndike could not tell, and neither could Guthrie. Yet a legend was perpetuated. Perhaps the acceptance of the legend had something to do with the lack of concerted research on punishment from 1930–1955. For example, psychologists were not then particularly adventuresome in their search for experimentally effective punishments.

Or, in addition to the legend, perhaps a bit of soft-heartedness is partly responsible for limiting our inventiveness. (The Inquisitors, the Barbarians, and the Puritans could have given us some good hints! They did not have electric shock, but they had a variety of interesting ideas, which, regrettably, they often put to practice.) We clearly need to study new kinds of punishments in the laboratory. For most psychologists, a punishment in the laboratory means electric shock. A few enterprising experimenters have used air blasts, the presentation of an innate fear releaser, or a signal for the coming omission of reinforcement, as punishments. But we still do not know enough about using these stimuli in a controlled fashion to produce either behavior supression, or a CER effect, or the facilitation of extinction. Many aversive states have gone unstudied. For example, conditioned nausea and vomiting is easy to produce, but it has not been used in the role of punishment. Even the brain stimulators, though they have since 1954 tickled brain areas that will instigate active escape learning, have not used this knowledge to study systematically the punishing effects of such stimulation on existing responses.

While the more humanitarian ones of us were bent on the discovery of new positive reinforcers, there was no such concerted effort on the part of the more brutal ones of us. Thus, for reasons that now completely escape me, some of us in the past were thrilled by the discovery that, under some limited conditions, either a light onset or a light termination could raise lever-pressing rate significantly, though trivially, above operant level. If one is looking for agents to help in the task of getting strong predictive power, and strong control of behavior, such discoveries seem not too exciting. Yet, in contrast, discoveries *already have* been made of the powerful aversive control of behavior. Clearly, we have been afraid of their implications. Humanitarian guilt and normal kindness are undoubtedly involved, as they should be. But I believe that one reason for our fear has been the widespread implication of the *neurotic syndrome* as a *necessary* outcome of all severe punishment procedures. A second reason has been the general acceptance of the behavioral phenomena of rigidity, inflexibility, or narrowed cognitive map, as *necessary* outcomes of experiments in which noxious stimuli have been used. I shall question *both* of these conclusions.

If one should feel that the Skinnerian generalizations about the inadequate effects of punishment on instrumental responses are tinged with a laudable, though thoroughly incorrect and unscientific, sentimentalism and softness, then, in contrast, one can find more than a lurid tinge in discussions of the effects of punishment on the *emotional* balance of the individual. When punishments are asserted to be ineffective controllers of instrumental behavior, they are, in contrast, often asserted to be devastating controllers of emotional reactions, leading to neurotic and psychotic symptoms, and to general pessimism, depressiveness, constriction of thinking, horrible psychosomatic diseases, and even death! This is somewhat of a paradox, I think. The convincing part of such generalizations is only their face validity. There *are* experiments, many of them carefully done, in which these neurotic outcomes were clearly observed. Gantt's (1944) work on neurotic dogs, Masserman's (1943) work on neurotic cats and monkeys, Brady's (1958) recent work on ulcerous monkeys, Maier's (1949) work on fixated rats, show some of the devastating consequences of the utilization of punishment to control behavior. The side effects are frightening, indeed, and should *not* be ignored! But there *must be* some rules, some principles, governing the appearance of such side effects, for they *do not* appear in all experiments involving the use of strong punishment or the elicitation of terror. In Yates' (1962) new book, *Frustration and Conflict,* we find a thorough discussion of punishment as a creator of conflict. Major attention is paid to the instrumental-response outcomes of conflict due to punishment. Phenomena such as rigidity, fixation, regression, aggression, displacement, and primitivization are discussed. Yates accepts the definition of neurosis developed by Maier and by Mowrer: self-defeating behavior oriented toward no goal, yet compulsive in quality. The behavioral phenomena that reveal neuroses are said to be fixations, regressions, aggressions, or resignations. But we are not told the necessary or sufficient experimental conditions under which these dramatic phenomena emerge.

Anyone who has tried to train a rat in a **T** maze, using food reward for a correct response, and shock to the feet for an incorrect response, knows that there *is* a period of emotionality during early training, but that, thereafter, the rat, when the percentage of correct responses is high, looks like a hungry, well-motivated, happy rat, eager to get from his cage to the experimenter's hand, and thence to the start box. Evidently, merely going through conflict is not a condition for neurosis. The rat is reliable, unswerving in his choices. Is he neurotic? Should this be called subservient resignation? Or a happy adjustment to an inevitable event? Is the behavior constricted? Is it a fixation, an evidence of behavioral rigidity? The criteria for answering such questions are vague today. Even if we should suggest some specific tests for rigidity, they lack face validity. For example, we might examine *discrimination reversal* as a test of *rigidity*. Do subjects who have received reward for the correct response, and punishment for the incorrect response, find it harder to reverse when the contingencies are reversed, as compared with subjects trained with reward alone? Or, we might try a *transfer test,* introducing our subject to a new maze, or to a new jumping stand. Would the previously punished subject generalize more readily than one not so punished? And if he did, would he then be *less discriminating* and thus neurotic? Or, would the previously punished subject generalize poorly and hesitantly, thus being *too discriminating,* and thus neurotic, too? What are the criteria for behavioral *malfunction* as a consequence of the use of punishment? When instrumental responses are used as the indicator, we are, alas, left in doubt!

The most convincing demonstrations of neurotic disturbances stemming from the use of punishment are seen in Masserman's (Masserman & Pechtel, 1953) work with monkeys. But here the criterion for neurosis is *not* based on instrumental responding. Instead, it is based on emotionality expressed in consummatory acts and innate impulses. Masserman's monkeys were frightened by a toy snake while they were eating. Feeding inhibition, shifts in food preferences, odd sexual behavior, tics, long periods of crying, were observed. Here, the criteria have a face validity that is hard to reject. Clearly, punishment was a dangerous and disruptive behavioral influence in Masserman's experiments. Such findings are consonant with the Freudian position postulating the pervasive influences of traumatic experiences, permeating all phases of the affective existence of the individual, and persisting for long time periods.

To harmonize all of the considerations I have raised concerning the conditions leading to neurosis due to punishment is a formidable task. My guess at the moment is that neurotic disturbances arise often in those cases where *consummatory* behavior or *instinctive* behavior is punished, and punished under *nondiscriminatory* control. But this is merely a guess, and in order for it to be adequately tested, Masserman's interesting procedures would have to be repeated, using discriminative stimuli to signalize when it is safe and not safe for the monkey. Such experiments should be carried out if we are to explore adequately the possible effects of punishment on emotionality. Another possibility is that the number of rewarded behavior alternatives in an otherwise punishing situation will determine the emotional aftereffects of punishments. We have seen that Whiting and Mowrer (1943) gave their rats a rewarding alternative, and the resulting behavior was highly reliable. Their rats remained easy to handle and eager to enter the experimental situation. One guess is that increasing the number of behavioral alternatives leading to a consummatory response will, in a situation where only one behavior alternative is being punished, result in reliable behavior and the absence of neurotic emotional manifestations. However, I suspect that matters cannot be that simple. If our animal subject is punished for Response A, and the punishment quickly elicits Response B, and then Response B is quickly rewarded, we have the stimulus contingencies for the establishment of a masochistic habit. Reward follows punishment quickly. Perhaps the subject would then persist in performing the punished Response A? Such questions need to be worked out empirically, and the important parameters must be identified. We are certainly in no position today to specify the necessary or sufficient conditions for experimental neurosis.

I have, in this talk, decried the stultifying effects of legends concerning punishment. To some extent, my tone was reflective of bias, and so I overstated some conclusions. Perhaps now it would be prudent to soften my claims.[4] I must admit that all is not lost! Recently, I have noted a definite increase in good parametric studies of the effects of punishment on several kinds of behavior. For example, the pages of the *Journal of the Experimental Analysis of Behavior* have, in the last 5 years, become liberally sprinkled with reports of punishment experiments. This is a heartening development, and though it comes 20 years delayed, it is welcome.

Summary

I have covered a great deal of ground here, perhaps too much for the creation of a clear picture. The major points I have made are as follows: *First, the effectiveness of punishment as a controller of instrumental behavior varies with a wide variety of known parameters.* Some of these are: (*a*) intensity of the punishment stimulus, (*b*) whether the response being punished is an instrumental one or a consummatory one, (*c*) whether the response is instinctive or reflexive, (*d*) whether it was established originally by reward or by punishment, (*e*) whether or not the punishment is closely associated in time with the punished response, (*f*) the temporal arrangements of reward and punishment, (*g*) the strength of the response to be punished, (*h*) the familiarity of the subject with the punishment being used, (*i*) whether or not a reward alternative is offered during the behavior-suppression period induced by punishment, (*j*) whether a distinctive, incompatible avoidance response is strengthened by omission of punishment, (*k*) the age of the subject, and (*l*) the strain and species of the subject.

Second, I have tried to show the theoretical virtues of considering active and passive avoidance learning to be similar processes, and have shown the utility of a two-process learning theory. I have described some examples of the application of findings in active avoidance-learning experiments to the creation of new punishment experiments and to the reanalysis of approach-avoidance conflict experiments.

Third, I have questioned persisting legends concerning both the ineffectiveness of punishment as an

4. Presidential addresses sometimes produce statements that may be plausible at the moment, but on second thought may seem inappropriate. In contrast to my complaints about inadequate research on punishment and the nature of active and passive avoidance learning are Hebb's (1960) recent remarks in his APA Presidential Address. He said: "The choice is whether to prosecute the attack, or to go on with the endless and trivial elaboration of the same set of basic experiments (on pain avoidance for example); trivial because they have added nothing to knowledge for some time, though the early work was of great value [p. 740]."

agent for behavioral change as well as the inevitability of the neurotic outcome as a legacy of all punishment procedures.

Finally, I have indicated where new experimentation might be especially interesting or useful in furthering our understanding of the effects of punishment.

If there is one idea I would have you retain, it is this: Our laboratory knowledge of the effects of punishment on instrumental and emotional behavior is still rudimentary—much too rudimentary to make an intelligent choice among conflicting ideas about it. The polarized doctrines are probably inadequate and in error. The popularized Skinnerian position concerning the inadequacy of punishment in suppressing *instrumental* behavior is, if correct at all, only conditionally correct. The Freudian position, pointing to pain or trauma as an agent for the pervasive and long-lasting distortion of *affective* behavior is equally questionable, and only conditionally correct.

Happily, there is now growing attention being paid to the effects of punishment on behavior, and this new development will undoubtedly accelerate, because the complexity of our current knowledge, and the perplexity it engenders, are, I think, exciting and challenging.

References

Adler, N., & Hogan, J. A. Classical conditioning and punishment of an instinctive response in *Betta splendens. Anim. Behav.,* 1963, *11,* 351–354.

Appel, J. B. Punishment and shock intensity. *Science,* 1963, *141,* 528–529.

Azrin, N. H. Some effects of two intermittent schedules of immediate and non-immediate punishment. *J. Psychol.,* 1956, *42,* 8–21.

Azrin, N. H. Punishment and recovery during fixed-ratio performance. *J. exp. Anal. Behav.,* 1959, *2,* 301–305.

Azrin, N. H., & Holz, W. C. Punishment during fixed-interval reinforcement. *J. exp. Anal. Behav.,* 1961, *4,* 343–347.

Beach, F. A., Conovitz, M. W., Steinberg, F., & Goldstein, A. C. Experimental inhibition and restoration of mating behavior in male rats. *J. genet. Psychol.,* 1956, *89,* 165–181.

Brady, J. V. Ulcers in "executive monkeys." *Scient. American,* 1958, *199,* 95–103.

Brogden, W. J. Acquisition and extinction of conditioned avoidance response in dogs. *J. comp. physiol. Psychol.,* 1949, *42,* 296–302.

Brown, J. S. Gradients of approach and avoidance responses and their relation to level of motivation. *J. comp. physiol. Psychol.,* 1948, *41,* 450–465.

Bugelski, B. R. *The psychology of learning.* New York: Holt, 1956.

Carlsmith, J. M. The effect of punishment on avoidance responses: The use of different stimuli for training and punishment. Paper read at Eastern Psychological Association, Philadelphia, April 1961.

Church, R. M. The varied effects of punishment on behavior. *Psychol. Rev.,* 1963, *70,* 369–402.

Deese, J. *The psychology of learning.* New York: McGraw-Hill, 1958.

Dinsmoor, J. A. Punishment: II. An interpretation of empirical findings. *Psychol. Rev.,* 1955, *62,* 96–105.

Estes, W. K. An experimental study of punishment. *Psychol. Monogr.,* 1944, *57* (3, Whole No. 263).

Gantt, W. H. *Experimental basis for neurotic behavior.* New York: Hoeber, 1944.

Guthrie, E. R. *The psychology of learning.* New York: Harper, 1935. (Rev. ed., 1952)

Hebb, D. O. The American revolution. *Amer. Psychologist,* 1960, *15,* 735–745.

Hess, E. H. Imprinting. *Science,* 1959, *130,* 133–141. (a)

Hess, E. H. Two conditions limiting critical age for imprinting. *J. comp. physiol. Psychol.,* 1959, *52,* 515–518. (b)

Holz, W., & Azrin, N. H. Discriminative properties of punishment. *J. exp. Anal. Behav.,* 1961, *4,* 225–232.

Holz, W. C., & Azrin, N. H. Interactions between the discriminative and aversive properties of punishment. *J. exp. Anal. Behav.,* 1962, *5,* 229–234.

Hunt, J. McV., & Schlosberg, H. Behavior of rats in continuous conflict. *J. comp. physiol. Psychol.,* 1950, *43,* 351–357.

Hunter, W. S. Conditioning and extinction in the rat. *Brit. J. Psychol.,* 1935, *26,* 135–148.

Imada, M. The effects of punishment on avoidance behavior. *Jap. Psychol. Res.,* 1959, *1,* 27–38.

Kamin, L. J. The delay-of-punishment gradient. *J. comp. physiol. Psychol.,* 1959, *52,* 434–437.

Karsh, E. B. Effects of number of rewarded trials and intensity of punishment on running speed. *J. comp. physiol. Psychol.*, 1962, *55*, 44–51.

Karsh, E. B. Changes in intensity of punishment: Effect on runway behavior of rats. *Science*, 1963, *140*, 1084–1085.

Kovach, J. K., & Hess, E. H. Imprinting: Effects of painful stimulation upon the following response. *J. comp. physiol. Psychol.*, 1963, *56*, 461–464.

Lichtenstein, F. E. Studies of anxiety: I. The production of a feeding inhibition in dogs. *J. comp. physiol. Psychol.*, 1950, *43*, 16–29.

Maier, N. R. F. *Frustration: The study of behavior without a goal.* New York: McGraw-Hill, 1949.

Masserman, J. M. *Behavior and neurosis.* Chicago: Univer. Chicago Press, 1943.

Masserman, J. M., & Pechtel, C. Neurosis in monkeys: A preliminary report of experimental observations. *Ann. N.Y. Acad. Sci.*, 1953, *56*, 253–265.

Miller, N. E. Liberalization of basic S-R concepts: Extensions to conflict behavior, motivation, and social learning. In S. Koch (Ed.), *Psychology: A study of a science.* Vol. 2. *Sensory, perceptual, and physiological formulations.* New York: McGraw-Hill, 1959. Pp. 196–292.

Miller, N. E. Learning resistance to pain and fear: Effects of overlearning, exposure, and rewarded exposure in context. *J. exp. Psychol.*, 1960, *60*, 137–145.

Miller, N. E., & Murray, E. J. Displacement and conflict-learnable drive as a basis for the steeper gradient of approach than of avoidance. *J. exp. Psychol.*, 1952, *43*, 227–231.

Moltz, H., Rosenblum, L., & Halikas, N. Imprinting and level of anxiety. *J. comp. physiol. Psychol.*, 1959, *52*, 240–244.

Mowrer, O. H. *Learning theory and behavior.* New York: Wiley, 1960.

Murray, E. J., & Berkun, M. M. Displacement as a function of conflict. *J. abnorm. soc. Psychol.*, 1955, *51*, 47–56.

Schlosberg, H. Conditioned responses in the white rat. *J. genet. Psychol.*, 1934, *45*, 303–335.

Skinner, B. F. *The behavior of organisms.* New York: Appleton-Century, 1938.

Skinner, B. F. *Walden Two.* New York: Macmillan, 1948.

Skinner, B. F. *Science and human behavior.* New York: Macmillian, 1953.

Skinner, B. F. *Cumulative record.* New York: Appleton-Century-Crofts, 1961.

Solomon, R. L., & Brush, E. S. Experimentally derived conceptions of anxiety and aversion In M. R. Jones (Ed.), *Nebraska Symposium on Motivation: 1956.* Lincoln: Univer. Nebraska Press, 1956.

Storms, L. H., Boroczi, C., & Broen, W. E. Punishment inhibits on instrumental response in hooded rats. *Science*, 1962, *135*, 1133–1134.

Storms, L. H., Boroczi, C., & Broen, W. E. Effects of punishment as a function of strain of rat and duration of shock. *J. comp. physiol. Psychol.*, 1963, *56*, 1022–1026.

Thorndike, E. L. *Human learning.* New York: Appleton-Century-Crofts, 1931.

Tolman, E. C., Hall, C. S., & Bretnall, E. P. A disproof of the law of effect and a substitution of the laws of emphasis, motivation, and disruption. *J. exp. Psychol.*, 1932, *15*, 601–614.

Turner, L. H., & Solomon, R. L. Human traumatic avoidance learning: Theory and experiments on the operant-respondent distinction and failures to learn. *Psychol. Monogr.*, 1962, *76*, (40, Whole No. 559).

Walters, G. C., & Rogers, J. V. Aversive stimulation of the rat: Long term effects on subsequent behavior. *Science*, 1963, *142*, 70–71.

Warden, C. J., & Aylesworth, M. The relative value of reward and punishment in the formation of a visual discrimination habit in the white rat. *J. comp. Psychol.*, 1927, *7*, 117–127.

Wendt, G. R. An interpretation of inhibition of conditioned reflexes as competition between reaction systems. *Psychol. Rev.*, 1936, *43*, 258–281.

Whiting, J. W. M., & Mowrer, O. H. Habit progression and regression—a laboratory study of some factors relevant to human socialization. *J. comp. Psychol.*, 1943, *36*, 229–253.

Woodworth, R. S., & Schlosberg, H. *Experimental psychology.* New York: Holt, 1954.

Yates, A. J. *Frustration and conflict.* New York: Wiley, 1962.

some recent studies of conflict behavior and drugs[1]

neal e. miller
rockefeller university

Clinical studies of mental disease indicate the extreme importance of fear and conflict, two factors which usually are closely interrelated. Studies of men in combat show clearly that practically all of the common symptoms of neuroses, and even psychoses, can be produced by intense fear and conflict. Similarly, experimental studies on animals show that fear and conflict can produce behavioral disturbances, and even psychosomatic symptoms such as stomach acidity, ulcers, cardiac symptoms, and increased susceptibility to infection. Even in normal life, fear and conflict contribute significantly to human physical and mental fatigue.

1. Work on this paper and on studies cited in it was supported by Grants M 647 and MY 2949 from the National Institute of Mental Health, United States Public Health Service. Reprinted from *American Psychologist*, 1961, Vol. 16, pp. 12–24. Copyright 1961 by the American Psychological Association, and reproduced by permission.

My earlier work on conflict behavior (Miller, 1944, 1959) was closely integrated by theory. I started with principles which had been abstracted from results of experiments in the simplified conditioning situation, and made a few additional assumptions. First, very simple deductions from these principles were tested in very simple experimental situations. Then, step by step, attempts were made to apply the joint action of a number of principles to more complex situations with additional experimental checks at each successive stage of development. The studies I am talking about here are related to the same theory; but they also attempt to investigate new variables which ultimately should be incorporated into the theory, after we have enough data to formulate reasonably probable principles. Since I am investigating a variety of such variables, the studies are somewhat heterogeneous.

In both the former work and these studies, I have benefited greatly by interaction with my students. The work I report here is that of the entire group in my laboratory.[2] It continues to be a great pleasure to work

2. In addition to those mentioned in the text, I want to acknowledge the help on various experiments of K. Gustav Ogren and Charles W. Alkire, who helped in the construction of the apparatus; Arlo K. Myers, Gordon H. Bower, who helped in a supervisory capacity; and the following who helped with the running of experimental animals: Nariyuki Agarie, Edward E. Etheridge, Elizabeth S. Jackson, Libby Michel, Phyllis Miller, Roberta Pritzker, Gerald Schwartz, Gail E. Tidd, Russell Tousley, Sylvia A. Wagner, and Hanna B. Weston.

with such wonderful groups of students and collaborators.

Effects of Sodium Amytal on Conflict

First, I shall describe some studies of effects of drugs on fear and conflict done in collaboration with Herbert Barry, III. One of our purposes is to study how performance in a number of experimental situations which presumably measure fear is changed by various drugs which presumably affect fear. We want to see whether fear behaves as a single unitary variable, or whether certain drugs have more effect on the crouching freezing pattern, while others have more effect on startle and avoidance responses, or whether the results are still more complex (Miller & Barry, 1960).

In the course of this work, we have devised a number of techniques for getting repeated measures of conflict behavior, so that each animal can be used as his own control, and so that a variety of drugs can be tested with the same group of animals.

Another of our purposes (which is the basis of the work to be exemplified here) is to make analytical studies of the behavioral effects of certain drugs which are definitely known to have interesting effects on human behavior. I shall illustrate our work by presenting some results of an analytical series of experimental studies still in progress on one of the drugs with interesting clinical effects, amobarbital sodium, commonly called sodium amytal. I believe that in a modest and incomplete way the studies of this drug illustrate a type of work which is needed on a variety of selected drugs, each of which has well-established, but different, psychological effects on the human subject.

A decade ago, John Dollard and I (1950) advanced the hypothesis that the therapeutic effects of this drug, which are especially notable in combat neuroses, are produced by reducing the avoidance component of an approach-avoidance conflict more than the approach one. In fairly extensive exploratory work on rats, Bailey and I (1952) were unable to demonstrate such an effect, but we did readily get the fear-reducing effect in an experiment on cats. In the current experiments on rats under the supervision of Barry, this drug has produced unusually consistent effects in ameliorating approach-avoidance conflict. The unexplained discrepancy with the early exploratory results on rats is puzzling and indicates the danger of generalizing too widely from observations of drug effects in a single experimental situation.

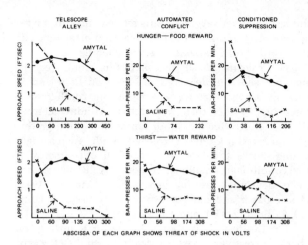

Fig. 1

Effects of an intraperitoneal injection of 20 mg/kg of amobarbital sodium (sodium amytal) administered to Sprague-Dawley albino rats 20 minutes before testing in six experiments on fear and conflict by different techniques described in the text.

Figure 1 shows the effects of an intraperitoneal injection of 20 mg/kg of amobarbital sodium, commonly called sodium amytal, on a variety of experimental tests of fear and conflict in the albino rat. Let me briefly describe the tests.

In the *telescope alley* test, on the first trial, the rats run 1 foot to the reward, where they never receive electric shock. (Therefore this trial is labeled "0" on the ordinate which indicates threat of shock.) On each successive trial, the rats are required to run an additional foot and occasionally receive the shocks at the goal which, when they occur, are stronger the longer the distance to the goal. Incidentally, the shocks in all of our experiments are given through a series resistance of approximately 200,000 ohms, which accounts for the high voltages. The current is 60 cycle ac.

In this test the cues for danger are primarily proprioceptive and visual. The response, which is running, involves considerable movement and is rewarded every trial.

In the *automated conflict* test, the rats press a bar for a reward on a variable interval schedule. The first 2 minutes are safe, but after that, an increasingly loud tone signals unpredictable shocks on the bar which, when they occur, are increasingly strong the louder the tone. For the last 2 minutes, the tone and shock are turned off. The cues for danger are primarily auditory, the test chamber severely limits movement, and the response of standing on the hind legs and pressing a bar is rewarded on a variable interval schedule.

The *conditioned suppression* test is similar except that the shock is delivered via the grid floor and is inescapable, so that we are measuring conflict with "freezing," rather than with active withdrawal from the bar. Except for the minor innovation of the gradually increasing tone correlated with increasingly strong shocks, this last test is identical, of course, with the conditioned emotional response (CER) which has been developed out of Estes and Skinner's (1941) classic paper and has been extensively used by Hunt (1956), Brady (1956), and others.

On the test trials shown in Figure 1, no electric shocks were given, so we are dealing with the effects of fear, rather than of pain plus fear. In order to control for any effects specific to the approach drive, animals in the experiments represented in the top row were motivated by hunger and rewarded by food, while those in the bottom row were motivated by thirst and rewarded by water.

It can be seen that the results under all of these various conditions were highly similar. Looking at the beginning of each curve, which represents performance with little or no fear, it can be seen that, in general, the amytal reduced performance below the placebo level. This part of the test acts as a control to show that the effects of the amytal were not simply to produce an increase in the approach drive, or to act as a general stimulant. As the rats encountered cues to which increasingly strong fear had been conditioned, the performance following placebo was markedly reduced. But the performance under sodium amytal was not affected nearly as much by the fear-inducing cues. Thus, amytal improved the performance under fear.

The fact that so similar results appear in tests involving different cues, different responses, and different drives, makes it unlikely that the effects are specific to the peculiarities of a certain testing situation. The remarkable agreement in the results of the six different experiments makes it clear that sodium amytal definitely reduced the relative strength of fear in our different conflict situations.

Having experimentally demonstrated a striking effect on rats consonant with clinical observations on people, the next step is to determine how this effect is produced. More precise knowledge of the detailed behavioral effects of this drug is needed in order to know

under what circumstances a fear-reducing effect can be expected to occur. It is also needed as a basis for relating behavioral effects to results secured with powerful new neurophysiological and biochemical techniques for studying the action of drugs on different parts of the brain.

PRIMACY OF HABIT VERSUS DIRECT
ACTION ON FEAR
In all of the preceding experiments, the amytal improved performance by reducing the relative strength of the fear-motivated habit. How was this effect achieved: directly by a selective action on the brain mechanisms involved in fear, or indirectly by other means? For example, in all of these experiments, as well as in all other experiments that I know of on the effects of drugs on conflict, the habit of approach was established first, and the habit of avoidance second. Perhaps the drug reduced the fear-motivated avoidance not because it has a selective effect on certain fear centers, but rather because it has a selective effect on the more recently established habit.

Perhaps there is something special about the first habit to be established in any situation that makes it more resistant to drug effects—and also to other interventions. In their trail blazing papers on primary inhibition, Szwejkowska (1959) and Konorski and Szwejkowska (1952) have shown that whether a cue is first presented in an excitatory or inhibitory role makes a great deal of difference in the ease of subsequent excitatory or inhibitory conditioning, even after several reversals of the role. Perhaps primacy is more important than we have realized. How can we test for its effects in our experiments on drugs?

In the simplest of a series of experiments on this problem, we trained an animal first to go right in a **T** maze and then to go to the left. After the second habit was fairly well established, we tested with injections of drug or saline. The sodium amytal produced an increase in errors which would be consistent with the primacy hypothesis. Since the errors did not reliably exceed the 50% that would be expected by chance, we were unable to discriminate a differential resistance of the first-established habit to the drug from a mere increase in random behavior.

In another experiment, we tried establishing the fear of the tone in a Skinner box first before we trained the animal to press a bar to secure food there. In the hope of attaching the fear specifically to the tone, and

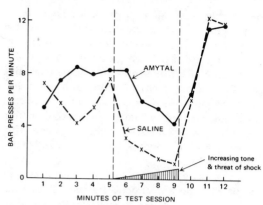

Fig. 2

In the conditioned suppression test, sodium amytal affects the habit motivated by fear rather than the habit established most recently. (The rats had learned to fear the tone before they learned to press the bar.)

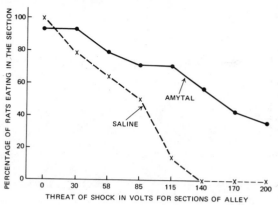

Fig. 3

In the shuttle alley, sodium amytal reduces the strength of the originally learned habit of avoiding electric shock associated with a flashing light more than it does that of the subsequently learned habit of advancing to eat pellets of food found in cups spaced at 1-foot intervals.

avoiding too much fear of the whole situation, we started out with weak shocks first and gradually increased them after the animal had a chance to learn the discrimination. This procedure apparently was reasonably successful, because it was not extraordinarily difficult subsequently to train the animals to eat and then to press the bar during silent periods in the Skinner box. Then we tested for the effects of sodium amytal. If this drug primarily affects fear, results should be similar to our previous ones, but if it primarily affects the most recent habit, our results should be completely reversed.

Figure 2 shows the results. You can see that the results were similar to our previous ones; the sodium amytal had the greater effect on fear, even though it was the first-established habit. In this experiment we may have had some residual fear of the general testing situation. Such fear would account for the low initial rate of bar pressing and for the fact that the amytal had some beneficial effect on performance even before the fear-evoking tone was sounded.

In another experiment on the same topic, we used a technique analogous to our telescope alley. We used a shuttle alley 8 feet long with a light bulb at either end. Five seconds after the light at one end started flashing, an electric shock was delivered through the sections of the grid floor. This shock was strongest at the lighted end and progressively weaker in farther sections, with

the one at the opposite end having no shock. In this way, we trained the rats to shuttle from one end of the alley to the other, always staying away from the flashing light. After they had learned this, we gave the hungry rats trials of being started at alternate ends of the darkened alley, and finding food pellets in tiny cups in the center of each 1-foot section. Then they were given trials with the light flickering at the far end from the start. On these trials shocks occurred on the grid at unpredictable times, being stronger, as before, nearer to the flashing light. The rat was taken out after he had been in the alley 2 minutes, or had taken the pellet in the section nearest the flashing light.

Following this training, the animals were given the drug and placebo tests. During these tests trials, no shock was actually given. The results are presented in Figure 3. It can be seen that under amytal, the animals approached farther toward the flashing light into sections with a higher threat of shock than they did after a placebo. Since the habit of approaching was established after the fear of the sections near the flashing light, we would expect exactly the *opposite* results if the main effect of the amytal had been to weaken the most recently established habit.

The results of these two different experiments indicate that the amytal did not produce its fear-reducing effects merely by weakening the more recently established habit.

Studies of Conflict Behavior and Drugs

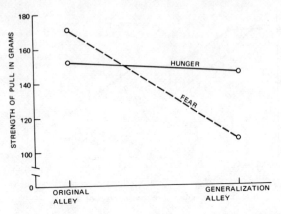

Fig. 4

The gradient of stimulus generalization of avoidance motivated by fear contrasted with that of approach motivated by hunger. (The strength of pull of each rat was measured twice in the same alley in which he was originally trained and twice in a different alley, with the sequence of testing balanced.) (From Murray & Miller, 1952)

STIMULUS CHANGE VERSUS DIRECT ACTION ON FEAR MECHANISM

As background for the next experiment, I shall remind you of some older results which extend the notion that the gradient of avoidance is steeper than that of approach from the original gradients in space, to gradients of stimulus generalization. Edward Murray and I (1952) trained one group of hungry rats, which wore harnesses attached to a string, to run down a wide white alley to secure food at the goal. We trained another similar group to run down the same alley to avoid electric shock by reaching an island of safety at the goal. Two more groups were similarly trained in a narrow black alley. Then half of each group was tested in the *same* alley in which they had been trained, and the other half was tested in the *other* alley for stimulus generalization. The rats were temporarily restrained halfway down the alley while their strength of pull was measured. You can see by Figure 4 that the gradient of stimulus generalization of avoidance was steeper and crossed that of approach. This means that a change in the stimulus situation weakens tendencies to avoid more than those to approach.

Doris Kraeling and I (Miller & Kraeling, 1952) tested the application of this principle to a conflict situation by training one group of hungry rats to run down the wide white alley, and another group to run down the narrow black alley to get food. Then, both groups were given increasingly strong shocks at the goal until the avoidance prevented them from reaching it. After this, one-third of each group was given test trials in the same alley, one-third in a somewhat different grey alley of intermediate width, and one-third in the opposite alley. As you can see from Figure 5, more of the rats reached the goal when tested in the different alleys than when tested in the same one. The change in cues had altered the balance of conflict in favor of approaching.

But this is exactly the same kind of effect that was produced by the sodium amytal. Perhaps this drug does not have a direct effect specific to the fear mechanism, but only affects fear indirectly by changing the stimulus situation. How can we test for this?

To test for this possibility, we performed another experiment in which we gave half of the animals their avoidance training in the normal state, as is customarily done, but gave the other half their avoidance training under the influence of the drug. Then half of each of these two groups was tested following isotonic saline, and the other half following drug injection. This experiment was performed in the telescope alley.

The 2 × 2 design and results are summarized in Table 1. Adding up the rows shows the effect of having

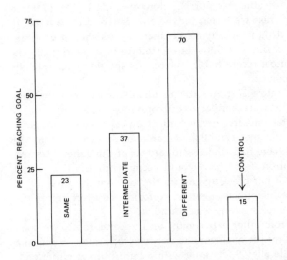

Fig. 5

Effects of stimulus generalization on an approach-avoidance conflict. More rats reached the goal when tested in a different alley than when tested in the one in which the approach and avoidance tendencies were originally established. (From Miller & Kraeling, 1952)

TABLE 1

Average Speed of Approach in the Last 6 Inches of the Telescope Alley during a Series of Tests for Fear without Shocks

Training	Testing		
	Amytal	Saline	Sum
Amytal	1.00	.82	1.82
Saline	1.14	.54	1.68
Sum	2.14	1.36	3.50

Note. Trials in which the rat failed to reach the goal are scored as zero. Speed of approach is in feet per second.

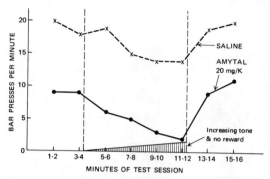

Fig. 6
Sodium amytal does not seem to reduce the decrement produced by a gradually increasing tone which has always been associated with nonreward in a Skinner box.

had the amytal during training. The effect is in the direction of fear-reduction, but is not reliable. Adding up the columns shows the effect of amytal during testing. The difference is larger and is statistically reliable. The superior performance during amytal shows that the drug has reduced fear even when any effects of stimulus change are completely balanced out. Finally, computing the interaction by comparing the two diagonals suggests that stimulus change did reduce fear somewhat in the groups that were changed, but the difference is not statistically reliable.

POSSIBLE EFFECTS OF AMYTAL ON DISCRIMINATION

Although the sodium amytal does not produce its apparently fear-reducing effect primarily by changing the stimulus situation, it is possible that it has another effect on cues. Perhaps it interferes in some way with the ability of the rat to discriminate the cues of danger. For example, it might make him less perceptive of presence or absence of the tone which signals presence or absence of the possibility of electric shocks in the Skinner box. In this case the behavior would be changed toward the average of that in the safe and dangerous conditions. Compared with the sober state, performance would be depressed then in the safe and improved in the dangerous conditions, which is exactly what we observed. The notion that this drug affects the subject's ability to discriminate is made plausible by the fact that one of its main effects is on the reticular activating system which is known to affect the perception of cues (Magoun, 1958). How can we check this possibility?

To test for this possibility, we trained a new group of rats in a different discrimination in the same apparatus. Instead of signaling shock, the same tone signaled that the bar no longer delivered food. After the rats had learned the discrimination which reduced their rate to approximately the same level as the shock did, we gave them tests with sodium amytal and other drugs.

If this different discrimination is not affected by the drug, it will show that the drug does not destroy the animal's ability to react discriminatively to the tone. If, on the other hand, we secure the same results as with fear, there will be two possibilities: (a) the drug may have disrupted the discrimination, or (b) the drug may have produced a direct reduction in the frustrational inhibition, presumably produced by the nonrewarded trials, in the same way that it is assumed to reduce the fear produced by the electric shocks.

Figure 6 shows that the amytal seemed to leave the discrimination relatively unaffected. The drug certainly did not produce the kind of improvement during the tone that we have seen in the experiments in which the tone was a cue for fear. These results seem to rule out the possibility that amytal destroys the rat's ability to perceive the dangerous cue itself. All of the differences on this graph are highly reliable. Perhaps the greater depressing effect of the drug during the nontone intervals in this experiment is due to the fact that there was no general fear of the experimental situation for it to relieve.

On thinking over this experiment, however, another possibility occurred to us. You will note that the onset of the tone does not produce an immediate large decrease in the rate. The difference seems to build up during the 8-minute interval during which

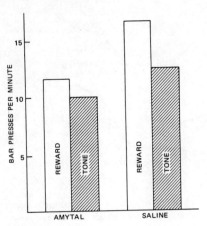

Fig. 7
Results of a test in which a 1-minute tone is the cue for non-reward, while a 1-minute silent period is the cue for a variable interval schedule averaging one reward a minute. Under these most stringent conditions in the Skinner box, the drug appears to reduce but does not eliminate the discrimination.

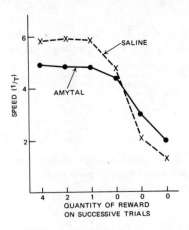

Fig. 8
In the frustration alley, amytal produces results similar to those in previous tests with fear (depicted in Figure 1), and different from those in the Skinner box (as depicted in Figures 6 and 7).

the loudness of the tone increases. Perhaps the nice dip in the curves of Figure 6 does not represent a discrimination at all, but merely the cumulative effects of the nonreinforced bar presses during the test period with tone.

In order to check on this possibility, we retrained the animals with the tone on at full intensity for 1-minute intervals, alternating with 1-minute silent intervals during which the customary schedule of reward was resumed. Since this schedule of reward was a 1-minute variable interval one, the reward would not be delivered during approximately half of the positive silent intervals. Therefore, one would not expect much extinction to occur during any given 1-minute non-rewarded negative interval with tone. Any difference between the tones and the silent periods would be due primarily to the learned discrimination that reward never occurs during the tone, but sometimes occurs during the silent period.

After the animals had learned this discrimination, each one was tested in a balanced order for effects of injections of sodium amytal versus control solutions. The results are presented in Figure 7. It can be seen that the results are similar to those of Figure 6 and different from those in our previous experiments in which the same cue is used for fear instead of for nonreward. Although the sodium amytal seems to have

reduced the discrimination, the difference between the rewarded silent period and the nonrewarded tone is still reliable. Furthermore, the difference between the experimental and the control groups is not reversed as it was when the response decrement was produced by fear instead of by nonreward.

We also ran a similar type of test in the alley situation. Instead of giving stronger shocks for trials with longer runs as we did in the telescope alley tests, we reduced the quantity of reward which was four pellets for the first trial of running the 1-foot length, two for the second trial of running the 2-foot length, one for the third trial, and zero for the fourth, fifth, and sixth trials. (Half of the animals had the opposite sequence of the large rewards for the long runs and the small ones for the short ones.) We called this the *frustration alley* test.

Figure 8 shows the results of this experiment. In this case you can see that the amytal speeded up running on the nonrewarded trials much as it did on the fear trials in Figure 1. Apparently, the amytal either counteracted the effects of frustration, or reduced the discriminability of the cues indicating that the trial was going to be nonrewarded.

This experiment and the immediately preceding two were designed to test the same thing, namely, the effects of amytal on the rat's ability to discriminate the cues used in preceding experiments on fear. The fact that the experiments in the Skinner box and in the alley yielded opposite results poses a dilemma. Are the effects related to possible differences in the degree to which the discriminations were learned, to the different cues used (distance versus tone), to the different types of responses required (running versus balancing on the hind legs and pressing a bar), to the different schedules of reinforcement (100% for the best distances in the alley and a 1-minute variable interval schedule, involving nonrewarded bar presses even without the tone in the Skinner box), or to yet other unsuspected differences between the two situations? We hope to perform soon more experiments to try to find out. In the meantime, we cannot be sure exactly what mixture of effects sodium amytal has.

The possibility that drugs may affect the subject's discriminative reaction to cues, makes it harder to interpret the results of complex experiments in which the same subjects are trained in a variety of different habits under the discriminative control of different stimuli, although such procedures also have their legitimate uses. We certainly shall want to proceed with our plan to test amytal (and the rest of our drugs) in simplified situations in which one group is trained only to approach motivated by hunger and another group is trained only to avoid motivated by fear, using the strength-of-pull technique (or possibly a strength-of-push technique) to measure the effects of the drug separately on each of these two tendencies acting singly.

We plan also to measure drug effects in a simple test of experimental extinction. Finally, dose-response studies are essential; they may help us better to analyze the effects of this drug.

TRANSFER OF FEAR-REDUCTION FROM DRUGGED TO SOBER STATE

If a drug produces a differential reduction in fear, by any one of a number of mechanisms, it may have some therapeutic usefulness as a chronic medication for people who need to have all of their fears reduced somewhat, or may help to tide a person over a transient situation which is producing too much general anxiety.

In many cases, however, it is necessary to reduce a specific unrealistic fear which is far too strong without producing an equivalent reduction in realistic fears, such as those of reckless driving. Since we cannot

expect any drug to have such a discriminative action tailored to the needs of the culture at a given moment in history, the patient can only be helped by retraining, or, in other words, psychotherapy. Even here, a temporary use of the drug might theoretically be useful in order to help the person to become able to practice the responses he needs to learn. But as John Dollard and I (1950) pointed out, such new learning under the influence of the drug will not be useful unless it ultimately can be transferred to the normal nondrugged state. Perhaps drugs differ in this significant aspect of their effectiveness. How can we test for this?

In one of the few studies on this problem, Hunt (1956) recently found that experimental extinction of fear under chlorpromazine did not transfer effectively to the normal state. But human patients usually are not merely extinguished on their fears; they also are rewarded for performing the correct response in spite of fear. Thus the approach-avoidance conflict situation seemed to me more relevant than simple experimental extinction. It also seemed more likely to show a positive transfer effect because the reward would be expected to add counterconditioning to the extinction of fear.

Hungry albino rats were trained to press a bar with food as a reward on a 100% schedule. Then the bar was electrified for unpredictable brief periods approximately half of the time. The strength of these shocks was increased until such a strong conflict was established that the rats would not press the bar.

After this conflict had been set up, the rats were given a retraining session in the apparatus with the shock turned off. During this session half of them had received a dose of amytal, and other half a placebo injection. Figure 9 shows the results. You can see that during the extinction session, labeled "Drug Test," more of the amytal than the control animals resumed pressing the bar. On another day, the rats were given post-drug tests to see whether the superiority during retraining with drug transferred to the normal nondrugged state. You can see that it did not. But the apparent inferiority of the drug group is not statistically reliable.

Figure 10 shows the results of a similar experiment with 2 mg/kg of chlorpromazine. Although the initial fear-reducing effects with this drug do not seem to be as striking as those with sodium amytal, there is less loss with transfer to the normal state. The superiority

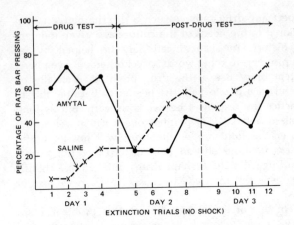

Fig. 9

The therapeutic effects of sodium amytal fail to transfer from the drugged to the nondrugged condition.

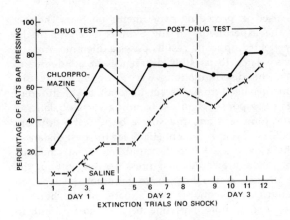

Fig. 10

While chlorpromazine (2 mg/kg intraperitoneally 45 minutes before the test) produces less initial improvement than does sodium amytal, more of the gain seems to persist during subsequent tests without drugs.

of the chlorpromazine group on the post-drug test approaches statistical reliability. We are performing dose-response studies essential to establish more definitely the apparent difference in transfer of the effects of these two drugs. If indeed there is less decrement in the transfer of training from the drugged to the normal state with chlorpromazine, this difference may be related to the fact that this drug has less extensive effects on the reticular formation than does sodium amytal.

Meanwhile, these experiments clearly show that it is unsafe to assume that therapeutic transfer will occur from the drugged to the nondrugged state. It is also unsafe to assume that the drug which produces the greatest effect on immediate performance will have the greatest ultimate effect on learning transferred to the normal state. Perhaps some drugs will be discovered which are markedly superior in this crucial respect. Such a drug could make a major contribution to psychotherapy.

Need for Basic Studies to Establish a Science of Psychopharmacology

The work I have just described is a progress report rather than a completed program. By now it should be clear that an adequate study of even certain aspects of the behavioral effects of a single drug is a major project. Nevertheless, I believe it is necessary for us to take the time to be analytical and precise in determining the exact behavioral effects of a variety of drugs already known in a general way to have interesting clinical ef-

fects. Then we should advance to the further step of trying to find lawful relationships between these behavioral effects and the action of the drug on different parts of the brain as determined by techniques of neurophysiology, biochemistry, and biophysics. Out of such work may come a better understanding of how the brain functions to control behavior. Out of such work may emerge a basic science of psychopharmacology. As I have said before, the principles of such a basic science should eventually supply a rational basis for practical applications to mental health in the same way that organic chemistry provides a rational basis for the synthesis of new compounds.

Can Conflict Be Specific to a Drive or to an Anticipatory Goal Response?

In addition to the work on the effects of drugs, my students and I have been doing a number of other experiments on conflict behavior. One of these experiments stems from the attempt to apply learning theory to problems of neuroses and psychotherapy (Dollard & Miller, 1950). We have assumed that fear and avoidance can be specifically attached to the cues involved in certain drives, and to the thoughts aroused by specific drives. Cheng Fayu and I tested this assumption in a situation in which approach responses were punished if motivated by one drive, but not if motivated by a different one. The experiment was designed to determine the role of cues from the drive, and also from distinctive anticipatory goal responses to the drive.

Rats were trained to run down a short alley, jump over a low hurdle, land on a platform recording their response, and then pass under a curtain which hid the reward in the goal box. On some days they were run only when hungry and on others only when thirsty. Half of the animals were given a series of progressively increasing shocks only on trials when they were hungry, the other half only when thirsty.

The foregoing part of the design was to determine the role of drive; the following part was to determine that of distinctive anticipatory goal responses. Half of each of these groups found dry food in the goal box on days when they were hungry and only water in the goal box on days when they were thirsty. For these animals, the distinctive goal responses of chewing or lapping would be expected to become anticipatory, and hence to provide distinctive cues in addition to those involved in the drive itself. According to our theory, anticipatory goal responses should serve primitive cue-producing functions similar to the much more sophisticated responses of labeling involved in human speech and thought (Miller, 1935).

The other half of each of these groups found sugar water in the same identical drinking spout on both days, and hence performed exactly the same goal response to either hunger or thirst. These animals were satiated on pure sugar before runs on thirst days. They would not be expected to be helped by cues from distinctive anticipatory goal responses.

The results are presented in Figure 11. The dotted lines in the graph show that the animals which were running to drink sugar water from the spout eventually learned not to run on the days when they were motivated by the dangerous drive, but to run when they were motivated by the acceptable drive. It should be noted that this experiment is superior to most others which have demonstrated reasonably rapid learning of a good discrimination between drives, in that the learning to respond to the cues from the drive is not confounded with learning to go to different places, or to get different goal objects which elicit different anticipatory goal responses.

The solid lines in the curve show the behavior of animals which were trained in the same way except that they received dry food when hungry and water when thirsty. It can be seen that these rats, which had the benefit of cues from distinctive anticipatory goal

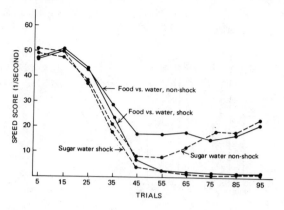

Fig. 11

In a conflict situation, the avoidance of exactly the same place can be made dependent upon the drive motivating approach. The discrimination is learned more quickly when the consummatory responses, and hence presumably the anticipatory goal responses, are made more distinctive.

responses, learned the discrimination faster. The difference is highly reliable. This is exactly what would be predicted from the assumption that Dollard and I have made that distinctive cue-producing responses facilitate the learning and performance of discriminative behavior. According to us it is the loss of these cue-producing responses that makes behavior following repression less adaptive (Dollard & Miller, 1950).

Does Fear Become Consolidated with Time?

In lay and clinical experience there are two schools of thought which make different assumptions concerning the setting or forgetting of fear after a traumatic event. One school of thought recommends that a person suffering a fear-inducing accident when practicing an activity, such as flying an airplane or riding a horse, should go back to it immediately before the fear has a chance to become set. The opposite school of thought recommends an immediate rest to allow the fear to subside. Of course, these human examples may be complicated by the effects of verbal rehearsal during the intervening intervals. Nevertheless, the notion has been advanced by a number of different people that a basic physiological process of consolidation occurs shortly after a new learning experience (Coons & Miller, 1960; Hebb, 1949). Thus it seemed worthwhile to Edgar Coons, James Faust, and me to investigate this problem with animals.

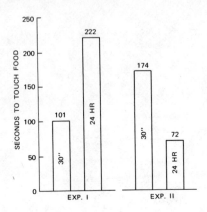

Fig. 12
Whether or not a 24-hour interval produces consolidation or forgetting of fear depends upon details of the experimental situation, which were designed to affect the degree to which the interval of time restored or altered the pattern of cues present when the traumatic shock was received.

In the first experiment, hungry rats received 30 trials at the rate of 5 a day running down an elevated strip to food. Then they were divided into two matched groups. On the first trial of the next day, upon touching the food, each rat received a traumatic electric shock at the goal and then was immediately removed to its home cage. Thirty seconds later the rats in the first group were returned to the runway for a test, while those in the second group were tested 24 hours later. The time required to touch food was recorded with a 5-minute maximum limit. It can be seen from the left-hand side of Figure 12 that the rats tested 24 hours later required twice as long to go back to touch the food as did those tested 30 seconds afterwards. Since the difference is highly reliable, we may conclude that the relative strength of avoidance, and hence presumably of fear, increased during the 24-hour interval immediately following the strong electric shock.

We have considered a number of hypotheses to explain these results. One is that the fear is consolidated during the interval. Another is that the excitement produced by the electric shock has a dynamogenic effect that increases the rat's tendency to run up to the goal immediately afterwards. Another is that under the particular conditions of this experiment, the stimulus conditions for the 30-second group differed more than did those for the 24-hour group from the

ones immediately preceding the strong shock. Then it follows that the greater stimulus change for the 30-second group should produce a greater decrement in avoidance than in approach, so that this group would reach the goal sooner.

To describe this stimulus-change hypothesis in more detail, let us note that, when the animals received their shock, it was the first trial of the day, and they had not received any immediately preceding shock. For these animals tested 24 hours later, it was again the first trial of the day, and as before, they had not received any immediately preceding shock. But for the 30-second group the conditions were different in that it was the second trial of the day and they had just received an electric shock. Assuming that some sort of after-effects from the immediately preceding trial and/or shock persist, these would be expected to change the stimulus situation. These changes should produce a greater decrement in the avoidance motivated by fear than in the approach motivated by hunger. Therefore, these animals should show relatively less avoidance.

How can we test this hypothesis? Suppose we change the conditions so that the two factors—an immediately preceding trial and an immediately preceding shock—make the training and test conditions more similar for the 30-second group instead of for the 24-hour one. Then, we will expect the direction of the difference of the two groups to be reversed. The other two hypotheses would not predict such a reversal.

To test this prediction, we ran additional animals in another experiment exactly similar to the foregoing one, except that, instead of giving them their shock in the runway on the first trial of the day, we gave it to them on the third trial. We also gave them a shock in a quite different apparatus 30 seconds before their shock trial in the alley. When these animals were being trained to avoid the goal by being shocked there, they had the stimulus aftereffects of an immediately preceding trial and shock. But when tested 24 hours later, they were in a somewhat different stimulus context of no immediately preceding trials and no immediately preceding shock. Therefore, we would expect their avoidance to be relatively weaker on this test 24 hours later, so that the results would be completely opposite to those of the preceding experiment.

The right-hand side of Figure 12 shows the results of the second experiment. It can be seen that the results are opposite to those in the first experiment. The difference is highly reliable (p < .01). Instead of being consolidated with time, the relative strength of fear was reduced in the second experiment. The stimulus-change hypothesis was confirmed. Under the conditions of these experiments, differences in the stimulus traces were shown to be more important than any setting or forgetting of fear with time.

The results of these two experiments impress us with the importance of trying to analyze the exact stimulus conditions under which the fear was originally established and those under which it is tested.

Learning Resistance to Stress

The final experiments I shall describe have to do with learning resistance to pain and fear in an approach-avoidance conflict situation. Can resistance to stressful situations be learned? If such learning is possible, what are the laws determining its effectiveness and generality?

In one experiment on this topic, which is reported in more detail elsewhere (Miller, 1960), albino rats were trained to run down an alley for food. Their criterion task was to continue running in spite of 400-volt electric shocks administered through a 250,000-ohm series resistance for .1 second immediately after they reached the goal. Some of these animals were introduced to the shock suddenly, others were given special training to resist the shock by receiving first mild shocks at the goal, followed by trials with shocks of gradually increasing strength.

The results are presented in Figure 13. You can see that the animals that had been habituated to gradually increasing shocks in the alley continued to run much faster than those in the sudden groups which had not received the same type of training.

Was the superior performance of the gradually habituated group a general effect of mere exposure to the shocks, or, as our theoretical analysis demanded, was it an effect dependent upon specific rewarded training in the criterion situation? This was tested by giving another group the same gradual habituation to the same shocks administered at a different time of day in a distinctive box outside of the alley. You can see that this group was not appreciably helped. Apparently, mere exposure to tough treatments will not necessarily improve resistance to stress in a different criterion situation.

As a control for the effect of additional training trials in the alley, we ran one group which was sud-

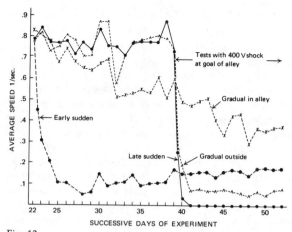

Fig. 13
Hungry rats may be trained to resist stress by continuing to run down an alley to a goal where they receive both food and electric shock. Under these conditions, previous overlearning of the habit of running to food decreases, rather than increases, resistance to stress. (From Miller, 1960)

denly exposed to 400-volt shocks at the goal on the same trial that the gradual group received its first mild shocks, and we ran another group which was suddenly exposed to the 400-volt shocks at the same time that the gradual group reached the level of 400 volts. As you have already seen, the performance of both of these groups was poorer than that of the rats receiving the gradually increasing shocks at the goal of the alley. But looking at the curves for these two groups immediately after the sudden shocks were introduced, we can see a surprising fact. The speed of the group shocked late in training falls off much more rapidly than that of the one shocked early in training. This difference, which is reliable at the .02 level of confidence, confirms earlier suggestive results in our laboratory by Eileen Karsh. It is directly contrary to the widely-held notion that over-training will increase resistance to stress.

The results of the foregoing experiment suggest that it should be feasible and profitable to analyze further at both the animal and human level, the laws governing the learning of resistance to stresses, such as pain, fear, fatigue, frustration, noise, nausea, and extremes of temperature.

Two of my colleagues, David Williams and Herbert Barry, III, have already performed an interesting experiment providing behavioral evidence for the counterconditioning of fear. Rats were trained on a variable interval schedule of food reward. On exactly the same variable interval schedule, they were given a gradually increasing series of electric shocks for pressing the bar. For one group the food and shock schedules were in phase, so that every time they got a shock, a pellet of food was promptly delivered; for the other group, the schedules were out of phase, so that they received the same number and distribution of shocks, but at times when food was not delivered. You should note that for each bar press in both groups, the probability of food or shock was equally great and equally unpredictable. Nevertheless, the correlation of shock with food apparently rendered shock less disrupting to the rat, because the animals in the in-phase group continued pressing through considerably higher levels of shock than those in the out-of-phase group.

At present we are trying to secure objective measures of the counterconditioning of physiological responses to pain, a phenomenon suggested by Pavlov (1927). If we succeed, we want to study this phenomenon in greater detail to determine how it is affected by factors such as strength of drive, amount and schedule of reward, and experimental extinction.

Summary
In the first part of this paper I have described a series of experiments analyzing how a drug with well-established clinical effects on human behavior may act to achieve some of these effects. Amobarbital sodium, commonly called sodium amytal, was the drug selected for this first series of experiments. As the first step, we established that we could produce in experiments on rats, effects which appear to parallel the fear-reducing effects of this drug in human conflict situations. These effects were repeated in experiments in three different types of apparatus with the approach motivated by two different drives.

In further experiments, we found that this fear-reducing effect was not primarily produced indirectly by drug induced changes in the stimulus situation. We also found that it was not primarily due to a greater effect of the drug on the more recently established habit of avoidance; similar effects were secured when avoidance was learned first.

One series of experiments suggested that the fear-reducing effects of the drug in the Skinner box were not due merely to interference with the rat's ability to discriminate the tone used as a cue for danger in that situation. But another experiment in the alley situation showed that the drug either did interfere with discrimination, or produced recovery from experimental extinction. Thus, although a number of indirect modes of action have been ruled out, we have not yet decisively narrowed down the drug's fear-reducing effects to a direct action on the fear mechanism.

Finally, we found that the beneficial effects of the sodium amytal on relearning in a conflict situation did not generalize from the drugged to the normal state. Chlorpromazine yielded more promising results on this crucial test. Dose-response studies are in progress to determine the generality of the difference between the drugs in this respect.

In another series of experiments we have seen that fear and conflict can be conditioned specifically to the cues of a given drive, so that whether or not a given response will elicit conflict can depend on the motivation for that response. When distinctive anticipatory goal responses are present, they improve the discrimination.

We have also seen that some conditions can produce an apparent consolidation of fear with the passing of time, while other conditions produce an apparent forgetting of fear. In these experiments, the crucial factor seems to be the extent to which the elapsed time changes or restores the cues present immediately before the traumatic electric shock.

Finally, we have seen that it is possible to increase the resistance to the stress of pain and fear by appropriate training. But one of the most obvious methods, overlearning, can reduce, rather than improve, the resistance of the habit to disruption by fear.

References
Bailey, C. J., & Miller, N. E. The effect of sodium amytal on an approach-avoidance conflict in cats. *J. comp. physiol. Psychol.*, 1952, *45*, 205–208.

Brady, J. V. Assessment of drug effects on behavior. *Science*, 1956, *123*, 1033–1034.

Coons, E. E., & Miller, N. E. Conflict versus consolidation of memory traces to explain "retrograde amnesia" produced by ECS. *J. comp. physiol. Psychol.*, 1960, *53*, 524–531.

Dollard, J., & Miller, N. E. *Personality and psychotherapy.* New York: McGraw-Hill, 1950.

Estes, W. K., & Skinner, B. F. Some quantitative properties of anxiety. *J. exp. Psychol.*, 1941, *29*, 390–400.

Hebb, D. O. *The organization of behavior*. New York: Wiley, 1949.

Hunt, H. F. Effects of drugs on emotional responses and abnormal behavior in animals. In, *Conference on drugs and psychiatry*. Washington, D. C.: National Research Council, 1956.

Konorski, J., & Szwejkowska, G. Chronic extinction and restoration of conditioned reflexes: IV. The dependence of the course of extinction and restoration of conditioned reflexes on the "history" of the conditioned stimulus. (The principle of the primacy of first training.) *Acta biol. exp.*, 1952, *16*, 95–113.

Magoun, H. W. *The waking brain*. Springfield, Ill.: Charles C. Thomas, 1958.

Miller, N. E. A reply to "sign-gestalt or conditioned reflex?" *Psychol. Rev.*, 1935, *42*, 280–292.

Miller, N. E. Experimental studies of conflict. In J. McV. Hunt (Ed.), *Personality and the behavior disorders*. New York: Ronald, 1944. Pp. 431–465.

Miller, N. E. Liberalization of basic S-R concepts: Extensions to conflict behavior, motivation and social learning. In S. Koch (Ed.), *Psychology: A study of a science*. Vol. 2. New York: McGraw-Hill, 1959. Pp. 196–292.

Miller, N. E. Learning resistance to pain and fear: Effects of overlearning, exposure, and rewarded exposure in context. *J. exp. Psychol.*, 1960, *60*, 137–145.

Miller, N. E., & Barry, H. Motivational effects of drugs: Methods which illustrate some general problems in psychopharmacology. *Psychopharmacologia*, 1960, *1*, 169–199.

Miller, N. E., & Kraeling, D. Displacement: Greater generalization of approach than avoidance in a generalized approach-avoidance conflict. *J. exp. Psychol.*, 1952, *43*, 217–221.

Murray, E. J., & Miller, N. E. Displacement: Steeper gradient of generalization of avoidance than of approach with age of habit controlled. *J. exp. Psychol.*, 1952, *43*, 222–226.

Pavlov, I. P. *Conditioned reflexes*. (Trans. by G. V. Anrep) London: Oxford Univer. Press, 1927.

Szwejkowska, G. The transformation of differentiated inhibitory stimuli into positive conditioned stimuli. *Acta biol. exp.*, 1959, *19*, 151–159.

perception, cognition, and language

the useful dimensions of sensitivity[1]

james j. gibson
cornell university

What I am going to talk about is the relation of sensing to perceiving. We have all believed that we understood the process of sensation fairly well and that only the process of perception gave us difficulties. But I am going to suggest on the contrary that a straightforward theory of perception is possible and that it is our understanding of sensation which is confused.

First let us make sure that there is really a problem in how to treat sensing and perceiving. Some psychologists now maintain that there is no difference between them in fact. The distinction has broken

1. This work was supported in part by the Office of Naval Research under Contract 401 (14) with Cornell University. Reprinted from *American Psychologist*, 1963, Vol. 18, pp. 1–15. Copyright 1963 by the American Psychological Association, and reproduced by permission. The theory suggested in this address is elaborated more fully in *The Senses Considered as Perceptual Systems*, Houghton-Mifflin, 1966.

down; they say it has no validity and we should forget it. I think that what they mean is this. An individual can make discriminations in many ways. We can say either that he is *sensitive to* many variables of stimulation or that he can *experience* many kinds of differences between things but what has importance, the argument goes, are only the facts of discrimination, not whether they are called sensory or perceptual. There is something valid in this argument. I would call it the experimentalist's position—stick to the facts and cut the cackle! It is enough to determine just what differences an animal, a child, or a man can respond to and what others he cannot. This limited aim of psychology might be called simple psychophysics (not metric psychophysics) and it is good experimental science. But it provides no explanation of how the individual keeps in touch with the environment around him. The problem of perception, then, the problem of contact with the environment, still remains.

The variables of sensory discrimination are radically different from the variables of perceptual discrimination. The former are said to be dimensions like quality, intensity, extensity, and duration, dimensions of hue, brightness, and saturation, of pitch, loudness, and timbre, of pressure, warmth, cold, and pain. The latter are dimensions of the environment, the variables of events and those of surfaces, places, objects, of other animals, and even of symbols. Perception involves meaning; sensation does not. To see a patch of color is not to see an object. To see the extensity of a color is not to see the *size* of an object, nor is seeing the form of a color the same as seeing the *shape* of an object. To see a darker patch is not to see a shadow on a surface. To see the magnification of a form in the field is not to see an approaching object, and to see the expansion of the whole field is not to observe one's own forward locomotion. To have a salty taste is not to taste salt, and to have a certain olfactory impression is not to smell, say, a mint julep. To feel an impression on the skin is not to feel an object, nor is having sensations of strain and pressure to feel the weight of an object. To feel a local pain is not to feel the pricking of a needle. To feel warmth on one's skin, is not to feel the sun on one's skin, and to feel cold is not to feel the coldness of the weather. To hear sound is not the same thing as to hear an event, nor is to hear an increasing loudness to hear the approach of a sounding object. Finally, let us note that having a difference of sound sensation in the two ears is by no means the same as to hear the direction of a sound. The last case is instructive, for we do not in fact have such binaural differences in sensory experience but we do localize sounds.

Having sensations is not perceiving, and this fact cannot be glossed over. Nevertheless, perceiving unquestionably depends on sensing *in some meaning of that term.* That is, it depends on sensitivity or the use of the sense organs. To observe, one must sense. The question I wish to raise is whether or not it is true that to observe one must have sensations.

I realize that any inquiry into the relation of sensing to perceiving raises the ghosts of formidable men. It is disconcerting to feel that Locke, Berkeley, and Hume are looking over one's shoulder, or that Kant and two generations of Mills are raising their eyebrows. A perceptual theorist can get into staggering muddles, and he does well to be cautious. Nevertheless, I have a set of hypotheses to propose and you may judge it both for internal contradictions and for conformity with the facts. My first suggestion, the general thesis, is that the useful dimensions of sensitivity are those that specify the environment and the observer's relation to the environment. There are other dimensions of sensitivity which do not specify such facts and relations, but they are not useful in this way, being only incidental to the activity of perception.

A whole set of correlative hypotheses go along with this radical thesis. They need to be understood before it begins to have plausibility, and the theory should be considered as a whole. The facts of sensory psychology and sense physiology are so varied and

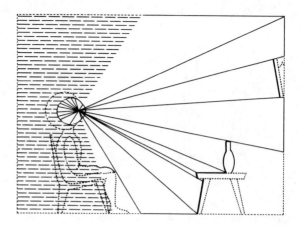

Fig. 1
Longitudinal section of the effective sector of an optic array.

voluminous that it is not easy to stand back and take a fresh look at the evidence. Moreover, each of us is apt to have his own private opinion about the data of his senses. But if you will suspend belief in the standard doctrine of sensation and question your favorite introspections, I hope to convince you that the explanation of sense perception is not as difficult and roundabout as it has always appeared to be.

Consider first the puzzle of perceptual constancy. I will not attempt to review the experiments measuring the tendency toward constancy which are limited to vision and which, in any case, are indecisive. Instead I will point to the general evidence for an invariance of perception with varying sensations. This invariance appears not only in vision but also in other senses, notably those excited by mechanical energy, hearing, and touch. The paradox of constancy—the "distal focusing of perception" as Egon Brunswik (1956) put it, is more than a matter of color, size, and shape constancy; it is the heart of the problem of useful sensitivity.

What enters the human eye at any given moment is a patchwork of visual sensations, a wide-angle cone of light rays. Figure 1 is a longitudinal section of such a wide-range cone. Whenever the eye moves to a new fixation point it will take in a new cone of rays. At any station point in the room there exists a complete optic array of available stimulation, the array being sampled and explored by new fixations. Figure 2 shows that if the *man* moves, instead of his eye moving, the pattern of the entering array is *transformed,* that is, every patch

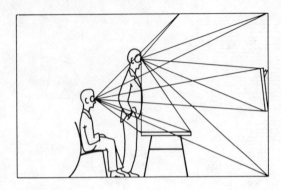

Fig. 2
Perspective transformation of the patchwork of an optic array due to change of viewpoint.

of color in the array changes form, and the patchwork as a whole is altered.

All this is simply the outcome of the laws of ambient light, or what may be called optical perspective (Gibson, 1961). The laws of *pictorial* perspective with which we are more familiar are a special case involving the sheaf of rays at a picture plane (Gibson, 1960b). Figure 3 is an illustration of so-called linear perspective on a picture.

The sensations of the visual field shift with every movement of the eye, and transform with every movement of the head. But, the perception of the room remains constant throughout. There is invariance of perception with varying sensations.

There are two kinds of seeing, I argue, one resulting in the experience of a visual field and the other in the experience of a visual world (Gibson, 1950). The field is bounded; the world is unbounded. The field is unstable; the world is stable. The field is composed of adjacent areas, or figures; the world is composed of

surfaces, edges, and depths, or solid objects and interspaces. The field is fluid in size and shape; the world is rigid in size and shape. As pure cases, they are distinct, although in many experimental situations the observer gets a compromise experience between the two extremes. However, these experimental situations are seldom ones in which the observer is free to explore a complete optic array with his eyes, and are never ones in which he is allowed to move about so as to obtain a series or family of perspectives.

The visual *field* ahead of the observer during locomotion expands in a sort of centrifugal flow governed by the laws of motion perspective. The visual *world* during locomotion is phenomenally quite rigid. Sensation varies but perception is invariant. To be sure, the observer sees his locomotion. The expansion of the field ahead *specifies* locomotion. This suggests a strange and radical hypothesis—that the visual sensation in this case is a symptom of kinesthesis, having reference to the self instead of the world, and that it has nothing to do with the visual perception of the world (Gibson, 1958).

Another case is that of the perception aroused by the perspective transformation of a silhouette in an otherwise empty field of view. As an experiment, this does not require a panoramic motion picture screen, and it can be carried out in a laboratory. There results a perception named stereokinesis, or the kinetic depth effect, or simply rigid motion in depth (Gibson & Gibson, 1957). Behind the translucent screen in such experiments, at an indefinite distance, there appears a virtual object moving in space. The form of the silhouette changes; the form of the phenomenal object remains invariant. The observer can see a change of form if he attends to the flat screen, but what he spontaneously reports is a rigid object. Ordinarily the transformation is seen as motion of the object, not as a sensation.

Another example is the familiar one that the color of the surfaces of the environment, including the white to black series, does not change as the illumination goes from brilliant to dim. The corresponding sensations, however, the film colors obtained by seeing a surface through an aperture, vary widely with illumination. The perception of whiteness is quite a different matter from the sensation of brightness. With the available stimulus of a complete optic array, the ambient light reflected from a whole layout of surfaces, one can detect the actual physical reflectance of each surface.

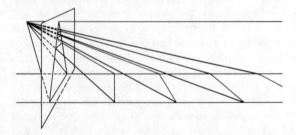

Fig. 3
The special case of a ray sheaf at a hypothetical picture plane.

The absolute luminous intensity of a color patch determines the sensation of brightness, but only if it is taken in isolation.

Finally, I remind you of the difference between the binocular sensations of objects in depth and the binocular perception of the depth of objects. When one attends to his visual sensations one can notice the doubling or diplopia of images in the field of view; crossed diplopia from here to the fixated object, and uncrossed diplopia beyond that point. This doubling changes with every change in convergence, especially as we look to or away from what our hands are doing. We ought to see nothing as single except what lies on the momentary horopter. But of course we see everything as single, that is, we perceive it so. There is a phenomenal unity of each object despite an ever-varying doubleness of its sensation.

Auditory perception, we say, is based on a different mode or department of sense from visual perception. But the paradox of invariant perception with varying sensations holds nevertheless. Consider those very peculiar and special sounds, the phonemes of speech. They are acoustically analysable, it is true, in terms of intensity, frequency, and the frequency spectrum, but their distinctive nature consists of higher-order variables which are now beginning to be specified. Phonemes are the same at quite different levels of pitch and loudness, and hence are phenomenally constant for the voices of men, or women, or children. Speech cannot only be voiced; it can also be murmured, shouted, whispered, or sung. It can be emitted in falsetto, or even by a sort of whistling, without completely destroying the distinctive features which define the phonemic units of speech. They are invariant with changes of auditory sensation.

Consider also the hypothetical sensations that a hearer would get during auditory localization—the different sense impressions or sense data from the two ears. The main stimulus differences are ones of intensity and time of onset. As we know from the experiments of Wallach (1940) and others, the hearer turns and tilts his head from side to side, as if exploring, when he hears an unseen event. For a repeating sound, this means that the relative loudness and onsets of sensation are continually changing during the head turning. But the perception is that of a fixed or constant direction of the sound in space. As a matter of fact there is no evidence to show that any man or animal every heard the changes of binaural sensations

when turning his head. There is no awareness of such a flux. Binaural disparity never becomes conscious as binocular disparity can (Rosenzweig, 1961). I prefer to believe that the binaural mechanism is an active system which responds to disparity and tends to react by nullifying it, that is, by pointing the head toward the source of sound. The system responds to the sound field in the air, and we are misled when we consider only the wave train entering each ear separately.

So much for hearing. It is the sense of touch, so-called, that provides the clearest examples of the invariance of perception with varying sensations. In the last two or three years I have been running a series of experiments to test the limits of what an observer can do by touching or feeling without vision, that is, to discover what he can detect or discriminate about surfaces, edges, interspaces, objects and motions in the neighborhood of his body. In these experiments we can compare the classical results obtained with passive punctate stimulation of the skin (intensity, locus, duality, and motion of a cutaneous impression or a pattern of such impressions) and the results obtained with the self-produced stimulation of touching. In general, an observer can perceive the properties of an object by active touch with quite surprising success. So also, of course, can a blind person. The following results come from a long series of observations (Gibson, 1962).

Rigidity. For example, when pressing on a rigid object with a finger, or squeezing it with the hand, there is an increase of sensation and then a decrease, or usually a flow of changing intensities. The perception, however, is of a constant rigidity of the surface. One simply feels the object. The impression on the skin as such is hard to detect. When one is touched *by* the same object instead of touching it, however, the variation of intensity is easy to detect. An observer can distinguish correctly between two protuberant surfaces, one rigid and the other yielding, when he presses them, but not when they are pressed on his passive skin.

Unity. When feeling one object between two fingers, only one object is felt, although two separated cutaneous sensations occur. This is a suprising fact when you consider it. The different local signs of these impressions have seemingly dropped out of the experience. The result is the same whether the object is held with two, three, four, or five fingers; the multiplicity of impressions on the skin has no effect on the perception of spatial unity of the object. It can be held by two hands and still be one object. It can be felt by many combinations of all 10 fingers, in rapidly changing combinations, and the perception of the object is all the better for it.

Stability. Active touch is exploratory and the observer tends to slide his finger over a corner or protuberance of a hidden object. The impression is then displaced over the skin and a feeling of tactile motion would be expected to occur. But the object is perceived to be stationary in space, and the tactile motion is not noticed. The perception is stable although the sensation is moving.

Weight. When one holds or lifts an object, the judgment of its weight is easier than when it is allowed simply to press downward against the skin of the supported resting hand. In active lifting, a whole set of additional inputs is involved. Besides the end organs of the skin and the deeper tissue, the receptors of the finger joints, wrist joints, and arm joints are excited, and the whole neuromuscular feedback system of the arm is activated. The flux and array of pressure sensations and articular sensations from a dozen or so joints ought to be of bewildering complexity. It probably would be if introspection could detect all that goes on in hefting a weight. But what the observer perceives is the mass of the object, unchanging despite the changing sensations. A weight comes to be as well or better perceived, in fact, when the object is shifted back and forth from one hand to the other. Something invariant emerges from this seeming mishmash of excitation. The perception is equivalent to that which accompanies the controlled and isolated sensory impressions of the standardized weight-lifting experiment.

Shape. . . . The haptic system of the exploring hand is sensitive to the variables of solid geometry, not those of plane geometry. It gets nothing of a flat picture, but it gets a great deal of the shape of a solid object. The hand can detect all of the following properties: the slant of a surface, the convexity or concavity of a surface, the edge or corner at the junction of two or more surfaces, and the separation of two edges, as our experiments demonstrate. Now it has always been assumed that the skin must be analogous to the retina— that it is a sensory mosaic which registers the form or pattern of the receptors excited. The skin and the retina can, in fact, do so when they are passively stimulated,

and this has been taken to be their basic or sensory function.

If the cutaneous form sense is the basis for the feeling of objective shape, however, an impossible paradox arises. The series of cutaneous pressure patterns with a pair of exploring hands is something like that of a kaleidoscope; it seemingly has no rationale, and no single pattern is ever like the shape of the object. Nevertheless, from the inputs of the skin and the joints together, from the sensory system if not from the sensations, a remarkably clear perception of shape arises. The phenomenal shape of the object is invariant although the phenomenal patterns of sense data fluctuate and vary from moment to moment.

Conclusion. From all these facts of vision, hearing, and touch we ought to conclude that sensations are not the cause of perceptions. This is a strange statement. But I am willing to draw this conclusion. Conscious sensory impressions and sense data in general are incidental to perception, not essential to it. They are occasionally symptomatic of perception. But they are not even necessary symptoms inasmuch as perception may be "sensationless" (as for example in auditory localization). Having a perception does not entail the having of sensations.

The difficulty in accepting this conclusion is how to explain sense perception *unless* by way of sensations. But there is a way out of this difficulty, and that is to distinguish two meanings of the word "sense." Sensitivity is one thing, sensation is quite another.

The first meaning refers to the effects of stimulation in general. The second refers to conscious impressions induced by certain selected variables of stimulation. We can now assert that in the first meaning sensory *inputs* are prerequisite to perception, but that in the second meaning sensory *impressions* are *not* prerequisite to perception. In other words the *senses* are necessary for perception but *sensations* are not. In order to avoid confusion it might be better to call the senses by a new term such as *esthesic system.* We can then distinguish between sensory perception and sensory experience, between perception as a result of stimulation and sensation as a result of stimulation. The variables of stimulation that cause the first must be different from those that cause the second. Likewise the dimensions of sensitivity to informative stimuli must be different from those to uninformative stimuli.

How is the invariance of perception with varying sensations to be explained? By higher-order variables of stimulation which are themselves invariant, and by the sensitivity of esthesic systems to such invariant information. This kind of sensitivity is useful to animals. It may be innate, or acquired, or a little of both—that is a question for experiment. We can study it directly. We do not have to solve the puzzle of how there can be invariance of perception despite varying sensations. We do not have to inquire how sensations might be converted into perceptions, or corrected, or compensated for, or how one set of sensations might reciprocally interact with another set. If the sensations are disposed of, the paradox of perceptual constancy evaporates. Clearly the hypothesis of stimulus invariants is crucial for this explanation, and I will have to return to it later. Note that with this approach, a seemingly useful tool of experimenters, the index of constancy, loses its meaning. It ceases to be a measure of perceptual achievement. The supposed baseline of this ratio, the "retinal" size, shape, or brightness, cannot be used in a computation of the achievement if it is not the basis of the perception. It falls in a different realm of discourse, and it simply is not commensurable with perceptual size, shape, or brightness.

What are sensations? We might well pause at this stage to consider what is being discarded. Just what are these experiences that the perceptual theorist should no longer appeal to? I suggested at the beginning that our understanding of sensations has always been obscure. The reason for this, I think, is that the term sensation has been applied to quite different things. Let us examine the various meanings of the word to be found in philosophy, psychology, and physiology.

1. The theoretical concept. Theories of perception, as already noted, have always assumed that sensations were the necessary occasions of perception; that they were entailed in perceiving. This is precisely the assumption that is being challenged by my distinction between sensation and sensitivity. Its plausibility comes only from the evidence that *stimuli* are the necessary occasions of perception. I shall argue that none of the kinds of experience which have been called sensory *requires* this theoretical assumption.

2. The experimentalist's concept. In psychophysical experiments the variables of sensation have been taken to be correlates of the variables of physical energy which the experimenter could apply to his observer. In

the past, the latter have tended to be those which were fundamental for physics proper, and which were controllable by borrowing the instruments of optics, acoustics, and mechanics. The favorite physical variables were intensity and frequency for wave energy, along with simple location or extension, and time or duration. But these dimensions of stimulation have little to do with the environment. They are fundamental for physics but not necessarily so for sense organs. The dimensions of available stimulation in a natural physical environment are of higher order than these, being variables of pattern and change. We are beginning to be able to control these natural stimulus variables. Note also that the stimuli of classical psychophysics are *applied* to a passive observer by an experimenter whereas the stimuli in perceptual psychophysics are *obtained* by an active observer (although the opportunities for obtainable stimulation are provided by the experimenter). The experiences resulting from these two situations are apt to be different, as the experiments on active touch demonstrate.

3. The physiological concept. The early physiologists discovered the receptor elements of the sense organs and assumed that these cells (rods, cones, hair cells, etc.) were the units of a receptor mosaic. Hence a sensation was taken to be a correlate of a single receptor, that is, the end organ of a nerve fiber. But we are now fairly sure, after recording from single fibers with microelectrodes, that the functional units of a sense organ are not the anatomical cells, but groupings of cells. It was also assumed, after Johannes Müller, that a specific mode or quality of sensation corresponded to any given nerve or fiber. But this generalization too, can no longer be supported since, for one thing, the same fiber can participate in different groupings and have thereby different receptive functions. When Müller insisted that the mind had no direct contact with the environment but only with the "qualities of the sensory nerves," he was confusing sensitivity with sensation. He assumed that the function of the senses was to provide sensations. He was right, surely, to maintain that perception depends on stimulation but wrong to maintain that it depends on the conscious qualities of sense. A sense *organ* has to be defined as a hierarchy of functional groupings of cells, and they are not always adjacent anatomically.

4. The analytic concept. The attempt to reduce consciousness to its lowest terms by introspection culmi-

nated in Titchener. A sensation was taken to be an irreducible experience not analysable into components—a simple datum. It is fair to say that the attempt failed. Sensations as combining elements are no longer advocated, although the elegance and force of the structuralist program was such that traces of it are still influential in psychology. Conscious perceptions *cannot* always be reduced to conscious sensations, as the Gestalt theorists have shown. It is clear that sensation in this meaning of the term is not prerequisite to perception.

5. The empiricist's concept. According to Locke and all the thinkers influenced by him, sense impressions are the original beginnings of perceptual experience prior to learning. They are innate, and pure sensations are had only by the new-born infant. They are without meaning and probably without reference to external objects. They are data for thought (or inference, or interpretation, or association, or other kinds of learning, either automatic or rational). What they are like has been the subject of endless inquiry, and this explains our strong curiosity about the first visual experiences of the congenitally blind after the operation for cataract. The theory that original experience was composed of sensations has always appealed to psychologists because the available alternatives, nativism and rationalism, implied either a faculty of perception or a faculty of reason. But we can reject sensation as the original beginning of perception and accept useful sensitivity as something present from the start of life without being driven into the arms of faculty psychology. We can also avoid the nagging difficulty that infants and young animals (and the cataract patients, in my opinion) do not, on the evidence, seem to have the bare and meaningless sensations that classical empiricism says they should have.

6. The concept of an experience with subjective reference. There is still another possible meaning of the term sensation. It is the meaning used in saying that a stomach-ache is sensory rather than perceptual. The same could be said of an afterimage as compared with an object, for it seems to refer more to the observer than it does to the outer world. In cases of passive tactual experience, the observer can feel either the impression on the skin as such or the object as such, depending on how he directs his attention. It is as if the phenomenal experience had both a subjective pole and an objective pole. Pain is ordinarily subjective (al-

though there may be some objective reference, e.g., a pin) and vision is ordinarily objective (although there can be a subjective aspect, e.g., dazzle), but all senses, in this view of the matter, carry both subjective and objective information. The observer's body, as well as his environment, can always be noted, together with the relation between them. The body and the world are different sources of stimulation; there is propriosensitivity as well as exterosensitivity. Sherrington was wrong only in supposing that there are separate proprioceptors and exteroceptors. All organs of sensitivity, I suggest, have this dual function.

Note that sensation considered as the subjective pole of experience is quite different from the other meanings of sensation. This is not the provider of data for perception or of messages or elements, nor is it the innate beginning of perception. This is a legitimate and useful meaning, but not the classical one—the basis of the experience of the external world.

Conclusion. Having examined the various kinds of experience that have been called sensory, I conclude that no one of them is required as the necessary occasion of perception. Several of them do undoubtedly occur in a man who introspects, or who serves as subject in an experiment, but the explanation of perception can dispense with all of them.

Reconstruction of a Theory of Perception

If sensitivity is distinguished from sensation, and if perception depends on the former but not the latter, we will have to make a fresh start on the explanation of perception. We will have to discard many cherished doctrines and formulas (like separate and distinct modalities of sense), to clarify and find words for new things (like stimulus patterns and transformations), and to devise new experimental methods (such as how to control stimulus information instead of traditional stimuli). What are the requirements of a theory of perception not mediated by sense data?

Obviously it will have to show that sensitivity, with or without accompanying sensations, is adequate for all the manifold properties of perception (Gibson, 1959). It will have to show that the afferent inputs to the nervous system of a child or a man are rich enough to explain the degree to which he is aware of the world (but the inputs are taken to be those of active systems, not passive receptors or even sense organs). It will have to show that there is information in available stimulation (but the potential stimuli are taken to be limitless in variables of higher order). It will have to show that there are constants in the flow of available stimulation in order to explain constancy. It will have to show that these invariants in the ambient light, sound, and mechanical contact, do in fact specify the objects which are their sources — that something in the proximal stimulus is specific to the distal stimulus (Gibson, 1960a). It will have to suggest how these invariants can be discovered by the activity of selective attention (but there are hints of such a mechanism in what we already know about sense-organ adjustments, so-called, and about the selective filtering of higher nerve centers). It will have to explain propriosensitivity (self-perception) along with exterosensitivity (object perception), but without appealing to the oversimplified doctrine of a special sense of kinesthesis.

Moreover, the theory will have to explain all the observations and experiments of past generations which seem to make it perfectly evident that the observer *contributes* meaning to his experience, that he *supplements* the data, and that significance *accrues* to sensation. I have assumed limitless information in available stimulation from the natural environment. Therefore, the explanation must be that the *experimenter* has limited the available information in all such experiments, or else that, in a natural situation, the available stimulus information is impoverished, as by darkness or a disadvantageous point of view. Psychologists are accustomed to use stimulus situations with impoverished, ambiguous, or conflicting information. These have been devised in the hope of revealing the constructive process taken to characterize *all* perception. In these special situations there must indeed occur a special process. It could appropriately be called *guessing*. But I would distinguish perceiving from guessing, and suggest that we investigate the first and try to understand the second by means of corollaries about deficient information.

The theory will have to provide an explanation of illusions, not only the optical ones but those of all the other channels of sensitivity. The postulates of stimulus information and stimulus ecology, however, suggest ways in which the various illusions can be, for the first time, classified into types and subtypes of misperception, with the reasons therefore. A proper description of the information in an optic array will necessarily include a description of the information in a picture, and the ambiguous, conflicting, equivocal, or

misleading information that can be incorporated in a picture. Note that illusions will be treated as special cases of perception, not as phenomena which might reveal the laws of the subjective process of perception.

Finally, the theory will have to be consistent with the known facts about social perception and all the information that has accumulated about the perception and learning of symbols and words. Here, you may think, a sensitivity theory of perception must surely fail. Even allowing that physiognomic and expressive character may have some basis in complex stimulation, words can have no meaning except that supplied by the perceiver. But this objection, cogent as it may sound, entirely misses the point. Once it is granted that stimuli may carry information, or have meaning, the whole theory of meaning is revolutionized, and we have to make a new start on it. Once it is granted that a child or a man can develop sensitivity to the invariants of the ecological stimulus environment it is no great step to admit that he can also learn to respond to the invariants of the social and the symbolic environments. The laws by which stimuli specify events and objects are not, of course, the rules or conventions by which chosen events or objects stand for others, but both are lawful. If animals and children can register perceptual meanings it is not suprising that children and adults can go on to register verbal meanings. However, just as the child does not first have a repertory of sensations and then attach meanings, so also he does not first hear a vocabulary of words and then attach meanings.

ROLE OF ATTENTION IN PERCEPTION

An entirely different picture of the senses has emerged. For this to happen, we had to suppose that their sole function was not to yield sensations. Instead of mere receptors, that is receivers and transducers of energy, they appear to be systems for exploring, searching, and selecting ambient energy. The sense organs are all capable of motor adjustment. Figure 4 is a diagram which supplements and alters the usual stimulus-response diagram. It shows on the left the modification of stimulation by reactions of the exteroceptive system, and on the right the modification of reactions by stimulation of the proprioceptive system. The latter is familiar nowadays under the name of feedback, that is, the neural loops essential for the control of behavior. But the loops on the left are just as essential as those on the right. The organism has two kinds of feedback, not one. There are two kinds of action, in fact, one being

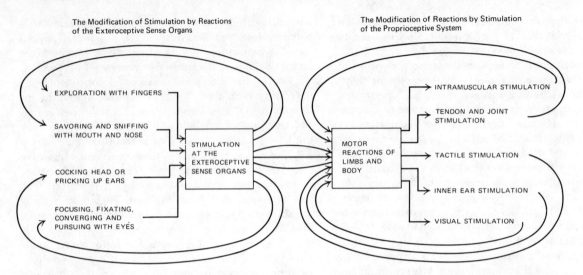

The Modification of Stimulation by Reactions of the Exteroceptive Sense Organs

The Modification of Reactions by Stimulation of the Proprioceptive System

Fig. 4
The feedback loops for exploring stimulation and those for controlling behavior. (The angular lines represent physical action; the curved lines represent neural action.

exploratory action and the other *performatory* action. Muscles can enhance perception as well as do work and some, like the eye muscles, have this function exclusively. The hands, mouth and nose, ears, and eyes are all in their own way active systems, as the body is. The primary reaction to pressure on the skin is exploration with the fingers. Chemicals at the nose and mouth first elicit sniffing and savoring. Sound at the ears causes head turning. Light at the eyes brings about focusing, fixating, converging, and exploring of the light. Note that the outcome of all these adjustments is to obtain stimulation or, rather, to obtain the maximum information from the available stimulation.

This new picture of the senses includes attention as part of sensitivity, not as an act of the mind upon the deliverances of the senses. Every esthesic system is an attentional system. Attention is not an intervening process, therefore, but one that starts at the periphery. It also continues to select and filter the already selected inputs at nerve centers, as we know both from introspection and from the evidence obtained by microelectrode recording.

PATTERN AND CHANGE OF STIMULATION
Consider the sense organs in the old way, each as a population of receptive units. We have thought of the retina, the skin, the tongue, and perhaps the olfactory epithelium as examples of a sensory surface, a mosaic. Even the Organ of Corti and the lining of the statocysts may be conceived in this way. But note, parenthetically, that the flat surface analogy does not hold at all for the articular sense, that is, the set of receptors for all the joints of the skeleton. The point is that any population of receptive units is capable of delivering a *simultaneous array of neural inputs* (although it is gratuitous or false to call this a two-dimensional pattern or picture, as we do for the retina and are tempted to do for the skin). Apart from this muddle, every sense, then, is a pattern sense. Equally, they are all capable of delivering *a sequence or stream of neural inputs of changes in the simultaneous pattern*. Every sense is therefore a transformation sense as well as a pattern sense.

Consider next the stimulation for these senses, the *proximal* stimulation. In every case it also is a simultaneous array and a successive flux. There are two kinds of order in stimulation, as I once put it, adjacent order and sequential order (Gibson, 1950). Pattern and change are characteristic of stimulation in general, unless it has been sterilized by an experimenter, and here is where the information lies. For example, pattern and change occur at the retina and the skin—even more at the dual retina and the two-handed skin, as the experiments reported have shown. They occur at the basilar membrane of the cochlea as, respectively, the momentary sound spectrum and the transients of sound; moreover the binaural disparity patterns change with head movement. The simultaneous pattern of input from all joints of the skeleton taken together is a highly intricate and interlocked configuration, yet its slightest transformation seems to be registered when the individual moves. Pattern and change occur at the gustatory and olfactory surfaces, and even for the statocysts and the semicircular canals. Pattern and change are universal.

Now, sensory physiologists have always recognized the importance of patterns of stimulation and tried to relate them to the sensory projection areas of the brain. What they have not understood is transformations of pattern. They have tried to imagine a cortical correlate of form, which is difficult enough (as witness Hebb's recent attempt to explain visual form perception, 1949), but not the changes of form which I have described. A tabulation may help to clarify the problem (Table 1).

TABLE 1

A Classification of Stimulus Variables for Perception

I. The unchanging stimulus array. *Unvarying variables*
Dimensions of pattern, form, and structure as such

II. The changing stimulus array. *Varying variables*
  A. Self-produced transformation—specifies *motion of self*
    1. With sense-organ exploration—control of *attention* (e.g., eye movement)
    2. With gross motor reactions—control of *performance* (e.g., locomotion)
  B. Other-produced transformation—specifies *motion of object*

III. The *invariants* in a changing stimulus array. *Invariant variables*
  Unchanging dimensions under transformation—specify *rigid surfaces and objects*

The motionless frozen observer with his eyes fixed on a motionless frozen world gets a pattern of stimulation from each of his senses (Type I stimulation) but the stimulation is hardly typical. The array at the eyes is comparable to a panoramic still picture. If he moves, or if something moves, the arrays change (at the eyes, the skin, and the joints, for instance) in specific ways or dimensions (Type II stimulation). I have worked out the dimensions of transformation for the eyes, and it

ought to be possible to do this for the other systems. Subjective movement and objective motion (A and B) normally yield different stimuli even at the eyes. The observer can see himself moving, as one does in automobile driving, and even see his own eye movements, as in observing the shifting of an afterimage, but these are perceptions with subjective reference. They are "proprioceptive." We might say that the stimuli are propriospecific, since they carry information about the self.

The third type of stimulus variable is crucial since it is taken to explain the invariance of object perception. Change of an array usually involves nonchange. Some order is preserved in every transformation. Neither at the eye nor the skin nor at any other organ does the energy scintillate, as it were, like the random flashing of the fireflies in a field. There are always invariant variables alongside the varying variables. They are specific to (but not copies of) the permanent properties of external things. It is not a paradox that perception should correspond to the distal object, although it depends on the proximal stimulus, if the object is in fact specified in the stimulus. The Ames demonstrations purporting to show that optical stimulation can *never* specify objects depend on a frozen array from which the invariants cannot emerge.

Consider the difference between *unvarying* and *invariant* variables of stimulation (Type I and Type III). In the former case the stimuli that would be invariant do not get separated off from those that would vary if the array underwent transformation. The frozen array, the case of continuous nontransformation, carries less information. The case is one that never occurs in life. A prolonged freezing of the pattern of stimulation on the retina or the skin, in fact, yields an input which soon fades away to nothing.

The normal world is sufficiently full of motions and events to make a stream of stimulation. But even without external motions a flow is produced. The normal activity of perception is to explore the world. We thus alter its perspectives, if events do not alter them for us. What exploration does is to isolate the invariants. The sensory system can separate the permanence from the change only if there is change.

In vision, we strive to get new perspectives on an object in order to perceive it properly. I believe that something analogous to this is what happens in the active exploratory touching of an object. The momentary visual perspectives, of course, are pictures or forms in the geometrical sense of that term whereas the momentary tactual perspectives are not. Nevertheless they are similar since, for an object of a given solid shape, any change of cutaneous pattern like any change of retinal pattern is *reversible*. The impression of the object on the skin, like its impression on the retina, can recur by a reversal of the act that transformed it. The successive patterns thus fall into a family of patterns which is specific to the object. I submit to Hebb the suggestion that the first problem in perceptual physiology is not how the brain responds to form as such, unvarying form, but instead how it responds to the invariant variables of changing form. I think we should attempt a direct physiological theory of object perception without waiting for a successful theory of picture perception.

INVARIANT PROPERTIES OF A CHANGING STIMULUS ARRAY

The crux of the theory of stimulation here proposed is the existence of certain types of permanence underlying change. These invariants are not, I think, produced by the acquiring of invariant responses to varying stimuli—they are *in* the stimuli at least potentially. They are facts of stimulus ecology, independent of the observer although dependent upon his exploratory isolation of them. This kind of order in stimulation is not created by the observer, either out of his past experience or by innate preknowledge. Just as the invariant properties of the physical world of objects are not constructed by the perceiver, so the invariant properties in available stimulation are not constructed by him. They are discoverable by the attentive adjustments of his sense organs and by the education of his attention.

Some of these stimulus invariants are extremely subtle. The ultimate subtleties of the information in stimulation may well be unlimited. But other invariants are quite simple and easily detected. The optical texture that specifies a physical surface (in contrast with the textureless patch that specifies an empty space) is invariant with illumination and under all transformations of perspective. Introspectively we say that one yields a surface color and the other a film color, but the spatial meaning is what counts, not the introspection. The textures of earth, air, and water are different, and the differences are constant. So are the differences that specify to the young of any species the fur, feathers, or face of the mother. The intensity and wave length of the light are irrelevant. The infant seems to be sensitive from the beginning, more or less, to such external stimuli as these. The tablet of his consciousness may be nearly blank at birth, as Locke believed, but the impressions that do appear are vague perceptions, not bare sensations. The earliest dimensions of sensitivity are useful ones.

Classical sense impressions, I think, are something of which only a human adult is aware. They tend to arise when he introspects, or when he tries to describe the content of experience, or the punctate momentary elements of perception, or when simple variables of physical energy are experimentally isolated for him by a psychologist, or when stimuli are applied to his receptors instead of his being allowed to obtain them for himself. Far from being original experiences, they are sophisticated ones; they depend on having had a great deal of past experience.

This is not to deny that perception alters with learning or depends upon learning. Instead it points to a different kind of learning from that we have previously conceived. Unquestionably the infant has to learn to perceive. That is why he explores with eyes, hands, mouth, and all of his organs, extending and refining his dimensions of sensitivity. He has to separate what comes from the world and what comes from himself. But he does not, I think, have to learn to convert sensations into perceptions.

References

Brunswik, E. *Perception and the representative design of experiments.* Berkeley: Univer. California Press, 1956.

Caviness, J. A., & Gibson, J. J. The equivalence of visual and tactual stimulation for the perception of solid forms. Paper read at Eastern Psychological Association, Atlantic City, April 1962.

Gibson, J. J. *The perception of the visual world.* Boston: Houghton Mifflin, 1950.

Gibson, J. J. Visually controlled locomotion and visual orientation in animals. *Brit. J. Psychol.*, 1958, 49, 182–194.

Gibson, J. J. Perception as a function of stimulation. In S. Koch (Ed.), *Psychology: A study of a science.* New York: McGraw-Hill, 1959, Pp. 457–501.

Gibson, J. J. The concept of the stimulus in psychology. *Amer. Psychologist*, 1960, 16, 694–703. (a)

Gibson, J. J. Pictures, perspective, and perception. *Daedalus*, 1960, *89*, 216–227. (b)

Gibson, J. J. Ecological optics. *Vision Res.*, 1961, *1*, 253–262.

Gibson, J. J. Observations on active touch. *Psychol. Rev.*, 1962, *69*, 477–491.

Gibson, J. J., & Gibson, E. J. Continuous perspective transformations and the perception of rigid motion. *J. exp. Psychol.*, 1957, *54*, 129–138.

Hebb, D. O. *The organization of behavior.* New York: Wiley, 1949.

Rosenzweig, M. R. Development of research on the physiological mechanisms of auditory localization. *Psychol. Bull.*, 1961, *58*, 376–389.

Wallach, H. The role of head movements and vestibular and visual cues in sound localization. *J. exp. Psychol.*, 1940, *27*, 339–368.

to perceive is to know[1]

w. r. garner
johns hopkins university

This paper is a progress report of research on perception in the broad sense. The experiments reported are chosen with the expectation that they will illustrate three aspects of perception. These three aspects are:

First, and most general, *to perceive is to know.* Perceiving is a cognitive process involving knowing, understanding, comprehending, organizing, even cognizing. Most of our current research on the topic would suggest that perceiving is responding, naming, discriminating, and analyzing. These psychological processes all exist, and it does not matter that they are *also* called perception. What does matter is that we study

1.   The research reported here has been supported by the Veterans Administration, the Office of Naval Research, and the National Institutes of Health. The preparation of this paper was supported by Grant No. MH11062 from the National Institute of Mental Health. Reprinted from *American Psychologist*, 1966, Vol. 21, pp. 11–19. Copyright 1966 by the American Psychological Association, and reproduced by permission.

perception as a cognitive process. As such, perception is much more closely related to classification, conceptualization, and free-recall learning than to sensory or discriminatory processes.

Second, *the factors known in perception are properties of sets of stimuli,* not properties of individual stimuli (to say nothing of the elements which make up these individual stimuli). Gestalt psychologists have emphasized that perception is concerned with organized wholes, not analyzed parts, but they were talking about the single stimulus. Yet a single stimulus can have no real meaning without reference to a set of stimuli, because the attributes which define it cannot be specified without knowing what the alternatives are.

It is convenient to think of three levels of stimulus set. There is the *single stimulus* itself, and often we do want to talk about it. But that stimulus has attributes whose combinations define a *total set,* and the real or assumed properties of this total are also the properties of the single stimulus. In addition, there is usually a *subset* of the total set, a subset which does not include all stimuli from the total set, but which does include the particular stimulus we are concerned about. This subset is redundant in some fashion, since it is smaller than the total set; and it has properties of its own which are not identical to those of the total set.

Now the important point is simply this: How the single stimulus is perceived is a function not so much of what it is, but is rather a function of what the total set and the particular subset are. The properties of the total set and the subset are also the perceived properties of the single stimulus, so we cannot understand the knowing of the single stimulus without understanding the properties of the sets within which it is contained.

Third, *to perceive is an active process*, one in which the perceiver participates fully. The perceiver does not passively *re*ceive information about his environment; rather, he actively *per*ceives his environment. Nor does he simply impose his organization on an otherwise unstructured world—the world is structured. But he does select the structure to which he will attend and react, and he even provides the missing structure on occasion. In particular, as we shall see, the perceiver provides his own total set and subset when these do not physically exist.

Free versus Constrained Classification

The first experiment I want to discuss was done in collaboration with Shiro Imai (Imai & Garner, 1965), and it is concerned with perceptual classification of sets of stimuli defined by different numbers and kinds of attributes. More specifically, we compared two types of classification task: a constrained classification, in which the experimenter specifies the attribute by which the subject is to classify; and a free classification, in which the subject chooses his own mode of classification.

The stimuli we used in this experiment are shown in Figure 1. Each stimulus consisted of a small card on which were placed two dots. The locations of these dots could be varied so as to produce three perceived attributes: *Position*, in that the pair of dots could be to the left or right of center; *Distance* between the dots, large or small; and *Orientation*, with rotation to the right or left of vertical. The two levels of each of the three attributes provide the eight possible stimuli in a set. In some cases the sets involved the various combinations of just pairs of these attributes, and such sets

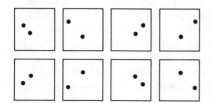

Fig. 1
Types of stimuli used in free and constrained classification (after Imai & Garner, 1965).

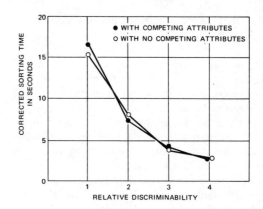

Fig. 2
Sorting times for decks of 32 cards as a function of relative discriminability of the criterion attribute, with and without the existence of competing attributes (from Imai & Garner, 1965).

contain four different stimuli. And in one situation the stimuli varied on just a single attribute.

Each attribute varied also in discriminability, which we changed by using larger or smaller differences in the two levels of the attribute. We used four degrees of discriminability for each attribute, as equally matched between attributes as we could make them, and we used the degrees of discriminability in all possible combinations to determine the effect of discriminability of attribute on classification.

Constrained classification. In the constrained-classification task the subject was required to sort a deck of 32 cards into two piles as fast as he could, and the attribute by which he was required to sort was specified by the experimenter. With this task the experimental result is the time required to sort the deck of cards.

The major result of this part of the experiment is shown in Figure 2. In this figure, a corrected sorting time is shown as a function of the relative discriminability (on the abscissa) of the attribute by which the subject was sorting. The drop in this function makes it quite clear that sorting is much faster with higher discriminability. So we do know that discriminability of attribute affects how well subjects can do in this constrained task.

The results for all three attributes have been combined in this figure because there were no differences between the attributes. So we also know that the discriminabilities of different attributes can at least be adjusted so that they are quite equivalent with regard to sorting speed.

But there are two functions shown here. One is the function obtained when the stimuli differed on just one attribute. The other function is for all conditions in which there were one or two competing attributes with different degrees of discriminability. All these other conditions have been combined because once again there were no differential effects: Neither the number nor the discriminability of the competing attributes had any effect on sorting speed.

Thus our conclusion is that only the discriminability of the differentiating or classifying attribute affects the nature of the perceived organization.

Free classification. In free classification, the task was somewhat different. A set of either four or eight stimuli (depending on whether two or three attributes were used) was placed in front of the subject, and he was simply required to arrange the stimuli into two groups. With this task we do not measure how well the subject can do what he is told to do, but rather we measure what in fact he does—that is, what attribute he classifies by.

Some of the results with free classification are shown in Table 1. On the bottom row is shown the percentage of times that subjects used each of the attributes in making the classification. Distance between dots was used nearly 50% of the time, Orientation was used nearly 40% of the time, and Position was used less than 10% of the time. Since all combinations of discriminabilities had been used in producing the stimulus sets, these results are due entirely to an overall preference of subjects to classify by some attributes rather than by others.

These preferences for attributes are not the same for all subjects, as is shown on the other three rows of

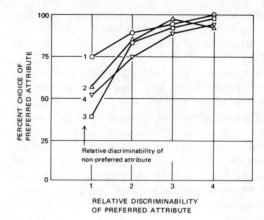

Fig. 3

Percentage choice of a preferred attribute in free classification as a function of its discriminability and the discriminability of a competing nonpreferred attribute (from Imai & Garner, 1965).

data. On the top row, 12 of the subjects preferred Distance, using it 69% of the time. On the second row, 8 of the subjects preferred Orientation, using it nearly 62% of the time. And on the third row, 4 subjects preferred both Distance and Orientation equally, using each of them about 40% of the time. No subject preferred Position as the classifying attribute.

So not only are there overall preferences for attributes, but there are also strong individual differences in these preferences. And I hasten to add that these individual differences are not correlated with equivalent differences in speed of sorting with the various attributes.

Still further results are shown in Figure 3. This graph shows data for all the cases where there were just four stimuli in the set; that is, there were just two attributes the subject could use to classify. For each set of stimuli we knew which attribute was preferred over the other on the average, and the discriminability of this attribute is shown on the abscissa. The discriminability of the nonpreferred attribute is shown separately for each of the curves; and the ordinate shows the percentage of times that the preferred attribute was actually chosen. Notice, on the right, that when the preferred attribute has high discriminability, it is chosen regardless of the discriminability of the nonpreferred attribute. However, on the left, where the preferred attribute has low discriminability, the discriminability of the nonpreferred attribute affects the choice, even to

TABLE 1

Percentage Choice of Attribute by Three Types of Subjects in Free Classification

Subject type	Attribute chosen			
	Distance	Orientation	Position	Other
D preferring (12)	69.0	22.3	5.3	3.4
O preferring (8)	22.8	61.9	12.2	3.1
DO preferring (4)	39.5	40.0	19.0	1.5
All subjects (24)	48.7	38.4	9.9	3.0

Note. From Imai and Garner (1965).

198

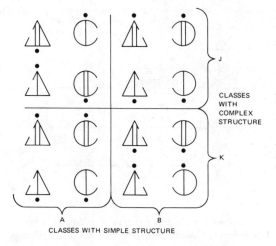

Fig. 4
Stimuli used in classification learning (after Whitman &
Garner, 1963).

the extent that it will be chosen more often than the
preferred attribute.

So this experiment has shown us that what the
subject can do is one thing, but that what he does do
is quite another. What he can do is to ignore all attributes of the stimulus which define a larger set except
the differentiating one, and he shows no performance
advantage of one attribute over another. What he does
do is to have definite and personal preferences for attributes, and his perceptual organization is affected by
all attributes defining the set of stimuli. To perceive is
to know—all properties of the stimulus set, not just
those immediately relevant to discrimination.

Classification Learning

The next experiment I shall discuss was done in collaboration with James Whitman (Whitman & Garner,
1963), and it concerns the learning of classifications.
This type of task is, in a sense, another form of constrained classification since the experimenter sets the
rules (that is, he defines the subsets or classes of
stimuli to be learned) and the subject is required to
perform according to these rules, even having to discover them.

The particular purpose of this experiment can most
easily be seen with reference to the stimuli actually
used, as shown in Figure 4. This total set of 16 stimuli
is formed from four dichotomous attributes: circle or
triangle; one vertical line or two; gap on the right or on

the left; and dot above or below. These 16 stimuli were
formed into two classes of 8 in two different ways, as
indicated in the figure.

First, notice the two classes formed by a vertical
separation. Each of these classes has an equal number
of each level of each attribute. For example, the class of
stimuli labeled "A" has four triangles and four circles,
and so does the remaining set of stimuli, those labeled
"B." The same is true for location of gap, number of
lines, and location of dot. In addition, within each of
these two classes one pair of attributes is perfectly correlated. Specifically, in the eight Class A stimuli, the
gap is always on the left of the triangle and on the right
of the circle. This same pair of attributes is also correlated in the Class B stimuli, except now the gap is on
the right of the triangle and on the left of the circle. The
structure have no pair correlations. To illustrate, in the
we know from a previous experiment (Whitman &
Garner, 1962) that subsets with these simple contingencies or correlations are easy to learn.

Now notice the classes formed with a horizontal
separation. Once again, each of the classes has an equal
number of each level of each attribute. So there is no
difference between the two methods of classification in
this regard. However, these classes with complex
structure have no pair correlations. To illustrate , in the
J class, half the time the gap is on the right of the circle
and half the time on the left, and the same is true for
the triangles. Nor is any other pair of attributes
correlated.

Now our specific experimental question was
whether the nature of the classification system affected
the ease of classification learning. But more importantly, we wanted to know whether the difference in
difficulty of learning (which we really knew to exist in
some cases at least) depended on how the stimuli were
presented to the subject. In particular, we wanted to
know whether presenting classes with simple structure
as intact groups, rather than as single stimuli, facilitated learning.

Both classes presented mixed. In the more-or-less traditional method used in concept or classification
learning, stimuli from both classes are presented singly
and in a mixed order, and this is one of the methods
we used. On each trial all 16 stimuli were presented,
with the stimuli randomly arranged in order, and with
each stimulus labeled. The subject read out the label—
the A or B, the J or K—on each stimulus card. At the
end of each trial, a shuffled deck of all 16 cards was

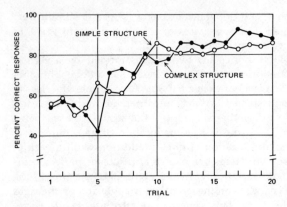

Fig. 5
Learning curves for simple and complex classifications when both classes are presented mixed (after Whitman & Garner, 1963).

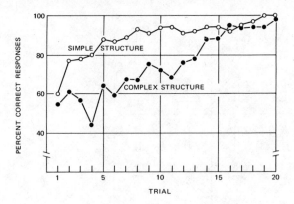

Fig. 6
Learning curves for simple and complex classifications when one class is presented alone (after Whitman & Garner, 1963).

handed to the subject, who was then required to sort them into the two separate classes.

The learning curves obtained with this method are shown in Figure 5. The percentage of correct responses is shown on the ordinate as a function of trials. These two curves cross and recross, and there is no significant difference between them. The conclusion with this method is that the nature of the structure in the subset does not affect the ease of learning.

One class presented alone. With the other method, we presented just one class of stimuli to the subject—either the A stimuli or the J stimuli, depending on which classification was being learned. Once again the subject read aloud the label on each stimulus, but the label that he read was always the same. The other stimuli were never shown to the subject on the presentation trials. After each trial, the subject was again given the full set of stimuli and required to sort them into the two classes.

The results with this method are shown in Figure 6. Here there is a very clear separation between the two curves, showing that the classification with simple structure is much easier to learn than the classification with complex structure. Incidentally, the bottom curve here is not significantly different from the two curves obtained with mixed stimulus presentation, so this method facilitates learning of the classification with simple structure, rather than making it more difficult with complex structure.

This last point is of some importance, because if we just look at learning of sets with simple structure and compare learning with the two methods of stimulus presentation, we see that learning improves when we show the subject only half the stimuli. This result does not seem reasonable unless we realize that the subjects are in fact learning sets of stimuli, not individual stimuli.

The conclusion is clear: People do perceive properties of sets of stimuli, and these properties affect ease of learning. But the stimuli must be presented so that it is clear to the subject what constitutes a single class or group or subset. If the stimuli are presented so that the subject must learn them as individual stimuli, he can do so, but then he cannot take advantage of some facilitating properties of sets.

Visual Pattern Perception
The next problem area I want to discuss involves two experiments, in which David Clement and Stephen Handel were my collaborators (Garner & Clement, 1963; Handel & Garner, 1966). The problem is to determine the nature of pattern goodness with visual patterns.

In my *Uncertainty and Structure* book (Garner, 1962) I discussed the relation between pattern goodness and the concept of redundancy, or its inverse uncertainty. Goodness is a concept appropriate to a particular pattern, not a subset of patterns. Nevertheless, I had

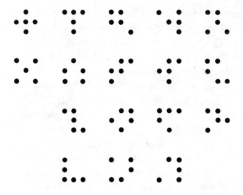

Fig. 7
Prototypical dot patterns used in experiments on pattern goodness. (Each of these patterns is 1 from a subset of 1, 4, or 8 patterns which are equivalent when rotated or reflected.)

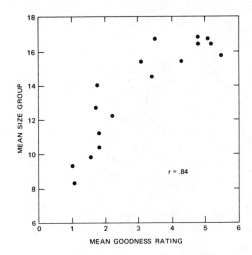

Fig. 8
Mean goodness rating versus mean size group for 17 dot patterns (after Garner & Clement, 1963).

suggested that the goodness of the single pattern is itself related to the size of a subset of patterns in which the particular pattern exists. This subset, however, is not defined objectively, or even by the experimenter, but rather is inferred by the subject. I had stated the specific hypothesis that good patterns come from small inferred subsets, and poor patterns come from large ones. These experiments are concerned with this hypothesis.

The kinds of stimuli used in these two experiments are shown in Figure 7. These stimulus patterns are produced by placing five dots in the cells of a 3×3 imaginary matrix. Although there are 126 patterns which can be formed in this manner, in our first experiment we used just 90 of them, eliminating those patterns in which a row or a column had no dot in it. These 90 patterns form several subsets of patterns by the objective rule that all patterns which can produce each other by rotation or reflection are to be considered as a single subset. In this figure, 1 pattern from each of the 17 such subsets is shown, and our data will be given for these 17 prototypical patterns.

In this first experiment, subjects did two things with these 90 patterns. One group of subjects rated each of the 90 patterns for goodness on a 7-point scale, and we obtained a mean rating for each of the patterns. Another group of subjects was required to sort the 90 patterns into approximately eight groups, keeping similar patterns in the same group. These subjects were

not, however, required to have all groups be of the same size, and in fact the measure we used for each pattern was the size of the group in which it had been placed. We used a mean size of group as the summary statistic for this second task.

Now we have for each of the 90 patterns a mean goodness rating and a mean size group, and the hypothesis states that these two measures should be correlated. The relation between these measures for the 17 prototypical patterns is shown in Figure 8. Here the mean goodness rating (with a small numerical rating meaning a good pattern) is shown on the abscissa, and the mean size group is on the ordinate. The correlation between these two measures is .84, which is quite high enough for us to conclude that the basic hypothesis is essentially correct: Good patterns come from small inferred subsets, and poor patterns come from large inferred subsets.

Nested or partitioned sets? Our basic conception of the different sizes of inferred subsets was as shown in Figure 9. Here the outer bound represents the total set of stimulus patterns, and the smaller regions inside represent the inferred subsets, whose sizes we obtained experimentally. Notice that these subsets differ in size, and are also mutually exclusive; that is, the subsets do not overlap each other. Subset A is, to illustrate, a small subset of good patterns, and Subset I is a

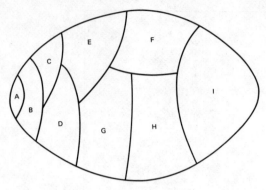

Fig. 9
A conception of subsets of unequal size produced by partitioning. (All subsets are mutually exclusive.)

large subset of different, poor patterns. This method of obtaining subsets from a total set is called partitioning, and it corresponds exactly to what we required our subjects to do, since they had to form different groups using all of the stimuli, and no stimulus was allowed to be in more than one group.

After this experiment had been completed, it occurred to us that there is at least one other highly possible way in which subjects can infer subsets of different sizes, and that is with the use of nested sets. A diagram of such a system of subsets is shown in Figure 10. In this conception, Set A includes Subset B and Subset C, and in fact all of the stimuli. Subset B includes Subset C and Subset D, and in fact all of the stimuli except those in Set A which do not overlap with Subset B; and likewise for Set C. In other words,

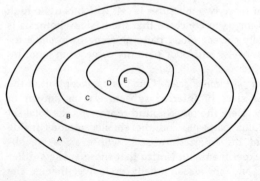

Fig. 10
A conception of subsets of unequal size produced by nesting. (Each subset includes all smaller ones.)

these sets form a kind of inclusive ordering with respect to size of set, since the most inclusive set will contain all stimuli, the next most will contain all but a few of those in the largest set, until finally the smallest set may well contain only a single stimulus.

This conception would have satisfied the requirements of the original hypothesis perfectly well, since all the hypothesis required is that inferred subsets have different sizes. In fact, if the nesting conception of the perceptual process is correct, our obtaining of such a high correlation between goodness and inferred subset size might have been a little fortunate, since in our experimental procedure we forced the subjects to partition, and the partitions formed from nonoverlapping parts need not vary in size.

A very plausible assumption allowed us to get at this problem with a quite different experimental technique. The technique was to obtain pattern "associates" by presenting one pattern to a subject as a stimulus and then asking him to produce one as an associate which was suggested by it, but not identical to it. We carried out this pattern-associates experiment with all of the 126 dot patterns which can be generated with five dots in the nine-cell matrix.

The assumption which makes this experimental procedure interpretable to the nesting conception is simply this: A pattern will be used as an associate to another stimulus pattern only if it lies in the smallest subset in which the stimulus pattern exists. To illustrate, suppose Stimulus x exists in Set A but not in B or any smaller set—that is, it exists in the outer ring. Its smallest subset is the total set, so any pattern in the total set can be used as an associate to it. Now suppose that Stimulus y exists in Subset B but not in that part of A which does not overlap B. Such a stimulus exists in both A and in B, but since B is the smaller subset, any associate must come from Subset B.

The consequence of this assumption is that the associates are unidirectional—they can go toward a smaller subset, but cannot go backward to a larger subset. If we are right that these smaller subsets contain the better patterns, then this assumption means that pattern associates will move toward good patterns. And the actual experimental result will be that some patterns (the poor ones) will have many other patterns as associates, while other patterns (the good ones) will have very few different associates.

The results we obtained with this association experiment are illustrated in Figure 11. In this figure each

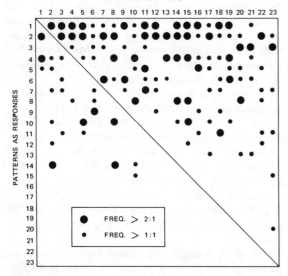

Fig. 11
The distribution of patterns used as associates to different patterns used as stimuli. (The filled circles indicate a greater than expected ratio of occurrences—after Handel & Garner, 1966).

column stands for a pattern used as a stimulus and each equivalent row for the same pattern used as a response. If our nesting idea is correct, it should be possible to arrange the order of the patterns so that practically all of the associates are above the diagonal line, that is, go toward better patterns, and the ordering shown here is the best that can be obtained with this criterion. (Again, incidentally, we are showing data for prototypical patterns rather than for each individual pattern.)

These actual results strongly confirm our hypothesis (with its working assumption). The small circles represent cells whose frequencies are greater than the expected value (assuming all associates equally likely) and the large circles represent cells where the expected frequency has been exceeded by a factor of 2. The vast majority of the associates are clearly unidirectional. Only with the lower numbered patterns—those presumably nested well within the total set—do we get apparent bi-directionality of associates. We must remember, however, that our technique is limited since subjects were required to produce an associate different from the stimulus. So

these bidirectional associates may be an artifact of our method.

The ordering of these stimulus patterns in this figure is based entirely on the association data. We also did obtain goodness ratings of the patterns, and the correlation between the orderings based on associations and those based on goodness ratings is .85. Thus, not only can we feel that the nesting conception is fundamentally correct, but we also know that it is related to pattern goodness.

Furthermore, both of these experiments show that sets and subsets of stimuli do exist for subjects even though we, as experimenters, present a single stimulus and want to act as though the single stimulus exists in isolation. The subject actively participates in the perceptual process by forming sets and subsets of stimuli and his perception of the individual stimulus is really perception of the properties of these sets.

Auditory Pattern Perception
The last experiment I shall describe concerns auditory pattern perception, and was done in collaboration with Fred Royer (Royer & Garner, 1966). In changing from visual pattern perception to auditory pattern perception, it is inevitable that we change from thinking of patterns as existing in space (which is the primary way in which visual patterns are perceived) to thinking of patterns as existing in time (which is the primary way in which auditory patterns are perceived).

The questions we undertook to investigate were: first, whether the concept of pattern complexity or goodness is appropriate to auditory temporal pattern perception; second, whether such pattern goodness is related to the size of an inferred subset of stimuli; and third, whether the difficulty of perceiving a perceptual organization or pattern is related to the complexity and the size of the inferred subset.

The stimuli we used consisted of dichotomous, qualitatively different elements (two different door buzzers worked quite well for us), presented in a rigidly fixed time schedule of two per second, and at the same intensity and duration. We worked with a basic sequence of eight elements, and actually used all of the 256 sequences which can be generated with dichotomous elements in sequences of eight. However, once a particular sequence was started, it continued indefinitely with no break at the end of the eight elements.

Three of the sequences used, and some results obtained with them, are shown in Figure 12. The three

PATTERN	UNCERTAINTY OF POINT OF RESPONSE (BITS)	AVERAGE RESPONSE DELAY	AVERAGE NO. ERRORS
G 11111000	1.45	20.5	0.34
K 11110010	2.02	33.4	1.59
T 11011010	2.73	48.8	3.34

Fig. 12
Response uncertainty, delay, and errors for three auditory temporal patterns (after Royer & Garner, 1966).

actual patterns are shown on the left, with the 0's and 1's standing for the two dichotomous elements or buzzers. These 256 different sequences, when repeated, reduce to a much smaller number, because on repetition many of the patterns become the same. To illustrate, Pattern G is shown here as 11111000. Another actual sequence is 11100011, but this sequence, when repeated, becomes exactly the same as Pattern G, and can be considered the same as Pattern G except that it is started at the third position of the pattern. Most of the 256 patterns are one of a subset of eight, all of which are the same with continued repetition, and the three patterns illustrated here are all of this type.

Our experimental procedure was moderately straightforward. We started a particular pattern and the subject was required simply to listen to it. As soon as he thought he could, he was to produce the pattern by pushing two telegraph keys in synchrony with the auditory pattern, which continued until the subject had been correct for two complete cycles.

We measured three things: Two of them are measures which reflect the difficulty of a pattern to a subject—first, the delay after the stimulus sequence had begun and before the subject attempted to respond, shown as the average response delay in the middle column; and second, the number of errors made after responding began, shown on the far right as an average per subject per sequence.

The third measure requires a slight explanation. Each pattern was started at each of its eight possible starting points, but there was no requirement that the subject begin responding at that particular point—he was free to begin responding at any point in the sequence. We noted the exact point in the sequence at which the subject started to respond. Not all subjects started at the same point, nor did the same subject start at the same point each time he heard a particular pattern but with a different stimulus starting point. So we have a distribution of beginning response points for each pattern, and the variability of this distribution was measured in bits of uncertainty. It is the measure shown in the first column of numbers.

This number tells us one of the things we want to know. There are not in fact 256 perceived temporal patterns, but considerably fewer, because all alternative modes of organization are not acceptable to subjects. But more important, it makes clear that the number of alternative modes of organization does vary from pattern to pattern, and by a substantial amount. These three patterns have uncertainties which are the equivalent of less than three alternative organizations for Pattern G, to about four for Pattern K, to almost seven for Pattern T.

So there is a difference in size of an inferred, or subjective, subset of patterns which is quite analogous to what we find with visual patterns. Furthermore, this size is obviously related to pattern complexity or goodness—so much so that we did not think it necessary to obtain direct goodness ratings of the various patterns. Good or simple auditory patterns have few alternative modes of organization; poor patterns have many alternative modes.

Now to return to our measures of perceptual difficulty. The average response delay does vary with complexity and uncertainty, being just over 20 elements for Pattern G and almost 49 elements for Pattern T. In like manner, the number of errors made after starting to respond varies from about one error for every three sequences with Pattern G to over three per sequence with Pattern T. So both delay and errors are highly correlated with each other, and either or both of them are highly correlated with the uncertainty of the point at which responding begins.

To summarize, there are simple and complex auditory temporal patterns. Simple patterns (good, in the Gestalt sense) are stable, have few alternative modes of perceptual organization, and are quickly organized with little error. Complex patterns are unstable, have many alternative modes of perceptual organization, are organized only after considerable time, and even after that are organized imperfectly. And again it is clear that the perceiver actively participates in the organizing process.

Conclusion

In conclusion, I hope that these experiments have illustrated for you that to perceive is to know. It is to know and comprehend the nature of a stimulus; it is to know the nature of the alternatives to a stimulus; and it is to know the structure and organization of sets of stimuli. Furthermore, the perception of stimuli as existing in sets and subsets is an active process for the perceiver, one in which he will define and organize sets of stimuli which he may never have experienced, if the nature of a stimulus clearly requires such an inference in order for it to be known.

References

Garner, W. R. *Uncertainty and structure as psychological concepts.* New York: Wiley, 1962.

Garner, W. R., & Clement, D. E. Goodness of pattern and pattern uncertainty. *Journal of Verbal Learning and Verbal Behavior,* 1963, 2, 446–452.

Handel, S., & Garner, W. R. The structure of visual pattern associates and pattern goodness. *Journal of Perception and Psychophysics,* 1966.

Imai, S., & Garner, W. R. Discriminability and preference for attributes in free and constrained classification. *Journal of Experimental Psychology,* 1965, *69,* 596–608.

Royer, F. L., & Garner, W. R. Response uncertainty and perceptual difficulty of auditory temporal patterns. *Journal of Perception and Psychophysics,* 1966.

Whitman, J. R. & Garner, W. R. Free recall learning of visual figures as a function of form of internal structure. *Journal of Experimental Psychology,* 1962, *64,* 558–564.

Whitman, J. R., & Garner, W. R. Concept learning as a function of form of internal structure. *Journal of Verbal Learning and Verbal Behavior,* 1963, *2,* 195–202.

the growth of mind[1]

jerome s. bruner
harvard university

These past several years, I have had the painful pleasure — and it has been both — of exploring two aspects of the cognitive processes that were new to me. One was cognitive development, the other pedagogy. I knew, as we all know, that the two were closely related, and it was my naive hope that, betimes, the relation would come clear to me. Indeed, 2 years ago when I first knew that in early September 1965 I would be standing here, delivering this lecture, I said to myself that I would use the occasion to set forth to my colleagues what I had been able to find out about this vexed subject, the relation of pedagogy and development. It seemed obvious then that in 2 years one could get to the heart of the matter.

1. Address of the President to the Seventy-Third Annual Convention of the American Psychological Association, Chicago, September 4, 1965. Reprinted from *American Psychologist*, 1965, Vol. 20, pp. 1007–1017. Copyright 1965 by the American Psychological Association, and reproduced by permission.

The 2 years have gone by. I have had the privilege of addressing this distinguished audience (Bruner, 1964) on some of our findings concerning the development of cognitive processes in children, and I have similarly set forth what I hope are not entirely unreasonable ideas about pedagogy (Bruner, 1966). I am still in a very deep quandary concerning the relation of these two enterprises. The heart of the matter still eludes me, but I shall stand by my resolve. I begin on this autobiographical note so that you may know in advance why this evening is more an exercise in conjecture than a cataloguing of solid conclusions.

What is most unique about man is that his growth as an individual depends upon the history of his species — not upon a history reflected in genes and chromosomes but, rather, reflected in a culture external to man's tissue and wider in scope than is embodied in any one man's competency. Perforce, then, the growth of mind is always growth assisted from the outside. And since a culture, particularly an advanced one, transcends the bounds of individual competence, the limits for individual growth are by definition greater than what any single person has previously attained. For the limits of growth depend on how a culture assists the individual to use such intellectual potential as he may possess. It seems highly unlikely — either empirically or canonically — that we have any realistic sense of the furthest reach of such assistance to growth.

The evidence today is that the full evolution of intelligence came as a result of bipedalism and tool using. The large human brain gradually evolved as a sequel to the first use of pebble tools by early near-man. To condense the story, a near-man, or hominid, with a slightly superior brain, using a pebble tool, could make out better in the niche provided by nature than a near-man who depended not on tools but on sheer strength and formidable jaws. Natural selection favored the primitive tool user. In time, thanks to his better chance of surviving and breeding, he became more so: The ones who survived had larger brains, smaller jaws, less ferocious teeth. In place of belligerent anatomy, they developed tools and a brain that made it possible to use them. Human evolution thereafter became less a matter of having appropriate fangs or claws and more one of using and later fashioning tools to express the powers of the larger brain that was also emerging. Without tools the brain was of little use, no matter how many hundred cubic centimeters of it there might be. Let it also be said that without the original programmatic capacity for fitting tools into a sequence of acts, early hominids would never have started the epigenetic progress that brought them to their present state. And as human groups stabilized, tools became more complex and "shaped to pattern," so that it was no longer a matter of reinventing tools in order to survive, but rather of mastering the skills necessary for using them. In short, after a certain point in human evolution, the only means whereby man could fill his evolutionary niche was through the cultural transmission of the skills necessary for the use of priorly invented techniques, implements, and devices.

Two crucial parallel developments seem also to have occurred. As hominids became increasingly bipedal, with the freed hands necessary for using spontaneous pebble tools, selection also favored those with a heavier pelvic bony structure that could sustain the impacting strain of bipedal locomotion. The added strength came, of course, from a gradual closing down of the birth canal. There is an obstetrical paradox here: a creature with an increasingly larger brain but with a smaller and smaller birth canal to get through. The resolution seems to have been achieved through the immaturity of the human neonate, particulary cerebral immaturity that assures not only a smaller head, but also a longer period of transmitting the necessary skills required by human culture. During this same period, human language must have emerged, giving man not only a new and powerful way of representing reality but also increasing his power to assist the mental growth of the young to a degree beyond anything before seen in nature.

It is impossible, of course, to reconstruct the evolution in techniques of instruction in the shadow zone between hominids and man. I have tried to compensate by observing contemporary analogues of earlier forms, knowing full well that the pursuit of analogy can be dangerously misleading. I have spent many hours observing uncut films of the behavior of free-ranging baboons, films shot in East Africa by my colleague Irven DeVore with a very generous footage devoted to infants and juveniles. I have also had access to the unedited film archives of a hunting-gathering people living under roughly analogous ecological conditions, the !Kung Bushman of the Kalahari, recorded by Laurance and Lorna Marshall, brilliantly aided by their son John and daughter Elizabeth.[2] I have also worked directly but informally with the Wolof of Senegal, observing children in the bush and in French-style schools. Even more valuable than my own informal observations in Senegal were the systematic experiments carried out later by my colleague, Patricia Marks Greenfield (1966).

Let me describe very briefly some salient differences in the free learning patterns of immature baboons and among !Kung children. Baboons have a highly developed social life in their troops, with well-organized and stable dominance patterns. They live within a territory, protecting themselves from predators by joint action of the strongly built, adult males. It is striking that the behavior of baboon juveniles is shaped principally by play with their peer group, play that provides opportunity for the spontaneous expression and practice of the component acts that, in maturity, will be orchestrated into either the behavior of the dominant male or of the infant-protective female. All this seems to be accomplished with little participation by any mature animals in the play of the juveniles. We know from the important experiments of Harlow and his colleagues (Harlow & Harlow, 1962) how devastating a disruption in development can be produced in subhuman primates by interfering with

2. I am greatly indebted to Irven DeVore and Educational Services Incorporated for the opportunity to view his films of free-ranging baboons, and to Laurance and Lorna Marshall for the opportunity to examine their incomparable archives. DeVore and the Marshalls have been generous in their counsel as well.

their opportunity for peer-group play and social interaction.

Among hunting-gathering humans, on the other hand, there is *constant* interaction between adult and child, or adult and adolescent, or adolescent and child. !Kung adults and children play and dance together, sit together, participate in minor hunting together, join in song and story telling together. At very frequent intervals, moreover, children are party to rituals presided over by adults—minor, as in the first haircutting, or major, as when a boy kills his first Kudu buck and goes through the proud but painful process of scarification. Children, besides, are constantly playing imitatively with the rituals, implements, tools, and weapons of the adult world. Young juvenile baboons, on the other hand, virtually never play with things or imitate directly large and significant sequences of adult behavior.

Note, though, that in tens of thousands of feet of !Kung film, one virtually never sees an instance of "teaching" taking place outside the situation where the behavior to be learned is relevant. Nobody "teaches" in our prepared sense of the word. There is nothing like school, nothing like lessons. Indeed, among the !Kung children there is very little "telling." Most of what we would call instruction is through showing. And there is no "practice" or "drill" as such save in the form of play modeled directly on adult models—play hunting, play bossing, play exchanging, play baby tending, play house making. In the end, every man in the culture knows nearly all there is to know about how to get on with life as a man, and every woman as a woman—the skills, the rituals and myths, the obligations and rights.

The change in the instruction of children in more complex societies is twofold. First of all, there is knowledge and skill in the culture far in excess of what any one individual knows. And so, increasingly, there develops an economical technique of instructing the young based heavily on *telling* out of context rather than *showing* in context. In literate societies, the practice becomes institutionalized in the school or the "teacher." Both promote this necessarily abstract way of instructing the young. The result of "teaching the culture" can, at its worst, lead to the ritual, rote nonsense that has led a generation of critics from Max Wertheimer (1945) to Mary Alice White (undated) of Teachers' College to despair. For in the detached school, what is imparted often has little to do with life

as lived in the society except insofar as the demands of school are of a kind that reflect *indirectly* the demands of life in a technical society. But these indirectly imposed demands may be the most important feature of the detached school. For school is a sharp departure from indigenous practice. It takes learning, as we have noted, out of the context of immediate action just by dint of putting it into a school. This very extirpation makes learning become an act in itself, freed from the immediate ends of action, preparing the learner for the chain of reckoning remote from payoff that is needed for the formulation of complex ideas. At the same time, the school (if successful) frees the child from the pace setting of the round of daily activity. If the school succeeds in avoiding a pace-setting round of its own, it may be one of the great agents for promoting reflectiveness. Moreover, in school, one must "follow the lesson" which means one must learn to follow either the abstraction of written speech—abstract in the sense that it is divorced from the concrete situation to which the speech might originally have been related—or the abstraction of language delivered orally but out of the context of an ongoing action. Both of these are highly abstract uses of language.

It is no wonder, then, that many recent studies report large differences between "primitive" children who are in schools and their brothers who are not: differences in perception, abstraction, time perspective, and so on. I need only cite the work of Biesheuvel (1949) in South Africa, Gay and Cole (undated) in Liberia, Greenfield (1966) in Senegal, Maccoby and Modiano (1966) in rural Mexico, Reich (1966) among Alaskan Eskimos.

What a culture does to assist the development of the powers of mind of its members is, in effect, to provide amplification systems to which human beings, equipped with appropriate skills, can link themselves. There are, first, the amplifiers of action—hammers, levers, digging sticks, wheels—but more important, the programs of action into which such implements can be substituted. Second, there are amplifiers of the senses, ways of looking and noticing that can take advantage of devices ranging from smoke signals and hailers to diagrams and pictures that stop the action or microscopes that enlarge it. Finally and most powerfully, there are amplifiers of the thought processes, ways of thinking that employ language and formation of explanation, and later use such languages as mathematics and logic and even find automatic servants to crank out the consequences. A culture is, then, a deviser, a repository, and a transmitter of amplification systems and of the devices that fit into such systems. We know very little in a deep sense about the transmission function, how people are trained to get the most from their potential by use of a culture's resources.

But it is reasonably clear that there is a major difference between the mode of transmission in a technical society, with its schools, and an indigenous one, where cultural transmission is in the context of action. It is not just that an indigenous society, when its action pattern becomes disrupted falls apart—at a most terrifying rate—as in uncontrolled urbanization in some parts of Africa. Rather, it is that the institution of a school serves to convert knowledge and skill into more symbolical, more abstract, more verbal form. It is this process of transmission—admittedly very new in human history—that is so poorly understood and to which, finally, we shall return.

There are certain obvious specifications that can be stated about how a society must proceed in order to equip its young. It must convert what is to be known— whether a skill or a belief system or a connected body of knowledge—into a form capable of being mastered by a beginner. The more we know of the process of growth, the better we shall be at such conversion. The failure of modern man to understand mathematics and science may be less a matter of stunted abilities than our failure to understand how to teach such subjects. Second, given the limited amount of time available for learning, there must be a due regard for saving the learner from needless learning. There must be some emphasis placed on economy and transfer and the learning of general rules. All societies must (and virtually all do) distinguish those who are clever from those who are stupid—though few of them generalize this trait across all activities. Cleverness in a particular activity almost universally connotes strategy, economy, heuristics, highly generalized skills. A society must also place emphasis upon how one derives a course of action from what one has learned. Indeed, in an indigenous society, it is almost impossible to separate what one does from what one knows. More advanced societies often have not found a way of dealing with the separation of knowledge and action—probably a result of the emphasis they place upon "telling" in their instruction. All societies must maintain interest among the young in the learning process, a minor problem

when learning is in the context of life and action, but harder when it becomes more abstracted. And finally, and perhaps most obviously, a society must assure that its necessary skills and procedures remain intact from one generation to the next—which does not always happen, as witnessed by Easter Islanders, Incas, Aztecs, and Mayas.[3]

Unfortunately, psychology has not concerned itself much with any of these five requisites of cultural transmission—or at least not much with four of them. We have too easily assumed that learning is learning is learning—that the early version of what was taught did not matter much, one thing being much like another and reducible to a pattern of association, to stimulus-response connections, or to our favorite molecular componentry. We denied there was a problem of development beyond the quantitative one of providing more experience, and with the denial, closed our eyes to the pedagogical problem of how to represent knowledge, how to sequence it, how to embody it in a form appropriate to young learners. We expended more passion on the part-whole controversy than on what whole or what part of it was to be presented first. I should except Piaget (1954), Köhler (1940), and Vygotsky (1962) from these complaints—all until recently unheeded voices.

Our neglect of the economy of learning stems, ironically, from the heritage of Ebbinghaus (1913), who was vastly interested in savings. Our nonsense syllables, our random mazes failed to take into account how we reduce complexity and strangeness to simplicity and the familiar, how we convert what we have learned into rules and procedures, how, to use Bartlett's (1932) term of over 30 years ago, we turn around

3. I have purposely left out of the discussion the problems of impulse regulation and socialization of motives, topics that have received extended treatment in the voluminous literature on culture and personality. The omission is dictated by emphasis rather than evaluation. Obviously, the shaping of character by culture is of great importance for an understanding of our topic as it bears, for example, upon culture-instilled attitudes toward the uses of mind. Since our emphasis is upon human potential and its amplification by culturally patterned instrumental skills, we mention the problem of character formation in passing and in recognition of its importance in a complete treatment of the issues under discussion.

on our own schemata to reorganize what we have mastered into more manageable form.

Nor have we taken naturally to the issue of knowledge and action. Its apparent mentalism has repelled us. Tolman (1951), who bravely made the distinction, was accused of leaving his organisms wrapt in thought. But he recognized the problem and if he insisted on the idea that knowledge might be organized in cognitive maps, it was in recognition (as a great functionalist) that organisms go somewhere on the basis of what they have learned. I believe we are getting closer to the problem of how knowledge affects action and vice versa, and offer in testimony of my conviction the provocative book by Miller, Galanter, and Pribram (1960), *Plans and the Structure of Behavior*.

Where the maintenance of the learner's interest is concerned, I remind you of what my colleague Gordon Allport (1946) has long warned. We have been so concerned with the model of driven behavior, with drive reduction and the *vis a tergo* that, again, until recently, we have tended to overlook the question of what keeps learners interested in the activity of learning, in the achievement of competence beyond bare necessity and first payoff. The work of R. W. White (1959) on effectance motivation, of Harlow and his colleagues (Butler, 1954; Harlow, 1953) on curiosity, and of Heider (1958) and Festinger (1962) on consistency begins to redress the balance. But it is only a beginning.

The invention of antidegradation devices, guarantors that skill and knowledge will be maintained intact, is an exception to our oversight. We psychologists have been up to our ears in it. Our special contribution is the achievement test. But the achievement test has, in the main, reflected the timidity of the educational enterprise as a whole. I believe we know how to determine, though we have not yet devised tests to determine, how pupils use what they learn to think with later in life — for there is the real issue.

I have tried to examine briefly what a culture must do in passing on its amplifying skills and knowledge to a new generation and, even more briefly, how we as psychologists have dealt or failed to deal with the problems. I think the situation is fast changing — with a sharp increase in interest in the conversion problem, the problems of economy of learning, the nature of interest, the relation of knowledge and action. We are, I believe, at a major turning point where psychology will once again concern itself with the design of methods of assisting cognitive growth, be it through the invention of a rational technology of toys, of ways of enriching the environment of the crib and nursery, of organizing the activity of a school, or of devising a curriculum whereby we transmit an organized body of knowledge and skill to a new generation to amplify their powers of mind.

I commented earlier that there was strikingly little knowledge available about the "third way" of training the skills of the young: the first being the play practice of component skills in prehuman primates, the second the teaching-in-context of indigenous societies, and the third being the abstracted, detached method of the school.

Let me now become highly specific. Let me consider a particular course of study, one given in a school, one we are ourselves constructing, trying out, and in a highly qualitative way, evaluating. It is for schools of the kind that exist in Western culture. The experience we have had with this effort, now in its third year, may serve to highlight the kinds of problems and conjectures one encounters in studying how to assist the growth of intellect in this "third way."

There is a dilemma in describing a course of study. One begins by setting forth the intellectual substance of what is to be taught. Yet if such a recounting tempts one to "get across" the subject, the ingredient of pedagogy is in jeopardy. For only in a trivial sense is a course designed to "get something across," merely to impart information. There are better means to that end than teaching. Unless the learner develops his skills, disciplines his taste, deepens his view of the world, the "something" that is got across is hardly worth the effort of transmission.

The more "elementary" a course and the younger its students, the more serious must be its pedagogical aim of forming the intellectual powers of those whom it serves. It is as important to justify a good mathematics course by the intellectual discipline it provides or the honesty it promotes as by the mathematics it transmits. Indeed, neither can be accomplished without the other. The content of this particular course is man: his nature as a species, the forces that shaped and continue to shape his humanity. Three questions recur throughout:

What is human about human beings?
How did they get that way?
How can they be made more so?

In pursuit of our questions we explore five matters, each closely associated with the evolution of man as a species, each defining at once the distinctiveness of man and his potentiality for further evolution. The five great humanizing forces are, of course, tool making, language, social organization, the management of man's prolonged childhood, and man's urge to explain. It has been our first lesson in teaching that no pupil, however eager, can appreciate the relevance of, say, tool making or language in human evolution without first grasping the fundamental concept of a tool or what a language is. These are not self-evident matters, even to the expert. So we are involved in teaching not only the role of tools or language in the emergence of man, but, as a necessary precondition for doing so, setting forth the fundamentals of linguistics or the theory of tools. And it is as often the case as not that (as in the case of the "theory of tools") we must solve a formidable intellectual problem ourselves in order to be able to help our pupils do the same. I should have said at the outset that the "we" I employ in this context is no editorial fiction, but rather a group of anthropologists, zoologists, linguists, theoretical engineers, artists, designers, camera crews, teachers, children, and psychologists. The project is being carried out under my direction at Educational Services, Incorporated, with grants from the National Science Foundation and the Ford Foundation.

While one readily singles out five sources of man's humanization, under no circumstances can they be put into airtight compartments. Human kinship is distinctively different from primate mating patterns precisely because it is classificatory and rests on man's ability to use language. Or, if you will, tool use enhances the division of labor in a society which in turn affects kinship. So while each domain can be treated as a separate set of ideas, their teaching must make it possible for the children to have a sense of their interaction. We have leaned heavily on the use of contrast, highly controlled contrast, to help children achieve detachment from the all too familiar matrix of social life: the contrasts of man versus higher primates, man versus prehistoric man, contemporary technological man versus "primitive" man, and man versus child. The primates are principally baboons, the prehistoric materials mostly from the Olduvai Gorge and Les Eyzies, the "primitive" peoples mostly the Netsilik Eskimos of Pelly Bay and the !Kung Bushmen. The materials, collected for our purposes, are on film, in story, in ethnography, in pictures and drawings, and principally in ideas embodied in exercises.

We have high aspirations. We hope to achieve five goals:

1. To give our pupils respect for and confidence in the powers of their own minds

2. To give them respect, moreover, for the powers of thought concerning the human condition, man's plight, and his social life

3. To provide them with a set of workable models that make it simpler to analyze the nature of the social world in which they live and the condition in which man finds himself

4. To impart a sense of respect for the capacities and plight of man as a species, for his origins, for his potential, for his humanity

5. To leave the student with a sense of the unfinished business of man's evolution

One last word about the course of study that has to do with the quality of the ideas, materials, and artistry—a matter that is at once technological and intellectual. We have felt that the making of such a curriculum deserved the best talent and technique available in the world. Whether artist, ethnographer, film maker, poet, teacher—nobody we have asked has refused us. We are obviously going to suffer in testing a Hawthorne effect of some magnitude. But then, perhaps it is as well to live in a permanent state of revolution.

Let me now try to describe some of the major problems one encounters in trying to construct a course of study. I shall not try to translate the problems into refined theoretical form, for they do not as yet merit such translation. They are more difficulties than problems. I choose them, because they are vividly typical of what one encounters in such enterprises. The course is designed for 10-year-olds in the fifth grade of elementary school, but we have been trying it out as well on the fourth and sixth grades better to bracket our difficulties.

One special point about these difficulties. They are born of trying to achieve an objective and are as much policy bound as theory bound. It is like the difference between building an economic theory about monopolistic practices and constructing policies for controlling monopoly. Let me remind you that modern economic theory has been reformulated, refined, and revived by having a season in policy. I am convinced that the psychology of *assisted growth, i.e., pedagogy,* will have to be forged in the policy crucible of curriculum making before it can reach its full descriptive power as theory. Economics was first through the cycle from theory to policy to theory to policy; it is happening now to psychology, anthropology, and sociology.

Now on to the difficulties. The first is what might be called *the psychology of a subject matter.* A learned discipline can be conceived as a way of thinking about certain phenomena. Mathematics is one way of thinking about order without reference to what is being ordered. The behavioral sciences provide one or perhaps several ways of thinking about man and his society—about regularities, origins, causes, effects. They are probably special (and suspect) because they permit man to look at himself from a perspective that is outside his own skin and beyond his own preferences—at least for awhile.

Underlying a discipline's "way of thought," there is a set of connected, varyingly implicit, generative propositions. In physics and mathematics, most of the underlying generative propositions like the conservation theorems, or the axioms of geometry, or the associative, distributive, and commutative rules of analysis are by now very explicit indeed. In the behavioral sciences we must be content with more implicitness. We traffic in inductive propositions: e.g., the different activities of a society are interconnected such that if you know something about the technological response of a society to an environment, you will be able to make some shrewd guesses about its myths or about the things it values, etc. We use the device of a significant contrast as in linguistics as when we describe the territoriality of a baboon troop in order to help us recognize the system of reciprocal exchange of a human group, the former somehow provoking awareness of the latter.

There is nothing more central to a discipline than its way of thinking. There is nothing more important in its teaching than to provide the child the earliest opportunity to learn that way of thinking—the forms of connection, the attitudes, hopes, jokes, and frustrations that go with it. In a word, the best introduction to a subject is the subject itself. At the very first breath, the young learner should, we think, be given the chance to solve problems, to conjecture, to quarrel as these are done at the heart of the discipline. But, you will ask, how can this be arranged?

Here again the problem of conversion. There exist ways of thinking characteristic of different stages of development. We are acquainted with Inhelder and Piaget's (1958) account of the transition from preoperational, through concrete operational, to propositional thought in the years from preschool through, say, high school. If you have an eventual pedagogical objective in mind, you can translate the way of thought of a discipline into its Piagetian (or other) equivalent appropriate to a given level of development and take the child onward from there. The Cambridge Mathematics Project of Educational Services, Incorporated, argues that if the child is to master the calculus early in his high school years, he should start work early with the idea of limits, the earliest work being manipulative, later going on to images and diagrams, and finally moving on to the more abstract notation needed for delineating the more precise idea of limits.

In "Man: A Course of Study," (Bruner, 1965) there are also versions of the subject appropriate to a particular age that can at a later age be given a more powerful rendering. We have tried to choose topics with this in mind: The analysis of kinship that begins with children using sticks and blocks and colors and whatnot to represent their own families, goes on to the conventional kinship diagrams by a meandering but, as you can imagine, interesting path, and then can move on to more formal and powerful componential analysis. So, too, with myth. We begin with the excitement of a powerful myth (like the Netsilik Nuliajik myth), then have the children construct some myths of their own, then examine what a set of Netsilik myths have in common, which takes us finally to Lévi-Strauss's (1963) analysis of contrastive features in myth construction. A variorum text of a myth or corpus of myths put together by sixth graders can be quite an extraordinary document.

This approach to the psychology of a learned discipline turns out to illuminate another problem raised earlier: the maintenance of interest. There is, in this approach, a reward in understanding that grows from the subject matter itself. It is easier to engineer this satisfaction in mathematics, for understanding is so utter in a formal discipline—a balance beam balances or it does not; therefore there is an equality or there is not. In the behavioral sciences the payoff in understanding cannot be so obviously and startlingly self-revealing. Yet, one can design exercises in the understanding of man, too—as when children figure out the ways in which, given limits of ecology, skills, and materials,

Bushmen hunt different animals, and then compare their predictions with the real thing on film.

Consider now a second problem: *how to stimulate thought in the setting of a school.* We know from experimental studies like those of Bloom and Broder (1950), and of Goodnow and Pettigrew (1955), that there is a striking difference in the acts of a person who thinks that the task before him represents a problem to be solved rather than being controlled by random forces. School is a particular subculture where these matters are concerned. By school age, children have come to expect quite arbitrary and, from their point of view, meaningless demands to be made upon them by adults—the result, most likely, of the fact that adults often fail to recognize the task of conversion necessary to make their questions have some intrinsic significance for the child. Children, of course, will try to solve problems if they recognize them as such. But they are not often either predisposed to or skillful in problem finding, in recognizing the hidden conjectural feature in tasks set them. But we know now that children in school can quite quickly be led to such problem finding by encouragement and instruction.

The need for this instruction and encouragement and its relatively swift success relates, I suspect, to what psychoanalysts refer to as the guilt-ridden over-suppression of primary process and its public replacement by secondary process. Children, like adults, need reassurance that it is all right to entertain and express highly subjective ideas, to treat a task as a problem where you *invent* an answer rather than *finding* one out there in the book or on the blackboard. With children in elementary school, there is often a need to devise emotionally vivid special games, story-making episodes, or construction projects to reestablish in the child's mind his right not only to have his own private ideas but to express them in the public setting of a classroom.

But there is another, perhaps more serious difficulty: the interference of intrinsic problem solving by extrinsic. Young children in school expend extraordinary time and effort figuring out what it is that the teacher wants—and usually coming to the conclusion that she or he wants tidiness or remembering or to do things at a certain time in a certain way. This I refer to as extrinsic problem solving. There is a great deal of it in school.

There are several quite straightforward ways of stimulating problem solving. One is to train teachers to want it and that will come in time. But teachers can be

encouraged to like it, interestingly enough, by providing them and their children with materials and lessons that *permit* legitimate problem solving and permit the teacher to recognize it. For exercises with such materials create an atmosphere by treating things as instances of what *might* have occurred rather than simply as what did occur. Let me illustrate by a concrete instance. A fifth-grade class was working on the organization of a baboon troop—on this particular day, specifically on how they might protect against predators. They saw a brief sequence of film in which six or seven adult males go forward to intimidate and hold off three cheetahs. The teacher asked what the baboons had done to keep the cheetahs off, and there ensued a lively discussion of how the dominant adult males, by showing their formidable mouthful of teeth and making threatening gestures had turned the trick. A boy raised a tentative hand and asked whether cheetahs always attacked together. Yes, though a single cheetah sometimes followed behind a moving troop and picked off an older, weakened straggler or an unwary, straying juvenile. "Well, what if there were four cheetahs and two of them attacked from behind and two from in front. What would the baboons do then?" The question could have been answered empirically—and the inquiry ended. Cheetahs *do not* attack that way, and so we do not know what baboons *might* do. Fortunately, it was not. For the question opens up the deep issues of what might be and why it is not. Is there a necessary relation between predators and prey that share a common ecological niche? Must their encounters have a "sporting chance" outcome? It is such conjecture, in this case quite unanswerable, that produces rational, self-consciously problem-finding behavior so crucial to the growth of intellectual power Given the materials, given some background and encouragement, teachers like it as much as the students.

I should like to turn now to the *personalization of knowledge.* A generation ago, the progressive movement urged that knowledge be related to the child's own experience and brought out of the realm of empty abstractions. A good idea was translated into banalities about the home, then the friendly postman and trashman, then the community, and so on. It is a poor way to compete with the child's own dramas and mysteries. A decade ago, my colleague Clyde Kluckhorn (1949) wrote a prize-winning popular book on anthropology with the entrancing title *Mirror for Man.* In some deep way, there is extraordinary power in "that mirror which other civilizations still hold up to us to recognize and study . . . [the] image of ourselves [Lévi-Strauss, 1965]." The psychological bases of the power are not obvious. Is it as in discrimination learning, where increasing the degree of contrast helps in the learning of a discrimination, or as in studies of concept attainment where a negative instance demonstrably defines the domain of a conceptual rule? Or is it some primitive identification? All these miss one thing that seems to come up frequently in our interviews with the children. It is the experience of discovering kinship and likeness in what at first seemed bizarre, exotic, and even a little repellant.

Consider two examples, both involving film of the Netsilik. In the films, a single nuclear family, Zachary, Marta, and their 4-year-old Alexi, is followed through the year—spring sealing, summer fishing at the stone weir, fall caribou hunting, early winter fishing through the ice, winter at the big ceremonial igloo. Children report that at first the three members of the family look weird and uncouth. In time, they look normal, and eventually, as when Marta finds sticks around which to wrap her braids, the girls speak of how pretty she is. That much is superficial—or so it seems. But consider a second episode.

It has to do with Alexi who, with his father's help, devises a snare and catches a gull. There is a scene in which he stones the gull to death. Our children watched, horror struck. One girl, Kathy, blurted out, "He's not even human, doing that to the seagull." The class was silent. Then another girl, Jennine, said quietly: "He's got to grow up to be a hunter. His mother was smiling when he was doing that." And then an extended discussion about how people have to do things to learn and even do things to learn how to feel appropriately. "What would you do if you had to live there? Would you be as smart about getting along as they are with what they've got?" said one boy, going back to the accusation that Alexi was inhuman to stone the bird.

I am sorry it is so difficult to say it clearly. What I am trying to say is that to personalize knowledge one does not simply link it to the familiar. Rather one makes the familiar an instance of a more general case and thereby produces awareness of it. What the children were learning about was not seagulls and Eskimos, but about their own feelings and preconceptions that, up to then, were too implicit to be recognizable to them.

Consider finally the problem of *self-conscious reflectiveness*. It is an epistemological mystery why tradi-

tional education has so often emphasized extensiveness and coverage over intensiveness and depth. We have already commented on the fact that memorizing was usually perceived by children as one of the high-priority tasks but rarely did children sense an emphasis upon ratiocination with a view toward redefining what had been encountered, reshaping it, reordering it. The cultivation of reflectiveness, or whatever you choose to call it, is one of the great problems one faces in devising curriculum. How lead children to discover the powers and pleasures that await the exercise of retrospection?

Let me suggest one answer that has grown from what we have done. It is the use of the "organizing conjecture." We have used three such conjectures—what is human about human beings, how they got that way, how they could become more so. They serve two functions, one of them the very obvious though important one of putting perspective back into the particulars. The second is less obvious and considerably more surprising. The questions often seemed to serve as criteria for determining where they were getting, how well they were understanding, whether anything new was emerging. Recall Kathy's cry: "He's not human doing that to the seagull." She was hard at work in her rage on the conjecture what makes human beings human.

There, in brief, are four problems that provide some sense of what a psychologist encounters when he takes a hand in assisting the growth of mind in children in the special setting of a school. The problems look quite different from those we encounter in formulating classical developmental theory with the aid of typical laboratory research. They also look very different from those that one would find in an indigenous society, describing how children picked up skills and knowledge and values in the context of action and daily life. We clearly do not have a theory of the school that is sufficient to the task of running schools—just as we have no adequate theory of toys or of readiness building or whatever the jargon is for preparing children to do a better job the next round. It only obscures the issue to urge that some day our classical theories of learning will fill the gap. They show no sign of doing so.

I hope that we shall not allow ourselves to be embarrassed by our present ignorance. It has been a long time since we have looked at what is involved in imparting knowledge through the vehicle of the school—

if ever we did look at it squarely. I urge that we delay no longer.

But I am deeply convinced that the psychologist cannot alone construct a theory of how to assist cognitive development and cannot alone learn how to enrich and amplify the powers of a growing human mind. The task belongs to the whole intellectual community: the behavioral scientists and the artists, scientists, and scholars who are the custodians of skill, taste, and knowledge in our culture. Our special task as psychologists is to convert skills and knowledge to forms and exercises that fit growing minds — and it is a task ranging from how to keep children free from anxiety and how to translate physics for the very young child into a set of playground maneuvers that, later, the child can turn around upon and convert into a sense of inertial regularities.

And this in turn leads me to a final conjecture, one that has to do with the organization of our profession, a matter that has concerned me greatly during this past year during which I have had the privilege of serving as your President. Psychology is peculiarly prey to parochialism. Left to our own devices, we tend to construct models of a man who is neither a victim of history, a target of economic forces, or even a working member of a society. I am still struck by Roger Barker's (1963) ironic truism that the best way to predict the behavior of a human being is to know where he is: In a post office he behaves post office, at church he behaves church.

Psychology, and you will forgive me if the image seems a trifle frivolous, thrives on polygamy with her neighbors. Our marriage with the biological sciences has produced a cumulation of ever more powerful knowledge. So, too, our joint undertakings with anthropology and sociology. Joined together with a variety of disciplines, we have made lasting contributions to the health sciences and, I judge, will make even greater contributions now that the emphasis is shifting to the problems of alleviating stress and arranging for a community's mental health. What I find lacking is an alignment that might properly be called the growth sciences. The field of pedagogy is one participant in the growth sciences. Any field of inquiry devoted to assisting the growth of effective human beings, fully empowered with zest, with skill, with knowledge, with taste is surely a candidate for this sodality. My friend Philip Morrison once suggested to his colleagues at Cornell that his department of physics grant a doctorate not only for work in theoretical, experimental, or applied physics, but also for work in pedagogical physics. The limits of the growth sciences remain to be drawn. They surely transcend the behavioral sciences cum pediatrics. It is plain that, if we are to achieve the effectiveness of which we as human beings are capable, there will one day have to be such a field. I hope that we psychologists can earn our way as charter members.

References

Allport, G. Effect: A secondary principle of learning. *Psychological Review*, 1946, *53*, 335–347.

Baker, R. On the nature of the environment. *Journal of Social Issues*, 1963, *19*, 17–38.

Bartlett, F. *Remembering*. Cambridge, England: Cambridge Univer. Press, 1932.

Biesheuvel, S. Psychological tests and their application to non-European peoples. *Yearbook of Education*. London: Evans, 1949. Pp. 87–126.

Bloom, B., & Broder, L. Problem solving processes of college students. *Supplementary Educational Monograph, No. 73.* Chicago: Univer. Chicago Press, 1950.

Bruner, J. The course of cognitive growth. *American Psychologist*, 1964, *19*, 1–15.

Bruner, J. Man: A course of study. *Educational Services Inc. Quarterly Report*, 1965, Spring-Summer, 3–13.

Bruner, J. *Toward a theory of instruction*. Cambridge: Harvard Univer. Press, 1966.

Butler, R. A. Incentive conditions which influence visual exploration. *Journal of Experimental Psychology*, 1954, *48*, 19–23.

Ebbinghaus, H. *Memory: A contribution to experimental psychology*. New York: Teachers College, Columbia University, 1913.

Festinger, L. A theory of cognitive dissonance. Stanford: Stanford Univer. Press, 1962.

Gay, J., & Cole, M. Outline of general report on Kpelle mathematics project. Stanford: Stanford University, Institute for Mathematical Social Studies, undated. (Mimeo)

Goodnow, Jacqueline, & Pettigrew, T. Effect of prior patterns of experience on strategies and learning sets. *Journal of Experimental Psychology*, 1955, *49*, 381–389.

Greenfield, Patricia M. Culture and conservation. In J. Bruner, Rose Olver, & Patricia M. Greenfield (Eds.), *Studies in cognitive growth*. New York: Wiley, 1966. Ch. 10.

Harlow, H., & Harlow, Margaret. Social deprivation in monkeys. *Scientific American*, 1962, November.

Harlow, H. F. Mice, monkeys, men, and motives. *Psychological Review*, 1953, *60*, 23–32.

Heider, F. *The psychology of interpersonal relations*. New York: Wiley, 1958.

Inhelder, Bärbel, & Piaget, J. *The growth of logical thinking*. New York: Basic Books, 1958.

Kluckhorn, C. *Mirror for man*. New York: Whittlesey House, 1949.

Köhler, W. *Dynamics in psychology*, New York: Liveright, 1940.

Lévi-Strauss, C. The structural study of myth. *Structural anthropology*. (Trans. by Claire Jacobson & B. Grundfest Scharpf) New York: Basic Books, 1963. Pp. 206–231.

Lévi-Strauss, C. Anthropology: Its achievements and future. Lecture presented at Bicentennial Celebration, Smithsonian Institution, Washington, D. C., September 1965.

Maccoby, M., & Modiano, Nancy. On culture and equivalence. In J. Bruner, Rose Olver, & Patricia M. Greenfield (Eds.), *Studies in cognitive growth*. New York: Wiley, 1966. Ch. 12.

Miller, G., Galanter, E., & Pribram, K. *Plans and the structure of behavior*. New York: Holt, 1960.

Piaget, J. *The construction of reality in the child*. New York: Basic Books, 1954.

Reich, Lee. On culture and grouping. In J. Bruner, Rose Olver, & Patricia M. Greenfield (Eds.), *Studies in cognitive growth*. New York: Wiley, 1966. Ch. 13.

Tolman, E. Cognitive maps in rats and men. *Collected papers in psychology*. Berkeley & Los Angeles: Univer. California Press, 1951. Pp. 241–264.

Vygotsky, L. *Thought and language*. (Ed. & trans. by Eugenia Hanfmann & Gertrude Vakar) New York: Wiley, 1962.

Wertheimer, M. *Productive thinking*. New York & London: Harper, 1945.

White, Mary A. The child's world of learning. Teachers College, Columbia University, undated. (Mimeo)

White, R. W. Motivation reconsidered: The concept of competence. *Psychological Review*, 1959, *66*, 297–333.

Some fields of psychology have for many years been dominated by ideas concerning the importance of rewards in the establishment and maintenance of behavior patterns. So dominant has this notion become, that some of our most ingenious theoretical thinking has been devoted to imagining the existence of rewards in order to explain behavior in situations where, plausibly, no rewards exist. It has been observed, for example, that under some circumstances an organism will persist in voluntarily engaging in behavior which is frustrating or painful. To account for such behavior it has, on occasion, been seriously proposed that the cessation of the frustration or pain is rewarding and thus reinforces the tendency to engage in the behavior.

I want to maintain that this type of explanation is not only unnecessary but also misleading. I certainly do *not* wish to say that rewards are unimportant, but I propose to show that the absence of reward or the existence of inadequate reward produces certain specific consequences which can account for a variety of phenomena which are difficult to deal with if we use our usual conceptions of the role of reward.

Before I proceed, I would like to say that most of the thinking and most of the experimental work which I will present are the result of collaboration between Douglas H. Lawrence and myself. Indeed, whatever you find interesting in what I say you may safely attribute primarily to him.

I will start my discussion in a rather roundabout manner with some remarks which concern themselves

the psychological effects of insufficient rewards[1]

leon festinger
new school for social research

primarily with some aspects of the thinking processes of human beings. Human thinking is sometimes a strange mixture of "plausible" and "magical" processes. Let us examine more closely what I mean by this. For example, imagine that a person knows that some event is going to occur, and that the person can do something to prepare himself to cope more adequately with the impending event. Under such circumstances it is very reasonable (perhaps you might even want to use the word "rational") for the person to do whatever is necessary in preparation for the coming event. Human thinking, however, also works in reverse. Consider a person who goes to a lot of trouble to prepare himself for a future event which might pos-

1. Reprinted from *American Psychologist*, 1961, Vol. 16, pp. 1–11. Copyright 1961 by the American Psychological Association, and reproduced by permission.

sibly occur. Such a person will subsequently tend to persuade himself that the event is rather likely to occur. There is nothing very plausible or rational about this kind of mental process—rather, it has almost a magical quality about it. Let me illustrate this briefly by describing an experiment recently conducted by Ruby Yaryan.[2]

Under the pretext of investigating the manner in which students study for examinations, she asked subjects to study a list of arbitrary definitions of symbols in preparation for a possible test. Two conditions were experimentally created for the subjects. Half of the subjects were told that, if they actually took the test, this list of definitions of the symbols would be in their possession during the test, and so, all that was necessary in preparation was to familiarize themselves with the list. This was, essentially, an "easy preparation" condition. That is, not much effort was required of the subjects in advance preparation for the test.

The other half of the subjects were told that, if they actually took the test, they would *not* have the list of definitions with them and so it was necessary for them to memorize the symbols and their definitions in preparation for the test. It is clear that this constitutes a much more "effortful preparation" condition. Considerable effort was required of these subjects in advance preparation for the possible test.

It was carefully explained to each subject that not everyone would actually have to take the test. Specifically, they were told that only half of the people in the experiment *would* take the test. It was also carefully explained that the selection of who would, and who would not, have to take the test had already been made in consultation with their teachers (the subjects were all high school girls). Nothing that happened during the experiment would affect whether or not they took the test—this had already been decided in advance for each of them.

After they finished studying the list of definitions, they were asked a number of questions to preserve the fiction that the experiment was concerned with study habits. Each subject was also asked to indicate how likely she thought it was that she, personally, would have to actually take the test. The results show, quite clearly, that subjects in the effortful preparation con-

2. Yaryan, R. B., & Festinger, L. The effect of preparatory action on belief in the occurrence of possible future events. Unpublished paper.

dition, on the average, thought it was more likely that they would have to take the test than did subjects in the easy preparation condition. In other words, those who were experimentally induced to engage in a lot of preparatory effort, persuaded themselves that the thing they were preparing themselves for would actually occur.

The relevance of this experiment to the problem of the effects of inadequate rewards will become clearer in the following example which illustrates the same psychological process. Consider some person who is strongly attracted to some goal. It is quite reasonable for this person to be willing to expend more effort, or to endure more pain, in order to reach the goal than he would be if he were less attracted. Once more, however, one finds the same process of reasoning in reverse. That is, if a person exerts a great deal of effort, or endures pain, in order to reach some ordinary objective, there is a strong tendency for him to persuade himself that the objective is especially valuable or especially desirable. An experiment conducted by Elliot Aronson and Judson Mills (1959) shows the effect quite nicely.

The subjects in the experiment by Aronson and Mills were college girls who volunteered to join small discussion groups. Each subject, when she appeared for the discussion group, was told that, instead of being put into a new group, she was being considered for inclusion in an ongoing group which had recently lost one of its members. However, the subject was told, because of the group's concern that the replacement be someone who would be able to discuss freely and openly, the experimenter had agreed to test the replacement before admitting her to the group. Some subjects were then given a very brief and not painful test while others were given a rather extended and embarrassing test. The experimenter then, of course, told each subject that she had done well and was admitted to the group. Thus, there were some subjects who had attained membership in the group easily and some subjects who had endured a painful experience in order to be admitted to the group.

The experimenter then explained to the subject that the discussion was carried on by means of an intercommunication system, each girl being in a separate room. She was brought into her room which contained a microphone and earphones. The experimenter told her that the others had already started and perhaps it would be best for her not to participate in the dis-

218

cussion this time but just to listen. Next meeting, of course, she would participate fully. Speaking into the microphone the experimenter then went through the illusion of introducing her to the three other girls in the group. He then "disconnected" the microphone and gave the subject the earphones to wear. The subject then listened for about 25 minutes to a tape recording of a rather dull and halting discussion. All subjects, of course, heard exactly the same tape recording thinking they were listening to the actual live group discussion.

When the discussion was finished, the experimenter explained to the subject that, after each meeting, each of the girls filled out a "post-meeting reaction form." She was then given a questionnaire to complete which asked a variety of questions concerning how interesting she had found the discussion to be, how much she liked the other members of the group, and other similar questions. The results show, as anticipated, that those subjects who had gone through a painful procedure in order to be admitted to the group thought the discussion was more interesting and liked the other group members better than did those who had gained admission to the group easily. In other words, we see the same process operating here as we noted in the previous experiment. If someone is somehow induced to endure embarrassment in order to achieve something, she then persuades herself that what she has achieved is valuable.

In both of the examples which I have discussed (and one could present many more examples of similar nature) a situation has been produced where the organism has two pieces of information (or cognitions) which do not fit together. In the first example, these two pieces of information were: (a) I have worked hard in preparation for an event. (b) The event is not too likely to occur. In the second example, the two cognitions which did not fit together were: (a) I have endured pain to attain an objective. (b) The objective is not very attractive. This kind of "nonfitting" relationship between two pieces of information may be termed a dissonant relation (Festinger, 1957). The reason, of course, that dissonance exists between these cognitions is that, psychologically, the obverse of one follows from the other. Psychologically, if an objective is very attractive, it follows that one would be willing to endure pain to attain it; or if the objective is not attractive, it follows that one does not endure pain to attain it. This specification of why a given relation between cognitions is dissonant also provides the clues to predicting specifically how the organism will react to the existence of the dissonance. Assuming that the organism will attempt to reduce the dissonance between the cognitions, there are obviously two major classes of ways in which this can be done. He can attempt to persuade himself that the pain which he endured was not really painful or he can attempt to persuade himself that the objective is very attractive.

I will not spend any more time than this in general theoretical discussion of the theory of dissonance and the reduction of dissonance. I hope that this small amount of general theoretical discussion will be enough to give context to the specific analysis of the psychological effects of insufficient rewards.

Let us consider in more detail what is suggested by the example of the experiment by Aronson and Mills and by the theory of cognitive dissonance. In that experiment the dissonance which was created was reduced by enhancing the value of the goal. This suggests that organisms may come to like and value things for which they have worked very hard or for which they have suffered. Looking at it from another aspect, one might say that they may come to value activities for which they have been inadequately rewarded. At first glance this may seem to contradict a widely accepted notion in psychology, namely, that organisms learn to like things for which they *have* been rewarded. In a sense it is contradictory, but not in the sense that it denies the operation of this widely assumed process. It does, however, state that another process also operates which is rather of an opposite character.

Let us analyze the situation with which we are concerned somewhat more carefully and more precisely. We are concerned with the dissonance between two possible cognitions. One of these is a cognition the organism has concerning his behavior, namely, I have voluntarily done something which, all other things being equal, I would avoid doing. The other is a cognition about the environment or about the result of his action, namely, the reward that has been obtained is inadequate. As we mentioned before, this dissonance can be reduced if the organism can persuade himself that he really likes the behavior in which he engaged or if he enhances for himself the value of what he has obtained as a result of his actions.

There is, of course, another way to reduce the dissonance, namely, for the organism to change his behavior. That is, having done something which resulted in an inadequate reward the organism can refuse to perform the action again. This means of reducing the dissonance is undoubtedly the one most frequently employed by organisms. If the organism obtains information which is dissonant with his behavior, he usually modifies his behavior so that it fits better what he knows concerning his environment. Here, however, I am going to consider only situations in which this means of reducing dissonance is not available to the organism. That is, I will consider only situations in which the organism is somehow tricked or seduced into continuing to engage in the activity in spite of the dissonance which is introduced. Under these circumstances we would expect one of the two previously mentioned dissonance reduction mechanisms to be used.

If one thinks for a while about the possible behavioral consequences of such a psychological process as we have described, an explanation suggests itself for the well known finding that resistance to extinction is greater after partial reward than after complete reward.

Before I explain this more adequately, I would like to digress for a moment. Since much of the research on the effects of partial reward has been done on rats, and since the experiments that Lawrence and I have done are also on rats, the question will inevitably arise as to whether or not I really think that rats have cognitions and that rats reduce dissonance the way humans do.

First for the matter of cognitions in rats: All that is meant by cognition is knowledge or information. It seems to me that one can assume that an organism has cognitions or information if one can observe some behavioral difference under different stimulus conditions. If the organism changes his behavior when the environment changes, then obviously he uses information about the environment and, equally obviously, can be said to have cognitions.

Now for the question of whether or not rats reduce dissonance as humans do: Although Lawrence keeps telling me that rats are smarter than humans, I suspect that the rat is a rather stupid organism and does not reduce dissonance nearly as effectively as the human being does. I suspect that the mechanisms available to the rat for dissonance reduction are very limited and that the amount of dissonance which gets effectively reduced is relatively small. Still, I suspect that they *do* reduce dissonance. At any rate, if we find that the theory of dissonance can make valid predictions for rat behavior, this will be evidence that they do, indeed, reduce dissonance.

Now to return to the matter of the increased resistance to extinction following partial reward. Let us examine what occurs, psychologically, during a series of trials on which the behavior of an organism is only occasionally rewarded. Imagine a hungry animal who dashes frantically down some runway and into some so-called "goal box" only to find that there is nothing there. The cognition that he has obtained nothing is dissonant with the cognition that he has expended effort to reach the goal box. If this state of affairs were continually repeated, as we all know, the animal would reduce the dissonance by refusing to go to the goal box, that is, he would change his behavior. But, in a partial reward situation, the animal is tricked into continuing to run to the goal box because an appreciable number of times that he goes there he does find food. But, on each nonrewarded trial dissonance is introduced when the animal finds the goal box empty. The assumed process of dissonance reduction would lead us to expect that, gradually, the animal develops some extra preference either for the activity or for the goal box itself. A comparable animal that was rewarded every time he ran to the goal box would not develop any such extra preference.

Consider the situation, then, when extinction trials begin. In addition to realizing that food is no longer present, the partially rewarded animal also has to overcome his extra preference before he stops going to the goal box. We would thus expect "extinction" to take longer for a partially rewarded animal than for an animal that was always rewarded. The magnitude of the difference should be far greater than just the slight effect which would exist if the 100% animal discovers more rapidly that the situation has changed.

If this explanation is correct, then the greater resistance to extinction following partial reward is a direct consequence of the process of dissonance reduction. This, of course, immediately suggests an extension of this line of reasoning to situations other than those involving partial reward. *Any* procedure which introduces dissonance during the training trials should similarly be expected to increase resistance to extinction since the same kind of dissonance reduction process should operate.

Let us, however, try to be precise about what kinds of procedures would introduce dissonance for an organism during training trials in an experiment. It is, fortunately, possible to define this operationally in a precise manner. Let us imagine that we test an organism in a single choice situation. In the case of a rat, for example, this might be simply an apparatus where, from the starting point the animal can turn either right or left. Let us further imagine that the organism we are testing is quite hungry and that, whichever alternative he chooses, he obtains food. We can, then, vary one at a time a variety of factors to discover what the organism will ordinarily avoid doing. One would, of course, find many such factors which would lead the organism not to choose the alternative with which that factor is associated. Dissonance will be created for the organism if he is somehow tricked into consistently engaging in an activity involving such a factor.

This may sound very involved so let me try to say it again, this time, a bit less abstractly. Imagine that we test rats in a simple left-right choice apparatus and, no matter whether the animal goes left or right, he obtains food. But, imagine that, if he goes left, the animal must swim through water to get to the food but, if he goes right, there is simply a short run down an alley to the food. Let us further imagine that, under such circumstances, the animal will consistently choose to go to the right, that is, he will avoid swimming through water. Armed with this knowledge concerning the behavior of the rat we can then assert the following: if one puts a rat in a situation where we somehow trick the rat into consistently swimming through water, dissonance will have been created.

Remembering what we have already said about the ways in which dissonance can be reduced in this kind of situation (provided that we are successful in tricking the organism into continuing to engage in the activity) we would then arrive at the following statement: any condition which the animal will avoid in the above mentioned test situation will increase resistance to extinction in a nonchoice situation.

Let us look at some of the data which exist which are relevant to this statement. We know that if a hungry rat is put in a situation where he has a choice between a goal box where he is rewarded 100% of the time and a goal box where he is rewarded only part of the time, he will fairly consistently go to the place where he is rewarded 100% of the time. And, of course, we also know that where no choice is involved, partial reward increases resistance to extinction. But there are other variables or conditions which should increase

resistance to extinction in a similar manner if our theoretical analysis is correct.

Consider the question of delay of reinforcement. Once more, thinking of our hypothetical test situation, we can be reasonably certain that a rat, if faced with a choice where one alternative led to immediate reward while the other alternative involved an appreciable delay before the rat was allowed to continue to the goal box to obtain food, the rat would rather consistently choose the alternative that led to immediate reward. We should then expect that, in a nonchoice situation, delay of reward should lead to greater resistance to extinction. Existing data show that this is indeed correct. Appreciable delay of reward does lead to greater resistance to extinction. I will briefly review some of the data which exist on delay of reward to give you some idea of the effect which is obtained.

The usual experiment that has been done on extinction following delay of reinforcement compares one condition in which the rats encounter no enforced delay between starting down a runway and obtaining food in the goal box with other conditions in which, on some trials, the rats are detained in a delay chamber before being allowed to proceed to the food. The usual period of delay which has been used has been about 30 seconds. Crum, Brown, and Bitterman (1951) and Scott and Wike (1956) both find that a group of rats delayed on half the trials shows much greater resistance to extinction than a group which was never delayed. In another experiment, Wike and McNemara (1957) ran three groups which differed in the percentage (and of course, number) of trials on which they were delayed. They find that the larger the percentage or number of trials on which the animal experiences delay, the greater is the resistance to extinction. The same kind of result is obtained by Fehrer (1956) who compared rats who were delayed for 20 seconds on *every* trial with ones who were never delayed. She also finds that delay results in increased resistance to extinction.

Before we proceed to other matters, I would like to briefly raise a question concerning one kind of explanation that has frequently, in one form or another, been offered to account for increased resistance to extinction after partial reward. The basis of this kind of explanation, whether it be in terms of expectancy, or conditioning of cues, or any of a number of other varieties, rests in pointing out that there is more similarity between acquisition and extinction for partial reward conditions than for 100% reward conditions. I would like to point out that this type of explanation is clearly not very useful in explaining the increased resistance to extinction after delay of reward. From the point of view of the explanation I am here proposing, however, partial reward and delay of reward clearly involve the same psychological processes.

Let us go on now to examine the matter of work and effort. I am sure it is fairly obvious to all of you now what I want to say about work and effort. If we return to a consideration of our hypothetical test situation we know that, given a choice between an effortless path to food and a path requiring expenditure of effort, the hungry animal will choose the effortless path rather regularly. Hence, in accordance with our analysis concerning dissonance and dissonance reduction, we would expect the requirement of greater effort during acquisition to lead to increased resistance to extinction.

It is surprising that, in spite of the relative consistency of results among the studies which exist in the literature, the effect of effort during acquisition on resistance to extinction has not been generally noted. People have rather tended to note the finding that the greater the effort required during extinction, the faster does extinction occur. But the data are also clear with respect to the effect of effort during acquisition. They show quite clearly that, holding effort during extinction constant, the more effort required during acquisition, the more resistance there is to extinction. The data from one of the more adequately controlled experiments will suffice to illustrate the effect.

Aiken (1957) reports an experiment in which the animal was required to press a panel in order to gain access to food. Some rats were required to exert little effort while others were required to exert considerable effort during training. Half of the animals in each condition were extinguished with the low effort requirement and half with the high effort requirement. Holding effort during extinction constant, the results show clearly that the average number of trials to a criterion of extinction was considerably greater for the high effort acquisition condition than for the low effort acquisition condition. Other experiments in the literature also show this same effect if one examines the data carefully. It should once more be pointed out that any explanation of this effect which depends upon a notion of similarity between acquisition and extinction conditions is clearly inadequate.

One could list many other specific conditions which, analyzed in the same way, would be expected to increase resistance to extinction. I have chosen the three preceding ones to discuss because reasonably good data concerning them exist in the literature. Now, however, I would like to return to a more thorough consideration of the partial reward situation.

I have stated that, on nonrewarded trials in a partial reward situation, dissonance is introduced into the animal's cognition when he realizes that there is no food available. The amount of dissonance can, of course, vary in magnitude. It is important for us to consider the operational variables which will affect the total magnitude of dissonance which is introduced in this manner. This total magnitude of dissonance, of course, will determine how much dissonance reduction occurs through the development of extra preferences (always assuming that the animal does not change his behavior) and hence will determine the resistance to extinction.

In the past, it has generally been assumed that the major operational variable affecting resistance to extinction is the ratio of reward. That is, the smaller the proportion of rewarded trials, the greater the resistance to extinction. However, one might reason that since dissonance is created for the animal on every nonrewarded trial, it seems plausible to suppose that the major operational variable which will affect the resistance to extinction is, rather, the sheer total number of nonrewarded trials which the animal has experienced rather than the ratio of nonreward. From the data in published experiments it is imposssible to assess whether or not this is correct since these two variables are completely confounded in the literature. Experiments on partial reward have always held constant either the number of rewarded trials or else the total number of trials that the animal experiences. It is clear, of course, that when either of these quantities is held constant, the number of nonrewarded trials is perfectly correlated with the ratio of nonreward and so the effects cannot be separated.

It is possible, perhaps, to get some hunch about this, however, from examining the results of experiments which have used rather few training trials. If we are correct, these experiments should show very weak effects of partial reward on resistance to extinction. Sheffield (1949), for example, using a total of 30 trials (only 15 nonrewarded trials) found very small differences between extinction after partial and complete reward. Wilson, Weiss, and Amsel (1955) and also Lewis (1956), replicating the Sheffield experiment almost exactly, also find such small differences that it requires an analysis of covariance to make them appear significant. However, Weinstock (1954), using a similar apparatus, but employing 75 training trials, finds huge and unmistakable differences.

It is unnecessary to belabor the matter by quoting many studies here since it is all a matter of hunch and impression. In general, when one goes through the literature one gets the impression that the experiments which show small effects after partial reward have tended to employ rather few trials. But comparison of this kind between different experiments done by different experimenters is a very shabby business at best since the variation from experimenter to experimenter can be quite large for unknown reasons. The question seemed important enough, however, so that Lawrence and I thought it worthwhile to do a study which could answer the question. The study was carried out through the kind efforts of John Theios. I would like to describe it to you briefly.

The general design of the study is very simple and does not differ in any essential way from the usual study which has been done on the effects of partial reward. The major difference was that we were primarily concerned with seeing the effects of the absolute number of nonrewarded trials and with being able to separate these effects from the effects of ratio of reward. We employed four different conditions of "number of unrewarded trials." Some groups experienced 0 unrewarded trials; some groups of animals experienced a total of 16 unrewarded trials in the apparatus; still other groups experienced a moderate number of unrewarded trials, namely, 27; and finally some groups were run who experienced very many unrewarded trials, namely, 72.

Within these conditions, by varying the total number of trials, different conditions of ratio of reward were set up. Some animals were run with 33% reward, others with 50% reward, and still others with 67% reward. Of course, it was not possible to vary the ratio of reward for animals in the condition of 0 unrewarded trials but the animals were run for varying numbers of trials anyhow. Figure 1 shows the total design. The numbers in the cells indicate the total number of trials after preliminary training which the animals in that

REWARD SCHEDULE	NUMBER OF UNREWARDED TRIALS			
	0	16	27	72
33%		24	43	108
50%		31	54	144
67%		48		216
100%	0 54 216			

Fig. 1
Total number of trials after preliminary training in partial reward experiment.

condition ran. During preliminary training, of course, all groups were rewarded 100% of the time. There were between 11 and 16 animals in each condition. It will be noted that we did not run a condition of 67% reward and 27 unrewarded trials. The reason for this is simple. We ran out of patience and decided this condition was not essential.

It will also be noted that three groups of 0 unrewarded trials were run so that the total number of trials brackets the entire range for the other groups.

Figure 2 shows the results of the experiment. Along the horizontal axis of the figure are indicated the various values of number of unrewarded trials which we employed and along the ordinate are the average number of trials to reach a criterion of extinction. Each circle on the figure represents the results for one of our

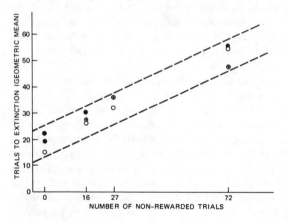

Fig. 2
Number of trials to extinction after partial reward.

experimental conditions. The empty circles represent the data for those with the fewest total number of trials. Thus, except for the 0 unrewarded trials conditions, these empty circles represent the data for the 33% reward conditions. Similarly, the dark circles represent the longest number of total trials and hence, for the partial reward groups, represent the 67% reward conditions.

It is clear from an examination of the figure that, holding constant the number of unrewarded trials, there were only slight differences among the different conditions of ratio of reward. On the other hand, the variable of total number of unrewarded trials has a large and significant effect. It would, indeed, seem that in these data the only variable affecting resistance to extinction after partial reward is the number of unrewarded trials. The results of the experiment are hence, quite consistent with the interpretations which we have made from the theory of dissonance.

These data are, of course, encouraging but certainly not conclusive. It would be nice to be able to have more direct evidence that nonreward tends to result in the development of extra preferences. From the point of view of obtaining such more direct evidence concerning the validity of our theoretical interpretation, the partial reward situation is not very adequate. For one thing, our theoretical analysis states that quite different processes occur, psychologically, on rewarded and on unrewarded trials. In a partial reward situation, however, the animal experiences both kinds of trials and, hence, an attempt to separate the effects of the two kinds of trials is bound to be indirect. And, of course, the possibility always exists that the increased resistance to extinction may depend upon some more or less complicated interaction between rewarded and unrewarded trials.

It would then be desirable to be able to compare pure conditions of reward and nonreward. That is, we could test the theory more adequately if we could compare the resistance to extinction of two groups of animals, one of which had always been rewarded in a given place, and the other of which had *never* been rewarded in that same place. This, of course, presents technical problems of how one manages to induce an animal to consistently go to a place where he never gets rewarded. This problem, however, can be solved by employing a variation of what is, essentially, a delay of reward experiment. With the very able assistance and hard work of Edward Uyeno we proceeded

to do a series of such experiments in an attempt to get more direct validation of our theoretical derivations. I would like to describe some of these experiments for you.

The apparatus we used was a runway with two boxes in addition to the starting box. The two boxes were, of course, quite easily distinguishable. We will refer to one of them as the end-box and to the other as the mid-box. From the starting place, the animal was to run through a section of alley to the mid-box and then through another section of alley to the end-box. One group of rats was fed on every trial in the mid-box and also fed on every trial in the end-box. We will refer to this group as the 100% reward condition. Another group of rats was never fed in the mid-box but, instead, was delayed there for the same amount of time that it took the other to eat its food. These animals then continued to the end-box where they were also fed on every trial. We will refer to this group as the 0% reward condition. The designations of 100% and 0% reward refer, of course, to the reward in the mid-box. Both groups were rewarded on every trial in the end-box and this, of course, is what induced the animals in the 0% reward condition to run consistently to a place where they were never rewarded.

The procedure which was employed in extinction was also somewhat different from the usual procedure in a delay of reward experiment. Because we were interested in comparing the two groups of animals in their willingness to go to the mid-box where one group had always, and the other group had never, been fed, we ran extinction trials only from the starting position to the mid-box. During extinction, of course, no food was present for either condition and after a short period of time in the mid-box the animals were returned to their home cage. Thus, from this experiment we have a better comparison of the effects of reward and of nonreward. Figure 3 shows the average running times for the two groups during extinction.

The figure shows the data for the first 30 extinction trials averaged in groups of 3 trials each. It is clear from the figure that there is a very marked difference between the two groups of animals. Those who were always fed in the mid-box start off running quite fast (reflecting their speed of running during acquisition) but slow down very rapidly. Those animals that were never fed in the mid-box start off more slowly (again reflecting their speed of running during acquisition) but they do not show as rapid a rate of extinction.

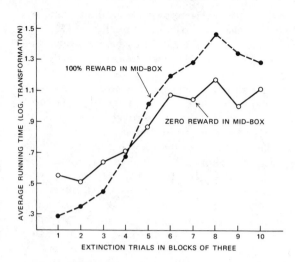

Fig. 3
Running time during extinction in single mid-box experiment.

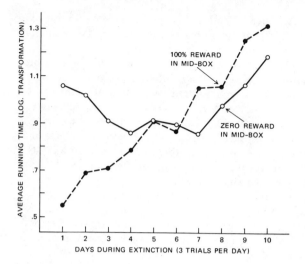

Fig. 4
Running time while satiated during extinction in single mid-box experiment.

Indeed, between the fourth and fifth blocks of trials the two curves cross over and thereafter the animals run considerably faster to a place where they have never been rewarded than they do to a place where they have always been rewarded.

One may certainly conclude from these data that increased resistance to extinction results from non-reward and that an explanation of the partial reward effect in terms of some interaction between reward and nonreward is not very tenable. Actually, in the experiment I have just described we ran a third group of animals which was rewarded 50% of the time in the mid-box and the results for these animals during extinction fall nicely mid-way between the two curves in Figure 3. The resistance to extinction of those who were never fed in the mid-box is greater than that of either of the other two groups of animals.

At the risk of being terribly repetitious, I would like to remind you at this point of the explanation I am offering for these data. Briefly, dissonance is introduced as a result of the insufficient reward or absence of reward. As long as the organism is prevented from changing his behavior, the dissonance tends to be reduced by developing some extra preference about something in the situation. The existence of this extra preference leads to the stronger inclination to continue running during extinction trials.

If this explanation is correct, however, one should be able to observe the effects of this extra preference even in a situation where all the motivation for food was removed. Indeed, it would seem that this would be a better test of this theoretical explanation. We consequently repeated the experiment I have just described to you with one modification. Three days were allowed to elapse between the end of acquisition and the beginning of extinction. During these 3 days food was always present in the cages so that by the time the extinction trials started the animals were quite well fed and not hungry. Food remained always available in their cages during the extinction period. In addition, during the 3 intervening days, each animal was placed for periods of time in the end-box without food being available there. In other words, there was an attempt to communicate to the animal that food was no longer available in the apparatus and anyhow the animals were not very motivated for food.

Extinction trials were, of course, run just from the starting box to the mid-box. Three trials were run each day and Figure 4 shows the results for the first 10 days of extinction. It is clear from an examination of the figure that the results are very similar to the previous results and are, in a sense, even stronger. Those animals who were always fed in the mid-box start off relatively fast and as extinction trials progress the curve shows steady and rather rapid increase in running time. In short, one obtains a familiar kind of extinction curve for these animals.

The group that was never fed in the mid-box, however, shows a very different pattern of behavior. They start off much more slowly than the other group but, for the first 4 days of extinction, they actually run faster than at the beginning. By the seventh day the two curves have crossed and thereafter the 0% reward group runs faster than the 100% reward group. It is also interesting to note that, for the 0% reward group, through the eighth day, one can see no evidence of any extinction having occurred at all. If one is inclined to do so, one can certainly see in these data some evidence that an extra preference of rather weak strength exists for the animals that were never rewarded in the mid-box.

We were sufficiently encouraged by these results so that we proceeded to perform what I, at least, regarded as a rather ambitious experiment. Before I describe the experiment, let me briefly explain the reasoning which lay behind it. It is plausible to suppose that the extra preference which the organism develops in order to reduce dissonance may be focused on any of a variety of things. Let me explain this by using the experiment I have just described as an illustration. Those animals who were never fed in the mid-box, and thus experienced dissonance, could have developed a liking for the activity of running down the alley to the mid-box, they could have developed a preference for some aspect of the mid-box itself, or they could have developed a preference for any of the things they did or encountered subsequent to leaving the mid-box. Experimentally, of course, there was no control over this.

It occurred to us, in thinking about this, that if the dissonance were reduced, at least to some extent, by developing a preference for something about the *place* where the dissonance was introduced, then it would be possible to show the same effects in a very well controlled experiment. In other words, if the dissonance introduced by absence of reward were reduced, at least in part, by developing some liking for the place where they were not rewarded, then one could compare two groups of animals, both of which experienced the identical amount of dissonance, but who would be expected to develop preferences for different places.

To do this we used the same basic technique as in the previous two experiments I have described but with an important modification. Instead of one mid-box, two mid-boxes were used. From the starting box the animals went to Mid-box A, from there to Mid-box B, and from there to the end-box where all animals received food on every trial. Two groups of animals were run in this experiment. Group A was delayed in Mid-box A for a period of time and then was allowed to run directly through Mid-box B to the end-box. Group B was allowed to run directly through Mid-box A but was delayed for a period of time in Mid-box B before being allowed to go to the end-box. In other words, both groups of animals had identical experience. The only difference between the groups lay in the particular box in which they were delayed. (All three boxes were, of course, quite distinctive.) For the extinction trials the animals were satiated as in the preceding experiment. For the extinction trials, the animals were run only from Box A to Box B. That is, during extinction the animals were placed directly into Box A, the door was then opened, and when they ran to Box B were removed to their home cage.

Thus, Group A during extinction was running away from the place where they had been delayed, while Group B was running to the place where they had been delayed. If some extra preference had developed for the place where they had been delayed, we would expect Group B to show more resistance to extinction than Group A. In short, during extinction, Group B should behave like the 0% reward groups in the previous experiments. Group A, however, should behave during extinction more like the 100% reward animals in the preceding experiments.

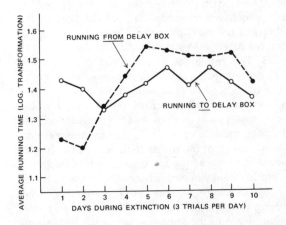

Fig. 5
Running time while satiated during extinction in double mid-box experiment.

Figure 5 shows the data for these two groups of animals for the first 10 days of extinction, three trials having been run on each day. The two curves in the figure must, by now, look very familiar to you. The same result is obtained as in the two previous experiments. The initial difference between the two groups again reflects their previous running speed in that section of the apparatus. During acquisition, Group B ran more hesitantly in the section between the two mid-boxes than did Group A. This difference, of course, still exists at the start of the extinction trials. Thereafter, however, Group A, which was running away from its delay box, rapidly increases its running time. Group B, which was running to its delay box, does not increase its time at all and shows no evidence of any extinction during 30 trials. By the fourth day of extinction, the two curves have crossed and thereafter Group B consistently runs faster than Group A.

If one looks carefully at all the data, I think one finds reasonable evidence that insufficient reward does lead to the development of extra preference. This extra preference, at least in the white rat, seems to be of a rather mild nature, but the magnitude of the effect is quite sufficient to account for the increased resistance to extinction after partial reward or after delay of reward.

Let us then briefly examine the implications of these findings and of the theory of dissonance for our traditional conception of how reward functions. It seems clear that the inclination to engage in behavior after extrinsic rewards are removed is not so much a function of past rewards themselves. Rather, and paradoxically, such persistence in behavior is increased by a history of nonrewards or inadequate rewards. I sometimes like to summarize all this by saying that rats and people come to love things for which they have suffered.

References

Aiken, E. G. The effort variable in the acquisition, extinction, and spontaneous recovery of an instrumental response. *J. exp. Psychol.*, 1957, 53, 47–51.

Aronson, E., & Mills, J. The effect of severity of initiation on liking for a group. *J. abnorm. soc. Psychol.*, 1959, 59, 177–181.

Crum, J., Brown, W. L. & Bitterman, M. E. The effect of partial and delayed reinforcement on resistance to extinction. *Amer. J. Psychol.*, 1951, 64, 228–237.

Fehrer, E. Effects of amount of reinforcement and of pre- and postreinforcement delays on learning and extinction. *J. exp. Psychol.*, 1956, 52, 167–176.

Festinger, L. *A theory of cognitive dissonance.* Evanston, Ill.: Row, Peterson, 1957.

Lewis, D. J. Acquisition, extinction, and spontaneous recovery as a function of percentage of reinforcement and intertrial intervals. *J. exp. Psychol.*, 1956, 51, 45–53.

Scott, E. D., & Wike, E. L. The effect of partially delayed reinforcement and trial distribution on the extinction of an instrumental response. *Amer. J. Psychol.*, 1956, 69, 264–268.

Sheffield, V. F. Extinction as a function of partial reinforcement and distribution of practice. *J. exp. Psychol.*, 1949, 39, 511–526.

Weinstock, S. Resistance to extinction of a running response following partial reinforcement under widely spaced trials. *J. comp. physiol. Psychol.*, 1954, 47, 318–322.

Wike, E. L., & McNemara, H. J. The effects of percentage of partially delayed reinforcement on the acquisition and extinction of an instrumental response. *J. comp. physiol. Psychol.*, 1957, 50, 348–351.

Wilson, W., Weiss, E. J., & Amsel, A. Two tests of the Sheffield hypothesis concerning resistance to extinction, partial reinforcement, and distribution of practice. *J. exp. Psychol.*, 1955, 50, 51–60.

some psychological studies of grammar[1]

george a. miller
rockefeller university

Language is a topic that psychologists have long discussed from many points of view. We have treated it as a system of cognitive categories, as a medium for self-expression or for persuasion, therapy, and education, as a tool for ordering and controlling our other mental operations, and in many other ways. The approach I want to take here, however, is to regard language as an extremely complicated human skill. My aspiration is to examine that skill in detail in the hope of learning something more about what it consists of and how it functions.

1. Presidential address delivered before the Eastern Psychological Association in Atlantic City, New Jersey, April 27, 1962. The preparation of this document was supported in part by the National Science Foundation (NSF G-16486). Reprinted from *American Psychologist*, 1962, Vol. 17, pp. 748–762. Copyright 1962 by the American Psychological Association, and reproduced by permission.

When psychologists talk about language as a skill they frequently emphasize problems of *meaning*. Learning what different utterances mean is, of course, a fundamental skill that any user of a language must acquire. But meaning is too large a problem to solve all at once; we are forced to analyze it into more manageable parts. Consequently, there is in psychology a long tradition of defining meaning in terms of *reference*—in terms of an arbitrary association between some referent and a vocal utterance—and then reducing reference in turn to a simple matter of *conditioning*. In that way many difficult problems of human language are transformed into simpler processes that can be studied in lower animals as well as in man, so the general similarities, rather than the specific differences between linguistic and other skills are emphasized.

I have no quarrel with that approach as long as we recognize that it treats only the simplest 1% of the psycholinguistic problem, and that our crucially important human skill in arranging symbols in novel and useful combinations is largely ignored by the successive reduction of language to meaning to reference to conditioning.

Our combinatorial power, which is so characteristically human, provides the psychological foundation for something that linguists usually call "grammar." I use the term defiantly, for I am fully aware that it is a grim and forbidding subject. It still reeks of the medieval trivium of grammar, logic, and rhetoric; it still reminds us vividly of all those endless and incomprehensible rules that our teachers tried to drum into us in grammar school. I wish I could gloss over it with some euphemism about "communication theory" or "verbal behavior," but, alas, I have no honest alternative but to admit that it is grammar that concerns me. It is grammar that is so significantly human, so specific to our species, so important for psychologists to understand more clearly. I do not in any sense wish to criticize psychological studies of the referential process, or of the intricate associative network that supports the referential process. My goal is rather to persuade psychologists, by argument and illustration, that there is much more to our linguistic skills than *just* the referential process. I do not see how we are going to describe language as a skill unless we find some satisfactory way to deal with grammar and with the combinatorial processes that grammar entails.

In order to illustrate what our linguistic skills are, I need to draw on certain basic concepts of modern linguistics. Fortunately, modern linguists have a somewhat different conception of grammar—a more scientific conception—than your English teacher had years ago. If I can communicate this newer conception of grammar well enough, perhaps it will revive some spark of interest that you may still have.

Consider a brief sample of the scientific approach to grammar. Let us choose a sentence so simple that we can have no trouble in analyzing it or in understanding the principles of analysis that are being used. Interesting sentences are much more complicated, of course, but the same principles are involved.

Take the sentence *Bill hit the ball.* To native speakers of English it is intuitively obvious that this sequence of words has a kind of structure, that some pairs of adjacent words are more closely related than others. For instance, *the ball* feels like a more natural unit than, say, *hit the.* One way to express that fact is to say that it is very easy to substitute a single word for *the ball,* but it is difficult to think of a single word for *hit the* that would not change the underlying structure of the sentence.

On the first line at the top of Table 1 is the original sentence, *Bill hit the ball.* On line 2 is the derived sentence, *Bill hit it,* which is formed by substituting *it* for *the ball.* On line 3 there is another substitution—*acted* instead of *hit it*—and so we obtain the sentence *Bill acted.*

This process, in one form or another, is called "constituent analysis" by modern linguists (Harris,

TABLE 1

Illustrating Constituent Analysis of a Simple Sentence

1	Bill	hit	the	ball
2	Bill	hit	it	
3	Bill	acted		

Bill	hit	the T	ball N
	V	NP_2	
NP_1	VP		

1946; Nida, 1948; Pike, 1943; Wells, 1947). As described so far, it may sound as though it depends on your perseverance in searching for alternative words to substitute for each constituent. We can generalize the procedure, however, by introducing specific names for the various kinds of constituent units. Such a use of names is indicated in the lower half of the table. *The* is an article (symbolized T) and *ball* is a noun (symbolized N); together they form a noun phrase (symbolized NP). The verb *hit* combines with the noun phrase to form a verb phrase (symbolized VP). And, finally, the initial noun phrase *Bill* combines with the verb phrase to form a grammatical sentence. Thus each type of constituent has its own name.

As soon as we try to deal abstractly with grammatical sentences, we become involved with these kinds of structured patterns. Obviously, we need some formal system to keep track of them. Several theoretical possibilities are currently available.

One way to deal with the constituent structure of a sentence is to use what linguists have come to call a *generative grammar* (Chomsky, 1956). The central idea was first developed for combinatorial systems in the study of formal logic (Post, 1936, 1944). Starting from a basic axiom, we apply rules of formation that permit us to rewrite the axiom in certain acceptable ways until we have finally derived the desired sentence. If the rules are formulated properly, only the grammatical sentences will be derivable; all other sentences will be ungrammatical.

Figure 1 illustrates how a small fragment of English grammar might be expressed in this manner. The basic axiom is S. The rewriting rules F1—7 permit us to form the sentence *Bill hit the ball* in a sequence of steps. First S is rewritten as $NP + VP$, according to rule F1. Then we

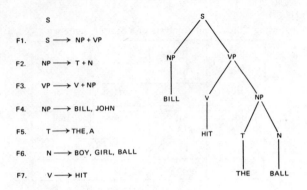

F1. S $\longrightarrow$ NP + VP

F2. NP $\longrightarrow$ T + N

F3. VP $\longrightarrow$ V + NP

F4. NP $\longrightarrow$ BILL, JOHN

F5. T $\longrightarrow$ THE, A

F6. N $\longrightarrow$ BOY, GIRL, BALL

F7. V $\longrightarrow$ HIT

Fig. 1

A fragment of English grammar, phrased in terms of rewriting rules, illustrating a generative grammar.

can rewrite *NP* as *Bill* according to rule F4. Since there is not any rule available for rewriting *Bill*, we are forced to stop at this point. We can, however, rewrite *VP* according to rule F3, thus getting *Bill* + *V* + *NP*. In this way we can proceed as indicated by the tree graph on the right until the desired sentence is derived. Note that the diagram of the derivation corresponds to the constituent structure that we saw in Table 1.

The set of rewriting rules on the left of Figure 1 can be conveniently referred to as the grammar, and the set of sentences that the grammar generates defines the language. It is an important feature of this kind of grammar that there are terminal symbols, symbols that cannot be rewritten, and these comprise what we ordinarily recognize as the vocabulary of the language. According to this way of representing it, the vocabulary is included in the grammar.

Most people, when they encounter a generative grammar for the first time, get an impression that it means we must always form our sentences from axiom to terminal symbols, that we must always decide what phrases we want before we can decide what words we want to use. That is not a necessary assumption, however. These rules of formation, and the trees that represent the structures of the grammatical sentences, are purely formal devices for representing word groupings. How a sentence is actually manufactured or understood by users of the language — what particular cognitive processes he performs — is not a linguistic problem, but a psychological one.

Just to suggest how the same structural properties can be formalized in a different manner, therefore, con-

sider briefly something that linguists have come to call a *categorial grammar* (Bar-Hillel, 1953; Lambek, 1958). This alternative was also borrowed from symbolic logic. (Cf. Ajdukiewicz, 1935.) According to this way of thinking about grammar, all the words and constituents must be classified into syntactic categories — corresponding roughly to what you may once have learned to call *parts of speech* — that, like chemical elements, are characterized by the ways they can combine with each other. I can make the reasoning clear most quickly, I think, by an example. In Figure 2 on the left is a small segment of the English vocabulary, alphabetized as it would be in any proper dictionary. Listed after each entry are a set of symbols that indicate the syntactic categories that the word belongs to. In order to use those category markers you must understand a simple fact about the way they cancel, namely, that left and right cancellation are distinct. The word *ball* belongs to the category $t \backslash n$ (read "t under n") and has the characteristic that when a member of t is placed to its left, the ts cancel, much as in ordinary algebra, leaving simply n. According to this way of representing the grammar, each word in the sentence is first replaced by its category symbol, then the category symbols are combined by left and right cancellation in all possible ways. If any result includes the single symbol s, then we know that we are dealing with a grammatical sentence; the order of cancellations indicates its underlying constituent structure. In the case of *Bill hit the ball*, the successive cancellations are shown on the right half of Figure 2.

There are obvious differences between categorial grammars and generative grammars. A categorial grammar starts with the words and works toward a

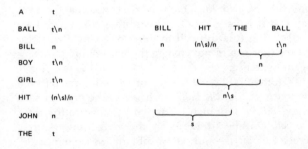

A	t
BALL	$t \backslash n$
BILL	n
BOY	$t \backslash n$
GIRL	$t \backslash n$
HIT	$(n \backslash s)/n$
JOHN	n
THE	t

Fig. 2

A fragment of English grammar, phrased in terms of rules of cancellation, illustrating a categorial grammar.

single symbol that represents a grammatical sentence; a generative grammar seems to move in the opposite direction. Notice also that the categorial system seems to have all its grammatical rules included in the dictionary, whereas the generative system does just the opposite and includes the dictionary in its grammatical rules. In spite of these superficial differences, however, it has been possible to show — by stating each type of system precisely and studying its formal properties — that they are equivalent in the range of languages that they are capable of characterizing (Bar-Hillel, Gaifman, & Shamir, 1960).

That is enough grammatical theory for the moment. It is time now to stop and ask whether there are any psychological implications to all this. Are these systems of rules nothing more than a convenient way to summarize linguistic data, or do they also have some relevance for the psychological processes involved? If human speech is a skilled act whose component parts are related to one another in the general manner that the linguists have been describing, what measurable consequences can we expect to find? What measurable effects would such skills have on our other psychological processes?

First, we might ask if there is any solid empirical evidence for the psychological reality of syntactic categories. One clear implication of these linguistic hypotheses would be that we must have our memory for the words of our language organized according to syntactic categories. Is there any evidence that such an organization exists? There is, of course. For example, psychologists who work with word associations have always claimed — although until recently they have done relatively little to explore the claim — that responses from adult subjects on a word-association test have a marked tendency to be members of the same syntactic category as are the stimuli that evoke them (Ervin, 1961). Certainly there is *some* lawful relation between the syntactic category of the stimulus word and the syntactic category of the response word, but exactly what the relation is may not be quite as simple as originally advertised. James Deese has recently begun to study the syntactic dimensions of word associations in considerable detail; in a few years we may be in a much better position to discuss these relations.

As further evidence for the psychological reality of syntactic categories, recall that our syntactic categories affect the way we memorize and remember new verbal materials. Here again everybody knows this relation

exists, but few studies have tried to exploit it. One example should indicate what I have in mind. Murray Glanzer (1962) has shown that in learning paired associates it is clearly easier for us to learn associations between nonsense syllables and content words (nouns, verbs, adjectives, adverbs) than it is to learn associations between nonsense syllables and function words (pronouns, prepositions, conjunctions). That is to say, YIG-FOOD and MEF-THINK can be associated more readily than TAH-OF and KEX-AND, etc.

Of particular interest in Glanzer's studies, however, was the fact that function words become easier to learn when they are placed in contexts that seem more suitable to them. For instance, when triplets consisting of syllable-word-syllable were used, then TAH-OF-ZUM and KEX-AND-WOJ are learned faster than are YIG-FOOD-SEB and MEF-THINK-JAT. The point, of course, is that in the triplet context the function words are more readily bound to the nonsense syllables because they seem to form natural syntactic constituents in that context.

Where do syntactic categories come from? The development of these categories is currently a matter of great concern and excitement to several psychologists. Here again I will mention only one example, just to indicate the sort of thing that is going on. In an effort to discover how children learn the syntactic categories, Martin Braine (1963) has recently used very simple artificial languages to explore a process he calls "contextual generalization." Contextual generalization resembles stimulus generalization, where the verbal context plays the role of the stimulus. Will a verbal response learned in one context generalize to other contexts? If so, the process might help to explain how children learn the syntactic categories. Braine has his subjects learn a few of the nonsense sentences in the artificial language, then tests generalization to other sentences that the learners have not seen before.

There are limits to what we can explain with a notion such as contextual generalization. Some of its inadequacies may become apparent below when we consider transformational aspects of grammar. However, this is not the time and I am not the person to review Braine's work in detail. I mention it merely to persuade you that the psychological problems posed by these simple grammatical concepts are indeed well defined and that with a little patience and ingenuity it is even possible to coax them into the psychological laboratory.

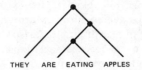 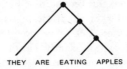

Fig. 3

Syntactic ambiguity arises when two different sentences are expressed by the same string of words.

One unavoidable fact about nonsense materials, however, is that they are nonsense; and artificial languages are inescapably artificial. I believe that the case for the psychological reality of these grammatical conventions might be strengthened if we would focus on the process of comprehension, rather than on the processes of learning and memory. In order to phrase the matter in a strong form, consider the following proposition: *We cannot understand a sentence until we are able to assign a constituent structure to it.*

Perhaps the simplest way to illustrate what I have in mind is to examine a sentence that is syntactically ambiguous. In Figure 3 we have an example of the sort that linguists like to consider: *They are eating apples* is really two sentences, even though both of them consist of exactly the same sequence of words. The sentence on the left would answer the question, *What are your friends doing?* The one on the right would answer the question, *Are those apples better for eating or for cooking?* On the basis of the linear sequence of words alone, however, we cannot tell which meaning is intended. Somehow, from the context, we must decide which syntactic structure is appropriate. Until we have decided on its structure, however, the sentence is ambiguous and we cannot completely understand its meaning. Thus, the proper functioning of our syntactic skill is an essential ingredient in the process of understanding a sentence. Again I emphasize that the problem of meaning involves a great deal more than the matter of reference.

For still another example of the psychological significance of syntactic structure let me draw on some of my own research on the perception of speech. Several years ago I participated in an experimental study showing that words can be perceived more accurately when they are heard in the context of a sentence than when they are pronounced separately as individual items on a list of test words (Miller, Heise, & Lichten, 1951). Those results are shown graphically in Figure 4,

where the percentage of the words that were heard correctly is plotted as a function of the signal-to-noise ratio. As you can see, the same words were heard more accurately in sentences than in isolation.

In 1951 when we first reported this observation we argued that a sentence context serves to narrow down the set of alternative words that the listener expects, and so makes the perceptual task of recognition just that much easier. I still believe that our original explanation was correct, as far as it went. But it did not go far enough. It left open the psychologically crucial question of exactly *how* the sentence context reduced the variety of alternatives.

Words in sentences are often slurred and pronounced carelessly, yet we found they were more accurately perceived; an explanation in terms of reduced alternatives might account for that, of course. But words in sentences also run together. A listener must segment the ongoing flow of sound in order to discover the word units, yet this extra operation seemed to be no burden; the explanation in terms of reduced alternatives says nothing at all about this extra operation of segmentation. And, perhaps, worst of all, the explanation seemed to imply that a listener makes separate, successive decisions about the identity of the separate, successive words he is hearing in the sentence. Since words can be spoken at a rate of two or three per second, the rate at which successive sets of alternative words must be conjured up, recognized, and replaced by the listener is really quite remarkable.

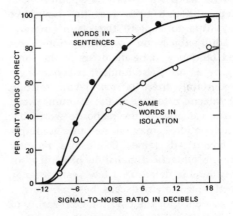

Fig. 4

The effect of sentence context on the intelligibility of words (from Miller, Heise, & Lichton, 1951).

232

In short, the more I thought about how the sentence context exerts its helpful influence, the more complicated it seemed.

In order to explore the matter further, therefore, we performed the following experiment (Miller, 1962): First, we drew up a list of 25 monosyllabic English words and divided it into five sublists of five words each, as shown in Table 2. These sublists are constructed in such a way that if you chose any words successively from sublists 1, 2, 3, 4, and 5, they will form a grammatical English sentence. The subjects in this experiment spent an entire summer with me—four afternoons a week—listening to these 25 words in the presence of a masking noise. To say they knew the lists perfectly is a gross understatement; before the summer was over we all were thoroughly sick of them.

TABLE 2

Five Subvocabularies Used to Explore the Perceptual Effects of Grammatical Context

1	2	3	4	5
Don	Brought	His	Black	Bread
He	Has	More	Cheap	Sheep
Red	Left	No	Good	Shoes
Slim	Loves	Some	Wet	Socks
Who	Took	The	Wrong	Things

We tested four separate conditions. The first two conditions provided a kind of control. In one case, successive words were selected from the entire set of 25 words in random order. In the second case, successive words were selected in random order from one of the five sublists of five words. The words were spoken in groups of five and heard by the listeners against a background of random masking noise. The listeners' responses were spoken aloud and individually recorded, so the tests did not need to be delayed in order to allow time for the listeners to write down their responses. As we had expected, the words were easier to recognize when they occurred as one of 5 alternatives than when they were one of 25 alternatives. Those two control conditions provided the calibration we needed for the two remaining experimental conditions.

In the third test condition, words were chosen from the subgroups successively so as to form grammatical sentences: *Don has no wet things*, for example. And in the fourth test condition, the order of the subgroups was reversed, so that the sequence of words was not grammatical: *things wet no has Don*, for example. Since these backward strings were based on exactly the same sublists of alternatives as were the sentences, we called them pseudosentences.

Our question, of course, was whether there would be any difference between the intelligibility of the sentences and the intelligibility of the pseudosentences. The answer was both yes and no. When we paused between successive strings of five words and gave the listeners a chance to think about what they had just heard, there was no difference; sentences and pseudosentences gave the same results, and both were the same as the results for the 5-word sublists.

When the test was speeded up, however, by eliminating the pauses between successive sentences, a difference appeared. Under time pressure we got the results shown in Figure 5. On the left the word intelligibility scores are plotted as a function of the signal-to-noise ratio for all four test conditions. The sentences and the 5-word vocabularies give one function; the pseudosentences and the 25-word vocabularies give another. On the right are the corresponding functions obtained when the scoring unit was the entire sentence, rather than the individual words.

The results with pseudosentences demonstrated that when time is short and words do not follow a familiar grammatical pattern, subjects are unable to exploit a narrower range of alternatives. They do not have time to hear each word separately, decide what it was, then anticipate the next set of alternatives, listen to the next word, etc. At slow speeds they had time to make separate decisions about each word, but not at the more rapid speeds that would be characteristic of normal, conversational speech. All they could do with the rapid pseudosentences was to treat the successive words as if they were chosen randomly from the larger set of 25 alternatives.

Thus it is possible to show that the sentence context does indeed serve to narrow the range of alternative words, but the mechanism involved seems to be more complicated than we had originally imagined. In addition to reducing the variety of competing alternatives, the sentence context also enables us to organize the flow of sound into decision units larger than individual words—perhaps into units similar to the linguist's constituents—and so to make our perceptual decisions about what we are hearing at a slower and more comfortable rate.

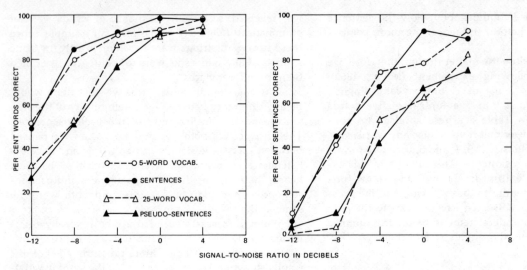

Fig. 5
Word intelligibility (left) and sentence intelligibility (right) scores indicate that under time pressure grammatical contexts facilitate speech perception and ungrammatical contexts do not, even though the number of different words involved is not altered by the context (after Miller, 1962).

In short, I am arguing that in ordinary conversation the functional unit of speech perception is usually larger than a single word or a single morpheme and more nearly the size and shape of a syntactic constituent. As long as we studied speech perception by using lists of words spoken in isolation, the existence of those larger units was not apparent. As soon as we begin to combine words into continuous sequences, however, we discover that the familiar grammatical sequences form unique and distinctive patterns of words. And that, of course, is just what a linguistic theory of syntactic structures would lead us to expect.

The experiment I have just described argues for the existence of perceptual units larger than a single word. It does not, however, argue in favor of any particular type of structure underlying those larger units. That is, it does not show that some form of grammatical structure must be preferred to, say, a Markovian structure of the kind that communication theorists talk about (Shannon, 1948, 1951).

In order to illustrate the psychological reality of these syntactic structures, we must consider the critical feature that these grammatical systems admit, but that Markovian structures do not—namely, the possibility of unlimited self-embedding (Chomsky, 1959). Again I will draw upon my own research, but now in the field of verbal learning and verbal memory.

One important feature of the grammatical rules that linguists have proposed is that they are recursive. That is to say, there is no limit to the number of times that the same rule can be applied in the derivation of a sentence. In general, three different kinds of recursiveness are permitted by our grammatical rules. In Figure 6 we see syntactic structures illustrating each of the three

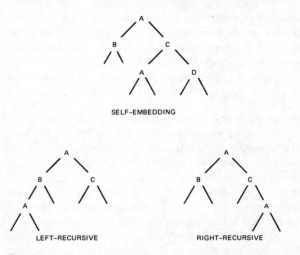

Fig. 6
Illustrating three types of recursive rules that permit an element of type A to be part of an element of type A.

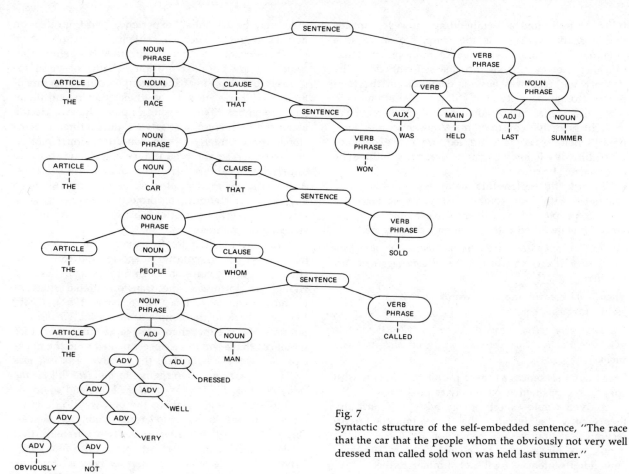

Fig. 7
Syntactic structure of the self-embedded sentence, "The race that the car that the people whom the obviously not very well dressed man called sold won was held last summer."

types: left-recursive, right-recursive, and self-embedding. All three are characterized by the fact that a given type of constituent—labeled "A" in this figure—can appear as a part of itself; where it appears—at the left end, at the right end, or in the middle—determines the type of recursiveness. In English, for example, a left-recursive construction would be *The obviously not very well dressed man is here*, or *John's father's car's roof's color is red*. Right-recursive structures can be strung out at great length; a famous example is *This is the cow with the crumpled horn that tossed the dog that worried the cat that killed the rat that ate the malt that lay in the house that Jack built*. This same sentence can be rephrased, however, to illustrate a self-embedded construction. We can build up the self-embedded version step by step:

The rat ate the malt,
The rat that the cat killed ate the malt,
The rat that the cat that the dog worried killed ate the malt,
The rat that the cat that the dog that the cow tossed worried killed ate the malt, etc.

It is farily clear that even though the self-embedded version is perfectly grammatical, it is far more complicated psychologically—harder to understand and to remember—than the right-recursive version.

There are some relatively profound reasons why this should be the case. A language that could be characterized entirely in terms of right-recursive rules could be described in terms of a Markov process (Chomsky, 1956; Chomsky & Miller, 1958). The possibility of unlimited self-embedding, however, means that a Markov system is too simple to serve as a grammar for a natural language. Of more practical significance, however, is the fact that self-embedding by its very nature places heavier demands on the temporary storage capacity of any device that attempts to cope with it—far heavier than do either left-recursive or right-recursive constructions. And, since our temporary memory is quite limited, we can experience great difficulty following grammatical rules in this type of syntactic structure.

In order to explore this matter we can take some sentences with very complicated syntactic structure and ask people to repeat them. For example, one sentence I have worked with is diagramed in Figure 7:

The race that the car that the people whom the obviously not very well dressed man called sold won was held last summer.

Then, as a control, the same words were arranged in a right-branching structure:

The obviously not very well dressed man called the people who sold the car that won the race that was held last summer.

I read such sentences as these to college students who tried to repeat them as accurately as possible.

As you would expect, on the basis of almost any theory of verbal learning that I can imagine, right-recursive sentences are easier for English-speaking people to repeat and to memorize than are self-embedded sentences. I will not summarize the quantitative results, but I think that some of the qualitative results are amusing. For example, after hearing the self-embedded sentence only once, subject may say:

The race—that the car—that the clearly not so well dressed man—saw—sold one—last summer?

The subjects who respond in this way are quite interesting; their intonation is characteristic of the recitation of a list of unrelated phrases, not the utterance of a sentence. And I was also interested to note that the number of items on the list would usually be about six or seven, close to the span of immediate memory for those subjects (Miller, 1956).

The second time such a subject hears the same sentence he may still recite it as though it were a list, but with somewhat more accurate recall of the individual items. By the second or third time through, however,

there may be an "Aha!" experience, and from then on he tries to give it a normal, sentence intonation.

These examples should indicate why I believe that sentences are not just arbitrary chains of vocal responses, but that they have a complex inner structure of their own. How we perceive them, understand them, and remember them depends upon what we decide about their structure. Just as we induce a three-dimensional space underlying the two-dimensional pattern on the retina, so we must induce a syntactic structure underlying the linear string of sounds in a sentence. And just as the student of space perception must have a good understanding of projective geometry, so a student of psycholinguistics must have a good understanding of grammar.

There is much more to grammar, however, than just the system of syntactic categories and constituent structure. Let me lapse once again into linguistics long enough to introduce the transformational rules of grammar (Chomsky, 1956, 1957; Harris, 1952a, 1952b, 1957). Go back to the simple sentence *Bill hit the ball.* But now observe that there are a large number of other sentences that seem to be closely related to it: the negative, *Bill didn't hit the ball;* the passive, *The ball was hit by Bill;* various interrogative forms, *Did Bill hit the ball?, What did Bill hit?, Who hit the ball?,* and so on.

Linguists disagree about the best way to describe these different kinds of relations among sentences. One opinion is that we learn "senctence frames" that we keep filed away in a sort of sentence-frame dictionary. The declarative, interrogative, affirmative, negative, active, passive, compound, complex, etc., sentence frames are all supposed to be learned separately and to have no intrinsic relation to one another. A second opinion agrees with the first in seeing no intrinsic relations among the various types of sentences, but argues that there are too many different frames to learn them all separately. The advocates of this second view say that there must be rules, similar to those we have just been discussing, that the talker can use actively to manufacture a grammatical frame as it is needed. But, according to this view, there is one set of rules for manufacturing active, declarative, affirmative sentences, another set of rules for manufacturing passive, declarative, affirmative sentences, etc.

On the other side of the argument are linguists who wish to describe the relations among these sentences in terms of explicit rules of transformation. One version of this view, which I favor, says that we do indeed have a scheme for manufacturing simple, active, declarative sentences, but we can apply rules of transformation to change them from active to passive, or from declarative to interrogative, or from affirmative to negative, or to combine them, etc. This transformational scheme shortens the statement of a grammar considerably, since many rules need be stated only once and need not be repeated for each separate type of sentence. And once you have admitted such rules to your grammar you quickly discover many uses for them.

Transformational rules are both complicated and powerful, however, so many linguists are reluctant to use them. There has been some esthetic disagreement about which kind of simplicity is more desirable in a linguistic theory. Is it better to have a long list of short rules, or a short list of long rules?

The arguments among linguists—who seem to rely heavily on their linguistic intuitions, on logical counterexamples, and on appeals to the economy and elegance of simplicity—can get rather bitter at times. And it is by no means obvious a priori that the most economical and efficient formal description of the linguistic data will necessarily describe the psychological process involved when we actually utter or understand a grammatical sentence. In the hope of providing a more experimental foundation to the argument, therefore, we have recently begun to test some of the psychological implications of a transformational linguistic theory. Our efforts to explore this aspect of linguistic skill are still tentative, however, so the two examples to be mentioned below are still in the enthusiastic stage and subject to revision as more data accumulate. But they will serve to support the main point, that an experimental approach to these matters is both possible and (potentially) rewarding.

Perhaps the simplest way to study grammatical transformations experimentally would be to tell a person what transformation to perform, then give him a sentence, and measure how long it takes him to make the transformation. We intend to explore the transformation process in just that way, but at the moment we are not prepared to report on the results. Instead, therefore, let me tell you about a more indirect method—a sentence-matching test—that Kathryn Ojemann McKean, Dan Slobin, and I have been using.

Our first assumption is that the more complicated a grammatical transformation is, the longer it will take people to perform it. The purpose of the test is to give subjects a set of sentences to transform and to see how many of them they can complete in a fixed interval of time. Of course, there is much more that we would like to know about the transformation than just how long it takes, but at least this is one way to begin.

One form of the test that we have used contains 18 basic, or kernel sentences: all of the sentences that can be formed by taking *Jane, Joe,* or *John* as the first word, *liked* or *warned* as the second word, and *the small boy, the old woman,* or *the young man* as the final phrase. In addition, we used the corresponding sets of 18 sentences that can be produced from those kernels by negative, passive, and passive-negative transformations. Thus, for example, *Joe liked the small boy* appears in the set of kernels; *Joe didn't like the small boy* appears in the set of negatives; *The small boy was liked by Joe* appears in the set of passives; and *The small boy wasn't liked by Joe* appears in the set of passive-negatives.

A test is constructed by taking two of these four sets of 18 sentences and asking people to pair them off. Take as an example the test that requires people to match passive sentences with their corresponding passive-negative forms. The test sheet looks something like Table 3. Half of the pairs are arranged with the passive sentences on the left, half with the passive-negative sentences on the left. This produces two lists, a left-hand list and a right-hand list, which are presented to the subject. Similar tests can be constructed for all the other pairs of sentence types.

Before the two lists of sentences are presented, the subject studies a sample pair of sentences that illustrates the desired transformation, and he prepares himself to perform the same transformation (or its inverse) on the test sentences. When the signal is given to start, he begins with the first sentence at the top of the left column, identifies its type and decides whether the transformation or its inverse is called for, performs the indicated transformation (or its inverse), searches for the transformed sentence in the right-hand column, then places the number of the transformed sentence to the left of the original sentence in the left-hand column. He continues in this way down the left-hand list until, at the end of one minute, he is instructed to stop. This general strategy is shown in Figure 8 by a flow chart.

TABLE 3

Example of a Sentence-Matching Test Designed to Study Transformations between Affirmative-Passive and Negative-Passive Sentences

____ The old woman was warned by Joe	1. The small boy wasn't warned by John
____ The small boy wasn't liked by Joe	2. The old woman wasn't warned by Jane
____ The young man was liked by John	3. The young man was warned by Jane
____ The old woman wasn't liked by Joe	4. The old woman wasn't warned by Joe
____ The young man wasn't warned by Jane	5. The old woman was liked by John
____ The small boy was liked by Jane	6. The small boy wasn't liked by John
____ The young man wasn't liked by Jane	7. The young man wasn't warned by John
____ The old woman was warned by Jane	8. The old woman was warned by John
____ The small boy wasn't warned by Joe	9. The young man wasn't warned by Joe
____ The small boy was warned by John	10. The small boy was warned by Jane
____ The young man was warned by John	11. The small boy was warned by Joe
____ The small boy wasn't warned by Jane	12. The small boy wasn't liked by Jane
____ The small boy was liked by John	13. The young man wasn't liked by John
____ The young man wasn't liked by Joe	14. The young man was liked by Jane
____ The young man was warned by Joe	15. The old woman was liked by Joe
____ The old woman was liked by Jane	16. The old woman wasn't liked by Jane
____ The old woman wasn't liked by John	17. The small boy was liked by Joe
____ The old woman wasn't warned by John	18. The young man was liked by Joe

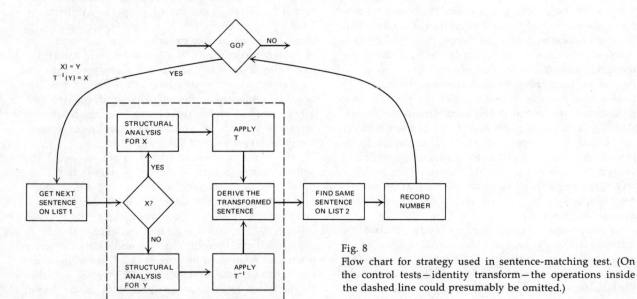

Fig. 8

Flow chart for strategy used in sentence-matching test. (On the control tests—identity transform—the operations inside the dashed line could presumably be omitted.)

As a control condition, six further tests required no transformations at all; the sentences in the left column were simply matched with the identical sentences in the right column (where the right column was the same one used in the corresponding experimental test). From these measurements on the identity transformation, therefore, we could estimate how long subjects required to read down the right-hand column, find the sentence they wanted, and write its number in the appropriate space. We assume that on these control tests the subject's strategy is just the same as on the experimental tests, except that the steps enclosed in dotted lines in Figure 8 — the transformational steps — can be omitted. Therefore, we can subtract the time spent searching and writing from the total time, and so can obtain an estimate of the time required to recognize, analyze, and transform the sentences.

We knew, of course, that subtracting reaction times involves some of the oldest pitfalls in psychology, and we would not have been terribly surprised if the results had been meaningless. Fortunately, we got fairly large and (we believe) sensible differences for the various kinds of transformations.

Consider what you might expect to get on the basis of various theories that grammarians have talked about. Linguists who look upon the four different sentence types as four separate, coordinate, and independent sentence frames would probably expect that moving between any two of them should be about as difficult as moving between any other two. This line of reasoning is depicted in Figure 9, where the letters indicate the various kinds of sentences — kernels, negatives, passives, and passive-negatives — and the lines between them indicate all the possible relations between them. A grammatical theory that says that all sentence frames are coordinate would assign the same difficulty to every one of those connecting lines. It is just one step from any type of sentence to any other type of sentence.

On the other hand, a transformational theorist would like to reduce those six direct relations to a pair of transformations, one for the affirmative-negative aspect and one for the active-passive aspect. This line of reasoning leads to Figure 10, where the lines indicate the direct results of applying a grammatical

Fig. 10
Graph indicating one-step transformations.

transformation. In this view of things, two steps are required to go between kernels and passive-negative sentences, or between passives and negatives. Therefore, a transformational theory leads us to expect that these diagonal relations will take longer to perform than the simpler, one-step relations.

Some data are given in Table 4. For each type of test, Table 4 gives the average number of sentences that our 60 subjects were able to transform and/or locate in one minute. The reciprocals give the time per sentence for the average subject. And in the right-hand column is the result we are looking for — the estimates (in seconds) of the time it took to perform the grammatical transformations.

It is apparent that some tests were easier than others. Look at the pattern: the top two of these estimated times involve only a negative transformation or

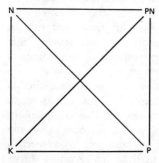

Fig. 9
Graph indicating six pairs of sentence types that can be formed with kernel sentences (K), negatives (N), passives (P), and passive-negatives (NP).

TABLE 4
The Mean Numbers of Sentences Matched Correctly in One Minute, with Transformations (Exper.) and Without (Contr.), is Used to Estimate the Average Transformation Time per Sentence ($N = 60$)

Test condition	Mean number of sentences correct		Time for average subject (secs.)		Estimated transformation times (secs.)
	Exper.	Contr.	Exper.	Contr.	
K: N	7.5	8.7	8.0	6.9	1.1
P: PN	5.5	6.4	10.5	9.3	1.2
K: P	8.1	10.1	7.4	5.9	1.5
PN: N	6.7	8.5	8.9	7.1	1.8
K: PN	6.9	10.0	8.7	6.0	2.7
N: P	5.6	8.4	10.7	7.2	3.5

its inverse; they seem to occur rather quickly. The second pair of these estimated times involves only the passive transformation or its inverse; these are slightly longer, which would agree with one's intuitive impression that the passive is a more complicated transformation. And, finally, the bottom two estimated times involve both the negative and the passive transformations; on the average, they are the slowest of all.

In their gross outline, therefore, these data support the transformational theorists. In their fine detail, however, they raise several interesting questions. Before we spend too much effort answering them, however, we had better make sure the data are correct. At the present time, therefore, we are trying to perfect our measuring instrument in order to obtain results accurate enough to test in detail some of the available linguistic theories about the transformational process.

There are, of course, many other psychological methods that we might use to test the validity of a transformational theory of grammar. One that I believe holds considerable promise has been proposed by Jacques Mehler; he has only begun to explore it, but already the results look interesting. His idea was to present a list of sentences for people to learn and to score the results in terms of the syntactic errors that they made. For example,

The typist has copied the paper is a kernel sentence;
The student hasn't written the essay is a negative sentence;
The photograph has been made by the boy is a passive sentence;
Has the train hit the car? is a query;
The passenger hasn't been carried by the airplane is a passive-negative sentence;
Hasn't the girl worn the jewel? is a negative query;
Has the discovery been made by the biologist? is a passive query; and
Hasn't the house been bought by the man? is a passive-negative query.

Other sets of sentences can easily be generated, of course, by permuting the kernels with the various transformations.

Mehler presents such a list of sentences—without the syntactic comments, of course—to his subjects, who then try to write them out word for word. He gives them five trials, scrambling the order on each trial.

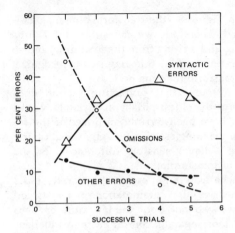

Fig. 11
Syntactic errors can be relatively common in the free recall of sentences that are of different types.

The first question, of course, is whether or not subjects make any syntactic errors in this situation. Mehler's preliminary results are shown in Figure 11. Errors have been grouped into three main classes: (a) errors of omission, (b) syntactic errors, and (c) other types of errors (which include the introduction of extraneous words and the confusion of two different sentences). As you can see from the figure, the probability that a sentence will be completely missing in recall decreases very rapidly, and the probability of semantic confusion is low and relatively constant. The bulk of the errors that people make on this task are of a syntactic nature—they recall the sentence, but they alter its syntactic form.

For several years now I have held rather stubbornly to the opinion that there is an operation called "recoding" that frequently plays an important role in remembering verbal materials. Let me develop this opinion into a specific hypothesis about Mehler's experiment.

The hypothesis is that what people remember is the kernel sentence, but that when you ask them to recite the original sentence exactly, they supplement their memory of the kernel with a footnote about the syntactic structure. This variant of Woodworth's "schema-plus-correction" method of recoding turns *Hasn't the girl worn the jewel?* into the kernel sentence *The girl has worn the jewel*, plus some kind of implicit code that—if remembered correctly—enables the

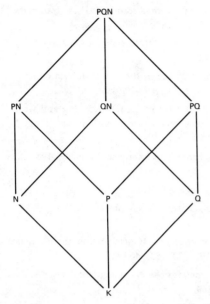

Fig. 12
Graph indicating relations among eight types of sentences formed by negative (N), passive (P), and interrogative (Q) transformations.

subject to make the necessary grammatical transformations when he is called upon to recite the original sentence.

The relations among the eight types of sentences that Mehler uses are indicated in Figure 12. The lines connect the types of sentences that would become confused if the subject remembered incorrectly just one of the three transformations that he has to keep track of. If my recoding hypothesis was correct, of course, I would expect most of the syntactic errors to involve just one of the three transformations, and two and three step errors would be relatively less frequent.

Before Mehler's data were analyzed I had expected to find a strong shift toward the recall of kernels. There is some tendency for people to favor kernel sentences when they recall, but it is insignificant and probably would not have been noticed at all if we had not been looking for it. What seems to happen, however, is actually simpler than I had expected. The subjects quickly get the impression that about half the sentences are negative, half are passives, half are questions; in recall, therefore, they try a little probability matching. If a transformation is forgotten, it is not

simply omitted; instead, a guess is made, based upon the overall impression of how often each transformation should be applied.

The upshot of this argument was that I constructed a very simple hypothesis, based on this kernel-plus-code idea, plus an absurd but convenient assumption that each of the four elements necessary for correct recall—that is to say, the kernel and the three transforms—was recalled independently of the other three. Thus the probability of a correct recall would be simply the product of the probabilities of recalling each of the four components, and the probability of one syntactic error would be the product of the probability of recalling the kernel and the probability of getting two transformations right and one wrong, and so forth. The simple result of this line of reasoning is the following equation. Given these definitions: k = probability of recalling the kernel; $p = 1 - q$ = probability of recalling transform; m = number of transforms to be recalled; P_i = probability of recall with i syntactic errors; then, on the assumption of independent recall of the kernels and the several transformations, we have:

$$P_i = k\binom{m}{m - i}p^{m-i}\,q^i.$$

Now by lumping together all of Mehler's 15 subjects on all trials for all sentences, we can estimate the necessary probabilities and then see if the assumption of independence will predict the observed distribution of errors. The results are shown in Table 5. The estimated probability of recalling the kernel was 0.66. The estimated probabilities for getting each of the transformations correct were all very close to 0.80, so that a single value was used for all three. And when we put these parameter values into the equation for P_i, we obtain fairly good agreement between data and hypothesis. Or to state the matter more carefully, on the basis of Mehler's preliminary evidence, we cannot reject the hypothesis that sentences were recoded and that each of the four components of the kernel-plus-code was remembered correctly or incorrectly independently of the others.

TABLE 5
Distribution of Syntactic Errors in Free Recall of Sentences

Errors: i	0	1	2	3
Calculated P_i	0.34	0.25	0.06	0.01
Obtained P_i	0.36	0.20	0.09	0.01

Here again our work has only begun and so my report of it is still colored by all the natural enthusiasm and prejudices that seem to accompany every programmatic statement. My colleagues and I now see syntactic structure as an important variable to explore. The logicians and linguists are currently defining the theoretical issues with great precision, so that the full range of our experimental and psychometric methods can be brought to bear. I am enthusiastically convinced that such studies have an important contribution to make to the science of psychology.

In the course of this work I seem to have become a very old-fashioned kind of psychologist. I now believe that mind is something more than a four-letter, Anglo-Saxon word — human minds exist and it is our job as psychologists to study them. Moreover, I believe that one of the best ways to study a human mind is by studying the verbal systems that it uses. But what I want most to communicate here is my strong conviction that such a program is not only important, but that it is also possible, even now, with the relatively crude and limited empirical weapons that we have already developed. In the years ahead I hope we will see an increasing flow of new and exciting research as more psychologists discover the opportunities and the challenge of psycholinguistic theory and research.

References

Ajdukiewicz, K. Die syntaktische Konnexität. *Stud. phil.*, 1935, *1*, 1–27.

Bar-Hillel, Y. A quasiarithmetical notation for syntactic description. *Language*, 1953, *29*, 47–58.

Bar-Hillel, Y., Gaifman, C., & Shamir, E. On categorial and phrase-structure grammars. *Bull. Res. Council Israel*, 1960, *9F*, 1–16.

Braine, M. D. S. On learning the grammatical order of words. *Psychol. Rev.*, 1963, *70*, 323–348.

Chomsky, N. Three models for the description of language. *IRE Trans. Inform. Theory*, 1956, *IT-2*, 113–124.

Chomsky, N. *Syntactic structures.* 's-Gravenhage: Mouton, 1957.

Chomsky, N. On certain formal properties of grammars. *Inform. Control*, 1959, *2*, 137–167.

Chomsky, N., & Miller, G. A. Finite state languages. *Inform. Control*, 1958, *1*, 91–112.

Ervin, S. M. Changes with age in the verbal determinants of word-association. *Amer. J. Psychol.*, 1961, *74*, 361–372.

Glanzer, M. Grammatical category: A rote learning and word association analysis. *J. verbal Learn. verbal Behav.*, 1962, *1*, 31–41.

Harris, Z. S. From morpheme to utterance, *Language*, 1946, *22*, 161–183.

Harris, Z. S. Discourse analysis. *Language*, 1952, *28*, 1–30. (a)

Harris, Z. S. Discourse analysis: A sample text. *Language*, 1952, *28*, 474–494. (b)

Harris, Z. S. Co-occurrence and transformation in linguistic structure. *Language*, 1957, *33*, 283–340.

Lambek, J. The mathematics of sentence structure. *Amer. math. Mon.*, 1958, *65*, 154–169.

Miller, G. A. The magical number seven, plus or minus two, *Psychol. Rev.*, 1956, *63*, 81–97.

Miller, G. A. Decision units in the perception of speech. *IRE Trans. Inform. Theory*, 1962, *IT-8*, 81–83.

Miller, G. A., Heise, G. A., & Lichten, W. The intelligibility of speech as a function of the context of the test materials. *J. exp. Psychol.*, 1951, *41*, 329–335.

Nida, E. A. The analysis of immediate constituents. *Language*, 1948, *24*, 168–177.

Pike, K. L. Taxemes and immediate constituents. *Language*, 1943, *19*, 65–82.

Post, E. L. Finite combinatory processes: Formulation I. *J. symb. Logic.* 1936, *1*, 103–105.

Post, E. L. Recursively enumerable sets of positive integers and their decision problems. *Bull. Amer. Math. Soc.*, 1944, *50*, 284–316.

Shannon, C. E. A mathematical theory of communication. *Bell Sys. tech. J.*, 1948, *27*, 379–423.

Shannon, C. E. Prediction and entropy of printed English. *Bell Sys. tech. J.*, 1951, *30*, 50–64.

Wells, R. S. Immediate constituents. *Language*, 1947, *23*, 81–117.

developmental psychology, personality, and psychotherapy

Love is a wondrous state, deep, tender, and rewarding. Because of its intimate and personal nature it is regarded by some as an improper topic for experimental research. But, whatever our personal feelings may be, our assigned mission as psychologists is to analyze all facets of human and animal behavior into their component variables. So far as love or affection is concerned, psychologists have failed in this mission. The little we know about love does not transcend simple observation, and the little we write about it has been written better by poets and novelists. But of greater concern is the fact that psychologists tend to give progressively less attention to a motive which pervades our entire lives. Psychologists, at least psychologists who write textbooks, not only show no interest in the origin and development of love or affection, but they seem to be unaware of its very existence.

The apparent repression of love by modern psychologists stands in sharp contrast with the attitude taken by many famous and normal people. The word "love" has the highest reference frequency of any word cited in Barlett's book of *Familiar Quotations*. It would appear that this emotion has long had a vast interest and fascination for human beings, regardless of the attitude taken by psychologists; but the quotations cited, even by famous and normal people, have a mundane redundancy. These authors and authorities have stolen love from the child and infant and made it the exclusive property of the adolescent and adult.

Thoughtful men, and probably all women, have speculated on the nature of love. From the developmental point of view, the general plan is quite clear:

the nature of love[1]

harry f. harlow
university of wisconsin

The initial love responses of the human being are those made by the infant to the mother or some mother surrogate. From this intimate attachment of the child to the mother, multiple learned and generalized affectional responses are formed.

Unfortunately, beyond these simple facts we know little about the fundamental variables underlying the formation of affectional responses and little about the mechanisms through which the love of the infant for the mother develops into the multifaceted response

1.   Address of the President at the sixty-sixth Annual Convention of the American Psychological Association, Washington, D.C., August 31, 1958. Reprinted from *American Psychologist*, 1958, Vol. 13, pp. 673–685. Copyright 1958 by the American Psychological Association, and reproduced by permission.

The researches reported in this paper were supported by funds supplied by Grant No. M-722, National Institutes of Health, by a grant from the Ford Foundation, and by funds received from the Graduate School of the University of Wisconsin.

patterns characterizing love or affection in the adult. Because of the dearth of experimentation, theories about the fundamental nature of affection have evolved at the level of observation, intuition, and discerning guesswork, whether these have been proposed by psychologists, sociologists, anthropologists, physicians, or psychoanalysts.

The position commonly held by psychologists and sociologists is quite clear: The basic motives are, for the most part, the primary drives—particularly hunger, thirst, elimination, pain, and sex—and all other motives, including love or affection, are derived or secondary drives. The mother is associated with the reduction of the primary drives—particularly hunger, thirst, and pain—and through learning, affection or love is derived.

It is entirely reasonable to believe that the mother through association with food may become a secondary-reinforcing agent, but this is an inadequate mechanism to account for the persistence of the infant-maternal ties. There is a spate of researches on the formation of secondary reinforcers to hunger and thirst reduction. There can be no question that almost any external stimulus can become a secondary reinforcer if properly associated with tissue-need reduction, but the fact remains that this redundant literature demonstrates unequivocally that such derived drives suffer relatively rapid experimental extinction. Contrariwise, human affection does not extinguish when the mother ceases to have intimate association with the drives in question. Instead, the affectional ties to the mother show a lifelong, unrelenting persistence and, even more surprising, widely expanding generality.

Oddly enough, one of the few psychologists who took a position counter to modern psychological dogma was John B. Watson, who believed that love was an innate emotion elicited by cutaneous stimulation of the erogenous zones. But experimental psychologists, with their peculiar propensity to discover facts that are not true, brushed this theory aside by demonstrating that the human neonate had no differentiable emotions, and they established a fundamental psychological law that prophets are without honor in their own profession.

The psychoanalysts have concerned themselves with the problem of the nature of the development of love in the neonate and infant, using ill and aging human beings as subjects. They have discovered the overwhelming importance of the breast and related this to the oral erotic tendencies developed at an age preceding their subjects' memories. Their theories range from a belief that the infant has an innate need to achieve and suckle at the breast to beliefs not unlike commonly accepted psychological theories. There are exceptions, as seen in the recent writings of John Bowlby, who attributes importance not only to food and thirst satisfaction, but also to "primary object-clinging," a need for intimate physical contact, which is initially associated with the mother.

As far as I know, there exists no direct experimental analysis of the relative importance of the stimulus variables determining the affectional or love responses in the neonatal and infant primate. Unfortunately, the human neonate is a limited experimental subject for such researches because of his inadequate motor capabilities. By the time the human infant's motor responses can be precisely measured, the antecedent determining conditions cannot be defined, having been lost in a jumble and jungle of confounded variables.

Many of these difficulties can be resolved by the use of the neonatal and infant macaque monkey as the subject for the analysis of basic affectional variables. It is possible to make precise measurements in this primate beginning at two to ten days of age, depending upon the maturational status of the individual animal at birth. The macaque infant differs from the human infant in that the monkey is more mature at birth and grows more rapidly; but the basic responses relating to affection, including nursing, contact, clinging, and even visual and auditory exploration, exhibit no fundamental differences in the two species. Even the development of perception, fear, frustration, and learning capability follows very similar sequences in rhesus monkeys and human children.

Three years' experimentation before we started our studies on affection gave us experience with the neonatal monkey. We had separated more than 60 of these animals from their mothers 6 to 12 hours after birth and suckled them on tiny bottles. The infant mortality was only a small fraction of what would have obtained had we let the monkey mothers raise their infants. Our bottle-fed babies were healthier and heavier than monkey-mother-reared infants. We know that we are better monkey mothers than are real monkey mothers thanks to synthetic diets, vitamins, iron extracts, penicillin, chloromycetin, 5% glucose, and constant, tender, loving care.

Fig. 1
Response to cloth pad by one-day-old monkey.

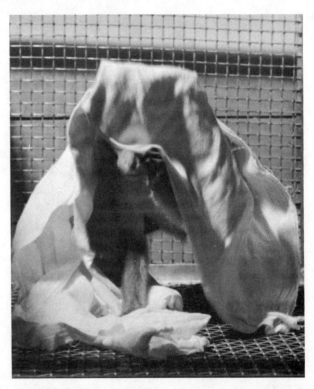

Fig. 2
Response to gauze pad by six-month-old monkey used in earlier study.

During the course of these studies we noticed that the laboratory-raised babies showed strong attachment to the cloth pads (folded gauze diapers) which were used to cover the hardware-cloth floors of their cages. The infants clung to these pads and engaged in violent temper tantrums when the pads were removed and replaced for sanitary reasons. Such contact-need or responsiveness had been reported previously by Gertrude van Wagenen for the monkey and by Thomas McCulloch and George Haslerud for the chimpanzee and is reminiscent of the devotion often exhibited by human infants to their pillows, blankets, and soft, cuddly stuffed toys. Responsiveness by the one-day-old infant monkey to the cloth pad is shown in Figure 1, and an unusual and strong attachment of a six-month-old infant to the cloth pad is illustrated in Figure 2. The baby, human or monkey, if it is to survive, must clutch at more than a straw.

We had also discovered during some allied observational studies that a baby monkey raised on a bare wire-mesh cage floor survives with difficulty, if at all, during the first five days of life. If a wire-mesh cone is introduced, the baby does better; and, if the cone is covered with terry cloth, husky, healthy, happy babies evolve. It takes more than a baby and a box to make a normal monkey. We were impressed by the possibility that, above and beyond the bubbling fountain of breast or bottle, contact comfort might be a very important variable in the development of the infant's affection for the mother.

At this point we decided to study the development of affectional responses of neonatal and infant monkeys to an artificial, inanimate mother, and so we built a surrogate mother which we hoped and believed would be a good surrogate mother. In devising this surrogate mother we were dependent neither upon the capriciousness of evolutionary processes nor upon mutations produced by chance radioactive fallout. Instead, we designed the mother surrogate in terms of modern human-engineering principles (Figure 3). We produced a perfectly proportioned, streamlined body stripped of unnecessary bulges and appendices. Redundancy in the surrogate mother's system was avoided by reducing the number of breasts from two to one and placing this unibreast in an upper-thoracic, sagittal position, thus maximizing the natural and known perceptual-motor capabilities of the infant

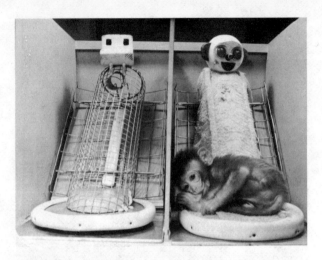

Fig. 3
Wire and cloth mother surrogates.

operator. The surrogate was made from a block of wood, covered with sponge rubber, and sheathed in tan cotton terry cloth. A light bulb behind her radiated heat. The result was a mother, soft, warm, and tender, a mother with infinite patience, a mother available twenty-four hours a day, a mother that never scolded her infant and never struck or bit her baby in anger. Furthermore, we designed a mother-machine with maximal maintenance efficiency since failure of any system or function could be resolved by the simple substitution of black boxes and new component parts. It is our opinion that we engineered a very superior monkey mother, although this position is not held universally by the monkey fathers.

Before beginning our initial experiment we also designed and constructed a second mother surrogate, a surrogate in which we deliberately built less than the maximal capability for contact comfort. This surrogate mother is illustrated in Figure 3. She is made of wire-mesh, a substance entirely adequate to provide postural support and nursing capability, and she is warmed by radiant heat. Her body differs in no essential way from that of the cloth mother surrogate other than in the quality of the contact comfort which she can supply.

In our initial experiment, the dual mother-surrogate condition, a cloth mother and a wire mother were placed in different cubicles attached to the in-

fant's living cage as shown in Figure 3. For four newborn monkeys the cloth mother lactated and the wire mother did not; and, for the other four, this condition was reversed. In either condition the infant received all its milk through the mother surrogate as soon as it was able to maintain itself in this way, a capability achieved within two or three days except in the case of very immature infants. Supplementary feedings were given until the milk intake from the mother surrogate was adequate. Thus, the experiment was designed as a test of the relative importance of the variables of contact comfort and nursing comfort. During the first 14 days of life the monkey's cage floor was covered with a heating pad wrapped in a folded gauze diaper, and thereafter the cage floor was bare. The infants were always free to leave the heating pad or cage floor to contact either mother, and the time spent on the surrogate mothers was automatically recorded. Figure 4 shows the total time spent on the cloth and wire mothers under the two conditions of feeding. These data make it obvious that contact comfort is a variable of overwhelming importance in the development of affectional responses, whereas lactation is a variable of negligible importance. With age and opportunity to learn, subjects with the lactating wire mother showed decreasing responsiveness to her and increasing responsiveness to the nonlactating cloth mother, a finding completely contrary to any interpretation of derived drive in which the mother-form becomes conditioned to hunger-thirst reduction. The persistence of these differential responses throughout 165 consecutive days of testing is evident in Figure 5.

One control group of neonatal monkeys was raised on a single wire mother, and a second control group was raised on a single cloth mother. There were no differences between these two groups in amount of milk

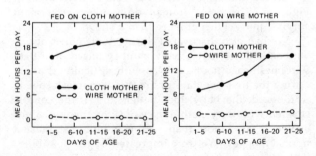

Fig. 4
Time spent on cloth and wire mother surrogates.

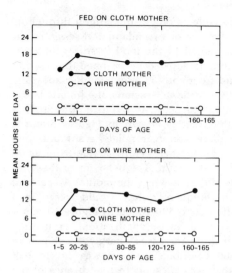

Fig. 5
Long-term contact time on cloth and wire mother surrogates.

ingested or in weight gain. The only difference between the groups lay in the composition of the feces, the softer stools of the wire-mother infants suggesting psychosomatic involvement. The wire mother is biologically adequate but psychologically inept.

We were not surprised to discover that contact comfort was an important basic affectional or love variable, but we did not expect it to overshadow so completely the variable of nursing; indeed, the disparity is so great as to suggest that the primary function of nursing as an affectional variable is that of insuring frequent and intimate body contact of the infant with the mother. Certainly, man cannot live by milk alone. Love is an emotion that does not need to be bottle- or spoon-fed, and we may be sure that there is nothing to be gained by giving lip service to love.

A charming lady once heard me describe these experiments; and, when I subsequently talked to her, her face brightened with sudden insight: "Now I know what's wrong with me," she said, "I'm just a wire mother." Perhaps she was lucky. She might have been a wire wife.

We believe that contact comfort has long served the animal kingdom as a motivating agent for affectional responses. . . .

One function of the real mother, human or subhuman, and presumably of a mother surrogate, is to provide a haven of safety for the infant in times of fear and danger. The frightened or ailing child clings to its mother, not its father; and this selective responsiveness in times of distress, disturbance, or danger may be used as a measure of the strength of affectional bonds. We have tested this kind of differential responsiveness by presenting to the infants in their cages, in the presence of the two mothers, various fear-producing stimuli such as a moving toy bear. A typical response to a fear stimulus is shown in Figure 6, and the data on differential responsiveness are presented in Figure 7. It is apparent that the cloth mother is highly preferred over the wire one, and this differential selectivity is enhanced by age and experience. In this situation, the variable of nursing appears to be of absolutely no importance: the infant consistently seeks the soft mother surrogate regardless of nursing condition.

Similarly, the mother or mother surrogate provides its young with a source of security, and this role or function is seen with special clarity when mother and child are in a strange situation. At the present time we

Fig. 6
Typical response to cloth mother surrogate in fear test.

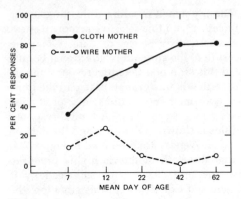

Fig. 7
Differential responsiveness in fear tests.

have completed tests for this relationship on four of our eight baby monkeys assigned to the dual mother-surrogate condition by introducing them for three minutes into the strange environment of a room measuring six feet by six feet by six feet (also called the "open-field test") and containing multiple stimuli known to elicit curiosity-manipulatory responses in baby monkeys. The subjects were placed in this situation twice a week for eight weeks with no mother surrogate present during alternate sessions and the cloth mother present during the others. A cloth diaper

was always available as one of the stimuli throughout all sessions. After one or two adaptation sessions, the infants always rushed to the mother surrogate when she was present and clutched her, rubbed their bodies against her, and frequently manipulated her body and face. After a few additional sessions, the infants began to use the mother surrogate as a source of security, a base of operations. As is shown in Figures 8 and 9, they would explore and manipulate a stimulus and then return to the mother before adventuring again into the strange new world. The behavior of these infants was quite different when the mother was absent from the room. Frequently they would freeze in a crouched position, as is illustrated in Figure 10. Emotionality indices such as vocalization, crouching, rocking, and sucking increased sharply, as shown in Figure 11. Total emotionality score was cut in half when the mother was present. In the absence of the mother some of the experimental monkeys would rush to the center of the room where the mother was customarily placed and then run rapidly from object to object, screaming and crying all the while. Continuous, frantic clutching of their bodies was very common, even when not in the crouching position. These monkeys frequently contacted and clutched the cloth diaper, but this action never pacified them. The same behavior occurred in the presence of the wire mother.

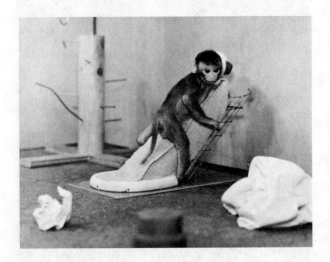

Fig. 8
Response to cloth mother in the open-field test.

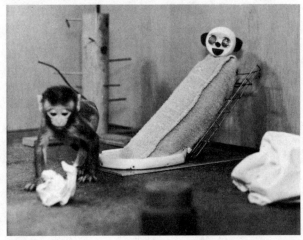

Fig. 9
Object exploration in presence of cloth mother.

248

Fig. 10
Response in the open-field test in the absence of the mother surrogate.

now have data indicating that neonatal monkeys show this same compulsive visual curiosity on their first test day in an adaptation of the Butler apparatus which we call the "love machine," an apparatus designed to measure love. Usually these tests are begun when the monkey is 10 days of age, but this same persistent visual exploration has been obtained in a three-day-old monkey during the first half-hour of testing. Butler also demonstrated that rhesus monkeys show selectivity in rate and frequency of door-opening to stimuli of differential attractiveness in the visual field outside the box. We have utilized this principle of response selectivity by the monkey to measure strength of affectional responsiveness in our infants in the baby version of the Butler box. The test sequence involves four repetitions of a test battery in which four stimuli—cloth mother, wire mother, infant monkey, and empty box—are presented for a 30-minute period on successive days. The first four subjects in the dual mother-surrogate group

No difference between the cloth-mother-fed and wire-mother-fed infants was demonstrated under either condition. Four control infants never raised with a mother surrogate showed the same emotionality scores when the mother was absent as the experimental infants showed in the absence of the mother, but the controls' scores were slightly larger in the presence of the mother surrogate than in her absence.

Some years ago Robert Butler demonstrated that mature monkeys enclosed in a dimly lighted box would open and reopen a door hour after hour for no other reward than that of looking outside the box. We

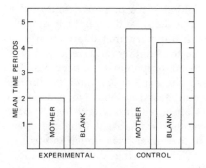

Fig. 11
Emotionality index with and without the presence of the cloth mother.

Fig. 12
Visual exploration apparatus.

The Nature of Love

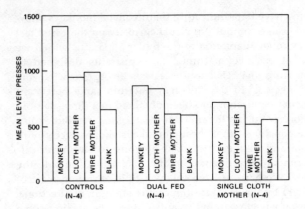

Fig. 13
Differential responses to visual exploration.

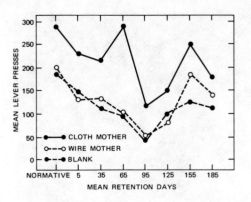

Fig. 14
Retention of differential visual-exploration responses.

were given a single test sequence at 40 to 50 days of age, depending upon the availability of the apparatus, and only their data are presented. The second set of four subjects is being given repetitive tests to obtain information relating to the development of visual exploration. The apparatus is illustrated in Figure 12. The data obtained from the first four infants raised with the two mother surrogates are presented in the middle graph of Figure 13 and show approximately equal responding to the cloth mother and another infant monkey, and no greater responsiveness to the wire mother than to an empty box. Again, the results are independent of the kind of mother that lactated, cloth or wire. The same results are found for a control group raised, but not fed, on a single cloth mother; these data appear in the graph on the right. Contrariwise, the graph on the left shows no differential responsiveness to cloth and wire mothers by a second control group, which was not raised on any mother surrogate. We can be certain that not all love is blind.

The first four infant monkeys in the dual mother-surrogate group were separated from their mothers between 165 and 170 days of age and tested for retention during the following 9 days and then at 30-day intervals for six successive months. Affectional retention as measured by the modified Butler box is given in Figure 14. In keeping with the data obtained on adult monkeys by Butler, we find a high rate of responding to any stimulus, even the empty box. But throughout the entire 185-day retention period there is a consistent and significant difference in response frequency to the cloth mother contrasted with either the wire mother or the empty box, and no consistent difference between wire mother and empty box.

Affectional retention was also tested in the open field during the first 9 days after separation and then at 30-day intervals, and each test condition was run twice at each retention interval. The infant's behavior differed from that observed during the period preceding separation. When the cloth mother was present in the post-separation period, the babies rushed to her, climbed up, clung tightly to her, and rubbed their heads and faces against her body. After this initial embrace and reunion, they played on the mother, including biting and tearing at her cloth cover; but they rarely made any attempt to leave her during the test period, nor did they manipulate or play with the objects in the room, in contrast with their behavior before maternal separation. The only exception was the occasional monkey that left the mother surrogate momentarily, grasped the folded piece of paper (one of the standard stimuli in the field), and brought it quickly back to the mother. It appeared that deprivation had enhanced the tie to the mother and rendered the contact-comfort need so prepotent that need for the mother overwhelmed the exploratory motives during the brief, three-minute test sessions. No change in these behaviors was observed throughout the 185-day period. When the mother was absent from the open field, the behavior of the infants was similar in the initial retention test to that during the preseparation tests; but they tended to show gradual adaptation to the open-field situation with repeated testing and, consequently, a reduction in their emotionality scores.

In the last five retention test periods, an additional test was introduced in which the surrogate mother was placed in the center of the room and covered with a clear Plexiglas box. The monkeys were initially disturbed and frustrated when their explorations and manipulations of the box failed to provide contact with the mother. However, all animals adapted to the situation rather rapidly. Soon they used the box as a place of orientation for exploratory and play behavior, made frequent contacts with the objects in the field, and very often brought these objects to the Plexiglas box. The emotionality index was slightly higher than in the condition of the available cloth mothers, but it in no way approached the emotionality level displayed when the cloth mother was absent. Obviously, the infant monkeys gained emotional security by the presence of the mother even though contact was denied.

Affectional retention has also been measured by tests in which the monkey must unfasten a three-device mechanical puzzle to obtain entrance into a compartment containing the mother surrogate. All the trials are initiated by allowing the infant to go through an unlocked door, and in half the trials it finds the mother present and in half, an empty compartment. The door is then locked and a ten-minute test conducted. In tests given prior to separation from the surrogate mothers, some of the infants had solved this puzzle and others had failed. The data of Figure 15 show that on the last test before separation there were no differences in total manipulation under mother-present and mother-absent conditions, but striking differences exist between the two conditions throughout the post-separation test periods. Again, there is no interaction with conditions of feeding.

The over-all picture obtained from surveying the retention data is unequivocal. There is little, if any, waning of responsiveness to the mother throughout this five-month period as indicated by any measure. It becomes perfectly obvious that this affectional bond is highly resistant to forgetting and that it can be retained for very long periods of time by relatively infrequent contact reinforcement. During the next year, retention tests will be conducted at 90-day intervals, and further plans are dependent upon the results obtained. It would appear that affectional responses may show as much resistance to extinction as has been previously demonstrated for learned fears and learned pain, and such data would be in keeping with those of common human observation.

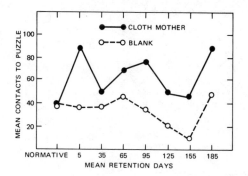

Fig. 15
Retention of puzzle manipulation responsiveness.

The infant's responses to the mother surrogate in the fear tests, the open-field situation, and the baby Butler box and the responses on the retention tests cannot be described adequately with words. For supplementary information we turn to the motion picture record. (At this point a 20-minute film was presented illustrating and supplementing the behaviors described thus far in the address.)

We have already described the group of four control infants that had never lived in the presence of any mother surrogate and had demonstrated no sign of affection or security in the presence of the cloth mothers introduced in test sessions. When these infants reached the age of 250 days, cubicles containing both a cloth mother and a wire mother were attached to their cages. There was no lactation in these mothers, for the monkeys were on a solid-food diet. The initial reaction of the monkeys to the alterations was one of extreme disturbance. All the infants screamed violently and made repeated attempts to escape the cage whenever the door was opened. They kept a maximum distance from the mother surrogates and exhibited a considerable amount of rocking and crouching behavior, indicative of emotionality. Our first thought was that the critical period for the development of maternally directed affection had passed and that these macaque children were doomed to live as affectional orphans. Fortunately, these behaviors continued for only 12 to 48 hours and then gradually ebbed, changing from indifference to active contact on, and exploration of, the surrogates. The home-cage behavior of these control monkeys slowly became similar to that of the animals raised with the mother surrogates from birth. Their manipulation and play on the cloth mother

The Nature of Love

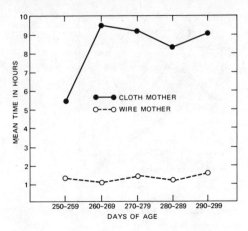

Fig. 16

Differential time spent on cloth and wire mother surrogates by monkeys started at 250 days of age.

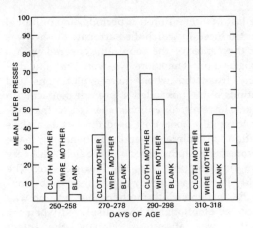

Fig. 17

Differential visual exploration of monkeys started at 250 days of age.

became progressively more vigorous to the point of actual mutilation, particularly during the morning after the cloth mother had been given her daily change of terry covering. The control subjects were now actively running to the cloth mother when frightened and had to be coaxed from her to be taken from the cage for formal testing.

Objective evidence of these changing behaviors is given in Figure 16, which plots the amount of time these infants spent on the mother surrogates. Within 10 days mean contact time is approximately nine hours, and this measure remains relatively constant throughout the next 30 days. Consistent with the results on the subjects reared from birth with dual mothers, these late-adopted infants spent less than one and one-half hours per day in contact with the wire mothers, and this activity level was relatively constant throughout the test sessions. Although the maximum time that the control monkeys spent on the cloth mother was only about half that spent by the original dual mother-surrogate group, we cannot be sure that this discrepancy is a function of differential early experience. The control monkeys were about three months older when the mothers were attached to their cages than the experimental animals had been when their mothers were removed and the retention tests begun. Thus, we do not know what the amount of contact would be for a 250-day-old animal raised from birth with surrogate mothers. Nevertheless, the magnitude of the differences and the fact that the contact-

time curves for the mothered-from-birth infants had remained constant for almost 150 days suggest that early experience with the mother is a variable of measurable importance.

The control group has also been tested for differential visual exploration after the introduction of the cloth and wire mothers; these behaviors are plotted in Figure 17. By the second test session a high level of exploratory behavior had developed, and the responsiveness to the wire mother and the empty box is significantly greater than that to the cloth mother. This is probably not an artifact since there is every reason to believe that the face of the cloth mother is a fear stimulus to most monkeys that have not had extensive experience with this object during the first 40 to 60 days of life. Within the third test session a sharp change in trend occurs, and the cloth mother is then more frequently viewed than the wire mother or the blank box; this trend continues during the fourth session, producing a significant preference for the cloth mother.

Before the introduction of the mother surrogate into the home-cage situation, only one of the four control monkeys had ever contacted the cloth mother in the open-field tests. In general, the surrogate mother not only gave the infants no security, but instead appeared to serve as a fear stimulus. The emotionality scorces of these control subjects were slightly higher during the mother-present test sessions than during the mother-absent test sessions. These behaviors were changed radically by the fourth post-introduction test approximately 60 days later. In the absence of the cloth mothers the emotionality index in this fourth test remains near the earlier level, but the score is reduced by half when the mother is present, a result strikingly similar to that found for infants raised with the dual mother-surrogates from birth. The control infants now show increasing object exploration and play behavior, and they begin to use the mother as a base of operations, as did the infants raised from birth with the mother surrogates. However, there are still definite differences in the behavior of the two groups. The control infants do not rush directly to the mother and clutch her violently; but instead they go toward, and orient around, her, usually after an initial period during which they frequently show disturbed behavior, exploratory behavior, or both.

That the control monkeys develop affection or love for the cloth mother when she is introduced into the cage at 250 days of age cannot be questioned. There is every reason to believe, however, that this interval of delay depresses the intensity of the affectional response below that of the infant monkeys that were surrogate-mothered from birth onward. In interpreting these data it is well to remember that the control monkeys had had continuous opportunity to observe and hear other monkeys housed in adjacent cages and that they had had limited opportunity to view and contact surrogate mothers in the test situations, even though they did not exploit the opportunities.

During the last two years we have observed the behavior of two infants raised by their own mothers. Love for the real mother and love for the surrogate mother appear to be very similar. The baby macaque spends many hours a day clinging to its real mother. If away from the mother when frightened, it rushes to her and in her presence shows comfort and composure. As far as we can observe, the infant monkey's affection for the real mother is strong, but no stronger than that of the experimental monkey for the surrogate cloth mother, and the security that the infant gains from the presence of the real mother is no greater than the security it gains from a cloth surrogate. Next year we hope to put this problem to final, definitive, experimental test. But, whether the mother is real or a cloth surrogate, there does develop a deep and abiding bond between mother and child. In one case it may be the call of the wild and in the other the McCall of civilization, but in both cases there is "togetherness."

In spite of the importance of contact comfort, there is reason to believe that other variables of measurable importance will be discovered. Postural support may be such a variable, and it has been suggested that, when we build arms into the mother surrogate, 10 is the minimal number required to provide adequate child care. Rocking motion may be such a variable, and we are comparing rocking and stationary mother surrogates and inclined planes. The differential responsiveness to cloth mother and cloth-covered inclined plane suggests that clinging as well as contact is an affectional variable of importance. Sounds, particularly natural, maternal sounds, may operate as either unlearned or learned affectional variables. Visual responsiveness may be such a variable, and it is possible that some semblance of visual imprinting may develop in the neonatal monkey. There are indications that this becomes a variable of importance during the course of infancy through some maturational process.

John Bowlby has suggested that there is an affectional variable which he calls "primary object following," characterized by visual and oral search of the mother's face. Our surrogate-mother-raised baby monkeys are at first inattentive to her face, as are human neonates to human mother faces. But by 30 days of age ever-increasing responsiveness to the mother's face appears—whether through learning, maturation, or both—and we have reason to believe that the face becomes an object of special attention.

Our first surrogate-mother-raised baby had a mother whose head was just a ball of wood since the baby was a month early and we had not had time to design a more esthetic head and face. This baby had contact with the blank-faced mother for 180 days and was then placed with two cloth mothers, one motionless and one rocking, both being endowed with painted, ornamented faces. To our surprise the animal would compulsively rotate both faces 180 degrees so that it viewed only a round, smooth face and never the painted, ornamented face. Furthermore, it would do this as long as the patience of the experimenter in re-orienting the faces persisted. The monkey showed no sign of fear or anxiety, but it showed unlimited persistence. Subsequently it improved its technique, compulsively removing the heads and rolling them into its cage as fast as they were returned. We are intrigued by this observation, and we plan to examine systematically the role of the mother face in the development of infant-monkey affections. Indeed, these observations suggest the need for a series of ethological-type researches on the two-faced female.

Although we have made no attempts thus far to study the generalization of infant-macaque affection or love, the techniques which we have developed offer promise in this uncharted field. Beyond this, there are few if any technical difficulties in studying the affection of the actual, living mother for the child, and the techniques developed can be utilized and expanded for the analysis and developmental study of father-infant and infant-infant affection.

Since we can measure neonatal and infant affectional responses to mother surrogates, and since we know they are strong and persisting, we are in a position to assess the effects of feeding and contactual schedules; consistency and inconsistency in the mother surrogates; and early, intermediate, and late maternal deprivation. Again, we have here a family of problems of fundamental interest and theoretical importance.

If the researches completed and proposed make a contribution, I shall be grateful; but I have also given full thought to possible practical applications. The socioeconomic demands of the present and the threatened socioeconomic demands of the future have led the American woman to displace, or threaten to displace, the American man in science and industry. If this process continues, the problem of proper child-rearing practices faces us with startling clarity. It is cheering in view of this trend to realize that the American male is physically endowed with all the really essential equipment to compete with the American female on equal terms in one essential activity: the rearing of infants. We now know that women in the working classes are not needed in the home because of their primary mammalian capabilities; and it is possible that in the foreseeable future neonatal nursing will not be regarded as a necessity, but as a luxury—to use Veblen's term—a form of conspicuous consumption limited perhaps to the upper classes. But whatever course history may take, it is comforting to know that we are now in contact with the nature of love.

the heterosexual affectional system in monkeys[1]

harry f. harlow
university of wisconsin

The inspiration for this address came from observational data obtained from seven guinea pigs—two males and three females in a colony and two females brought in temporarily. Observations were provided by my ten-year-old daughter Pamela. These observations were made with love and endearment, and the behavior observed was endearment and love. Furthermore, these observations were made at a level of objectivity difficult for an adult to attain in this field.

Male and female guinea pigs are very fond of each other. They stare blissfully into the limpid pink or ruby or midnight-blue pools of each other's eyes. They nuzzle and they cuddle and the end production is not characterized by rush or rape. After all, one does not have to hurry if there is no hurry to be had. This, Pamela has witnessed several times. A caged, virgin adult female was brought by a friend for mating. Twirp, Pamela's large, black, gentle male, was put into the cage with the new female. He purred, nuzzled her, brushed up against her, smelled and licked her, and gradually conquered the frightened animal. A half-hour later they were snuggled up next to each other, peaceful and content, and they lived in bliss for several weeks until another friend brought in her female and Twirp repeated his patient, gentle approach. Twirp has convinced me that some male guinea pigs, at least, are endowed with an innate sense of decency, and I am happy to say that this is the way most male monkeys behave. I presume that there are some men who have as deep a depth of dignity as guinea pigs.

The guest stands, unfortunately, ended peaceful coexistence in the colony. For many months the five adult guinea pigs had lived amiably in one large cage, with Twirp in command and the second male playing second fiddle. While Twirp was host to the visiting females, White Patch commanded the permanent harem. When Twirp was reintroduced to the colony cage, it took but ten seconds to discover that he would not be tolerated. White Patch bared his teeth and

1. This research was supported by funds received from the Graduate School of the University of Wisconsin, from the Ford Foundation, and from Grant M-4528, National Institutes of Health. Reprinted from *American Psychologist*, 1962, Vol. 17, pp. 1–9. Copyright 1962 by the American Psychological Association, and reproduced by permission.

lunged at Twirp, and to save the males, a new cage was acquired.

This led to various divisions of the females and led Pamela to discover particular male guinea pigs like particular female guinea pigs, and they squeal piteously when separated, even when the female is so bulging with babies that she can offer the male nothing in terms of drive reduction. Particular female guinea pigs like particular male guinea pigs. Tastes seem fairly stable, for even after weeks of peaceful residence with the unfavored male, the female will still attempt to get to her favorite male, and after weeks of quiet residence with unfavored females, the male will still try to get to his favorite female.

The females, like the males, defend their rights. In the happy one-cage days two females were separated from the group to care for their litters. White Thrush, in an advanced stage of pregnancy, lived alone with the males. When Chirp was returned to the colony cage after three weeks of maternal chores, both males approached enthusiastically, making friendly gestures. But Hell hath no fury like a female guinea pig spurned, and White Thrush would not tolerate infidelity. She hissed at Chirp, and lunged, and as Chirp fled from the cage, White Thrush pursued, teeth bared. The males also pursued, clucking and purring in anticipation. The males won, and White Thrush sulked the rest of the day. Guinea pigs apparently have a well-developed heterosexual affectional system.

Sex behavior in the guinea pig has been intensively investigated, and there are exhaustive studies on what has been called the sex drive, but I know of no previous mention of or allusion to the guinea pig's heterosexual affectional system. No doubt this stems from the paradigm which has been established for research in this area.

In a typical experiment a male guinea pig and a female guinea pig in estrus are taken from their individual cages, dropped into a barren chamber and observed for 15 minutes. In such a situation there is a high probability that something is going to happen and that it will happen rapidly and repeatedly. The thing that happens will be reliable and valid, and all that one needs to do to score it is to count. It is my suggestion that from this time onward it be known as the "flesh count." Sometimes I wonder how men and women would behave if they were dropped naked into a barren chamber with full realization that they had only fifteen minutes to take advantage of the opportu-

nities offered them. No doubt there would be individual differences, but we would obtain little information on the human heterosexual affectional system from such an experiment.

Sex is not an adventitious act. It is not here today and gone tomorrow. It starts with the cradle, and as a part of the human tragedy it wanes before the grave. We have traced and are tracing the development of the heterosexual affectional system in monkeys.

We believe that the heterosexual affectional system in the rhesus monkey, like all the other affectional systems, goes through a series of developmental stages—an infantile heterosexual stage, a preadolescent stage, and an adolescent and mature heterosexual stage. Although these stages are in considerable part overlapping and cannot be sharply differentiated in time, we would think of the infantile stage as lasting throughout the first year and being characterized by inadequate and often inappropriate sexual play and posturing. The preadolescent stage, beginning in the second year and ending in the third year in the female and the fourth year in the male, is characterized by adequate and appropriate sexual play and posturing, but incompleteness. The adolescent and adult stage is characterized by behaviors which are similar in form but give rise to productive outcomes which are also reproductive.

Since in this paper sex is an unavoidable issue, we present illustrations of normal adult macaque monkey

Fig. 1
Initial response to female sexual-present posture. The male subsequently accepted the invitation.

sex behavior. Sexual invitation may be initiated by the female, as in Figure 1, by a present pattern with buttocks oriented toward the male, tail elevated, and the female looking backward with a fear-grimace (not threat) pattern involving flattened ears and lip smacking. As you can see, this pattern need not involve rape nor even rush on the part of the male. The male may also solicit, as in the case of the animal in the foreground of Figure 2; this animal has assumed a posture soliciting either grooming or more intimate favors. These patterns seldom elicit violent, uncontrolled, reflex behaviors. Normal male and female overt sex behavior is shown in Figure 3, the male having assumed the complex sex posture involving ankle clasp, dorsoventral mounting, and clasp of the female's buttocks. The partner demonstrates the complete female sexual pattern of elevating the buttocks, lowering the head, and looking backward. There have been millions of rhesus monkeys for millions of years, and there will be more in the future.

We have traced the development of the infantile heterosexual stage during the first year of life in two test situations using observational techniques. One is our playroom, illustrated in Figure 4, which consists of a room 8 ft. high with 36 feet of floor space. In this room are a platform, ladder, revolving wheel, and flying rings to encourage the infants' adaptation to a three-dimensional world, and there is an assortment of puzzles and toys for quieter activities. Two groups of four infants each, half of each group male and half

Fig. 3
Normal male and female sexual positioning.

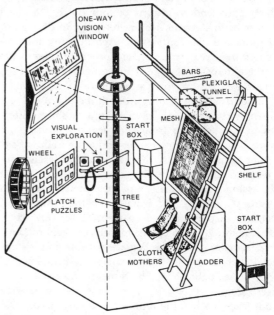

Fig. 4
Playroom test situation.

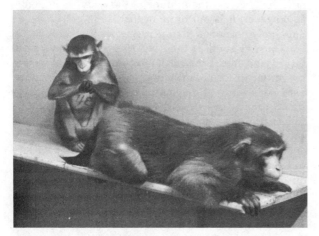

Fig.2
Initial response to male sexual-present posture. The female (No. 48) subsequently approached and groomed the male.

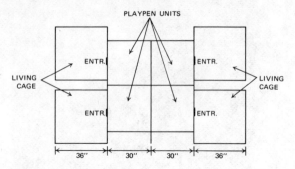

Fig. 5
Playpen test situation.

Fig. 6
Immature male and female sexual posturing, playroom observation.

female, have been observed in the playroom daily over many months. The second apparatus is shown in Figure 5. This is the playpen situation, and it consists of four large living cages and adjoining pens. Each living cage houses a mother and infant, and a three-inch by five-inch opening in the wall between cage and playpen units enables the infants to leave the home cage at any time but restrains the mothers. The playpen units are separated by wire-mesh panels which are removed one or two hours a day to allow the infants to interact in pairs during the first 180 days and both in pairs and in groups of four during the next half-year of life. Again, we are referring to data gathered from two playpen setups, each housing four infants and their real or surrogate mothers. Insofar as the infantile heterosexual stage is concerned, it makes little or no difference from which situation we take our data.

The outstanding finding in both the playroom and playpen is that male and female infants show differences in sex behavior from the second month of life onward. The males show earlier and more frequent sex behavior than do females, and there are differences in the patterns displayed by the sexes. The males almost never assume the female sex-posture patterns, even in the earliest months. The females, on the other hand, sometimes display the male pattern of sex posturing, but this is infrequent after ten months of age. Predominantly, females show the female pattern and exceptional instances are to other females, not males. Frequency of sex behavior for both males and females increases progressively with age. There is no latency period—except when the monkeys are very tired.

The early infantile sexual behaviors are fragmentary, transient, and involve little more than pas-sivity by the female and disoriented grasping and thrusting by the male. Thus, the male may thrust at the companion's head in a completely disoriented manner or laterally across the midline of the body, as in Figure 6. However, it is our opinion that these behaviors are more polymorphous than perverse.

Thus, as soon as the sexual responses can be observed and measured, male and female sexual behaviors differ in form. Furthermore, there are many other behaviors which differ between males and females as soon as they can be observed and measured. Figure 7 shows the development of threat responses by males and females in the playroom, and these differences are not only statistically significant, but they also have face validity. Analysis of this behavior shows that males threaten other males and females but that females are innately blessed with better manners; in particular, little girl monkeys do not threaten little boy monkeys.

The withdrawal pattern—retreat when confronted by another monkey—is graphed for the playroom in Figure 8, and the significance is obvious. Females evince a much higher incidence of passive responses,

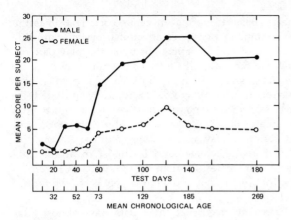

Fig. 7
Frequency of threat responses by males and females in the
playroom.

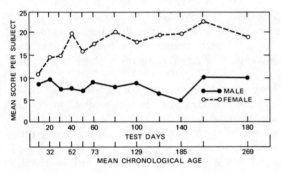

Fig. 8
Frequency of withdrawal responses by males and females in
the playroom.

which are characterized by immobility with buttocks
oriented toward the male and head averted, and a similar pattern, rigidity, in which the body is stiffened
and fixed.

In all probability the withdrawal and passivity
behavior of the female and the forceful behavior of the
male gradually lead to the development of normal sex
behaviors. The tendency for the female to orient away
from the male and for the male to clasp and tussle at
the female's buttocks predisposes the consorts to
assume the proper positions. The development of the
dorsally oriented male sex-behavior pattern as observed in the playroom situation is shown in Figure 9
and may be described as a composite yearning and
learning curve.

Infant male and female monkeys show clear-cut
differences in behavior of far greater social significance
than neonatal and infantile sex responses. Grooming
patterns, which are basic to macaque socialization,
show late maturation, but as is seen in Figure 10, when
they appear, they sharply differentiate the two sexes.
Caressing is both a property and prerogative of the

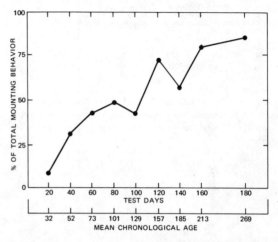

Fig. 9
Percentage of all male mounts (immature and mature) in the
playroom that shows dorsal orientation (mature pattern).

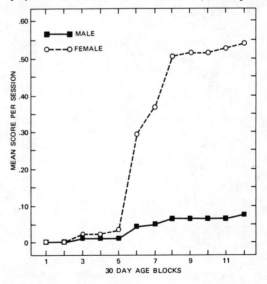

Fig. 10
Frequency of grooming responses made by males and females
in the playroom.

Heterosexual Affectional System in Monkeys

259

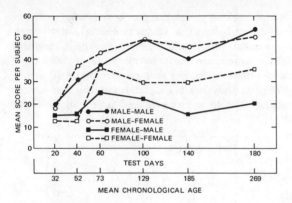

Fig. 11
Frequency of play-initiations by males and females to monkeys of the same (male-male, female-female) and other sex (male-female, female-male). Observations are from the playroom.

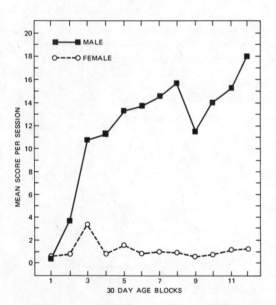

Fig. 12
Frequency of occurrence of "rough-and-tumble" play for two males and two females in the playroom through the first year of life.

females. Basic to normal macaque socialization is the infant-infant or peer-peer affectional system, and this arises out of and is dependent upon the play patterns which we have described elsewhere and only mention here. As is shown in the solid lines of Figure 11, play behavior in the playroom is typically initiated by males, seldom by females. However, let us not belittle the female, for they also serve who only stand and wait. Contact play is far more frequent among the males than the females and is almost invariably initiated by the males. Playpen data graphed in Figure 12 show that real rough-and-tumble play is strictly for the boys.

I am convinced that these data have almost total generality to man. Several months ago I was present at a school picnic attended by 25 second-graders and their parents. While the parents sat and the girls stood around or skipped about hand in hand, 13 boys tackled and wrestled, chased and retreated. No little girl chased any little boy, but some little boys chased some little girls. Human beings have been here for two million years, and they'll probably be here two million more.

These secondary sex-behavior differences probably exist throughout the primate order, and, moreover, they are innately determined biological differences regardless of any cultural overlap. Because of their nature they tend automatically to produce sexual segregation during middle and later childhood, but fortunately this separation is neither complete nor permanent. Behavioral differences may very well make it easy through cultural means to impose a sexual latency period in the human being from childhood to puberty. We emphasize the fact that the latency period is not a biological stage in which primary sex behavior is suppressed, but a cultural stage built upon secondary behavioral differences.

We believe that our data offer convincing evidence that sex behaviors differ in large part because of genetic factors. However, we claim no originality for the discovery of intersex behavioral differences. In 1759 Laurence Sterne in his book *Tristram Shandy* described male and female differences at the most critical period in Tristram Shandy's development; indeed, it would not be possible to conceive of a more critical period.

"Pray, my dear, quoth my mother, *have you not forgot to wind up the clock? —— Good G——!* cried my father, making an exclamation, but taking care to

moderate his voice at the same time——*Did ever woman, since the creation of the world, interrupt a man with such a silly question?"*[2]

Men and women have differed in the past and they will differ in the future.

It is possible that the listener has been dismayed by the frequent reference to sex and the relatively infrequent reference to affection. Out of these infantile behavior patterns, both sexual and non-sexual, develop the affectional bonds and the social ordering that appear to be important or even essential to the full development of the heterosexual affectional system of macaques. Traumatic affectional errors, both transient and prolonged, may have devastating effects upon subsequent social and sexual behaviors.

For some years we have been attempting to establish experimental neuroses in infant monkeys by having them live on unfriendly and inconsistent mother surrogates. One preparation was a rejecting mother that on schedule or demand separated her baby when a wire frame embedded in her spun-nylon covering was displaced violently upward and backward. The baby was disturbed, but as soon as the frame was returned to its resting position, the baby returned to cling to its surrogate mother as tightly as ever. Next we developed an air-blast mother with a series of nozzles down the entire center of her body which released compressed air under high pressure—an extremely noxious stimulus to monkeys. The blasted baby never even left the mother, but in its moments of agony and duress, clung more and more tightly to the unworthy mother. Where else can a baby get protection? Apparently our infant had never read Neal Miller's theory that avoidance gradients are precipitous and approach gradients gradual and tenuous, for love conquered all.

We next devised a shaking mother, which on schedule or demand shook her infant with unconscionable violence until its teeth chattered. The infant endured its tribulations by clinging more and more tightly. At the present time we believe we may be on the threshold of success through Jay Mowbray's creation of the porcupine mother, which extrudes brass

2. Sterne, Laurence. *The life and opinions of Tristram Shandy, Gentleman.* J. A. Work (Ed.), New York: The Odyssey Press, 1940, p. 5.

spikes all over its ventral surface. Preliminary studies on two infants suggest that they are emotionally disturbed. Whether or not we eventually succeed, the fact remains that babies are reluctant to develop experimental neuroses, and at one time we even wondered if this were possible.

During the time that we were producing these evil mothers, we observed the monkeys which we had separated from their mothers at birth and raised under various mothered and nonmothered conditions. The first 47 baby monkeys were raised during the first year of life in wire cages so arranged that the infants could see and hear and call to other infants but not contact them. Now they are five to seven years old and sexually mature. As month after month and year after year have passed, these monkeys have appeared to be less and less normal. We have seen them sitting in their cages strangely mute, staring fixedly into space, relatively indifferent to people and other monkeys. Some clutch their heads in both hands and rock back and forth—the autistic behavior pattern that we have seen in babies raised on wire surrogates. Others, when approached or even left alone, go into violent frenzies of rage, grasping and tearing at their legs with such fury that they sometimes require medical care.

Eventually we realized that we had a laboratory full of neurotic monkeys. We had failed to produce neurotic monkeys by thoughtful planning and creative research, but we had succeeded in producing neurotic monkeys through misadventure. To err is human.

Because of housing pressures some of these monkeys and many of our surrogate-raised monkeys lived in pairs for several years while growing to sexual maturity, but we have seldom seen normal sex behavior, and we certainly have not had the validating criterion of newborn baby monkeys. Instead, these monkeys treat each other like brother and sister, proving that two can live in complete propinquity with perfect propriety as long as no one cares.

Their reason for being, as we saw it, was to produce babies for our researches, and so at this point we deliberately initiated a breeding program which was frighteningly unsuccessful. When the older, wire-cage-raised males were paired with the females at the peak of estrus, the introduction led only to fighting, so violent and vicious that separation was essential to survival. In no case was there any indication of normal sex behavior. Frequently the females were the aggressors; even the normal praying mantis waits until the sex act is completed.

Pairing such cloth-surrogate-raised monkeys as were sexually mature gave little better end results. Violent aggression was not the rule, and there was attempted sex behavior, but it was unreproductive since both the male and female behaviors were of the infantile type we have already described.

At this point we took the 17 oldest of our cage-raised animals, females showing consistent estrous cycles and males obviously mature, and engaged in an intensive re-education program, pairing the females with our most experienced, patient, and gentle males, and the males with our most eager, amiable, and successful breeding females. When the laboratory-bred females were smaller than the sophisticated males, the girls would back away and sit down facing the males, looking appealingly at these would-be consorts. Their hearts were in the right place, but nothing else was. When the females were larger than the males, we can only hope that they misunderstood the males' intentions, for after a brief period of courtship, they would attack and maul the ill-fated male. Females show no respect for a male they can dominate.

The training program for the males was equally unsatisfactory. They approached the females with a blind enthusiasm, but it was a misdirected enthusiasm. Frequently the males would grasp the females by the side of the body and thrust laterally, leaving them working at cross purposes with reality. Even the most persistent attempts by these females to set the boys straight came to naught. Finally, these females either stared at the males with complete contempt or attacked them in utter frustration. It became obvious that they, like their human counterpart, prefer maturer men. We realized then that we had established, not a program of breeding, but a program of brooding.

We had in fact been warned. Our first seven laboratory-born babies were raised in individual cages while being trained on a learning test battery. William Mason planned to test their social behaviors subsequently, and great care had been taken to keep the babies socially isolated and to prevent any physical contacts. Neonatal baby monkeys require 24-hour-a-day care, and infant monkeys need ministrations beyond a 40-hour week. We had assigned the evening care to Kathy, a maternal bit of fluff who had worked for several years as a monkey tester while studying to become an elementary school teacher.

Checking on his wards one night near 10 p.m., Mason found Kathy sitting on the floor surrounded by seven baby monkeys, all eight of the primates playing happily together. Before the horrified scientist could express his outrage, Kathy had risen to her full height of five feet two. Already anticipating the carping criticisms which he was formulating, she shook her finger in his face and spoke with conviction: "Dr. Mason, I'm an education student and I know that it is improper and immoral to blight the social development of little children. I am right and you are wrong!"

Although we were angry with Kathy, we did think there was a certain humor in the situation and we did not worry about our monkeys. We simply transferred Kathy to an office job. Alas, she could not have been more right and we could not have been more wrong! We have already described the social-sexual life of these 7 monkeys and the next 40 to come.

Two years later we had more than theoretical reasons to be disturbed because Mason tested a group of these isolation-raised monkeys, then between 2.5 and 3.5 years of age, and found evidence of severe social abnormalities, which might be described as a sociopathic syndrome. He matched the laboratory-raised monkeys on the basis of weight and dentition patterns with monkeys that had been born and raised in the wild for the first 12 to 18 months, then captured and subjected to various kinds of housing and caging treatments for the next year or two. In the test situations the laboratory-raised monkeys, as compared with feral monkeys, showed infantile sexual behavior, absence of grooming, exaggerated aggression, and absence of affectional interaction as measured by cooperation.

We are now quite certain that this sociopathic syndrome does not stem from the fact that the baby monkeys were raised in the laboratory but from *how* they were raised in the laboratory. Our infants raised in the laboratory by real monkey mothers and permitted opportunity for the development of normal infant-infant affection demonstrate normal male and female sexual behavior when they enter the second year of life. Furthermore, our playroom and playpen studies show that infant monkeys raised on cloth mothers but given the opportunity to form normal infant-infant affectional patterns, also develop normal sexual responses.

In a desperate attempt to assist a group of 18 three- to four-year-old cloth-surrogate-raised monkeys, half of them males and half females, we engaged in a group-psychotherapy program, placing these animals for two months on the monkey island in the Madison Zoo. Their summer vacation on the enchanted island was not without avail, and social grooming responses rapidly developed and were frequent in occurrence. After a few days of misunderstanding, patterns of social ordering developed, and a number of males and females developed friendship patterns. Unfortunately, sexual behavior was infrequent, and the behavior that was observed was completely inadequate—at least from our point of view. In desperation we finally introduced our most experienced, most patient, and most kindly breeding male, Smiley (the male in Figures 1 and 2), and he rapidly established himself as king of the island and prepared to take full advantage of the wealth of opportunity which surrounded him. Fortunately, the traumatic experiences he encountered with unreceptive females have left no apparent permanent emotional scars, and now that he has been returned to our laboratory breeding colony, he is again making an important contribution to our research program. If normal sexual behavior occurred, no member of our observational team ever saw it, and had a female become pregnant, we would have believed in parthenogenesis.

But let us return to the monkeys that we left on the island and the older ones that we left in their cages. A year has passed, and the frustrations that both we and our monkeys experienced are in some small part nothing but a memory. We constructed larger and more comfortable breeding cages, and we designed a very large experimental breeding room 8 feet by 8 feet by 8 feet in size with appropriate platforms and a six-foot tree. Apparently we designed successful seraglios for I can report that not all love's labors have been lost. It does appear that the males are completely expendable unless they can be used in a program of artificial insemination. Certainly we can find no evidence that there is a destiny that shapes their ends unless some Skinnerite can help us with the shaping process. We have, however, had better success with some of the females, particularly the females raised on cloth surrogates.

Even so, one of the wire-cage-raised females is a mother and another is pregnant. Three cloth-surrogate females are mothers and four or five are expectant. We give all the credit to three breeding males. One, Smiley, does not take "no" for an answer. Smiley has a way with females. Patient, gentle, and persuasive, he has overcome more than one planned program of passive resistance. One female did not become pregnant until the fifth successive month of training. Month after month she has changed, and now she is mad about the boy. Male No. 342 behaves very much like Smiley. Even when females threaten him, he does not harm them. Given time, he has been able to overcome more than one reluctant dragon, and he is a master of the power of positive suggestion.

Breeding male No. 496 has helped us greatly, particularly with the younger, cloth-surrogate-raised females. His approach differs from that of Smiley and No. 342. His technique transcends seduction, and in contract bridge terms it may be described as an approach-forcing system.

Combining our human and male-monkey talents, we are winning the good fight and imparting to naive and even resistant female monkeys the priceless gift of motherhood. Possibly it is a Pyrrhic victory. As every scientist knows, the solution of one scientific problem inevitably leads to another and this is our fate. Month after month female monkeys that never knew a real mother, themselves become mothers—helpless, hopeless, heartless mothers devoid, or almost devoid, of any maternal feeling.

three faces of intellect[1]

j. p. guilford
university of southern california

Before anything else, I should like to express my deep appreciation to Mrs. Walter V. Bingham for making this lecture possible and also to the committee of the American Psychological Association for inviting me to be the 1959 lecturer. I shall attempt as much as possible to make the lecture a suitable tribute to the distinguished psychologist whom we commemorate on this occasion. Appreciation is also due to those at Stanford University who have made the local arrangements. The selection of Stanford University for the scene of the lecture is a most natural one, in view of the lectureship's aim to honor institutions that have made outstanding contributions to the furtherance of methods for the recognition of talent. It is very noteworthy that twice before this university has been indirectly honored by the selection of Lewis M. Terman as the first Walter V. Bingham lecturer and the selection of Edward K. Strong, Jr. as the lecturer in 1958.

1. The Walter V. Bingham Memorial Lecture given at Stanford University on April 13, 1959. Reprinted from *American Psychologist*, 1959, Vol. 14, pp. 469–479. Copyright 1959 by the American Psychological Association, and reproduced by permission.

My subject is in the area of human intelligence, in connection with which the names of Terman and Stanford have become known the world over. The Stanford Revision of the Binet intelligence scale has been the standard against which all other instruments for the measurement of intelligence have been compared. The term IQ or intelligence quotient has become a household word in this country. This is illustrated by two brief stories.

A few years ago, one of my neighbors came home from a PTA meeting, remarking: "That Mrs. So-And-So, thinks she knows so much. She kept talking about the 'intelligence *quota*' of the children; 'intelligence *quota*'; imagine. Why, everybody knows that IQ stands for 'intelligence *quiz*.'"

The other story comes from a little comic strip in a Los Angeles morning newspaper, called "Junior Grade." In the first picture a little boy meets a girl, both apparently about the first-grade level. The little girl remarks, "I have a high IQ." The little boy, puzzled, said, "You have a what?" The little girl repeated, "I have a high IQ," then went on her way. The little boy, looking thoughtful, said, "And she looks like such a nice little girl, too."

It is my purpose to speak about the analysis of this thing called human intelligence into its components. I do not believe that either Binet or Terman, if they were still with us, would object to the idea of a searching and detailed study of intelligence, aimed toward a better understanding of its nature. Preceding the development of his intelligence scale, Binet had done much research on different kinds of thinking activities and apparently recognized that intelligence has a number of aspects. It is to the lasting credit of both Binet and

Terman that they introduced such a great variety of tasks into their intelligence scales.

Two related events of very recent history make it imperative that we learn all we can regarding the nature of intelligence. I am referring to the advent of the artificial satellites and planets and to the crisis in education that has arisen in part as a consequence. The preservation of our way of life and our future security depend upon our most important national resources: our intellectual abilities and, more particularly, our creative abilities. It is time, then, that we learn all we can about those resources.

Our knowledge of the components of human intelligence has come about mostly within the last 25 years. The major sources of this information in this country have been L. L. Thurstone and his associates, the wartime research of psychologists in the United States Air Forces, and more recently the Aptitudes Project[2] at the University of Southern California, now in its tenth year of research on cognitive and thinking abilities. The results from the Aptitudes Project that have gained perhaps the most attention have pertained to creative-thinking abilities. These are mostly novel findings. But to me, the most significant outcome has been the development of a unified theory of human intellect, which organizes the known, unique or primary intellectual abilities into a single system called the "structure of intellect." It is to this system that I shall devote the major part of my remarks, with very brief mentions of some of the implications for the psychology of thinking and problem solving, for vocational testing, and for education.

The discovery of the components of intelligence has been by means of the experimental application of the method of factor analysis. It is not necessary for you to know anything about the theory or method of factor analysis in order to follow the discussion of the components. I should like to say, however, that factor analysis has no connection with or resemblance to psychoanalysis. A positive statement would be more helpful, so I will say that each intellectual component or factor is a unique ability that is needed to do well in a certain class of tasks or tests. As a general principle we find that certain individuals do well in the tests of a certain class, but they may do poorly in the tests of another class. We conclude that a factor has certain

2. Under Contract N6onr-23810 with the Office of Naval Research (Personnel and Training Branch).

properties from the features that the tests of a class have in common. I shall give you very soon a number of examples of tests, each representing a factor.

The Structure of Intellect
Although each factor is sufficiently distinct to be detected by factor analysis, in very recent years it has become apparent that the factors themselves can be classified because they resemble one another in certain ways. One basis of classification is according to the basic kind of process or operation performed. This kind of classification gives us five major groups of intellectual abilities: factors of cognition, memory, convergent thinking, divergent thinking, and evaluation.

Cognition means discovery or rediscovery or recognition. Memory means retention of what is cognized. Two kinds of productive-thinking operations generate new information from known information and remembered information. In divergent-thinking operations we think in different directions, sometimes searching, sometimes seeking variety. In convergent thinking the information leads to one right answer or to a recognized best or conventional answer. In evaluation we reach decisions as to goodness, correctness, suitability, or adequacy of what we know, what we remember, and what we produce in productive thinking.

A second way of classifying the intellectual factors is according to the kind of material or content involved. The factors known thus far involve three kinds of material or content: the content may be figural, symbolic, or semantic. Figural content is concrete material such as is perceived through the senses. It does not represent anything except itself. Visual material has properties such as size, form, color, location, or texture. Things we hear or feel provide other examples of figural material. Symbolic content is composed of letters, digits, and other conventional signs, usually organized in general systems, such as the alphabet or the number system. Semantic content is in the form of verbal meanings or ideas, for which no examples are necessary.

When a certain operation is applied to a certain kind of content, as many as six general kinds of products may be involved. There is enough evidence available to suggest that, regardless of the combinations of operations and content, the same six kinds of products may be found associated. The six kinds of products are: units, classes, relations, systems, transfor-

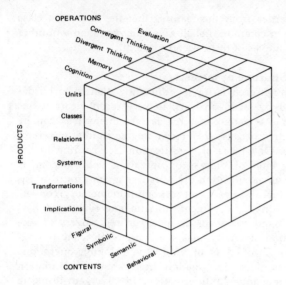

Fig. 1
A cubical model representing the structure of intellect.

mations, and implications. So far as we have determined from factor analysis, these are the only fundamental kinds of products that we can know. As such, they may serve as basic classes into which one might fit all kinds of information psychologically.

The three kinds of classifications of the factors of intellect can be represented by means of a single solid model, shown in Figure 1. In this model, which we call the "structure of intellect," each dimension represents one of the modes of variation of the factors.[3] Along one dimension are found the various kinds of operations, along a second one are the various kinds of products, and along the third are various kinds of content. Along the dimension of content a fourth category has been added, its kind of content being designated as "behavioral." This category has been added on a purely theoretical basis to represent the general area sometimes called "social intelligence." More will be said about this section of the model later.

In order to provide a better basis for understanding the model and a better basis for accepting it as a picture of human intellect, I shall do some exploring of it with you systematically, giving some examples of

3. For an earlier presentation of the concept, see Guilford (1956).

tests. Each cell in the model calls for a certain kind of ability that can be described in terms of operation, content, and product, for each cell is at the intersection of a unique combination of kinds of operation, content, and product. A test for that ability would have the same three properties. In our exploration of the model, we shall take one vertical layer at a time, beginning with the front face. The first layer provides us with a matrix of 18 cells (if we ignore the behavioral column for which there are as yet no known factors) each of which should contain a cognitive ability.

THE COGNITIVE ABILITIES
We know at present the unique abilities that fit logically into 15 of the 18 cells for cognitive abilities. Each row presents a triad of similar abilities, having a single kind of product in common. The factors of the first row are concerned with the knowing of units. A good test of the ability to cognize figural units is the Street Gestalt Completion Test. In this test, the recognition of familiar pictured objects in silhouette form is made difficult for testing purposes by blocking out parts of those objects. There is another factor that is known to involve the perception of auditory figures — in the form of melodies, rhythms, and speech sounds — and still another factor involving kinesthetic forms. The presence of three factors in one cell (they are conceivably distinct abilities, although this has not been tested) suggests that more generally, in the figural column, at least, we should expect to find more than one ability. A fourth dimension pertaining to variations in sense modality may thus apply in connection with figural content. The model could be extended in this manner if the facts call for such an extension.

The ability to cognize symbolic units is measured by tests like the following:

Put vowels in the following blanks to make real words:
P___W___R
M___RV___L
C___RT___N

Rearrange the letters to make real words:
R A C I H
T V O E S
K L C C O

The first of these two tests is called Disemvoweled Words, and the second Scrambled Words.

The ability to cognize semantic units is the well-known factor of verbal comprehension, which is best measured by means of a vocabulary test, with items such as:

Gravity means_____
Circus means_____
Virtue means_____

From the comparison of these two factors it is obvious that recognizing familiar words as letter structures and knowing what words mean depend upon quite different abilities.

For testing the abilities to know classes of units, we may present the following kinds of items, one with symbolic content and one with semantic content:

Which letter group does not belong?
XECM   PVAA   QXIN   VTRO

Which object does not belong?
clam   tree   oven   rose

A figural test is constructed in a completely parallel form, presenting in each item four figures, three of which have a property in common and the fourth lacking that property.

The three abilities to see relationships are also readily measured by a common kind of test, differing only in terms of content. The well-known analogies test is applicable, two items in symbolic and semantic form being:

JIRE   :   KIRE   : :   FORA   :   KORE   KORA   LIRE   GORA   GIRE
poetry : prose : : dance : music walk sing talk jump

Such tests usually involve more than the ability to cognize relations, but we are not concerned with this problem at this point.

The three factors for cognizing systems do not at present appear in tests so closely resembling one another as in the case of the examples just given. There is nevertheless an underlying common core of logical similarity. Ordinary space tests, such as Thurstone's Flags, Figures, and Cards or Part V (Spatial Orientation) of the Guilford-Zimmerman Aptitude Survey (GZAS), serve in the figural column. The system involved is an order or arrangement of objects in space. A system that uses symbolic elements is illustrated by the Letter Triangle Test, a sample item of which is:

```
        —
   d    —
 b   e    —
a  c   f    ?
```

What letter belongs at the place of the question mark?

The ability to understand a semantic system has been known for some time as the factor called general reasoning. One of its most faithful indicators is a test composed of arithmetic-reasoning items. That the phase of understanding only is important for measuring this ability is shown by the fact that such a test works even if the examinee is not asked to give a complete solution; he need only show that he structures the problem properly. For example, an item from the test Necessary Arithmetical Operations simply asks what operations are needed to solve the problem:

A city lot 48 feet wide and 149 feet deep costs $79,432. What is the cost per square foot?

A. add and multiply
B. multiply and divide
C. subtract and divide
D. add and subtract
E. divide and add

Placing the factor of general reasoning in this cell of the structure of intellect gives us some new conceptions of its nature. It should be a broad ability to grasp all kinds of systems that are conceived in terms of verbal concepts, not restricted to the understanding of problems of an arithmetical type.

Transformations are changes of various kinds, including modifications in arrangement, organization, or meaning. In the figural column for the transformations row, we find the factor known as visualization. Common measuring instruments for this factor are the surface-development tests, and an example of a different kind is Part VI (Spatial Visualization) of the GZAS. A test of the ability to make transformations of meaning, for the factor in the semantic column, is called Similarities. The examinee is asked to state several ways in which two objects, such as an apple and an orange, are alike. Only by shifting the meanings of both is the examinee able to give many responses to such an item.

In the set of abilities having to do with the cognition of implications, we find that the individual goes beyond the information given, but not to the extent of what might be called drawing conclusions. We may say that he extrapolates. From the given information he expects or foresees certain consequences, for example. The two factors found in this row of the cognition matrix were first called "foresight" factors. Foresight in connection with figural material can be tested by means of paper-and-pencil mazes. Foresight in connection with ideas, those pertaining to events, for example, is indicated by a test such as Pertinent Questions:

In planning to open a new hamburger stand in a certain community, what four questions should be considered in deciding upon its location?

The more questions the examinee asks in response to a list of such problems, the more he evidently forsees contingencies.

THE MEMORY ABILITIES

The area of memory abilities has been explored less than some of the other areas of operation, and only seven of the potential cells of the memory matrix have known factors in them. These cells are restricted to three rows: for units, relations, and systems. The first cell in the memory matrix is now occupied by two factors, parallel to two in the corresponding cognition matrix: visual memory and auditory memory. Memory for series of letters or numbers, as in memory span tests, conforms to the conception of memory for symbolic units. Memory for the ideas in a paragraph conforms to the conception of memory for semantic units.

The formation of associations between units, such as visual forms, syllables, and meaningful words, as in the method of paired associates, would seem to represent three abilities to remember relationships involving three kinds of content. We know of two such abilities, for the symbolic and semantic columns. The memory for known systems is represented by two abilities very recently discovered (Christal, 1958). Remembering the arrangement of objects in space is the nature of an ability in the figural column, and remembering a sequence of events is the nature of a corresponding ability in the semantic column. The differentiation between these two abilities implies that a person may be able to say where he saw an object on a page, but he might not be able to say on which of several pages he saw it after leafing through several pages that included the right one. Considering the blank rows in the memory matrix, we should expect to find abilities also to remember classes, transformations, and implications, as well as units, relations, and systems.

THE DIVERGENT-THINKING ABILITIES

The unique feature of divergent production is that a *variety* of responses is produced. The product is not completely determined by the given information. This is not to say that divergent thinking does not come into play in the total process of reaching a unique

conclusion, for it comes into play wherever there is trial-and-error thinking.

The well-known ability of word fluency is tested by asking the examinee to list words satisfying a specified letter requirement, such as words beginning with the letter "s" or words ending in "-tion." This ability is now regarded as a facility in divergent production of symbolic units. The parallel semantic ability has been known as ideational fluency. A typical test item calls for listing objects that are round and edible. Winston Churchill must have possessed this ability to a high degree. Clement Attlee is reported to have said about him recently that, no matter what problem came up, Churchill always seemed to have about ten ideas. The trouble was, Attlee continued, he did not know which was the good one. The last comment implies some weakness in one or more of the evaluative abilities.

The divergent production of class ideas is believed to be the unique feature of a factor called "spontaneous flexibility." A typical test instructs the examinee to list all the uses he can think of for a common brick, and he is given eight minutes. If his responses are: build a house, build a barn, build a garage, build a school, build a church, build a chimney, build a walk, and build a barbecue, he would earn a fairly high score for ideational fluency but a very low score for spontaneous flexibility, because all these uses fall into the same class. If another person said: make a door stop, make a paper weight, throw it at a dog, make a bookcase, drown a cat, drive a nail, make a red powder, and use for baseball bases, he would also receive a high score for flexibility. He has gone frequently from one class to another.

A current study of unknown but predicted divergent-production abilities includes testing whether there are also figural and symbolic abilities to produce multiple classes. An experimental figural test presents a number of figures that can be classified in groups of three in various ways, each figure being usable in more than one class. An experimental symbolic test presents a few numbers that are also to be classified in multiple ways.

A unique ability involving relations is called "associational fluency." It calls for the production of a variety of things related in a specified way to a given thing. For example, the examinee is asked to list words meaning about the same as "good" or to list words meaning about the opposite of "hard." In these instances the response produced is to complete a relationship, and semantic content is involved. Some of our present experimental tests call for the production of varieties of relations, as such, and involve figural and symbolic content also. For example, given four small digits, in how many ways can they be related in order to produce a sum of eight?

One factor pertaining to the production of systems is known as expressional fluency. The rapid formation of phrases or sentences is the essence of certain tests of this factor. For example, given the initial letters:

W_____ c_____ e_____ n_____

with different sentences to be produced, the examinee might write "We can eat nuts" or "Whence came Eve Newton?" In interpreting the factor, we regard the sentence as a symbolic system. By analogy, a figural system would be some kind of organization of lines and other elements, and a semantic system would be in the form of a verbally stated problem or perhaps something as complex as a theory.

In the row of the divergent-production matrix devoted to transformations, we find some very interesting factors. The one called "adaptive flexibility" is now recognized as belonging in the figural column. A faithful test of it has been Match Problems. This is based upon the common game that uses squares, the sides of which are formed by match sticks. The examinee is told to take away a given number of matches to leave a stated number of squares with nothing left over. Nothing is said about the sizes of the squares to be left. If the examinee imposes upon himself the restriction that the squares that he leaves must be of the same size, he will fail in his attempts to do items like that in Figure 2. Other odd kinds of solutions are introduced in other items, such as overlapping squares and squares within squares, and so on. In another variation of Match Problems the examinee is told to produce two or more solutions for each problem.

A factor that has been called "originality" is now recognized as adaptive flexibility with semantic material, where there must be a shifting of meanings. The examinee must produce the shifts or changes in meaning and so come up with novel, unusual, clever, or farfetched ideas. The Plot Titles Test presents a short story, the examinee being told to list as many appropriate titles as he can to head the story. One story is about a missionary who has been captured by cannibals in Africa. He is in the pot and about to be boiled when a princess of the tribe obtains a promise for his

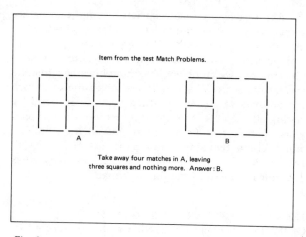

Fig. 2

A sample item from the test Match Problems. The problem in this item is to take away four matches and leave three squares. The solution is given.

release if he will become her mate. He refuses and is boiled to death.

In scoring the test, we separate the responses into two categories, clever and nonclever. Examples of nonclever responses are: African Death, Defeat of a Princess, Eaten by Savages, The Princess, The African Missionary, In Darkest Africa, and Boiled by Savages. These titles are appropriate but commonplace. The number of such responses serves as a score for ideational fluency. Examples of clever responses are: Pot's Plot, Potluck Dinner, Stewed Parson, Goil or Boil, A Mate Worse Than Death, He Left a Dish for a Pot, Chaste in Haste, and A Hot Price for Freedom. The number of clever responses given by an examinee is his score for originality, or the divergent production of semantic transformations.

Another test of originality presents a very novel task so that any acceptable response is unusual for the individual. In the Symbol Production Test the examinee is to produce a simple symbol to stand for a noun or a verb in each short sentence, in other words to invent something like pictographic symbols. Still another test of originality asks for writing the "punch lines" for cartoons, a task that almost automatically challenges the examinee to be clever. Thus, quite a variety of tests offer approaches to the measurement of originality, including one or two others that I have not mentioned.

Three Faces of Intellect

269

Abilities to produce a variety of implications are assessed by tests calling for elaboration of given information. A figural test of this type provides the examinee with a line or two, to which he is to add other lines to produce an object. The more lines he adds, the greater his score. A semantic test gives the examinee the outlines of a plan to which he is to respond by stating all the details he can think of to make the plan work. A new test we are trying out in the symbolic area presents two simple equations such as $B - C = D$ and $z = A + D$. The examinee is to make as many other equations as he can from this information.

THE CONVERGENT-PRODUCTION ABILITIES

Of the 18 convergent-production abilities expected in the three content columns, 12 are now recognized. In the first row, pertaining to units, we have an ability to name figural properties (forms or colors) and an ability to name abstractions (classes, relations, and so on). It may be that the ability in common to the speed of naming forms and the speed of naming colors is not appropriately placed in the convergent-thinking matrix. One might expect that the thing to be produced in a test of the convergent production of figural units would be in the form of figures rather than words. A better test of such an ability might somehow specify the need for one particular object, the examinee to furnish the object.

A test for the convergent production of classes (Word Grouping) presents a list of 12 words that are to be classified in four, and only four, meaningful groups, no word to appear in more than one group. A parallel test (Figure Concepts Test) presents 20 pictured real objects that are to be grouped in meaningful classes of two or more each.

Convergent production having to do with relationships is represented by three known factors, all involving the "eduction of correlates," as Spearman called it. The given information includes one unit and a stated relation, the examinee to supply the other unit. Analogies tests that call for completion rather than a choice between alternative answers emphasize this kind of ability. With symbolic content such an item might read:

pots   stop   bard   drab   rats $\overset{?}{\rule{1.5em}{0.4pt}}$

A semantic item that measures eduction of correlates is:

The absence of sound is ―――――.

Incidentally, the latter item is from a vocabulary-completion test, and its relation to the factor of ability to produce correlates indicates how, by change of form, a vocabulary test may indicate an ability other than that for which vocabulary tests are usually intended, namely, the factor of verbal comprehension.

Only one factor for convergent production of systems is known, and it is in the semantic column. It is measured by a class of tests that may be called ordering tests. The examinee may be presented with a number of events that ordinarily have a best or most logical order, the events being presented in scrambled order. The presentation may be pictorial, as in the Picture Arrangement Test, or verbal. The pictures may be taken from a cartoon strip. The verbally presented events may be in the form of the various steps needed to plant a new lawn. There are undoubtedly other kinds of systems than temporal order that could be utilized for testing abilities in this row of the convergent-production matrix.

In the way of producing transformations of a unique variety, we have three recognized factors, known as redefinition abilities. In each case, redefinition involves the changing of functions or uses of parts of one unit and giving them new functions or uses in some new unit. For testing the ability of figural redefinition, a task based upon the Gottschaldt figures is suitable. Figure 3 shows the kind of item for such a test. In recognizing the simpler figure within the structure of a more complex figure, certain lines must take on new roles.

In terms of symbolic material, the following sample items will illustrate how groups of letters in given words must be readapted to use in other words. In the test Camouflaged Words, each sentence contains the name of a sport or game:

I did not know that he was ailing.
To beat the Hun, tin goes a long way.

For the factor of semantic redefinition, the Gestalt Transformation Test may be used. A sample item reads:

From which object could you most likely make a needle?
A. a cabbage
B. a splice
C. a steak
D. a paper box
E. a fish

The convergent production of implications means the drawing of fully determined conclusions from given

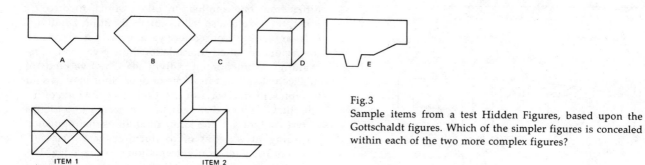

Fig.3
Sample items from a test Hidden Figures, based upon the Gottschaldt figures. Which of the simpler figures is concealed within each of the two more complex figures?

information. The well-known factor of numerical facility belongs in the symbolic column. For the parallel ability in the figural column, we have a test known as Form Reasoning, in which rigorously defined operations with figures are used. For the parallel ability in the semantic column, the factor sometimes called "deduction" probably qualifies. Items of the following type are sometimes used.

Charles is younger than Robert
Charles is older than Frank
Who is older: Robert or Frank?

EVALUATIVE ABILITIES

The evaluative area has had the least investigation of all the operational categories. In fact, only one systematic analytical study has been devoted to this area. Only eight evaluative abilities are recognized as fitting into the evaluation matrix. But at least five rows have one or more factors each, and also three of the usual columns or content categories. In each case, evaluation involves reaching decisions as to the accuracy, goodness, suitability, or workability of information. In each row, for the particular kind of product of that row, some kind of criterion or standard of judgment is involved.

In the first row, for the evaluation of units, the important decision to be made pertains to the identity of a unit. Is this unit identical with that one? In the figural column we find the factor long known as "perceptual speed." Tests of this factor invariably call for decisions of identity, for example, Part IV (Perceptual Speed) of the GZAS or Thurstone's Identical Forms. I think it has been generally wrongly thought that the ability involved is that of cognition of visual forms. But we have seen that another factor is a more suitable candidate for this definition and for being in the very first cell of the cognitive matrix. It is parallel to this evaluative ability but does not require the judgment of identity as one of its properties.

In the symbolic column is an ability to judge identity of symbolic units, in the form of series of letters or numbers or of names of individuals.

Are members of the following pairs identical or not:
825170493____825176493
dkeltvmpa____dkeltvmpa
C. S. Meyerson____C. E. Meyerson

Such items are common in tests of clerical aptitude.

There should be a parallel ability to decide whether two ideas are identical or different. Is the idea expressed in this sentence the same as the idea expressed in that one? Do these two proverbs express essentially the same idea? Such tests exist and will be used to test the hypothesis that such an ability can be demonstrated.

No evaluative abilities pertaining to classes have as yet been recognized. The abilities having to do with evaluation where relations are concerned must meet the criterion of logical consistency. Syllogistic-type tests involving letter symbols indicate a different ability than the same type of test involving verbal statements. In the figural column we might expect that tests incorporating geometric reasoning or proof would indicate a parallel ability to sense the soundness of conclusions regarding figural relationships.

The evaluation of systems seems to be concerned with the internal consistency of those systems, so far as we can tell from the knowledge of one such factor. The factor has been called "experiential evaluation," and its representative test presents items like that in Figure 4 asking "What is wrong with this picture?" The things wrong are often internal inconsistencies.

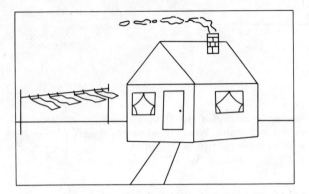

Fig. 4
A sample item from the test Unusual Details. What two things are wrong with this picture?

A semantic ability for evaluating transformations is thought to be that known for some time as "judgment." In typical judgment tests, the examinee is asked to tell which of five solutions to a practical problem is most adequate or wise. The solutions frequently involve improvisations, in other words, adaptations of familiar objects to unusual uses. In this way the items present redefinitions to be evaluated.

A factor known first as "sensitivity to problems" has become recognized as an evaluative ability having to do with implications. One test of the factor, the Apparatus Test, asks for two needed improvements with respect to each of several common devices, such as the telephone or the toaster. The Social Institutions Test, a measure of the same factor, asks what things are wrong with each of several institutions, such as tipping or national elections. We may say that defects or deficiencies are implications of an evaluative kind. Another interpretation would be that seeing defects and deficiencies are evaluations of implications to the effect that the various aspects of something are all right.[4]

Some Implications of the Structure of Intellect

FOR PSYCHOLOGICAL THEORY
Although factor analysis as generally employed is best designed to investigate ways in which individuals

4. For further details concerning the intellectual factors, illustrative tests, and the place of the factors in the structure of intellect, see Guilford (1959).

differ from one another, in other words, to discover traits, the results also tell us much about how individuals are alike. Consequently, information regarding the factors and their interrelationships gives us understanding of functioning individuals. The five kinds of intellectual abilities in terms of operations may be said to represent five ways of functioning. The kinds of intellectual abilities distinguished according to varieties of test content and the kinds of abilities distinguished according to varieties of products suggest a classification of basic forms of information or knowledge. The kind of organism suggested by this way of looking at intellect is that of an agency for dealing with information of various kinds in various ways. The concepts provided by the distinctions among the intellectual abilities and by their classifications may be very useful in our future investigations of learning, memory, problem solving, invention, and decision making, by whatever method we choose to approach those problems.

FOR VOCATIONAL TESTING
With about 50 intellectual factors already known, we may say that there are at least 50 ways of being intelligent. It has been facetiously suggested that there seem to be a great many more ways of being stupid, unfortunately. The structure of intellect is a theoretical model that predicts as many as 120 distinct abilities, if every cell of the model contains a factor. Already we know that two cells contain two or more factors each, and there probably are actually other cells of this type. Since the model was first conceived, 12 factors predicted by it have found places in it. There is consequently hope of filling many of the other vacancies, and we may eventually end up with more than 120 abilities.

The major implication for the assessment of intelligence is that to know an individual's intellectual resources thoroughly we shall need a surprisingly large number of scores. It is expected that many of the factors are intercorrelated, so there is some possibility that by appropriate sampling we shall be able to cover the important abilities with a more limited number of tests. At any rate, a multiple-score approach to the assessment of intelligence is definitely indicated in connection with future vocational operations.

Considering the kinds of abilities classified as to content, we may speak roughly of four kinds of intelligence. The abilities involving the use of figural information may be regarded as "concrete" intelligence. The people who depend most upon these abilities deal with concrete things and their properties. Among these people are mechanics, operators of machines, engineers (in some aspects of their work), artists, and musicians.

In the abilities pertaining to symbolic and semantic content, we have two kinds of "abstract" intelligence. Symbolic abilities should be important in learning to recognize words, to spell, and to operate with numbers. Language and mathematics should depend very much upon them, except that in mathematics some aspects, such as geometry, have strong figural involvement. Semantic intelligence is important for understanding things in terms of verbal concepts and hence is important in all courses where the learning of facts and ideas is essential.

In the hypothesized behavioral column of the structure of intellect, which may be roughly described as "social" intelligence, we have some of the most interesting possibilities. Understanding the behavior of others and of ourselves is largely nonverbal in character. The theory suggests as many as 30 abilities in this area, some having to do with understanding, some with productive thinking about behavior, and some with the evaluation of behavior. The theory also suggests that information regarding behavior is also in the form of the six kinds of products that apply elsewhere in the structure of intellect, including units, relations, systems, and so on. The abilities in the area of social intelligence, whatever they prove to be, will possess considerable importance in connection with all those individuals who deal most with other people: teachers, law officials, social workers, therapists, politicians, statesmen, and leaders of other kinds.

FOR EDUCATION

The implications for education are numerous, and I have time just to mention a very few. The most fundamental implication is that we might well undergo transformations with respect to our conception of the learner and of the process of learning. Under the prevailing conception, the learner is a kind of stimulus-response device, much on the order of a vending machine. You put in a coin, and something comes out. The machine learns what reaction to put out when a certain coin is put in. If, instead, we think of the learner as an agent for dealing with information, where information is defined very broadly, we have

something more analogous to an electronic computer. We feed a computer information; it stores that information; it uses that information for generating new information, either by way of divergent or convergent thinking; and it evaluates its own results. Advantages that a human learner has over a computer include the step of seeking and discovering new information from sources outside itself and the step of programming itself. Perhaps even these steps will be added to computers, if this has not already been done in some cases.

At any rate, this conception of the learner leads us to the idea that learning is discovery of information, not merely the formation of associations, particularly associations in the form of stimulus-response connections. I am aware of the fact that my proposal is rank heresy. But if we are to make significant progress in our understanding of human learning and particularly our understanding of the so-called higher mental processes of thinking, problem solving, and creative thinking, some drastic modifications are due in our theory.

The idea that education is a matter of training the mind or of training the intellect has been rather unpopular, wherever the prevailing psychological doctrines have been followed. In theory, at least, the emphasis has been upon the learning of rather specific habits or skills. If we take our cue from factor theory, however, we recognize that most learning probably has both specific and general aspects or components. The general aspects may be along the lines of the factors of intellect. This is not to say that the individual's status in each factor is entirely determined by learning. We do not know to what extent each factor is determined by heredity and to what extent by learning. The best position for educators to take is that possibly every intellectual factor can be developed in individuals at least to some extent by learning.

If education has the general objective of developing the intellects of students, it can be suggested that each intellectual factor provides a particular goal at which to aim. Defined by a certain combination of content, operation, and product, each goal ability then calls for certain kinds of practice in order to achieve improvement in it. This implies choice of curriculum and the choice or invention of teaching methods that will most likely accomplish the desired results.

Considering the very great variety of abilities revealed by the factorial exploration of intellect, we are in a better position to ask whether any general intellectual skills are now being neglected in education and whether appropriate balances are being observed. It is often observed these days that we have fallen down in the way of producing resourceful, creative graduates. How true this is, in comparison with other times, I do not know. Perhaps the deficit is noticed because the demands for inventiveness are so much greater at this time. At any rate, realization that the more conspicuously creative abilities appear to be concentrated in the divergent-thinking category, and also to some extent in the transformation category, we now ask whether we have been giving these skills appropriate exercise. It is probable that we need a better balance of training in the divergent-thinking area as compared with training in convergent thinking and in critical thinking or evaluation.

The structure of intellect as I have presented it to you may or may not stand the test of time. Even if the general form persists, there are likely to be some modifications. Possibly some different kind of model will be invented. Be that as it may, the fact of a multiplicity of intellectual abilities seems well established.

There are many individuals who long for the good old days of simplicity, when we got along with one unanalyzed intelligence. Simplicity certainly has its appeal. But human nature is exceedingly complex, and we may as well face that fact. The rapidly moving events of the world in which we live have forced upon us the need for knowing human intelligence thoroughly. Humanity's peaceful pursuit of happiness depends upon our control of nature and of our own behavior; and this, in turn, depends upon understanding ourselves, including our intellectual resources.

References

Christal, R. E. Factor analytic study of visual memory. *Psychol. Monogr.*, 1958, 72, No. 13 (Whole No. 466).

Guilford, J. P. The structure of intellect. *Psychol. Bull.*, 1956, 53, 267–293.

Guilford, J. P. *Personality.* New York: McGraw-Hill, 1959.

Years ago I ventured to present a paper before the Ninth International Congress at New Haven (G. W. Allport, 1931). It was entitled "What Is a Trait of Personality?" For me to return to the same topic on this honorific occasion is partly a sentimental indulgence, but partly too it is a self-imposed task to discover whether during the past 36 years I have learned anything new about this central problem in personality theory.

In my earlier paper I made eight bold assertions. A trait, I said,

1. Has more than nominal existence.
2. Is more generalized than a habit.
3. Is dynamic, or at least determinative, in behavior.
4. May be established empirically.
5. Is only relatively independent of other traits.
6. Is not synonymous with moral or social judgment.
7. May be viewed either in the light of the personality which contains it, or in the light of its distribution in the population at large.

To these criteria I added one more:

8. Acts, and even habits, that are inconsistent with a trait are not proof of the nonexistence of the trait.

While these propositions still seem to me defensible they were originally framed in an age of psychological innocence. They now need reexamination in the light of subsequent criticism and research.

Criticism of the Concept of Trait

Some critics have challenged the whole concept of trait. Carr and Kingsbury (1938) point out the danger of reifi-

traits revisited[1]

gordon w. allport (1897–1967)
harvard university

cation. Our initial observation of behavior is only in terms of adverbs of action: John behaves aggressively. Then an adjective creeps in: John has an aggressive disposition. Soon a heavy substantive arrives, like William James' cow on the doormat: John has a trait of aggression. The result is the fallacy of misplaced concreteness.

The general positivist cleanup starting in the 1930s went even further. It swept out (or tried to sweep out) all entities, regarding them as question-begging redundancies. Thus Skinner (1953) writes:

When we say that a man eats *because* he is hungry, smokes a great deal *because* he has the tobacco habit, fights *because* of the instinct of pugnacity, behaves brilliantly *because* of his intelligence, or plays the piano well *because* of his musical ability, we seem to be referring to causes. But on analysis these phrases prove to be merely redundant descriptions [p. 31].

1. Reprinted from *American Psychologist*, 1966, Vol. 21, pp. 1–10. Copyright 1966 by the American Psychological Association, and reproduced by permission.

It is clear that this line of attack is an assault not only upon the concept of trait, but upon all intervening variables whether they be conceived in terms of expectancies, attitudes, motives, capacities, sentiments, or traits. The resulting postulate of the "empty organism" is by now familiar to us all, and is the scientific credo of some. Carried to its logical extreme this reasoning would scrap the concept of personality itself—an eventuality that seems merely absurd to me.

More serious, to my mind, is the argument against what Block and Bennett (1955) called "traitology" arising from many studies of the variability of a person's behavior as it changes from situation to situation. Every parent knows that an offspring may be a hellion at home and an angel when he goes visiting. A businessman may be hardheaded in the office and a mere marshmallow in the hands of his pretty daughter.

Years ago the famous experiment by La Piere (1934) demonstrated that an innkeeper's prejudice seems to come and go according to the situation confronting him.

In recent months Hunt (1965) has listed various theories of personality that to his mind require revision in the light of recent evidence. Among them he questions the belief that personality traits are the major sources of behavior variance. He, like Miller (1963), advocates that we shift attention from traits to interactions among people, and look for consistency in behavior chiefly in situationally defined roles. Helson (1964) regards trait as the residual effect of previous stimulation, and thus subordinates it to the organism's present adaptation level.

Scepticism is likewise reflected in many investigations of "person perception." To try to discover the traits residing within a personality is regarded as either naive or impossible. Studies, therefore, concentrate only on the *process* of perceiving or judging, and reject the problem of validating the perception and judgment. (Cf. Tagiuri & Petrullo, 1958.)

Studies too numerous to list have ascribed chief variance in behavior to situational factors, leaving only a mild residue to be accounted for in terms of idiosyncratic attitudes and traits. A prime example is Stouffer's study of *The American Soldier* (Stouffer et al., 1949). Differing opinions and preferences are ascribed so far as possible to the GI's age, marital status, educational level, location of residence, length of service, and the like. What remains is ascribed to "attitude." By this procedure personality becomes an appendage to demography (see G. W. Allport, 1950). It is not the integrated structure within the skin that determines behavior, but membership in a group, the person's assigned roles—in short, the prevailing situation. It is especially the sociologists and anthropologists who have this preference for explanations in terms of the "outside structure" rather than the "inside structure" (cf. F. H. Allport, 1955, Ch. 21).

I have mentioned only a few of the many varieties of situationism that flourish today. While not denying any of the evidence adduced I would point to their common error of interpretation. If a child is a hellion at home, an angel outside, he obviously has two contradictory tendencies in his nature, or perhaps a deeper genotype that would explain the opposing phenotypes. If in studies of person perception the process turns out to be complex and subtle, still there would be no perception at all unless there were something out there to perceive and to judge. If, as in Stouffer's studies, soldiers' opinions vary with their marital status or length of service, these opinions are still their own. The fact that my age, sex, social status help form my outlook on life does not change the fact that the outlook is a functioning part of me. Demography deals with distal forces—personality study with proximal forces. The fact that the innkeeper's behavior varies according to whether he is, or is not, physically confronted with Chinese applicants for hospitality tells nothing about his attitude structure, except that it is complex, and that several attitudes may converge into a given act of behavior.

Nor does it solve the problem to explain the variance in terms of statistical interaction effects. Whatever tendencies exist reside in a person, for a person is the sole possessor of the energy that leads to action. Admittedly different situations elicit differing tendencies from my repertoire. I do not perspire except in the heat, nor shiver except in the cold; but the outside temperature is not the mechanism of perspiring or shivering. My capacities and my tendencies lie within.

To the situationist I concede that our theory of traits cannot be so simpleminded as it once was. We are now challenged to untangle the complex web of tendencies that constitute a person, however contradictory they may seem to be when activated differentially in various situations.

On the Other Hand

In spite of gunfire from positivism and situationism, traits are still very much alive. Gibson (1941) has pointed out that the "concept of set or attitude is nearly universal in psychological thinking." And in an important but neglected paper—perhaps the last he ever wrote—McDougall (1937) argued that *tendencies* are the "indispensable postulates of all psychology." The concept of *trait* falls into this genre. As Walker (1964) says trait, however else defined, always connotes an enduring tendency of some sort. It is the structural counterpart of such functional concepts as "expectancy," and "goal-directedness."

After facing all the difficulties of situational and mood variations, also many of the methodological hazards such as response set, halo, and social desirability, Vernon (1964) concludes, "We could go a long way towards predicting behavior if we could assess these stable features in which people differ from one another [p. 181]." The powerful contributions of Thurstone, Guilford, Cattell, and Eysenck, based on factor analysis, agree that the search for traits should provide eventually a satisfactory taxonomy of personality and of its hierarchical structure. The witness of these and other thoughtful writers helps us withstand the pessimistic attacks of positivism and situationism.

It is clear that I am using "trait" as a generic term, to cover all the "permanent possibilities for action" of a generalized order. Traits are cortical, subcortical, or postural dispositions having the capacity to gate or guide specific phasic reactions. It is only the phasic aspect that is visible; the tonic is carried somehow in the still mysterious realm of neurodynamic structure. Traits, as I am here using the term, include long-range sets and attitudes, as well as such variables as "perceptual response dispositions," "personal constructs," and "cognitive styles."

Unlike McClelland (1951) I myself would regard traits (i.e., some traits) as motivational (others being merely stylistic). I would also insist that traits may be studied at two levels: (*a*) dimensionally, that is as an aspect of the psychology of individual differences, and (*b*) individually, in terms of *personal dispositions*. (Cf. G. W. Allport, 1961, Ch. 15.) It is the latter approach that brings us closest to the person we are studying.

As for factors, I regard them as a mixed blessing. In the investigations I shall soon report, factorial analysis, I find, has proved both helpful and unhelpful. My principal question is whether the factorial unit is idiomatic enough to reflect the structure of personality as the clinician, the counselor, or the man in the street apprehends it. Or are factorial dimensions screened so extensively and so widely attenuated—through item selection, correlation, axis manipulation, homogenization, and alphabetical labeling—that they impose an artifact of method upon the personal neural network as it exists in nature?

A Heuristic Realism

This question leads me to propose an epistemological position for research in personality. Most of us, I suspect, hold this position although we seldom formulate it even to ourselves. It can be called a *heuristic realism*.

Heuristic realism, as applied to our problem, holds that the person who confronts us possesses inside his skin generalized action tendencies (or traits) and that it is our job scientifically to discover what they are. Any form of realism assumes the existence of an external structure ("out there") regardless of our shortcomings in comprehending it. Since traits, like all intervening variables, are never directly observed but only inferred, we must expect difficulties and errors in the process of discovering their nature.

The incredible complexity of the structure we seek to understand is enough to discourage the realist, and to tempt him to play some form of positivistic gamesmanship. He is tempted to settle for such elusive formulations as: "If we knew enough about the situation we wouldn't need the concept of personality"; or "One's personality is merely the way other people see one"; or "There is no structure in personality but only varying degrees of consistency in the environment."

Yet the truly persistent realist prefers not to abandon his commitment to find out what the other fellow is really like. He knows that his attempt will not wholly succeed, owing partly to the complexity of the object studied, and partly to the inadequacy of present methods. But unlike Kant who held that the *Ding an Sich* is doomed to remain unknowable, he prefers to believe that it is at least partly or approximately knowable.

I have chosen to speak of *heuristic* realism, because to me special emphasis should be placed on empirical methods of discovery. In this respect heuristic realism goes beyond naive realism.

Taking this epistemological point of view, the psychologist first focuses his attention on some limited slice of personality that he wishes to study. He then selects or creates methods appropriate to the empirical testing of his hypothesis that the cleavage he has in mind is a trait (either a dimensional trait or a personal disposition). He knows that his present purposes and the methods chosen will set limitations upon his discovery. If, however, the investigation achieves acceptable standards of validation he will have progressed far toward his identification of traits. Please note, as with any heuristic procedure the process of discovery may lead to important corrections of the hypothesis as originally stated.

Empirical testing is thus an important aspect of heuristic realism, but it is an empiricism restrained throughout by rational considerations. Galloping empiricism, which is our present occupational disease, dashes forth like a headless horseman. It has no rational objective; uses no rational method other than mathematical; reaches no rational conclusion. It lets the discordant data sing for themselves. By contrast heuristic realism says, "While we are willing to rest our case for traits on empirical evidence, the area we carve out for study should be rationally conceived, tested by rational methods; and the findings should be rationally interpreted."

Three Illustrative Studies

It is now time for me to illustrate my argument with sample studies. I have chosen three in which I myself have been involved. They differ in the areas of personality carved out for study, in the methods employed, and in the type of traits established. They are alike, however, in proceeding from the standpoint of heuristic realism. The presentation of each study must of necessity be woefully brief. The first illustrates what might be called *meaningful dimensionalism;* the second *meaningful covariation;* the third *meaningful morphogenesis.*

DIMENSIONS OF VALUES

The first illustration is drawn from a familiar instrument, dating almost from the stone age, *The Study of Values* (Allport & Vernon, 1931). While some of you have approved it over the years, and some disapproved, I use it to illustrate two important points of my argument.

First, the instrument rests on an a priori analysis of one large region of human personality, namely, the region of generic evaluative tendencies. It seemed to me 40 years ago, and seems to me now, that Eduard Spranger (1922) made a persuasive case for the existence of six fundamental types of subjective evaluation of *Lebensformen.* Adopting this rational starting point we ourselves took the second step, to put the hypothesis to empirical test. We asked: Are the six dimensions proposed—the *theoretic,* the *economic,* the *esthetic, social, political,* and *religious*—measurable on a multidimensional scale? Are they reliable and valid? Spranger defined the six ways of looking at life in terms of separate and distinct ideal types, although he did not imply that a given person belongs exclusively to one and only one type.

It did not take long to discover that when confronted with a forced-choice technique people do in fact subscribe to all six values, but in widely varying degrees. Within any pair of values, or any quartet of values, their forced choices indicate a reliable pattern. Viewed then as empirical continua, rather than as types, the six value directions prove to be measurable, reproducible, and consistent. But are they valid? Can we obtain external validation for this particular a priori conception of traits? The test's *Manual* (Allport & Vernon, 1931) contains much such evidence. Here I would add a bit more, drawn from occupational studies with women subjects. (The evidence for men is equally good.) The data in Table 1 are derived partly from the *Manual,* partly from Guthrie and McKendry (1963) and partly from an unpublished study by Elizabeth Moses.

TABLE 1

Mean Scores for Occupational Groups of Women: Study of Values

	Female collegiate norms	Graduate nurses training for teaching	Graduate students of business administration	Peace Corps teachers
	$N = 2.475$	$N = 328$	$N = 77$	$N = 131$
Theoretical	36.5	40.2	37.3	40.6
Economic	36.8	32.9	40.4	29.9
Esthetic	43.7	43.1	46.8	49.3
Social	41.6	40.9	35.0	41.2
Political	38.0	37.2	41.8	39.7
Religious	43.1	45.7	38.7	39.2

For present purposes it is sufficient to glance at the last three columns. For the *theoretic* value we note that the two groups of teachers or teachers in preparation select this value significantly more often than do graduate students of business administration. Conversely the young ladies of business are relatively more *economic* in their choices. The results for the *esthetic* value probably reflect the higher level of liberal arts background for the last two groups. The *social* (philanthropic) value is relatively low for the business group, whereas the *political* (power) value is relatively high. Just why nurses should more often endorse the *religious* value is not immediately clear.

Another study of external validation, showing the long-range predictive power of the test is an unpublished investigation by Betty Mawardi. It is based on a follow-up of Wellesley graduates 15 years after taking the Study of Values.

Table 2 reports the significant deviations (at the 5% level or better) of various occupational groups from the mean scores of Wellesley students. In virtually every case we find the deviation meaningful (even necessary) for the occupation in question. Thus women in business are significantly high in *economic* interests; medical, government, and scientific workers in *theoretical*; literary and artistic workers in *esthetic*; social workers in *social*; and religious workers in *religious* values.

One must remember that to achieve a relatively high score on one value, one must deliberately slight others. For this reason it is interesting to note in the table the values that are systematically slighted in order to achieve a higher score on the occupationally relevant value. (In the case of social workers it appears that they "take away" more or less uniformly from other values in order to achieve a high social value.)

Thus, even at the college age it is possible to forecast in a general way modal vocational activity 15 years hence. As Newcomb, Turner, and Converse (1965) say, this test clearly deals with "inclusive values" or with "basic value postures" whose generality is strikingly broad. An evaluative posture toward life saturates, or guides, or gates (choose your own metaphor) specific daily choices over a long expanse of years.

One reason I have used this illustration of trait research is to raise an important methodological issue. The six values are not wholly independent. There is a slight tendency for theoretic and esthetic values to covary; likewise for economic and political values; and so too with social and religious. Immediately the thought arises, "Let's factor the whole matrix and see what orthogonal dimensions emerge." This step has been taken several times (see *Manual*); but always with confusing results. Some investigators discover that fewer than six factors are needed—some that we need more. And in all cases the clusters that emerge seem strange and unnamable. Here is a case, I believe, where our empiricism should submit to rational restraint. The traits as defined are meaningful, reliably measured, and validated. Why sacrifice them to galloping gamesmanship?

COVARIATION: RELIGION AND PREJUDICE
Speaking of covariation I do not mean to imply that in restraining our empirical excesses we should fail to explore the patterns that underlie covariation when it seems reasonable to do so.

Take, for example, the following problem. Many investigations show conclusively that on the broad average church attenders harbor more ethnic prejudice

TABLE 2

Significant Deviations of Scores on the Study of Values for Occupational Groups of Wellesley Alumnae from Wellesley Mean Scores

Occupational groups	N	Theoretical	Economic	Esthetic	Social	Political	Religious
Business workers	64	Lower	Higher				
Medical workers	42	Higher	Lower			Lower	
Literary workers	40	Higher	Lower	Higher			
Artistic workers	37			Higher	Lower		
Scientific workers	28	Higher		Lower			
Government workers	24	Higher			Lower		Lower
Social workers	26				Higher		
Religious workers	11					Lower	Higher

than nonattenders. (Some of the relevant studies are listed by Argyle, 1959, and by Wilson, 1960.) At the same time many ardent workers for civil rights are religiously motivated. From Christ to Gandhi and to Martin Luther King we note that equimindedness has been associated with religious devoutness. Here then is a paradox: Religion makes prejudice; it also unmakes prejudice.

First we tackle the problem rationally and form a hypothesis to account for what seems to be a curvilinear relation. A hint for the needed hypothesis comes from *The Authoritarian Personality* (Adorno, Frenkel-Brunswik, Levinson, & Sanford, 1950) which suggests that acceptance of institutional religion is not as important as the *way* in which it is accepted. Argyle (1959) sharpens the hypothesis. He says, "It is not the genuinely devout who are prejudiced but the conventionally religious [p. 84]."

In our own studies we have tentatively assumed that two contrasting but measurable forms of religious orientation exist. The first form we call the *extrinsic* orientation, meaning that for the churchgoer religious devotion is not a value in its own right, but is an instrumental value serving the motives of personal comfort, security, or social status. (One man said he went to church because it was the best place to sell insurance.) Elsewhere I have defined this utilitarian orientation toward religion more fully (G. W. Allport, 1960, 1963). Here I shall simply mention two items from our scale, agreement with which we assume indicates the extrinsic attitude:

What religion offers me most is comfort when sorrows and misfortune strike.

One reason for my being a church member is that such membership helps to establish a person in the community.

By contrast the *intrinsic* orientation regards faith as a supreme value in its own right. Such faith strives to transcend self-centered needs, takes seriously the commandment of brotherhood that is found in all religions, and seeks a unification of being. Agreement with the following items indicates an intrinsic orientation:

My religious beliefs are what really lie behind my whole approach to life.

If not prevented by unavoidable circumstances, I attend church, on the average (more than once a week) (once a week) (two or three times a month) (less than once a month).

This second item is of considerable interest, for many studies have found that it is the irregular attenders

TABLE 3

Correlations between Measures of Religious Orientation among Churchgoers and Various Prejudice Scales

Denominational sample	N	r
Unitarian	50	
Extrinsic—anti-Catholicism		.56
Intrinsic—anti-Catholicism		−.36
Extrinsic—anti-Mexican		.54
Intrinsic—anti-Mexican		−.42
Catholic	66	
Extrinsic—anti-Negro		.36
Intrinsic—anti-Negro		−.49
Nazarene	39	
Extrinsic—anti-Negro		.41
Intrinsic—anti-Negro		−.44
*Mixed**	207	
Extrinsic—anti-Semitic		.65

*From Wilson (1960).

who are by far the most prejudiced (e.g., Holtzmann, 1956; Williams, 1964). They take their religion in convenient doses and do not let it regulate their lives.

Now for a few illustrative results in Table 3. If we correlate the extrinsicness of orientation with various prejudice scales we find the hypothesis confirmed. Likewise, as predicted, intrinsicness of orientation is negatively correlated with prejudice.

In view of the difficulty of tapping the two complex traits in question, it is clear from these studies that our rationally derived hypothesis gains strong support. We note that the trend is the same when different denominations are studied in relation to differing targets for prejudice.

Previously I have said that empirical testing has the ability to correct or extend our rational analysis of patterns. In this particular research the following unexpected fact emerges. While those who approach the intrinsic pole of our continuum are on the average less prejudiced than those who approach the extrinsic pole, a number of subjects show themselves to be disconcertingly illogical. They accept both intrinsically worded items and extrinsically worded items, even when these are contradictory, such as:

My religious beliefs are what really lie behind my whole approach to life.

Though I believe in my religion, I feel there are many more important things in my life.

It is necessary, therefore, to inspect this sizable group of muddleheads who refuse to conform to our neat religious logic. We call them "inconsistently proreligious." They simply like religion; for them it has "social desirability" (cf. Edwards, 1957).

The importance of recognizing this third mode of religious orientation is seen by comparing the prejudice scores for the groups presented in Table 4. In the instruments employed the lowest possible prejudice score is 12, the highest possible, 48. We note that the mean prejudice score rises steadily and significantly from the intrinsically consistent to the inconsistently proreligious. Thus subjects with an undiscriminated proreligious response set are on the average most prejudiced of all.

TABLE 4

Types of Religious Orientation and Mean Prejudice Scores

| | Mean prejudice scores | | | |
	Consistently extrinsic	Consistently intrinsic	Moderately inconsistent (proreligion)	Extremely inconsistent (proreligion)
Anti-Negro	28.7	33.0	35.4	37.9
Anti-Semitic	22.6	24.6	28.0	30.1

Note. N = 309, mixed denominations. All differences significant at .01 level.

Having discovered the covariation of prejudice with both the extrinsic orientation and the "pro" response set, we are faced with the task of rational explanation. One may, I think, properly argue that these particular religious attitudes are instrumental in nature; they provide safety, security, and status—all within a self-serving frame. Prejudice, we know, performs much the same function within some personalities. The needs for status, security, comfort, and a feeling of self-rightness are served by both ethnic hostility and by tailoring one's religious orientation to one's convenience. The economy of other lives is precisely the reverse: It is their religion that centers their existence, and the only ethnic attitude compatible with this intrinsic orientation is one of brotherhood, not of bigotry.

This work, along with the related investigations of Lenski (1963), Williams (1964), and others, signifies that we gain important insights when we refine our

conception of the nature of the religious sentiment and its functions. Its patterning properties in the economy of a life are diverse. It can fuse with bigotry or with brotherhood according to its nature.

As unfinished business I must leave the problem of nonattenders. From data available it seems that the unchurched are less prejudiced on the average than either the extrinsic or the inconsistent churchgoers, although apparently more prejudiced on the average than those whose religious orientation is intrinsic. Why this should be so must form the topic of future research.

PERSONAL DISPOSITIONS:
AN IDIOMORPHIC APPROACH

The final illustration of heuristic realism has to do with the search for the natural cleavages that mark an individual life. In this procedure there is no reference to common dimensions, no comparison with other people, except as is implied by the use of the English language. If, as Allport and Odbert (1936) have found, there are over 17,000 available trait names, and if these may be used in combinations, there is no real point in arguing that the use of the available lexicon of a language necessarily makes all trait studies purely nomothetic (dimensional).

A series of 172 published *Letters from Jenny* (G. W. Allport, 1965) contains enough material for a rather close clinical characterization of Jenny's personality, as well as for careful quantitative and computational analysis. While there is no possibility in this case of obtaining external validation for the diagnosis reached by either method, still by employing both procedures an internal agreement is found which constitutes a type of empirical validation for the traits that emerge.

The *clinical* method in this case is close to common sense. Thirty-nine judges listed the essential characteristics of Jenny as they saw them. The result was a series of descriptive adjectives, 198 in number. Many of the selected trait names were obviously synonymous; and nearly all fell readily into eight clusters.

The *quantitative* analysis consisted of coding the letters in terms of 99 tag words provided by the lexicon of the General Inquirer (Stone, Bales, Namenwirth, & Ogilvie, 1962). The frequency with which these basic tag words are associated with one another in each letter forms the basis for a factor analysis (see G. W. Allport, 1965, p. 200).

Table 5 lists in parallel fashion the clusters obtained by clinical judgment based on a careful reading

TABLE 5

Central Traits in Jenny's Personality as Determined by Two Methods

Common-sense traits	Factorial traits
Quarrelsome-suspicious ⎫ Aggressive ⎬	Aggression
Self-centered (possessive)	Possessiveness
Sentimental	⎧ Need for affiliation ⎨ Need for family acceptance
Independent-autonomous	Need for autonomy
Esthetic-artistic	Sentience
Self-centered (self-pitying)	Martyrdom
(No parallel)	Sexuality
Cynical-morbid	(No parallel)
Dramatic-intense	("Overstate")

of the series, along with the factors obtained by Jeffrey Paige in his unpublished factorial study.

In spite of the differences in terminology the general paralleling of the two lists establishes some degree of empirical check on both of them. We can say that the direct common-sense perception of Jenny's nature is validated by quantification, coding, and factoring. (Please note that in this case factor analysis does not stand alone, but is tied to a parallel rational analysis.)

While this meaningful validation is clearly present, we gain (as almost always) additional insights from our attempts at empirical validation of the traits we initially hypothesize. I shall point to one instance of such serendipity. The tag words (i.e., the particular coding system employed) are chiefly substantives. For this reason, I suspect, *sexuality* can be identified by coding as a minor factor; but it is not perceived as an independent quality by the clinical judges. On the other hand, the judges, it seems, gain much from the running style of the letters. Since the style is constant it would not appear in a factorial analysis which deals only with variance within the whole. Thus the common-sense traits *cynical-morbid* and *dramatic-intense* are judgments of a pervading expressive style in Jenny's personality and seem to be missed by factoring procedure.

Here, however, the computer partially redeems itself. Its program assigns the tag "overstate" to strong words such as *always, never, impossible,* etc., while words tagged by "understate" indicate reserve,

caution, qualification. Jenny's letters score exceedingly high on overstate and exceedingly low on understate, and so in a skeletonized way the method does in part detect the trait of dramatic intensity.

One final observation concerning this essentially idiomorphic trait study. Elsewhere I have reported a small investigation (G. W. Allport, 1958) showing that when asked to list the "essential characteristics" of some friend, 90% of the judges employ between 3 and 10 trait names, the average number being 7.2. An "essential characteristic" is defined as "any trait, quality, tendency, interest, that you regard as of major importance to a description of the person you select." There is, I submit, food for thought in the fact that in these two separate studies of Jenny, the common-sense and the factorial, only 8 or 9 central traits appear. May it not be that the essential traits of a person are few in number if only we can identify them?

The case of Jenny has another important bearing on theory. In general our besetting sin in personality study is irrelevance, by which I mean that we frequently impose dimensions upon persons when the dimensions fail to apply. (I am reminded of the student who was told to interview women patients concerning their mothers. One patient said that her mother had no part in her problem and no influence on her life; but that her aunt was very important. The student answered, "I'm sorry, but our method requires that you tell about your mother." The *method* required it, but the *life* did not.)

In ascribing a list of traits to Jenny we may seem to have used a dimensional method, but such is not the case. Jenny's traits emerge from her own personal structure. They are not imposed by predetermined but largely irrelevant schedules.

Conclusion

What then have I learned about traits in the last 4 decades? Well, I have learned that the problem cannot be avoided—neither by escape through positivism of situationism, nor through statistical interaction effects. Tendencies, as McDougall (1937) insisted, remain the "indispensable postulates of all psychology."

Further, I have learned that much of our research on traits is overweighted with methodological preoccupation; and that we have too few restraints holding us to the structure of a life as it is lived. We find ourselves confused by our intemperate empiricism which often yields unnamable factors, arbitrary codes, unintelligible interaction effects, and sheer flatulence from our computers.

As a safeguard I propose the restraints of "heuristic realism" which accepts the common-sense assumption that persons are real beings, that each has a real neuro-psychic organization, and that our job is to comprehend this organization as well as we can. At the same time our profession uniquely demands that we go beyond common-sense data and either establish their validity or else—more frequently—correct their errors. To do so requires that we be guided by theory in selecting our trait slices for study, that we employ rationally relevant methods, and be strictly bound by empirical verification. In the end we return to fit our findings to an improved view of the person. Along the way we regard him as an objectively real being whose tendencies we can succeed in knowing—at least in part—beyond the level of unaided common sense. In some respects this recommended procedure resembles what Cronbach and Meehl (1955) call "construct validation," with perhaps a dash more stress on external validation.

I have also learned that while the major foci of organization in a life may be few in number, the network of organization, which includes both minor and contradictory tendencies, is still elusively complex.

One reason for the complexity, of course, is the need for the "inside" system to mesh with the "outside" system—in other words, with the situation. While I do not believe that traits can be defined in terms of interaction effects (since all tendencies draw their energy from within the person), still the vast variability of behavior cannot be overlooked. In this respect I have learned that my earlier views seemed to neglect the variability induced by ecological, social, and situational factors. This oversight needs to be repaired through an adequate theory that will relate the inside and outside systems more accurately.

The fact that my three illustrative studies are so diverse in type leads me to a second concession: that trait studies depend in part upon the investigator's own purposes. He himself constitutes a situation for his respondents, and what he obtains from them will be limited by his purpose and his method. But this fact need not destroy our belief that, so far as our method and purpose allow, we can elicit real tendencies.

Finally, there are several problems connected with traits that I have not here attempted to revisit. There are, for example, refinements of difference between trait, attitude, habit, sentiment, need, etc. Since these are all inside tendencies of some sort, they are for the present occasion all "traits" to me. Nor am I here exploring the question to what extent traits are motivational, cognitive, affective, or expressive. Last of all, and with special restraint, I avoid hammering on the distinction between common (dimensional, nomothetic) traits such as we find in any standard profile, and individual traits (personal dispositions) such as we find in single lives, e.g., Jenny's. (Cf. G. W. Allport, 1961, Ch. 15, also 1962.) Nevitt Sanford (1963) has written that by and large psychologists are "unimpressed" by my insisting on this distinction. Well, if this is so in spite of 4 decades of labor on my part, and in spite of my efforts in the present paper—I suppose I should in all decency cry "uncle" and retire to my corner.

References

Adorno, T. W., Frenkel-Brunswik, Else, Levinson, D. J., & Sanford, R. N. *The authoritarian personality.* New York: Harpers, 1950.

Allport, F. H. *Theories of perception and the concept of structure.* New York: Wiley, 1955.

Allport, G. W. What is a trait of personality? *Journal of Abnormal and Social Psychology,* 1931, 25, 368–372.

Allport, G. W. Review of S. A. Stouffer et al., *The American soldier. Journal of Abnormal and Social Psychology,* 1950, 45, 168–172.

Allport, G. W. What units shall we employ? In G. Lindzey (Ed.), *Assessment of human motives.* New York: Rinehart, 1958.

Allport, G. W. Religion and prejudice. In, *Personality and social encounter.* Boston: Beacon Press, 1960. Ch. 16.

Allport, G. W. *Pattern and growth in personality.* New York: Holt, Rinehart & Winston, 1961.

Allport, G. W. The general and the unique in psychological science. *Journal of Personality,* 1962, 30, 405–422.

Allport, G. W. Behavioral science, religion and mental health. *Journal of Religion and Health,* 1963, 2, 187–197.

Allport, G. W. (Ed.) *Letters from Jenny.* New York: Harcourt, Brace & World, 1965.

Allport, G. W., & Odbert, H. S. Trait-names: A psycholexical study. *Psychological Monographs,* 1936, 47 (1, Whole No. 211).

Allport, G. W., & Vernon, P. E. *A study of values.* Boston: Houghton-Mifflin, 1931. (Reprinted: With G. Lindzey, 3rd ed., 1960.)

Argyle, M. *Religious behaviour.* Glencoe, Ill.: Free Press, 1959.

Block, J., & Bennett, Lillian. The assessment of communication. *Human Relations,* 1955, *8,* 317–325.

Carr, H. A., & Kingsbury, F. A. The concept of trait. *Psychological Review,* 1938, *45,* 497–524.

Cronbach, L. J., & Meehl, P. E. Construct validity in psychological tests. *Psychological Bulletin,* 1955, *52,* 281–302.

Edwards, A. L. *The social desirability in personality assessment and research.* New York: Dryden Press, 1957.

Gibson, J. J. A critical review of the concept of set in contemporary experimental psychology. *Psychological Bulletin,* 1941, *38,* 781–817.

Guthrie, G. M., & McKendry, Margaret S. Interest patterns of Peace Corps volunteers in a teaching project. *Journal of Educational Psychology,* 1963, *54,* 261–267.

Helson, H. *Adaptation-level theory.* New York: Harper & Row, 1964.

Holtzman, W. H. Attitudes of college men toward nonsegregation in Texas schools. *Public Opinion Quarterly,* 1956, *20,* 559–569.

Hunt, J. McV. Traditional personality theory in the light of recent evidence. *American Scientist,* 1965, *53,* 80–96.

La Piere, R. Attitudes *vs.* actions. *Social Forces,* 1934, 230–237.

Lenski, G. *The religious factor.* Garden City, N. Y.: Doubleday, 1961.

McClelland, D. C. *Personality.* New York: Dryden Press, 1951.

McDougall, W. Tendencies as indispensable postulates of all psychology. In, *Proceedings of the XI International Congress on Psychology: 1937.* Paris: Alcan, 1938. Pp. 157–170.

Miller, D. R. The study of social relationships: Situation, identity, and social interaction. In S. Koch (Ed.), *Psychology: A study of a science.* Vol. 5. *The process areas, the person, and some applied fields: Their place in psychology and the social sciences.* New York: McGraw-Hill, 1963. Pp. 639–737.

Newcomb, T. M., Turner, H. H., & Converse, P. E. *Social psychology: The study of human interaction.* New York: Holt, Rinehart & Winston, 1965.

Sanford, N. Personality: Its place in psychology. In S. Koch (Ed.), *Psychology: A study of a science.* Vol. 5. *The process areas, the person, and some applied fields: Their place in psychology and in science.* New York: McGraw-Hill, 1963, Pp. 448–592.

Skinner, B. F. *Science and human behavior.* New York: Macmillan, 1953.

Spranger, E. *Lebensformen.* (3d ed.) Halle: Niemeyer, 1922. (Translated: P. Pigors. *Types of men.* Halle: Niemeyer, 1928.)

Stone, P. J., Bales, R. F., Namenwirth, J. Z., & Ogilvie, D. M. The general inquirer: A computer system for content analysis and retrieval based on the sentence as a unit of information. *Behavioral Science,* 1962, *7*(4), 484–498.

Stouffer, S. A., et al. *The American soldier.* Princeton: Princeton Univer. Press, 1949. 2 vols.

Tagiuri, R., & Petrullo, L. *Person perception and interpersonal behavior.* Stanford: Stanford Univer. Press, 1958.

Vernon, P. E. *Personality assessment: A critical survey.* London: Methuen, 1964.

Walker, E. L. Psychological complexity as a basis for a theory of motivation and choice. In D. Levine (Ed.), *Nebraska symposium on motivation: 1964.* Lincoln: Univer. Nebraska Press, 1964.

Williams, R. M., Jr. *Strangers next door.* Englewood Cliffs, N.J.: Prentice-Hall, 1964.

Wilson, W. C. Extrinsic religious values and prejudice. *Journal of Abnormal and Social Psychology,* 1960, *60,* 286–288.

This paper will be concerned with an examination of the incest taboo with particular attention being paid to theories of the origin of the taboo, the implications of the taboo for psychological development, and the relation between these observations and the current status of psychoanalytic theory.

The existence of prohibitions against nuclear incest (and by this I mean sexual relations between members of the nuclear family other than mother with father) long has been observed to be one of the few regularities in complex human behavior that transcends time and culture. The presence of such taboos appears to be almost exceptionless, and they are much more than ideal cultural patterns, inasmuch as the overt incidence of incest is believed generally to be very low. Given the extreme rarity of significant behavioral regularities that occur across all cultures, it is not surprising that anthropologists have shown intense interest in the study of this phenomenon. In contrast, one of the instigations for the present talk is the relative sparseness of interest on the part of psychologists, other than psychoanalysts, in incest and its psychological significance.

Explanation of the incest taboo has attracted dozens of strongly partisan anthropological and sociological theorists who have attributed the phenomenon to a wide variety of simple and complex determinants. Moreover, this is an area of theorizing that has proven appealing to far more than its reasonable share of theorists who believe in what Gordon Allport has referred to as "simple and sovereign" formulations. It is a rare

some remarks concerning incest, the incest taboo, and psychoanalytic theory[1]

gardner lindzey[2]
university of texas

1. Address of the President to the Seventy-Fifth Annual Convention of the American Psychological Association, Washington, D. C., September 2, 1967. Reprinted from *American Psychologist*, 1967, Vol. 22, pp. 1051–1059. Copyright 1967 by the American Psychological Association, and reproduced by permission.

2. I am grateful for the valuable advice of Leslie Segner, H. D. Winston, Carol Ryan, Sheldon C. Reed, and Irving I. Gottesman. Preparation of the manuscript was facilitated by Grant MH 14076 from the National Institute of Mental Health. I appreciate the cooperation of the Institute for Sexual Research of Indiana University, in providing data reported in this paper.

incest theorist who is willing to entertain seriously a multiplicity of instigating and sustaining events, even though available facts point strongly in this direction. Examination of the merits and flaws of each of these theories would be time consuming, tedious, and an act of covert hostility toward any captive audience. Instead, I propose to examine one particular set of determinants (the biological) which I believe by itself provides a *sufficient* explanation of the origin of the taboo. At the same time, I do not intend to imply that other mechanisms such as family cohesiveness, Malinowski (1927), developmental immunization, Fox (1962), Wolf (1966), demographic-ecological factors, Slater (1959), enhancement of role learning, Parsons (1954), or the emergence of adaptive social structures, White (1948) may not have played some determining part. In my judgment, however, most of these factors are likely to occupy a more significant role in explaining the *maintenance* of the taboo rather than its origin.

Very simply the formulation I am advancing argues that the biological consequence of inbreeding is a decrease in fitness. This decrement in fitness is present in all animals, but it is particularly pronounced in the case of man for a number of reasons including his slowness in reaching sexual maturity and his limited number of offspring. Given this lowered fitness a human group practicing incest operates at a selective disadvantage in competition with outbreeding human groups and ultimately would be unlikely to survive. Conversely, a group which prohibited inbreeding (presumably through some form of the incest taboo) would be at an advantage in comparison to groups that permitted inbreeding. I assume that in the process of dealing with the problems posed by stable and intimate personal interactions, different human groups initially devised a variety of patterns of mating and family relations, with these variations determined by ecological factors, random factors, and other determinants that we can not hope to specify. Given this variation, however, one might expect over time that natural selection would lead to preservation of societies that practiced outbreeding (incest taboo) and elimination of those societies that favored, or were neutral to, the practice of incest. Consequently, what eventually remains is a substantial amount of variability in marriage rules and kinship structure across cultures, but with all varieties providing the basic minimum of outbreeding imposed by natural selection.

It should be understood that this formulation does not imply that early man necessarily understood the consequences of inbreeding when the incest taboo was established. Natural selection acting upon either morphological or behavioral characters is not mediated ordinarily by awareness on the part of the individual organism. Nonetheless, many of the deleterious consequences of human inbreeding are sufficiently rare, dramatic, and early in appearance (for example, albinism, some forms of mental deficiency, deaf-mutism, and major physical malformations such as dwarfism) so it is not altogether unlikely that in some cases the connection between incest and abnormality may have been noted by primitive man. Indeed an unpublished examination of incest myths in the Human Relations Area Files (Segner & Collins, 1967) revealed that in roughly one-third of the myths involving incest, deformed offspring or infertility were a consequence of the union. Such a substantial degree of association suggests that on occasion some degree of biological insight may well have accompanied the origin of the taboo.

Early scientific theories concerning the origins of the incest taboo emphasized biological or genetic explanations of the phenomenon, as illustrated by the formulations of Westermarck (1894) and the distinguished anthropologist, Lewis Morgan (1907). However, these positions were based upon pre-Mendelian conceptions of the process of inheritance, and inevitably they have been largely discredited by modern advances in the field of genetics. In spite of these early theories, and common belief among nonscientific observers, the negative effects of inbreeding are not widely accepted, or understood, by behavioral scientists today. Present day counterparts of the biological approach to understanding the incest taboo are few in number, and perhaps are best represented by the points of view of Aberle, Bronfenbrenner, Hess, Miller, Schneider, and Spuhler (1963) and Ember (1961) which are consistent in many important respects with the position advocated here.

Just what is the theory and evidence suggesting that inbreeding results in a reduction of fitness? The most relevant concepts here are *heterosis* or hybrid vigor—which refers to the relatively greater rate of growth, size, fertility, and comparable characters in hybrids when compared to their parents; and its mirror image—*inbreeding depression*, which designates the tendency of closely inbred animals to show a decline in such components of fitness as fertility and resistance to disease.

The most general theoretical observation that can be made in regard to the maladaptiveness of inbreeding concerns its effects upon genetic variability. Given nuclear incest (brother-sister or parent-child mating) it is commonly agreed (Falconer, 1960; Wright, 1933) that each successive generation of inbreeding leads to not less than a 19% reduction in degree of heterozygosis (number of chromosomal loci occupied by different alleles). With a few simplifying assumptions, this trend implies that approximately 20 generations of such inbreeding will produce individuals who are at the asymptote for homozygosity—that is to say, at each locus all alleles are identical. The fact that the paired chromosomes present identical alleles to be included in the genome of the individual offspring means that environmental forces have very limited opportunity to exercise selection in favor of particular genotypes. Consequently, changes in selection pressure, including cultural changes, would encounter a population or breeding group that was rigidly specified and relatively incapable of varied biological response to environmental demands. This is true in spite of a potentially greater variability in the individual organism's response to environmental variation (Lerner, 1954). As all of this suggests, genetic diversity is the raw material upon which changing environmental settings operate to select the biological variations that make the organism better adapted to its environment. Because inbreeding reduces this variability, it may be seen as interfering with the normal evolutionary process and to be powerfully maladaptive for the groups involved.

A further relevant formulation concerns the capacity in a heterozygotic condition for dominant genes to mask or suppress the action of deleterious or lethal recessive genes. It is generally accepted that since mutations, spontaneously occurring genetic changes, are continuously occurring, the genes resulting from mutations are ordinarily deleterious, because those mutations that lead to adaptive alleles already will have been retained through selection in the past (Dobzhansky, 1952). Moreover, those mutations leading to deleterious genes that are dominant would be phenotypically expressed and hence immediately subjected to negative selection, with the result that they would disappear. Deleterious genes that are recessive, however, would be maintained at some constant proportion because they would not be exposed to selection when paired with dominant genes. Thus, it is reasoned, and there is strong supporting empirical evidence (Lerner, 1958; Morton, 1961), that recessive genes are generally maladaptive in their effects. In addition, we know that inbreeding will have the effect of increasing the likelihood that recessive alleles will be paired with other recessive alleles and thus their deleterious or lethal effects will be given expression. In brief, inbreeding eliminates or minimizes the masking of deleterious recessive genes by dominant genes, a process which occurs frequently in the normal, outbred state.

A final consideration is that groups of genes, commonly called polygenes, that have a combined effect upon the phenotype may have been jointly selected for over time because of their mutual (epistatic) and interacting positive effects. These balanced or coadapted systems, which represent a kind of genetic homeostasis (Lerner, 1954), are readily disrupted by inbreeding with a resultant loss in adaptiveness or fitness. It should be noted that some observers, especially Lerner (1954), have considered that even aside from the factors just discussed, homozygosity is intrinsically maladaptive. This view suggests that there is a level or balance of homozygosity below which the individual or group is severely penalized by a decreased likelihood of survival regardless of the nature of the specific recessive genes involved. As Gottesman (1965) has remarked, nature may not only abhor a vacuum but also a homozygote.

Thus, there are a variety of theoretical reasons for anticipating that inbreeding will have maladaptive effects. Let us turn now to the most pertinent empirical data suggesting the negative impact of inbreeding. Findings in regard to morphological and reproductive heterosis have been available for many years concerning a variety of characters and types of subjects (Dinsley, 1963; Falconer, 1960; Gowan, 1952; Lerner, 1954). For example, it has been shown for the mouse that hybrids generally have larger litters (Green, 1931); live longer (Gates, 1926); are larger (Law 1938; Marshak, 1936); and are more resistant to disease. With chickens, hybrids have been shown to exceed the relatively inbred parental strains in egg size, hatchability of fertile eggs, number of eggs laid, and body size in adulthood. Comparable demonstrations have been made for many other species including rats, honey bees, silkworms, and drosophila.

It is only very recently, however, that we have begun to obtain firm evidence concerning behavioral heterosis. During the past 10 years a number of studies from our own laboratory and elsewhere have produced results suggesting or demonstrating that relatively heterozygous animals are superior to their homozygous counterparts in terms of such behavioral characters as appetitive learning (Winston, 1964), aversive learning (Winston, 1964), exploratory behavior (Bruell, 1964b), and activity (Bruell, 1964a; Mordkoff & Fuller, 1959). Although such findings are not observed for all behavioral attributes, they appear highly characteristic of those traits that are plausibly linked to natural selection and evolution. I believe that all of these results provide factual, although indirect, evidence for the folly of a social system that includes no proscription against incest.

Most interesting of the modern evidence are the findings that imply a strong buffering effect of heterosis upon the negative effects of noxious, early experience. The first of these studies was carried out in our laboratory by Winston (1963, 1964) using *Mus musculus,* or the common house mouse, as the target population. In this experiment the highly homozygous members of three inbred strains were subjected in infancy to an intense, high frequency, auditory stimulus. The maze learning of these groups in adulthood was found to be inferior to that of control animals not subjected to the intense, noxious stimulus. In contrast, when outbred and heterozygous F_1 animals, produced by crossing the three strains, were exposed to infantile trauma and compared with controls in their adult learning capacity, there were no observed differences. Thus, it appeared that the heterotic condition had the effect of introducing a damping or buffering effect that minimized the maladaptive consequences of noxious, early experience. This general finding has been replicated partially, under somewhat different conditions, in another laboratory, by Henderson (1966, 1967). He also found that for some treatment conditions infantile treatments that produced adult effects in inbred mice did not produce such effects in their hybrid offspring. If such findings could be generalized to human populations, they might imply that the relatively inbred and relatively homozygous creature would operate at a markedly impaired level of functioning, because of the increased probability that negative early experiences would have a disabling or impairing effect upon adult adjustment. These findings are consistent with a large amount of evidence (Dinsley, 1963) indicating that

homozygotes generally are more influenced by environmental variation than comparable heterozygotes.

Parenthetically it should be noted that there is considerably less than consensus in the animal literature as to whether the effects of noxious, infantile stimulation upon adult behavior are benign or malignant (Dennenberg,. 1962; Hall & Whiteman, 1951; Levine, 1962; Lindzey, Lykken, & Winston, 1960; Lindzey, Winston, & Manosevitz, 1963). Undoubtedly one of the poorly controlled parameters that has contributed to these confusing, and variable, findings has been variation in the degree of heterozygosity of animals under study.

There is ample evidence from a wide variety of sources for the operation of inbreeding depression in lower animals (Dinsley, 1963; Falconer, 1960; Lerner, 1954, 1958). Characters such as rate of growth, resistance to disease, physical size, life span, and fertility are all negatively influenced by inbreeding. These findings are consistent across many different species including mice, swine, poultry, sheep, and cattle. Such effects are most marked in connection with fertility and viability of offspring, with the result that in many species inbreeding typically leads to failure to reproduce and loss of the strain in a relatively short number of generations.

Although controlled evidence for heterosis is very difficult to obtain for human subjects, there are considerable data bearing upon the effects of inbreeding (consanguinity) on fitness. These findings provide strong evidence of inbreeding depression. The data are most compelling in the case of disease entities such as phenylketonuria, amaurotic idiocy, and albinism where, under conditions of consanguineous marriages, the incidence of the disorders departs markedly from population figures. Among the many relevant studies in this area (cf. Morton, 1958, 1961; Morton, Crow, & Muller, 1956; Penrose, 1938; Schull, 1958; Stern, 1960; Sutter, 1958) perhaps the most impressive is the extensive investigation by Schull and Neel (1965). This study involved the comparison of offspring from more than 2,300 consanguineous marriages with the offspring of over 2,000 nonconsanguineous marriages. It was facilitated by the fact that in Japan approximately 5% of all marriages are between first cousins (Okazaki, 1941). The data were collected in Nagasaki and Hiroshima, and in selection of the samples and analysis of the data every effort was made to minimize the potential contribution of contaminating factors such as socioeconomic status. When the inbred sample was compared to an outbred group, there was clear, although not dramatic, evidence for inbreeding depression in incidence of loss of child during pregnancy, mortality in the first year of life, age at which child first walked and talked, visual and auditory acuity, physical stature, measures of neuromuscular and intellectual functioning (IQ), and incidence of major physical defects. It is worth emphasis that these effects were observed with a sample subjected to much less intense inbreeding than that involved in parent-child or brother-sister reproduction.

The findings most directly relevant to our present interest resulted from a very recent study by Adams and Neel (1967) in which they compared the children of 18 nuclear incest matings (12 brother-sister and 6 father-daughter) with 18 control matings, rather closely matched with the incest group for age, weight, stature, intelligence, and socioeconomic status. At the end of 6 months they found that of the 18 children of an incestuous union, five had died; two were severely mentally retarded, were subject to seizures, and had been institutionalized; one had a bilateral cleft palate; and three showed evidence of borderline intelligence (estimated IQ 70). Thus, only 7 of the 18 children were considered free of pathology and ready for adoption. On the other hand, none of the 18 control children had died or were institutionalized, none was severely mentally retarded, only one had a major physical defect, and 15 were considered ready for adoption. Roughly comparable findings have been observed in an unpublished study by Sheldon C. Reed.

Perhaps it should be noted that the impressive and growing body of empirical findings (for example, Gottesman & Shields, 1966; Kringlin, 1966) concerning genetic variation and mental disorder has general implications for the maladaptiveness of incestuous matings. If any of the various genetic theories of schizophrenia, especially the autosomal recessive theory of Kallman (1953), should prove to be consistent with reality, it alone would provide powerful reasons for inhibiting or minimizing the incidence of inbreeding among humans.

A number of writers (for example, Aberle et al., 1963; Murdock, 1949) have implied that under some conditions, or with some species, inbreeding may produce a superior strain or race of animals. I know of no evidence to support this contention and there is much evidence to the contrary. Such animals may be superior in regard to one or a few characters, particu-

larly if there has been controlled selection for these characters, but they regularly suffer the general loss of fitness that is a dependable consequence of lowered genetic variability.

Thus, there is compelling theoretical rationale, and a variety of empirical data at both human and lower-animal levels, to imply that the consequences of inbreeding are sufficiently strong and deleterious to make it unlikely that a human society would survive over long periods of time if it permitted, or encouraged, a high incidence of incest. In this sense, then, one may say that the incest taboo (whatever other purposes it may serve) is biologically guaranteed.

Given this biological mandate against inbreeding, one may ask whether the resultant prohibition is likely to be the basis for inducing serious conflict. Here the essential question is: Do we have evidence for the existence of strong and pervasive incestuous impulses that would be interfered with by such a taboo?

One may argue persuasively that the mere universal existence of the incest taboo, together with the powerful affects or emotions that are associated with its violation, constitute convincing evidence for the existence of a set of general tendencies that are being denied. It seems unlikely that there would have been universal selection in favor of such a taboo if there were not rather widespread impulses toward expression of the prohibited act. Cultures seldom focus upon the inhibition of behavior which few individuals feel compelled to display.

It should be mentioned, although not emphasized, that there is substantial clinical support in the raw material of therapeutic exchanges and case histories for the existence of incestuous impulses. Indeed, although I know of no controlled investigation, my impression from contact with clinicians and dream investigators is that overt incestuous dreams are by no means uncommon. To this infirm evidence can be appended the central and recurrent role that has been assigned to incestuous relations in the world of the theater and novel from the time of Sophocles until today. Even among nonliterate societies incest themes have occupied a prominent position because of their extremely high frequency in myths, as several studies (Kluckhohn, 1960; Moore, 1964) have shown.

More dramatic and undeniable evidence of the existence of incestuous impulses is presented by the occurrence of consummated incest. In spite of the strong and universal operation of the incest taboo, there is a detectable, although small, incidence of overt acts. The figure generally referred to in the literature is less than one case per million persons in modern western societies (Riemer, 1940; Weinberg, 1955). This index is obviously an extreme underestimation in view of the fact that it refers to reported or detected cases, and it seems evident that the majority of such cases go unreported and/or undetected by persons other than the participants.

Surprisingly enough the best available evidence has not been introduced in such discussions in the past. I am referring here to data collected by Kinsey, Gebhard, and their collaborators (Gebhard, Gagnon, Pomeroy, & Christenson, 1965; Kinsey, Pomeroy, & Martin, 1948; Kinsey, Pomeroy, Martin, & Gebhard, 1953). There are two relevant sets of data, one collected from a group of over 3,500 subjects who were imprisoned for sexual offenses and the other a noncriminal sample of almost 12,000, comprising the large number of subgroups included in the main Kinsey study. For the criminals the incidence of incest was roughly 30 cases for each 1,000 persons in the sample, while in the noncriminal group the incidence was approximately 5 cases for each 1,000 persons. Even for these groups the available figures may be taken as substantial understatements (since forgetting and voluntary deception would be expected to play some significant role). Nevertheless, they vastly exceed the customarily cited index of "less than one case per million." More important, when this appreciable incidence is viewed against the background of powerful inhibiting forces, it provides strong support for the existence of frequent, if not invariable, incestuous impulses. It is worth further note that although the figures conventionally cited indicate that father-daughter incest is most common, the Kinsey-Gebhard data indicate that in the general population brother-sister incest is five times as common as the next most common variety (father-daughter relations).

Another relevant data domain is the substantial evidence indicating that personal attractiveness and interpersonal choice are mediated, or determined, by similarity in attitudes, values, needs, and background factors (Lindzey & Byrne, 1968). To all of this can be added the relatively massive literature indicating that positive social choice is strongly facilitated by physical or geographic proximity (for example, Festinger, Schachter, & Back, 1950). These findings clearly support the contention that heterosexual choice within the family would be the easiest and most congruent alternative for most or many individuals. Likewise the evidence indicating homogeneity in mate selection (Tharp, 1963) far outweighs the occasional support advanced for a need-complementarity hypothesis (Winch, 1955). Again it seems that most of what we know about assortative mating in the human suggests that in the absence of the incest taboo, mate selection within the nuclear family would be a high frequency choice. The evidence in regard to association and mating preference at a lower animal level is somewhat more mixed (Beck & Lucas, 1963; Cairns, 1966; Mainardi, 1965; Mainardi, Marsan, & Pasquali, 1965; Warriner, Lemmon, & Ray, 1963), but again there is considerable hard data suggesting that like prefers and copulates with like.

I have suggested thus far, that an examination of available data, leavened only modestly with speculation, implies that the evolutionary achievement of the incest taboo (a biological necessity) has resulted in the imposition of a developmental crisis upon the human organism. An immature individual, endowed with only limited capacity for diverse and integrated adaptive acts, is faced with the imperative that he must reorganize and channel in new directions his sexual impulses—one of the most powerful of human motives. The image that I am attempting to convey is one of an organism that is wired for sexual choice along dimensions of proximity and similarity, encountering a society or culture that is necessarily programmed for destruction or inhibition of these natural tendencies. Moreover, the person first encounters this fundamental opposition at a time when he is poorly equipped to devise mediating and compromising patterns of response.

What I am asserting is—if the biological necessity of outbreeding led to the evolution of a set of prohibitions against this powerful tendency, the operation of these negative sanctions against an almost equally strong countertendency could well constitute a psychological dilemma of enormous consequence. To use a geological analogy, as Freud was wont to do, the conflict over resolution of the incestuous impulses may constitute a kind of psychological fault, about which present and future failures in adjustment are most likely to hover or appear.

We have just examined a behavioral paradox—the seemingly natural tendency to select a breeding partner who is similar and familiar, and the universal existence of a taboo that prohibits the selection of those partners who best fit these criteria. Let us turn now to a theoretical paradox posed by the enormous and pervasive impact of psychoanalytic theory upon the entire breadth of the behavioral sciences and the formal inelegance, imprecision, and factual lack of warrant of much of psychoanalytic theory. As you may suspect, I am about to suggest that resolution of the theoretical paradox could be rooted in the theory's acceptance of, indeed its emphasis upon, the behavioral paradox.

What can be said concerning the relevance of the incest taboo for psychoanalytic theory and vice versa? It is commonplace knowledge that Freud early in his career (1912–13) provided a theoretical account of the origins of the incest taboo. This highly speculative formulation is of no particular interest to us here, except as tangible evidence of the extent to which Freud was concerned with incest and the taboo prohibiting it. Of more concern is the fact that the most essential features of psychoanalytic theory (and I refer here to the Oedipus complex, the theory of psychosexual development, and the theories of psychopathology) are inextricably linked to the assumption that there are powerful incestuous impulses present in all humans and that the core developmental problem, faced by parent and child alike, is the redirection of these impulses. One need only remember that the Oedipus complex does nothing more than identify the universal and vital importance of incestuous motives and their fateful confrontation with the taboo inhibiting them, to accept this intimate association between the theory and matters pertaining to incest. I will not take the time to provide any extensive documentation of this point since it is self-evident from even a casual examination of Freud's theoretical writings (see, for example, Freud, 1923, 1926, 1940).

Thus, one may say that almost all that is most central and vital in classical psychoanalytic theory is related to the incest taboo and its consequences for psychological development. I believe it is not an overstatement to suggest that Freud himself viewed the conceptual identification of this conflict and its psychological implications as ranking with the distinction between primary process and secondary process as the most original and significant of his theoretical contributions. Indeed, in one of his final theoretical papers he reasoned that "if psychoanalysis could boast of no other achievement than the discovery of the repressed Oedipus Complex that alone would give it a claim to be included among the precious new acquisitions of mankind [Freud, 1940, pp. 192–193]."

Clearly, I am suggesting that if my general line of reasoning has any validity it would be possible for Freud to be wrong about all or many of the details of behavior, to be imprecise, to be metaphorical, to be limited in his domain of data, to be biased in many of his observations, to fail to appreciate the contribution of experimental science, to be swayed by personal problems and situational events, to be unduly influenced by faulty ethnology and transient cultural norms, to follow the lure of an archaic set of neurological formulations, and still to have more impact than others simply because of his powerful insights concerning incest. If the incest taboo has indeed created a basic conflict and consequent developmental frailty that characterizes all mankind, and if only Freud successfully identified this state of affairs, it should come as no surprise that psychoanalytic theory possesses a kind of transcendental vigor that guarantees wide applicability, pertinence, and impact.

Many of the criticisms of psychoanalysis have centered about cultural relativity, and, it should be noted, we are emphasizing here a component of behavior, and of the theory, that is literally and unquestionably transcultural. Such observations could reasonably have the effect of disarming some of the fiercest critics of psychoanalytic theory.

The suggestion that Freud's uniquely influential position among modern psychological theorists may rest upon his success in identifying a developmental crisis of crucial importance that was ignored or minimized by other theorists, may be viewed, in part, as an argument for the relative importance of classical psychoanalysis as opposed to the many derivative or revisionist positions. It implies that the fundamental contributions of the theory have to do with sexuality, early experience, and the Oedipus complex. Thus, the most seminal and far reaching aspects of the theory are linked to those features of Freud's thought that are most often modified or deleted by friendly and hostile believers in change. This is not to imply that psychoanalytic theory, new or old, represents even a remotely satisfactory theory of behavior. Whatever the ultimate importance may prove to be of specific psychoanalytic concepts and assumptions, no sentient person could defend the theory in any existing form as even crudely simulating a comprehensive and fully adequate theory of behavior. Nor is there a viable alternative that currently can be defended strongly on these same grounds.

In closing, I would like to confess that just as I believe in the givenness of human incestuous impulses and the evolutionary necessity of inhibiting them, so too do I believe in the intrinsic merit of the crude, early formulations of Freud. It appears to me that in the very process of making psychoanalytic theory more acceptable and congruent with general psychology (I am referring here to the work of such important figures as Heinz Hartmann, Ernst Kris, Erik Erikson, and David Rapaport) it is more or less guaranteed that the potent and distinctive features of the theory will be minimized or eliminated. The net result is a more palatable but a less powerful set of ideas.

References

Aberle, D., Bronfenbrenner, U., Hess, E., Miller, D., Schneider, D., & Spuhler, J. The incest taboo and the mating patterns of animals. *American Anthropologist*, 1963, *65*, 253–265.

Adams, M. S., & Neel, J. V. Children of incest. *Pediatrics*, 1967, *40*, 55–62.

Beck, S. L., & Lucas, J. J. Breeding characteristics of two strains of mice in a competitive situation. *Genetics*, 1963, *48*, 833.

Bruell, J. H. Heterotic inheritance of wheel running in mice. *Journal of Comparative and Physiological Psychology*, 1964, *58*, 159–163. (a)

Bruell, J. H. Inheritance of behavioral and physiological characters of mice and problems of heterosis. *American Zoologist*, 1964, *4*, 125–138. (b)

Cairns, R. B. Attachment behavior of mammals. *Psychological Review*, 1966, *73*, 409–426.

Dennenberg, V. H. The effects of early experience. In E. S. E. Hafez (Ed.), *The behaviour of domestic animals*. Baltimore: Williams & Wilkins, 1962. Pp. 109–138.

Dinsley, M. Inbreeding and selection. In W. Lane-Petter (Ed.), *Animals for research*. London: Academic Press, 1963. Pp. 235–259.

Dobzhansky, T. Nature and origin of heterosis. In J. W. Gowen (Ed.), *Heterosis*. Ames: Iowa State College Press, 1952. Pp. 218–223.

Ember, M. The incest taboo and the nuclear family. Paper presented at the meeting of the American Anthropological Association, Philadelphia, November 1961.

Falconer, D. S. *Introduction to quantitative genetics*. New York: Ronald Press, 1960.

Festinger, L., Schachter, S., & Back, K. *Social pressure in informal groups: A study of human factors in housing*. New York: Harper, 1950.

Fox, J. R. Sibling incest. *British Journal of Sociology*, 1962, *13*, 128–150.

Freud, S. Totem and taboo. In J. Strachey (Ed.), *Standard edition of the complete psychological works of Sigmund Freud*. Vol. 13. (Orig. publ. 1912–13) London: Hogarth, 1955. Pp. 1–161.

Freud, S. Inhibitions, symptoms and anxiety. In J. Strachey (Ed.), *The standard edition of the complete psychological works of Sigmund Freud*. Vol. 20. (Orig. publ. 1926) London: Hogarth, 1959. Pp. 87–172.

Freud, S. The ego and the id. In J. Strachey (Ed.), *The complete psychological works of Sigmund Freud*. Vol. 19. (Orig. publ. 1923) London: Hogarth, 1961. Pp. 3–66.

Freud, S. An outline of psychoanalysis. In J. Strachey (Ed.), *The standard edition of the complete psychological works of Sigmund Freud*. Vol. 23. (Orig. publ. 1940) London: Hogarth, 1964. Pp. 144–207.

Gates, W. H. The Japanese waltzing mouse: Its origin, heredity and relation to the genetic characters of other varieties of mice. (No. 337) Washington, D. C.: Carnegie Institution, 1926. Pp. 83–138.

Gebhard, P. H., Gagnon, J. H., Pomeroy, W. B., & Christenson, C. V. *Sex offenders: An analysis of types*. New York: Harper & Row, 1965.

Gottesman, I. I. Personality and natural selection. In S. G. Vandenberg (Ed.), *Methods and goals in human behavior genetics*. New York: Academic Press, 1965. Pp. 63–74.

Gottesman, I. I., & Shields, J. The twins of schizophrenics: 16 years of consecutive admissions to a psychiatric clinic. *Diseases of the nervous system*, (Monogr. Suppl.) 1966, *27*, 11–19.

Gowan, J. W. (Ed.) *Heterosis*. Ames: Iowa State College Press, 1952.

Green, C. V. Size inheritance and growth in a mouse species cross *(Mus musculus X Mus bactrianus):* I. Litter size. *Journal of Experimental Zoology*, 1931, *58*, 237–246.

Hall, C. S., & Whiteman, P. H. The effects of infantile stimulation upon later emotional stability in the mouse. *Journal of Comparative and Physiological Psychology*, 1951, *44*, 61–66.

Henderson, N. D. Inheritance of reactivity to experimental manipulation in mice. *Science*, 1966, *153*, 651–652.

Henderson, N. D. Prior treatment effects on open field behaviour of mice: A genetic analysis. *Animal Behaviour*, 1967, *15*, 364–376.

Kallmann, F. J. *Heredity in health and mental disorder.* New York: Norton, 1953.

Kinsey, A. C., Pomeroy, W. B., & Martin, C. E. *Sexual behavior in the human male.* Philadelphia: Saunders, 1948.

Kinsey, A. C., Pomeroy, W. B., Martin, C. E., & Gebhard, P. H. *Sexual behavior in the human female.* Philadelphia: Saunders, 1953.

Kluckhohn, C. Recurrent themes in myth and myth making. In H. A. Murray (Ed.), *Myth and myth making.* New York: Braziller, 1960. Pp. 46–60.

Kringlin, E. Schizophrenia in twins. *Psychiatry*, 1966, *122*, 809–818.

Law, L. W. Studies on size inheritance in mice. *Genetics*, 1938, *23*, 399–422.

Lerner, I. M. *Genetic homeostasis.* London: Oliver & Boyd, 1954.

Lerner, I. M. *The genetic basis of selection.* New York: Wiley, 1958.

Levine, S. Psychophysiological effects of infantile stimulation. In E. L. Bliss (Ed.), *Roots of behavior.* New York: Hoeber, 1962. Pp. 246–253.

Lindzey, G., & Byrne, D. Measurement of social choice and interpersonal attractiveness. In G. Lindzey & E. Aronson (Eds.), *Handbook of social psychology.* Vol. 2. (2nd ed.) Reading, Mass.: Addison-Wesley, 1968.

Lindzey, G., Lykken, D. T., & Winston, H. D. Infantile trauma, genetic factors, and adult temperament. *Journal of Abnormal and Social Psychology*, 1960, *61*, 7–14.

Lindzey, G., Winston, H., & Manosevitz, M. Early experience, genotype, and temperament in *Mus musculus. Journal of Comparative and Physiological Psychology*, 1963, *56*, 622–629.

Mainardi, D. Un esperimento nuovo sul determinismo delle preferenze sessuali nell femmina di topo (*Mus musculus domesticus*). *Bool Zool.*, 1965, *32*.

Mainardi, D., Marsan, M., & Pasquali, A. Assenza di preferenze sessuali tra ceppi nel maschio di *Mus musculus* domesticus. *Instituto Lombardo*, (Rend, Sc.) 1965, *B99*, 26–34.

Malinowski, B. *Sex and repression in savage society.* London: Routledge, Kegan Paul, 1927.

Marshak, A. Growth differences in reciprocal hybrids and cytoplasmic influence on growth in mice. *Journal of Experimental Zoology*, 1936, *72*, 497–510.

Moore, S. F. Descent and symbolic filiation. *American Anthropologist*, 1964, *66*, 1308–1321.

Mordkoff, A. M., & Fuller, J. L. Heritability in activity within inbred and cross-bred mice: A study in behavior genetics. *Journal of Heredity*, 1959, *50*, 6–8.

Morgan, L. *Ancient society.* New York: Holt, 1907.

Morton, N. E. Empirical risks in consanguineous marriages: Birth weight, gestation time, and measurements of infants. *American Journal of Human Genetics*, 1958, *10*, 344–349.

Morton, N. E. Morbidity of children from consanguineous marriages. In A. G. Steinberg (Ed.), *Progress in medical genetics.* New York: Grune & Stratton, 1961.

Morton, N. E., Crow, J. F., & Muller, H. J. An estimate of the mutational damage in man from data on consanguineous marriages. *Proceedings of the National Academy of Science*, 1956, *42*, 855–863.

Murdock, G. P. *Social structure.* New York: Macmillan, 1949.

Okazaki, A. *Kekkon to jinkō.* Tokyo: Chikura Shobo, 1941.

Parsons, T. The incest taboo in relation to social structure and the socialization of the child. *British Journal of Sociology*, 1954, *5*, 101–117.

Penrose, L. S. A clinical and genetical study of 1,280 cases of mental defect. *Great Britain Medical Research Council, Special Report Series*, 1938, *229*, 1–159.

Riemer, S. A research note on incest. *American Journal of Sociology*, 1940, *45*, 554–565.

Schull, W. J. Empirical risks in consanguineous marriages: Sex ratio, malformation, and viability. *American Journal of Human Genetics*, 1958, *10*, 294–343.

Schull, W. J., & Neel, J. V. *The effects of inbreeding on Japanese children.* New York: Harper & Row, 1965.

Segner, L., & Collins, A. Cross-cultural study of incest myths. Unpublished manuscript, University of Texas, 1967.

Slater, M. Ecological factors in the origin of incest. *American Anthropologist*, 1959, *61*, 1042–1059.

Stern, C. *Principles of human genetics.* (2nd ed.) San Francisco: Freeman, 1960.

Sutter, J. *Recherches sur les effects de la consanguinité chez l'homme.* Lons-le-Saunier: Declume Press, 1958.

Tharp, R. G. Psychological patterning in marriage. *Psychological Bulletin*, 1963, *60*, 97–117.

Warriner, C. C., Lemmon, W. B., & Ray. T. S. Early experience as a variable in mate selection. *Animal Behaviour*, 1963, *11*, 121.

Weinberg, S. K. *Incest behavior.* New York: Citadel, 1955.

Westermarck, E. *The history of human marriage.* London: Macmillan, 1894.

White, L. The definition and prohibition of incest. *American Anthropologist,* 1948, *50,* 416–435.

Winch, R. F. The theory of complementary needs in mate selection: Final results on the test of general hypotheses. *American Sociological Review,* 1955, *20,* 552–555.

Winston, H. Influence of genotype and infantile trauma on adult learning in the mouse. *Journal of Comparative and Physiological Psychology,* 1963, *56,* 630–635.

Winston, H. Heterosis and learning in the mouse. *Journal of Comparative and Physiological Psychology,* 1964, *57,* 279–283.

Wolf, A. P. Childhood association, sexual attraction, and the incest taboo: A Chinese case. *American Anthropologist,* 1966, *68,* 883–898.

Wright, S. Inbreeding and homozygosis. *Proceedings National Academy of Sciences,* 1933, *19,* 411–420.

I would like to take you with me on a journey of exploration. The object of the trip, the goal of the search, is to try to learn something of the *process* of psychotherapy, or the *process* by which personality change takes place. I would warn you that the goal has not yet been achieved and that it seems as though the expedition has advanced only a few short miles into the jungle. Yet perhaps if I can take you with me, you will be tempted to discover new and profitable avenues of further advance.

The Puzzle of Process

My own reason for engaging in such a search seems simple to me. Just as many psychologists have been interested in the invariant aspects of personality — the unchanging aspects of intelligence, temperament, personality structure — so I have long been interested in the invariant aspects of *change* in personality. Do personality and behavior change? What commonalities exist in such changes? What commonalities exist in the conditions which precede change? Most important of all, what is the process by which such change occurs?

Puzzling over this problem of getting at the process has led me to realize how little objective research deals with process in any field. Objective research slices through the frozen moment to provide us with an exact picture of the interrelationships which exist at that moment. But our understanding of the ongoing movement — whether it be the process of fermentation, or the circulation of the blood, or the process of atomic

a process conception of psychotherapy[1]

carl r. rogers
western behavioral science institute

fission — is generally provided by a theoretical formulation, often supplemented, where feasible, with a clinical observation of the process. I have thus come to realize that perhaps I am hoping for too much to expect that research procedures can shed light directly upon the process of personality change. Perhaps only theory can do that.

A REJECTED METHOD

When I determined, more than a year ago, to make a fresh attempt to understand the manner in which such change takes place, I first considered various ways in which the experience of therapy might be described in terms of some other theoretical framework. There was

1. Reprinted from *American Psychologist*, 1958, Vol. 13, pp. 142–149. Copyright 1958 by the American Psychological Association, and reproduced by permission.

much that was appealing in the field of communication theory, with its concepts of feedback, input and output signals, and the like. There was the possibility of describing the process of therapy in terms of learning theory or in terms of general systems theory. As I studied these avenues of understanding, I became convinced that it would be possible to translate the process of psychotherapy into any one of these theoretical frameworks. It would, I believe, have certain advantages to do so. But I also became convinced that, in a field so new, this is not what is most needed.

I came to a conclusion which others have reached before: in a new field perhaps what is needed first is to steep oneself in the *events*, to approach the phenomena with as few preconceptions as possible, to take a naturalist's observational, descriptive approach to these events, and to draw forth those low-level inferences which seem most native to the material itself.

THE MODE OF APPROACH
So, for the past year, I have used the method which so many of us use for generating hypotheses, a method which psychologists in this country seem so reluctant to expose or comment on. I used myself as a tool. I have spent many hours listening to recorded therapeutic interviews—trying to listen as naively as possible. I have endeavored to soak up all the clues I could capture as to the process, as to what elements are significant in change. Then I have tried to abstract from that sensing the simplest abstractions which would describe them. Here I have been much stimulated and helped by the thinking of many of my colleagues, but I would like to mention my special indebtedness to Eugene Gendlin, William Kirtner, and Fred Zimring, whose demonstrated ability to think in new ways about these matters has been particularly helpful and from whom I have borrowed heavily.

The next step has been to take these observations and low-level abstractions and formulate them in such a way that testable hypotheses can readily be drawn from them. This is the point I have reached. I make no apology for the fact that I am reporting no empirical investigations of these formulations. If past experience is any guide, then I may rest assured that, if the formulations I am about to present check in any way with the subjective experience of other therapists, then a great deal of research will be stimulated, and in a few years there will be ample evidence of the degree of truth and falsity in the statements which follow.

A BASIC CONDITION
If we were studying the process of growth in plants, we would assume certain constant conditions of temperature, moisture, and sunlight in forming our conceptualizations of the process. Likewise in conceptualizing the process of personality change in psychotherapy, I shall assume a constant and optimal set of conditions for facilitating this change. I have recently tried to spell out these conditions in some detail (7). For our present purpose, I believe I can state this assumed condition in one word. Throughout the discussion which follows, I shall assume that the client experiences himself as being fully *received*. By this I mean that, whatever his feelings—fear, despair, insecurity, anger; whatever his mode of expression—silence, gestures, tears, or words; whatever he finds himself being in this moment, he senses that he is psychologically *received*, just as he is, by the therapist. There is implied in this term the concept of being understood, empathically, and the concept of acceptance. It is also well to point out that it is the client's experience of this condition which makes it optimal, not merely the fact of its existence in the therapist.

In all that I shall say, then, about the process of change, I shall assume as a constant an optimal and maximum condition of being received.

THE EMERGING CONTINUUM
In trying to grasp and conceptualize the process of change, I was initially looking for elements which would mark or characterize change itself. I was thinking of change as an entity and searching for its specific attributes. What gradually emerged in my understanding as I exposed myself to the raw material of change was a continuum of a different sort than I had conceptualized before.

Individuals move, I began to see, not from a fixity or homeostasis through change to a new fixity, though such a process is indeed possible. But much the more significant continuum is from fixity to changingness, from rigid structure to flow, from stasis to process. I formed the tentative hypothesis that perhaps the qualities of the client's expression at any one point might indicate his position on this continuum, might indicate where he stood in the process of change.

Seven Stages of Process
I gradually developed this concept of a continuum of process, discriminating seven stages in it, with

examples from recorded therapeutic interviews illustrating the qualities of the process at each stage. It would be quite impossible to give all of this crude scale here, but I shall try to suggest something of its nature by describing very briefly Stages 1 and 2, to illustrate the lower end of the continuum, and describing more fully Stages 5, 6, and 7, to fill in the upper end of the scale.[2]

FIRST STAGE

The individual in this stage of fixity and remoteness of experiencing is not likely to come voluntarily for therapy. However, I can to some degree describe the characteristics of this stage:

There is an unwillingness to communicate self. Communication is only about externals.

Feelings and personal meanings are neither recognized as such nor owned.

Personal constructs (to use Kelly's helpful term, 4) *are extremely rigid.*

Close and communicative relationships are construed as dangerous.

No problems are recognized or perceived at this stage.

There is no desire to change.

There is much blockage of internal communications.

Perhaps these brief statements will convey something of the psychological fixity of this end of the continuum. The individual has little or no recognition of the ebb and flow of the feeling life within him. He construes his experience rigidly in terms of the past. He is (to borrow the term of Gendlin and Zimring) structure-bound in his manner of experiencing, reacting to now "by finding it to be like a past experience and then reacting to that past, feeling *it*" (3). The individual at this stage represents stasis, fixity, the opposite of flow or change.

SECOND STAGE OF PROCESS

When the person in the first stage can experience himself as fully received, then the second stage follows. We seem to know very little about how to provide the experience of being received for the person in the first stage, but it is occasionally achieved in play or group

2. An amplification of this paper, giving the whole scale with more extended illustrations, may be obtained from the author by those who are interested in using it for research purposes.

therapy where the person can be exposed to a receiving climate, without himself having to take any initiative, for a long enough time to experience himself *as received.* In any event where he does experience this, then a slight loosening and flowing of symbolic expression occurs, which tends to be characterized by the following:

Expression begins to flow in regard to nonself topics.

Ex. "I guess that I suspect my father has often felt very insecure in his business relations."[3]

Problems are perceived as external to self.

Ex. "Disorganization keeps cropping up in my life."

There is no sense of personal responsibility in problems.

Ex. This is illustrated in the above excerpt.

Feelings are described as unowned, or sometimes as past objects.

Ex. Counselor: "If you want to tell me something of what brought you here. . . ." Client: "The symptom was—it was—just being very depressed." This is an excellent example of the way in which internal problems can be perceived and communicated about as entirely external. She is not saying "I am depressed" or even "I was depressed." Her feeling is handled as a remote, unowned object, entirely external to self.

Feelings may be exhibited, but are not recognized as such or owned.

Experiencing is bound by the structure of the past.

Ex. "I suppose the compensation I always make is, rather than trying to communicate with people or have the right relationship with them, to compensate by, well, shall we say, being on an intellectual level." Here the client is beginning to recognize the way in which her experiencing is bound by the past. Her statement also illustrates the remoteness of experiencing at this level. It is as though she were holding her experience at arm's length.

Personal constructs are rigid, and unrecognized as being constructs, but are thought of as facts.

Ex. "I can't ever do anything right—can't ever finish it."

Differentiation of personal meanings and feelings is very limited and global.

3. The many examples used as illustrations are taken from recorded interviews, unless otherwise noted. For the most part, they are taken from interviews which have never been published, but a number of them are taken from the report of two cases in a chapter of a forthcoming book (6).

The preceding example is a good illustration. "I can't *ever*" is one instance of a black and white differentiation, as is also the use of " ight" in this absolute sense.

Contradictions may be expressed, but with little recognition of them as contradictions.

Ex. "I want to know things, but I look at the same page for an hour."

As a comment on this second stage of the process of change, it might be said that a number of clients who voluntarily come for help are in this stage, but we (and probably therapists in general) have a very minimal degree of success in working with them. This seems, at least, to be a reasonable conclusion from Kirtner's study (5), though his conceptual framework was somewhat different. We seem to know too little about the ways in which a person at this stage may come to experience himself as "received."

THE FIFTH STAGE

I shall omit any description of Stages 3 and 4. Each involves a further loosening of symbolic expression in regard to feelings, constructs, and self. These stages constitute much of psychotherapy. But going beyond these stages, we can again mark a point on the continuum and call it Stage 5. If the client feels himself received in his expressions, behaviors, and experiences at the third and fourth stage, then this sets in motion still further loosenings, and the freedom of organismic flow is increased. Here I believe we can again delineate crudely the qualities of this phase of the process:

Feelings are expressed freely as in the present.

Ex. "I expected kinda to get a severe rejection—this I expect all the time . . . somehow I guess I even feel it with you. . . . It's hard to talk about because I want to be the best I can possibly be with you." Here feelings regarding the therapist and the client in relationship to the therapist, emotions often most difficult to reveal, are expressed openly.

Feelings are very close to being fully experienced. They "bubble up," "seep through," in spite of the fear and distrust which the client feels at experiencing them with fullness and immediacy.

Ex. Client is talking about an external event. Suddenly she gets a pained, stricken look. Therapist: "What—what's hitting you now?" Client: "I don't know. (She cries) . . . I must have been getting a little too close to something I didn't want to talk about." The feeling has almost seeped through into awareness, in spite of her.

There is a beginning tendency to realize that experiencing a feeling involves a direct referent.

The example just cited illustrates this in part. The client knows she has experienced something, knows she is not clear as to what she has experienced. But there is also the dawning realization that the referent of these vague cognitions lies within her, in an organismic event against which she can check her symbolization and her cognitive formulations. This is often shown by expressions that indicate the closeness or distance the individual feels from this referent.
Ex. "I really don't have my finger on it. I'm just kinda describing it."

There is surprise and fright, rarely pleasure, at the feelings which "bubble through."

Ex. Client, talking about past home relationships, "That's not important any more. Hmm. [Pause] That was somehow very meaningful—but I don't have the slightest idea why. . . . Yes, that's it! I can forget about it now and—why, it *isn't* that important. Wow! All that miserableness and stuff!"

There is an increasing ownership of self feelings, and a desire to be these, to be the "real me."

Ex. "The real truth of the matter is that I'm not the sweet, forbearing guy that I try to make out that I am. I get irritated at things. I feel like snapping at people, and I feel like being selfish at times; and I don't know why I should pretend I'm *not* that way." This is a clear instance of the greater degree of acceptance of all feelings.

Experiencing is loosened, no longer remote, and frequently occurs with little postponement.

There is little delay between the organismic event and the full subjective living of it. A beautifully precise account of this is given by a client. Ex. "I'm still having a little trouble trying to figure out what this sadness—and the weepiness—means. I just know I feel it when I get close to a certain kind of feeling—and usually when I do get weepy, it helps me to kinda break through a wall I've set up because of things that have happened. I feel hurt about something and then automatically this kind of shields things up and then I feel like I can't really touch or feel *anything* very much . . . and if I'd be *able* to feel, or could *let* myself feel the instantaneous feeling when I'm hurt, I'd immediately start being weepy right then, but I can't."

Here we see him regarding his feeling as an inner referent to which he can turn for greater clarity. As he senses his weepiness, he realizes that it is a delayed and partial experiencing of being hurt. He also recognizes that his defenses are such that he can not, at this point, experience the event of hurt when it occurs.

The ways in which experience is construed are much loosened. There are many fresh discoveries of personal constructs as constructs, and a critical examination and questioning of these.

Ex. A man says: "This idea of needing to please people—of having to do it—that's really been kind of a basic assumption of my life (he weeps quietly). It's kind of, you know, just one of the very unquestioned axioms that I *have* to please. I have no choice. I just *have to.*" Here he is clear that this assumption has been a construct, and it is evident that its unquestioned status is at an end.

There is a strong and evident tendency toward exactness in differentiation of feelings and meanings.

A client speaks of "Some tension that grows in me, or some hopelessness, or some kind of incompleteness—and my life actually is very incomplete right now. . . . I just don't know. Seems to be, the closest thing it gets to, is *hopelessness.*" Obviously he is trying to capture the exact term which for him symbolizes his experience.

There is an increasingly clear facing of contradictions and incongruences in experience.

Ex. "My conscious mind tells me I'm worthy. But someplace inside I don't believe it. I think I'm a rat—a no-good. I've no faith in my ability to do anything."

There is an increasing quality of acceptance of self-responsibility for the problems being faced, and a concern as to how he has contributed.
There are increasingly freer dialogues within the self—an improvement in, and reduced blockage of, internal communication.

Sometimes these dialogues are verbalized. Ex. "Something in me is saying: 'What more do I have to give up? You've taken so much from me already.' This is *me* talking to *me*—the *me* way back in there who talks to the *me* who runs the show. It's complaining now, saying, 'You're getting too close! Go away!' "

I trust that the examples I have given of this fifth phase of the process continuum will make several points clear. In the first place, this phase is several hundred psychological miles from the first stage described. Here many aspects of the client are in flow, as against the rigidity of the first stage. He is very much closer to his organic being, which is always in process. He is much closer to being in the flow of his feelings. His constructions of experience are decidedly loosened and repeatedly being tested against referents and evidence within and without. Experience is much more highly differentiated, and thus internal communication, already flowing, can be much more exact.

As a general comment on the description thus far, it would be my observation that a person is never wholly at one or another stage of the process. There is, however, a general consistency in his manner of ex-

periencing and expressing. Thus, a client who is generally at Stage 2 or 3 seems unlikely to exhibit any behaviors characteristic of Stage 5. This is especially true if we limit observations to a single defined area of related personal meanings in the client. Then I would hypothesize that there will be considerable regularity, that Stage 3 would rarely be found before Stage 2, that Stage 4 would rarely follow Stage 2 without Stage 3 intervening. Such tentative hypotheses can, of course, be put to empirical test.

THE SIXTH STAGE
If I have been able to communicate some feeling for the scope and quality of the increased loosening, at each stage, of feeling, experiencing, and construing, then we are ready to look at the next stage, which appears, from observation, to be a very crucial one. Let me see if I can convey what I perceive to be its characteristic qualities.

Assuming that the client continues to be fully received in the therapeutic relationship, then the characteristics of Stage 5 tend to be followed by a very distinctive and often dramatic phase. It is characterized as follows:

A feeling which has previously been "stuck," has been inhibited in its process quality, is experienced with immediacy now.
A feeling flows to its full result.
A present feeling is directly experienced with immediacy and richness.
This immediacy of experiencing, and the feeling which constitutes its content, are accepted. This is something which is, not something to be denied, feared, struggled against.

All the preceding sentences attempt to describe slightly different facets of what is, when it occurs, a clear and definite phenomenon. It would take recorded examples to communicate its full quality, but I shall try to give an illustration without benefit of recording. A somewhat extended excerpt from the eightieth interview with a young man may communicate the way in which a client comes into Stage 6.

Client: "I could even conceive of it as a possibility that I could have a kind of tender concern for me. . . . Still, how could *I* be tender, be concerned for *myself*, when they're one and the same thing? But yet I can *feel* it so clearly. . . . You know, like taking care of a child. You want to give it this and give it that. . . . I can kind of clearly see the purposes for somebody else . . . but I can never see them for . . . myself, that I could do this for me, you know. Is it possible that I can really want to take care of myself, and make that a major purpose of my life? That means I'd have to deal with the whole world as if I were guardian of the most cherished and most wanted possession, that this *I* was between this precious *me* that I wanted to take care of and the whole world. . . . It's almost as if I *loved* myself—you know—that's strange—but it's true." Therapist: "It seems such a strange concept to realize. Why, it would mean I would face the world as though a part of my primary responsibility was taking care of this precious individual who is me—whom I love." Client: "Whom I care for—whom I feel so *close* to. Woof!! That's another *strange* one." Therapist: "It just seems *weird*." Client: "Yeah. It hits rather close somehow. The idea of my loving me and the taking care of me. [His eyes grow moist] That's a very, very nice one—very nice."

The recording would help to convey the fact that here is a feeling which had never been able to flow in him, which is experienced with immediacy, in this moment. It is a feeling which flows to its full result, without inhibition. It is experienced acceptantly, with no attempt to push it to one side or to deny it.

There is a quality of living subjectively in the experience, not feeling about it.

The client, in his *words*, may withdraw enough from the experience to feel about it, as in the above example, yet the recording makes it clear that his words are peripheral to the experiencing which is going on within him and in which he is living. The best communication of this in his words is "Woof!! That's another *strange* one."

Self as an object tends to disappear.

The self, at this moment, *is* this feeling. This is a being in the moment, with little self-conscious awareness, but with primarily a reflexive awareness, as Sartre terms it. The self *is*, subjectively, in the existential moment. It is not something one perceives.

Experiencing, at this stage, takes on a real process quality.

One client, a man who is approaching this stage, says that he has a frightened feeling about the source of a lot of secret thoughts in himself. He goes on: "The butterflies are the thoughts closest to the surface. Underneath there's a deeper flow. I feel very removed from it all. The deeper flow is like a great school of fish moving under the surface. I see the ones that break through the surface of the water—sitting with my fishing line in one hand, with a bent pin on the end of it—trying to find a better tackle—or better yet, a way of diving in. That's the scary thing. The image I get is that *I* want to be one of the fish myself." Therapist: "You want to be down there flowing along, too."

Though this client is not yet fully experiencing in a process manner, and hence does not fully exemplify this sixth point on the continuum, he foresees it so clearly that his description gives a real sense of its meaning.

Another characteristic of this stage of process is the physiological loosening which accompanies it.

Moistness in the eyes, tears, sighs, muscular relaxation are frequently evident. Often there are other physiological concomitants. I would hypothesize that in these moments, had we the measures for it, we would discover improved circulation, improved conductivity of nervous impulses. An example of the "primitive" nature of some of these sensations may be indicated in the following excerpt:

The client, a young man, has expressed the wish his parents would die or disappear. "It's kind of like wanting to wish them away, and wishing they had never been. . . . And I'm so ashamed of myself because then they call me, and off I go—swish! They're somehow still so strong. I don't know. There's some umbilical—I can almost feel it inside me—swish" [and he gestures, plucking himself away by grasping at his navel]. Therapist: "They really do have a hold on your umbilical cord." Client: "It's funny how real it feels . . . like a burning sensation, kind of, and when they say something which makes me anxious I can feel it right here [pointing]. I never thought of it quite that way." Therapist: "As though, if there's a disturbance in the relationship between you, then you do just feel it as though it was a strain on your umbilicus." Client: "Yeah, kind of like in my gut here. It's so hard to define the feeling that I feel there."

Here he is living subjectively in the feeling of dependence on his parents. Yet it would be inaccurate to say that he is perceiving it. He is *in* it, experiencing it as a strain on his umbilical cord.

In this stage, internal communication is free and relatively unblocked.

I believe this is quite adequately illustrated in the examples given. Indeed the phrase "internal communication" is no longer quite correct; for, as each of these examples illustrates, the crucial moment is a moment of integration, in which communication between different internal foci is no longer necessary, because they become *one*.

The incongruence between experience and awareness is vividly experienced as it disappears into congruence.
The relevant personal construct is dissolved in this experiencing moment, and the client feels cut loose from his previously stabilized framework.

I trust these two characteristics may acquire more meaning from the following example. A young man has been having difficulty getting close to a certain unknown feeling. "That's almost exactly what the feeling is, too—it was that I was living so much of my life, and seeing so much of my life, in terms of being *scared* of something." He tells how his professional activities are just to give him a little safety and "a little world where I'll be secure, you know. And for the same reason. [Pause] I was kind of letting it seep through. But I also tied it in with you and with my relationship with you, and one thing I feel about it is fear of its going away. [His tone changes to role-play more accurately his feeling.] Won't you let me have this? I kind of *need* it. I can be so lonely and scared without it." Therapist: "M-hmm, m-hmm. 'Let me hang on to it because I'd be terribly scared if I didn't!' . . . It's a kind of pleading thing too, isn't it?" Client: "I get a sense of—it's this kind of pleading little boy. It's this gesture of begging" [putting his hands up as if in prayer]. Therapist: "You put your hands in kind of a supplication." Client: "Yeah, that's right. 'Won't you do this for me?' kind of. Oh, that's terrible! Who, *me? Beg?* . . . That's an emotion I've never felt clearly at all—something I've never been. . . . [Pause] . . . I've got such a confusing feeling. One is, it's such a wondrous feeling to have these new things come out of me. It amazes me so much each time, and there's that same feeling, being scared that I've so much of this. [Tears] . . . I just don't know myself. Here's suddenly something I never realized, hadn't any inkling of—that it was some *thing* or some *way* I wanted to be."

Here we see a complete experiencing of his pleadingness, and a vivid recognition of the discrepancy between this experiencing and his concept of himself. Yet this experiencing of discrepancy exists in the moment of its disappearance. From now on he *is* a person who feels *pleading*, as well as many other feelings. As this moment dissolves the way he has construed himself, he feels cut loose from his previous world—a sensation which is both wondrous and frightening.

The moment of full experiencing becomes a clear and definite referent.

The examples given should indicate that the client is often not too clearly aware of what has "hit him" in these moments. Yet this does not seem too important because the event is an entity, a referent, which can be returned to, again and again if necessary, to discover more about it. The pleadingness, the feeling of "loving myself" which are present in these examples, may not prove to be exactly as described. They are, however, solid points of reference to which the client can return until he has satisfied himself as to what they are. It is, perhaps, that they constitute a clear-cut physiological event, a substratum of the conscious life, which the client can return to for investigatory purposes. Gendlin has called my attention to this significant quality of experiencing as a referent. He is endeavoring to build an extension of psychological theory on this basis (2, especially Chap. 7).

Differentiation of experiencing is sharp and basic.

Because each of these moments is a referent, a specific entity, it does not become confused with anything else. The process of sharp differentiation builds on it and about it.

In this stage there are no longer "problems," external or internal. The client is living, subjectively, a phase of his problem. It is not an object.

I trust it is evident that in any of these examples it would be grossly inaccurate to say that the client perceives his problem as internal or is dealing with it as an internal problem. We need some way of indicating that he is further than this and, of course, enormously far in the process sense from perceiving his problem as external. The best description seems to be that he neither perceives his problem nor deals with it. He is simply living some portion of it knowingly and acceptingly.

I have dwelt so long on this sixth definable point on the process continuum because I see it as a highly crucial one. My observation is that these moments of immediate, full, accepted experiencing are in some sense almost irreversible. To put this in terms of the examples, it is my observation and hypothesis that with these clients, whenever a future experiencing of the same quality and characteristics occurs, it will necessarily be recognized in awareness for what it is: a tender caring for self, an umbilical bond which makes him a part of his parents, or a pleading small-boy dependence, as the case may be. And, it might be remarked in passing, once an experience is fully in awareness, fully accepted, then it can be coped with effectively, like any other clear reality.

THE SEVENTH STAGE

In those areas in which the sixth stage has been reached, it is no longer so necessary that the client be fully received by the therapist, though this still seems helpful. However, because of the tendency for the sixth stage to be irreversible, the client often seems to go on into the seventh and final stage without much need of the therapist's help. This stage occurs as much outside of the therapeutic relationship as in it and is often reported, rather than experienced, in the therapeutic hour. I shall try to describe some of its characteristics as I feel I have observed them:

New feelings are experienced with immediacy and richness of detail, both in the therapeutic relationship and outside.
The experiencing of such feelings is consciously used as a clear referent.
There is a growing and continuing sense of acceptant ownership of these changing feelings, a basic trust in his own process.

This trust is not primarily in the conscious processes which go on, but rather in the total organismic process. One client puts it: "I seem to work best when my conscious mind is only concerned with facts and letting the analysis of them go on by itself without paying any attention to it."

Experiencing has lost almost completely its structure-bound aspects and becomes process experiencing—that is, the situation is experienced and interpreted in its newness, not as the past.

An example in a very specific area is given by a client in a follow-up interview as he explains the different quality that has come about in his creative work. It used to be that he tried to be orderly. "You begin at the beginning and you progress regularly through to the end." Now he is aware that the process in himself is different. "When I'm working on an idea, the whole idea develops like the latent image coming out when you develop a photograph. It doesn't start at one edge and fill in over to the other. It comes in *all over*. At first all you see is the hazy outline, and you wonder what it's going to be; and then gradually something fits here and someting fits there, and pretty soon it all comes clear—all at once." It is obvious that he has not only come to trust this process, but that he is experiencing it as it *is*, not in terms of some past.

The self becomes increasingly simply the subjective and reflexive awareness of experiencing. The self is much less frequently a perceived object and much more frequently something confidently felt in process.

An example may be taken from the same follow-up interview with the client quoted above. In this interview, because he is reporting his experience since therapy, he again becomes aware of himself as an object; but it is clear that this has not been the quality of his day-by-day experience. After reporting many changes, he says: "I hadn't really thought of any of these things in connection with therapy until tonight. ... [Jokingly] Gee! maybe something *did* happen. Because my life since *has* been different. My productivity has gone up. My confidence has gone up. I've become brash in situations I would have avoided before. And also, I've become less brash in situations where I would have become very obnoxious before." It is clear that only afterward does he realize what his self as an object has been.

Personal constructs are tentatively reformulated, to be validated against further experience, but even then to be held loosely.

A client describes the way in which such a construct changed, between interviews, toward the end of therapy: "I don't know what [changed], but I definitely feel different about looking back at my childhood, and some of the hostility about my mother and father has evaporated. I substituted for a feeling of resentment about them a sort of acceptance of the fact that they did a number of things that were undesirable with me. But I substituted a sort of feeling of interested excitement that—gee—now that I'm finding out what was wrong, *I* can do something about it—correct their mistakes." Here the way in which he construes his experience with his parents has been sharply altered.

Internal communication is clear, with feelings and symbols well matched, and fresh terms for new feelings.
There is the experiencing of effective choice of new ways of being.

Because all the elements of experience are available to awareness, choice becomes real and effective. Here a client is just coming to this realization: "I'm trying to encompass a way of talking that is a way out of being scared of talking. Perhaps just kind of thinking out loud is the way to do that. But I've got so *many* thoughts I could only do it a little bit. But maybe I could let my talk be an expression of my thoughts, instead of just trying to make the proper noises in each situation." Here he is sensing the possibility of effective choice, perhaps approaching this seventh stage rather than being in it.

By no means all clients move this far on the continuum; but when this seventh stage is reached, it involves us in another dimension. For it will be evident that the client has now incorporated the quality of motion, of flow, of changingness into every aspect of his psychological life. He will therefore continue to be a continually changing person, experiencing with freshness and immediacy in each new situation, responding to its newness with real and accepted feelings, and construing its meaning in terms of what it *is*, not in terms of some past experience.

Recapitulation

I have tried to sketch, in a crude and preliminary manner, the flow of a process of change which occurs when a client experiences himself as being received, welcomed, understood as he is. This process involves several threads, separable at first, becoming more of a unity as the process continues.

This process involves a loosening of feelings. From feelings which are unrecognized, unowned, unexpressed, the client moves toward a flow in which everchanging feelings are experienced in the moment, knowingly and acceptingly, and may be accurately expressed.

The process involves a change in the manner of experiencing. From experiencing which is remote in time from the organic event, which is bound by the structure of experience in the past, the client moves toward a manner of experiencing which is immediate, which interprets meaning in terms of what is, not what was.

The process involves a loosening of the cognitive maps of experience. From construing experience in rigid ways which are perceived as external facts, the client moves toward developing changing, loosely held construings of meaning in experience, constructions which are modifiable by each new experience.

The process involves a change in the self. From being a self which is not congruent with experience, the client moves through the phase of perceiving self as an object, to a self which is synonymous with experience, being the subjective awareness of that experience.

There are other elements, too, involved in the process: movement from ineffective to effective choice, from fear of relationships to freely living in relationship, from inadequate differentiation of feelings and meanings to sharp differentiation.

In general, the process moves from a point of fixity, where all these elements and threads are separately discernible and separately understandable, to the flowing peak moments of therapy in which all these threads become inseparably woven together. In the new experiencing with immediacy which occurs at such moments, feeling and cognition interpenetrate, self is subjectively present in the experience, volition is simply the subjective following of a harmonious balance of organismic direction. Thus, as the process reaches this point, the person becomes a unity of flow, of motion. He has changed; but, what seems most significant, he has become an integrated process of changingness.

References

1. Bergman, D. V. Counseling method and client responses. *J. consult. Psychol.*, 1951, *15*, 216–224.

2. Gendlin, E. The function of experiencing in symbolization. Unpublished doctoral dissertation, Univer. of Chicago, 1958.

3. Gendlin, E., & Zimring, F. The qualities or dimensions of experiencing and their change. *Counseling Center Discussion Papers*, 1955, *1*, No. 3. (Univer. of Chicago Counseling Center)

4. Kelly, G. A. *The psychology of personal constructs.* Vol. I. A theory of personality. New York: Norton, 1955.

5. Kirtner, W. L. Success and failure in client-centered therapy as a function of personality variables. Unpublished master's thesis, Univer. of Chicago, 1955.

6. Lewis, M. K., Rogers, C. R., & Shlien, J. M. Two cases of time-limited client-centered psychotherapy. In A. Burton (Ed.), *Case studies of counseling and psychotherapy.* New York: Prentice-Hall.

7. Rogers, C. R. The necessary and sufficient conditions of therapeutic personality change. *J. consult. Psychol.*, 1957, *21*, 95–103.

social behavior

---

reconciling conflicting results derived from experimental and survey studies of attitude change[1]

carl i. hovland (1912–1961)
yale university

Two quite different types of research design are characteristically used to study the modification of attitudes through communication. In the first type, the *experiment*, individuals are given a controlled exposure to a communication and the effects evaluated in terms of the amount of change in attitude or opinion produced. A base line is provided by means of a control group not exposed to the communication. The study of

1. Reprinted from *American Psychologist*, 1959, Vol. 14, pp. 8–17. Copyright 1959 by the American Psychological Association, and reproduced by permission.

Gosnell (1927) on the influence of leaflets designed to get voters to the polls is a classic example of the controlled experiment.

In the alternative research design, the *sample survey*, information is secured through interviews or questionnaires both concerning the respondent's exposure to various communications and his attitudes and opinions on various issues. Generalizations are then derived from the correlations obtained between reports of exposure and measurements of attitude. In a variant of this method, measurements of attitude and of exposure to communication are obtained during repeated interviews with the same individual over a period of weeks or months. This is the "panel method" extensively utilized in studying the impact of various mass media on political attitudes and on voting behavior (cf., e.g., Kendall & Lazarsfeld, 1950).

Generalizations derived from experimental and from correlational studies of communication effects are usually both reported in chapters on the effects of mass media and in other summaries of research on attitude, typically without much stress on the type of study from which the conclusion was derived. Close scrutiny of the results obtained from the two methods, however, suggests a marked difference in the picture of communication effects obtained from each. The object of my paper is to consider the conclusions derived from these two types of design, to suggest some of the factors responsible for the frequent divergence in results, and then to formulate principles aimed at reconciling some of the apparent conflicts.

Divergence

The picture of mass communication effects which emerges from correlational studies is one in which few individuals are seen as being affected by communications. One of the most thorough correlational studies of the effects of mass media on attitudes is that of Lazarsfeld, Berelson, and Gaudet published in *The People's Choice* (1944). In this report there is an extensive chapter devoted to the effects of various media, particularly radio, newspapers, and magazines. The authors conclude that few changes in attitudes were produced. They estimate that the political positions of only about 5% of their respondents were changed by the election campaign, and they are inclined to attribute even this small amount of change more to personal influence than to the mass media. A similar evaluation of mass media is made in the recent chapter in the *Handbook of Social Psychology* by Lipset and his collaborators (1954).

Research using experimental procedures, on the other hand, indicates the possibility of considerable modifiability of attitudes through exposure to communication. In both Klapper's survey (1949) and in my chapter in the *Handbook of Social Psychology* (Hovland, 1954) a number of experimental studies are discussed in which the opinions of a third to a half or more of the audience are changed.

The discrepancy between the results derived from these two methodologies raises some fascinating problems for analysis. This divergence in outcome appears to me to be largely attributable to two kinds of factors: one, the difference in research design itself; and, two, the historical and traditional differences in general approach to evaluation characteristic of researchers using the experimental as contrasted with the correlational or survey method. I would like to discuss, first, the influence these factors have on the estimation of overall effects of communications and, then, turn to other divergences in outcome characteristically found by the use of the experimental and survey methodology.

Undoubtedly the most critical and interesting variation in the research *design* involved in the two procedures is that resulting from differences in definition of exposure. In an experiment the audience on whom the effects are being evaluated is one which is fully exposed to the communication. On the other hand, in naturalistic situations with which surveys are typically concerned, the outstanding phenomenon is the limitation of the audience to those who *expose themselves* to the communication. Some of the individuals in a captive audience experiment would, of course, expose themselves in the course of natural events to a communication of the type studied; but many others would not. The group which does expose itself is usually a highly biased one, since most individuals "expose themselves most of the time to the kind of material with which they agree to begin with" (Lipset et al., 1954, p. 1158). Thus one reason for the difference in results between experiments and correlational studies is that experiments describe the effects of exposure on the whole range of individuals studied, some of whom are initially in favor of the position being advocated and some who are opposed, whereas surveys primarily describe the effects produced on those already in favor of the point of view advocated in the communication. The amount of change is thus, of course, much smaller in surveys. Lipset and his collaborators make this same evaluation, stating that:

As long as we test a program in the laboratory we always find that it has great effect on the attitudes and interests of the experimental subjects. But when we put the program on as a regular broadcast, we then note that the people who are most influenced in the laboratory tests are those who, in a realistic situation, do not listen to the program. The controlled experiment always greatly overrates effects, as compared with those that really occur, because of the self-selection of audiences (Lipset et al., 1954, p. 1158).

Differences in the second category are not inherent in the design of the two alternatives, but are characteristic of the way researchers using the two methods typically proceed.

The first difference within this class is in the size of the communication unit typically studied. In the majority of survey studies the unit evaluated is an entire program of communication. For example, in studies of political behavior an attempt is made to assess the effects of all newspaper reading and television viewing on attitudes toward the major parties. In the typical experiment, on the other hand, the interest is usually in some particular variation in the content of the communications, and experimental evaluations much more frequently involve single communications. On this point results are thus not directly comparable.

Another characteristic difference between the two methods is in the time interval used in evaluation. In the typical experiment the time at which the effect is observed is usually rather soon after exposure to the communication. In the survey study, on the other hand, the time perspective is such that much more remote effects are usually evaluated. When effects decline with the passage of time, the net outcome will, of course, be that of accentuating the effect obtained in experimental studies as compared with those obtained in survey researches. Again it must be stressed that the difference is not inherent in the designs as such. Several experiments, including our own on the effects of motion pictures (Hovland, Lumsdaine, & Sheffield, 1949) and later studies on the "sleeper effect" (Hovland & Weiss, 1951; Kelman & Hovland, 1953), have studied retention over considerable periods of time.

Some of the difference in outcome may be attributable to the types of communicators characteristically used and to the motive-incentive conditions operative in the two situations. In experimental studies communications are frequently presented in a classroom situation. This may involve quite different types of factors from those operative in the more naturalistic communication situation with which the survey researchers are concerned. In the classroom there may be some implicit sponsorship of the communication by the teacher and the school administration. In the survey studies the communicators may often be remote individuals either unfamiliar to the recipients, or outgroupers clearly known to espouse a point of view opposed to that held by many members of the audience. Thus there may be real differences in communicator credibility in laboratory and survey researches. The net effect of the differences will typically be in the direction of increasing the likelihood of change in the experimental as compared with the survey study.

There is sometimes an additional situational difference. Communications of the type studied by survey researchers usually involve reaching the individual in his natural habitat, with consequent supplementary effects produced by discussion with friends and family. In the laboratory studies a classroom situation with low postcommunication interaction is more typically involved. Several studies, including one by Harold Kelley reported in our volume on *Communication and Persuasion* (Hovland, Janis, & Kelley, 1953), indicate that, when a communication is presented in a situation which makes group membership salient, the individual is typically more resistant to counternorm influence than when the communication is presented under conditions of low salience of group membership (cf. also, Katz & Lazarsfeld, 1955, pp. 48–133).

A difference which is almost wholly adventitious is in the types of populations utilized. In the survey design there is, typically, considerable emphasis on a random sample of the entire population. In the typical experiment, on the other hand, there is a consistent overrepresentation of high school students and college sophomores, primarily on the basis of their greater accessibility. But as Tolman has said: "college sophomores may not be people." Whether differences in the type of audience studied contribute to the differences in effect obtained with the two methods is not known.

Finally, there is an extremely important difference in the studies of the experimental and correlational variety with respect to the type of issue discussed in the communications. In the typical experiment we are interested in studying a set of factors or conditions which are expected on the basis of theory to influence the extent of effect of the communication. We usually deliberately try to find types of issues involving attitudes which are susceptible to modification through communication. Otherwise, we run the risk of no measurable effects, particularly with small-scale experiments. In the survey procedures, on the other hand, socially significant attitudes which are deeply rooted in prior experience and involve much personal commitment are typically involved. This is especially true in voting studies which have provided us with so many of our present results on social influence. I shall have considerably more to say about this problem a little later.

The differences so far discussed have primarily concerned the extent of overall effectiveness indicated by the two methods: why survey results typically show little modification of attitudes by communication while experiments indicate marked changes. Let me now turn to some of the other differences in generalizations derived from the two alternative designs. Let me take as the second main area of disparate results the research on the effect of varying distances between the position taken by the communicator and that held by the recipient of the communication. Here it is a matter of comparing changes for persons who at the outset closely agree with the communicator with those for others who are mildly or strongly in disagreement with him. In the naturalistic situation studied in surveys the typical procedure is to determine changes in opinion following reported exposure to communication for individuals differing from the communicator by varying amounts. This gives rise to two possible artifacts. When the communication is at one end of a continuum, there is little room for improvement for those who differ from the communication by small amounts, but a great deal of room for movement among those with large discrepancies. This gives rise to a spurious degree of positive relationship between the degree of discrepancy and the amount of change. Regression effects will also operate in the direction of increasing the correlation. What is needed is a situation in which the distance factor can be manipulated independently of the subject's initial position. An attempt to set up these conditions experimentally was made in a study by Pritzker and the writer (1957). The method involved preparing individual communications presented in booklet form so that the position of the communicator could be set at any desired distance from the subject's initial position. Communicators highly acceptable to the subjects were used. A number of different topics were employed, including the likelihood of a cure for cancer within five years, the desirability of compulsory voting, and the adequacy of five hours of sleep per night.

The amount of change for each degree of advocated change is shown in Fig. 1. It will be seen that there is a fairly clear progression, such that the greater the

amount of change advocated the greater the average amount of opinion change produced. Similar results have been reported by Goldberg (1954) and by French (1956).

But these results are not in line with our hunches as to what would happen in a naturalistic situation with important social issues. We felt that here other types of response than change in attitude would occur. So Muzafer Sherif, O. J. Harvey, and the writer (1957) set up a situation to simulate as closely as possible the conditions typically involved when individuals are exposed to major social issue communications at differing distances from their own position. The issue used was the desirability of prohibition. The study was done in two states (Oklahoma and Texas) where there is prohibition or local option, so that the wet-dry issue is hotly debated. We concentrated on three aspects of the problem: How favorably will the communicator be received when his position is at varying distances from that of the recipient? How will what the communicator says be perceived and interpreted by individuals at varying distances from his position? What will be the amount of opinion change produced when small and large deviations in position of communication and recipient are involved?

Three communications, one strongly wet, one strongly dry, and one moderately wet, were employed. The results bearing on the first problem, of *reception*, are presented in Fig. 2. The positions of the subjects are indicated on the abscissa in letters from A (extreme dry) to H (strongly wet). The positions of the communication are also indicated in the same letters, *B* indicating a strongly dry communication, *H* a strongly wet, and *F* a moderately wet. Along the ordinate there is plotted the percentage of subjects with each position on the issue who described the communication as "fair" and "unbiased." It will be seen that the degree of distance between the recipient and the communicator greatly influences the evaluation of the fairness of the communication. When a communication is directed at the pro-dry position, nearly all of the dry subjects consider it fair and impartial, but only a few per cent of the wet subjects consider the identical communication fair. The reverse is true at the other end of the scale. When an intermediate position is adopted, the percentages fall off sharply on each side. Thus under the present conditions with a relatively ambiguous communicator one of the ways of dealing with strongly

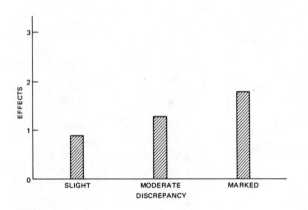

Fig. 1
Mean opinion change score with three degrees of discrepancy (deviation between subject's position and position advocated in communication). [From Hovland & Pritzker, 1957]

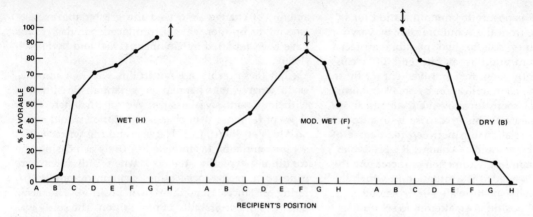

Fig. 2

Percentage of favorable evaluations ("fair", "unbiased," etc.) of wet (H), moderately wet (F), and dry (B) communications for subjects holding various positions on prohibition. Recipients' positions range from A (very dry) to H (very wet). Position of communications indicated by arrow. [From Hovland, Harvey, & Sherif, 1957]

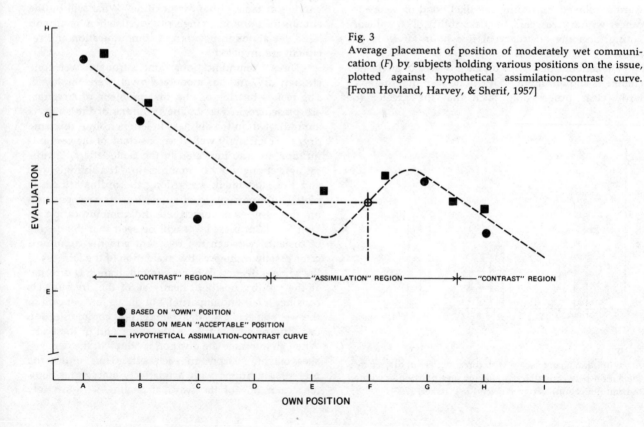

Fig. 3

Average placement of position of moderately wet communication (F) by subjects holding various positions on the issue, plotted against hypothetical assimilation-contrast curve. [From Hovland, Harvey, & Sherif, 1957]

discrepant positions is to *discredit* the communicator, considering him unfair and biased.

A second way in which an individual can deal with discrepancy is by distortion of what is said by the communicator. This is a phenomenon extensively studied by Cooper and Jahoda (1947). In the present study, subjects were asked to state what position they thought was taken by the communicator on the prohibition question. Their evaluation of his position could then be analyzed in relation to their own position. These results are shown in Fig. 3 for the moderately wet communication. It will be observed that there is a tendency for individuals whose position is close to that of the communicator to report on the communicator's position quite accurately, for individuals a little bit removed to report his position to be substantially more like their own (which we call an "assimilation effect"), and for those with more discrepant positions to report the communicator's position as more extreme than it really was. This we refer to as a "contrast effect."

Now to our primary results on opinion change. It was found that individuals whose position was only slightly discrepant from the communicator's were influenced to a greater extent than those whose positions deviated to a larger extent. When a wet position was espoused, 28% of the middle-of-the-road subjects were changed in the direction of the communicator, as compared with only 4% of the drys. With the dry communication 14% of the middle-of-the-roaders were changed, while only 4% of the wets were changed. Thus, more of the subjects with small discrepancies were changed than were those with large discrepancies.

These results appear to indicate that, under conditions when there is some ambiguity about the credibility of the communicator and when the subject is deeply involved with the issue, the greater the attempt at change the higher the resistance. On the other hand, with highly respected communicators, as in the previous study with Pritzker using issues of lower involvement, the greater the discrepancy the greater the effect. A study related to ours has just been completed by Zimbardo (1959) which indicates that, when an influence attempt is made by a strongly positive communicator (i.e., a close personal friend), the greater the discrepancy the greater the opinion change, even when the experimenter made a point of stressing the great importance of the subject's opinion.

The implication of these results for our primary problem of conflicting results is clear. The types of issues with which most experiments deal are relatively uninvolving and are often of the variety where expert opinion is highly relevant, as for example, on topics of health, science, and the like. Here we should expect that opinion would be considerably affected by communications and furthermore that advocacy of positions quite discrepant from the individual's own position would have a marked effect. On the other hand, the types of issues most often utilized in survey studies are ones which are very basic and involve deep commitment. As a consequence small changes in opinion due to communication would be expected. Here communication may have little effect on those who disagree at the outset and function merely to strengthen the position already held, in line with survey findings.

A third area of research in which somewhat discrepant results are obtained by the experimental and survey methods is in the role of order of presentation. From naturalistic studies the generalization has been widely adopted that primacy is an extremely important factor in persuasion. Numerous writers have reported that what we experience first has a critical role in what we believe. This is particularly stressed in studies of propaganda effects in various countries when the nation getting across its message first is alleged to have a great advantage and in commercial advertising where "getting a beat on the field" is stressed. The importance of primacy in political propaganda is indicated in the following quotation from Doob:

The propagandist scores an initial advantage whenever his propaganda reaches people before that of his rivals. Readers or listeners are then biased to comprehend, forever after, the event as it has been initially portrayed to them. If they are told in a headline or a flash that the battle has been won, the criminal has been caught, or the bill is certain to pass the legislature, they will usually expect subsequent information to substantiate this first impression. When later facts prove otherwise, they may be loath to abandon what they believe to be true until perhaps the evidence becomes overwhelming (Doob, 1948, pp. 421–422).

A recent study by Katz and Lazarsfeld (1955) utilizing the survey method compares the extent to which respondents attribute major impact on their decisions about fashions and movie attendance to the presentations to which they were first exposed. Strong primacy effects are shown in their analyses of the data.

We have ourselves recently completed a series of experiments oriented toward this problem. These are reported in our new monograph on *Order of Presentation in Persuasion* (Hovland, Mandell, Campbell, Brock, Luchins, Cohen, McGuire, Janis, Feierabend, & Anderson, 1957). We find that primacy is often *not* a very significant factor when the relative effectiveness of the first side of an issue is compared experimentally with that of the second. The research suggests that differences in design may account for much of the discrepancy. A key variable is whether there is exposure to both sides or whether only one side is actually received. In naturalistic studies the advantage of the first side is often not only that it is first but that it is often then the only side of the issue to which the individual is exposed. Having once been influenced, many individuals make up their mind and are no longer interested in other communications on the issue. In most experiments on order of presentation, on the other hand, the audience is systematically exposed to both sides. Thus under survey conditions, self-exposure tends to increase the impact of primacy.

Two other factors to which I have already alluded appear significant in determining the amount of primacy effect. One is the nature of the communicator, the other the setting in which the communication is received. In our volume Luchins presents results indicating that, when the same communicator presents contradictory material, the point of view read first has more influence. On the other hand, Mandell and I show that, when two different communicators present opposing views successively, little primacy effect is obtained. The communications setting factor operates similarly. When the issue and the conditions of presentation make clear that the points of view are controversial, little primacy is obtained.

Thus in many of the situations with which there had been great concern as to undesirable effects of primacy, such as in legal trials, election campaigns, and political debate, the role of primacy appears to have been exaggerated, since the conditions there are those least conducive to primacy effects: the issue is clearly defined as controversial, the partisanship of the communicator is usually established, and different communicators present the opposing sides.

Time does not permit me to discuss other divergences in results obtained in survey and experimental studies, such as those concerned with the effects of repetition of presentation, the relationship between level of intelligence and susceptibility to attitude change, or the relative impact of mass media and personal influence. Again, however, I am sure that detailed analysis will reveal differential factors at work which can account for the apparent disparity in the generalizations derived.

Integration

On the basis of the foregoing survey of results I reach the conclusion that no contradiction has been established between the data provided by experimental and correlational studies. Instead it appears that the seeming divergence can be satisfactorily accounted for on the basis of a different definition of the communication situation (including the phenomenon of self-selection) and differences in the type of communicator, audience, and kind of issue utilized.

But there remains the task of better integrating the findings associated with the two methodologies. This is a problem closely akin to that considered by the members of the recent Social Science Research Council summer seminar on *Narrowing the Gap Between Field Studies and Laboratory Studies in Social Psychology* (Riecken, 1954). Many of their recommendations are pertinent to our present problem.

What seems to me quite apparent is that a genuine understanding of the effects of communications on attitudes requires both the survey and the experimental methodologies. At the same time there appear to be certain inherent limitations of each method which must be understood by the researcher if he is not to be blinded by his preoccupation with one or the other type of design. Integration of the two methodologies will require on the part of the experimentalist an awareness of the narrowness of the laboratory in interpreting the larger and more comprehensive effects of communication. It will require on the part of the survey researcher a greater awareness of the limitations of the correlational method as a basis for establishing casual relationships.

The framework within which survey research operates is most adequately and explicitly dealt with by Berelson, Lazarsfeld, and McPhee in their book on *Voting* (1954). The model which they use, taken over by them from the economist Tinbergen, is reproduced in the top half of Fig. 4. For comparison, the model used by experimentalists is presented in the lower half of the figure. It will be seen that the model used by the survey researcher, particularly when he employs the

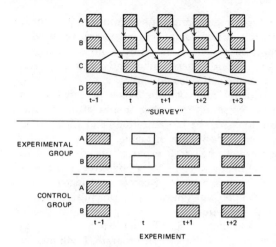

Fig. 4

Top half: "Process analysis" schema used in panel research. (Successive time intervals are indicated along abscissa. Letters indicate the variables under observation. Arrows represent relations between the variables. [From Berelson, Lazarsfeld, & McPhee, 1954]

Bottom half: Design of experimental research. (Letters on vertical axis again indicate variables being measured. Unshaded box indicates experimentally manipulated treatment and blank absence of such treatment. Time periods indicated as in top half of chart.)

"panel" method, stresses the large number of simultaneous and interacting influences affecting attitudes and opinions. Even more significant is its provision for a variety of "feedback" phenomena in which consequences wrought by previous influences affect processes normally considered as occurring earlier in the sequence. The various types of interaction are indicated by the placement of arrows showing direction of effect. In contrast the experimentalist frequently tends to view the communication process as one in which some single manipulative variable is the primary determinant of the subsequent attitude change. He is, of course, aware in a general way of the importance of context, and he frequently studies interaction effects as well as main effects; but he still is less attentive than he might be to the complexity of the influence situation and the numerous possibilities for feedback loops. Undoubtedly the real life communication situation is better described in terms of the survey type of model. We are all familiar, for example, with the interactions in which attitudes predispose one to acquire certain

types of information, that this often leads to changes in attitude which may result in further acquisition of knowledge, which in turn produces more attitude change, and so on. Certainly the narrow question sometimes posed by experiments as to the effect of knowledge on attitudes greatly underestimates these interactive effects.

But while the conceptualization of the survey researcher is often very valuable, his correlational research design leaves much to be desired. Advocates of correlational analysis often cite the example of a science built on observation exclusively without experiment: astronomy. But here a very limited number of space-time concepts are involved and the number of competing theoretical formulations is relatively small so that it is possible to limit alternative theories rather drastically through correlational evidence. But in the area of communication effects and social psychology generally the variables are so numerous and so intertwined that the correlational methodology is primarily useful to suggest hypotheses and not to establish casual relationships (Hovland et al., 1949, pp. 329–340; Maccoby, 1956). Even with the much simpler relationships involved in biological systems there are grave difficulties of which we are all aware these days when we realize how difficult it is to establish through correlation whether eating of fats is or is not a cause of heart disease or whether or not smoking is a cause of lung cancer. In communications research the complexity of the problem makes it inherently difficult to derive causal relationships from correlational analysis where experimental control of exposure is not possible. And I do not agree with my friends the Lazarsfelds (Kendall & Lazarsfeld, 1950) concerning the effectiveness of the panel method in circumventing this problem since parallel difficulties are raised when the relationships occur over a time span.

These difficulties constitute a challenge to the experimentalist in this area of research to utilize the broad framework for studying communication effects suggested by the survey researcher, but to employ well controlled experimental design to work on those aspects of the field which are amenable to experimental manipulation and control. It is, of course, apparent that there are important communication problems which cannot be attacked directly by experimental methods. It is not, for example, feasible to modify voting behavior by manipulation of the issues discussed by the opposed parties during a particular campaign. It is not feasible to assess the effects of communications over a very long span of time. For example, one cannot visualize experimental procedures for answering the question of what has been the impact of the reading of *Das Kapital* or *Uncle Tom's Cabin*. These are questions which can be illuminated by historical and sociological study but cannot be evaluated in any rigorous experimental fashion.

But the scope of problems which do lend themselves to experimental attack is very broad. Even complex interactions can be fruitfully attacked by experiment. The possibilities are clearly shown in studies like that of Sherif and Sherif (1953) on factors influencing cooperative and competitive behavior in a camp for adolescent boys. They were able to bring under manipulative control many of the types of interpersonal relationships ordinarily considered impossible to modify experimentally, and to develop motivations of an intensity characteristic of real-life situations. It should be possible to do similar studies in the communication area with a number of the variables heretofore only investigated in uncontrolled naturalistic settings by survey procedures.

In any case it appears eminently practical to minimize many of the differences which were discussed above as being not inherent in design but more or less adventitiously linked with one or the other method. Thus there is no reason why more complex and deeply-involving social issues cannot be employed in experiments rather than the more superficial ones more commonly used. The resistance to change of socially important issues may be a handicap in studying certain types of attitude change; but, on the other hand, it is important to understand the lack of modifiability of opinion with highly-involving issues. Greater representation of the diverse types of communicators found in naturalistic situations can also be achieved. In addition, it should be possible to do experiments with a wider range of populations to reduce the possibility that many of our present generalizations from experiments are unduly affected by their heavy weighting of college student characteristics, including high literacy, alertness, and rationality.

A more difficult task is that of experimentally evaluating communications under conditions of self-selection of exposure. But this is not at all impossible in theory. It should be possible to assess what demographic and personality factors predispose one to expose oneself to particular communications and then to utilize experimental and control groups having these characteristics. Under some circumstances the evaluation could be made on only those who select themselves, with both experimental and control groups coming from the self-selected audience.

Undoubtedly many of the types of experiments which could be set up involving or simulating naturalistic conditions will be too ambitious and costly to be feasible even if possible in principle. This suggests the continued use of small-scale experiments which seek to isolate some of the key variables operative in complex situations. From synthesis of component factors, prediction of complex outcomes may be practicable. It is to this analytic procedure for narrowing the gap between laboratory and field research that we have devoted major attention in our research program. I will merely indicate briefly here some of the ties between our past work and the present problem.

We have attempted to assess the influence of the communicator by varying his expertness and attractiveness, as in the studies by Kelman, Weiss, and the writer (Hovland & Weiss, 1951; Kelman & Hovland, 1953). Further data on this topic were presented earlier in this paper.

We have also been concerned with evaluating social interaction effects. Some of the experiments on group affiliation as a factor affecting resistance to counternorm communication and the role of salience of group membership by Harold Kelley and others are reported in *Communication and Persuasion* (Hovland et al., 1953).

Starting with the studies carried out during the war on orientation films by Art Lumsdaine, Fred Sheffield, and the writer (1949), we have had a strong interest in the duration of communication effects. Investigation of effects at various time intervals has helped to bridge the gap between assessment of immediate changes with those of longer duration like those involved in survey studies. More recent extensions of this work have indicated the close relationship between the credibility of the communicator and the extent of postcommunication increments, or "sleeper effects" (Hovland & Weiss, 1951; Kelman & Hovland, 1953).

The nature of individual differences in susceptibility to persuasion via communication has been the subject of a number of our recent studies. The generality of persuasibility has been investigated by Janis and collaborators and the development of persuasibility in children has been studied by Abelson and Lesser. A volume concerned with these audience factors to which Janis, Abelson, Lesser, Field, Rife, King, Cohen, Linton, Graham, and the writer have contributed will appear under the title *Personality and Persuasibility* (1959).

Lastly, there remains the question on how the nature of the issues used in the communication affects the extent of change in attitude. We have only made a small beginning on these problems. In the research reported in *Experiments on Mass Communication,* we showed that the magnitude of effects was directly related to the type of attitude involved: film communications had a significant effect on opinions related to straight-forward interpretations of policies and events, but had little or no effect on more deeply intrenched attitudes and motivations. Further work on the nature of issues is represented in the study by Sherif, Harvey, and the writer (1957) which was discussed above. There we found a marked contrast between susceptibility to influence and the amount of ego-involvement in the issue. But the whole concept of ego-involvement is a fuzzy one, and here is an excellent area for further work seeking to determine the theoretical factors involved in different types of issues.

With this brief survey of possible ways to bridge the gap between experiment and survey I must close. I should like to stress in summary the mutual importance of the two approaches to the problem of communication effectiveness. Neither is a royal road to wisdom, but each represents an important emphasis. The challenge of future work is one of fruitfully combining their virtues so that we may develop a social psychology of communication with the conceptual breadth provided by correlational study of process and with the rigorous but more delimited methodology of the experiment.

References

Berelson, B. R., Lazarsfeld, P. F., & McPhee, W. N. *Voting: A study of opinion formation in a presidential campaign.* Chicago: Univer. Chicago Press, 1954.

Cooper, Eunice, & Jahoda, Marie. The evasion of propaganda: How prejudiced people respond to antiprejudice propaganda. *J. Psychol.,* 1947, *23,* 15–25.

Doob, L. W. *Public opinion and propaganda.* New York: Holt, 1948.

French, J. R. P., Jr. A formal theory of social power. *Psychol. Rev.,* 1956, *63,* 181–194.

Goldberg, S. C. Three situational determinants of conformity to social norms. *J. abnorm. soc. Psychol.,* 1954, *49,* 325–329.

Gosnell, H. F. *Getting out the vote: An experiment in the stimulation of voting.* Chicago: Univer. Chicago Press, 1927.

Hovland, C. I. Effects of the mass media of communication. In G. Lindzey (Ed.), *Handbook of social psychology.* Vol. II. *Special fields and applications.* Cambridge, Mass.: Addison-Wesley, 1954. Pp. 1062–1103.

Hovland, C. I., Harvey. O. J., & Sherif, M. Assimilation and contrast effects in reactions to communication and attitude change. *J. abnorm. soc. Psychol.,* 1957, *55,* 244–252.

Hovland, C. I., Janis, I. L., & Kelley, H. H. *Communication and persuasion.* New Haven: Yale Univer. Press, 1953.

Hovland, C. I., Lumsdaine, A. A., & Sheffield, F. D. *Experiments on mass communication.* Princeton: Princeton Univer. Press, 1949.

Hovland, C. I., Mandell, W., Campbell, Enid H., Brock, T., Luchins, A. S., Cohen, A. R., McGuire, W. J., Janis, I. L., Feierabend, Rosalind L., & Anderson, N. H. *The order of presentation in persuasion.* New Haven: Yale Univer. Press, 1957.

Hovland, C. I., & Pritzker, H. A. Extent of opinion change as a function of amount of change advocated. *J. abnorm. soc. Psychol.,* 1957, *54,* 257–261.

Hovland, C. I., & Weiss, W. The influence of source credibility on communication effectiveness. *Publ. opin. Quart.,* 1951, *15,* 635–650.

Janis, I. L., Hovland, C. I., Field, P. B., Linton, Harriett, Graham, Elaine, Cohen, A. R., Rife, D., Abelson, R. P., Lesser, G. S., & King, B. T. *Personality and persuasibility.* New Haven: Yale Univer. Press, 1959.

Katz, E., & Lazarsfeld, P. F. *Personal influence,* Glencoe, Ill.: Free Press, 1955.

Kelman, H. C., & Hovland, C. I. "Reinstatement" of the communicator in delayed measurement of opinion change. *J. abnorm. soc. Psychol.,* 1953, *48,* 327–335.

Kendall, Patricia L., & Lazarsfeld, P. F. Problems of survey analysis. In R. K. Merton & P. F. Lazarsfeld (Eds.), *Continuities in social research: Studies in the scope and method of "The American Soldier."* Glencoe, Ill.: Free Press, 1950. Pp. 133–196.

Klapper, J. T. *The effects of mass media.* New York: Columbia Univer. Bureau of Applied Social Research, 1949. (Mimeo.)

Lazarsfeld, P. F., Berelson, B., & Gaudet, Hazel. *The people's choice*. New York: Duell, Sloan, & Pearce, 1944.

Lipset, S. M., Lazarsfeld, P. F., Barton, A. H., & Linz, J. The psychology of voting: An analysis of political behavior. In G. Lindzey (Ed.), *Handbook of social psychology*. Vol. II. *Special fields and applications*. Cambridge, Mass.: Addison-Wesley, 1954. Pp. 1124–1175.

Maccoby, Eleanor E. Pitfalls in the analysis of panel data: A research note on some technical aspects of voting. *Amer. J. Sociol.*, 1956, *59*, 359–362.

Riecken, H. W. (Chairman) Narrowing the gap between field studies and laboratory experiments in social psychology: A statement by the summer seminar. *Items Soc. Sci. Res. Council*, 1954, *8*, 37–42.

Sherif, M., & Sherif, Carolyn W. *Groups in harmony and tension: An integration of studies on intergroup relations*. New York: Harper, 1953.

Zimbardo, P. G. Involvement and communication discrepancy as determinants of opinion change. Unpublished doctoral dissertation, Yale University, 1959.

Not long ago, Henry Murray (1962), in an address entitled, "The Personality and Career of Satan," gibed at psychologists for undertaking Satan's task of shattering man's faith in his own potentialities:

Man is a computer, an animal, or an infant. His destiny is completely determined by genes, instincts, accidents, early conditioning and reinforcements, cultural and social forces. Love is a secondary drive based on hunger and oral sensations or a reaction formation to an innate underlying hate. . . . If we psychologists were all the time, consciously or unconsciously, intending out of malice to reduce the concept of human nature to its lowest common denominators . . . then we might have to admit that to this extent the Satanic spirit was alive within us [p. 53].

Isidor Chein (1962), too, sides with the humanist against the scientist in psychology.

among psychologists whose careers are devoted to the advancement of the science, the prevailing image of Man is that of an impotent reactor. . . . He is implicitly viewed as robot. . . .

The opening sentence of *Ethical Standards of Psychologists* is that, "the psychologist is committed to a belief in the dignity and worth of the individual human being." . . .

But what kind of dignity can we attribute to a robot [p. 3]?

The issue is not, however, whether the *findings* of social science do and should have an influence on how we run our lives and think about ourselves, an influence to a certain extent inevitable and, to some, desirable. The real issue is whether our social model of man—the model we use for running society—and our scientific model or models—the ones we use for

the obstinate audience: the influence process from the point of view of social communication[1]

raymond a. bauer
graduate school of business administration, harvard university

running our subjects—should be identical. That the general answer should be "No," I learned when working on my doctoral thesis (Bauer, 1952), which was a chronology of Soviet attempts to keep the social and scientific models of man in line with each other, for I became soberly aware then of the delicacy and complexity of the relationship of the social and the scientific models of man.

1. Revision of a paper read at Western Psychological Association, Santa Monica, California, April 1963. Reprinted from *American Psychologist*, 1964, Vol. 19, pp. 319–328. Copyright 1964 by the American Psychological Association, and reproduced by permission.

I shall here discuss the relationship of these two models in the area of social communication. I shall set up two stereotypes. First, the social model of communication: The model held by the general public, and by social scientists when they talk about advertising, and somebody else's propaganda, is one of the exploitation of man by man. It is a model of one-way influence: The communicator *does* something to the audience, while to the communicator is generally attributed considerable latitude and power to do what he pleases to the audience. This model is reflected—at its worst—in such popular phrases as "brainwashing," "hidden persuasion," and "subliminal advertising."

The second stereotype—the model which *ought* to be inferred from the data of research—is of communication as a transactional process in which two parties each expect to give and take from the deal approximately equitable values. This, although it *ought* to be the scientific model, is far from generally accepted as such, a state of affairs on which W. Phillips Davison (1959) makes the comment:

the communicator's audience is not a passive recipient—it cannot be regarded as a lump of clay to be molded by the master propagandist. Rather, the audience is made up of individuals who demand something from the communications to which they are exposed, and who select those that are likely to be useful to them. In other words, they must get something from the manipulator if he is to get something from them. A bargain is involved. Sometimes, it is true, the manipulator is able to lead his audience into a bad bargain by emphasizing one need at the expense of another or by representing a change in the significant environment as greater than it actually has been. But audiences, too, can drive a hard bargain. Many communicators who have been widely disregarded or misunderstood know that to their cost [p. 360].

Davison does not contend that all the exchanges are equitable, but that the inequities may be on either side. He only implies that neither the audience nor the communicator would enter into this exchange unless each party expected to "get his money's worth," at least most of the time. After all, Davison is not speaking as a social philosopher nor as an apologist for the industry, but as an experienced researcher trying to make sense out of the accumulated evidence.

Whether fortunately or unfortunately, social criticism has long been associated with the study of communication. The latter was largely stimulated by the succession of exposés of propaganda following World War I, particularly of the munitions-makers' lobby and of the extensive propaganda of the public utilities. There was also social concern over the new media, the movies and radio, and the increasingly monopolistic control of newspapers. Propaganda analysis, which is what research communication was called in those days, was occupied with three inquiries: the structure of the media (who owns and controls them, and what affects what gets into them); content analysis (what was said and printed); and propaganda techniques (which are the devil's devices to influence people). In this period, *effects* for the most part were not studied: They were taken for granted. Out of this tradition evolved Laswell's (Smith, Laswell, & Casey, 1946) formulation of the process of communication that is the most familiar one to this day: "Who says what, through what channels [media] of communication to whom [with] what . . . results [p. 121]." This apparently self-evident formulation has one monumental built-in assumption: that the initiative is exclusively with the communicator, the effects being exclusively on the audience.

While the stimulus and the model of research on communication were developing out of the analysis of propaganda, survey research, relatively independently, was evolving its technology in the commercial world of market research and audience and leadership measurement. As is well known, Crossley, Gallup, and Roper each tried their hands at predicting the 1936 presidential election and whipped the defending champion, the *Literary Digest*. By 1940, Lazarsfeld was ready to try out the new technology on the old model with a full-scale panel study of the effects of the mass media on voting in a national election, having tested his strategy in the New Jersey gubernatorial race in 1938.

The results of this study, again, are well known. Virtually nobody in the panel changed his intention, and most of the few who did so attributed it to personal influence (Lazarsfeld, Berelson, & Gaudet, 1948). The mass media had had their big chance—and struck out. Negative results had been reached before but none which had been demonstrated by such solid research. A number of equally dramatic failures to detect effects of campaigns carried on in the mass media followed, and by the end of the decade Hyman and Sheatsley (1947) were attempting to explain why. No one could take the effects of communication for granted.

As a matter of fact a considerable number of the sociologists studying communication grew discouraged with inquiring into the immediate effects of the mass media, and went looking for "opinion leaders," "influentials," the "web of influence," and so on. At the same time, a few here and there began doing something we now call "functional studies." They were curious to know how the audience was behaving.

In the meantime, at just about the time that the students of the effect of communication in a natural setting were beginning to wonder if communication ever had effects, experimental studies were burgeoning under essentially laboratory conditions. Experiments had been conducted before, but the tradition of experimenting on the effects of communication was vastly enhanced by the War Department's Information and Education Division, and after the war by Hovland and his associates at Yale (Hovland, Lumsdaine, & Sheffield, 1949). The Yale group's output, and that of colleagues and students of Kurt Lewin, account for a very high proportion of the experimental work on the subject in the past 2 decades.

The experimenters generally had no trouble conveying information or changing attitudes. Of course nobody stopped to record very explicitly the main finding of all the experiments: that communication, given a reasonably large audience, varies in its impact. It affects some one way, some in the opposite way, and some not at all. But nevertheless the experimenters got results.

By the end of the 'fifties it was quite clear that the two streams of investigation needed reconciling, and Carl Hovland (1959) did so. More recently, pursuing the same theme, I stated Hovland's major point as being that the audience exercises much more initiative outside the laboratory than it does in the experimental situation (Bauer, 1962). The audience selects what it will attend to. Since people generally listen to and read things they are interested in, these usually are topics on which they have a good deal of information and fixed opinions. Hence the very people most likely to attend to a message are those most difficult to change; those who can be converted do not look or listen. A variety of studies attribute to this circumstance alone: the fact that actual campaigns have often produced no measurable results, while quite marked effects could be produced in a laboratory.

Two favorite problems of the laboratory experimenters take on quite a different aspect when considered in a natural setting. One is the question of the order of presentation of arguments. Is it an advantage to have your argument stated first (the so-called law of primacy) or stated last (the so-called law of recency)? In a laboratory the answer is complex but it may be quite simple in a natural situation: He who presents his argument first may convert the audience and they in turn may exercise their oft-exercised prerogative of not listening to the opposing case. Hence to have the first word rather than the last could be decisive in the real world, but for a reason which may seem irrelevant to the relative merits of primacy versus recency.

Of course, another important variable is the credibility of the source. By creating an impression of the credibility of the stooge or experimenter in the laboratory, it is often possible to convert a person to a position far removed from his original one. But in real life, the audience usually does its own evaluation of sources, and at a certain point sometimes arrives at a result quite the opposite of that reached experimentally. If the audience is confronted with a communicator trying to convert it to a position opposed to its own, it is likely to see him as "biased," and the like, and come away further strengthened in its own convictions.

It was quite clear from Hovland's piece, and should have been even earlier, that the characteristic behavior of the audience in its natural habitat is such as to bring about crucial modifications of the results seen in the laboratory. In general, these modifications are strongly in the direction of suppressing effect.

In a sense, Joseph Klapper's 1960 book, *The Effects of Mass Communication*, marks the end of an era. Twenty years earlier, a social scientist would have taken effects for granted and specified the devices the propagandist employed to achieve them. But Klapper (1960) makes statements like these: "[my position] is in essence a shift *away* from the tendency to regard mass communication as a necessary and sufficient cause of audience effects, toward a view of the media as influences, working amid other influences, in a total situation [p. 5]." He sees communications as operating through mediating factors—group membership, selective exposure, defense mechanisms—"such that they typically render mass communication a contributory agent, but not the sole cause in a process of reinforcing the existing conditions. (Regardless of the condition in question ... the media are more likely to reinforce [it] than to change) [p. 8]." Change takes place, according to Klapper, in those rare circumstances when mediating forces are inoperative, when they are occasionally mobilized to facilitate change, or in certain residual situations. He reviews the literature on the effect of variation in content, mode of presentation, media, and so on, but rather than taking effects for granted, he searches for the exceptional case in which the mass media change rather than fortify and entrench.

Klapper recommends what he calls the "phenomenalistic" and others have called the functional approach. The study of communication has traditionally (although not exclusively) been conducted from the point of view of the *effects intended by the communicator*. From this perspective, the disparity between actual and intended results has often been puzzling. The answer has come increasingly to be seen in entering the phenomenal world of the audience and studying the functions which communication serves. The failure in research to this point has been that the audience has not been given full status in the exchange: The intentions of its members have not been given the same attention as those of the communicator.

Some will argue that these generalizations do not hold true of advertising. They do. But until now no one has undertaken to match the effects of communication in various areas according to comparable criteria and against realistic expectation.

Actually much more is expected of the campaigns with which academic psychologists are associated than is expected of commercial promotion. For example, a paper on governmental informational campaigns concluded with these words (Seidenfeld, 1961): "while people are willing to walk into a drugstore and buy low calorie preparations and contraceptives, they are not very anxious to take shots for protection against polio or attend a clinic dealing with sexual hygiene." By the author's own figures, 60% of the public had had one or more polio shots and 25% had had the full course of four. According to his expectations, and probably ours, these were hardly satisfactory accomplishments.

Yet, what about the highly advertised product, low in calories, with which he was comparing polio inoculations? Presumably he had heard that it was a smashing commercial success, or had seen some dollar volume figure on gross sales. Actually, it was being bought by 4% of the market—and 60% and even 25% are larger figures than 4%. Our unacknowledged expectations must be reckoned with.

These differences in expectation and criteria produce much confusion, usually on the side of con-

vincing people that commercial campaigns are more successful than others. Yet, consistently successful commercial promotions convert only a very small percentage of people to action. No one cigarette now commands more than 14% of the cigarette market, but an increase of 1% is worth $60,000,000 in sales. This means influencing possibly .5% of all adults, and 1% of cigarette smokers. This also means that a successful commercial campaign can alienate many more than it wins, and still be highly profitable.

Equally misleading is the frequent reference to percentage increase on some small base. This device has been a particular favorite of both the promoters and the critics of motivation research: One party does it to sell its services, the other purportedly to warn the public; both exaggerate the effect. Thus, for example, the boast, "a 300% increase in market share," means that the product increased; but it may easily be from 1% of the market to 3%. Or we may have a 500% gain in preference for "the new package" over the old one. That there is that much consensus in the esthetic judgment of the American public is a matter of interest, but it tells nothing about the magnitude of consequences on any criterion in which we are interested. I have made some computations on the famous Kate Smith war-bond marathon, which elicited $39 million in pledges. Kate Smith moved apparently a maximum of 4% of her audience to pledge to buy bonds; the more realistic figure may be 2%! In the commercial world this is a rather small effect as judged by some expectations, but yet an effect which often adds up to millions of dollars.

But commercial promotions often do not pay their way. The word is currently being circulated that a mammoth corporation and a mammoth advertising agency have completed a well-designed experiment that proves the corporation has apparently wasted millions of dollars on promoting its corporate image. Some studies have shown that an increase in expenditures for advertising has, under controlled experimental conditions, produced a decrease in sales.

The truth is now out: that our social model of the process of communication is morally asymmetrical; it is concerned almost exclusively with inequities to the advantage of the initiators, the manipulators. From the social point of view this may be all to the good. The answer to the question whether our social and scientific models should be identical is that there is no reason why we should be equally concerned with inequities in either direction; most of us consider it more important to protect the weak from the powerful, than vice versa. However, no matter how firmly committed to a morally asymmetrical social model, investigators should note that inequities fall in either direction and in unknown proportions.

The combination of this asymmetry and the varying expectations and criteria mentioned earlier fortifies the model of a one-way exploitative process of communication. And it is probably further reinforced by the experimental design in which the subject is seen as *re*acting to conditions established by the experimenter. We forget the cartoon in which one rat says to another: "Boy, have I got this guy trained! Every time I push this bar he gives me a pellet of food." We all, it seems, believe that *we* train the *rats*. And while the meaning of "initiative" in an experimental situation may be semantically complicated, the experimenter is usually seen there as *acting* and the subjects as *reacting*. At the very least and to all appearances, the experimental design tends to entrench the model of influence flowing in one direction.

The tide is, in fact, turning, although as a matter of fact, it is difficult to say whether the final granting of initiative to the audience, which seems to be imminent, is a "turn" or a logical extension of the research work of the past 25 or 30 years. Obviously Davison and Klapper and others, such as the Rileys, Dexter and White, Charles Wright, and Talcott Parsons, regard their position as the logical conclusion of what has gone before rather than a drastic inversion. So-called "functional" studies are increasing in volume, and appear now to be a matter of principle. In any event, Dexter and White (1964), the editors of a reader whose title is *People, Society and Mass Communications*, are firmly committed to this point of view and have organized the book upon it.

Traditionally, the name "functional studies" has been applied to any work concerned with a range of consequences wider than or different from those intended by the communicator. Two early classics, both done in the 'forties, are studies of listening to daytime radio serials: one by Herta Herzog (1944), and the other by Warner and Henry (1948). They established that women used the radio serials as models for their behavior in real life. In the late 'forties, Berelson (1949) studied how people reacted to not having newspapers during a strike, work which Kimball (1959) replicated in the newspaper strike of 1948. The variety of func-

tions the newspapers proved to serve is amazing, including the furnishing of raw material for conversation. "The radio is no substitute for the newspaper. I like to make intelligent conversation [Kimball, 1959, p. 395]." There was also research on the adult following of comics (Bogart, 1955), children's use of TV (Maccoby, 1954), and the reading of *Mad* magazine (Winick, 1962).

From a cursory glimpse, one concludes that early functional studies suffered from a tendency to focus on the deviant. Or, put another way, functional or motivational analysis (motivation research can be regarded as a subdivision of functional analysis) was ordinarily evoked only when the stereotyped model of economic rational man broke down. The findings advanced scientific knowledge but did little to improve the image of man in the eyes of those committed to a narrow concept of economic rationality. We may well argue that the social scientists' model of man is in reality broader, more scientifically based, and even more compassionate; but the public may not think so.

Thus, the early functional studies added to knowledge of the process of communication by including effects intended by the audience. There is a question, however, as to what they did to the social model of the process. Certainly the work of motivation research was written up in such a way as to confirm the exploitative model. But more recent functional studies focus on ordinary aspects of communication, and present the audience in a more common, prosaic, and, therefore, more sensible light.

Meanwhile, new trends have been developing in psychological research on communication. Until about a decade ago, the failure of experimental subjects to change their opinions was regarded as a residual phenomenon. Little systematic or sympathetic attention was paid to the persistence of opinion. The considerable volume of recent research using what the Maccobys (Maccoby & Maccoby, 1961) call a homeostatic model is dominated by theories based on the psychology of cognition, Heider's balance theory, Festinger's dissonance theory, Osgood and Tannenbaum's congruity theory, and Newcomb's strain for symmetry. While the proponents of each theory insist on adequate grounds on their distinctiveness, all agree that man acts so as to restore equilibrium in his system of belief. In any event, homeostatic studies do finally accord some initiative to the audience. Specifically, they reveal individuals as deliberately seeking out information on persons either to reinforce shaken convictions or consolidate those recently acquired. Festinger, for example, is interested in the reduction of dissonance following upon decisions—which means he views people as reacting to their own actions as well as to the actions of others. This influx of new ideas and new research is a valuable and welcome addition to both the theory and practice of social communication.

Restoring cognitive equilibrium is, however, only one of the tasks for which man seeks and uses information. Furthermore, the homeostatic theories, while according initiative to the audience, make it peculiarly defensive. They do little to counteract the notion of a one-way flow of influence—although it must be conceded that a scientific model is under no moral obligation to correct the defects, if any, of the social model.

Much is gained by looking upon the behavior of the audience as full-blown problem solving. Such a viewpoint requires the assumption that people have more problems to solve than simply relating to other people and reducing their psychic tension, among them being the allocation and conservation of resources.

The mass media have long been criticized because they facilitate escape from the responsibilities of the real world. But Katz and Foulkes (1962) point out that if man is to cope adequately with his environment, he must on occasion retreat to gather strength. Hence, escape per se is not a bad thing: It is socially approved to say, "Be quiet! Daddy is sleeping," although not yet approved to say, "Be quiet! Daddy is drinking." They take a generally irresponsibly handled problem of social criticism and convert it into one of the allocation and conservation of resources. It would take close calculation to decide whether an hour spent drinking beer in front of the TV set would, for a given individual, result in a net increase or decrease in his coping effectively with the environment. Yet, while the data they require are manifestly unattainable, their very way of posing the problem raises the level of discourse.

The necessity for taking explicit cognizance of the audience's intention was forced on us when we were studying Soviet refugees. We knew that virtually every Soviet citizen was regularly exposed to meetings at which were conveyed a certain amount of news, the party line on various issues, and general political agitation and indoctrination. In free discussion our respondents complained endlessly of the meetings so we knew they were there. But when we asked them, "From what sources did you draw most of your infor-

mation about what was happening?" only 19% specified them, in contrast to 87% citing newspapers, 50% citing radio, and another 50% word of mouth (Inkeles & Bauer, 1959, p. 163). Gradually the obvious dawned on us; our respondents were telling us where they learned what *they* wanted to know, not where they learned what the regime wanted them to know.

A similar perplexity arose with respect to the use of word-of-mouth sources of information. It was the least anti-Soviet of our respondents who claimed to make most use of this unofficial fountain of information. Rereading the interviews, and further analysis, unraveled the puzzle. It was the people most involved in the regime, at least in the upper social groups, who were using word-of-mouth sources the better to understand the official media, and the better to do their jobs (Inkeles and Bauer, 1959, p. 161)! As a result we had to conduct analysis on two levels, one where we took into account the intentions of the regime, the other, the intentions of the citizen. Thus, viewed from the vantage point of the regime's intention, the widespread dependence upon word of mouth was a failure in communication. From the point of view of the citizen and what he wanted, his own behavior made eminent sense.

At the next stage, we benefited from the looseness of our methods, the importance of the people we were studying, and from highly imaginative colleagues from other disciplines. We were studying the processes of decision, communication, and the like, in the business and political community. As we studied "influence" by wandering around and getting acquainted with the parties of both camps, and kept track of what was going on, the notion of a one-way flow became preposterous. A Congressman, for example, would snort: "Hell, pressure groups? I have to roust 'em off their fat rears to get them to come up here." It also became clear that men in influential positions did a great deal to determine what sort of communication was directed toward them (Bauer, Pool, & Dexter, 1963). At this juncture, Ithiel de Sola Pool crystallized the proposition that the audience in effect influences the communicator by the role it forces on him. This idea became the organizing hypothesis behind the Zimmerman and Bauer (1956—this experiment was replicated by Schramm & Danielson) demonstration that individuals process new information as a function of their perceived relationship to future audiences. Specifically, they are less likely to remember information that would conflict with the audience's views than they are to remember information to which the audience would be hospitable.

The final crystallization of my present views began several years ago when a decision theorist and I together reviewed the studies by motivation researchers of the marketing of ethical drugs to doctors. Surprisingly, I found the level of motivation discussed in these reports quite trivial, but the reports provided perceptive cognitive maps of the physician's world and the way he went about handling risk. The now well-known studies of the adoption of drugs by Coleman, Menzel, and Katz (1959) contributed data consistent with the following point: Physicians become increasingly selective in their choice of information as risk increases either because of the newness of the drug or difficulty in assessing its effects. Thereupon, a group of Harvard Business School students (in an unpublished manuscript) established by a questionnaire survey that as the seriousness of the disease increased, physicians were increasingly likely to prefer professional to commercial sources of information.

Parenthetically with respect to the Coleman, Menzel, and Katz (1959) studies whose data I said are "consistent with" the notion of risk handling: I am convinced that this way of thinking is wholly compatible to the authors. Yet their presentation is sufficiently dominated by the prevailing view of "social influence" as a matter of personal compliance that one cannot be entirely sure just where they do stand.

Why doesn't the physician always prefer professional to commercial sources of information? The physician is a busy man whose scarcest resources are time and energy, two things which commercial sources of information, on the whole, seem to help him conserve. Even so, he is selective. Let us assume two components in the choice of source of information: social compliance and the reduction of risk. Consider, then, that the doctor may be influenced by his liking either for the drug company's salesman who visits his office, or for the company itself. We may assume that, of these two components of influence, social compliance will be more associated with his sentiments toward the salesman and risk reduction with the company's reputation.

In a study conducted with the Schering Corporation (Bauer, 1961), I found that in the case of relatively riskless drugs, the correlation of preference for drugs with preference for salesman and for company was about equal. However, with more hazardous drugs—and with large numbers of subjects—preference for the company carried twice the weight of preference for the salesmen: The physicians selected the source closest associated with reduction of risk.

In the latest and fullest development of this point of view, Cox (1962) asked approximately 300 middle-class housewives to evaluate the relative merits of "two brands" of nylon stockings (Brand N & Brand R) as to over-all merits and as to each of 18 attributes. After each rating the subject was asked to indicate how confident she was in making it. The subjects then listened to a tape-recorded interview with a supposed salesgirl who stated that Brand R was better as to 6 attributes, whereupon they were asked to judge the stockings again and to evaluate the salesgirl and their confidence in rating her. Finally, they completed a questionnaire which included three batteries of questions on personality, one of which was a measure of self-confidence.

The findings of interest here bear upon personality and persuasibility. Male subjects low in generalized self-confidence are generally the more persuasible. Females are more persuasible in general but on the whole this is not correlated with self-confidence or self-esteem.

The reigning hypotheses on the relationship of self-confidence to persuasibility have been based either on the concept of ego defense (Cohen, 1959) or social approval (Janis, 1954), and Cox chose to add *perceived self-confidence in accomplishing a task*. He was dealing, then, with two measures of self-confidence: generalized self-confidence, presumably an attribute of "personality"; and specific self-confidence, that is, perceived confidence in judging stockings.

It has been suggested that the reason that in women personality has not been found correlated with persuasibility is that the issues used in experiments have not been important to them. And importance may account for the strong relationship Cox found when he gave them the task of rating stockings. That he was testing middle-class housewives may be why the relationship was curvilinear. (That is to say, his subjects may have covered a wider range of self-confidence than might be found in the usual experimental groups.) Women with *medium* scores on the test of self-confidence were the most likely to alter their rating of the stockings in the direction recommended by the salesgirl; those scoring *either* high or low were less likely to accept her suggestion. As a matter of fact, counter-suggestibility apparently crept in among the women low in self-confidence; those who rated lowest were almost three times as likely as the others to change in the *opposite* direction. Since these findings were replicated in three independent samples, ranging from 62 to 144 subjects, there is little reason to question them for this type of person and situation. The differences were both significant and big.

The curvilinear relationship was not anticipated and any explanation must, of course, be ad hoc. One might be that, faced with the difficult task of judging between two identical stockings and the salesgirl's flat assertion that one was better than the other, the women tacitly had to ask themselves two questions: Do I need help? Am I secure enough to accept help? Accordingly, the subjects most likely to accept the salesgirl's suggestion would be those with little enough self-confidence to want help, but still with enough to accept it. As an explanation, this is at least consistent with the curvilinear data and with the apparent countersuggestibility of the subjects with little self-confidence.

This explanation, however, should not apply to individuals confident of their ability to perform the task. And this turned out to be the case. Among the subjects confident they could perform the *specific* task, generalized self-confidence played little or no role. The usual notions of social compliance and ego defense were virtually entirely overridden by the subject's confidence in her handling of the task—a conclusion which is supported, no matter how the data are combined.

My intention in telling this is to present a promising experiment in regarding the audience as being involved in problem solving. As already suggested theories of social communication are caught between two contrasting models of human behavior. One we may call the "influence" model: One person does something to another. We have partially escaped from the simplest version of it, and now regard the audience as influenced only in part, and in the other part solving problems of ego defense or of interpersonal relations. Meanwhile, there is the always endemic model of economic rationality which in one or another of its forms sees man as maximizing some tangible value. This latter, very simple problem-solving model we spontaneously use when we *judge* behavior, particularly with respect to whether it is rational or sensible or dignified. Thus ironically, we use the influence model, or the modified influence model, to explain why people do what they do, but we use the economist's problem-solving model for evaluating the behavior. There is scarcely a surer way of making people look foolish!

There is no reason why the two models should not be seen as complementary rather than antagonistic. But the fusion has not taken place to any conspicuous degree in the mainstream of research, as can be seen most clearly in literature on informal communication and personal influence. There are two major traditions from which this literature has developed (Rogers, 1962): One, that of the heartland of social communication, stresses social compliance and/or social conformity. The other tradition, that of rural sociology, is concerned with how farmers acquire knowledge useful in their day-to-day problems. While the two have in certain respects become intermeshed after some decades of isolation, overtones of social compliance and conformity persist in the social-psychological literature. There is little reference to problem solving.

The students of one of my colleagues who had read a standard treatment of the role of reference groups in buying behavior discussed it entirely without reference to the fact that the consumers might want to eat the food they bought!

The virtue of Cox's data is that they enable us to relate the problem-solving dimensions of behavior to social relationships and ego defense. It is interesting that—in this study—the more "psychological" processes come into play only at the point at which felt self-confidence in accomplishing the task falls below a critical point. Thus, tendency to accept the suggestions of the alleged salesgirl in Cox's experiment must be seen as a function of both ability to deal with the task and personality.

The difficulty of the task may either fortify or suppress the more "social-psychological" processes, depending on the specific circumstances. Thus, study of drug preference shows that as the task gets easier, the individual can indulge in the luxury of concurring with someone whom he likes, whereas when risk is great he has to concentrate on the risk-reducing potentialities of the source of information.

Thus the full-blown, problem-solving interpretation of the behavior of an audience in no sense rules out the problems with which students of communication have recently concerned themselves: ego defense and social adjustment. As a matter of fact, such problems seem explorable in a more profitable fashion if, simultaneously, attention is paid to the more overt tasks for which people use information. Yet, while there has been a consistent drift toward granting the audience more initiative, it cannot be said that the general literature on communication yet accords it a full range of intentions.

Of course, the audience is not wholly a free agent: It must select from what is offered. But even here, the audience has influence, since it is generally offered an array of communications to which it is believed it will be receptive. The process of social communication and of the flow of influence in general must be regarded as a transaction. "Transactionism," which has had a variety of meanings in psychology, is used here in the sense of an exchange of values between two or more parties; each gives in order to get.

The argument for using the transactional model for *scientific* purposes is that it opens the door more fully to exploring the intention and behavior of members of the audience and encourages inquiry into the influence of the audience on the communicator by specifically treating the process as a two-way passage. In addition to the influence of the audience on the communicator, there seems little doubt that influence also operates in the "reverse" direction. But the persistence of the one-way model of influence discourages the investigation of both directions of relationship. With amusing adroitness some writers have assimilated the original experiment of Zimmerman and Bauer to established concepts such as reference groups, thereby ignoring what we thought was the clear implication of a two-way flow of influence.

At our present state of knowledge there is much to be said for the transactional model's pragmatic effect on research, but at the same time it is the most plausible description of the process of communication as we know it. Yet there seems to be a tendency to assume that words such as "transaction," "reciprocity," and the like imply exact equality in each exchange, measured out precisely according to the value system and judgment of the observer. This is nonsense. Obviously there are inequities, and they will persist, whether we use our own value systems as observers or if we have perfect knowledge of the people we observe.

The rough balance of exchange is sufficiently equitable in the long run to keep *most* individuals in our society engaged in the transactional relations of communication and influence. But some "alienated" people absent themselves from the network of communication as do, also, many businessmen who have doubts about the money they spend on advertising. The alienation is by no means peculiar to one end of the chain of communication or influence.

This point of view may be taken as a defense of certain social institutions such as advertising and the mass media. There is a limited range of charges against which *impotence* may indeed be considered a defense. Once more, ironically, both the communicator and the critic have a vested interest in the exploitative model. From the point of view of the communicator, it is reassuring that he will receive *at least* a fair return for his efforts; to the critic, the exploitative model gratifies the sense of moral indignation.

References

Bauer, R. A. *The new man in Soviet psychology.* Cambridge: Harvard Univer. Press, 1952.

Bauer, R. A. Risk handling in drug adoption: The role of company preference. *Publ. Opin. Quart.,* 1961, 25, 546–559.

Bauer, R. A. The initiative of the audience. Paper read at New England Psychological Association, Boston, November, 1962.

Bauer, R. A., Pool, I. de Sola, & Dexter, L. A. *American business and public policy.* New York: Atherton Press, 1963.

Berelson, B., What missing the newspaper means. In P. F. Lazarsfeld & F. N. Stanton (Eds.), *Communications research,* 1948–1949. New York: Harper, 1949. Pp. 111–129.

Bogart, L. Adult talk about newspaper comics. *Amer. J. Sociol.,* 1955, 61, 26–30.

Chein, I. The image of man. *J. soc. Issues,* 1962, 18, 36–54.

Cohen, A. R. Some implications of self-esteem for social influence. In C. I. Hovland & I. L. Janis (Eds.), *Personality and persuasibility.* New Haven: Yale Univer. Press, 1959. Pp. 102–120.

Coleman, J., Menzel, H., & Katz, E. Social processes in physicians' adoption of a new drug. *J. chron. Dis.,* 1959, 9, 1–19.

Cox, D. F. Information and uncertainty: Their effects on consumers' product evaluations. Unpublished doctoral dissertation, Harvard University, Graduate School of Business Administration, 1962.

Davison, W. P. On the effects of communication. *Publ. Opin. Quart.,* 1959, 23, 343–360.

Dexter, L. A., & White, D. M. (Eds.), *People, society and mass communications.* Glencoe, Ill.: Free Press, 1964.

Herzog, Herta. What do we really know about daytime serial listeners? In P. F. Lazarsfeld & F. N. Stanton (Eds.), *Radio research, 1942–1943.* New York: Duell, Sloan & Pearce, 1944. Pp. 3–33.

Hovland, C. I. Reconciling conflicting results derived from experimental survey studies of attitude change. *Amer. Psychologist,* 1959, *14*, 8–17.

Hovland, C. I., Lumsdaine, A. A., & Sheffield, F. D. *Experiments in mass communication.* Princeton: Princeton Univer. Press, 1949.

Hyman, H. H., & Sheatsley, P. B. Some reasons why information campaigns fail. *Publ. Opin. Quart.,* 1947, *11*, 412–423.

Inkeles, A., & Bauer, R. A. *The Soviet citizen.* Cambridge: Harvard Univer. Press, 1959.

Janis, I. L. Personality correlates of susceptibility to persuasion. *J. Pers.,* 1954, *22*, 504–518.

Katz, E., & Foulkes, D. On the use of the mass media for "escape." *Publ. Opin. Quart.,* 1962, *26*, 377–388.

Kimball, P. People without papers. *Publ. Opin. Quart.,* 1959, *23*, 389–398.

Klapper, J. *The effects of mass communication.* Glencoe, Ill.: Free Press, 1960.

Lazarsfeld, P. F., Berelson, B., & Gaudet, Hazel. *The people's choice.* New York: Columbia Univer. Press, 1948.

Maccoby, Eleanor E. Why do children watch T.V.? *Publ. Opin. Quart.,* 1954, *18*, 239–244.

Maccoby, N., & Maccoby, Eleanor E. Homeostatic theory in attitude change. *Pub. Opin. Quart.,* 1961, *25*, 535–545.

Murray, H. A. The personality and career of Satan. *J. soc. Issues,* 1962, *18*, 1–35.

Rogers, E. M. *Diffusion of innovations.* Glencoe, Ill.: Free Press, 1962.

Seidenfeld, M. A. Consumer psychology in public service and government. In R. W. Seaton (Chm.), Consumer psychology: The growth of a movement. Symposium presented at American Psychological Association, New York, September 1961.

Smith, B. L., Laswell, H. D., & Casey, R. D. *Propaganda, communication and public opinion.* Princeton: Princeton Univer. Press, 1946.

Warner, W. L., & Henry, W. E. The radio daytime serial: A symbolic analysis. *Genet. Psychol. Monogr.,* 1948, *37*, 3–71.

Winick, C. Teenagers, satire and *Mad. Merrill-Palmer Quart.,* 1962, *8*, 183–203.

Zimmerman, Claire, & Bauer, R. A. The effects of an audience on what is remembered. *Publ. Opin. Quart.,* 1956, *20*, 238–248.

What possible connection might there be between the pristine beauty of the memory drum and the rough and tumble world of juvenile delinquency? I shall attempt to show that these seemingly different worlds can be bridged, and that this is possible in terms of concepts related to modeling and observational learning. In the process of doing this, I shall describe an ongoing investigation of psychological variables which bear upon the problem of the prevention and control of juvenile delinquency. The subjects of the investigation are institutionalized delinquents. The basic hypothesis underlying the investigation is that systematic exposure to meaningful identification models can have a discernible and salutary influence in modifying the behavior of the acting-out teen-ager.

The significance of this topic is obvious. Few social problems rival juvenile delinquency as a source of concern and urgency. The general public has called stridently—at times, even with terror—for the development of procedures for the control of crime and delinquency and for the prevention of recidivism. Professional workers often become dismayed at the apparent failure of extant and traditional cognitively oriented "talking therapy" to modify the undesirabe behavior of juvenile and adult criminals.

The research which I shall describe is an outgrowth of social learning theory and research dealing with the process of observational learning. Sociological and clinical evidence relating to the behavior of crime and delinquency have also influenced its development. My present work with delinquents is a cognitively complex

verbal learning, modeling, and juvenile delinquency [1]

irwin g. sarason
university of washington

1. This paper is based on talks given since June 1967. The research which it reports has been supported by grants from the Department of Health, Education and Welfare's Social and Rehabilitation Service, the National Science Foundation, and the National Institute of Mental Health. Victor J. Ganzer and I have worked closely on every phase of this research. I am indebted to Ganzer for reviewing this manuscript and providing several helpful suggestions. Robert Tropp, Supervisor of Institutional Services, and William Callahan, Superintendent of Cascadia Juvenile Reception-Diagnostic Center, have contributed to the conduct of the research described in this paper. The following assistants have contributed importantly to this research: David Barrett, Peter Carlson, Duane Dahlum, Richard Erickson, Robert Howenstine, Robert Kirk, David Snow. Reprinted from *American Psychologist*, 1968, Vol. 23, pp. 254–266. Copyright 1968 by the American Psychological Association, and reproduced by permission.

product and sibling (believe it or not!) of another, and more venerable, ongoing research interest in the relationship of anxiety and the observation of models to learning and performance. In order to present a realistic account, not only of the series of delinquency experiments, but of their genesis as well, I shall begin by tracing the relationship between the research on anxiety and modeling, using college students as subjects, and the study of juvenile delinquents from an observational learning point of view. After laying the groundwork for applying the concept of modeling to an effort at modifying the behavior of juvenile delinquents, I shall describe the methods and results of two studies which have already been completed. Finally, I shall briefly outline the goals and methods of our presently ongoing major study.

Test Anxiety, the Observation of Models, and Verbal Learning

Over the past 15 years, considerable research has been carried out which relates to an interfering response interpretation of one type of anxiety, test anxiety. Test anxiety may be viewed as an inferred class of internal responses consisting of self-oriented thoughts and emotional reactions. This form of anxiety may be conceptualized as a specific situationally relevant aspect of the general construct of anxiety. The highly test-anxious individual is one who is especially prone to become preoccupied with himself, his inadequacies, and the impression he makes on others. These preoccupations may be viewed as interfering with many ongoing activities, such as intellectual performance, concerning which he might be evaluated. These are some of the items which comprise the 37-item Test Anxiety Scale:

(T) While taking an important exam I find myself thinking of how much brighter the other students are than I am.

(T) As soon as an exam is over, I try to stop worrying about it, but I just can't.

(F) If I knew I was going to take an intelligence test, I would feel confident and relaxed beforehand.

(F) I really don't see why some people get so upset about tests.

(T) During tests, I find myself thinking of the consequences of failing.

(T) After important tests I am frequently so tense that my stomach gets upset.

(T) I start feeling very uneasy just before getting a test paper back.

(F) When taking a test, my emotional feelings do not interfere with my performance.

The highly test-anxious person can be operationally defined as one who admits to tension, worry, and feeling upset before, during, and after taking tests. He appears to be excessively fearful of failure. While virtually all people are challenged and made anxious by the possibility of being evaluated by others, he seems not to have developed an adequate repertory of coping responses appropriate for use in testing situations, and often remains at the level of rumination and fear.

While all aspects of this construct of test anxiety have not been explored and verified, considerable support for it does exist. Relevant evidence includes the following: (a) Under personally threatening or highly motivating test-oriented conditions (for example, ego-involving instructions, "You are now going to take an intelligence test") high test-anxious scorers tend to perform at a lower level than do low test-anxious scorers. (b) Differences due to test anxiety under high motivational conditions seem to be greatest on difficult or complex tasks. (c) Under neutral conditions (for example, preperformance instructions which do not emphasize the evaluation of subjects' performance) differences among persons varying in scores on test-anxiety questionnaires tend to be small or nonexistent. However, some studies involving performance on highly complex tasks have found low-anxious subjects to be generally superior to high-anxious subjects. (d) When low-anxious scorers have been found to be superior to high-anxious scorers in verbal learning experiments, it has also been found that the latter are much more resistant than the former to making guesses early in performance.

Illustrative of the relationship of test anxiety and orienting instructions to performance are the following findings of two verbal learning experiments using difficult stimulus materials. Table 1 shows the number of correct responses by blocks for high and low test-anxiety scorers under an instructional condition which emphasized that subjects' performance would be evaluated and would provide indices of their intelligence. As the table shows, the low are consistently superior to the high test-anxious scorers.

Table 2 shows the performance of high and low test-anxiety groups under neutral and reassurance conditions. Under the latter condition subjects are told that the task on which they are to perform is extremely

TABLE 1

Experiment I: Mean Number of Correct Responses for Trial Blocks (Five Trials per Block) for High and Low Test Anxiety Scale (TAS) Subjects under High Motivating Conditions

Group	Trial blocks					
	N	1	2	3	4	5
High TAS	32	3.3	15.7	28.3	42.0	52.0
Low TAS	32	6.0	21.7	34.7	49.8	62.0

difficult, and that they should not worry about the many errors which they will make. Table 2 shows that under the neutral condition the two anxiety groups performed quite similarly. Under reassurance, the superiority of the high to the low test-anxious group is sizable and significant.

TABLE 2

Experiment II: Mean Number of Correct Responses for Trial Blocks (Five Trials per Block) for High and Low Test Anxiety Scale (TAS) Subjects under Neutral and Reassurance Conditions

Group	Trial blocks					
	N	1	2	3	4	5
High TAS-neutral	10	11.0	27.7	45.5	56.6	69.9
High TAS-reassurance	10	8.3	22.0	35.9	47.0	63.4
Low TAS-reassurance	10	6.6	17.1	24.3	35.7	45.8

It appears to me that available results suggest that scores on test anxiety scales do reflect the tendency of individuals to show disruption in performance when the testing and evaluative aspects of situations are emphasized. I have suggested that highly anxious people are particularly sensitive to cues which have evaluative connotations. It seems possible also that highly anxious persons strive especially strongly for environmental cues which might assist them in their problem solving.

This cue-seeking behavior of highly anxious persons has been studied in verbal conditioning experiments in which subjects are asked simply to describe themselves. These studies have shown that high test-anxious scorers tend to describe themselves in

more negative terms than do low-anxious scorers. This finding is, of course, not especially surprising. What is particularly relevant for our present concern is that high test-anxious persons seem to show a stronger response to reinforcement (for example, "mm-hm") than do low test-anxious scorers. That is, their frequency of emission of response classes increases at a greater rate as a function of reinforcement than is true for low-anxious subjects. This response is even stronger if subjects are told that their self-descriptions are part of an evaluative psychiatric interview. The role of reinforcement has been studied in verbal learning experiments, and their results suggest also that the performance of high-anxious subjects is more strongly and favorably influenced by experimenters' utterances of "good" than is the performance of low-anxious scorers.

Tying together the results of experiments on performance in verbal learning situations and on self-description in a free verbalization setting, it would seem that high test-anxious subjects are adversely affected by evaluative stress. However, at least under certain circumstances, their strong cue-seeking needs may contribute to increased vigilance with regard to possibly helpful elements in the environment. If this interpretation is correct, it would appear that research on anxiety, verbal learning, and intellectual performance have emphasized only part of the anxiety story. We know quite a bit about the detrimental effects of heightened motivation stress on behavior. For example, detrimental to the performance of high-anxious persons are the degrees to which (a) the situation is introduced as a personally threatening one, (b) the task is difficult and complex, and (c) the situation does not provide cues which might give direction for the person's efforts.

On the other hand, there has not been nearly as much emphasis on conditions which might facilitate performance. I have mentioned that events such as the experimenters' uttering "good" at appropriate points during subjects' verbal learning or self-descriptions seemed to be facilitative cues. There is another type of potential behavior-influencing cue which, a few years ago, seemed to me to deserve experimental investigation.

These cues are the behavior of others. For example, it is possible that some highly anxious people are anxious because in their development they were exposed to the behavior of significant persons who displayed anxiety in certain types of situations. Looking at it more positively, a child whose parents enjoy and play readily with animals is less likely to develop anxieties about animals than a child whose parents are frightened of and avoid animals. Recent research has shown that several types of social and emotional responses can be strengthened simply through observation of another person, a model, emitting responses. For example, Bandura's work has shown that as a consequence of their observation of models' aggressive and moral behavior, children's frequencies of emission of these types of responses increase.[2] Studies of vicarious reinforcement have shown that observation of another person receiving reinforcement can have a significant influence on behavior. Social psychologists, because of their interest in social relationships among observers and the observed, have also investigated a number of aspects of the problem of the effects on behavior of observing others. For example, it has been found that the tendency to empathize with an observed individual varies as a function of characteristics attributed to that person. While examples from everyday life suggest that observation of a model can influence intellectual performance, there has been relatively less emphasis in research on this relationship than on that between the observation of others and social and emotional responses (for example, hitting a doll).

I have felt that aspects of the research on anxiety referred to earlier may have important implications for the study of the effects of observing the behavior of models on one's own behavior. Assume that subjects are performing in a verbal learning experiment. If a highly test-anxious person were given an opportunity to observe someone else perform on a memory drum before he was asked to perform, two possibilities seem pertinent. First, the opportunity to observe another person or model perform might give the subject a chance to become more familiar with a new situation.

The subject might come to feel more sure of himself as a result of observing another person cope with a novel situation. Second, the opportunity to observe a model might provide him with cues that would be useful to him in his performance. For example, observing a model approach a task in an orderly and business-like manner could suggest useful tactics to a subject. This might serve to dispel some of his anxiety. Similarly, observing models receive praise and reinforcement for performing adequately might have a salutary effect on subjects' attitudes and behavior.

In the experiment which has served as a prototype for a series of verbal learning experiments, high, middle, and low test-anxiety groups composed of female college students served as subjects. Four of seven experimental conditions required the use of models. These were the four observational conditions:

1. Observation condition: Under this condition the subject observed a model "learn" a difficult list according to the usual serial position curve. A synchronously running memory drum was present in the observation room. After observation, the subject performed on the model's list.

2. Reverse observation condition: Under the condition the subject observed a model "learn " a difficult list according to a partially inverted or reversed serial position curve, i.e., material in the middle of the list was "learned" more quickly than material at the ends. Following observation, the subject performed on a different list and then on the model's list.

3. Observation–drum absent condition: This condition resembled the observation condition described above. However, while an opportunity to observe the model was provided, the subject was not shown the memory drum material upon which the model performed. Following observation, the subject performed on the two lists. This condition represents a check on the effects of observing only the model's behavior.

4. Rating condition: Under this condition the subject was asked to observe carefully the behavior of a "subject" (the model) in the other room. The subject was asked to attend carefully to and rate the degree to which the "other subject" was relaxed, attentive, or upset during her performance. The aim of this condition was to determine the effects of observation when emphasis is not placed on the task but on specified aspects of the model's behavior.

2. Interesting empirical and theoretical questions are posed by situations in which the model, instead of making an approach or copying response, makes an avoidant, fear-exhibiting response. Whether or not these types of responses will be imitated by observers is unclear at the present time, but, as I have already suggested, anxiety may develop in this way.

There were three conditions which did not involve observation of a model:

5. Orientation condition: Under this condition the subject was met by the experimenter and taken directly to the experimental room. The experimenter then proceeded to show the subject the memory drum apparatus, demonstrate how it works, and illustrate the method by which the experimenter recorded the subject's responses. After this, the subject performed on the two lists of disyllable words. The aim of this condition was to determine whether or not detailed orientation to the task at hand would be more facilitative for high- than for middle- and low-anxious scorers.

6. Task observation condition: Under this condition, the subject did not observe a model perform on a verbal learning task. Instead, she was given the opportunity, prior to performance on the two lists, to observe the same items to which models had responded in the four modeling conditions described above. This condition represents a check on the possibility that any facilitative efforts of the four modeling conditions might be due simply to the opportunity to observe verbal learning material rather than the opportunity to observe the behavior of a model who is acquiring verbal learning material.

7. Control condition: The subject was brought to the experimental room and then learned the two lists.

The research was carried out in such a way that it was possible to compare the reactions of groups differing in test anxiety to these seven experimental conditions.

Although some of the findings were complex, there were two major results of relevance to our present concern: one is that the observation and reverse-observation conditions led to superior performance over all other conditions in the experiment, and, second, subjects at the higher end of the test-anxiety continuum showed greater responsiveness to observational opportunities than did scorers at the lower end of the distribution. It is theoretically relevant to note that preperformance reassurance designed to allay learners' anxiety and observational opportunities has been found to have similar effects on performance.

Studies recently completed have added to our understanding of observational learning. They suggest that subjects perform differently depending upon the particular aspects of the behavior of the model under observation. Subjects who observe models who guess a

great deal in the course of performing on the experimental task do more guessing and perform at a higher level than those who do not observe guessing models. In general, high test-anxious groups seem to be more responsive to observational opportunities.

One contribution of these verbal learning experiments is the impetus that they provide for the investigation of modeling effects in a variety of performance and learning situations. Observing others in a novel situation may serve to increase task familiarity and to reduce the apprehension of an individual when he enters that situation. In addition, observing others may provide the observer with helpful cues for his own behavior. It would seem necessary, now, to begin to explore intensively the nature of observational cues and the effects of observational experiences on cognitive processes. One practical possibility is that manipulation of the composition of learning and social groups could have salutary effects on members' behavior. For example, underachieving college students might be given the opportunity to reside in dormitory units alongside more competent and successful students. Or, socially disadvantaged children might be given the opportunity to attend school with more fortunate children. What sorts of vicarious benefits might accrue to the underachiever or disadvantaged pupil in such a situation? Might observation by students of filmed models be an effective means of education? Might it be an especially effective means for certain students, such as those characterized by high test anxiety? The value of further experimentation on the modeling process in intellectual performance resides in the possibility of uncovering variables which have potent effects on learning and on achievement. This experimentation is relevant both to the development of the theory of observational learning and to the enhancement of educational opportunities (Sarason, Pederson, & Nyman).

The Delinquency Leap
Let us turn at this point to the seemingly only abstract relationship between verbal learning studies of relatively well-put-together college students and the behavior of acting-out youth. I shall not inflict upon you the complex and, no doubt, at least in part, poorly wired cognitive circuitry which made this connection. In fact, in candor, I shall admit that as the verbal learning research proceeded I simply became increasingly interested in the question: Might observational

opportunities prove to be a useful behavior-modification vehicle with persons who display behavior problems?

The behavior of juvenile delinquents is clearly a serious social problem. It seemed an appropriate focus for approaching the question of behavior modification, for a number of reasons. The major one is that a good bit of juvenile delinquency need not be viewed in terms of a mental illness conception. Rather, it can be seen as a reflection of inadequate learning experiences. The delinquent is someone who has fallen out of the mainstream of his culture; he is someone who is deficient in socially acceptable and adaptive behavior. His deviant behavior may be viewed as part of a rebellion against societal norms and as a failure to have introjected socially useful ways of responding. This failure, it seemed to me, comes about as a result of inadequate opportunities to observe, display, and, subsequently, receive reinforcement for socially useful behavior. This interpretation is consistent with empirical evidence, social learning theory, sociological theories such as those dealing with differential association, and clinical observations.

These considerations, together with the social importance of the problem of juvenile delinquency, contributed to development of the research which I shall now describe. I should point out that one determinant of the decision to study delinquents was that two groups of delinquents could be compared: those which are characterized by moderate to strong degrees of anxiety and those where anxiety is relatively absent (for example, as in many cases of character disorders). Thus, the research on delinquency really was not just a product of poorly wired cognitive circuitry. It is being carried out in order to find out the generality of the verbal learning research which I have described. Are anxious juvenile delinquents more responsive to observational opportunities than those who are low in anxiety?

The specific foci of our investigation were the vocational and educational plans of juvenile offenders, their motivations, interests, attitudes towards work, and their meager repertory of socially appropriate behavior. Our hypothesis is that systematic exposure to identification models who exhibit relevant socially appropriate behavior can have a salutary and positive influence in changing the behavior of the juvenile offender.

The project began in the fall of 1966. It was an obviously necessary first step to establish a good working relationship with the personnel at the locus of our research, the Cascadia Juvenile Reception-Diagnostic Center, located in Tacoma, Washington. Meetings were held with supervisory and staff members of the administration, psychology, education, recreation, and social service departments, and with the personnel of the cottages in which the research was to be conducted. Concurrently, time was spent learning the details of the diagnostic process, educational programs, and schedules to which delinquents at Cascadia are subjected during their stay at the institution and in determining the extent to which portions of the institution's diagnostic data and information could be utilized for research purposes. Within a relatively short period of time it became clear that both cooperation with and support of the project characterized every level of Cascadia's personnel.

Cascadia's cottages, in each of which 20-25 children reside, are staffed by a Supervising Group Life Counselor, an Assistant Counselor, and four staff counselors. These six persons staff the cottage in shifts round the clock. The children at Cascadia represent a 100% sample of children committed to the Department of Institutions by the juvenile courts of Washington. Approximately 1,700 cases per year are seen at Cascadia.

The models were clinical psychology graduate students (I shall have more to say about this fact later on). An early activity of the project was the development of the project's research assistants' skills in role playing and working with groups. Meetings, discussions, and practice sessions were devoted to maximizing the assistants' effectiveness as models, with emphasis on techniques appropriate for a population of adolescents.

At the outset of the research it was felt that three requirements would have to be met in order to attain our objectives. These requirements were:

1. Modeling opportunities afforded adolescent delinquents would have to be provided under controlled conditions.
2. Relevant comparison and control conditions would have to be investigated.
3. Objective behavioral indices would have to be developed in order to determine the efficacy of our experimental procedures.

The work of the first year was concerned with meeting these requirements. This initial period was also used for pilot work dealing with several specific questions, including these:

1. What types of observational opportunities would be interesting and ego involving for juvenile delinquents?
2. How should models behave toward the subjects in order to maximize the effects of observational opportunities?
3. What sorts of control groups are needed?
4. What specific types of dependent variables should be obtained in order to assess the effects of modeling opportunities?

It soon became clear to us that the more objective and uncomplicated the modeling situation is, the greater its applicability to various kinds of situations and the more useful and practical it will be to others as a rehabilitation aid. We concluded that two ingredients were needed for modeling opportunities to be effective: (a) an objectively describable modeling situation and (b) good rapport between models and subjects—the models must be liked by the subjects and must be objects with whom boys would want to identify.

Early preliminary studies led us to the conclusion that, while the models should interact informally with subjects in Cascadia's cottages, modeling sessions should be clearly labeled and easily discriminable situations. We have spent much time working on these situations and training our research assistants to be effective models and empathic, reinforcing individuals.

Preliminary work with several dozen subjects resulted in the development of a series of 15 modeling sessions to which Cascadia's delinquent boys were exposed. All of these sessions were explained to them as opportunities to develop more effective ways of coping with problems that are important and common for people like themselves. A practical problem-solving atmosphere was created during each session. This initial orientation was given to the boys:

First, let's all introduce ourselves, start with me. I'm Mr. —————— and this is Mr. —————— (boys introduce themselves). We are working with small groups of boys here at Cascadia. We are doing something new to show you some different ways of handling common situations and problems that will happen in your lives. The situations we'll work with

and emphasize are often particularly important for fellows like yourselves. We say this because just the fact that you're going through an institution will have important effects on your lives, and we want to work with you to teach you better ways of handling some of these effects. In other words, we want to work together with you to teach you new ways to handle problem situations. These are situations which we feel will be of importance to you in the future. They are things that probably all of you will run into from time to time and we think that you can benefit from learning and practicing different ways to act in these situations.

The way we want to do this isn't by lecturing or advising you. Having people watch others doing things and then discussing what has been done is a very important way and a useful way to learn. It is easy to learn how to do something just by observing someone else doing it first. Often times, just explaining something to someone isn't nearly as effective as actually doing it first while the other person watches. For example, it is easier to learn to swim, or repair a car, if you have a chance to watch someone else doing it first.

We think that small groups, working together, can learn a lot about appropriate ways of doing things just by playing different roles and watching others play roles. By role, we mean the particular part a person acts or plays in a particular situation—kind of like the parts actors play in a movie scene, only this will be more realistic. These roles will be based on actual situations that many young people have trouble with, like how to control your anger, or resist being pressured into doing destructive things by friends. Other roles are directly related to fellows like yourselves who have been in an institution. These are stituations such as your review board, or the ways you can best use the special skills of your parole counselor to help you after you leave here. Things like this are things that not everyone can do well. We want to emphasize better ways of doing these things and coping with similar problems which will be important in the future for most of you. Everyone in the group will both play the roles for themselves and watch others playing the same roles. This is like acting, only it is realistic because it involves situations in which you might really find yourselves. We feel that the situations are realistic because they are based on the real experiences of a lot of fellows who have gone through Cascadia.

There are seven of us here at Cascadia who are working in these small groups. We are not on the Cascadia staff. We are here because we are interested in working with fellows like yourselves and in helping you improve your skills in how you approach the situations I've just described. Since we are not on the Cascadia staff, we do not have anything to do with the decisions made concerning you or where you will go after leaving here. We do not share any of our information with the regular staff. Everything this group does or talks about is kept strictly confidential and isn't available to or used by the staff in any way at all.

This group is one of several we have been working with here on ————— Cottage. Each group meets three times a week for about 40 minutes at a time. This same group will meet together each week during the time you are all here at Cascadia, but different ones of us will be with this group on different days. We will be playing different roles in different situations on each day. This is how we will do it. First, we will describe the situation to you. Then we will play out the roles that are involved. We want you to watch us and then take turns in pairs, playing the same roles yourselves. We will also discuss how everyone does and what is important about the particular roles or situations and how they may be related to your lives. We will want you to stick closely to the roles as we play them but also add your own personal touch to your role. As you will see, it is important that we all get involved in this as much as we can. The more you put yourself into the role you play, the more realistic it will be to you and to the rest of the group. We see these scenes as examples of real situations that you will all find yourselves in sometime, and it is important to play them as realistically as possible. We will outline each scene as we go along.

Also, each meeting will be tape-recorded. We use these tape-recordings for our own records of how each group proceeds. These tapes are identified by code numbers and no one's name actually appears in the tape. The tapes are confidential too, and will be used only by us. As we said, none of this information is used by the regular staff.

Before going any further, we want to give you an example of what we're talking about. Mr. ————— and I will play two roles which involve a scene that has really gone on right here on your cottage. This scene is based on information we got from a cottage counselor and other boys who have been on this cottage. This situation involves a common cottage problem and we will show you some things that can be done about it.

Each session had a particular theme, e.g., applying for a job, resisting temptations by peers to engage in antisocial acts, taking a problem to a teacher or parole counselor, foregoing immediate gratifications in order to lay the groundwork for more significant gratifications in the future. In each situation, an emphasis was placed on the generality of the appropriate behaviors being modeled in order to emphasize their potential usefulness. An example of one of these situations is the job interview scene, in which roles are played by an interviewer and a job applicant. The dialogue emphasizes the kinds of questions an interviewer might ask and the various positive, coping responses an interviewee is expected to make. Also, such factors as proper appearance, mannerisms, honesty, and interest are stressed.

Job Interview Scene

Introduction: Having a job can be very important. It is a way that we can get money for things we want to buy. It is a way we can feel important because we are able to earn something for ourselves through our own efforts. For this same reason, a job can make us feel more independent. Getting a job may not always be easy. This is especially true of jobs that pay more money and of full-time jobs. A job may be important to guys like you who have been in an institution because it gives you a way of showing other people that you can be trusted, that you can do things on your own, that you are more than just a punk kid. However, because you've been in trouble, you may have more trouble than most people getting a job. In the scene today you'll have a chance to practice applying for a job and being interviewed by the man you want to work for. Being interviewed makes most people tense and anxious because interviewers often ask questions which are hard to answer. After each of you has been interviewed, we'll talk about the way it felt and about what to do about the special problems that parolees may face in getting jobs.

SCENE Ia

A boy who is on parole from Cascadia is applying for a job at a small factory in his home town. He is 18 and has not finished high school but hopes to do so by going to school at night. Obviously, the boy has a record. This will come up during the interview. Pay careful attention to how he handles this problem. This is a two part scene; first, we'll act out the job interview, then a part about another way of convincing an employer that you want a job.

(Mr. Howell is seated at his desk when George knocks on the door.)

Howell. "Hello. Have a seat. I'm Mr. Howell, and your name?"

(Mr. Howell rises—shakes hands.)

George. "George Smith."

Howell. "Have a seat, George."

(Both sit down.)

"Oh yes, I have your application right here. There are a few questions I'd like to ask you. I see that you have had some jobs before; tell me about them."

George. "They were just for the summer because I've been going to school. I've worked on some small construction jobs and in a food processing plant."

Howell. "Did you ever have any trouble at work, or ever get fired?"

George. "No trouble, except getting used to the work the first couple of weeks. I did quit one job—I didn't like it."

Howell. "I see that you have only finished half your senior year in high school. You don't intend to graduate?"

George. (showing some anxiety) "Yes, I do. I intend to go to night school while I'm working. It may take me a year or so, but I intend to get my diploma."

Howell. "How did you get a year behind?"

George. "I've been out of school for awhile because I've been in some trouble. Nothing really serious."

Howell. "I'd like to know just what kind of trouble you've had, serious or not."

George. "Well, I was sent to Cascadia for six weeks but I'm out on parole now. I just got out a couple of weeks ago. One of the reasons I want a job is to help keep me out of trouble."

Howell. "What kind of trouble were you involved in?"

George. "A friend and I stole some car parts and parts off an engine. I guess we were pretty wild. I'm not running around like that any more though."

Howell. "You sound like you think you can stay out of trouble now. Why do you think so?"

George. "In those six weeks at Cascadia I thought about myself and my future a whole lot, and realized it was time to get serious about life and stop goofing off. I know I haven't been out very long yet, but my parole counselor is helping me with the problems that come up. I'm trying to stay away from the guys that I got into trouble with. I really think that if I could get a job and be more on my own it would help a lot."

Howell. "Yes, I think you're probably right—but, I'm afraid we don't have any openings right now. I'll put your application on file though and let you know if anything turns up. I have several other applications too, so don't be too optimistic."

George. "All right. Thank you."

(George stands and starts to leave as he says this line.)

SCENE Ib
Introduction. It is now two weeks later. George has called back several times to see if an opening has occurred. He now stops by to check again.

(George knocks on Mr. Howell's door.)

Howell. "Come in."

George. (enters room while speaking) "I stopped by to see whether you had an opening yet."

Howell. "You certainly don't want me to forget you do you?"

George. "No sir, I don't. I really want a job, I think its the best thing for me to do now."

Howell. "You know, I believe you. I wasn't so sure at first. It's pretty easy for a guy who has been in trouble to say that he's going to change and then do nothing about it. But the way you've been coming here and checking with me so often, I think you're really serious about it."

George. "Yes, sir, I am. I started night school this week. I think I'll be able to get my diploma in a year. So, if I had a job now I'd be all set."

Howell. "Well, I've got some good news for you, George. I have an opening for a man in the warehouse and I think you can handle the job if you want it."

George. "Yes, very much. When do you want me to start?"

Howell. "Tomorrow morning at 7:30."

George. "O.K."

Howell. "I'll take you out there now and introduce you to Mr. Jones, who will be your supervisor."

SCENE Ic
Introduction. Same as Scene Ib.

(George knocks on Mr. Howell's door.)

Howell. "Come in."

George. "I stopped by to see whether you had an opening yet."

(enters room while speaking)

Howell. "You sure are persistent. Have you tried other places?"

George. "Sure, I'm checking back on them too. Getting a good job isn't easy."

Howell. (uncomfortably) "Ah, well, look. We're not going to have a place for you here. I wouldn't want you to waste your time coming back again. We can't use you."

George. (rises to go) "Well . . . (pause) . . . O.K. Thanks for your trouble. Look, what's up? I know that your company is hiring other fellows like me right now."

Howell. "Er . . . that's true. Uh, I'm afraid that we have a company policy not to hire anyone with a record."

George. "How come? That dosen't sound fair to me."

Howell. "Well, er, ahem . . . that's just the company's policy. I'm sorry, but my hands are tied. There's nothing I can do about it."

George. "Well, I would have appreciated knowing that right away."

Howell. "I'm really sorry. I can see you're trying . . . I hope you get a job."

George. "Well, do you know of a place that could use me? Since you're in personnel, maybe you've heard something."

Each subject played George's role. At the end of the session, these discussion points were emphasized:

1. Importance of presenting oneself well. Getting a job is "selling yourself" too. In both scenes the boy takes the initiative instead of waiting around passively for things to happen.

2. How to deal with the fact that you have a record. Here, the boy had to admit to having a record because of the time in school gap. If he had lied, the interviewer would have caught this and formed the impression of dishonesty. Discuss the possibility of cases when telling about a record is unnecessary. Situational factors are very important.

3. It is understandable to feel anxious when being interviewed, because getting the job is important.

4. Persistence is a trait employers like. In this case, it is an important reason why the kid got the job.

Each session was attended by six persons. Two models (advanced graduate students in clinical psychology, especially interested in the field of delinquency) and four boys between the ages of 15½ and 18 years. A session began by one of the models setting the stage. He defined the topic for the session and the scene which everyone present would role play. Following this introduction, the two models would act out the scene which had previously been carefully planned. For example, one model might play a parole counselor and the other might play the role of the delinquent parolee. One pair of subjects would then act out the same scene. Following this, soft drinks[3] would be served, during which time a discussion of the various aspects and the strengths and weaknesses of the scene as acted out by the subjects would take place. After this, the other subjects would act out the same scene.

Our procedures were arrived at after a number of preliminary runs. They gave every indication of being interesting to the boys, who seemed to accept the modeling situations as they were presented to them: learning opportunities designed to enhance their ability to cope with situations that, for them, are problem areas.

We did our first pilot study in the winter of 1967. The general aims of this investigation were threefold: (a) to compare the relative effectiveness of a modeling approach and a more traditional role-playing approach as behavior-modification techniques with a suitable control (no treatment) group, (b) to assess the adequacy and efficiency of our dependent behavioral and attitudinal measures and rating scales which we had as-

sembled, and (c) to assess the feasibility of the research design and procedures employed prior to initiation of a major experimental effort.

As I have mentioned, in one of our groups the subjects were exposed to the modeling sessions described above. Another group, the control group, received neither the modeling experience nor any other kind of special treatment. The role-playing group was a comparison group similar to the modeling group except that the same roles were only verbally described to the boys, who then spontaneously enacted them. That is, the subjects were not given the opportunity to observe models handle particular problem situations first. But these boys did have an opportunity to act out the several scenes.

In the spring of 1967 we did an additional study which was similar to the first one except that in the spring the subjects were exposed to lengthier modeling sequences and more detailed group discussions than those employed in the winter procedure. No role playing was used in the spring study. The spring scenes were revised in a number of respects, and a greater emphasis was placed on the personal meaning of the group meetings to the subjects. Also, in the spring study, at the conclusion of the experimental sequence, the boys made up and acted out one scene in the group meeting.

In both studies, we looked at a number of dependent variables. Some of our measures were obtained prior to beginning the modeling and role-playing sequences. Some measures were obtained both before and after, and some measures were obtained only after the subjects had gone through the modeling and role-playing sequences. Our measures consisted of subjects' self-reports and data from the Cascadia staff. Two self-ratings were forms of the semantic differential and Wahler's Self-Description Inventory. The semantic differential consisted of concepts and words such as "me as I am," "me as I would like to be," "man," "work." These were rated on a 7-point scale along 11 bipolar dimensions. The Self-Description Inventory contained an assortment of positive and negative self-descriptive items, for example, "has a good sense of humor," "am often depressed or unhappy." These statements are evaluated in terms of the mean score of all favorable items endorsed versus the mean score of unfavorable items endorsed.

Cottage staff supplied two kinds of pre- and post-ratings. One was a Behavior Rating Scale which all staff

---

3. One of our major findings thus far is that teen-aged institutionalized delinquents do not like Fresca!

filled out on each boy. The scale consisted of 25 items describing different types of behavior, for example, table manners, lying, self-control. Each item was checked on a 9-point scale from high to low. The second rating, the Weekly Behavior Summary, included seven categories of behavior, for example, peer relationships, staff relationships, and work detail performance. Ratings were made for each boy after his initial 10 days on the cottage, and again just prior to his discharge from Cascadia. The two main post measures were taken from Cascadia Review Board decisions. These were the diagnosis of the boy and the Review Board placement decisions, that is, where the boy was to be sent from Cascadia. A breakdown of diagnostic categories was made on the basis of neurotic versus character disorder and combinations of these categories. Placement ratings were assigned numerical scores on the basis of rank ordering of possible placements along the dimension of most to least favorable for boys of the type seen at Cascadia.

The following have been our major findings. There has been a consistent tendency for experimental boys to show less discrepancy between "me as I would like to be" and "me as I am now," than control subjects. One of the most suggestive findings is that boys who have received the modeling condition became more personally *dissatisfied* with themselves as their stay at Cascadia proceeded. Control subjects, on the other hand, became more *satisfied* with themselves as their stay in Cascadia proceeded. At this point the meaning of these results is not immediately obvious. But one strong possibility is that untreated delinquents in an institution are initially anxious because of the strangeness of being in the institutional environment for the first time. As they adapt and "rest up," their anxiety level goes down and they, therefore, become more self-satisfied. If this is true, it may be that the experimental procedures we have been employing have been successful in stirring up the treated boys at Cascadia. If so, this has important theoretical implications, since the process of observational learning may be much more complex than simply observing someone else making a response and then attempting to replicate that response. Ignored thus far in research on observational learning has been what might be called cognitive modeling or the cognitive aspect of the modeling process. Our results concerning self-satisfaction suggest that lessened defensiveness and greater willingness to admit to having problems and difficulties have charac-

terized the responses of the experimental, but not the control, boys.

In general, the findings for our two pilot studies showed that boys who were members of our experimental groups showed more change in their behavior and attitudes than did matched control groups of boys who did not participate. The results were strongest and most positive in the case of the modeling groups, and second in order of potency was the role-playing condition. We obtained numerous kinds of ratings by cottage personnel of the behavior of our subjects. Overall, the experimental subjects were rated as showing more positive behavior change than control subjects. It should be noted that our groups had been matched for: (a) age, (b) intelligence level, and (c) severity and chronicity of delinquency. In addition, our data permit us to compare boys varying along the anxiety-sociopathy dimension. In view of our verbal learning research this dimension is of great interest to us. Preliminary analyses have suggested that boys who are characterized by high degrees of anxiety and neuroticism respond most favorably to observational opportunities. Table 3 provides data which support this conclusion. Thus far, our studies of the behavior of juvenile delinquents seem consistent with the verbal learning findings.

TABLE 3

Numbers of High and Low Test-Anxious Subjects Showing Either Change or No (or Negative) Change in Behavior Ratings

Subjects	Experimental group		Control group	
	Positive change	No or negative change	Positive change	No or negative change
High test anxiety	11	2	4	7
Low test anxiety	5	5	6	6

Note. Winter 1967 study.

One interesting difference between the winter and spring studies was that some of our results were much stronger for the winter study than for the spring one. This was true even though we felt at the time that most of our conditions were far superior in the spring study. In looking at our procedures we noted an important difference between the winter and spring studies. In the winter there were virtually no discussions following the modeling sessions, whereas discussion did follow the role-playing sessions. In the spring there were rather extensive discussion periods after the modeling sessions. One possibility which has occurred to us is that there may be something like a Zeigarnik effect at work; that is, when discussion follows either the modeling or the role-playing activity, subjects may achieve a degree of closure by virtue of the discussion. On the other hand, in the winter study no opportunity for closure was provided. It is possible that the winter study's seemingly "less smooth" procedure may, in fact, be better in that when questions are left unanswered adolescents tend to continue to come to grips with them after the experimental session is over.

We have been challenged and encouraged by the results of our pilot work and have just begun an experiment which will probably take 10 to 12 months to complete. It involves better defined conditions, larger Ns, and more reliable dependent measures than we had for our pilot studies. Also, we have formulated procedures for following up the Cascadia boys a year after they leave that institution. These dependent measures will include a number of specific indices of vocational and educational adjustment. Will the various groups differ in the level of jobs which they got? How many of them will be repeat offenders? How many of them will finish high school?

Not surprisingly, some of the procedures which we are now employing are different from those of our pilot studies. There are two which I should briefly mention. One is that we are using a comparison group different from the role-playing group which I have described. This change grew out of a need to achieve more fully the original aim of the research. This was to develop a behavior-modification procedure which would be both simple and direct. Since psychotherapy is a frequent technique employed with delinquents, we decided to use, for comparison purposes, a procedure more similar to psychotherapy than was that of role playing. This procedure will consist of guided group discussion meetings. Subjects in guided discussion groups of our experiment will have the same number of sessions as the modeling groups will have. In addition, the content of each session will be similar. That is, while the modeling group will act out a job interview scene, the guided discussion groups will discuss the problems posed by and solutions to the problems of job interviews. What follows suggests the orientation given to boys in the guided discussion groups. They are the guidelines which the group leaders follow in introducing the guided discussion sessions to the boys.

First, let's all introduce ourselves, starting with me. I'm Mr. —————— and this is Mr. —————— (boys introduce themselves). We are working with small groups of boys here at Cascadia. During the times we meet together, we will be talking about common situations and problems that happen in your lives. The situations we'll work with are often particularly important for fellows like yourselves. We say this because just the fact that you're going through an institution will have important effects on your lives, and we want to work with you by discussing some of these effects. In other words, we want to work together with you in talking about problem situations. These are situations which we feel will be of importance to you in the future. They are things that probably all of you will run into from time to time, and we think you can benefit from talking and thinking about them.

The way we want to do this isn't by lecturing or advising you. Your talking about these situations is an important way to learn. Often we don't take time to think about things that get us into trouble, or about situations that make us feel bad. It's kind of disturbing to think about it in the first place, and it's also hard to pull out words to describe what's going on. In the group you will find that you have experiences in common and you can help each other think through what happens.

We think that groups working together can help each member of the group learn a lot about what makes him tick . . . just by talking frankly about the topic. The topics will be real situations that many young people have trouble with: controlling your anger, or being pressured into doing destructive things by friends. Sometimes we will talk about the situations you fellows have to cope with as persons who have been in an institution. There are situations such as your Review Board, or the experiences you have had with your probation officer and anticipate having with your parole counselor when you get out of here. Subjects like this are often not carefully talked about and we think that the time we spend together talking about them will be important in the future for most of you. We use four rules in these groups: (1) One person talks at a time; (2) everyone contributes to the discussion; (3) what goes on here won't be taken outside the group—it will be confidential and not used by staff; and (4) no ranking—constructive criticism and comments are good, but ranking doesn't help anyone.

There are seven of us here at Cascadia who are working in these small groups. We are not on the Cascadia staff. We are here because we are interested in working with fellows like yourselves and in helping you understand yourselves and your experiences better. We want to emphasize that we are not connected with the Cascadia staff. Since we are not on the staff, we do not have anything to do with the decisions made concerning you or where you will go after leaving here. We do not share any of our information with the regular staff.

Everything this group does or talks about is kept strictly confidential and isn't available to or used by the staff in any way at all.

This group is one of several we have been working with on _____ cottage. Each group meets four times a week for about 40 minutes at a time. This same group will meet together each week during the time you are all here at Cascadia, but different ones of us will be with this group on different days. We will meet on _____, _____, _____, and _____. We will be talking about different situations on each day. This is how we will do it: First, we will describe the situation to you. Then we will turn the hour over to you except for the comments and questions we will add to the discussion from time to time. You can share with each other any experiences you have had, describe your feelings about what has happened, also question and make comments to each other. There is no certain way the discussion must go . . . it is pretty much up to what you think will be useful.

Also, each meeting will be tape-recorded. We use these tape-recordings for our own records of how each group proceeds. These tapes are identified by code numbers and no one's name actually appears on the tape. The tapes are confidential, too, and will be used only by us here. As we said, none of this information is used by the regular staff.

Before going on any further, we want to give you an example of what we're talking about. Mr. _____ will describe a situation here on your cottage, etc. . .

The following are our guidelines for the guided discussion group, analogue of the Job Interview Scene. The guidelines are those employed by the group leaders.

Having a job can be very important. It is a way to get money for things we need, but it is also a way to earn something for ourselves through our own efforts and it makes us feel more independent. Getting a job isn't easy. Today we want to talk about some of the things involved in getting jobs. Also, since you fellows have been in trouble with the law, you may have some extra problems getting jobs that other young fellows wouldn't have. We can talk about that too. Let's start today by finding out what sorts of jobs you fellows have had (ask each person in the group to describe the kinds of jobs he has had in the past).

A very important part of getting a job is, of course, the job interview. There are lots of ways to handle a job interview, so let's talk about that for awhile.

The leader then asks the boys what sort of interviews they have had, if any, and what kinds of questions were asked and how they handled these questions. He asks others to comment on each boy's discussion. He begins a discussion about what kinds of things are important in an interview, for example, how should one look, what does it mean when an interviewer says,

"We'll keep your application and call you." He raises the question of applying for more than one job at a time. There is a discussion of how each boy deals with the question of his record, whether or not he admits it, and, if not, why.

Besides employing the guided group discussions, the other new element in our major experiment is the introduction of closed-circuit television as a means of increasing the numbers of exposures subjects will have to observational opportunities. I mentioned earlier that our modeling sessions seemed to be successful in stirring up the boys. This suggested that, while the modeling sessions seemed to contribute to a desirable step forward for them, they needed more observational trials in order to strengthen their prosocial repertoires. Therefore, we are increasing the number of modeling sessions, and, in addition, we are televising them and playing them back to the boys. This will give them an opportunity, not only to observe others (models and peers), but also to observe themselves. Since the use of television is part of the experimental design, it will be used with half of the modeling and half of the guided discussion groups, which will enable us to assess its effectiveness as a behavior-modification technique. Another of our interests in video taping the modeling sessions is ultimately to carry out a study to determine the relative effectiveness of live modeling sessions and video-taped sessions.

There is one problem which we shall not study directly in our present experiment. We hope to study it in the future. That problem concerns the personal characteristics of the models. Our models are primarily middle class psychologists in training. They have some very positive characteristics: more than a little psychological *savoir faire*, and a deep interest in helping mixed-up people. We have seriously considered the possibility that the best models would be those who are more peerlike for delinquent boys. Within the institutional setting in which we are now working the use of peer models adminstratively and practically is not possible. It is interesting, however, that the Cascadia staff itself has made an effort in the recent past to use former delinquents as cottage personnel. This was done on the assumption that "Cascadia graduates" who had righted themselves might more easily establish rapport with delinquent boys than cottage personnel with other characteristics. The outcome of this effort was quite negative, because people who had been in Cascadia and who had managed to overcome the tendency towards delinquency often harbored quite negative attitudes toward delinquent boys. This seems analogous to the oft-observed situation in which people who have grown up in quite poverty-stricken environments may become quite unsympathetic and often antagonistic to their poor brethren when they reach the level of the *nouveau riche*. We hope soon to enter the planning stage of a study, to be carried out in the community, that would systematically explore characteristics of models as variables in achieving behavior modification among delinquents.

To summarize briefly, we have come to two conclusions. First, observational opportunities seem to be potentially powerful behavior-modification influences, and, second, it is important to have a proper respect for the complexities of the process of observational learning. Modeling is a potentially valuable behavior-modification vehicle, but there is much empirical and theoretical ground to be broken in understanding, developing, and validating its various ramifications.

References

Sarason, I. G. Test anxiety, experimental instructions, and verbal learning. Paper presented at the meeting of the American Psychological Association, New York, Septmeber 1961. (*American Psychologist*, 1961, *16*, 374, abstract)

Sarason, I. G., Pederson, A. M., & Nyman, B. A. Test anxiety and the observation of models. *Journal of Personality*,

In this presentation I would like to discuss a quite recent approach to the problem of modifying values and behavior. I will be discussing both the formation of values in children (commonly known as socialization) and the modification of value-related behavior in adults.

Let us begin with children. In the process of raising children, most parents are primarily concerned with two basic goals. The first of these is that of preventing the child from performing specific and momentary acts that are destructive, dangerous, and otherwise undesirable—like clobbering his younger brother, spreading blueberry jam on the new drapes, or dashing across a busy street in the midst of traffic. The second is concerned with instilling in the young child a permanent and enduring set of values which will enable him to live in society without breaking too many laws or violating too many cultural mores.

How can parents best achieve these goals? It would be wonderful if we could reason with the child—that is, convince him by rational and persuasive argument why it is not nice to beat up on his younger brother. But, as Aristotle observed 2000 years ago, even many adults cannot be taught by reasonable arguments; this is certainly true when applied to the four-year-old. Less rational techniques must be employed—techniques which involve rewarding or punishing the child. Most child psychologists are in agreement in advocating rewards, both in the form of concrete incentives and in the form of praise and approval, as a means of "reinforcing" desirable behavior. Psycholo-

cognitive dissonance as it affects values and behavior[1]

elliot aronson
the university of texas at austin

gists generally feel that rewarding desirable behavior is much more effective than punishing undesirable behavior. Thus, they recommend that we should reward Johnny for being kind to his little brother as opposed to punishing him for being unkind to his little brother. But parents (even those of us who happen to be psychologists!) are well aware of the fact that punishment or the threat of punishment is often necessary and, when judiciously used, can be an effective means of controlling the behavior of very young children.

1. Excerpted from an address given to the Council for the Advancement of Science Writing in New Brunswick, New Jersey. Portions of this address were published under the title of "Try a Little Dissonance" in the *New York Times Magazine*, Part I, September 11, 1966. The preparation of this paper was supported by a grant from the National Institutes of Health.

Let us take a closer look at threats of punishment as a technique. These threats usually take the form of spankings or denial of priviliges. A reasonable question is one of degree—in order to be most effective, how severe should a threat of punishment be? It stands to reason that if we want to prevent a child from performing a mischievous act, the more severe the threat, the greater the likelihood that he will comply—at least *while the threatening parent is standing there watching him.* And that's the problem: for while severe threats are effective in achieving the first major goal of parents (that of preventing momentary undesirable behavior), they have proved useless in helping the child develop a set of values. For example, child psychologists find that those parents who are most severe in punishing a child's aggressive behavior tend to have children who, although relatively unaggressive in the presence of their parents, are veritable hellions in the schoolyard where their parents are not present to punish them. It is unfortunate that those techniques which are best at preventing momentary infractions are ineffective as a means of imparting basic values. Moreover, of these two goals, it would appear that the latter is the more important, if for no other reason than the fact that it is more efficient—for once a child has developed a set of values, parents (and society) can afford to relax their vigil. If a child has not yet learned to respect the rights of others, we must be continually on our toes, armed with candies or threats, to see to it that Johnny doesn't slug his younger brother or infringe on his rights in other ways. Once the child has developed these values, he will refrain from these behaviors—not because of fear of punishment, but because he wants to. It would certainly be a much more efficient way to run a family (or a society) if we could somehow find a way to imbue young children with complex values; if we could get them to refrain from slugging their younger brothers because they had come to dislike slugging smaller children.

In the past few years we have been conducting psychological experiments which may have an important bearing on this problem. These experiments have been derived from and inspired by the theory of cognitive dissonance which was proposed by Leon Festinger (1957) and which I have recently revised and extended (Aronson, 1969). Before describing these experiments, let me first present a brief description of the theory. Stated in its simplest form, this theory suggests that when a person simultaneously holds two incompatible ideas (cognitions), dissonance occurs. This creates internal tension. Such tension is unpleasant, and the individual tries to diminish it by reducing the dissonance. This can be done by changing one idea (cognition) or the other to bring them closer together and make them more compatible.

For example, if a person has the cognition that he smokes cigarettes and reads that cigarette smoking leads to lung cancer, he experiences cognitive dissonance. His cognition that he is smoking is dissonant with his cognition that cigarette smoking might cause cancer. He can reduce this dissonance in a number of ways. Perhaps the most direct would be to stop smoking; the cognition that cigarette smoking causes cancer is perfectly compatible (consonant) with *not* smoking. Although this is the most direct way to reduce dissonance, it is not the easiest course of action to take—as many of us have discovered. Consequently, most people attempt to reduce dissonance by working on the other cognition—that is, by making cigarette smoking seem less silly. Perhaps we will try to belittle the evidence linking cigarette smoking to cancer ("Most of the data were gathered on rodents, not people"); or we might associate with other cigarette smokers ("If Sam, Jack, and Harry smoke, then it can't be very dangerous"); or we might smoke filter-tipped cigarettes and delude ourselves with the notion that the filter traps the cancer-producing materials; or we might convince ourselves that smoking is an important and highly pleasurable activity ("I'd rather have a shorter but more enjoyable life than a longer, unenjoyable one"); or we might actually make a virtue out of smoking by developing a romantic, devil-may-care picture of ourselves, flaunting danger by smoking. These behaviors are all acts of "self-justification" and, indeed, cognitive dissonance theory is largely concerned with man's attempt to justify his own behavior—to make his actions appear to be reasonable and rational, after the fact. One of the primary ways of reducing dissonance is through this technique, which the psychoanalysts refer to as rationalization.

What does all this have to do with instilling a permanent set of values in young children? Just this: Children are people too; there is every reason to suspect that they experience cognitive dissonance and attempt to reduce it in much the same way that adults do. As mentioned above, in the course of interacting with their children from day to day, parents typically threaten or punish them in order to curtail or prevent them from performing dangerous or undesirable actions. Thus, if a parent came upon his five-year-old in the act of beating up a younger brother, the parent might threaten to punish him in order to get him to stop. The key question is, how do we utilize these situations in order to build a permanent set of values? Let us imagine that each parent has at his disposal a range of punishments from an extremely mild rebuff on the one hand (for example, a stern look) to an extremely severe punishment on the other hand (a very stern look, accompanied by a severe spanking, forcing the child to stand in the corner for two hours, and depriving him of television privileges for a month). As mentioned previously, the more severe the threat, the greater the likelihood that he will stop beating up his little brother at that moment, *while his parent is watching him;* however, he may very well hit his brother again as soon as the parent turns his back.

But suppose instead that the parent threatens him with a very mild punishment—a punishment which was just barely severe enough to get him to stop aggressing at that moment. In either case—under threat of severe punishment or of mild punishment—the child is experiencing dissonance; he is aware that he is not beating up on his little brother while also aware that he wants to. When the little brother is present, the child has the urge to beat him up and, when he refrains, he asks himself, in effect, "how come I'm not beating up my little brother?" Under severe threat he has a ready answer: "I know damn well why I'm not beating up my little brother. I'm not beating him up because if I do, the giant standing over there (my father) is going to knock the hell out of me, stand me in the corner, and keep me from watching television for a month." In effect, the severe threat of punishment has provided the child with justifications for not beating up his brother, *at that moment, while he's being watched.*

But consider the child in the mild threat situation; he experiences dissonance too. He asks himself, in effect, "How come I'm not beating up my little brother?" But the difference is that he doesn't have a good answer—because, by definition, the threat, while barely severe enough to get the child to refrain momentarily, is so mild that it does not provide a superabundance of justification. In effect, the child is *not* doing something he *likes* to do—and while he has some justification, he lacks complete justification. In this situation he continues to experience dissonance. There is no simple way for him to reduce it by blaming

his inaction on a severe threat. He must, therefore, find reasons consonant with not hitting his little brother. Much like the cigarette smoker in the earlier example, the child must find a way to justify the fact that he is *not* aggressing against his little brother. The best way is to try to convince himself that he really doesn't like to beat his brother up, that he didn't want to do it in the first place, that beating up little kids is not fun. The less severe the threat, the less the "external" justification; the less the external justification, the greater the need for internal justification. Internal justifications are a long step toward the development of a permanent value.

To test this idea, I performed an experiment at the Harvard University nursery school in collaboration with my colleague, Dr. J. Merrill Carlsmith. In our experiment, for ethical reasons, we did not try to change important and basic values like aggression; i.e., we felt that parents might not approve of our changing important values. Instead, we chose a trivial and unimportant aspect of behavior—toy preference. We first asked four and five-year-old children to rate the attractiveness of several toys; then we chose one that a child considered to be quite attractive, and we told him he couldn't play with it. For one-half of the children we threatened mild punishment for transgression—"I would be a little annoyed"; with the other half, we threatened more severe punishment—"I would be very angry. I would have to take all of my toys and go home and never come back again. I would think you were just a baby." After that, we left the room and allowed the children to play with the other toys—and to resist the temptation of playing with the forbidden one. All of the children *did* resist the temptation—none played with the forbidden toy. On returning to the room we remeasured the attractiveness of all of the toys. Our results were both striking and exciting. Those children who underwent a mild threat now found the toy *less* attractive than before. In short, lacking adequate justification for refraining from playing with the toy, they succeeded in convincing themselves that they hadn't played with it *because they didn't really like it.* On the other hand, the toy did *not* become less attractive for those who were severely threatened. These children continued to rate the forbidden toy as highly desirable—indeed, some even found it more desirable than they had before the threat. The children in the severe threat condition had good external reasons for not playing with the toy (the severe threat itself); they therefore had no need to find additional reasons (like that the toy was no longer attractive); consequently, they continued to like the toy.

Our experiment has been repeated successfully and extended by other psychologists at different universities across the United States. The most dramatic of these experiments is one conducted by Dr. Jonathan Freedman (1965) of Stanford University. The exciting aspect of Freedman's study is that he showed that this effect is a long-lasting one. In his experiment, he repeated our procedure with minor changes. The crucial toy was a battery-powered robot which was, by far, the most attractive to all the children. Freedman forbade the children from playing with the mechanical robot, using mild threats for some and severe threats for others.

After some 23 to 64 days had elapsed, different experimenters came to the classroom under totally unrelated circumstances to administer a psychological test. They tested the students in the same room that was used by Freedman—the original toys were rather carelessly strewn about. After each experimenter had administered one test to a child, she told him that she would have to score it and might want to ask him some questions about it later—and while he was waiting, if he wanted to, he could amuse himself by playing with some of the toys lying around.

Freedman's results are consistent with our own. The overwhelming majority of the children who had been mildly threatened weeks earlier *did not* play with this inherently attractive toy; on the other hand, the great majority of the children who had been severely threatened *did,* in fact, play with the toy. In sum, a severe threat was not effective in inhibiting subsequent behavior—but the effect of one *mild* threat succeeded in inhibiting "undesirable" behavior for as long as 64 days! The beauty of this technique is that the child did not come to devalue this behavior (playing with the toy) because some adult told him it was undesirable; rather, he convinced *himself* that it was undesirable.

As I mentioned early in this presentation, the theory of cognitive dissonance is not limited to the area of the socialization of children—it also has a great deal to say about the modification of adult values, attitudes and behavior. I would like to discuss one experimental situation which I feel has important ramifications in this regard. I conducted this experiment in collaboration with Dr. David Mettee at the University of Texas (1968). The experiment is involved with inducing individuals to commit an immoral act or to resist the temptation to commit an immoral act.

Before I describe the experiment, I will present the theoretical rationale behind it. This can be stated in one sentence: All other things being equal, people tend to behave in a manner which is consistent with their self esteem. Thus, if a person is made to feel that he is a decent, worthwhile person, and is subsequently placed in a moral dilemma, he is more likely to behave morally than if he were made to feel that he is worthless as a person. The cognition "I am a decent person" is consistent with decent behavior and inconsistent with immoral behavior. The cognition "I am a worthless person" is consistent with immoral behavior and inconsistent with decent behavior.

In our experiment we attempted to modify a person's self concept (temporarily) in the following manner: College students were asked to fill out a personality inventory. Subsequently, they were given false information about the outcome of this inventory. On an individual basis, each student was given false, prearranged information about the results of this personality test. One third of the students were given positive feedback; specifically, they were told that the test indicated that they were mature, rational, interesting, etc. One third of the students were given negative feedback; they were told that the test indicated that they were relatively immature, irrational, rather shallow, etc. One third of the students were not given any information about the results of the test—they were informed that the inventory had not yet been scored.

Immediately afterwards, the students were scheduled to participate in an experiment which had no apparent relationship to the personality inventory and which was conducted by a different psychologist. As a part of this second experiment, the subjects participated in a game of cards against some of their fellow students. This was a gambling game in which students were allowed to bet money and were told that they could keep whatever money they won. In the course of the game, the subjects were presented with a few opportunities to cheat in a situation where it seemed impossible that they could be detected. The crucial situation was arranged so that if the students were to decide *not* to cheat, they would certainly lose—whereas if they decided to cheat, they would be certain to win a sizable sum of money.

Let me elaborate on this card-playing situation. The game is called "blackjack" (sometimes known as "21"). In this game, each player is dealt as many cards as he needs in an attempt to achieve a face value which totals 21—or to approach a total of 21 without exceeding that score. Thus, a 7, a 4, and a 10 would be a perfect score; likewise, a 5, a 3, a 6, and a 7 would be a winning combination. Since obtaining 21 itself is relatively rare, a score of 19 or 20 is usually sufficient to win. If a player's total exceeds 21, he automatically loses. A player whose cards total 14 or 15 will almost always decide to draw an additional card in the hope of increasing his score without exceeding 21. In the experiment, the subjects were separated from one another and from the experimenter by plywood walls. The cards (and money) were slipped to (and from) the player through a narrow opening at the bottom of his wall. The players were told that the cards would be dealt to them not by a person, but by a mechanical dealing machine. This machine was demonstrated to them. They were informed that the machine had not as yet been perfected and occasionally blundered. Specifically, they were told the mistake the machine might make would be to deal two cards simultaneously instead of one. If this occurred, the subjects were asked to slide the bottom-most card back through the opening since that was not their rightful card.

In the course of the game, the experimenter provided each subject with the opportunity and the temptation to cheat. This was accomplished in the following way: Imagine a player with cards totaling 13. Naturally he requests an additional card. "Whoops," the "machine" blunders and presents the player with two cards. His rightful card is a 10, which would cause him to lose; his illegitimate card is an 8, which would guarantee victory. A subject's decision to keep the illegitimate but winning card was our measure of cheating. In this situation the subjects were led to feel that they could not be detected because of the privacy provided by the booth and because of their belief that the cards were being distributed by an impersonal machine. In actuality, however, the experimenter was able to determine whether or not a person cheated because it was the experimenter who really distributed the cards rather than the machine.

Our results demonstrated that those students who had previously received information designed to raise their self esteem showed little inclination to cheat; i.e., they cheated slightly less frequently than the students

in the control condition (who received no prior information about their personalities). On the other hand, those students who had previously received information designed to lower their self esteem cheated more frequently than the students in the control condition. The difference in cheating between the subjects in the two experimental conditions was statistically reliable. It should be noted that, although our procedure caused some discomfort to ⅓ of the subjects, it was only temporary. A complete explanation of the procedure was presented to all subjects at the close of the experiment and whatever discomfort they felt was alleviated.

TABLE 1

Number of People Cheating at Least Once as a Function of Self Esteem

Condition	Cheat	Never cheat
Low Self Esteem	13	2
Control	9	6
High Self Esteem	6	9

Note. $\chi^2_{LHC} = 7.00$, $df = 2$, $p < .05$.
$\chi^2_{LH} = 5.17$, $df = 1$, $p < .03$.

The results of this experiment are quite provocative, especially when one takes into consideration the fact that one of the unique aspects of this study was the non-specific nature of the self concept manipulation. That is, in the "personality evaluation" that the subjects received, they were not told anything about themselves which would lead them to infer that they were moral-honest or immoral-dishonest people. Rather, as you will recall, they were told things designed to raise or reduce their self esteem in general—concretely, that they were uninteresting and immature people or interesting and mature people. The social implications of these findings would appear to be of some importance. The results suggest that people who have a high opinion of themselves are less prone to perform any activities which are generally dissonant with their opinion. Looking at the other side of this coin, our results indicate that it is easier for a person with a low self concept to commit acts of a criminal nature. Moreover, it may be that the common thread running through the complex variables involved in successful socialization is that of differential development of self esteem. Granted that most children become aware of what behavior is approved (moral) or disapproved (immoral), the development of high self esteem in the individual may be crucial in his choosing a moral rather than an immoral mode of behavior. This discussion is highly speculative, however, and further experimentation is necessary before its validity can be determined.

References

Aronson, E. The theory of cognitive dissonance: a current perspective. In L. Berkowitz (Ed.), *Advances in experimental social psychology*, Vol. 4 New York: Academic Press, 1969 (in press).

Aronson, E., & Carlsmith, J. M. Effect of the severity of threat on the devaluation of forbidden behavior. *J. abnorm. soc. Psychol.*, 1963, *66*, 584–588.

Aronson, E., & Mettee, D. R. Dishonest behavior as a function of differential levels of induced self-esteem. *J. Pers. soc. Psychol.*, 1968, *9*, 121–127.

Festinger, L. *A theory of cognitive dissonance.* Evanston, Ill.: Row, Peterson, 1957.

Freedman, J. L. Long-term behavioral effects of cognitive dissonance. *J. exp. soc. Psychol.*, 1965, *1*, 145–155.

What one hears and what one sees of southern race relations today are sharply divergent. Consider some of
the things that occur in interviews with white
Southerners.

"As much as my family likes TV," confided a
friendly North Carolina farmer, "we always turn the
set off when they put them colored people on." But as
the two of us were completing the interview, a series of
famous Negro entertainers performed on the bright,
21-inch screen in the adjoining room. No one in-
terrupted them.   •

A rotund banker in Charleston, South Carolina,
was equally candid in his remarks: "Son, under no
conditions will the white man and the black man ever
get together in this state." He apparently preferred to
ignore the government sponsored integration at his
city's naval installation, just a short distance from his
office.

Another respondent, this time a highly educated
Chattanooga businessman, patiently explained to me
for over an hour how race relations had not changed at
all in his city during the past generation. As I left his
office building, I saw a Negro policeman directing
downtown traffic. It was the first Negro traffic cop I
had ever seen in the South.

The South today is rife with such contradictions;
social change has simply been too rapid for many
Southerners to recognize it. Such a situation commands the attention of psychologists — particularly
those in the South.

social psychology and desegregation research[1]

thomas f. pettigrew
harvard university

There are many other aspects of this sweeping
process that should command our professional attention. To name just two, both the pending violence
and the stultifying conformity attendant with desegregation are uniquely psychological problems. We might
ask, for instance, what leads to violence in some desegregating communities, like Little Rock and Clinton,
and not in others, like Norfolk and Winston-Salem? A

1.   This paper was given as an invited address at the Annual
Meeting of the Southeastern Psychological Association, Atlanta, Georgia, March 31, 1960. The author wishes to express
his appreciation to Gordon W. Allport of Harvard University,
E. Earl Baughman of the University of North Carolina, and
Cooper C. Clements of Emory University for their
suggestions. Reprinted from *American Psychologist*, 1961, Vol.
16, pp. 105–112. Copyright 1961 by the American Psychological
Association, and reproduced by permission.

multiplicity of factors must be relevant and further research is desperately needed to delineate them; but tentative early work seems to indicate that desegregation violence so far has been surprisingly "rational." That is, violence has generally resulted in localities where at least some of the authorities give prior hints that they would gladly return to segregation if disturbances occurred; peaceful integration has generally followed firm and forceful leadership.[2]

Research concerning conformity in the present situation is even more important. Many psychologists know from personal experience how intense the pressures to conform in racial attitudes have become in the present-day South; indeed, it appears that the first amendment guaranteeing free speech is in as much peril as the fourteenth amendment. Those who dare to break consistently this conformity taboo must do so in many parts of the South under the intimidation of slanderous letters and phone calls, burned crosses, and even bomb threats. Moreover, this paper will contend that conformity is the social psychological key to analyzing desegregation.

It is imperative that psychologists study these phenomena for two reasons: first, our psychological insights and methods are needed in understanding and solving this, our nation's primary internal problem; second, this process happening before our eyes offers us a rare opportunity to test in the field the psychological concomitants of cultural stress and social change. Thus I would like in this paper to assess some of the prospects and directions of these potential psychological contributions.

Role of Social Science in the Desegregation Process to Date

The role of social science, particularly sociology and psychology, in the desegregation process has been much publicized and criticized by southern segregationists.[3] Many of these critics apparently think that

sociology is synonymous with socialism and psychology with brainwashing. In any event, their argument that we have been crucially important in the Supreme Court desegregation cases of the fifties is based largely on the reference to seven social science documents in Footnote 11 of the famous 1954 *Brown vs. Board of Education* decision. It would be flattering for us to think that our research has had such a dramatic effect on the course of history as segregationists claim, but in all truth we do not deserve such high praise.

In making their claim that the 1954 decision was psychological and not legal, the segregationists choose to overlook several things. The 1954 ruling did not come suddenly "out of the blue"; it was a logical continuation of a 44-year Supreme Court trend that began in 1910 when a former private in the Confederate Army, the liberal Edward White, became Chief Justice (Logan, 1956). When compared to this backdrop, our influence on the 1954 ruling was actually of only footnote importance. Furthermore, the language and spirit of the 1896 *Plessy vs. Ferguson*, separate-but-equal decision, so dear to the hearts of segregationists, were as immersed in the jargon and thinking of the social science of that era as the 1954 decision was of our era. Its 1896, Sumnerian argument that laws cannot change "social prejudices" (Allport, 1954, pp. 469–473) and its use of such social Darwinism terms as "racial instincts" and "natural affinities" lacked only a footnote to make it as obviously influenced by the then current social science as the 1954 ruling.

A final reason why we do not deserve the flattering praise of the segregationists is our failure to make substantial contributions to the process since 1954. The lack of penetrating psychological research in this area can be traced directly to three things: the lack of extensive foundation support, conformity pressures applied in many places in the South that deter desegregation research, and the inadequacy of traditional psychological thinking to cope with the present process. Let us discuss each of these matters in turn.

A few years ago Stuart Cook (1957) drew attention to the failure of foundations to support desegregation research; the situation today is only slightly improved. It appears that a combination of foundation fears has produced this situation. One set of fears, as Cook noted, may stem from concern over attacks by southern Congressmen on their tax free status; the other set may stem from boycotts carried out by some segregationists against products identified with the foundations. In

2. Clark (1953) predicted this from early border-state integration, and a variety of field reports have since documented the point in specific instances.

3. For instance, once-liberal Virginius Dabney (1957, p. 14), editor of the *Richmond Times-Dispatch,* charged that "the violence at Little Rock ... never would have happened if nine justices had not consulted sociologists and psychologists, instead of lawyers, in 1954, and attempted to legislate through judicial decrees."

any case, this curtailment of funds is undoubtedly one reason why social scientists have so far left this crucial process relatively unstudied. Recently, however, a few moderate sized grants have been made for work in this area; hopefully, this is the beginning of a reappraisal by foundations of their previous policies. And it is up to us to submit competent research proposals to them to test continually for any change of these policies.

It is difficult to assess just how much damage has been done to desegregation research in the South by segregationist pressures. Probably the number of direct refusals to allow such research by southern institutions outside of the Black Belt has actually been small. More likely, the greatest harm has been rendered indirectly by the stifling atmosphere which prevents us from actually testing the limits of research opportunities. Interested as we may be in the racial realm, we decide to work in a less controversial area. Perhaps it is less a matter of courage than it is of resignation in the face of what are thought to be impossible barriers. If these suspicions are correct, there is real hope for overcoming in part this second obstacle to desegregation research.

In some situations, there should be little resistance. In racially integrated veterans' hospitals, for instance, much needed personality studies comparing Negro and white patients should be possible. In other situations, the amount of resistance to race research may be less than we anticipate. Since Little Rock, many so-called "moderates" in the South, particularly businessmen, have become more interested in the dynamics of desegregation. This is not to say that they are more in favor of racial equality than they were; it is only to suggest that the bad publicity, the closing of schools, and the economic losses suffered by Little Rock have made these influential Southerners more receptive to objective and constructive research on the process. It is for this reason that it is imperative the limits for the southern study of desegregation be tested at this time.

Finally, psychological contributions to desegregation research have been restricted by the inadequacy of traditional thinking in our discipline. More specifically, the relative neglect of situational variables in interracial behavior and a restricted interpretation and use of the attitude concept hinder psychological work in this area.

The importance of the situation for racial interaction has been demonstrated in a wide variety of settings. All-pervasive racial attitudes are often not involved; many individuals seem fully capable of immediate behavioral change as situations change. Thus in Panama there is a divided street, the Canal Zone side of which is racially segregated and the Panamanian side of which is racially integrated. Biesanz and Smith (1951) report that most Panamanians and Americans appear to accommodate without difficulty as they go first on one side of the street and then on the other. Likewise in the coal mining county of McDowell, West Virginia, Minard (1952) relates that the majority of Negro and white miners follow easily a traditional pattern of integration below the ground and almost complete segregation above the ground. The literature abounds with further examples: southern white migrants readily adjusting to integrated situations in the North (Killian, 1949), northern whites approving of employment and public facility integration but resisting residential integration (Reitzes, 1953), etc. Indeed, at the present time in the South there are many white Southerners who are simultaneously adjusting to bus and public golf course integration and opposing public school integration. Or, as in Nashville, they may have accepted school integration but are opposing lunch counter integration.

This is not to imply that generalized attitudes on race are never invoked. There are some Panamanians and some Americans who act about the same on both sides of the Panamanian street. Minard (1952) estimated about two-fifths of the West Virginian miners he observed behave consistently in either a tolerant or an intolerant fashion both below and above ground. And some whites either approve or disapprove of all desegregation. But these people are easily explained by traditional theory. They probably consist of the extremes in authoritarianism; their attitudes on race are so generalized and so salient that their consistent behavior in racial situations is sometimes in defiance of the prevailing social norms.

On the other hand, the "other directed" individuals who shift their behavior to keep in line with shifting expectations present the real problem for psychologists. Their racial attitudes appear less salient, more specific, and more tied to particular situations. Conformity needs are predominantly important for these people, and we shall return shortly to a further discussion of these conformists.

One complication introduced by a situational analysis is that interracial contact itself frequently leads to the modification of attitudes. A number of studies of racially integrated situations have noted dramatic attitude changes, but in most cases the changes involved specific, situation linked attitudes. For example, white department store employees become more accepting of Negroes in the work situation after equal status, integrated contact but not necessarily more accepting in other situations (Harding & Hogrefe, 1952). And *The American Soldier* studies (Stouffer, Suchman, DeVinney, Star, & Williams, 1949) found that the attitudes of white army personnel toward the Negro as a fighting man improve after equal status, integrated contact in combat, but their attitudes toward the Negro as a social companion do not necessarily change. In other words, experience in a novel situation of equal status leads to acceptance of that specific situation for many persons. Situations, then, not only structure specific racial behavior, but they may change specific attitudes in the process.

One final feature of a situational analysis deserves mention. Typically in psychology we have tested racial attitudes in isolation, apart from conflicting attitudes and values. Yet this is not realistic. As the desegregation process slowly unfolds in such resistant states as Virginia and Georgia, we see clearly that many segregationist Southerners value law and order, public education, and a prosperous economy above their racial views. Once such a situation pits race against other entrenched values, we need to know the public's hierarchy of these values. Thus a rounded situational analysis requires the measures of racial attitudes in the full context of countervalues.[4]

A second and related weakness in our psychological approach is the failure to exploit fully the broad and dynamic implications of the attitude concept. Most social psychological research has dealt with attitudes as if they were serving only an expressive function; but racial attitudes in the South require a more complex treatment.

In their volume, *Opinion and Personality*, Smith, Bruner, and White (1956) urge a more expansive interpretation of attitudes. They note three attitude functions. First, there is the *object appraisal* function; attitudes aid in understanding "reality" as it is defined by the culture. Second, attitudes can play a *social ad-*

justment role by contributing to the individual's identification with, or differentiation from, various reference groups. Finally, attitudes may reduce anxiety by serving an expressive or *externalization* function.

Externalization occurs when an individual . . . senses an analogy between a perceived environmental event and some unresolved inner problem . . . [and] adopts an attitude . . . which is a transformed version of his way of dealing with his inner difficulty (pp. 41–44). (Reprinted with permission of John Wiley & Sons, Inc.)

At present the most fashionable psychological theories of prejudice — frustration-aggression, psychoanalytic, and authoritarianism — all deal chiefly with the externalization process. Valuable as these theories have been, this exclusive attention to the expressive component of attitudes has been at the expense of the object appraisal and social adjustment components. Moreover, it is the contention of this paper that these neglected and more socially relevant functions, particularly social adjustment, offer the key to further psychological advances in desegregation research.[5]

The extent to which this psychological concentration on externalization has influenced the general public was illustrated recently in the popular reaction to the swastika desecrations of Jewish temples. The perpetrators, all agreed, must be juvenile hoodlums, or "sick," or both. In other words, externalization explanations were predominantly offered.[6] Valid though these explanations may be in many cases, is it not also evident that the perpetrators were accurately reflecting the anti-Semitic norms of their subcultures? Thus their acts and the attitudes behind their acts are socially adjusting for these persons, given the circles in which they move.

Much less the public, some sociologists, too, have been understandably misled by our overemphasis on externalization into underestimating the psychological analysis of prejudice. One sociologist (Rose, 1956) categorically concludes:

4. A popular treatment of this point has been made by Zinn (1959).

5. Though this paper emphasizes the social adjustment aspect of southern attitudes toward Negroes, the equally neglected object appraisal function is also of major importance. Most southern whites know only lower class Negroes; consequently their unfavorable stereotype of Negroes serves a definite reality function.

6. Such explanations also serve for many anti-Semitic observers as an ego-alien defense against guilt.

There is no evidence that ... any known source of "prejudice" in the psychological sense is any more prevalent in the South than in the North (p. 174).

Two others (Rabb & Lipset, 1959) maintain firmly:

the psychological approach, as valuable as it is, does not explain the preponderance of people who engage in prejudiced behavior, but do *not* have special emotional problems (p. 26).

Both of these statements assume, as some psychologists have assumed, that externalization is the only possible psychological explanation of prejudice. These writers employ cultural and situational norms as explanatory concepts for racial prejudice and discrimination, but fail to see that conformity needs are the personality reflections of these norms and offer an equally valid concept on the psychological level. To answer the first assertion, recent evidence indicates that conformity to racial norms, one "known source of prejudice," is "more prevalent in the South than in the North." To answer the second assertion, strong needs to conform to racial norms in a sternly sanctioning South, for instance, are *not* "special emotional problems." Psychology is not just a science of mental illness nor must psychological theories of prejudice be limited to the mentally ill.

Conformity and Social Adjustment in Southern Racial Attitudes

Evidence of the importance of conformity in southern attitudes on race has been steadily accumulating in recent years. The relevant data come from several different research approaches; one of these is the study of anti-Semitism. Roper's (1946, 1947) opinion polls have twice shown the South, together with the Far West, to be one of the least anti-Semitic regions in the United States. Knapp's (1944) study of over 1,000 war rumors from all parts of the country in 1942 lends additional weight to this finding. He noted that anti-Semitic stories constituted 9% of the nation's rumors but only 3% of the South's rumors. By contrast, 8.5% of the southern rumors concerned the Negro as opposed to only 3% for the nation as a whole. Consistent with these data, too, is Prothro's (1952) discovery that two-fifths of his white adult sample in Louisiana was quite favorable in its attitudes toward Jews but at the same time quite unfavorable in its attitudes toward Negroes. But if the externalization function were predominant in southern anti-Negro attitudes, the South should also be highly anti-Semitic. Externalizing bigots do not select out just the Negro; they typically reject all out-groups, even, as Hartley (1946) has demonstrated, outgroups that do not exist.

Further evidence comes from research employing the famous F Scale measure of authoritarianism (Adorno, Frenkel-Brunswik, Levinson, & Sanford, 1950). Several studies, employing both student and adult samples, have reported southern F Scale means that fall well within the range of means of comparable nonsouthern groups (Milton, 1952; Pettigrew, 1959; Smith & Prothro, 1957). Moreover, there is no evidence that the family pattern associated with authoritarianism is any more prevalent in the South than in other parts of the country (Davis, Gardner, & Gardner, 1941; Dollard, 1937). It seems clear, then, that the South's heightened prejudice against the Negro cannot be explained in terms of any regional difference in authoritarianism. This is not to deny, however, the importance of the F Scale in predicting individual differences; it appears to correlate with prejudice in southern samples at approximately the same levels as in northern samples (Pettigrew, 1959).

The third line of evidence relates conformity measures directly to racial attitudes. For lack of a standardized, nonlaboratory measure, one study defined conformity and deviance in terms of the respondents' social characteristics (Pettigrew, 1959). For a southern white sample with age and education held constant, potentially conforming respondents (i.e., females or church attenders) were *more* anti-Negro than their counterparts (i.e., males or nonattenders of church), and potentially deviant respondents (i.e., armed service veterans or political independents) were *less* anti-Negro than their counterparts (i.e., nonveterans or political party identifiers). None of these differences were noted in a comparable northern sample. Furthermore, Southerners living in communities with relatively small percentages of Negroes were less anti-Negro than Southerners living in communities with relatively large percentages of Negroes, though they were *not* less authoritarian. In short, respondents most likely to be conforming to cultural pressures are more prejudiced against Negroes in the South but not in the North. And the percentage of Negroes in the community appears to be a fairly accurate index of the strength of these southern cultural pressures concerning race.

Thus all three types of research agree that conformity to the stern racial norms of southern culture is unusually crucial in the South's heightened hostility toward the Negro.[7] Or, in plain language, it is the path of least resistance in most southern circles to favor white supremacy. When an individual's parents and peers are racially prejudiced, when his limited world accepts racial discrimination as a given of life, when his deviance means certain ostracism, then his anti-Negro attitudes are not so much expressive as they are socially adjusting.

This being the case, it is fortunate that a number of significant laboratory and theoretical advances in the conformity realm have been made recently in our discipline. Solomon Asch's (1951) pioneer research on conformity, followed up by Crutchfield (1955) and others, has provided us with a wealth of laboratory findings, many of them suggestive for desegregation research. And theoretical analyses of conformity have been introduced by Kelman (1958, 1961), Festinger (1953, 1957), and Thibaut and Kelley (1959); these, too, are directly applicable for desegregation research. Indeed, research in southern race relations offers a rare opportunity to test these empirical and theoretical formulations in the field on an issue of maximum salience.

Consider the relevance of one of Asch's (1951) intriguing findings. Asch's standard situation, you will recall, employed seven pre-instructed assistants and a genuine subject in a line judgment task. On two-thirds of the judgments, the seven assistants purposely reported aloud an obviously incorrect estimate; thus the subject, seated eighth, faced unanimous pressure to conform by making a similarly incorrect response. On approximately one-third of such judgments, he yielded to the group; like the others, he would estimate a 5-inch line as 4 inches. But when Asch disturbed the unanimity by having one of his seven assistants give the correct response, the subjects yielded only a tenth, rather than a third, of the time. Once unanimity no longer existed, even when there was only one supporting colleague, the subject could better withstand the pressure of the majority to conform. To carry through the analogy to today's crisis in the South, obvious 5-inch lines are being widely described as 4 inches. Many Southerners, faced with what appears to be solid unanimity, submit to the distortion. But when even one respected source—a minister, a newspaper editor, even a college professor—conspicuously breaks the unanimity, *perhaps* a dramatic modification is achieved in the private opinions of many conforming Southerners. Only an empirical test can learn if such a direct analogy is warranted.

Consider, too, the relevance of recent theoretical distinctions. Kelman (1958, 1961), for example, has clarified the concept of conformity by pointing out that three separate processes are involved: *compliance, identification,* and *internalization*. Compliance exists when an individual accepts influence not because he believes in it, but because he hopes to achieve a favorable reaction from an agent who maintains surveillance over him. Identification exists when an individual accepts influence because he wants to establish or maintain a satisfying relationship with another person or group. The third process, internalization, exists when an individual accepts influence because the content of the behavior itself is satisfying; unlike the other types of conformity, internalized behavior will be performed without the surveillance of the agent or a salient relationship with the agent. It is with this third process that Kelman's ideas overlap with authoritarian theory.

We have all witnessed illustrations of each of these processes in the acceptance by Southerners of the region's racial norms. The "Uncle Tom" Negro is an example of a compliant Southerner; another example is furnished by the white man who treats Negroes as equals only when not under the surveillance of other whites. Identification is best seen in white Southerners whose resistance to racial integration enables them to be a part of what they erroneously imagine to be Confederate tradition. Such identifiers are frequently upwardly mobile people who are still assimilating to urban society; they strive for social status by identifying with the hallowed symbols and shibboleths of the South's past. Southerners who have internalized the white supremacy dictates of the culture are the real racists who use the issue to gain political office, to attract resistance group membership fees, or to meet personality needs. Southerners with such contrasting bases for their racial attitudes should react very differently toward desegregation. For instance, compliant whites can be expected to accept desegregation more readily than those who have internalized segregationist norms.

---

7.   Similar analyses of South African student data indicate that the social adjustment function may also be of unusual importance in the anti-African attitudes of the English in the Union (Pettigrew, 1958, 1960).

On the basis of this discussion of conformity, I would like to propose a new concept: *the latent liberal.* This is not to be confused with the cherished southern notion of the "moderate"; the ambiguous term "moderate" is presently used to describe everything from an integrationist who wants to be socially accepted to a racist who wants to be polite. Rather, the latent liberal refers to the Southerner who is neither anti-Semitic nor authoritarian but whose conformity habits and needs cause him to be strongly anti-Negro. Through the processes of compliance and identification, the latent liberal continues to behave in a discriminatory fashion toward Negroes even though such behavior conflicts with his basically tolerant personality. He is at the present time *illiberal* on race, but he has the personality potentiality of becoming liberal once the norms of the culture change. Indeed, as the already unleashed economic, legal, political, and social forces restructure the South's racial norms, the latent liberal's attitudes about Negroes will continue to change. Previously cited research suggests that there are today an abundance of white Southerners who meet this latent liberal description; collectively, they will reflect on the individual level the vast societal changes now taking place in the South.

Some Suggested Directions for Future Psychological Research on Desegregation[8]

We are in serious need of research on the Negro, both in the North and in the South. Most psychological research in this area was conducted during the 1930s and directed at testing racists' claims of Negro inferiority. But the most sweeping advances in American Negro history have been made in the past generation, requiring a fresh new look—particularly at the Negro personality.

Two aspects of this research make it complex and difficult. In the first place, the race of the interviewer is a complicating and not as yet fully understood factor. Further methodological study is needed on this point. Moreover, special problems of control are inherent in this research. Not only are there some relatively unique variables that must be considered (e.g., migration history, differential experience with the white community, etc.), but such simple factors as education are

8. For other suggestions, see the important analysis of desegregation by Cook (1957).

not easy to control. For instance, has the average graduate of a southern rural high school for Negroes received an education equal to the average graduate of such a school for whites? No, in spite of the South's belated efforts to live up to separate-but-equal education, available school data indicate that the graduates have probably not received equivalent educations. Yet some recent research on Negro personality has been based on the assumption that Negro and white education in the South are equivalent (e.g., Smith & Prothro, 1957).

Fortunately, the Institute for Research in the Social Sciences at the University of North Carolina has embarked on a large study of many of these content and methodological problems. It is to be hoped that their work will stimulate other efforts.

Some of the most valuable psychological data now available on desegregation have been collected by public opinion polls. But typically these data have been gathered without any conceptual framework to guide their coverage and direction.

For example, one of the more interesting poll findings is that a majority of white Southerners realize that racial desegregation of public facilities is inevitable even though about six out of seven strongly oppose the process (Hyman & Sheatsley, 1956). The psychological implications of this result are so extensive that we would like to know more. Do the respondents who oppose desegregation but accept its inevitability have other characteristics of latent liberals? Are these respondents more often found outside of the Black Belt? Typically, we cannot answer such questions from present poll data; we need to build into the desegregation polls broader coverage and more theoretical direction.

The third direction that psychological research in desegregation could usefully take concerns measurement. Save for the partly standardized F Scale, we still lack widely used, standardized field measures of the chief variables in this realm. Such instruments are necessary both for comparability of results and for stimulation of research; witness the invigorating effects on research of the F Scale, the Minnesota Multiphasic Inventory, and the need achievement scoring scheme. Mention of McClelland's need achievement scoring scheme should remind us, too, that projective and other indirect techniques might answer many of these measurement requirements—especially for such sensitive and subtle variables as conformity needs.

Finally, the definitive interdisciplinary case study of desegregation has yet to be started. Properly buttressed by the necessary foundation aid, such a study should involve comparisons before, during, and after desegregation of a wide variety of communities. The interdisciplinary nature of such an undertaking is stressed because desegregation is a peculiarly complex process demanding a broad range of complementary approaches.

Any extensive case project must sample three separate time periods: before a legal ruling or similar happening has alerted the community to imminent desegregation, during the height of the desegregating process, and after several years of accommodation. Without this longitudinal view, desegregation as a dynamic, ongoing process cannot be understood. This time perspective, for instance, would enable us to interpret the fact that an overwhelming majority of Oklahoma whites in a 1954 poll sternly objected to mixed schools, but within a few years has accepted without serious incident integrated education throughout most of the state (Jones, 1957).

A carefully selected range of communities is required to test for differences in the process according to the characteristics of the area. Recent demographic analyses and predictions of the South's school desegregation pattern (Ogburn & Grigg, 1956; Pettigrew, 1957; Pettigrew & Campbell, 1960) could help in making this selection of communities. Comparable data gathered in such a selected variety of locations would allow us to pinpoint precisely the aspects of desegregation unique to, say, a Piedmont city, as opposed to a Black Belt town.

Compare the potential value of such a broad research effort with the limited case studies that have been possible so far. Low budget reports of only one community are the rule; many of them are theses or seminar projects, some remain on the descriptive level, all but a few sample only one time period, and there is almost no comparability of instruments and approach. A comprehensive case project is obviously long overdue.

This has been an appeal for a vigorous empirical look at southern race relations. Despite segregationists' claims to the contrary, social psychological contributions to desegregation research have been relatively meager. There are, however, grounds for hoping that this situation will be partly corrected in the near future — particularly if psychologists get busy.

Foundations appear to be re-evaluating their previous reluctance to support such research. And we can re-evaluate our own resignation in the face of barriers to conduct investigations in this area; the tragedy of Little Rock has had a salutary effect on many influential Southerners in this respect.

Recognition of the importance of the situation in interracial behavior and the full exploitation of the attitude concept can remove inadequacies in the traditional psychological approach to the study of race. In this connection, an extended case for considering conformity as crucial in the Negro attitudes of white Southerners was presented and a new concept — the latent liberal — introduced. One final implication of this latent liberal concept should be mentioned. Some cynics have argued that successful racial desegregation in the South will require an importation of tens of thousands of psychotherapists and therapy for millions of bigoted Southerners. Fortunately for desegregation, psychotherapists, and Southerners, this will not be necessary; a thorough repatterning of southern interracial behavior will be sufficient therapy in itself.

References

Adorno, T. W., Frenkel-Brunswik, Else, Levinson, D. J., & Sanford, N. *The authoritarian personality.* New York: Harper, 1950.

Allport, G. W. *The nature of prejudice.* Cambridge, Mass.: Addison-Wesley, 1954.

Asch, S. E. Effects of group pressure upon the modification and distortion of judgments. In H. Guetzkow (Ed.), *Groups, leadership and men.* Pittsburgh: Carnegie, 1951.

Biesanz, J., & Smith, L. M. Race relations of Panama and the Canal Zone. *Amer. J. Sociol.,* 1951, *57,* 7–14.

Clark, K. B. Desegregation: An appraisal of the evidence. *J. soc. Issues,* 1953, *9,* 1–76.

Cook, S. W. Desegregation: A psychological analysis. *Amer. Psychologist,* 1957, *12,* 1–13.

Crutchfield, R. S. Conformity and character. *Amer. Psychologist,* 1955, *10,* 191–198.

Dabney, V. The violence at Little Rock. *Richmond Times-Dispatch,* 1957, *105,* September 24, 14.

Davis, A., Gardner, B., & Gardner, Mary. *Deep South.* Chicago: Univer. Chicago Press, 1941.

Dollard, J. *Caste and class in a southern town.* New Haven: Yale Univer. Press, 1937.

Festinger, L. An analysis of compliant behavior. In M. Sherif & M. O. Wilson (Eds.), *Group relations at the crossroads.* New York: Harper, 1953.

Festinger, L. *A theory of cognitive dissonance.* Evanston, Ill.: Row, Peterson, 1957.

Harding, J., & Hogrefe, R. Attitudes of white department store employees toward Negro co-workers. *J. soc. Issues,* 1952, *8,* 18–28.

Hartley, E. L. *Problems in prejudice.* New York: King's Crown, 1946.

Hyman, H. H., & Sheatsley, P. B. Attitudes toward desegregation. *Scient. Amer.,* 1956, *195,* 35–39.

Jones, E. City limits. In D. Shoemaker (Ed.), *With all deliberate speed.* New York: Harper, 1957.

Kelman, H. C. Compliance, identification, and internalization: Three processes of attitude change. *J. conflict Resolut.,* 1958, *2,* 51–60.

Kelman, H. C. *Social influence and personal belief.* New York: Wiley, 1961.

Killian, L. W. Southern white laborers in Chicago's West Side. Unpublished doctoral dissertation, University of Chicago, 1949.

Knapp, R. H. A psychology of rumor. *Publ. opin. Quart.,* 1944, *8,* 22–37.

Logan, R. W. The United States Supreme Court and the segregation issue. *Ann. Amer. Acad. Pol. Soc. Sci.,* 1956, *304,* 10–16.

Milton, O. Presidential choice and performance on a scale of authoritarianism. *Amer. Psychologist,* 1952, *7,* 597–598.

Minard, R. D. Race relations in the Pocahontas coal field. *J. soc. Issues,* 1952, *8,* 29–44.

Ogburn, W. F., & Grigg, C. M. Factors related to the Virginia vote on segregation. *Soc. Forces,* 1956, *34,* 301–308.

Pettigrew, T. F. Demographic correlates of border-state desegregation. *Amer. sociol. Rev.,* 1957, *22,* 683–689.

Pettigrew, T. F. Personality and sociocultural factors in intergroup attitudes: A cross-national comparison. *J. conflict Resolut.,* 1958, *2,* 29–42.

Pettigrew, T. F. Regional differences in anti-Negro prejudice. *J. abnorm. soc. Psychol.,* 1959, *59,* 28–36.

Pettigrew, T. F. Social distance attitudes of South African students. *Soc. Forces,* 1960, *38,* 246–253.

Pettigrew, T. F., & Campbell, E. Q. Faubus and segregation: An analysis of Arkansas voting. *Publ. opin. Quart.,* 1960, *24,* 436–447.

Prothro, E. T. Ethnocentrism and anti-Negro attitudes in the deep South. *J. abnorm. soc. Psychol.,* 1952, *47,* 105–108.

Rabb, E., & Lipset, S. M. *Prejudice and society.* New York: Anti-Defamation League of B'nai B'rith, 1959.

Reitzes, D. C. The role of organizational structures: Union versus neighborhood in a tension situation. *J. soc. Issues,* 1953, *9,* 37–44.

Roper, E. United States anti-Semites. *Fortune,* 1946, *33,* 257–260.

Roper, E. United States anti-Semites. *Fortune,* 1947, *36,* 5–10.

Rose, A. M. Intergroup relations vs. prejudice: Pertinent theory for the study of social change. *Soc. Probl.,* 1956, *4,* 173–176.

Smith, C. U., & Prothro, J. W. Ethnic differences in authoritarian personality. *Soc. Forces,* 1957, *35,* 334–338.

Smith, M. B., Bruner, J. S., & White, R. W. *Opinion and personality.* New York: Wiley, 1956.

Stouffer, S. A., Suchman, E. A., DeVinney, L. C., Star, Shirley A., Williams, R. M., Jr. *Studies in social psychology in World War II.* Vol. 1. *The American soldier: Adjustment during army life.* Princeton: Princeton Univer. Press, 1949.

Thibaut, J. W., & Kelley, H. H. *The social psychology of groups.* New York: Wiley, 1959.

Zinn, H. A fate worse than integration. *Harper's,* 1959, *219,* August, 53–56.

review of evidence relating to effects of desegregation on the intellectual performance of negroes[1]

irwin katz
university of michigan

This is a review of evidence regarding the effects of educational desegregation on the scholastic achievement of Negroes. It focuses on the problem of identi-

1. This paper was prepared at the request of the Society for the Psychological Study of Social Issues because of the social importance of the problem. The author wishes to express his gratitude to John R. P. French for his warm encouragement and helpful suggestions during the preparation of this paper. Thanks are due also to my many colleagues who read and commented on an earlier draft. Reprinted from *American Psychologist*, 1964, Vol. 19, pp. 381–399. Copyright 1964 by the American Psychological Association, and reprinted by permission.

fying the important situational determinants of Negro performance in the racially mixed classroom. Only a few studies have dealt directly with this problem, so that much of the evidence to be surveyed is only inferential. Included are the following: reports on the academic progress of Negro children attending integrated schools, evidence on aspects of the minority child's experience in desegregation that presumably affect his motivation to learn, relevant research on the behavioral effects of psychological stress, and, finally, a series of experiments on Negro productivity in biracial settings.

Negro Americans. In this paper the term "Negro Americans" refers to a minority segment of the national population that is more or less distinguishable on the basis of skin color, hair texture, etc., and that occupies a subordinate position in American culture. The extent of subordination varies in different regions and localities, but usually includes some degree of restriction on educational and economic opportunities, as well as social exclusion by whites and an attribution by whites of intellectual inferiority. While the term "race" will be used for convenience, no meaning is intended other than that of distinctiveness of appearance and commonality of experience; the issue of whether there are consequential differences in the genetic endowment of Negroes and whites will not be considered. Thus the present discussion should be more or less applicable to any American minority group whose status is similar to that of Negroes.

Desegregation. Educational desegregation is a politico-legal concept referring to the elimination of racial separation within school systems. As such it embraces a great variety of transitional situations having diverse effects upon the scholastic performance of Negro children. The meaning of desegregation has been broadened in recent years to include the reduction of racial clustering due to factors other than legal discrimination—i.e., de facto segregation. A number of recent court decisions in the North have ruled that "racial imbalance" in a school (a predominance of minority-group children) constitutes de facto segregation (United States Commission on Civil Rights, 1962a, 1962b). Also described as de facto segregation by various social scientists are the racially homogeneous classes often found in schools where children are grouped according to ability (Deutsch, 1963; Dodson, 1962; Tumin, 1963).

The present concern is mainly with instances of desegregation that are marked by a substantial increase in the proportion of white peers, or both white peers and adult authorities, in the immediate environment of the Negro student. (In the South integration with white classmates is usually also the occasion of initial contacts with white teachers, while in the North the proportion of white teachers may be high even in schools where Negro students predominate.) Almost invariably in this type of desegregation experience the minority group child is confronted with higher educational standards than prevail in segregated Negro schools (United States Commission on Civil Rights, 1962a, 1962b). Both aspects of the Negro's experience—change in the racial environment and exposure to relatively high academic standards—are likely to have important influences on his scholastic motivation.

Postulated Situational Determinants of Negro Performance in Desegregation

Social threat. Social threat refers to a class of social stimulus events that tend to elicit anxious expectations that others will inflict harm or pain. One may assume that novel types of contact with white strangers possess a social-threat component for members of a subordinated minority group. The degree of threat should be a direct function of (*a*) the amount of evidence of white hostility (or the extent to which evidence of white friendliness is lacking) and (*b*) the amount of power possessed by whites in the contact situation, as shown by their numerical predominance,

control of authority positions, etc. It seems likely that Negro children would be under some degree of social threat in a newly integrated classroom. Mere indifference on the part of white peers may frustrate their needs for companionship and approval, resulting in lowered self-esteem and the arousal of impulses to escape or aggress. In more extreme instances, verbal harassment and even physical hazing may elicit strong fear responses. These external threats are likely to distract the minority child from the task at hand, to the detriment of performance.

In addition, psychological theory suggests that the Negro's own covert reactions to social threat would constitute an important source of intellectual impairment. In discussing the effect of psychological stress on the learning of skills, Deese (1962) mentions distraction by the internal stimuli of autonomic activation, as well as disruption of task responses by neuromuscular and other components of the stress reaction. Mandler and Sarason (1962) and others call attention to the disruptive role of task-irrelevant defensive responses against anxiety. Spence (1958) and Taylor (1963) propose that anxiety, conceptualized as drive, increases intratask response competition. And according to Easterbrook (1959), emotion lowers efficiency on complex tasks by narrowing the range of cue utilization. Also relevant is Bovard's (1959) hypothesis of a specific physiological mechanism to account for the apparent lowering of the stress threshold under conditions of social isolation.

Another way in which social threat may impair performance is by causing Negro children to abandon efforts to excel in order not to arouse further resentment and hostility in white competitors. That is, the latter may possess what French and Raven (1960) refer to as "coercive power." When academic success is expected to instigate white reprisals, then any stimulus which arouses the motive to achieve should also generate anxiety, and defensive avoidance of such stimuli should be learned. This response pattern would not be wholly nonadaptive in a situation where a small number of Negro students stood relatively powerless against a prejudiced white majority—if one assumes that evidence of Negro intellectual competence might have an ego-deflating effect on these white students. The Group for the Advancement of Psychiatry (1957) has put the matter this way:

A feeling of superior worth may be gained merely from the existence of a downgraded group. This leads to an unrealistic and unadaptive kind of self-appraisal based on invidious comparison rather than on solid personal growth and achievement . . . [p. 10].

Finally with regard to possible social threat emanating from a white teacher—given the prestige of the adult authority, any expression by a white teacher of dislike or devaluation, whether through harsh, indifferent, or patronizing behavior, should tend to have unfavorable effects on Negro performance similar to those just described, and perhaps of even greater intensity.

Social facilitation. When the minority newcomer in a desegregated school is accepted socially by his white classmates, his scholastic motivation should be influenced favorably. It was noted earlier that achievement standards tend to be higher in previously all-white schools than in Negro schools. From studies based on white subjects, it is apparent that individuals are responsive to the standards of those with whom they desire to associate (reviewed by Bass, 1961; French & Raven, 1960; Thibaut & Kelley, 1959). That Negro children want friendship with white age mates was shown by Horowitz (1936), Radke, Sutherland, and Rosenberg (1950), and Yarrow (1958). Another study, by Criswell (1939), suggests that Negro children in racially mixed classrooms accept white prestige but increasingly withdraw into their own group as a response to white rejection. Thus, if their desire for acceptance is not inhibited or destroyed by sustained unfriendliness from white children, Negro pupils should tend to adopt the scholastic norms of the high-status majority group. Experimental support for this supposition comes from Dittes and Kelley (1956), who found with white college students that private as well as public adherence to the attitudinal standards of a group were highest among persons who had experienced a fairly high degree of acceptance from the group, with a possibility of gaining even fuller acceptance, while those who received a low degree of acceptance showed little genuine adherence to group norms.

Friendliness and approval on the part of white teachers should be beneficial to Negro motivation by increasing the incentive strength of scholastic success. Assuming that white teachers have more prestige for the minority child than do Negro teachers, the prospect of winning their approval should be more attractive. Hence, when such approval can be expected as a reward for good performance, motivation should be favorably influenced.

Probability of success. When the minority child is placed in a school that has substantially higher scholastic standards than he knew previously, he may become discouraged and not try to succeed. This common sense proposition is derivable from Atkinson's (1958a) theory of the motivational determinants of risk taking and performance. For individuals in whom the tendency to approach success is stronger than the tendency to avoid failure, task motivation is assumed to be a joint function of the subjective probability of achieving success and the incentive value of success. From a postulated inverse relationship between the latter two variables (assuming external influences on incentive strength are held constant) he derives a hypothesis that the strength of motivation is at a maximum when the probability of success is .50, and diminishes as this probability approaches zero or unity. The hypothesis is supported by findings on arithmetic performance of white college students (Atkinson, 1958b), and white elementary-school children (Murstein & Collier, 1962), as well as on digit-symbol performance of white high-school students (Rosen, 1961). (In these studies, the effect occurred regardless of whether subjects had scored relatively high or low on a projective personality measure of the motive to approach success.) It follows that if the Negro newcomer perceives the standards of excellence in a desegregated school as being substantially higher than those he encountered previously, so that the likelihood of his attaining them seems low, his scholastic motivation will decline.

Failure threat. Failure threat is a class of stimulus events in an achievement situation which tend to elicit anxious expectations of harm or pain as a consequence of failure. High probability of failure does not by itself constitute failure threat—it is necessary also that the failure have a social meaning. Thus in Atkinson's formulation, the negative incentive strength of failure varies inversely with the subjective probability of failure, so that fear of failure is most strongly aroused when the probability of failure is at an intermediate level. This leads to the paradoxical prediction that as the probability of failure increases beyond .50, fear of failure declines. The paradox is resolved when one recognizes that Atkinson's model deals only with that component of incentive strength that is determined by the apparent difficulty of the task. Sarason, Davidson, Lighthall, Waite, and Ruebush (1960) call attention to the important influence of anticipated disapproval by parents and teachers on the negative valence of failure. (While their primary interest is in test anxiety as a personality variable, their discussion seems applicable to the present problem of identifying situational determinants of fear of failure.) Presumably, the child's belief that his failure to meet prevailing standards of achievement will bring adult disapproval is relatively unaffected by his own perception of the difficulty of a given task. Hence, fear of disapproval should increase as it becomes more probable—i.e., as the subjective probability of failure increases. Sarason and his associates suggest that a high expectancy of failure arouses strong unconscious hostility against the adults from whom negative evaluation is foreseen. The hostility is turned inward against the self in the form of self-derogatory attitudes, which strengthen the expectation of failure and the desire to escape the situation. Distraction by these and other components of emotional conflict may cause a decrement in the child's performance.

Reports on Academic Achievement of Negroes in Desegregated Schools

There is a dearth of unequivocal information about Negro performance in desegregated schools. A number of factors have contributed to this situation.

1. Many desegregated school systems have a policy of racial nonclassification, so that separate data for Negroes and whites are not available.

2. Where total elimination of legal segregation has occurred, it has usually been accompanied by vigorous efforts to raise educational standards in *all* schools; hence the effects of desegregation per se are confounded with the effects of improved teaching and facilities.

3. In several Southern states only small numbers of highly selected Negro pupils have been admitted to previously all-white schools, and since before-after comparisons of achievement are not usually presented, reports of "satisfactory" adjustment by these Negro children shed little light on the question of relative performance.

Taking the published information for what it is worth, most of its presents a favorable picture of Negro academic adjustment in racially mixed settings. Stallings (1959) has reported on the results of achievement testing in the Louisville school system in 1955-56, the year prior to total elimination of legal segregation, and

again 2 years later. Gains were found in the median scores of all pupils for the grades tested, with Negroes showing greater improvement than whites. The report gave no indication of whether the gains for Negroes were related to amount of actual change in the racial composition of schools. Indeed, Stallings stated, "The gains were greater where Negro pupils remained by choice with Negro teachers." A later survey on Louisville by Knowles (1962) indicated that Negro teachers had not been assigned to classrooms having white students during the period covered by Stallings' research. This means that the best Negro gains observed by Stallings were made by children who *remained in segregated classrooms*, and can only be attributed to factors *other* than desegregation, such as a general improvement in educational standards.

In both Washington and Baltimore, where legal segregation was totally abolished in 1954, the United States Commission on Civil Rights found "some evidence that the scholastic achievement of Negroes in such schools has improved, and no evidence of a resultant reduction in the achievement of white students [*Southern School News, 1960*]." A detailed account of academic progress in the Washington schools since 1954 has been given by Hansen (1960). The results of a city-wide testing program begun in 1955 indicated year-to-year gains in achievement on every academic subject tested at every grade level where the tests were given. The data were not broken down by race. As in the case of Louisville, it seems reasonable to attribute these gains primarily to an ambitious program of educational improvement rather than to racial mixing. For several years the Washington schools have had a steadily increasing predominance of Negro pupils (over 76% in 1960); this, combined with a four-track system of homogeneous ability grouping which has the effect of concentrating Negroes in the lower tracks, has resulted in a minimal desegregation experience for the majority of Negro children.

Little relevant data have been published on other Southern states where desegregation has been initiated. In 1960, 12 administrators of desegregated school systems testified at a Federal hearing on whether integration had damaged academic standards (United States Commission on Civil Rights, 1960). They unanimously replied in the negative, but only one official (from Louisville) mentioned gains in the achievement of Negro pupils. Reports of widespread academic failure on the part of desegregated Negro children are rare. Among those that have appeared recently is one by Day (1962) on Chapel Hill, North Carolina. Referring to a total of about 45 Negroes in predominantly white schools, he stated that the experience of 2 years of desegregation has shown "a disturbing portion of Negro children attending desegregated schools have failed to keep pace with their white classmates. . . . The question remains as to how to raise the achievement of Negro pupils disadvantaged by their home background and lack of motivation [p. 78]." Wyatt (1962) quoted the Superintendent of Schools in Nashville, Tennessee, as stating there was substantially more difficulty with Negro students entering desegregated situations in the upper grades. The official ascribed most of the difficulties to problems of social adjustment, although the cumulative effect of the generally lower achievement in the Negro schools was credited with some responsibility for the situation.

The academic achievement of Negro graduates of segregated Southern high schools who attended integrated colleges has been reviewed by the National Scholarship Service and Fund for Negro Students (NSSFNS, 1963). In a period of 15 years, NSSFNS helped over 9,000 Negro students to enrol in interracial colleges, situated mostly in the North. The report stated:

Tabulations of the academic progress of former NSSFNS counselees and scholarship holders show that 5.6% of these students had a scholastic average of A or A—; 50.3% B+, B, or B—; 32.4% C+, C, or C—; and .7% D or below. Not listing grades were 11%. Fewer than 5% withdrew from college for any reason. This record of college success of an educationally and economically underprivileged group is far above the national average, which shows an over 40% incidence of dropouts from all causes [p. 9].

It should be noted that these students were carefully selected by NSSFNS for their academic qualifications. Nonetheless, the NSSFNS experience demonstrates that qualified Southern Negro youth can function effectively in predominantly white colleges of good quality. Later, there will be mention of additional material on these students which suggests that academic success was associated with social acceptance on the campus.

Evidence of Desegregation Conditions That May Be Detrimental to the Performance of Negroes

It was proposed that the achievement motivation of Negro children in desegregation may be strongly influenced by the social behavior of their white classmates and teachers (social threat and facilitation), by their level of expectancy with regard to academic success (probability of success), and by their perception of the social consequences of failure (failure threat). In this section, evidence about conditions of desegregation that are assumed to have unfavorable effects will be considered. The focusing on negative factors is not meant to suggest that conditions favorable to Negro performance are lacking in present-day situations of desegregation, but rather that the former have received more attention from social scientists — apparently because they are more salient.

SOCIAL REJECTION AND ISOLATION

The rationale for assuming that social rejection is detrimental to the minority child's academic behavior has already been discussed. To what extent are Negroes rejected by white classmates? It is clear that this varies greatly from one community to another. The bulk of early studies on the racial attitudes of white school children in the North indicated that from an early age they expressed strong preference for their own racial group (e.g., Criswell, 1939; Horowitz, 1936; Radke et al., 1950; Radke, Trager, & Davis, 1949). Two examples of desegregation that was highly stressful for Negro children have been described by a psychiatrist, Coles (1963). He writes of the first Negroes to enter white schools in Atlanta and New Orleans:

When they are in school they may experience rejection, isolation, or insult. They live under what physicians would consider to be highly stressful circumstances . . . [p. 4].

During a school year one can see among these children all of the medical and psychiatric responses to fear and anxiety. One child may lose his appetite, another may become sarcastic and have nightmares. Lethargy may develop, or excessive studying may mark the apprehension common to both. At the same time one sees responses of earnest and effective work. . . . Each child's case history would describe a balance of defenses against emotional pain, and some exhaustion under it, as well as behavior which shows an attempt to challenge and surmount it [p. 5].

Out of 13 original students who were studied during the first 2 years of integration, and 47 who became involved in integration 1 year later and were studied during the second year, "only one child has really succumbed to emotional illness." Coles does not present a systematic analysis of the various specific sources of fear and anxiety, but he suggests that worries about school work were of less importance than reactions to the prejudice of white children. Nor does he present adequate information about academic success, merely noting that very few learning difficulties "were insurmountable."

Severe stress due to social rejection has been experienced also by Negro students at various newly desegregated colleges and universities in the South. For example, several months after entering the University of Mississippi as its first Negro student, during which time he was often in considerable physical danger, James Meredith emphasized that rejection and social isolation were the most difficult features of his experience. He referred to himself as "the most segregated Negro in the world" despite his enrolment at the University. "Through it all," he said, "the most intolerable thing has been the campaign of ostracising me [*Southern School News*, 1963]."

Two Negro students who initiated integration at the University of Georgia experienced rejection and isolation during their entire 2-year enrolment (Trillin, 1964).

As Hamilton [Holmes] began his final ten-week quarter at Georgia, he had never eaten in a University dining hall, studied in the library, used the gymnasium, or entered the snack bar. He had no white friends outside the classroom. No white student had ever visited him and he had never visited one of them [p. 83].

The other student, Charlayne Hunter, eventually entered into friendly relationships with several white classmates, and was generally in the company of other students when walking to and from classes or eating on campus. However, she remained totally ostracized in the dormitory where she occupied a room by herself. She suffered from stomach trouble off and on during her entire stay at the University. Both Negroes have since graduated, Holmes with a distinguished academic record. Charlayne Hunter is now married to a white Southerner who was a fellow student at the University.

Desegregation under more favorable conditions has been investigated by Yarrow (1958). Comparable groups of Negro and white children of both sexes were observed in segregated and desegregated summer camps during 2-week sessions. The campers were from low-income families in Southern and Border states. The biracial camps had integrated adult staffs that were highly motivated to "make desegregation work." It was found that the behavior of children in segregated and integrated groups was quite similar. An initial tendency for both white and Negro children to prefer white friends lessened during the 2-week period studied. Satisfaction with the camp experience, as indicated by the percentage of children who expressed a desire that the camp session be extended, was somewhat higher in the desegregated camps. However, there were also indications of social conflict and emotional tension associated with the integration process. In older groups (ages 12 and 13) white children initially directed almost twice as much aggression toward Negro cabin mates as toward white age peers. At the beginning of contact 29% of all actions by white campers toward Negroes were hostile. On the other hand, Negro children of all ages aggressed more against one another than against whites. Overt manifestations of white prejudice tended to diminish during the 2-week period. Nonetheless, tension symptoms appeared in almost twice as many children in desegregated as in segregated groups (71% compared with 38%). Frequencies were the same for Negroes and whites. But Negro children in desegregation were more likely to manifest covert or internalized signs of distress (enuresis, fears, nightmares, withdrawal, physical symptoms) than those that were more overt (fighting, generally disruptive behavior, obscene language, complaining). Of the Negro campers showing tension, 85% showed reactions of the covert type. For the white children showing tension, neither covert nor overt responses predominated. That Negroes were particularly fearful of white disapproval is suggested by their oversensitiveness in desegregation to aggressive and dominative behavior in other Negroes, and their denial of such impulses in themselves. Both reactions are further evidence of a tendency to conceal tensions in the presence of whites.

Regarding the relevance of this study to school integration, it should be noted that the total period of interracial contacts was brief, but peer interactions were probably more intimate and intense than the usual classroom contacts. A generally favorable picture of race relations in Southern integrated schools is presented in a recent article by a journalist, Tanner (1964):

On the social side, younger white and Negro children attending desegregated classes seem to accept each other better than the older ones. Negro and white youngsters can be seen playing together on the slides and swings of almost any desegregated Southern elementary school's playground. At Nashville's Buena Vista Elementary School, Negro boys have won two of the three positions of captain on the school's safety patrol. And in Birmingham, often called the most segregated U.S. city, a Negro boy was chosen vice president of a sixth grade class that was desegregated last fall.

Even in desegregated high schools, some Negroes win quick social acceptance. When a lone Negro was admitted to the 10th grade of one high school in a small Texas town, he was elected vice president of the class his first day. A Negro also has become president of Oklahoma City's integrated Central High School student council.

One investigation has shown that experiences of social acceptance are associated with academic success. In the earlier-mentioned NSSFNS program of placing qualified Negro graduates of Southern high schools in Northern integrated colleges, it was found that those who participated in extracurricular activities, dated, and had a satisfactory number of friends got better marks than those who did not (NSSFNS, 1960). Though this finding is merely correlational, it is consistent with the proposition that acceptance by white peers is beneficial to the achievement motivation of Negro students.

FEAR OF COMPETITION WITH WHITES

It was suggested that low expectation of success is an important detrimental factor in the performance of minority children attending integrated schools. The evidence is strong that Negro students have feelings of intellectual inferiority which arise from an awareness of actual differences in racial achievement, or from irrational acceptance of the white group's stereotype of Negroes.

Inadequacy of previous training. The low quality of segregated Negro education is well documented. Plaut (1957) has summarized the overall situation:

Negroes, furthermore, have long been aware that most of their schools in the South, and often the *de facto* segregated schools in the North, are rundown, poorly staffed, and short-handed. Second- and third-rate schooling for Negroes leaves them without the ability to compete with white students and robs them of the initiative to compete. Even the 1955 Speaker of the Georgia House of Representatives admitted recently that "Negro education in Georgia is a disgrace. What the Negro child gets in the sixth grade, the white child gets in the third" [p. 51].

A few specific instances of educational disparity at the grade-school level will be cited. Findley (1956) found in testing for achievement in the Atlanta schools that from 40% to 60% of white pupils met the standards set by the top 50% of a national sample on the

different tests; but only 2% to 10% of Negro pupils met this standard on the various tests. In Tennessee, according to Wyatt (1962) Negro students averaged 1½ to 2 years behind grade level when transferred to biracial schools in the upper grades. In earlier grades, transfers performed satisfactorily. The same report described the status of Negro and white teachers in a Tennessee urban area. Only 49% of 901 academically qualified Negro teachers passed the National Teachers Examination; among white teachers, more than 97% of 783 qualified teachers passed the test. The Tennessee survey showed that the academic retardation of the segregated Negro elementary-school pupil is progressive.

The situation in northern Virginia was summarized by Mearns (1962) in a report written for the United States Commission on Civil Rights:

The Negroes themselves have recognized that the achievement gap exists, but the only obvious reaction among most Negroes is reluctance to transfer to white schools. The question is raised as to whether Negroes really obtain a better education in desegregated schools where they must compete with better prepared, highly motivated white students. Frustration and failure engulf the ill-prepared Negro pupils . . . [pp. 209–210].

Other data indicate that the racial gap in achievement continues to widen through high school and college. Roberts (1963) pointed out that less than 3% of Negro graduates of segregated high schools would meet the standards of nonsegregated colleges. Roberts estimated that not more than 10 to 15% of Negro American college youth were capable of exceeding the threshold-level score on the American Council on Education test that was recommended by the President's Commission (100 on the 1947 edition).

Even in the urban North, where schools are legally integrated, the education afforded Negroes tends to be inadequate. Deutsch (1960), for example, found that in time samples of classroom activity, from 50% to 80% of all classroom time in New York City elementary schools with predominantly Negro, lower-class children was "devoted to disciplining and various essentially non-academic tasks." By comparison, only 30% of classroom time was given over to such activities in elementary schools attended mainly by white children of roughly similar economic status.

The foregoing material indicates that when grade-a-year plans of desegregation are adopted, it is obviously desirable from an educational standpoint to begin integration at the lowest grade and work upward. However, many Southern school systems are on grade-a-year plans of reverse order, with integration starting in the twelfth grade and proceeding down.

Unrealistic inferiority feelings. Apparently, the Negro child's feeling of intellectual inferiority is based not only on reality experience, but reflects an emotional accommodation to the demeaning role in American culture that has been imposed upon his racial group by the dominant white majority. The Group for the Advancement of Psychiatry (1957) has summarized the observations of numerous investigators of Negro personality:

Wherever segregation occurs, one group, in this instance the Negroes, always suffers from inferior social status. The damaging effects of this are reflected in unrealistic inferiority feelings, a sense of humiliation, and constriction of potentialities for self-development. This often results in a pattern of self-hatred and rejection of one's own group, sometimes expressed by antisocial behavior toward one's own group or the dominant group. These attitudes seriously affect the levels of aspiration, the capacity to learn, and the capacity to relate in interpersonal situations [p. 10].

Two experiments with Negro male college students suggest the marked extent to which loss of confidence when competing with whites can over-ride reality. Preston and Bayton (1941) found that when students at a Negro college were told that their own scores on intellectual tasks were the same as the average scores of white students, they tended to set their goal levels lower on the next few trials than they did when told that their scores equalled those of other Negro students. The results can be interpreted on the basis of Atkinson's (1958a) theory of goal-setting behavior. Assuming that the Negro subject's motive to succeed tended to be stronger than his motive to avoid failure, he should have set his goal where the probability of success was .50. When a given level of performance was said to represent the white norm its apparent difficulty became greater than when it was supposed to represent the Negro norm, hence the goal level at which the expectancy of success was .50 tended to be lower immediately following the announcement of these norms. In an investigation of small biracial work terms at a Northern university, Katz and Benjamin (1960) observed that Negro students who had actually scored as well as their white teammates on various intellectual tasks afterwards rated their own performance as inferior. Here knowledge of white performance levels apparently influenced the Negro subjects' cognitions of their own *actual* performance, rather than just their estimations of *future* performance.

In an experiment suggested by Whyte's (1943) observations of status influence in a white streetcorner gang, Harvey (1953) had members of white high-school cliques take turns on a dart-throwing task. After several practice trials, the boys openly estimated their own and their companions' future performance. Guesses were directly related to social rank in the group. Only boys of lowest rank showed a tendency to *under*estimate own performance. Moreover, they were expected by those of middle and high status to perform more poorly than they actually did. It should be noted that it is unclear from Harvey's results whether rank influenced perception of own ability or merely what one was willing to say in front of higher-ranking clique mates who had coercive power (French & Raven, 1960) to keep those of lesser rank "in their place."

Experiments on Stress and Performance

Earlier some situational factors were described that presumably are detrimental to Negro academic achievement: social threat, low expectancy of success, and failure threat. Also, evidence was presented (some of it inferential) of their occurrence in actual situations of racial integration. A good deal of experimentation having to do with the influence of these factors on verbal and motor performance has been stimulated by the concept of psychological stress. Applezweig and Moeller (1957) proposed a definition of stress which focuses on the condition of the individual: Stress occurs when a motive or need is strongly aroused and the organism is unable to respond in such a way as to reduce its motivation. Deese (1962) finds it more useful to define stress as a class of stimulus events that elicit a set of correlated responses, among which are feelings of discomfort. He points out that the effects of stress on performance are specific to particular components of the performance under consideration—i.e., responses to stress may be either compatible or incompatible with the responses required in a given task.

Early studies of stress and performance did not employ the type of analytic comparison of stress responses and dimensions of ability in specific skills that

Deese suggests. The general trend of findings on verbal performance (reviewed by Lazarus, Deese, & Osler, 1952) has been that stress impairs efficiency on relatively complex and difficult tasks, while on simple tasks stress has sometimes been shown to improve performance. The types of stress that have been used in experiments include failure feedback or threat of failure, exposure to highly difficult tasks (often under time pressure), annoying or painful stimulation such as electric shock, distraction such as flashing lights or noises, disapproval or disparagement.

Many investigations have employed stress inductions that apparently aroused fear of failure. For example, using 9-year-old boys, Lantz (1945) observed an impairment of Stanford-Binet scores following a failure experience, but no such effect after a successful experience. An examination by Lantz of the differential effects of this failure experience upon the various subjects indicated that tasks requiring visual or rote memory were not affected, while those involving reasoning or thinking suffered a decrement. In other studies that were reviewed by Lazarus, Deese, and Osler failure stress produced decrements in scores on the following verbal-symbolic tasks: learning and recall of nonsense syllables, digit-symbol substitution, arithmetic, recognition of briefly exposed sentences, sentence formation, and digit span. Similar effects were obtained on various types of perceptual-motor performance (e.g., card sorting, reaction time).

Turning to some representative studies of stress not directly involving failure, Barker, Dembo, and Lewin (1941) observed regression in the mental age of nursery-school children, as measured by the constructiveness of their play, when the children were frustrated by being denied access to attractive toys. Stress associated with the blocking of hostile impulses against an instigating agent (a teacher who arbitrarily disregarded the expressed desire of students) was found by Goldman, Horwitz, and Lee (1954) to impair performance on three tasks: retention of learned material, digit span, and problem solving. Laird (1923) reported loss of body steadiness in college students who were "razzed" by future fraternity brothers while working on simple motor tasks. Klein (1957) found that a strong task-irrelevant drive (thirst) caused a reduction in the accuracy of visual size judgments; and Callaway and Thompson (1953) obtained a similar effect when their subjects were required to hold one foot in a bucket of ice water.

During the past decade much research has been done on the role of personality factors in reactions to stress, with particular focus on the role of individual differences in chronic anxiety as measured by Taylor's Manifest Anxiety scale and Mandler and Sarason's Test Anxiety Questionnaire. A lengthy review of this work would fall outside the scope of this paper, inasmuch as the primary concern here is with *situational* factors that affect Negro performance. Yet it is of interest to note the general pattern of experimental results. Greater decrements due to stress are found in the performance of high-anxious individuals than in the performance of subjects lower in the anxiety-score distribution. These studies have been reviewed by Sarason (1960) and Taylor (1963).

Speculating about underlying physiological processes in stress, Bovard (1959) places the organizing center of bodily-emotional responses to stress in the posterior and medial hypothalamus. Of particular interest are his hypotheses that (a) activity in the anterior hypothalamus tends to inhibit or dampen posterior activity, and (b) excitation in the anterior hypothalamus is produced by certain types of social stimuli. *Thus an organism's vulnerability to stress depends upon the nature of its social environment.* Bovard reviewed studies which suggest that the presence of companions or members of the same species has a supportive effect under stress. At the human level it has been observed that separation from the family and evacuation from London was more stressful for London children than enduring the bombings with their family (Titmuss, 1950). Mandlebaum (1952) and Marshall (1951) dealt with the importance of social contact among soldiers in resisting battle stress. Research at Boston Psychopathic Hospital (1955) has shown that lysergic acid diethylamide (LSD) taken in a group situation results in less anxiety and inappropriate behavior than when taken individually. Schachter (1959) reported that fear, as well as hunger, increased the affiliative tendency in college students; and Wrightsman (1960) found that being with others in a similar plight was anxiety reducing for students who were first-born or only children.

Similar phenomena have been observed at the animal level. Liddell (1950) found that the presence or absence of the mother goat determined whether young goats would develop an experimental neurosis in a conditioning situation. In experiments with rats, animals tested together under stressful conditions gave less fear response (Davitz & Mason, 1955) and had less resultant ulceration (Conger, Sawrey, & Turrell, 1957) than animals tested alone. Similarly, monkeys showed fewer fear responses in a strange situation when another monkey was present (Mason, 1960). Monkeys raised in total isolation from age peers were deficient in normal defensive responses to environmental threat (Harlow & Harlow, 1962).

If Bovard's theory is correct, the extreme social isolation that is often experienced by Negroes in predominantly white environments would weaken their resistance to other stress conditions, such as might arise from the inherent difficulty of academic work, time pressure, financial problems, etc.

Various theories have been invoked to account for the tendency of stress to reduce efficiency on complex tasks, but to facilitate performance, or have no effect, on simple tasks. Sarason and others (Child, 1954; Mandler & Sarason, 1952; Sarason et al., 1960) have dealt primarily with the effects of individual differences in vulnerability to failure stress. They emphasize the interference that occurs when expectation of failure generates anxiety which, in turn, acts as an internal stimulus for defensive, task-irrelevant responses. Similarly, Deese (1962) mentions task interference from responses to the internal stimuli of stress-induced autonomic activity.

Some writers have concerned themselves with the effect of drive on specific characteristics of task-relevant behavior. Thus Easterbrook (1959) postulates an inverse relationship between drive level and the range of cue utilization. Complex tasks require a relatively broad awareness of cues for optimal efficiency, whereas simple tasks by definition require apprehension of only a few cues for successful responding. Hence, when drive is very high (as in stress), relevant cues will be missed on hard tasks, but more closely attended to on easy tasks. Hullian theory, as developed with respect to anxiety drive and learning by Spence, Taylor, and others, deals with the energizing effect of drive on task responses. As strength of drive increases the number of habitual response tendencies that can be elicited in a given task increases also. When activation is strong (as in stress) intratask response competition is heightened. The theory is supported by the results of experiments in which high and low scorers on Taylor's Manifest Anxiety scale were required to learn competitional and noncompetitional paired-word lists (reviewed by Spence, 1958; Taylor, 1963). Thus Easter-

brook and the Hullians have each dealt with a particular component of a great number of tasks, and have tried to predict either favorable or detrimental effects of stress from the presence or absence of this component.

Discussing the effects of stress on perceptual-motor skills, Deese (1963) points out the need for systematic analysis of (a) the characteristics of motor arousal under stress, in relation to (b) the dimensions of psychomotor abilities that are requisite for various task performances. Both Deese and Spence (1958) mention that a fundamental weakness of present thinking about the effects of stress on *verbal* learning is that not enough dimensions of verbal skills have yet been explored to know what kinds of effects to look for.

Summarizing this section, there is a considerable amount of experimental evidence that types of stress which may be present in desegregation (as varieties of social threat and failure threat) impair certain kinds of verbal and perceptual-motor learning. However, there does not exist at present any comprehensive system of variables for predicting the specific effects of different conditions of stress on the Negro child's performance of various academic tasks.

Experiments on Negro Performance in Biracial Situations[2]

In recent years this author and his associates have been engaged in a series of experiments on the intellectual productivity of Negro male college students in situations involving white peers and/or white authority figures. The general aim of the research is the identification of underlying psychological factors that have either favorable or detrimental effects on Negro efficiency. In connection with the interpretation of the results that are now to be presented there evolved the set of postulated situational determinants of performance that were discussed in an earlier section of this paper.

BIRACIAL TEAMS

In two exploratory studies, conducted at a Northern university (Katz & Benjamin, 1960; Katz, Goldston, & Benjamin, 1958), various cognitive and motor tasks were assigned to groups composed of two Negro

2. All of the research by the author and his associates that is reviewed in this section was conducted under Contract Nonr 285 (24) between the Office of Naval Research and New York University.

students and two white students. Initially the men were total strangers. They worked together in several sessions for a total of 12½ hours. In general, it was found that Negroes displayed marked social inhibition and subordination to white partners. When teams were engaged in cooperative problem solving, Negro subjects made fewer proposals than did whites, and tended to accept the latter's contributions uncritically. On all tasks combined, Negroes made fewer remarks than did whites, and spoke more to whites, proportionately, than to one another. White men, on the other hand, spoke more to one another, proportionately, than to the Negroes. These behaviors occurred even when group members could expect a monetary bonus for good teamwork, and were informed that their abilities were higher than those of subjects in other teams. Moreover, in the second experiment Negro and white partners were matched on intelligence, and were even made to display equal ability on certain group tasks (by means of secret manipulation of tasks). Yet on a terminal questionnaire Negroes ranked whites higher on intellectual performance, preferred one another as future work companions, and expressed less satisfaction with the group experience than did whites.

The findings on Negro behavior may have been a result of (a) social threat (i.e., Negroes were fearful of instigating white hostility through greater assertiveness), (b) low task motivation in confrontation with white achievement standards (as derived earlier from Atkinson's model), or (c) failure threat (high expectancy of failure combined with anxious anticipation of disapproval and rejection by white peers and the white experimenter). The experimental data provide no basis on which to reject any of these factors as irrelevant.

In the next experiment, Katz and Cohen (1962) attempted to modify Negro behavior toward white partners in the direction of greater assertiveness and autonomy. It was predicted that (a) when Negroes were compelled to achieve on a task that was performed cooperatively with a white peer, they would subsequently display an increased amount of achieving behavior on another shared task of different content, and (b) Negro subjects who were not compelled to achieve on the first task would show an opposite tendency. Negro-white student dyads at a Northern university engaged in cooperative solving of problems adapted from the Raven Progressive Matrices. Some of the problems were made easy, to insure that both participants would perceive the correct

answer. On other problems the subject unknowingly received different information, so that one person had an insoluble version. Each subject had the easy version half the time. On every problem partners had to agree on a single team answer, after which the experimenter announced the correct solution. Before and after the problem-solving experience a disguised measure of social influence between the two men was obtained on a task which required group estimates of certain quantitative characteristics of briefly exposed photographs (e.g., the number of paratroopers in the sky).

In a control condition, the rules of the problem-solving situation did not require that each person openly propose an answer to every problem. It was found that Negroes tended to accept passively the suggestions of their white companions *even when they held the easy version and the teammate had to be in error.* Regarding intellectual efficiency, the private responses of Negroes, which they wrote down before each discussion began, showed *more errors than were made on the same problems at an earlier, individual testing session.* White subjects, on the other hand, made *fewer* private errors than they had made previously. As a consequence of the problem-solving experience in the control condition, Negroes showed increased social compliance on the picture estimations.

In an "assertion-training" condition the men were given their answer sheets from the previous session when they had worked alone. On every problem the two partners were required to read aloud their previous answers before negotiating a team reply. Thus, Negro subjects had the experience of openly announcing correct solutions in about half of all instances of disagreement (both men read off approximately the same number of correct answers). In the subsequent interactions over picture estimation there was an *increase* in the amount of influence Negroes had over the white partner. Further, Negro subjects were now inclined to accept the other person's influence only to the extent that he had displayed superior accuracy on previous pictures.

Thus, unless *forced* to express opinions at variance with those of a white peer, Negro students tended to suppress their own ideas in deference to the other person, and to show increased compliance on another task. But when they were *forced* to act independently on one task, they achieved greater autonomy in the second situation. The responses of white subjects on a postexperimental questionnaire indicate there may have been some hostility aroused against Negro partners who displayed intellectual competence. After working in the assertion-training condition whites tended to downgrade the Negro's performance and to accept him less as a future co-worker. However, since there were no all-white control groups, it is not known whether these reactions of white subjects were specifically interracial.

The results suggest that Negro submissiveness with the white companion was an effect primarily of social threat, and that probability of success was a relatively unimportant factor. As already mentioned, in both the assertion-training and control condition disagreement was experimentally arranged on almost all problems, with random alternation between partners in the assignment of easy and insoluble versions (on a few items *both* men had either easy or hard versions). Also, after each team decision the experimenter announced the correct answer (fictitious when both men had hard items) so that subjects could check the accuracy of their own private response and of the solution the partner had openly proposed. While there was a stable tendency in control teams for whites to make slightly fewer private errors than Negroes (all partners had been matched on pretest scores), it is doubtful that the average race difference of about two private errors on 49 items could have been discriminated by the average Negro subject. Hence the relative accuracy of own and partner's solutions was much the same for Negro subjects in the two experimental conditions, and the only difference between conditions was that in assertion training the Negro subject was forced to *disagree openly* with the partner. The disinhibiting effect of this experience on the Negro subject's behavior on another task seems attributable to a reduction in anxiety about instigating white hostility.

THE EFFECT OF INDUCED THREAT IN
DIFFERENT RACIAL ENVIRONMENTS

In the next experiment, Katz and Greenbaum (1963) examined more directly the influence of threat on Negro verbal performance by systematically varying the level of threat in different racial environments. Individual Negro students at a predominantly Negro college in the South were given a digit-symbol substitution task in the presence of two strangers who were both either white or Negro—an adult administrator and a confederate who pretended to be another student working on the same task. In order to minimize the amount of uncontrolled threat implicit in the white condition, there was no social interaction between the Negro subject and his white peer, and the task was described as a research instrument of no evaluative significance.

In addition to the variation of racial environment, the students were exposed to a condition of either high or low threat. Since the purpose of the threat variation was to determine whether individual Negroes were more vulnerable to debilitative effects of stress when they were alone with whites than when they were with other Negroes, it seemed desirable to use a threat stimulus that would not lead to intentional suppression of responses, by changing the social meaning of the task situation. The experimenters used an announcement that severe electric shock (high-threat condition) or mild electric shock (low-threat condition) would be administered to the subject and the co-worker at random times during the task. No shocks were actually delivered.

The results indicated that Negro students' scores on the digit-symbol task depended upon the particular combination of stress and racial-environment conditions under which they worked. When only mild shock was threatened they performed better in the presence of whites than of other Negroes. But when told to expect strong shock their efficiency in the Negro condition improved, while in the white condition it went down. Apparently, the prospect of successful competition against a white peer, and of approval from a white authority figure, had greater incentive strength than the corresponding prospect in the all-Negro situation. This is reasonable on the assumption that the whites (particularly the experimenter) had higher prestige for the subject than their Negro counterparts. Since in all experimental conditions the instructions for the task played down its intellectual significance, Negro subjects in the white-environment–low-shock threat condition would not have experienced strong failure threat. Hence, they could respond to the stronger incentive strength of success in the white condition.

There are a number of ways of looking at the effects of shock threat. First, if Negro subjects cared more about performing well in the white condition they would have been more fearful lest the strong shock disrupt their task responses (failure threat). The expected stimulus would thus become more salient and distracting. An upward spiral of debilitation could then be set in motion as distraction and fear made the task seem more difficult, and this in turn aroused further emotion. Subjects in the Negro environment, on the other hand, had a relatively relaxed attitude toward the task in the low-threat condition (*too* relaxed for good performance). Hence they would not have been fearful of possible decrements due to shock, but perhaps just enough concerned to work harder than before. Also relevant to these data is Bovard's earlier-mentioned notion that the ability to withstand stress is strengthened by the presence of familiar social stimuli that have nurturant associations (in this case other Negroes).

The Hullian conception of the energizing effect of drive is also applicable. Efficiency declined in the white condition because the subject's initial stimulation in this racial environment, in combination with the additional stimulation of the strong shock threat, produced a total drive strength that exceeded the optimum for the assigned task. In the Negro condition, initial stimulation was relatively low, so that the increment in arousal due to strong threat brought the total drive level closer to the optimum than it had been under mild threat.

EFFECTS OF IQ VERSUS NON-IQ INSTRUCTIONS
In a follow-up on the preceding experiment, Katz, Roberts, and Robinson (in press) investigated the effects of three factors on Negro students' efficiency; the race of the task administrator, the difficulty of the task, and the evaluative significance of the task. All subjects were students at a Southern Negro college. Half of them were tested individually by a Negro adult and the other half were tested by a white adult. In addition, one-third of the total sample worked on a relatively easy digit-symbol code, one-third were given a code of medium difficulty, and one-third had to do a relatively hard code. In order to attach a relatively nonthreatening significance to the situation, the task was described as a research instrument for studying eye-hand coordination, a nonintellectual characteristic. Unlike the Katz and Greenbaum experiment, there was no experimental confederate who posed as a second subject. The findings were consistent with results obtained in the low-threat condition of the earlier study—Negro subjects worked more efficiently when tested by a white adult than when tested by a Negro adult. However, the favorable influence of the white

administrator was apparent only on the most difficult of the three tasks. On the two easier codes there were no statistically reliable differences in achievement associated with the skin color of the experimenters. Apparently the easier tasks were too simple to reflect the differences in motivation.

Then two additional groups of Negro students were tested by the same Negro and white administrators on the most difficult task only. But instead of being told that the task measured eye-hand coordination, it was presented to these subjects as a test of intelligence. Now the subjects did not attain higher scores in the presence of a white experimenter; rather, the effect of the IQ instructions was to slightly elevate performance with a Negro tester and to lower scores markedly in the white-tester group, so that the means for both testers were at about the same level. Thus in this experiment, making the most difficult task relevant to intellectual ability had effects not unlike those of strong threat in the previous study by Katz and Greenbaum. On the assumption that intellectual instructions were more highly motivating than the motor-test instructions, one can again apply the Hullian interpretation that motivation in the IQ-test–white-administrator treatment was excessive.

More directly relevant is Atkinson's (1958a) conception of motivation as a joint function of the subjective probability and incentive value of success, which was discussed earlier. Assuming again that a white experimenter has higher prestige for the Negro student than does a Negro experimenter, the prospect of eliciting the white person's approval would be more attractive. It follows that when the likelihood of winning approval by scoring well is equally high whether the tester is Negro or white, the subject will work harder for the white person. Thus in this experiment Negro students performed better with a white adult than with a Negro adult when the task was supposed to assess an ability which Negroes are not stereotyped as lacking (eye-hand coordination). Presenting the task as an intelligence test ought to have raised the incentive value of achievement in both racial conditions, with perhaps an even greater increment occurring when the experimenter was white (since *intellectual* approval by a white adult might be uniquely gratifying to the Negro students' self-esteem).

But suppose that on the intellectual task the Negro subject saw very little likelihood of meeting the white experimenter's standard of excellence. Unless the incentive strength of success increased enough to counter-balance the drop in subjective probability, Atkinson's model would predict a reduction in task motivation. As an additional source of impairment in this situation, low expectancy of success could have aroused fear of earning the white tester's *dis*approval (failure threat).

Turning now to the situation where the tester is Negro, there is no reason to assume that the subject's expectation of success would be markedly lower when the task was described as intellectual than when it was presented as a motor test. In both instances the racial identity of the tester would tend to suggest to the subject that he was to be compared with other Negroes. Accordingly, performance with the Negro tester ought to go up under IQ instructions. The fact that it rose only slightly in our experiment may be ascribed to the subject's unclarity about the tester's frame of reference for evaluating his score. That is, he was not actually informed whether he would be compared with norms for Negro students only, or with norms for *all* college students. The next study deals directly with this issue.

EFFECTS OF VARIATIONS IN
ANTICIPATED COMPARISON
Katz, Epps, and Axelson (1964) investigated the effects on Negro students' digit-symbol performance of being told that they would be compared intellectually with other Negro students, or with white students. Hard and easy versions of the digit-symbol task were administered to different groups of students at a Southern Negro college under three different instructions: no test, scholastic aptitude test with own college norms, and scholastic aptitude test with national (i.e., predominantly white) college norms. Scores in all three conditions were reliably different from one another, with highest achievement occurring in the Negro-norms condition, intermediate achievement in the white-norms condition, and lowest achievement when no comparison was expected. These differences tended to be larger on the hard task than on the easy one.

Again referring to Atkinson's model, Negro performance was lowest in the no-test condition because of low incentive, while the difference between the two test conditions was due to higher subjective probability of success (closer to .50) when Negro subjects believed they were competing with members of their own race than when they expected to be compared with whites.

White students from a nearby state university were tested under comparable instructions on the hard task only. It was found that scores of the two norms groups—i.e., own college and national—did not differ, and *both* groups were more efficient than subjects in the no-comparison condition.

Future research can determine the usefulness of this application of Atkinson's theory for understanding Negro behavior in integrated schools. For example, the present formulation predicts that if the subjective probability of success were held constant, Negro subjects would perform *better* on certain types of intellectual test when the administrator was white than when he was Negro, or when they were competing with white peers rather than with Negro peers.

A PILOT EXPERIMENT ON THE EFFECT OF
PROBABILITY FEEDBACK
In a recent pilot study (unpublished), done in preparation for a larger experiment, students at a Southern Negro college were individually given a digit-symbol task by a white administrator under two conditions of probability of success. All subjects performed an initial trial under instructions that the task measured intelligence. Upon completing the first trial, every subject was informed that his final score would be compared with racially integrated norms. Half of all the subjects were told, in addition, that on the basis of their first-trial scores there was a statistical probability of about 60% that their final scores would exceed the mean for their age group. Then a second trial was administered to everyone. It was found that subjects who were given the probability information performed better on the second trial than those who were not. This preliminary investigation gives further weight to the suggestion that the perceived probability of success is an important determinant of Negro reactions to competition with whites.

EMOTIONAL REACTIONS TO TEST SITUATIONS
Another line of investigation has to do with the appraisal of Negro subjects' emotional reactions to various test situations. In connection with the earlier discussion of failure threat, reference was made to the research of Sarason and his associates (Sarason, 1960; Sarason et al., 1960) on emotional factors in the test-taking behavior of white school children. In their view,

the child who chronically experiences anxiety when tested is reacting with strong unconscious hostility to the adult tester, who he believes will in some way pass judgment on his adequacy. The hostility is not openly expressed, but instead is turned inward against the self in the form of self-derogatory attitudes, which strengthen the child's expectation of failure and his desire to escape the situation. Thus he is distracted from the task before him by his fear of failure and his impulse to escape.

Sarason has not as yet presented direct evidence that situations of adult evaluation arouse hostility in highly test-anxious children. However, in clinical studies by Lit (1956), Kimball (1952), and Harris (1961), difficulty in expressing aggression openly was found to be associated with scholastic underachievement. Rosenwald (1961) found that students who were relatively unwilling to give aggressive responses on a projective test showed greater impairment in solving anagrams after a hostility induction than did students who showed less inhibition of aggression on the projective test. Mention has been made of a study by Goldman, Horwitz, and Lee (1954), which demonstrated an association between the degree to which strong hostility against an instigator was denied expression and the amount of disruption of intellectual functioning.

These studies are pertinent to the problem of Negro children's learning efficiency in integrated classrooms, because these children often have to suppress strong hostility. It was seen that Yarrow (1958) found a much higher incidence of covert symptoms of emotional disturbance in Negro children than in white children at a desegregated summer camp. White children, it will be recalled, aggressed openly against their Negro cabin mates, but the latter did not respond in kind. Rather, they tended to deny aggressive impulses in themselves and to show heightened alertness to aggressive behavior in other Negro children. Another investigator who has reported stronger trends toward denial of hostile impulses in Negro children than in white children is Karon (1958), who examined individual personality by means of a projective technique, the Picture Arrangement Test.

It was suggested earlier that when the administrator of an intellectual test is white, or when comparison with white peers is anticipated, Negro subjects tend to become fearful of failure. Anticipation of failure would tend to generate feelings of victimization and

covert hostility against the white tester. Since hostility against white authorities is dangerous, the hostile impulse would be strongly inhibited. Katz, Robinson, Epps, and Waly undertook to find out whether suppression of hostile responses occurs when a white adult makes Negro students take an intelligence test. Negro male students at a segregated high school in the South were given a test of aggression disguised as a concept-formation test. It consisted of 58 four-word items, with instructions to "circle the word that does not belong with the others." In half of the items one word had aggressive meaning, one word was nonaggressive, and two words were ambiguous. Hence the subject could choose either a hostile or a neutral concept. Two equivalent forms of the test were administered on successive days. On the first day it was given informally to all subjects by a Negro teacher. The following day the entire sample was divided into four groups, each of which was tested by either a white or a Negro adult stranger, with instructions that described the task as either an intelligence test or a research instrument.

The results show that when neutral instructions were used on the second day, average scores in both the white-tester and Negro-tester groups were the same as on the pretest. But in the intelligence-test condition, hostility scores *increased* over the previous day when the experimenter was a Negro, and they *decreased* when the experimenter was white. The authors' interpretation is that both administrators instigated hostile impulses in the subjects when they announced that the task would be used to evaluate intelligence; when the adult authority was a Negro person, students revealed their annoyance by responding to the aggressive connotations of ambiguous words, but when the adult was a white person, the need to deny hostile feelings resulted in avoidance of aggressive word meanings. (The "denial" interpretation is of course inferential, since the results merely show that hostility scores in the white-adult—IQ-test condition went down; there was no *direct* evidence of increased emotional conflict in this condition.)

Assuming that these findings actually reflect variations in ability to express hostile impulses under different testing conditions, they furnish an interesting clue as to the nature of emotional processes attendant upon the disruption of Negro students' performance in the white-adult—IQ-test condition of an earlier experiment (Katz, Roberts, & Robinson).

Summary

This paper brings together evidence relating to the effect of school desegregation on the academic performance of young Negroes. Negro Americans are defined as a subordinated minority group, and the focus of attention is on their adjustment in schools where white age peers and teachers predominate. In situations of this type there appear to be a variety of favorable and detrimental influences on Negro performance.

Low probability of success—where there is marked discrepancy in the educational standards of Negro and white schools, or where feelings of inferiority are acquired by Negro children outside the school, minority-group newcomers in integrated classrooms are likely to have a low expectancy of academic success; consequently, their achievement motivation should be low. *Social threat*—given the prestige and power of the white majority group, rejection of Negro students by white classmates or teachers should tend to elicit emotional responses (fear, anger, and humiliation) that are detrimental to intellectual functioning. *Failure threat*—when academic failure entails disapproval by significant others (parents, teachers, and perhaps also classmates), low expectancy of success should elicit emotional responses that are detrimental to performance.

On the other hand, *acceptance* of Negroes by white peers and adults should have a *social facilitation* effect upon their ability to learn, by motivating them to adhere to white standards of academic performance; anticipation that high performance will win white approval should endow scholastic success with *high-incentive value*.

Reports on the academic progress of Negro children in desegregated schools are on the whole inadequate for drawing any conclusions about the effects of biracial environments upon Negro performance. However, other types of evidence indicate that any or all of the situational factors mentioned above may be operative in specific instances. Research on psychological stress generally supports the assumption that social threat and failure threat are detrimental to complex learning.

Experiments on Negro male college students by the author and his associates have shown that in work teams composed of Negro and white students of similar intellectual ability, Negroes are passively compliant, rate their own performance as inferior even when it is not, and express less satisfaction with the team experience than do their white companions. These results are seen as due to social threat and/or failure threat. Later studies have sought to identify specific situational determinants of Negro behavior in biracial settings.

Forcing Negro subjects into attempts to influence nonhostile white partners in problem solving had the effect of increasing their ascendancy on another task with the same white partner, apparently mainly through reduction of their fear of instigating hostility.

Experimentally creating a verbal-task situation that was low in both social threat and failure threat resulted in better performance by Negroes in the presence of whites than in the presence of other Negroes, suggesting that the incentive value of success was greater in the white environment. But when threat of strong electric shock was introduced, the white setting became less favorable to performance than the Negro one. Thus *vulnerability* to stress was greater in the white condition, even though it was not apparent until a strong explicit threat was introduced.

The evaluative significance of a verbal task (e.g., whether it was described as a perceptual-motor test or an intellectual test) interacted with race of the tester in determining Negro performance, in a manner consistent with the notions that (a) the incentive value of success was higher with a white tester than with a Negro tester, and (b) the probability of success was lower with a white tester than with a Negro tester only when the task was defined intellectually.

Anticipated intellectual comparison with Negro peers was found to produce a higher level of verbal performance than anticipated comparison with white peers, in accordance with the assumption that the subjective probability of success was lower when the expected comparison was with whites. Also, performance was facilitated when a white tester raised the subject's expectancy of attaining a white standard of performance by giving him suitable "information" about his score on a previous trial.

Finally, suppression of hostile impulses appeared to occur in Negro students who were tested by a white adult, but not in those who were tested by a Negro adult.

Further research is needed to clarify the effects of the various situational factors mentioned above on the cognitive functioning of Negroes in biracial settings. However, it is possible even now to point out some implications for educational practice of the findings that have been reviewed.

Implications for Educational Practice

The foregoing is relevant to a number of recent suggestions by social scientists on ways to foster movement toward equal education for all children (e.g., Klopf & Laster, 1963):

1. Educational standards of Negro schools should be raised to the level of white schools, so that minority-group children who transfer to previously all-white schools will have a reasonable chance of succeeding academically. This means, among other things, that the quality of training received by Negro teachers and the criteria used in selecting them for jobs must be raised to white levels, and racial integration of school faculties must be carried out.

2. Programs should be instituted for contacting parents and helping them to understand what they can do to prepare children for schooling, and to foster achievement once children are in school.

3. There should be in-service training of teachers and other personnel in newly integrated schools to develop awareness of the emotional needs of children in biracial situations. The training should include the imparting of techniques for helping children get acquainted with one another.

4. The widely accepted practice of assigning children to homogeneous ability groups (the "track" system) should either be abandoned entirely or modified to afford maximum opportunity for periodic re-evaluation of potentiality. Ability grouping tends inevitably to freeze teachers' expectations as well as children's own self-images, hence it is particularly dangerous to intellectual development in the early grades.

5. Where grade-a-year plans of desegregation are adopted, the process should begin at the lowest grades, where Negro children have the smallest educational handicap and where unfavorable racial attitudes are least strongly learned.

References

Applezweig, M. H., & Moeller, G. The role of motivation in psychological stress. *Off. Naval Res. tech. Rep.*, 1957, No. 3.

Atkinson, J. W. Motivational determinants of risk taking behavior. In J. W. Atkinson (Ed.), *Motives in fantasy, action, and society*. New York: Van Nostrand, 1958. Pp. 322–340. (a)

Atkinson, J. W. Towards experimental analysis of human motives in terms of motives, expectancies, and incentives. In J. W. Atkinson (Ed.), *Motives in fantasy, action, and society*. New York: Van Nostrand, 1958. Pp. 288–305. (b)

Barker, R., Dembo, Tamara, & Lewin, K. Frustration and regression: An experiment with young children. *U. Ia. Stud. Child Welf.*, 1941, *18*, No. 1.

Bass, B. M. Conformity, deviation, and a general theory of interpersonal behavior. In I. A. Berg & B. M. Bass (Eds.), *Conformity and deviation*. New York: Harper, 1961. Pp. 38–100.

Boston Psychopathic Hospital. Experimental psychoses. *Scient. American*, 1955, *192*(6), 34–39.

Bovard, E. W. The effects of social stimuli on the response to stress. *Psychol. Rev.*, 1959, *66*, 267–277.

Callaway, E., & Thompson, S. V. Sympathetic activity and perception. *Psychosom. Med.*, 1953, *15*, 443–455.

Child, I. L. Personality. In C. P. Stone & Q. McNemar (Eds.), *Annual Review of Psychology*. Stanford, Calif.: Annual Reviews, 1954. Pp. 149–170.

Coles, R. *The desegregation of southern schools: A psychiatric study*. New York: Anti-Defamation League, 1963.

Conger, J. J., Sawrey, W. L., & Turrell, E. S. An experimental investigation of the role of social experience in the production of gastric ulcers in hooded rats. *Amer. Psychologist*, 1957, *12*, 410. (Abstract)

Criswell, Joan H. A sociometric study of race cleavage in the classroom. *Arch. Psychol., N.Y.*, 1939, No. 235.

Davitz, J. R., & Mason, D. J. Socially facilitated reduction of a fear response in rats. *J. comp. physiol. Psychol.*, 1955, *48*, 149–151.

Day, R. E. Part 2, North Carolina. In United States Commission on Civil Rights, *Civil Rights U.S.A.—public schools, Southern states*. Washington, D.C.: United States Government Printing Office, 1962. Pp. 57–104.

Deese, J. Skilled performance and conditions of stress. In R. Glaser (Ed.), *Training research and education*. Pittsburgh: Univer. Pittsburgh Press, 1962. Pp. 199–222.

Deutsch, M. Minority group and class status as related to social and personality factors in scholastic achievement. *Soc. Appl. Anthropol. Monogr.*, 1960, No. 2.

Deutsch, M. Dimensions of the school's role in the problems of integration. In G. J. Klopf & I. A. Laster (Eds.), *Integrating the urban school*. New York: Teachers College, Columbia University, Bureau of Publications, 1963. Pp. 29–44.

Dittes, J. E., & Kelley, H. H. Effects of different conditions of acceptance upon conformity to group norms. *J. abnorm. soc. Psychol.*, 1956, *53*, 100–107.

Dodson, D. Statement read at *Conference before the United States Commission on Civil Rights: Fourth annual education conference on problems of segregation and desegregation of public schools*. Washington, D.C.: United States Commission on Civil Rights, 1962. Pp. 137–141.

Easterbrook, J. A. The effect of emotion on cue utilization and the organization of behavior. *Psychol. Rev.*, 1959, *66*, 183–201.

Findley, W. G. *Learning and teaching in Atlanta public schools.* Princeton, N.J.: Educational Testing Service, 1956.

French, J. R. P., Jr., & Raven, B. The bases of social power. In D. Cartwright & A. Zander (Eds.), *Group dynamics.* (2nd ed.) Evanston, Ill.: Row Peterson, 1960. Pp. 607–623.

Goldman, M., Horwitz, M., & Lee, F. J. Alternative classroom standards concerning management of hostility and effects on student learning. *Off. Naval Res. tech. Rep.*, 1954.

Group for the Advancement of Psychiatry. *Psychiatric aspects of school desegregation.* New York: GAP, 1957.

Hansen, C. F. The scholastic performances of Negro and white pupils in the integrated public schools of the District of Columbia. *Harvard educ. Rev.*, 1960, *30*, 216–236.

Harlow, H. F., & Harlow, Margaret K. Social deprivation in monkeys. *Scient. American*, 1962, *207*(5), 136–146.

Harris, I. *Emotional blocks to learning.* Glencoe, Ill.: Free Press, 1961.

Harvey, O. J. An experimental approach to the study of status relations in informal groups. *Amer. sociol. Rev.*, 1953, *18*, 357–367.

Horowitz, E. The development of attitudes toward the Negro. *Arch. Psychol., N.Y.*, 1936, No. 194.

Karon, B. P. *The Negro personality: A rigorous investigation of the effects of culture.* New York: Springer, 1958.

Katz, I., & Benjamin, L. Effects of white authoritarianism in biracial work groups. *J. abnorm. soc. Psychol.*, 1960, *61*, 448–456.

Katz, I., & Cohen, M. The effects of training Negroes upon cooperative problem solving in biracial teams. *J. abnorm. soc. Psychol.*, 1962, *64*, 319–325.

Katz, I. Epps, E. G., & Axelson, L. J. Effect upon Negro digit-symbol performance of anticipated comparison with whites and with other Negroes. *J. abnorm. soc. Psychol.*, 1964, *69*.

Katz, I., Goldston, Judith, & Benjamin, L. Behavior and productivity in biracial work groups. *Hum. Relat.*, 1958, *11*, 123–141.

Katz, I., & Greenbaum, C. Effects of anxiety, threat, and racial environment on task performance of Negro college students. *J. abnorm. soc. Psychol.*, 1963, *66*, 562–567.

Katz, I., Roberts, S. O., & Robinson, J. M. Effects of difficulty, race of administrator, and instructions on Negro digit-symbol performance. *J. abnorm. soc. Psychol.*

Katz, I., Robinson, J. M., Epps, E. G., & Waly, Patricia. Effects of race of experimenter and test vs. neutral instructions on expression of hostility in Negro boys. *J. soc. Issues.*

Kimball, Barbara. Sentence-completion technique in a study of scholastic underachievement. *J. consult. Psychol.*, 1952, *16*, 353–358.

Klein, G. S. Need and regulation. In M. R. Jones (Ed.), *Nebraska symposium on motivation: 1957.* Lincoln: Univer. Nebraska Press, 1957. Pp. 224–274.

Klopf, G. J., & Laster, I. A. (Eds.) *Integrating the urban school.* New York: Teachers College, Columbia University, Bureau of Publications, 1963.

Knowles, L. W. Part 1, Kentucky. In United States Commission on Civil Rights, *Civil Rights U.S.A. — public schools, Southern states.* Washington, D.C.: United States Government Printing Office, 1962. Pp. 19–56.

Laird, D. A. Changes in motor control and individual variations under the influence of "razzing." *J. exp. Psychol.*, 1923, *6*, 236–246.

Lantz, Beatrice. Some dynamic aspects of success and failure. *Psychol. Monogr.*, 1945, *59*(1, Whole No. 271).

Lazarus, R. S., Deese, J., & Osler, Sonia F. The effects of psychological stress upon performance. *Psychol. Bull.*, 1952, *49*, 293–317.

Liddell, H. Some specific factors that modify tolerance for environmental stress. In H. G. Wolff, S. G. Wolf, Jr., & C. C. Hare (Eds.), *Life stress and bodily disease.* Baltimore: Williams & Wilkins, 1950. Pp. 155–171.

Lit, J. Formal and content factors of projective tests in relation to academic achievement. *Dissert. Abstr.*, 1956, *16*, 1505–1506. (Order No. 16,311)

Mandlebaum, D. G. *Soldier groups and Negro soldiers.* Berkeley: Univer. California Press, 1952.

Mandler, G., & Sarason, S. B. A study of anxiety and learning. *J. abnorm. soc. Psychol.*, 1952, *47*, 166–173.

Marshall, S. L. A. *Men against fire.* Washington, D.C.: Combat Forces Press, 1951.

Mason, W. A. Socially mediated reduction in emotional responses of young rhesus monkeys. *J. abnorm. soc. Psychol.,* 1960, *60,* 100–104.

Mearns, E. A., Jr. Part 4, Virginia. In United States Commission on Civil Rights, *Civil Rights U.S.A.—public schools, Southern states.* Washington, D.C.: United States Government Printing Office, 1962. Pp. 155–217.

Murstein, B. I., & Collier, H. L. The role of the TAT in the measurement of achievement as a function of expectancy. *J. proj. Tech.,* 1962, *26,* 96–101.

National Scholarship Service and Fund for Negro Students. *Annual report 1959-1960.* New York: NSSFNS, 1960.

National Scholarship Service and Fund for Negro Students. *Annual report 1962-1963.* New York: NSSFNS, 1963.

Plaut, R. L. *Blueprint for talent searching.* New York: National Scholarship Service and Fund for Negro Students, 1957.

Preston, M. G., & Bayton, J. A. Differential effect of a social variable upon three levels of aspiration. *J. exp. Psychol.,* 1941, *29,* 351–369.

Radke, Marian, Sutherland, Jean, & Rosenberg, Pearl. Racial attitudes of children. *Sociometry,* 1950, *13,* 154–171.

Radke, Marian, Trager, Helen G., & Davis, Hadassah. Social perceptions and attitudes of children. *Genet. psychol. Monogr.,* 1949, *40,* 327–447.

Roberts, S. O. Test performance in relation to ethnic group and social class. Report, 1963, Fisk University, Nashville. (Mimeo)

Rosen, M. Valence, expectancy, and dissonance reduction in the prediction of goal striving. *Dissert. Abstr.,* 1961, *21,* 3846. (Order No. 61-2062)

Rosenwald, G. The assessment of anxiety in psychological experiments. *J. abnorm. soc. Psychol.,* 1961, *63,* 666–673.

Sarason, I. G. Empirical findings and theoretical problems in the use of anxiety scales. *Psychol. Bull.,* 1960, *57,* 403–415.

Sarason, S. B., Davidson, K. S., Lighthall, F. F., Waite, R. R., & Ruebush, B. K. *Anxiety in elementary school children.* New York: Wiley, 1960.

Schachter, S. *The psychology of affiliation.* Stanford: Stanford Univer. Press, 1959.

Southern School News. Untitled. *Sth. sch. News,* 1960 (Aug.), *7,* 6(Cols. 1–2).

Southern School News. Untitled. *Sth. sch. News,* 1963 (Apr.), *9,* 11(Col.2).

Spence, K. W. A theory of emotionally based drive (D) and its relation to performance in simple learning situations. *Amer. Psychologist,* 1958, *13,* 131–141.

Stallings, F. H. A study of the immediate effects of integration on scholastic achievement in the Louisville Public Schools. *J. Negro Educ.,* 1959, *28,* 439–444.

Tanner, J. C. Integration in action. *Wall Street J.,* January 26, 1964, *64,* 1.

Taylor, Janet A. Drive theory and manifest anxiety. In Martha T. Mednick & S. A. Mednick (Eds.), *Research in personality.* New York: Holt, Rinehart & Winston, 1963. Pp. 205–222.

Thibaut, J., & Kelley, H. H. *The social psychology of groups.* New York: Wiley, 1959.

Titmuss, R. M. *Problems of social policy.* London, England: His Majesty's Stationery Office & Longmans, Green, 1950.

Trillin, C. *An education in Georgia.* New York: Viking Press, 1964.

Tumin, M. The process of integration. In G. J. Klopf & I. A. Laster (Eds.), *Integrating the urban school.* New York: Teachers College, Columbia University, Bureau of Publications, 1963. Pp. 13–28.

United States Commission on Civil Rights. *Second annual conference on education, Gatlinburg, Tenn.* Washington, D.C.: United States Government Printing Office, 1960.

United States Commission on Civil Rights. *Civil Rights U.S.A.—public schools, cities in the North and West.* Washington, D. C.: United States Government Printing Office, 1962. (a)

United States Commission on Civil Rights. *Civil Rights U.S.A.—public schools, Southern states.* Washington, D.C.: United States Government Printing Office, 1962. (b)

Whyte, W. F. *Street corner society; the social structure of an Italian slum.* Chicago: Univer. Chicago Press, 1943.

Wrightsman, L. S., Jr. Effects of waiting with others on changes in level of felt anxiety. *J. abnorm. soc. Psychol.,* 1960, *61,* 216–222.

Wyatt, E. Part 3, Tennessee. In United States Commission on Civil Rights, *Civil Rights U.S.A.—public schools, Southern states.* Washington, D.C.: United States Government Printing Office, 1962. Pp. 105–130.

Yarrow, Marian R. (Issue Ed.) Interpersonal dynamics in a desegregation process. *J. soc. Issues,* 1958, *14*(1, entire issue).